How to Use This Book

This book provides a well-grounded background in VBScript. The motivated reader can cover the material in 21 days, progressing from beginning fundamentals to more advanced topics by the end of the three-week period. The book is intended for use with a browser so that you can attempt the examples as you cover the material. However, the material was written so that it will also be clear and easy to learn if you use it without a computer.

Ideally, you can cover this book at the rate of a chapter a day. Each day covers a specific topic of importance. Every day builds on the days that precede it, so the best approach to the material is a sequential one. Each week provides a new plateau of experience. The weekly material is covered at the beginning of each seven-day period and briefly reviewed again at the end of each week to put it all in context.

This book is accompanied by a CD-ROM that contains an overview of each day's material and the sample programs for each day. The main overview page has been especially constructed to make it very easy for you to follow the material and interactively view the samples from each day at the same time as you work your way through the book. The material is all available in HTML format to be viewed in your browser, but since it is on the CD-ROM, your browser won't have to go across the Internet to find it! Make sure to start by dragging the main page of the sample program overview, Default.htm on the CD-ROM, into your browser. Then you will have all the links and summaries right in front of you to experience firsthand everything described in the book. And of course, keep in mind that you can use the View | Source option of the browser to look at the source code behind all the examples.

Experienced Visual Basic and Internet users might find that they can also use the book as a handy reference resource by referring only to the days of interest. However, VBScript has so many nuances, small as well as large, that you should make an effort to understand them all to fully appreciate what the language can do. Reading the book cover-to-cover is recommended to all who can afford the time. Spending 21 days of focused effort is an ideal way to cover the material. If you have to digest the material more slowly because of time constraints, don't worry. Continue to make sequential headway at your own pace. In any case, the effort you invest in working your way through this book should pay off. The end result will be that you're ready to leverage the full strength of VBScript to create your own powerful, dynamic, and active Web pages.

Teach
Yourself
VBScript®
in 21 Days

Teach Yourself
VBSCRIPT®
in 21 Days

Keith Brophy
Timothy Koets

201 West 103rd Street
Indianapolis, Indiana 46290

From Keith to Sue, and from Tim to Michelle.

Copyright © 1996 by Sams.net Publishing

International Standard Book Number: 1-57521-120-3

Library of Congress Catalog Card Number: 96-68236

99 98 97 96   4 3 2 1

Interpretation of the printing code: The rightmost double-digit number is the year of the book's printing; the rightmost single-digit, the number of the book's printing. For example, a printing code of 96-1 shows that the first printing of the book occurred in 1996.

Composed in AGaramond and MCPdigital by Macmillan Computer Publishing

Printed in the United States of America

Trademarks

President, Sams Publishing Richard K. Swadley
Acquisitions Manager Greg S. Wiegand
Managing Editor Cindy Morrow
Marketing Manager John Pierce
Assistant Marketing Manager Kristina Perry

Acquisitions Editor
Christopher Denny

Development Editor
Anthony Amico

Software Development Specialist
Steve Straiger

Production Editors
Kitty Wilson
Kris Simmons

Copy Editors
Kate Shoup
Colleen A. Williams

Technical Reviewer
Greg Guntle

Editorial Coordinator
Bill Whitmer

Technical Edit Coordinator
Lynette Quinn

Editorial Assistants
Carol Ackerman
Andi Richter
Rhonda Tinch-Mize

Cover Designer
Tim Amrhein

Book Designer
Gary Adair

Copy Writer
Peter Fuller

Production Team Supervisor
Brad Chinn

Production
Mary Ann Abramson,
Georgiana Briggs, Cheryl Dietsch,
Michael Dietsch, Chris
Livengood, Paula Lowell, Mike
Henry, Dana Rhodes, Andy Stone

Overview

Appendixes

Contents

Foreword

A popular saying in the Internet development arena nowadays states that if a technology is more than three months old, it's obsolete! This sentiment is perhaps exaggerated for effect, but it does underscore a very significant change the industry is undergoing. New software technologies and breakthroughs are coming at a breakneck, leapfrog pace. Staying current is more of a challenge than ever before. Picking the technologies that will be here to stay, as opposed to pretenders to the throne, has never been tougher.

If you have a copy of this book, though, we think you've picked a winner. VBScript opens up a world of possibilities for the environments you apply it to—Web pages in particular. You can create smart, active, and interactive Web pages with VBScript with unparalleled ease. It is difficult to appreciate the full power and impact of this new scripting language without a good resource to back it up. It's been our aim to get such a resource into your hands as soon as possible. The "under-construction dust" is just settling as this book goes to print, but already it is clear that a capable, stable, mature product has emerged.

Microsoft, like many companies in the opinionated Internet fray, has its detractors. As a large, high-profile company and somewhat of a late arrival onto the Internet scene, its technologies are the focus of great anticipation and in some corners, even skepticism. The skepticism has been unfounded. Microsoft has delivered a scripting language that is easy to use, flexible, powerful, and secure. The most prominent home of the original release of this language is the browser, which is the main focus of this book. However, you can certainly expect it to become integral to many more products as the future unfolds. VBScript is a technology that is here to stay. As the waves of technology change in the exciting months and years ahead, it is a safe bet that VBScript will be riding the tide. To some extent, the course of many other of the vessels traveling the sea might be changed because of VBScript.

Keith and Tim
July 1996

NOTE ▶ This book is based on a stable beta version of Internet Explorer 3.0 and Visual Basic, Scripting Edition (also called VBScript). We've expended a lot of effort to ensure that it is as accurate as possible. However, if any discrepancies between the material covered here and the official product release of Internet Explorer 3.0 and VBScript come to light, they will be fully documented and available online. Refer to Appendix B, "Information Resources," for information on how to obtain the latest updates, if any, from Macmillan Publishing's Sams.net site (`http://www.mcp.com/samsnet`).

Disclaimer from the Publisher

The information contained in this book is subject to the following disclaimers:

1. The information in this book is based on a beta that is subject to change.
2. Microsoft does not endorse the content of this book, nor will it provide support for the beta product.
3. You can visit Microsoft's Web site at `http://www.microsoft.com/vbscript` for up-to-date information about Visual Basic, Scripting Edition, and `http://www.microsoft.com/intdev` for related ActiveX information and software.

Acknowledgments

We would like to thank Sams.net for the opportunity to tackle a topic that we view as a very important, exciting step in software evolution. Along with this, we extend a special thanks to Chris Denny for his help and support all along the way; Tony Amico, our key development editor; Kitty Wilson, our ever-patient production editor; Greg Guntle, technical editor; and the rest of the great Sams team behind us. Appreciation is similarly extended to the great gang at CNS, our Internet service provider and the best "voice of experience" we've found on rapidly evolving Internet connectivity issues.

We'd also like to thank our colleagues at X-Rite, Incorporated, where we develop software by day. Although this book is a project independent of the company, we certainly benefit in knowledge and spirit from our daily association with such a fine group of co-workers. Thanks especially to Steve Peterson for encouraging a view toward the leading edge of technology.

Thanks also to our friends and families. Without them, the book couldn't have come about. After spending much time on the last book saying, "It's gonna be a long time before we do this again," something unexpected happened. A fantastic topic coaxed us out of retirement and made liars of us within just a few months, and there we were, doing it again. This book came during busy times in our lives. During the time the book was written, we dealt with sick cockatiels (Tim), rescuing kids locked in the bathroom and taking them to the circus (Keith), wedding preparations (Tim), the Boston Marathon (Keith), busy work schedules (Tim and Keith), and then the wedding itself (Tim and Michelle)! We strove very hard for quality in this book and felt we never sacrificed in this regard. We did sacrifice time with family and friends, who nevertheless were right there behind us every step of the way. So much credit goes to them all.

Much thanks and love from Keith to Sue and from Tim to Michelle. This book is dedicated to them.

Keith adds: Thanks to my wife, Sue, for assisting with so many aspects of the book preparations in addition to being there every step of the way. Thanks also to Ginger, Mom, and Dad, not only for the support in general, but also for making the kids the world's happiest grandkids. To Ginny, Emma, and Ben, who are still waiting on that pool to go up, to family and friends who are wondering when my hair will stop looking so ruffled, and to special running comrades who are waiting for me to stop complaining that I'm out of shape: Thanks for understanding. Another book has been borne into the world, and we think it's an important one.

Tim adds: Thanks also to my wife, Michelle, for being so understanding and supportive during the busy time of wedding preparations and beginning a new life together. She has been patient and tolerant of those evenings when I had to spend an inordinate amount of time in the den at my computer and when my schedule got a bit hectic. She has been a terrific partner, and I look forward to a wonderful life together with her. Thanks also to our pet cockatiel, Buddy Bird, who not only provided me with some great examples in the book, but was a great companion on those lonely days when Michelle was at work. We also thank our parents for their support all through the years, both past and present.

About the Authors

Keith Brophy

Keith Brophy has many years of experience in the design, development, and testing of software systems. He is currently a software release coordinator for X-Rite, Incorporated, a leading worldwide provider of color and appearance quality control software and instrumentation in Grandville, Michigan. Prior to that, he was a lead software developer for IBM's System Integration and Federal Systems divisions in the Washington, D.C., area and worked on a wide variety of systems. His experience includes building Internet systems in the "pre-Web" era. During this time, he also was responsible for various operating system, performance, and graphical user interface research and development projects. He has taught in various venues, including Northern Virginia Community College and as the advanced Visual Basic adjunct faculty member at Grand Rapids Community College.

Mr. Brophy, along with Mr. Koets, co-authored *Visual Basic 4 Performance Tuning and Optimization* (Sams 1996) and was a contributing author for *Visual Basic 4.0 Unleashed* (Sams 1995). He also served as technical editor on *Real-World Programming with Visual Basic* (Sams 1995) and the revised edition of *Teach Yourself Visual Basic 4 in 21 Days* (Sams 1995). He has a B.S. in computer science from the University of Michigan in Ann Arbor and an M.S. in information systems from Strayer College in Washington, D.C. Mr. Brophy is the founder of DoubleBlaze Software Consortium (`www.DoubleBlaze.com`), an ActiveX Internet research and development company involved in endeavors such as research for this book.

Timothy Koets

Timothy Koets is a software engineer at X-Rite, Incorporated, a leading worldwide provider of color and appearance quality control software and instrumentation in Grandville, Michigan. Prior to this, Mr. Koets was a computer systems engineer in the Systems Engineering and Integration division of Martin Marietta in the Washington, D.C., area. In addition to developing Visual Basic applications, Mr. Koets has experience in many other areas including Visual C++, computer networking, client/server application design, parallel processing, and performance analysis. He, too, has previous experience building pre-Web systems that were Internet aware. Mr. Koets is an adjunct faculty member at Grand Rapids Community College, where he teaches advanced Visual Basic, and has prior teaching experience ranging from computer programming and engineering laboratory classes to Lotus Notes training courses.

Mr. Koets, along with Mr. Brophy, co-authored *Visual Basic 4 Performance Tuning and Optimization* (Sams 1996) and was a contributing author for *Visual Basic 4.0 Unleashed* (Sams 1995). He has a B.S. in electrical engineering and an M.S. in electrical engineering from Michigan Technological University in Houghton, Michigan. Mr. Koets is the founder of Cockatiel Software, an Internet research and development company that is an affiliate of DoubleBlaze Software Consortium (`www.doubleblaze.com`).

Tell Us What You Think!

As a reader, you are the most important critic of and commentator on our books. We value your opinion and want to know what we're doing right, what we could do better, what areas you'd like to see us publish in, and any other words of wisdom you're willing to pass our way. You can help us make strong books that meet your needs and give you the computer guidance you require.

Do you have access to CompuServe or the World Wide Web? Then check out our CompuServe forum by typing GO SAMS at any prompt. If you prefer the World Wide Web, check out our site at http://www.mcp.com.

NOTE

> If you have a technical question about this book, call the technical support line at 800-571-5840, ext. 3668.

As the team leader of the group that created this book, I welcome your comments. You can fax, e-mail, or write me directly to let me know what you did or didn't like about this book—as well as what we can do to make our books stronger. Here's the information:

Fax: 317-581-4669

E-mail: programming_mgr@sams.mcp.com

Mail: Greg Wiegand
          Comments Department
          Sams Publishing
          201 W. 103rd Street
          Indianapolis, IN 46290

Introduction

How important is VBScript to the future of computing? How important is it to you? Does it give you new capabilities that you can't get in other languages, or is it just another choice in a sea laden with confusing buzzwords? If you've pondered questions like these, you're not alone. VBScript is one of the most exciting new players in the rapidly expanding universe of technologies loosely termed the Internet. The purpose of this book is to teach you how to use VBScript. As a brief prerequisite to that journey, consider why VBScript is such an important part of the Web page development arsenal. Perhaps the best way to understand the potential of this future-centered technology is to take a look at how far the Internet has come. You might find that you have been involved in many of the trends leading up to the advent of VBScript without even realizing it, just as the authors have been.

A little over a decade ago, one of the authors was producing Department of Defense software and the reams of documentation that go along with it. One of the requirements in putting together this documentation stipulated that it should be generated in a markup language called *SGML*. This markup language was quite cumbersome. For example, it required that each heading start with an h1 tag and each paragraph with a p tag. Eventually, this project came to an end, and it seemed that this memory was just a relic of the past. Then, along came the World Wide Web. Behold: The World Wide Web is based on a page description language inherited to a large extent from SGML! The tag-oriented approach for Web pages succeeded precisely because it leaves the work of presenting Web pages to the browser. This approach provides an efficient, low-overhead means for communicating across the Internet because it enables the information sent across the network to be content-centered while the browser takes care of the cosmetic details on its own.

About a decade ago, another important change in the computer industry began. The mainframe-centered computing world, where all work was performed on a central computer, was quickly being replaced by a more distributed model. Users could now do some of the work locally, using the horsepower of their own PCs rather than the mainframe. For example, an accountant could now do much of her work in a spreadsheet on her own PC, rather than vie for time on an overloaded mainframe to perform accounting analyses.

Once users had more computing power in front of them, they could take advantage of that power with a graphical user environment. Windows filled this need, but the next big problem was creating the Windows applications themselves. In the early days when C was the only viable language alternative, Windows program development required such degrees of experience and development time that Windows programming was out of the reach of many. It was also quite difficult to integrate other commercial components into applications. Visual Basic came forward to fill these voids. Because of its ease of use and component integration capability, Visual Basic achieved widespread acceptance over the course of the next few years and releases. Some even claim that this language, which did not exist a decade ago, is now the world's most popular programming language.

That brings us to the very recent past. The Web provides a way to deliver content across the Internet to client computers, often PCs, using the tag-oriented HTML language. A page is sent from some host computer for an end user to look at. The browser on the end user's computer has the job of presenting the information. What if more complex processing is needed in conjunction with a page? Suppose you want to trigger a series of simple financial calculations from a Web page. The HTML language doesn't provide such support. For a while, the only way to do this was to use an approach similar to the old mainframe approach— send requests back to the host computer and make it perform the processing. Then came the advent of JavaScript. With JavaScript, when the browser on a client computer presents the page to the user, it can also act on the embedded JavaScript instructions to perform smart processing. However, it takes experience to develop JavaScript programs, which are some- what like C++ in nature. If you are a new programmer or one of the million or more programmers whose background is Visual Basic, you'd require a certain amount of effort to get up to speed on the JavaScript language.

Development for this very exciting environment required a language that not all could easily master. Sound like a familiar problem to you? It did to Microsoft, too, and in the process of inventing a comprehensive Internet strategy, Microsoft reinvented, or at least reengineered, the wheel. Visual Basic, Scripting Edition was its answer to these problems. VBScript, a subset of its parent, Visual Basic, is an easy-to-use language that is a cinch to integrate and provides an easy path to incorporate components.

If this brief history of the Internet and the reasons why VBScript came about are new to you, don't worry—you can take comfort in the fact that the currents of change are flowing in the right direction to make your Web page development easier than ever before. As to the "how" of VBScript, we'll tell you everything you need to know about using VBScript in the pages ahead.

Step-by-step, we will teach you how to use Visual Basic, Scripting Edition to its fullest potential. You will also see how to take advantage of powerful intrinsic controls, ActiveX controls, Java applets, and other objects through VBScript. During this journey, we will cut through all the Internet jargon and buzzwords, helping you to clearly understand how all the pieces of the Internet fit together and how you can participate in this new way of sharing information. We won't bore you with all kinds of information on the Internet that you don't need, nor will we give you just a cookbook of techniques. Rather, this book will give you the ability to creatively and expressively use VBScript to write impressive, powerful, useful Web pages.

Who Should Read This Book

This book is for you if you find yourself in one of the following categories:

- ☐ You've seen what's on the Web, and you want to contribute your own content.
- ☐ You represent a company that wants to make its presence known on the Internet in a powerful yet productive way.
- ☐ You're an information developer, and you want to learn how the Web can help you present your information online.
- ☐ You're a Visual Basic programmer who wants to create Web pages on the Internet without learning yet another programming language.
- ☐ You've used HTML to create Web pages, but you find it too limiting.
- ☐ You've mastered HTML and CGI and want to move beyond the limited capabilities of static Web pages. You want to use VBScript to bind programs around your pages, making your Web pages more dynamic.
- ☐ You've used other scripting languages, such as JavaScript, and you're interested in using a simpler language to accomplish your goals.

What This Book Contains

This book is intended to be completed in 21 days—one chapter per day—although the pace is really up to you. We have designed the book as a teacher would teach a course. We start with the basics and continue to introduce more of the language to you as the chapters progress. By the end of the first week, you will be creating your first VBScript Web page. As you work through the chapters, you will continue to design Web pages using VBScript that will become increasingly more powerful. In the second and third weeks, you will be exploring the more advanced features VBScript provides. In addition to instruction, we will furnish an abundance of examples, as well as exercises for you to try. You can learn a great deal by reading, but only when you try building a few VBScript Web pages of your own can you become truly experienced.

- ☐ During Week 1, you get a general overview of the Internet, the World Wide Web, Web browsers, and the languages available to develop Web pages. You will learn how to create variables, how to use operators to put variables to use, and the overall syntax of VBScript. Finally, you'll see a Web page incorporating useful VBScript code that will bring the Web page to life!
- ☐ During Week 2, you will be introduced to ActiveX controls. ActiveX controls enable you to present your Web page to the user in a very powerful way. You will also learn about intrinsic controls and objects. Then you will learn how to control

the user interface, process and interpret user input, work with mathematical functions, and extend VBScript capabilities in various ways.

☐ During Week 3, you will learn about even more powerful capabilities of VBScript. You will learn more about handling dates, strings, and mathematical functions. You will be exposed to advanced concepts about ActiveX control objects and intrinsic browser objects. You'll learn about script-based strategies to generate data on the client, validate it, and then provide it to the server for storage. You'll also learn key debugging and porting skills. At the completion of this week's material, you will have the well-rounded background needed to tackle all aspects of VBScript development.

With this book, you will become comfortable enough with VBScript to design and implement powerful Web pages of your own and become confident in your abilities to use it effectively—all in three weeks or less!

What You Need Before You Start

Because this is a book about creating Web pages, we assume that you are already able to access and use the Internet. You should have a World Wide Web browser that supports VBScript, such as Microsoft's Internet Explorer 3.0, and you should be somewhat familiar with it. (Steps to obtain such a browser are provided on Day 1.) A basic knowledge of the other Internet services such as electronic mail, FTP, Telnet, Usenet news, and Gopher is not necessary for working through this book, but it may be helpful for your future page development, particularly if you want your Web pages to interact with these services. As is true whenever you learn a new programming language, the more experience you have with programming, the better. Don't worry, though, if programming is new to you; you should be able to write VBScript code with a minimal amount of previous programming experience. Our objective is to begin from the ground up, and we do not assume you are an expert programmer. After all, VBScript is not designed just for experts, but for anyone interested in building active Web pages quickly—you don't necessarily have to be a computer language guru.

You're now ready to begin the first chapter on your journey of learning how to use VBScript. We're excited about showing you the potential of this new, exciting language. The journey will be well worth the effort.

WEEK 1

At a Glance

This book is intended to show you how to use VBScript as a powerful tool to extend the capabilities of environments such as World Wide Web pages. This week will provide you with a look at where VBScript fits in the context of the World Wide Web. You will also see some basic scripts and cover plenty of the fundamentals of building your own VBScript code. A browser that hosts VBScript will enable you to run the examples and build the programs described in the book. This week provides details on where to get such a browser, if you don't have one already, and shows VBScript pages you can run in that browser.

Where You Are Going

This week will begin with a brief look at what the Internet and the World Wide Web are really all about. That context is necessary to fully understand the evolution and purpose of VBScript, which is covered in detail. This week gives you a taste of the overall essence and capabilities of VBScript. Then the attention turns to specific fundamentals that you must master to use the language effectively. The lessons explain and demonstrate the use of variables in VBScript. This is followed by a close look at the operators available in the language and how to use them. Next, you'll examine control structures. Finally, this week provides a clear description of how to use procedures in VBScript. With the fundamentals provided during this week, you'll be ready to tackle more advanced topics and script programs in the weeks to follow.

Day **1**

Introducing VBScript and the World Wide Web

VBScript. Maybe you've heard it's a tool that lets you build more powerful Web pages. Perhaps you've heard it called the "JavaScript killer" because it's easier to use. You might simply know it as an Internet buzzword. Whatever your motivations, the fact that you're reading this book indicates that you want to know what VBScript is all about.

You've come to the right place! VBScript is an exciting, powerful tool at the center of the rapid Internet information revolution. In this book, you will find everything you need to know to get started. Before you start learning about how VBScript works, you should know a little bit about how the Internet phenomenon began and how VBScript fits into the big picture. It's so easy to get lost in a sea of terminology and acronyms. This lesson cuts through the jargon and helps prepare you for the exciting journey ahead of you—understanding and learning how to use VBScript to its fullest. Questions answered in this lesson include the following:

☐ What is the Internet, and why is it so popular?

☐ What is the World Wide Web, and how does it fit in to the Internet?

☐ What are Web browsers, and how are they used?

☐ What are the most popular and widely used browsers available today?

☐ What are Web pages, and how are they created?

☐ What is Microsoft's ActiveX technology, and how does it relate to the Web?

☐ How does VBScript fit in when creating a Web page?

☐ What are Java and CGI, and where do they fit in?

☐ How are Web pages sent over the Internet?

If you are already familiar with these concepts, you might want to skip ahead to Day 2, "The Essence of VBScript," which discusses how VBScript and Hypertext Markup Language (HTML) work together with the Web browser to present a Web page to the user.

The Internet and the World Wide Web

The Internet, which has come to serve over 20 million users worldwide, had relatively humble beginnings. It began as a rather obscure network called ARPANET—a network used by the Department of Defense, its contractors, and defense researchers. The ARPANET proved very useful and powerful, so much so that over time it grew tremendously. Soon, a more general network called the Internet was created with the same philosophy as ARPANET, only with a broader scope. In the late 1980s, the Internet spread across universities around the world and became more and more popular among researchers in the academic community.

As the popularity of the Internet increased, so did its size. Starting in its earlier days, users became increasingly aware of the benefits of specific services such as electronic mail and the ability to transfer files. Over time, the incredible potential of the Internet for sharing and distributing information became apparent as more and more people started using it. The National Science Foundation, which had almost completely funded the Internet in the United States until 1991, lifted its ban of commercial traffic on the Internet in 1991 and dropped most of its funding. This gave the Internet much more widespread exposure and opened the door to many more commercial ventures. Since then, the Internet has grown in incredible proportions. Given the current and potential growth of the Internet, you can't afford not to learn about the Internet, especially if you are a part of corporate America.

Now that corporations and the telecommunication giants are becoming more interested in the Internet, the Internet is maturing at an unprecedented rate. Organizations ranging from product vendors and standards bodies to the National Science Foundation, which helps support the backbone of the Internet that carries all of the information between the Internet and its hosts, are developing standards and security mechanisms that should take the Internet to new heights. Consider, for instance, the capability to receive real-time voice and video so that you can see the person you're talking to or the capability to order a pizza and watch a movie using the Internet. The possibilities are unlimited. Your ability to leverage its benefits for your company or personal use will become increasingly valuable as the Internet is exposed to more and more people across the world.

What is the Internet, really? The Internet, simply put, is like a vast ocean of computers across the world connected together by a network of cables. Figure 1.1 shows a simplified diagram of how the Internet is constructed.

Figure 1.1.

A simplified view of the Internet.

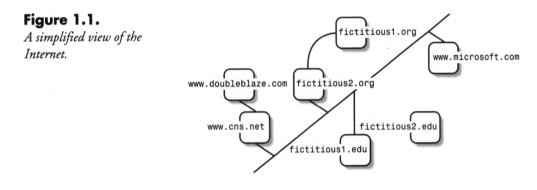

Because all these computers are connected as shown in Figure 1.1, a computer connected to the network can gain access to any of the others, providing a seemingly infinite amount of information to the user. Suppose, for example, that you are a bird lover who lives in Detroit. You want to get information on how to teach your cockatiel to sing. A computer down in Miami has just what you want—a bird lover's consortium, where people all over the world come to share information about birds. Using the Internet, you could connect to that computer as Figure 1.2 shows.

Figure 1.2.

Internet connection to the bird consortium.

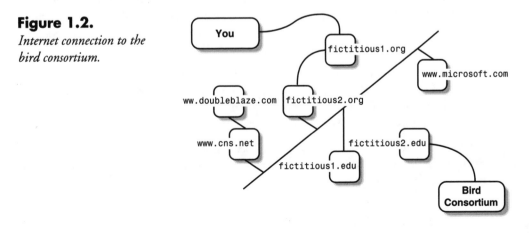

In this example, your computer sends information from your computer's modem, through your telephone line, out to a series of cables that provide access to all of the computers on the Internet. The Internet simply has to route the information from your computer to the computer in Miami—the one you want to access. As long as the Internet provides a valid route, you can send and receive information from this specific computer. If you want to exchange information with another computer in addition to the one in Miami, you are free to do so. The Internet provides this capability for you; all you need to know is the address of the computer you want to exchange information with. The Internet does all the rest.

NEW TERM   An *Internet address* is used to identify a computer connected to the Internet. Every address must be unique, since the computer represented by that address is unique to the Internet. Names are registered through the Network Information Center (`rs.internic.net`) to ensure uniqueness. Internet addresses can be represented in terms of textual domain names, such as `www.doubleblaze.com`; or in terms of the corresponding address, called an IP address, such as `205.132.48.237`. *Uniform resource locators*, or URLs, incorporate Internet addresses to indicate the network location of a Web page or other network resource.

The details of the illustration could vary because there are so many different possible routes to connect one computer to another on the Internet. If, for example, you are at work or school rather than at home, you might already be at a computer directly attached to the Internet. In that case, connecting with a modem might not be necessary. Furthermore, once you're on the Internet, you can trade information using a variety of approaches ranging from Web browsers or electronic mail to transferring files.

How do people use the Internet? The Internet is used for sending and receiving electronic mail, exchanging files, reading and participating in news groups, and obtaining information in general. In the bird consortium example, you have a variety of options at your disposal once you're connected to the Web site. You can browse a Web page filled with information on cockatiels or participate in a news group discussion of cockatiel mating habits. You might find a reference to a public file containing research on cockatiel schizophrenia and then download the file to your computer. You could even send e-mail to the president of the National Cockatiel Mating Society, given the correct address. Well, you get the point.

The best way to describe the Internet is to list the services it provides. The Internet has a wide variety of services available to the user. Often, a service on the Internet is called a *protocol*. A protocol is simply a set of rules for communication. Each service has its own special set of rules to accomplish its goals more easily. The following list describes some of the major services:

NEW TERM   A *protocol* is a set of rules for communicating across the Internet. Both parties know and follow the rules for sending and receiving information, making meaningful communication possible.

☐ Electronic mail: E-mail is a very simple and direct way to exchange messages targeted for particular users on the Internet.

1

☐ File Transfer Protocol (FTP): This protocol enables users connected to the Internet to exchange files with other users by sending them to and receiving them from Internet sites.

☐ Telnet: This protocol enables a user to connect to another computer on the Internet. With the appropriate privileges, this protocol could, for example, allow you to connect to the university's administration computer from the computer in your dorm room and then enter commands that are carried out on the administrative computer (such as changing all your grades to A's).

☐ Gopher: This protocol enables Internet users to access topical information from servers that support the Gopher protocol. This protocol, along with Telnet and FTP, is among the older protocols of the Internet. One of the services Gopher provides is the ability for users to search for information on the Internet by providing a list of news group topics. Users can then quickly and easily access the news groups of their choice from this list.

☐ Hypertext Transfer Protocol (HTTP): This protocol, the backbone of the World Wide Web, enables users to send and receive information from Internet servers in the form of documents, or *pages,* written using the Hypertext Markup Language (HTML). The user who receives the document, often called the *client,* can then use a *browser* or other form of software that recognizes the HTML language to view the contents of the document. Through a browser, the user can even access some of the other protocols, such as Telnet or FTP. HTTP and the World Wide Web can thereby facilitate access to the important protocols under one easy-to-use interface. If the user wants maximum flexibility in FTP file exchanges, he'd likely use the FTP protocol directly. On the other hand, the user can browse Web pages and easily locate FTP files from within the familiar browser interface if no advanced use is needed. This ease of use in sharing Web page information and working with the Internet protocols has been central to the widespread acceptance and popularity of the World Wide Web.

NEW TERM A *browser* is a software program used to view HTML documents within the World Wide Web.

The World Wide Web is by far the most talked-about service on the Internet today. As you can see, it is only one of many services available to the user. This goal of this book is to teach you how to use VBScript to enhance Web pages. Because Web pages are used within the World Wide Web, we will be focusing on this Internet service. If, however, you want your users to have access to these other services from within your Web pages, you should become familiar with the other protocols as well. Suppose, for example, you want to be able to initiate an FTP session so that the user of your Web page can transfer a file; before you can do so, you need to know what FTP does and how to use it. You can learn more about these other Internet services and the Internet in general by reading *The Internet Unleashed 1996* by Sams.net Publishing.

The World Wide Web is an information system that brings together data from many of the other Internet services under one set of protocols. The World Wide Web began in March 1989 when a group of high-energy physics research groups wanted a new protocol for distributing information on the Internet. The European Laboratory for Particle Physics, or CERN, actually proposed the standards, and a consortium of organizations, called the W3 Consortium, was created for continuing to develop the standards. The consortium put together a set of protocols for the World Wide Web by creating the Hypertext Markup Language, or HTML. HTML is the underlying standard and means by which information is exchanged in the World Wide Web. In addition, various browser developers, most prominently Netscape and Microsoft, have at times extended HTML with their own additions. Essentially, the World Wide Web consists of HTML documents, or Web pages, which are delivered by Web servers and can be interpreted by Web clients, or *browsers*. The next section discusses the Web clients that actually interpret these HTML documents for the user.

Browsing the World Wide Web

As was stated in the previous section, users view information within the World Wide Web by using Web browsers. Before you begin designing the Web pages themselves, you need to be acquainted with the tools people use to view them. Users who access the Internet are not limited to a specific type of computer. It's no surprise, then, that a wide variety of computers and operating systems are supported by Web browsers, including Windows for personal computers, Macintosh for Apple's Macintosh computers, X Window for UNIX systems, and more. How does a browser work? The primary goal of a Web browser is to send and receive data from the Web server that provides the Web page. The underlying markup language used to define the content of pages in the World Wide Web is HTML. Therefore, the server sends the Web page in the HTML markup language, and the browser interprets that HTML code, presenting the page to the user. The next section discusses HTML in detail. Right now, take a look at the most commonly used browsers available today.

Mosaic

Mosaic, created by NCSA at the University of Illinois, was the first full-color, graphical browser available for the Internet. Because it was the first of its kind, Mosaic was the first glimpse many users got of the World Wide Web and likely fired the imagination of many a potential Web page designer. Before Netscape was introduced and dominated the market, Mosaic was the most popular browser available. Figure 1.3 shows a Mosaic session in Microsoft Windows.

Like most browsers today, Mosaic supports all of the popular Internet services, including FTP, Gopher, and Telnet, just to name a few. Mosaic is available for Microsoft Windows,

Macintosh, and X Window, titled WinMosaic, MacMosaic, and XMosaic, respectively. At the time of this printing, you can obtain each version via FTP at `ftp://ftp.ncsa.uiuc.edu/Mosaic`. A special version of Mosaic for CompuServe called CompuServe Mosaic-Spry was also available for CompuServe users at the time of this printing. Mosaic-Spry contains special features that tie together CompuServe and the Internet. For example, users can access CompuServe from within Mosaic-Spry through the use of a menu. This is convenient for CompuServe users who want to switch back and forth between CompuServe and the Internet.

Figure 1.3.

Mosaic for Microsoft Windows.

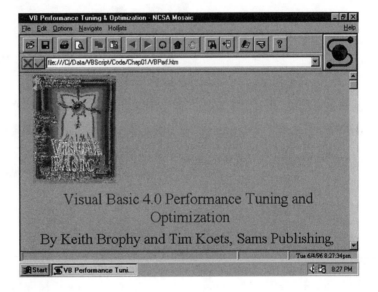

Netscape Navigator

Netscape Navigator, created by Netscape Corporation, is by far the most popular browser available today. One of the primary reasons for its success is that it is considerably faster than Mosaic, the once dominant browser. It also provides additional features that Mosaic does not have. Netscape is available on Windows, Macintosh, and X Window platforms. Figure 1.4 illustrates the main screen of a Netscape session.

Netscape is one of several browsers currently available that supports the Java language. The most recent version of Netscape contains specific extensions to HTML that provide much more control over the look and feel of a Web page. Many of these extensions were initially only supported by Netscape, although Microsoft's Internet Explorer 3.0 now supports many as well. Programmers who design Web pages using these extensions must remember that they will not operate with browsers that do not support them. At the time of this printing, you could obtain the latest copy of Netscape directly from the Netscape Communications FTP sites. Due to the popularity of this browser, there are almost 20 FTP sites available for downloading the Netscape browser. The addresses are `ftp://ftpx.netscape.com/`, where *x* is a number from 2 through 20, depending on the site you wish to access.

Figure 1.4.

Netscape for Microsoft Windows.

Internet Explorer

Internet Explorer is Microsoft's contribution to the Web browser community. The Internet Explorer is based on Microsoft's ActiveX technology and is available for Windows, Windows NT, and Macintosh platforms. As this browser gains acceptance while Microsoft expands its Internet efforts, Internet Explorer might challenge Netscape for domination of the browser market for Windows users. One significant capability of the Internet Explorer is that it supports embedded intrinsic and ActiveX controls within Web pages, which VBScript can interact with. This very important characteristic will be expanded upon in Days 8, "Intrinsic HTML Form Controls," 9, "More Intrinsic HTML Form Controls," 10, "An Introduction to Objects and ActiveX Controls," and 11, "More ActiveX Controls." Figure 1.5 shows Internet Explorer at work.

Microsoft's Internet Explorer was the first browser to support VBScript. As a result, Internet Explorer is used for most of the examples in this book. If you don't already have a copy, you should obtain one. Here are the steps you should follow to do so:

☐ First, download and install Microsoft's Internet Explorer 3.0. At the time of this printing, Internet Explorer 3.0 was still in beta and was available at `http://www.microsoft.com/ie`. Microsoft plans to provide Internet Explorer 3.0 with the Windows 95 Upgrade Pack slated for release in the fall of 1996. Until then, Microsoft's working beta is the only option available, and you must connect to Microsoft's Web site to download it.

Figure 1.5.

The Internet Explorer
Web browser.

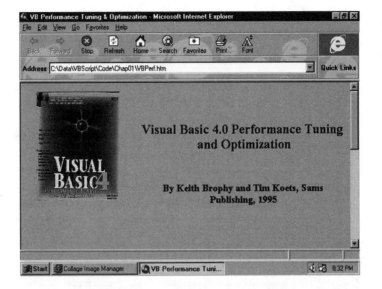

☐ In order to use ActiveX controls together with VBScript for the examples in this book, you must have access to the ActiveX controls used. Pages can be constructed to download the required controls from Microsoft's server when needed. However, to use the examples in this book with the beta Internet Explorer 3.0 you should initially download and install Microsoft's ActiveX Control Pack to obtain all the required controls at one time. At the time of this printing, the ActiveX Control Pack was still in beta and was available at `http://www.microsoft.com/ie/appdev/controls`. Microsoft plans to provide a complete suite of ActiveX controls with the Windows 95 Upgrade Pack slated for release in the fall of 1996. Until then, Microsoft's working beta is the only option available, and you must connect to Microsoft's Web site to download it.

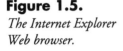

NOTE

Be sure you have Internet Explorer Version 3.0. Earlier versions of Internet Explorer do not support VBScript. If you have attempted to use VBScript before the official release of Internet Explorer 3.0, you had to use a beta copy available in the ActiveX Control Pack. With the release of the Windows 95 Upgrade Pack, you will be provided the official release of Internet Explorer.

NOTE Make sure you have the latest version of ActiveX controls on your system when using VBScript. Earlier versions of the ActiveX Control Kit may not work properly with the latest version of the Internet Explorer and VBScript.

The Internet Explorer capabilities are expected to eventually become an integrated part of future Microsoft Windows operating environments, and the underlying Internet services it requires will be built directly into the operating system. This means that in the future every user of Microsoft Windows will have easy access to these browser features and the corresponding VBScript support. This is one of the reasons that the Internet Explorer browser is viewed as a very strategic development platform when targeting Web page development, even though it currently has a significantly smaller share of the market than the Netscape browser.

Other Browsers

A variety of additional browsers are available, and because the Internet is evolving so rapidly, other new browsers may have come into existence since this book was printed. The core language capabilities of VBScript should be consistent under any browser that supports it because the definition of the language doesn't change and isn't dependent on the browser. However, VBScript can take advantage of the browser environment objects as well, and this may vary from browser to browser. The only requirement is that the browser supports VBScript. For any browser developer or provider who makes the request, Microsoft will provide a free license to the VBScript run-time code and even the source code so that they can make their browsers recognize and cooperate with VBScript. If you want more information on these efforts, refer to the VBScript white paper located on Microsoft's VBScript Web site, `http://www.microsoft.com/vbscript`. You can also refer to *The World Wide Web Unleashed 1996* (Sams.net Publishing) to learn more about other popular Internet browsers.

The Elements of the World Wide Web

The overall concept of the World Wide Web is an easy one to grasp once it's had some time to sink in. If you're a newcomer to the Web scene, getting the first, clear glimpse of the concepts can be a challenge! You've heard the old saying, "A picture's worth a thousand words." That's especially true when these words are an alphabet soup of protocols, buzzwords, and technologies. If you consider the simple analogy that follows, the concept of the World Wide Web should quickly come into focus. (See Figure 1.6.)

Figure 1.6.

Sending a Web page to a client.

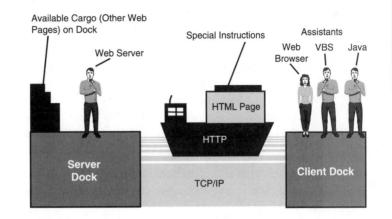

The two docks have a ship sailing from one dock to the other. The dock on the left is referred to as the "server dock" and the one on the right is the "client dock." The owner of the client dock wants to get some cargo from the server dock. The owner of the client dock sends over a ship and tells the captain of the ship to ask the server dock for a specific type of cargo. Once the ship gets over to the server dock, the worker on the server dock that handles such requests—the "Web server"—loads up the cargo that the client wants. The worker on the server dock knows that special unloading and handling will be needed once the cargo arrives at its destination, so he attaches those instructions to the cargo. Then, the ship sails on its way back over to the client.

When the ship arrives back at the client dock, a worker called the "Web browser" unloads the cargo. It turns out that the Web browser can unload cargo, but she doesn't know how to read the special instructions. Fortunately for her, a couple of assistants are on the dock to handle any special instructions that come their way. The Web browser, along with the assistants, Java and VBScript, unloads the cargo and then presents it to the owner of the client dock. The task is complete.

In real life, a similar sequence of events occurs. When you want to see a Web page, for instance, you first load your browser and then specify the name and address of the Web page you want to view, often referred to as a *uniform resource locator,* or URL. Once you've entered the URL, the browser connects to the server on which that Web page is found and asks the server to send over the Web page. Using the analogy, this is where the owner of the client dock sends a ship to the server dock requesting cargo. In the same way the cargo sits on the dock, a Web page resides on a server. To send a copy of the Web page over to the client, the Web page must travel across the Internet to the client. In the analogy, you can't get the cargo from the server dock to the client dock without two things—a ship to transport the cargo and water for the ship to travel through. Likewise, data can't get from one host to another on the Internet without a transport mechanism and a pathway for that transfer to take place.

NEW TERM A *uniform resource locator (URL)* is an address that identifies a resource on the Web.

As with any analogy, you can only take things so far. One thing to keep in mind when using this analogy is that, in reality, a Web page is not actually moved from one site to another. A *copy* of the page is sent from the server to the client. Picture an unlimited supply of stock on the dock where copies are lifted onto the ship whenever requested. The inventory won't get depleted. However, just as a dock can get very busy and arriving ships might have to wait their turn, a busy server can get overloaded and be slow in responding to Web page requests.

Now, take a look at each element of the Internet that works together to get a Web page from a server to a client. It's really not that complicated once you see how all the pieces fit together.

TCP/IP: The Way Data Moves Through the World Wide Web

The water in the ship analogy is representative of the Internet's means for communication, called the *Transmission Control Protocol/Internet Protocol,* or TCP/IP. TCP/IP takes care of successfully routing the information from one site to another. The beauty of the World Wide Web is that you, the user, are shielded from most of these inner workings. The protocol sets up an address for each site called an *IP address.* The IP address consists of four 8-bit numbers separated by dots and is sometimes called the *dot address.* For example, the address of the Internet site that holds information about this book and any late-breaking updates is 205.132.48.137. An IP address typically identifies a network card to which a connection is made; as a result, each IP address must be unique. TCP/IP also establishes for every server entity on the Internet an *IP machine name.* The name www.doubleblaze.com, which corresponds to 205.132.48.137, is one example of an IP machine name. The IP machine name is part of the URL that you enter into your browser when you want to view a Web page. When you type the URL, which includes the machine name, into the browser, the name is resolved by returning an IP address for the browser to connect to. All of this is transparent to the user. All you have to do is enter the URL of the Web page you want to see. Taken together, all the components of TCP/IP work together to get you to where you want to go on the Internet, much like the water in our analogy.

HTTP: The Way Data Is Transported Through the World Wide Web

The ship in the analogy represents the *Hypertext Transfer Protocol,* or HTTP. You typically enter http as the first part of any URL on the World Wide Web. HTTP is the protocol that enables Web clients and Web servers to communicate over TCP/IP. HTTP consists of a set

1

of rules by which data such as HTML documents, represented by the cargo on the ship, gets transmitted between Web clients and Web servers. The cargo carried by the ship in Figure 1.6 can consist of Web pages, which are HTML documents, as well as other data. It matters little to the ship what type of cargo it is carrying; the job of the ship is simply to get the cargo from one dock to the other without damaging the cargo. Likewise, the goal of HTTP is to work with TCP/IP to get the data from the server to the client free from corruption.

NEW TERM The *Hypertext Transfer Protocol (HTTP)* is a protocol used to transfer HTML documents across the World Wide Web. HTTP is the native protocol of the Web.

HTML: The Language of the World Wide Web

As mentioned in the previous section, one type of cargo the ship can carry is HTML documents. HTML documents, or Web pages, are the most common type of cargo that HTTP sends through the World Wide Web. It is easy to get HTML confused with HTTP. Keep in mind that HTTP is the set of rules used to transport HTML documents as well as other data. The analogy in Figure 1.6 should help you to keep these concepts straight. We will explore the structure of HTML much more in Day 2, where you will learn how to embed VBScript code into an HTML document. Consider the analogy once again: Once the cargo arrives at the dock, it must be unloaded. This is the job of the attendant standing at the dock— call that person the Web browser. This attendant presents the cargo to the customer. Likewise, the real Web browser takes the HTML code and makes it presentable on-screen to the user. This is how the user is then able to see the Web page. HTML and the information viewed by the user can be extended using ActiveX controls, VBScript, and other languages such as Java.

Extending the World Wide Web with VBScript

In Figure 1.6, the Web page cargo has special unloading instructions attached to it. These special instructions aren't written in a language the Web browser can understand, so she can't handle them directly. Fortunately, the Web browser has a couple of assistants on the dock with her whose job it is to handle these special instructions. When the cargo gets to the dock, the Web browser passes these special instructions to the assistants, who in turn help her handle the cargo.

In the ship analogy, these special instructions attached to the HTML document represent the interpreters for scripting languages such as VBScript and JavaScript. When you design a Web page, you package these special instructions in the form of code inside the HTML document. Then, when the Web page gets to the client, the Web browser has to be able to recognize the special instructions and have those assistants on-hand to process them.

JavaScript behaves similarly to VBScript in that it uses an interpreter to take the special instructions and execute them on the client computer. The scripting tools differ, however, in that Java is somewhat based on C/C++, whereas VBScript is based on Visual Basic. Furthermore, each tool has a different set of features and capabilities. A great number of Internet users who want to develop Web pages and already use Visual Basic will find VBScript extremely easy to use. Even those who have never used Visual Basic will find VBScript easy to learn as compared to the more complex C++-like language of JavaScript.

Microsoft ActiveX and ActiveX Controls

In an effort to facilitate development of Internet Web pages and applications, Microsoft introduced a set of standards, definitions, and beta software components called the ActiveX Development Kit in early 1996. This set of technologies marked a major technology focus affecting many areas of World Wide Web–related client and server technology as well as Windows itself. ActiveX is a framework that includes VBScript, ActiveX documents, ActiveX controls, and other layers and technology specifications as well. Within this new framework, it is easy to make the once static pages on the Web active. A page can essentially become a blend of HTML, embedded Java or VBScript, and ActiveX controls, OLE controls, and Java applets that the code language interacts with.

Microsoft's OLE (object linking and embedding) controls had been in use in the Windows world for some time prior to the introduction of the ActiveX terminology. OLE controls provide powerful, component-based capabilities and are easily incorporated into other programs through the OLE communication, control, data storage, and automation protocol. The ActiveX control technology specification is the new generation of OLE controls. While many ActiveX controls are being developed specifically for Internet-related purposes, ActiveX controls are not restricted to just Internet purposes.

The ActiveX Internet client technology first appeared in Microsoft Internet Explorer 3.0. VBScript is a part of this technology, so it can interact with ActiveX controls. By taking advantage of ActiveX controls, you can greatly extend the power of your Web pages. Many ActiveX controls are available from Microsoft, and any other developer can produce his own ActiveX controls. The end result is a wealth of building blocks that you can blend with VBScript into a powerful, active Web page. A significant part of being an effective VBScript programmer, then, is knowing how to leverage these controls.

Extending the World Wide Web with CGI

Thus far, discussion has focused on scripting tools that reside on the client's computer, interpreting special instructions intended to extend the functionality of a Web page. In addition to residing on the client, a certain type of scripting tool can also reside on the server.

Although scripting tools on the server serve a different purpose from those on the client, they are often very useful and sometimes necessary for advanced Web pages—for instance, when a user has a Web page that enables her to perform a search for pages that contain a keyword she supplies to the page. The HTML document itself isn't capable of doing a search because it doesn't know what's contained in other Web pages. Assume, however, that the server contains an entire database of Web pages. It would be convenient for the client page to have the server perform the search and report back the results. Doing so requires that the client request such a search from the server. The *Common Gateway Interface*, or CGI, was created for that purpose. ISAPI, OLE ISAPI, and IDC are somewhat similar technologies that can be used with Microsoft NT Server scripts. For now, we'll limit the focus to CGI, although the communication concepts described largely hold true to the other technologies as well. Refer to the familiar analogy of a ship sailing between two docks. The analogy so far is based on the server sending out information to the client in response to standard requests for cargo. In this case, however, you want the client to request from the server special information that must be custom-made. Once the server creates this cargo, it sends it to the client. The server can either send a standard Web page or special information requested by CGI that the server creates. Figure 1.7 shows the modified analogy.

NEW TERM The *Common Gateway Interface (CGI)* is a standard that allows programs to interface with the Web servers. This gives Web users the ability to interact with Web server programs in order to accomplish useful tasks such as database storage and retrieval.

Figure 1.7.

Sending a CGI script to the server.

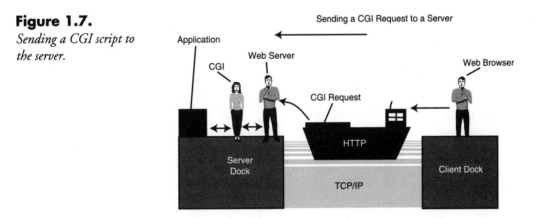

In this case, the Web browser places the request for special cargo on the ship, the ship then transports the request to the Web server, and the Web server unloads the request and passes it on to CGI for special processing. Once CGI gets the request, it determines the application it needs to call and calls it. Sometimes, the application is like a toolbox that enables the Web server to handcraft brand new cargo to send back to the client. The application gets the data and returns it to CGI, which then passes the results over to the Web server. The Web server then takes the results and passes them back to the Web browser.

CGI, like HTTP, is a protocol that is explicitly designed to interact with an HTTP server. Through a CGI request, the client can request that the server start a CGI script or application, pass parameter data to it, and then return the result from the application. CGI scripts can be written for a variety of servers with languages such as Perl, TCI, or the UNIX shell for UNIX-based platforms. On many Windows-based HTTP servers, a CGI extension layer called WinCGI also makes it possible to call Visual Basic programs. ISAPI, OLE ISAPI, and IDC are other high-performance technologies that can be used for NT Server scripting solutions. OLE ISAPI, like WinCGI, makes it easy to build a Visual Basic program that serves as a server-side script. All such scripting tools work very closely with HTTP servers. Once the server application has done the required work and obtained results, those results can be passed back to the client as HTML text. The server must therefore be able to exchange information with both the client and the application on the server using the CGI protocol.

CGI makes it possible for Web page users to ask the server to perform operations not available to the client. In order to maintain security, VBScript can only perform operations within the Web page; it cannot, for example, store data on the client, nor can it directly store data back on the server to a remote database. Typically, a Web page will rely on CGI services to get data back to the server. On the server's end, CGI capabilities complement the processing of VBScripts on the client's end. For example, a VBScript might process and validate user input, and then CGI might be used to store that data in the host database on the server.

As you can see, CGI and similar technologies offer a very powerful capability to make pages interact with the server. As you learn to use VBScript, you will begin to see the potential for such technologies as they work together with VBScript to enhance a Web page. With the combined power of VBScript and CGI or ISAPI, the programmatic possibilities behind a Web page are virtually unlimited!

The term *script* is commonly used in several contexts when talking about Web pages. VBScript can be used to build "intelligent" Web pages that carry out processing on the user's computer when the user views a page. JavaScript offers similar capabilities. These are called *Web page scripts*.

You can also have *server-side scripts* that carry out action on the server where the Web page files reside. These server-side scripts can be triggered into action by actions on the user's computer when viewing a page, if a page is set up accordingly. Regular Visual Basic (that is, Visual Basic 4.0), among other languages, can be used to write such server-side scripts. It can be expected that eventually VBScript will also be supported on the server and can be used to provide server-side scripting.

The focus of this book is on Web page scripts written in VBScript for the Internet Explorer browser environment. However, the information presented here about VBScript will be of use in dealing with scripts in other environments as well.

NOTE

This book is based on the beta release of Internet Explorer 3.0. Certain features may change with the release of the final product. Late-breaking update information on the final product may be available under the Macmillan Publishing site `www.mcp.com` (then follow the Sams.net selections). This information may also be found under the CNS server at `www.doubleblaze.com/vbs21day`.

Summary

The Internet is an exciting forum that makes it possible for users to access virtually an infinite supply of information. This lesson presents you with an overview of the Internet and, specifically, the World Wide Web. Reading it, you first learned a bit about what the Internet is and why it's so popular. Then, you learned about the variety of services the Internet has to offer—in particular, the World Wide Web. This lesson discusses the World Wide Web, pointing out how the World Wide Web fits into the Internet. Furthermore, the lesson gives you a brief but comprehensive overview of the major browsers on the market today. The lesson then shows you, with the help of an analogy, all of the pieces of the World Wide Web and how they all fit together to get information from one place to another. Specifically, the lesson discusses how ActiveX and VBScript fit into the scheme of the Internet and, particularly, the World Wide Web. On the days that follow, we will discuss VBScript itself, showing you how to embed script into HTML code and extend the power and capabilities of Web pages.

Q&A

Q Does any browser that supports HTML also support VBScript?

A Not necessarily, although some day almost all of the popular browsers should. Since VBScript is a new technology, it may take some time before all browsers support it. As VBScript becomes more popular, browser developers will want to respond to the demands of Web page designers and Web users, and VBScript will become widely supported!

Q Does VBScript replace HTML?

A Absolutely not. HTML is the foundation upon which Web pages are built. VBScript complements an already existing Web page by making it more powerful and extending its capabilities. You will get first-hand experience at seeing how VBScript enhances Web pages as you continue reading this book.

Q Why can't VBScript access files on the client system?

A The ability of VBScript to directly access files on the client computer presents a huge security risk. A Web page could, for example, use VBScript to delete or modify files on a client computer—a chance nobody would likely want to take. Furthermore, VBScript is intended to work with OLE and Internet OLE Controls that live inside a Web page. VBScript is not intended to venture beyond the Web page except through these controls. CGI can be used for that type of interaction on the server, and CGI has much better mechanisms for security.

Workshop

If you haven't already done so, install and become familiar with as many browsers as you can. Pay particular attention to the Microsoft Internet Explorer, since this browser will be used for most of the examples in this book. The more familiar you are with the browsers available for the Internet, the more you will appreciate what the World Wide Web provides you and what you can do with VBScript.

Quiz

NOTE Refer to Appendix C, "Answers to Quiz Questions," for the answers to these questions.

1. What are the most popular services available on the Internet?
2. What is the name of the language on which Web pages are built?
3. Is VBScript a part of this language? If not, how does VBScript run?

□ Is VBScript easy to learn?

□ What do I have to know to use VBScript?

□ What software or tools do I need to use it?

□ How secure is VBScript?

□ How does it compare to Visual Basic and Visual Basic for Applications?

You will also find several examples of Web pages that use VBScript so that you can see just how powerful and revolutionary VBScript really is. Think of today as a friendly introduction to the world of Internet programming with VBScript. You won't get hit with a lot of techno-jargon in this lesson, but you will see just what you can do with this new and exciting language.

What Is VBScript?

When the World Wide Web first became popular, HTML was the only language program-mers could use to create Web pages. They soon learned that HTML was quite limited in what it could do. It presented the user with a "page" of information, but the Web page and the user had a limited amount of interaction; it was like reading the front page of a newspaper on a computer monitor. Now most computer users, whether they use Windows, Macintosh, UNIX, or a combination of the three, are accustomed to graphical applications that provide interaction. They're used to clicking buttons, entering values into text boxes, and choosing from menus. The only way to get useful work done with a computer is to interact with it. The first generation of Web pages provided information to the users, but the users could not interact with the Web the way they could with their word processors. The interaction available to them required that they send the data to the server, where all the "smarts" were provided. The results were then sent back to the Web page. This interaction required a great deal of extra time, effort, and overhead, and the interface presented to the user was very constrained compared to the applications they were accustomed to using.

Fortunately, the builders of the Internet and the World Wide Web could see these limitations. They soon realized that if the user was denied the capability to interact with the Web page, it would become little more than a collection of information, much like a library of books. Although that collection is very useful, users demand more from their computers than what they could get elsewhere. The capabilities of HTML began to grow and become more powerful. Soon, designers began to realize that they needed more than just HTML to make the Internet accessible and useful to the masses. Corporations who wanted to develop enterprise solutions or make money off the Internet also began to put pressure on designers to give them something more.

These demands have resulted in a continued improvement of HTML, the emergence of browsers such as Internet Explorer that tap into the power of HTML, and the advent of scripting languages such as VBScript. To understand what a *scripting language* is, think

2

Week 1

Day 2

The Essence of VBScript

You've probably seen and heard a lot of excitement surrounding Microsoft's new Internet development platform and suite of Internet tools. This new technology is indeed very exciting to almost everyone in the computer industry today. When any new technology emerges, it takes time for the technology to "settle down." The creators of the technology first fill the airwaves with hype and send out beta copies of what they're working on. Finally, a solid release of the product emerges, and builders can actually start making full use of the technology that has been discussed for so long. After that, it takes a certain amount of time for the intended users of that technology to adjust to how it works and how to use it.

If you've heard a lot about VBScript and what it can do but you've been bombarded with so much new information that it's hard to absorb it all, you're not alone. Today's lesson was written for you! It will clearly and methodically explain to you the essence of VBScript—that is, what it's all about. Rather than drop a load of technical bombs that only a rocket scientist can understand, I explain in plain English why VBScript is exciting and what it can do for you. Here is a list of some of the questions I will answer today:

☐ What is VBScript?

☐ What can it do?

of HTML as an airport runway. You can get where you need to go on the ground, but you have an entire sky to travel through above you. Scripting languages are like the airplanes that make it possible for you to lift off the ground. They extend the capabilities of the Web much like an airplane extends the capabilities of man so he can travel through the sky. A script lets the page become an active, dynamic piece of software rather than a static piece of content.

NEW TERM A *scripting language* is a type of programming language used to provide control in another host environment. It is interpreted rather than compiled. This means that a program built with a scripting language must be run in the environment that contains the scripting language's interpreter and cannot be run as a stand-alone application.

HTML can't interpret a scripting language itself, but it knows enough to call the interpreter of the scripting language to carry out the interpretation. This enables you to go above and beyond HTML, using any browser-supported scripting language you want to extend the Web page. With scripting languages such as VBScript, the limitations of HTML disappear; the opportunities are now limited only by the scripting language itself! Although other scripting languages are bound to emerge, two widely used scripting languages in existence today are JavaScript and VBScript. Both of these languages can be embedded in a Web page, and if the browser supports them, they provide the path to smart, active programs that are part of that page.

With HTML, you can place controls such as buttons and text boxes on a Web page. Without a scripting language such as VBScript, any actions the user takes on the controls of a Web page must be sent back to the Web page server. They cannot be handled at the user's computer. Furthermore, the amount of control and flexibility available without a scripting language is very limited. With VBScript, you not only can link up to controls on the Web page, but you can also write code to respond to what the user does with those controls. If, for example, a Web page contains a command button, you can write VBScript code that gets executed immediately when the user clicks that button. An example of such a code segment might look like the following:

```
Sub Button_OnClick
    ' The message below will be displayed when the user clicks on the button
    Msgbox "This button was clicked"
End Sub
```

Button is the name of the button, and OnClick is the event that the user causes to occur when he or she clicks the button. You can supply code, such as the message statement shown here, to be executed every time the user clicks the button. The MsgBox statement, which will be covered in more detail on Day 14, "Working with Documents and User Interface Functions," simply presents a message box to the user. This example is simple, but it shows how VBScript code can give a page the capability to respond immediately to user actions. Rather than present the user with a lifeless Web page, VBScript breathes life into Web pages, making them dynamic, responsive, intelligent, and interactive.

What Can VBScript Do?

VBScript lets the user interact with a Web page rather than simply view it. There are many possible scenarios for this interaction. For instance, this capability to interact makes it possible for Web pages to ask questions and respond to how the user answers them. VBScript can then take input from the user and check the data to make sure it is valid or meets certain criteria. Then, it can put an Internet server to work either by actually storing the data or causing some action to take place on the server based on the information given. For example, VBScript could respond to a user's request for an airline reservation. It could read in the data, check to make sure all fields have been filled out and that the phone number and zip code are in a valid format, inform the user of the estimated price, and then notify the server of the reservation. All these tasks could be carried out by the code in the Web page that was downloaded across the Internet as it sits on the user's client PC. The server in turn would make sure there is an open slot for the customer for when he wants a ticket and then book the flight and get tickets out in the mail to the customer.

Interaction can also be helpful in advertising services or products to a user. Through an interactive survey, you can target exactly what the potential customer is looking for. Imagine, for example, a series of Web pages that ask you all kinds of questions about your dream car, along with what you want to spend, and then give you a series of vehicles that match your criteria. Rather than dealing with a pushy salesperson, you can take your time on the Internet and carefully research the facts. When you go to the dealer, you can be specific and avoid having to wrestle with a salesperson.

In this type of example, VBScript can play an important role in many ways, including validating data, pricing, providing impressive multimedia feedback, and initiating data storage. You can use VBScript to sequence the questions based on responses. For example, if a user indicates he wants a van, VBScript can generate an input box asking him how many seats he wants. Throughout the data entry process, VBScript can make sure the user enters a valid order, address, and method of payment, and it can even present him with a pie chart of how much of the cost goes toward the base price and how much goes toward extras. The generation of the bar graph can be accompanied by the sound of a trumpet fanfare. The possibilities are endless.

VBScript can also perform calculations on data, such as computing the cost of an item after taking into account the sales tax. Often, calculations on a Web page are useful in providing the user a way of figuring out what he wants to do, or perhaps giving the user some sort of result he is seeking. In this way, your Web page enables the user to walk away with more than a mere presentation of fixed information. You could, for example, allow the user to choose what luxury items he wants on a car and, as the luxury items are selected, keep adjusting the overall cost. The user could spend as much time as he wants and choose as many combinations as he likes until the perfect combination of features versus price is calculated. How often can you do that at a car dealership?

By utilizing other technologies such as CGI, VBScript code can even initiate order placement for that item in the computer of the company that is selling the item. If the script determines all criteria for a valid order are met, it can place the order. Otherwise, it can generate an error message. Using script logic, it could even place the order on a different server, depending on which type of car was requested, and provide an estimated time frame for delivery based on a rules-of-thumb calculation for that type of order. Visual Basic can carry out virtually anything you can think of that a traditional application could carry out. Even in areas where Visual Basic can't directly cause some action such as writing to the server database or playing a sound file, it can achieve these results indirectly by making use of CGI scripts or sound controls, for example. Visual Basic becomes the application behind the Web page that the user views and interacts with.

Another important aspect of this programming model is that you can also use the intrinsic HTML form controls and Microsoft's ActiveX controls with VBScript to give Web pages an attractive look and feel. Intrinsic HTML form controls, which are discussed in Days 8, "Intrinsic HTML Form Controls," and 9, "More Intrinsic HTML Form Controls," provide the Web page developer with a standard set of controls similar to those used in the Windows environment. ActiveX controls, which are discussed in Days 10, "An Introduction to Objects and ActiveX Controls," and 11, "More ActiveX Controls," consist of useful controls such as graphs and charts, labels that can be rotated 360 degrees, "new" banners that can remain on a Web page for however many days you want, a timer control that enables you to time events on Web pages, a pre-load control that lets you load bitmaps and other time-consuming parts of a Web page before it gets displayed, and so on. These controls further enhance Web pages to give them a professional, polished look. They also provide pages with smarter interactive response because the control characteristics can be controlled dynamically by a Visual Basic program. For example, your code can generate a new graph based on the user's input on a page.

You can also use Microsoft's vast array of OLE controls in VBScript, which opens up a whole world of possibilities for Web pages. Designers can now place ActiveX custom controls directly on Web pages in the Windows environment. OCXs, the forerunner of ActiveX controls, have made languages such as Visual Basic incredibly powerful because programmers can take an OCX that performs some task for them, such as displaying a calendar on the screen, and "glue" that component into the application. They don't have to create code to put a calendar on the screen; the OCX already does that for them. Likewise, programmers can now put an ActiveX control on a Web page and access the control through VBScript. The goal is to make Web pages capable of what a regular Windows application can do. There are some restrictions on what can be achieved due to security (addressed in Day 21, "Security, Stability, and Distributed Source Control Issues"), but the technology is rapidly moving in that direction. The Internet might someday be the "platform" that all our applications rest upon and work within.

In addition to using ActiveX controls, the current beta version of VBScript can also tie other applications into a Web page through OLE automation technology. For example, with the appropriate object declarations, you could tie an Excel spreadsheet into your Web page so that when the user clicks on the spreadsheet, Microsoft Excel runs and loads the spreadsheet for you to edit. Now, not only can you work within a Web page, but you can bring other applications into the Web page that can be activated at the click of a mouse button. This capability to tie other applications to a Web page lets you show virtually anything on a Web page; the only requirement is that the applications you want to link to a page support the OLE automation standard.

With VBScript and the right controls, you can even create 3-D animation effects, making your Web page come alive with moving objects in response to certain events. You can use animation to make cars careen across the screen, butterflies fly across your Web page, or arrows move and point to where you want the user to interact with the Web page. Although this might seem quite esoteric, animation does help attract the users' attention and makes them feel like they're working with a living, breathing entity. They're more likely to explore your Web page and stay tuned in to it when a lot of neat animated effects grab their attention.

The component incorporation capabilities of VBScript introduce some special considerations and trade-offs in page design. A Web page that includes VBScript code that interacts with Excel and Microsoft Word, as well as the currently Windows-specific ActiveX controls, is not one that can be fully distributed over the Internet with all the support software. It also might not run easily on any platform and operating system that could use it. On the other hand, such a page would be very powerful for Internet or intranet users who fit the target user profile. At the other end of the spectrum, a page that incorporates VBScript to carry out a series of calculations can be a perfect Internet citizen, fully downloadable over the Internet and running on a variety of platforms and operating systems. In this respect, the flavor and tone of your VBScript Web pages depends largely on how you want to leverage it. This is an important theme that we discuss throughout the remaining days' lessons.

> **NOTE** Microsoft may support ActiveX controls on other environments such as the PowerMac in the future, but they are currently supported only in the Windows environment.

In order to gain a more complete understanding of how VBScript works with browsers, controls, and objects, consider the simple model shown in Figure 2.1.

In this model, the innermost box is where the core language of the scripting language resides (in this case VBScript). Other languages such as JavaScript could be placed in this box as well. This core language cannot be run alone—it must be provided with a host that supports it. This leads to the second, larger box in the figure.

Figure 2.1.

A simple diagram of the VBScript-host model.

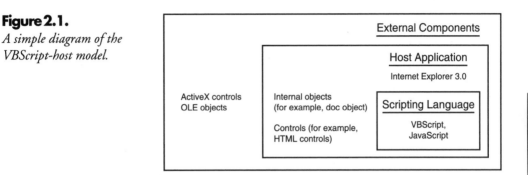

2

The second, larger box represents the host program that runs the scripting language. At the time of this printing, VBScript could be used with Microsoft Internet Explorer 3.0, which in this case would be the host. While the host may vary, the core VBScript language stays the same. In other words, the VBScript language is the same regardless of the host, whether it be Internet Explorer or any other product. The host may contain a set of internal objects and controls, such as the case with Internet Explorer 3.0. For example, you can access Internet Explorer's *document object* from VBScript, which will be discussed further on Day 10. You can also access Internet Explorer's intrinsic HTML controls through VBScript (this is discussed on Day 8). Any scripting language, such as JavaScript, has the same type and level of access to these browser objects and controls as does VBScript.

The third box represents components external to the browser but available in the Windows environment, such as ActiveX controls, OLE controls, and objects such as OLE automation servers. VBScript can access these controls and objects through the browser, as illustrated by Figure 2.1. In order for VBScript to access a control at this level, it must be linked through the host. Each link of the chain must be complete before VBScript can access any objects or controls throughout the chain. Since the browser is a secure environment, the user will be presented with appropriate warnings before a control is used by a script if default browser options are in place.

It's important to remember that any scripting language operates using this model. JavaScript, another powerful scripting language, would occupy the same position in the figure as VBScript does. This means that any scripting language has access to the browser's controls and objects as well as the system's controls and objects if supported by the browser.

The variety of controls and technologies that surround the World Wide Web is likely to increase dramatically over the next several years. Although it can be quite dizzying to keep up with the changes and new controls on the market, it's an exciting time to be a part of the Internet revolution. Now that you have a glimpse of the power of VBScript and the technologies that surround it, take a look at the examples in the next section. They will help you see some of what VBScript is capable of!

Some Examples of VBScript in Action

To help you appreciate and understand the power that VBScript gives you, I provide three simple examples in this lesson. Each example is on the CD-ROM that accompanies this book. You might want to load them into your browser and take a look at them for yourself. All of the examples presented here are very simple, but they help give you a taste of what lies ahead for you in building your own Web pages.

NOTE

You can run samples in this book over the Internet as well as from the CD-ROM provided with the book. Refer to Appendix B, "Information Resources," for details on where to find the samples on the World Wide Web.

Example #1: The DiscoTec Web Page

Imagine, for the moment, that you're the proud owner of a music store, and business is booming. You're always interested in more business, and you see tremendous potential in the Internet to help you sell your product. In fact, you want to do more than simply advertise; you want your customers to be able to figure the cost of the music they want to order over the Internet! This first example shows what you can do to make that possible. Take a look at the Web page shown in Figure 2.2, where you see a "costing form" page that lets the user calculate the cost of an order of music.

Figure 2.2.

The DiscoTec Web page.

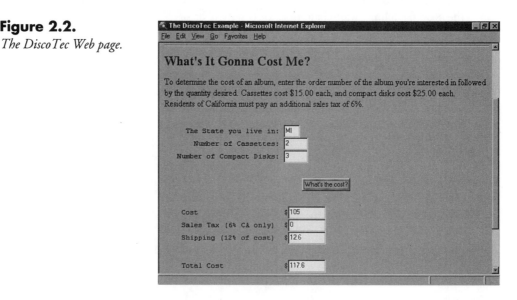

This page appears to the user after you have presented him or her with one or more pages showing the selection of music you offer. You could even get fancy and show a picture of each album cover and, when the user clicks on the cover, play a sample of the music contained on the album. You will see more about the concepts of using controls for such purposes on Days 10 and 11.

As you can see, the user enters his home state along with the number of cassettes or compact discs he wants. Then he clicks the What's the Cost? button. When the user clicks this button, the Web browser initiates VBScript code that calculates the cost for shipping and handling, adds in the sales tax, and presents the user with the total cost.

NOTE   This Web page, named discotec.htm, can be found on the CD-ROM that accompanies this book.

Listing 2.1 shows the Web page source code, which includes the VBScript code that gets executed when the user clicks the What's the Cost? button.

Listing 2.1. The HTML source code for the DiscoTec Web page.

```
<HTML>

<HEAD>
<TITLE>The DiscoTec Example</TITLE>
</HEAD>

<BODY>

<H1>
<A HREF="http://www.mcp.com"><IMG  ALIGN=BOTTOM
SRC="../shared/jpg/samsnet.jpg" BORDER=2></A>
<EM>The DiscoTec Music Company</EM></H1>
<HR>

<H2>What's It Gonna Cost Me?</H2>
<P>To determine the cost of an album, enter the order number of the album
you're interested in followed by the quantity desired. Cassettes cost
$15.00 each, and compact disks cost $25.00 each. Residents of California must
pay an additional sales tax of 6%.

<PRE>
     The State you live in: <INPUT NAME="txtState" SIZE=2>
        Number of Cassettes: <INPUT NAME="txtCassettes" SIZE=5>
   Number of Compact Disks: <INPUT NAME="txtDisks" SIZE=5>

</PRE>
```

continues

Listing 2.1. continued

```
<CENTER><B><INPUT TYPE=BUTTON VALUE="What's the cost?" NAME="cmdCost">
</B></CENTER>

<PRE>
    Cost                      $<INPUT NAME="txtCost" SIZE=10>
    Sales Tax (6% CA only)    $<INPUT NAME="txtTax" SIZE=10>
    Shipping (12% of cost)    $<INPUT NAME="txtShipping" SIZE=10>
<BR>
    Total Cost                $<INPUT NAME="txtTotal" SIZE=10>
</PRE>

<HR>

<center>
From <em>Teach Yourself VBScript in 21 Days</em> by
<A HREF="../shared/info/keith.htm">Keith Brophy</A> and
<A HREF="../shared/info/tim.htm">Tim Koets</A><br>
Return to <a href="..\default.htm">Content Overview</A><br>
Copyright 1996 by SamsNet<br>
</center>

<SCRIPT LANGUAGE="VBScript">
<!-- Option Explicit

    Sub cmdCost_OnClick()

        Dim State
        Dim Cassettes
        Dim Disks
        Dim Cost
        Dim Tax
        Dim Shipping
        Dim Total

        Cassettes = txtCassettes.Value
        Disks = txtDisks.Value
        State = txtState.Value

        If Cassettes = "" Then
           Cassettes = 0
        Else
           Cassettes = CInt(Cassettes)
        End If

        If Disks = "" Then
           Disks = 0
        Else
           Disks = CInt(Disks)
        End If

        If Cassettes + Disks = 0 Then
           MsgBox "You must enter at least one cassette or disk."
           Exit Sub
        End If
```

```
    Cost = 15.00 * Cassettes + 25.00 * Disks

    If State = "CA" Then
        Tax = Cost * 0.06
    Else
        Tax = 0
    End If

    Shipping = Cost * 0.12

    Total = Cost + Tax + Shipping

    txtCost.Value = Cost
    txtTax.Value = Tax
    txtShipping.Value = Shipping
    txtTotal.Value = Total

  End Sub

-->
</SCRIPT>

</BODY>
</HTML>
```

ANALYSIS   If the code doesn't make any sense to you, don't worry—it doesn't have to yet. You can see, however, that a fairly small amount of code is needed to do the calculations for the total cost of the items, and it's all accomplished on the user's computer. Without a scripting language, this kind of application would be impossible on the user's computer; the data would have to be transmitted back to the server, calculated there, and sent back. That would take considerably more time because of all the delay in getting the information back and forth, not to mention the overhead required to carry out the transaction.

One of the powerful benefits of VBScript is its capability to ensure the validity of the data the user enters. Suppose, for example, that the user enters a negative number for the quantity of an item. Obviously, this is an invalid amount. Fortunately, VBScript can validate the data the user enters. If, for example, the user doesn't enter a quantity either for cassettes or CDs, the message shown in Figure 2.3 appears when the user tries to calculate the cost.

This example shows you how you can make a Web page intelligent with VBScript. In addition to presenting a Web page that shows simple text and graphics, you can also truly interact with the Web page. Not only can you retrieve and process data entered by the user, but you can also perform checks to make sure the information he enters is valid, and if it isn't valid, you can take the steps necessary to make sure he enters the information correctly.

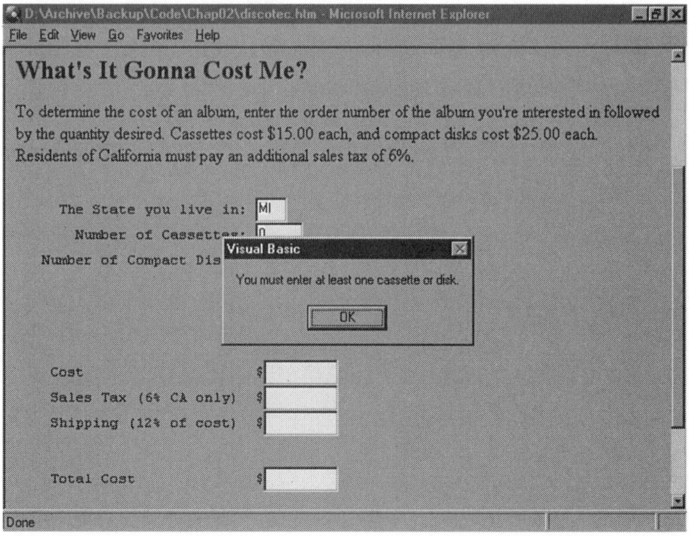

Figure 2.3.
What happens when the user forgets to enter the quantity.

Example #2: The Pace Pal

This next example of VBScript is very useful to a runner, jogger, or walker. You can use the Web page in this example to calculate your pace from a running, jogging, or walking workout. All the user has to do is enter the distance traveled and the time it took to travel that distance. Then, VBScript code calculates the pace and displays it back to the user. Figure 2.4 shows the Web page.

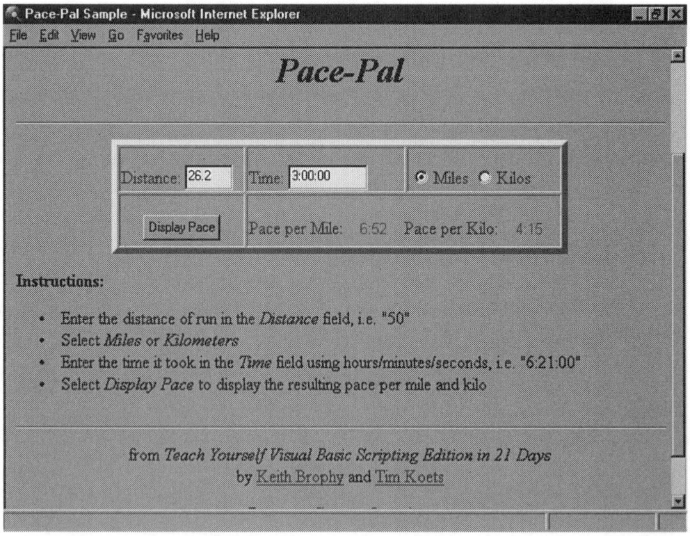

Figure 2.4.
The Pace-Pal Web page.

Figure 2.4 shows a text box where the user enters the distance traveled. He must choose the units of travel as either miles or kilometers. Notice the two special controls to the left of the text box. You use these special controls, called *radio buttons*, to limit the user to selecting one of the choices. VBScript can interact fully with controls such as these. You are not merely limited to text boxes and buttons as in the first example. Radio buttons, along with other important controls, will be discussed on Day 8.

Having entered the distance, the user then enters the time in the designated text box. Once the data is entered correctly, the user clicks the Display Pace button, which starts the calculation of the runner's pace. The result is displayed in miles and kilometers as shown on the page. This example once again shows you the benefits of VBScript. The pace calculation can be done entirely on the user's computer with no Internet involvement. Once the page is loaded into the browser, VBScript does the rest. You could, in fact, even disconnect from the Internet and use this page offline.

NOTE
> This Web page, named `pacepal.htm`, is also on the CD-ROM that comes with the book.

This example shows you how you can design Web pages to assist the user in some way. In a sense, a Web page can become an application delivered over the Internet. Before the Web page phenomenon grew so popular, you would probably write such an application using C or BASIC. Then, you might distribute the application as shareware. With the World Wide Web and VBScript, however, anyone who uses the Internet has instant access to your application, and it appears very attractively on a Web page. If you want to share your application with friends across the country, it's much easier for you to point them all to your Web page rather than send each of them a copy of it.

Example #3: The Bird Feeder

The last example today is a simple Web page that provides assistance to the user and helps advertise a product at the same time. This Web page is targeted to your average cockatiel owner. It determines just how much bird seed you need to feed your cockatiel each day over the next month. By the way, this example is purely fictitious, so please don't base your own cockatiel's diet on the results! Figure 2.5 shows the Web page.

This simple Web page asks the user for the age, sex, activity level, and weight of your cockatiel. Notice that when you enter the sex of the bird, you can only choose Male or Female through the use of the special radio button controls. When you enter the activity level of the bird, you can choose from a variety of selections that are contained in a special control called a *list box*. The list box gives you the ability to select one of several choices, but you cannot enter a new choice like you can in a text box. On Day 8, you will learn more about list box controls and how to use them.

Figure 2.5.

The Bird Feeder Web page.

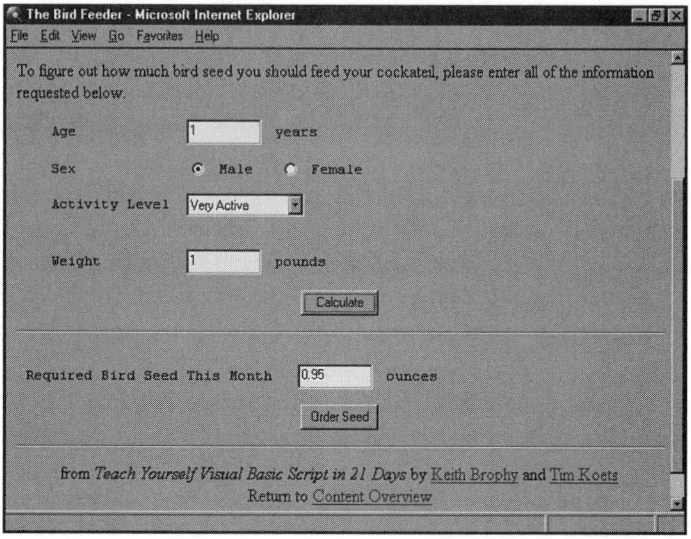

When you click the Calculate button, VBScript performs some simple calculations to determine the amount of bird seed required. The formula used to calculate this amount is in no way scientific and should not be considered valid if you want to use this on your own bird. It's just a fictitious example to show you what you can do with VBScript. Still, it shows you the potential of providing this service to the public. If you were selling bird seed, this Web page might be just enough of a convenience for the user to click the handy little Order Seed button at the bottom of the Web page!

NOTE

This Web page, named birdfeed.htm, is also on the CD-ROM that comes with the book.

These examples show only a fraction of what you can do with VBScript. All these examples involve taking input from the user, processing that input, and providing the results back to the user on the Web page. As you progress through the book, you will see how to use ActiveX controls, OLE, Java applets, CGI, animation, sound, and other useful features to make Web pages even more powerful. If you've used the Internet for a while, you can begin to appreciate just how useful VBScript really is. We've come a long way from the static text-and-graphic Web pages, and the journey has only begun.

Learning VBScript

VBScript is much easier to learn than programming languages such as C/C++ and other scripting languages such as Java. Derived from the BASIC language, VBScript should not be difficult for anyone who has done computer programming before. If you have done no programming whatsoever, it might take you a bit more time to come up to speed, but rest assured—you will. The most effective way to learn VBScript is to read this book and practice creating your own Web pages with VBScript. Reading a book is never enough unless it is accompanied with experience and practice. Fortunately, this book doesn't just tell you how to use VBScript; it shows you how and gives you exercises to try on your own. You can count on the fact that you will get knowledge and experience as a result of working through this book.

You need to know how to do two things before you begin to write VBScript code. First, you need to know how to use a browser and navigate through the World Wide Web. Second, you should be somewhat familiar with the Microsoft Windows environment and how to navigate your way through a Windows application, or have equivalent experience in another graphical user interface (GUI) environment. If you want to use VBScript to design Web pages, chances are you already have a browser and are quite capable of using it. You are probably very familiar with GUI applications as well. If so, the only remaining obstacle is learning how to program with VBScript. The more programming you have done in the past, the better you'll pick up on VBScript, especially if you've written programs using Visual Basic or Visual Basic for Applications. If you've never written a computer program, don't worry: You don't need a programming background to use this book.

To start working with VBScript, you need several things: a browser that supports VBScript, the VBScript run-time interpreter, access to required controls, and an editor or other tool to help you assemble Web pages or edit HTML documents. The first step is to obtain a browser that includes VBScript run-time support if you do not already have one. Microsoft's Internet Explorer 3.0 beta was the first publicly available browser that provided support for VBScript. This browser is available free of charge from Microsoft. At the time this was written, you could obtain Internet Explorer 3.0 from `http://www.microsoft.com/ie`.

The VBScript run-time interpreter will usually be included with any browser that supports VBScript. This is the case with Internet Explorer 3.0. If you obtain the browser and install it, you have everything you need to run VBScript, including the run-time interpreter. No separate installation is required to provide run-time capabilities. You don't need to obtain any other pieces. However, you might want to refer to the location `http://www.microsoft.com/vbscript` if you want a general description of run-time capabilities beyond that provided in this book. The run-time interpreter for VBScript is license free, just like Internet Explorer. Even if other browsers incorporate the VBScript run-time interpreter, Microsoft does not charge a licensing fee to the end user or the company that produces the browser. Therefore, it is a safe bet that the VBScript interpreter will be widely distributed with most browsers in the future.

If you've obtained Internet Explorer 3.0, you're nearly all set to run VBScript programs. You also will need ActiveX controls from Microsoft for many of the samples in this book. Pages can be set up with control definitions to automatically download required controls from across the Internet. However, for best results we recommend downloading the entire ActiveX control collection from Microsoft before proceeding with the samples in the book. This also allows you to work with the samples from the book's CD-ROM without being connected to the Internet. At the time of this printing, you could go to www.microsoft.com/intdev and do a search on ActiveX controls to find information about downloading the Control Pack. You will need these controls to use the book's samples.

Once you get set up, you can directly load the book VBScript pages from the CD-ROM or visit the Microsoft samples over the Internet (at www.microsoft.com/vbscript), or from any other site for that matter, and the VBScript capabilities will work right in front of you. If you're merely an end user of the Web, that's all you need to enjoy the power of VBScript programs. If you are a VBScript programmer—in other words, you want to edit VBScript programs or create your own from scratch—then you need one more tool, a Web page editing tool. Such a tool should not only let you generate Web pages, but it should also enable you to embed VBScript code into those pages. Fortunately, most tools provide this capability. As long as you can enter text insertion mode and type text directly into your page as you create it, you can insert VBScript statements. You can use many different tools to accomplish this. They range from the Windows Notepad, a simple text editor, to more sophisticated tools such as Internet Assistant, a utility that incorporates itself into Microsoft Word and enables you to quickly and easily build Web pages.

Another available tool for use in Web page design with VBScript is Microsoft's ActiveX Control Pad. This tool is an HTML text editor that allows you to insert HTML and ActiveX controls automatically into your HTML documents with the help of a wizard. Figure 2.6 shows the beta version of the ActiveX Control Pad in action.

The editor has a great deal of additional features that aid in editing Web pages and incorporating VBScript and JavaScript into them. You will learn more about the ActiveX Control Pad and ActiveX controls in general starting on Day 10.

Another useful capability from Microsoft is the Layout Control forms interface. This, together with Internet Explorer's incorporation of 2-D layout for HTML, makes it possible to position elements and controls anywhere on a page in a form-like fashion much like in Visual Basic. The layout takes place in a separate file that the layout control incorporates into your main page when that page is loaded. This approach is discussed in more detail on Day 18, "Advanced User Interface and Browser Object Techniques."

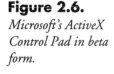

Figure 2.6.
*Microsoft's ActiveX
Control Pad in beta
form.*

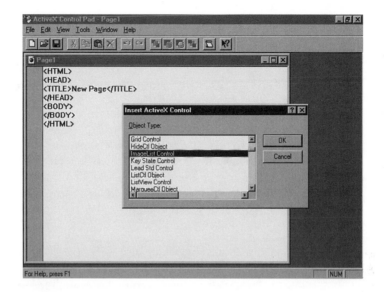

2

Security and VBScript

One of the many questions people have when learning about VBScript is, "How secure is it?" VBScript was designed as a subset of the Visual Basic language. When you look at the language and compare it to VBScript, you essentially see a stripped-down version of Visual Basic. The designers took any part of Visual Basic that could cause VBScript to be unsafe and insecure and eliminated it. The end result of their work is a language that is safe and "lighter" than its parent, Visual Basic.

When people think about safety and the Internet, their concerns are often valid. The Internet has just recently become popular to the masses, and companies are starting to think of ways to make money on the Internet. This brings to mind images of users entering credit card numbers, making banking and shopping transactions, and paying for other services. Obviously, before such activities can take place, the Internet must be secure. Otherwise, people simply won't want to take the chance of their credit card numbers being intercepted or some secure password being used to access their accounts. The World Wide Web and Internet consortia are working very hard to establish security mechanisms for the Internet. Rest assured; this will be an area of intense interest in the short term until security issues can be firmly resolved.

Those who use VBScript are also likely to be concerned about security. They want to make sure that VBScript does not open the door for a devious Web page to do damage to their computer systems in any way. The most common type of computer damage most users fear is the multitude of viruses that are transmitted to computers when files are downloaded from an Internet server and modified on the user's computer. Other possible damage includes a

Web page that, for some reason, causes the loss of data on the client's computer system or otherwise causes the computer to crash. Nothing is more frustrating to the user than to have five applications open and lose all the data because of a computer crash. Although multitasking systems such as Windows 95, Windows NT, and UNIX make that less likely to occur than the Windows operating system did, it is still an unfortunate possibility in some cases.

VBScript prevents these and other potential security and safety problems by eliminating the cause of such problems entirely. First of all, it is not possible to read and write files or databases in the normal fashion in VBScript. This might seem like quite a limitation, and it is indeed limiting, but this stops up a very large security leak. Damage could come to a user's computer through a Web page that opens and modifies a file or perhaps deletes a file on the user's computer. As a result, it is not possible for VBScript to modify files on the user's computer using conventional methods.

The second area of safety is making sure VBScript will not cause the computer to crash. If there is an important exchange of information happening in a Web page, the user would certainly not want the computer to crash due to an ill-formed script. It's a safe assumption that the designers of VBScript made this less likely by avoiding any code that could potentially cause a crash. It's impossible to state outright that a VBScript program cannot crash because absolutes in the world of computers are rare. It certainly is possible, however, to say that VBScript is very safe and robust and not likely to crash in and of itself.

The design of VBScript properly reflects the goal to prevent security leaks and ensure safety with VBScript, but the story does not end there. VBScript works together with ActiveX controls, intrinsic HTML controls, OCXs, and OLE objects within a Web page. VBScript has no control over what goes on when the code that composes such controls executes. All VBScript "sees" when working with a control or object is the interface that control provides. It is conceivable that a control could, for example, modify a file. VBScript doesn't modify the file—the control does. Although VBScript can't be faulted for causing damage to a user's system, it cannot be responsible for any controls or OLE objects it works with. This is true of security issues as well as stability.

If a control were written with some sort of a glitch or bug inside of it, it could cause a computer to crash or, at the very least, cause the Web page to not function properly. Again, the problem does not lie in VBScript itself but in the control it interfaces with. A Web page is only as stable as its least stable component. If a buggy control is included on a Web page, the potential of that Web page to become unstable is equal to the stability of that control. Therefore, it is very important to choose controls that will work as bug free as possible with any browser or any platform the Web page is run on.

Microsoft's Internet Explorer 3.0 is a good example of the current state of browser security. Internet Explorer contains a feature called Safe Content that makes sure that no unknown programs or components can be downloaded to the user's computer by a Web page without the user's consent. See Figure 2.7 for Internet Explorer 3.0 beta's security dialog for programs you receive within Web pages from the Internet.

Figure 2.7.

The Microsoft Internet Explorer 3.0 (beta) Program Security dialog.

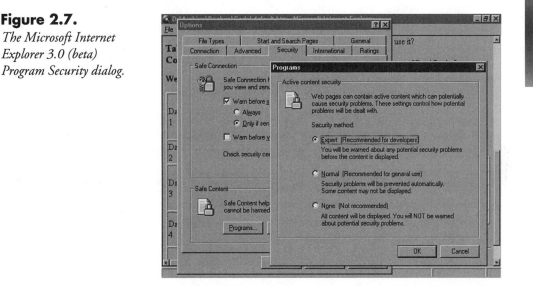

As you can see, you have the option of choosing Expert, which warns you about any security problems before a Web page is displayed; Normal, which automatically prevents security problems by not displaying content that causes security violations; and None, which displays all contents without worrying about security violations. With the current beta version of Internet Explorer 3.0, you should use either Expert or None when working with VBScript Web pages that contain ActiveX controls. This Expert setting will inform you whenever an object is required by the Web page or if a scripting language changes the properties of an existing control on a Web page. These safeguards are an example of part of an evolving process of making Web browsers more secure in an environment of rapidly growing objects, controls, and scripting languages.

You may wish to set this setting to None while using the samples in this book on the CD-ROM. These samples only make use of Microsoft ActiveX controls. Since your browser can run these locally from the CD-ROM, you don't even have to be on the Internet to progress through the samples and can be sure that you are working in a safe computing environment. Once you go out on the real Internet, any page can cause a control to be downloaded, and all bets are off! It is recommended that you use Expert when visiting pages you are not well acquainted with. Microsoft has provided a framework for certifying and identifying trusted controls so you can only choose to work with known commodity controls. This is discussed more fully on Day 21.

Industry approaches are continuing to rapidly develop in the arena of Web security, particularly in the area of component distribution and security. These issues will be addressed later in considerably more detail on Day 21. For now, it is important to understand that security considerations have shaped the capabilities inherent in the VBScript language.

VBScript Versus Visual Basic and Visual Basic for Applications

Many programmers who are interested in VBScript have used either Visual Basic or Visual Basic for Applications. If you are included in that group, you most likely know that VBScript is a subset of Visual Basic. You've probably also heard from Microsoft that if you already know Visual Basic or Visual Basic for Applications, you already know VBScript. Yes, well—sort of. You know what you could do, but you might not be sure what you cannot do.

One of the first striking differences between VBScript and Visual Basic is that Visual Basic has a design-time environment. When you run Visual Basic, you get an attractive editing environment where you can craft forms and write code using an interactive shell. When you work with VBScript, on the other hand, you have no such environment. VBScript code "lives" within an HTML document, which is a plain text file. At the time of this printing, neither Microsoft nor any other large commercial vendor has a design environment that lets users create VBScript code like Visual Basic does. This is due, in part, to the way in which VBScript works. Visual Basic code creates Windows applications that operate in and of themselves. On the other hand, VBScript code works inside of HTML documents and runs along with HTML. Even though VBScript is an interpreted language as is its parent, you must create VBScript code manually. Some tools are already emerging to overcome this limitation. Microsoft's ActiveX Control Pad, for example, helps overcome the tedious work of inserting controls and editing HTML code by providing a more sophisticated editing tool than Notepad. This tool is currently available for free and can be located by doing a search at www.microsoft.com/intdev. The tool provides for automatic insertion of control object definitions, and it provides a layout editor. The layout editor lets you lay out pages interactively, much like Visual Basic 4.0, and stores the results in a separate file for the layout control to integrate on your page. The ActiveX Control Pad even provides a Script wizard that lets you define scripts through an interactive high-level interface rather than by entering source code statements. Since the focus in this book is on helping you understand all the details of VBScript, however, we steer clear of the higher-level tools, which can shield you from some of the underlying details. We want you to learn those details! Therefore, the samples here are presented at the source code level and can be entered with a text editor such as Notepad. After you gain a well-grounded knowledge of VBScript, you might choose to progress to some of the higher-level tools.

The other primary difference between VBScript and Visual Basic aside from development environments is the language itself. As mentioned previously, many of the commands, keywords, and data types that are supported in Visual Basic are not supported in VBScript. Rather than provide a list of specifics in this lesson, we summarize all the differences between VBScript and Visual Basic in Appendix A, "VBScript Syntax Quick Reference." You'll notice quite a number of differences. If you've used Visual Basic in the past and you think you can use exactly the same code in VBScript, you will probably be surprised. It's important to understand how the languages differ. On Day 20, "Porting Between Visual Basic and VBScript," you will see how to properly port code from Visual Basic over to VBScript. Knowing what will and will not port is essential to that process. Day 20 will give you the information you need to make the transition as painless as possible.

Summary

Today you have been given a taste of what VBScript can do for you. The lesson begins by telling you a bit more about VBScript and what it does. You have learned that VBScript enables you to accomplish tasks otherwise impossible in HTML, and you can often do them with a small, simple amount of code. You have also been introduced to many of the technologies that surround the World Wide Web and VBScript, including CGI, ActiveX controls, intrinsic HTML form controls, OLE objects, OCXs, and so on. All these accompanying technologies help make your Web pages even more powerful and useful in ways never before possible. VBScript acts as a "glue" that helps you integrate all these components together. VBScript keeps the components together and working with each other, much like cartilage helps keep our bones moving freely and cooperatively.

You have seen several examples of VBScript in action. The purpose of these examples is to show you some of the things VBScript can do. The examples are by no means advanced or even very sophisticated, but they do help convey some of the exciting and powerful possibilities at your fingertips. The examples today are centered around getting information from the user, processing that information, and then displaying the information back to the user. As you progress through this book, you will learn how to manage this flow of information and make your Web pages very useful to your users. You want them to have a productive, fun, and exciting time working with your Web pages, and you will learn the tools and techniques to accomplish that.

After providing a taste of what VBScript can do, today's lesson discusses some of the questions people have about this new language. You have learned what tools and programs you need to get started with VBScript. You must have a browser that includes VBScript run-time support, such as Microsoft's Internet Explorer 3.0, to use VBScript pages. Any text editor will suffice to create or modify pages.

The lesson then discusses the safety and security of VBScript. There has been a lot of discussion recently about Internet security in the industry. VBScript is a very safe language because it prevents a Web page from accessing any of the data on your computer. Furthermore, the language itself is very safe. It is not easy to cause a VBScript program to crash or otherwise interrupt the normal flow of a Web page or its browser. Security is discussed in detail on Day 21.

Finally, today's lesson provides information for programmers who have used VBScript's parent product, Visual Basic. The lesson discusses the similarities and differences between the languages and what the Visual Basic or Visual Basic for Applications programmer should expect when working with VBScript. This subject is also discussed in detail on Day 20. As the lesson points out, those who have programmed in Visual Basic or Visual Basic for Applications will realize that VBScript is a subset of Visual Basic and Visual Basic for Applications. In other words, many of the commands in Visual Basic and Visual Basic for Applications do not exist in VBScript. This makes VBScript more stable, safe, and efficient. Stripped of the weight of its parent, VBScript can perform very efficiently and reliably in the browser.

Today's lesson gives you an overview of VBScript, its capabilities, what you need to know to learn it and use it, how safe and secure it is, and how it differs from its parent. Tomorrow, you will learn more about where VBScript is supported and, in particular, how it is supported. You will learn how VBScript is "connected" to a browser, and you will also write your first VBScript program.

Q&A

Q You mentioned that VBScript acts like "glue" to bind components together on a Web page. What do you mean by the term "glue"?

A The term "glue" is borrowed from VBScript's parent, Visual Basic. Controls and objects placed on a Web page can be linked together using VBScript. For example, you can use VBScript to respond and execute code when a user clicks a command button that places text in a text box control. In this way, you can create a "fabric" that makes all the components work together the way you intend. This applies not only to simple intrinsic controls, but also to more sophisticated objects such as Java applets, ActiveX controls, and other objects.

Q When a user is working with a Web page, what's so important about having the Web page execute code on the user's computer? Why can't all the code execute on the server?

A The most significant benefit of being able to execute code on the user's computer rather than the server is that first, it eliminates all the extra Internet traffic required between the client and the server; second, it relieves the server from the burden of performing the processing that the client could do itself. To the user, this means the Web page will be more peppy and responsive. To Internet users as a whole, this means less traffic and better response time. To the owners of the Internet servers, it means less work they have to handle on their servers and the more people they can serve at once who access those servers.

Q I've never done any programming at all. I just want to be able to write Web pages without going through a lot of hassle and learning time. Will it take me a long time to learn VBScript?

A If ever there was an easy language to learn, VBScript is it. Unlike more complicated scripting languages such as Java, VBScript is derived from one of the easiest-to-learn languages used for programming today. One could argue that the simplicity of VBScript comes at the expense of power and functionality. Power and simplicity have always been competing goals. VBScript gives the programmer a reasonable trade-off, however, because it is sufficiently powerful for sophisticated Web page applications, yet it is safe enough and easy enough for the beginner to learn quickly.

Q If VBScript is secure, but other components within a Web page might not be, how can I be sure a Web page won't damage my system when I load it into my browser and work with it?

A Security is a concern that is foremost on the minds of Internet developers and solutions providers. The bottom line is that market and corporate pressures will force control vendors and solution providers to make sure their controls do not contain security threats. Industry movements underway to clearly establish the identity of components (discussed further on Day 21) will further these efforts. At the very least, any possibility of such threats should be fully documented to the programmer and the users of the Web page before they have a chance of doing any potential damage.

Workshop

Take each of the examples presented today, and knowing what you know now about what VBScript can do, make a list of additional ideas and suggestions for these pages. Are there other Web pages you can create that will help make these examples more useful? Is there anything you can add to the Web pages to make them more powerful? When you've finished reading this book, take another look at these examples and ask yourself these questions again.

Quiz

NOTE   Refer to Appendix C, "Answers to Quiz Questions," for the answers to these questions.

1. What major capability does a scripting language give to a Web page?
2. Name a few of the surrounding technologies that can be "glued" together using VBScript.
3. What aspects of VBScript make it safe so that a Web page using VBScript cannot destroy or corrupt information on a user's computer?
4. Where did the VBScript language originate?
5. What do you need to write VBScript code or use Web pages that contain VBScript code?

Day 3

Extending the Power of Web Pages with VBScript

Now that you've seen what the World Wide Web is and what VBScript can do within it, it's time to learn how to put VBScript to work within the Web. Because VBScript is a new technology and the World Wide Web is evolving so rapidly, VBScript will continue to be supported in more and more browsers, tools, and components as time goes on. Today, you will be presented with an overview of most of the major browsers, tools, and components that have been or will soon be released. As you have read in Day 2, "The Essence of VBScript," VBScript works together with Web browsers, but VBScript language can potentially be used with a variety of other tools, components, and services as well.

In addition to showing you many of the places VBScript is or will be supported, this lesson focuses its attention on just how VBScript is implemented in Web browsers. After a general discussion of hosting environments, the rest of the book will focus on browser implementations of VBScript since that is by far its most popular use. This lesson, therefore, shows you the general structure of an HTML document as well as how to embed VBScript in that document. The specific details needed to embed your first script are covered, starting with which tags to use for an embedded script. That is followed by discussion of how to delimit script code in comments so it is correctly handled by VBScript-aware browsers and ignored by non–VBScript-aware browsers. Finally, script insertion rules and the framework for a simple script are outlined. At the end of the lesson, you'll have the opportunity to create your first Web page using HTML and VBScript together. By the end of the lesson you will have a good understanding of where you can use VBScript both now and in the future. You will also know how to get a browser to recognize and work with VBScript.

How VBScript Enhances Browsers and HTML

VBScript enhances Web browsers in a variety of helpful and significant ways. Web browsers are able to read and interpret HTML code, formatting the text and other data in a Web page based on the specifications of the browser. HTML was originally written to address content of a document while allowing the browser itself to worry about how to present the output to the user. As such, it is a relatively simple language that is quite limited in its power. One of its biggest limitations was the inability to support *interaction* with a Web page as fully as users have come to expect from computer-run applications. For instance, people who use sophisticated word processors such as Microsoft Word or MacWrite might come to expect the user-friendly atmosphere of menus, toolbars, and dialogs that help accomplish various tasks. When working with a Web page built only using HTML, the user is very limited in what he or she can do. Various controls can be placed on a form, but the Web page input must be submitted back to the server in order to perform any processing. This restriction usually makes Web pages fairly rigid in their interactive capabilities.

Web pages built entirely on HTML usually require the user to set a series of controls, such as check boxes and text fields. Typically an entire form's worth of data is supplied at a time. After filling in fields on a form, the user can click on a button, usually called Submit, and the contents of the Web page are sent back to the server. No work is done on the client's computer other than displaying the Web page to the user. All the intelligent work and processing must be done on the server. This not only increases the amount of traffic required on the Internet, but it also denies the user the ability to interact with the Web page. If, for example, the Web page was used to take a survey, HTML would not be able to validate the user's input. In other words, the Web page wouldn't be able to make sure that what the user was entering was valid. Rather, the user could enter a bunch of invalid data and send it to the server, only for the server to turn around and send the contents back, or simply give up and force the user to start over.

With VBScript, however, the Web page has its own intelligence. VBScript can, for example, make sure that what a user enters is valid before it is sent back to the server. This eliminates the need for all the extra traffic, not to mention the delay the user must experience in waiting for the information to get there. One immediate benefit for the user is that the overall Web page experience becomes much more enjoyable from faster, more responsive Web pages. Furthermore, many effects, such as multimedia and animation, that are limited, if not nonexistent, in HTML, can be performed relatively easily using VBScript to enhance the Web page experience.

Another great strength of VBScript is its capability to act as a "glue tool" that can integrate other components on a Web page like a fabric. Components such as OLE objects, ActiveX controls, Java applets, intrinsic HTML form controls, and VRML controls can all be tied together and controlled using VBScript. This same capability also made Visual Basic the tool it is today. To you, it means that all the components you obtain for Web pages can be quickly and easily brought together and controlled using a single language.

Therefore, VBScript enhances the power of browsers and HTML because it gives the Web page a higher degree of interaction with the user, allows for processing on the user's computer rather than only on the server, provides the user with more control over the Web page, and acts as glue to bind together various Internet components that can serve the user.

Where VBScript Is Supported

VBScript can be supported and used in any browser distributed with VBScript run-time support, as well as with a variety of other tools and components. This section briefly reviews some of the environments where VBScript is hosted, before turning to the specifics of how to make VBScript work in HTML browsers.

Web Browsers

At the time of this writing, support for VBScript was planned for many browsers. Microsoft Internet Explorer 3.0 supports VBScript today. It is expected that the other major browsers will follow suit, especially when VBScript gains enough popularity that market conditions and user pressures force the issue. Netscape's Navigator is the browser with the largest market share. Speculation has been that an add-on might materialize to provide support for VBScript in this environment. If and when that move occurs, then VBScript will become virtually a *de facto* standard in the browser arsenal, and would likely be a part of all serious browsers from then on.

Microsoft's Internet Explorer is the focus of the discussion in the remainder of this book, since that is the most established VBScript platform. If you use VBScript in another environment, recognize and take comfort in the fact that VBScript should work essentially the same everywhere. No matter which browser your script runs in, consistent behavior of the core language can be expected. The run-time interpreter, the engine that interprets and processes the language, will behave the same since it will be derived from the same Microsoft VBScript source code wherever it is found.

If a browser or tool vendor ports VBScript to a different environment, they can license the source code free of charge from Microsoft and modify it to work in that other environment. But even the modified version must meet Microsoft's criteria for VBScript conformance. There also may be slight variations in the objects that a host, such as a browser, makes available to VBScript to manipulate. Aside from these differences, though, the language and behavior of VBScript will be consistent from one implementation to another.

Microsoft's Internet Explorer already contains the Visual Basic run-time interpreter. Versions for 16- and 32-bit Windows will become available, as well as versions for the Macintosh and UNIX-based computers. This cross-platform support of VBScript through the Internet Explorer will not restrict VBScript users to the Windows environment, as did Visual Basic and Visual Basic for Applications. Furthermore, Microsoft will provide the Internet Explorer for free to users across these platforms.

So what does it mean to say that a browser supports VBScript? Later in this lesson, you will see the answer to this question and understand what it takes for VBScript to run within a browser. But first, consider some nonbrowser environments where VBScript will also be hosted.

Other Internet Tools

In addition to Web browsers, a variety of other tools for the Internet will benefit from VBScript support. The first case to consider is custom controls, which can be used as building blocks for standard applications. A variety of companies produce browser controls for Windows applications, for example, that allow developers to build their own Web browsers or incorporate some browser functionality into their applications. If, for example, a designer is building an application for a company, she may want to make the application "Internet aware" and provide a browser interface to the World Wide Web from within the application itself. A browser component such as this could potentially be made to support VBScript code as well. This would give application developers who incorporate browsers into their own applications the ability to support Web pages that use VBScript.

VBScript is also supported in services not directly related to Web browsers. Microsoft's Internet Information Server product is one example. The Internet Information Server enables computers where Web pages permanently reside to share their pages with the rest of the Internet. The product works in conjunction with Windows NT to deliver Web pages across the Internet in response to a user's request. VBScript is even used to glue server-side solutions together just like it can be used to glue Web page components and logic together.

VBScript support has also been projected for WebObjects, a dynamic Web page tool from Next Software, Inc. WebObjects is a tool that can be used for rapid development of sophisticated Web server solutions. Another area where VBScript can be used is Microsoft's ActiveVRML environment (see www.microsoft.com/intdev/avr). The *Virtual Reality Modeling Language,* or VRML, is quickly becoming very popular on the World Wide Web. VRML allows designers to create a three-dimensional world rather than fixed Web pages. The user can then navigate through this world, much like one would walk through a house, to explore its contents. VBScript can interact with Microsoft's *ActiveVRML* through standard events and properties of an ActiveVRML viewer ActiveX control. VBScript support for VRML control will help enhance its power and give the Web user even more visually appealing ways to interact with information.

NEW TERM   *Virtual Reality Modeling Language* is a language used to present a three-dimensional, graphical world to the Web user.

Why is VBScript so prevalent? Precisely because it was intended to be. Microsoft designed VBScript to be a general-purpose scripting language. It was not intended to be constrained just to HTML Web pages. To the contrary, it is specified in such a way that it can easily be incorporated as a smart programming language into any application. Microsoft provides the VBScript run-time license and source code free of charge to any software manufacturer who wants to take his product and make it VBScript aware.

Assume, for example, that you are marketing your own spreadsheet software. You want to give your customers a way to write macros that can interact with the contents of a spreadsheet based on instructions provided by the customer. One of the best ways to do this would be to incorporate VBScript run-time support. Then, you've extended the capabilities of your product by giving your customers an easy way to control the spreadsheet. It costs you, the manufacturer, virtually nothing, since you did it by leveraging Microsoft code. Models of this sort will continue to facilitate the growth of VBScript into arenas beyond just that of the Web page.

Microsoft announced plans to license its more extensive Visual Basic engine, called VBA, or Visual Basic for Applications, a few months after announcing the licensing plans for VBScript. A software provider could incorporate VBA into their product much the way they could incorporate VBScript. The difference is that VBA is a higher-end product, with more function, options, and bulk. VBA 5 has a development environment that can be called from the application that incorporates it, for example. VBScript, on the other hand, is designed to be lightweight, fast, and simple. Since it is derived from VBA, and is in fact a proper subset of VBA, the languages are very similar. Which will most vendors incorporate? Time will tell. Given that VBScript can be licensed for free, which is not the case with VBA, and its speed and simplicity advantages, it is a safe bet that you will continue to see VBScript spread into more and more applications.

As these examples show, the applications for VBScript are potentially broad. And VBScript can be targeted for networks other than the World Wide Web. It can also be useful in intranet applications, in a sense running over a private mini-Web. The intranet is a scaled version of the Internet that is contained within an organization—an intranet's corporation is equivalent to the Internet's world. VBScript can be used in such cases as well, since the same technology can be used in the intranet as is used in the Internet. In fact, VBScript may be especially well suited to the intranet, since very sophisticated solutions can be crafted on a powerful set of front-end Web pages and corresponding customer-made business rules as determined by the organization. The problems of distribution and support of components might be easier to handle when those components are shared just within the organization rather than the entire Internet. VBScript could make such a strategy more feasible.

The possibilities for using VBScript are numerous. Still, by far the most common desire for VBScript today is to use it to make great Web pages. This book uses VBScript within the Web browser. It also restricts the use of VBScript to preliminary versions of Microsoft's Internet Explorer 3.0 running within Windows 95. Keep in mind, however, that the concepts you learn in this book can be applied in any of the platforms or within any of the tools that support VBScript. You will now see specifically how VBScript is supported within a browser. Once you gain this knowledge, you will be able to create your first VBScript program!

Embedding VBScript in an HTML Document

Since the focus of this book is on placing VBScript code within HTML documents, you need to first of all know how an HTML document is constructed. This section will give you an overview of that structure, as well as a list of the most important HTML keywords you need to recognize when placing VBScript code in a document. Then, you will actually learn how to embed this code and see a working example of a Web page that uses VBScript.

The Structure of an HTML Document

An HTML document is a simple text file. While its simplicity makes it ideal for transmission across the Web, it can often be an inconvenience for the programmer. Until fairly recently, if you wanted to create an HTML document, you pretty much had to type it all in yourself. Now, however, programs are emerging on the market and in the Internet that help "manufacture" an HTML document for you. They put in all the tedious keywords and other code elements for you, allowing you to focus on your objective and not get sidetracked by the syntax and other details. Still, even with an HTML editor, you must at some point examine the raw HTML document. This is particularly true when you work with VBScript.

When you write VBScript code, you need to open the HTML document in a text editor, such as the Microsoft's Notepad or ActiveX Control Pad utility, and write your code within that program. It is quite likely that utilities to help you write VBScript code will continue to emerge once VBScript is used on a widespread scale. In any case, regardless of the tool used, you need to have an understanding of the underlying structure of an HTML document to effectively and properly use VBScript.

To begin with, an HTML document consists of a series of elements called *tags*. Tags help to block off portions of the Web page for some specific purpose. For example, you use a tag to tell the browser that you are about to enter VBScript code. Then, you use another tag to tell the browser you're finished.

NEW TERM   A *tag* is a special formatting code used to create an HTML element. That element can then be recognized by a program that reads HTML, such as a browser.

The first tag required in an HTML document is used to help define the structure of the document. It is called the *HTML tag*, and it indicates that the file is an HTML file. Even though VBScript is not HTML *code*, it does live inside the HTML *document*, and this tag is simply explaining to the browser what kind of document it is. A tag in HTML is surrounded by the < and > symbols. Therefore, the HTML tag is designated as <HTML>.

NEW TERM   An *HTML document* is a list of HTML instructions that constitute a Web page. These instructions are represented as standard lines of text with the appropriate HTML tags.

This marks the beginning of the HTML document. When the HTML document is finished, usually at the end of the file, another tag is needed to complete the section. The first tag is called an *opening tag* because it tells the browser that whatever the tag represents, in this case the fact that the document is an HTML document, is now in effect. The tag that tells the browser that a condition previously put into effect is now finished is called the *ending tag*. Ending tags contain a slash character (/), followed by the text in the starting tag. Thus, the ending tag for the <HTML> starting tag is simply </HTML>.

Your HTML document is therefore structured in this format:

```
<HTML>
… your code
</HTML>
```

The beginning and ending tags surround the contents within the tags. An HTML document is divided into two main parts—the *head* and the *body*. Each of these sections has its own tag to designate it—the head section using the <HEAD> tag and the body section using the <BODY> tag. The head section of an HTML document contains elements that serve as a "prologue" to the rest of the document. Such elements can include the title, comments telling who wrote the page, and any other introductory information you want to appear at the top of a document. The body of the document is where the main parts of an HTML document—

such as text, the controls, pictures, and so on—are stored. This makes the general format of an HTML document

```
<HTML>
<HEAD>
… head content
</HEAD>
<BODY>
… body content
</BODY>
</HTML>
```

Note that the head and body tags consist of opening and closing tags. It is very important to include both tags in your document.

Important HTML Keywords

While it is not the purpose of this book to teach you how to use HTML, this section lists some of the more familiar and important keywords that are used in an HTML document. If you don't know HTML at all, you need to become somewhat familiar with it. You might consider Lemay's *Teach Yourself Web Publishing with HTML 3.2, Professional Reference Edition* by Sams.net Publishing. It will teach you everything you need to know to create basic Web pages. You might also want to keep an eye on Microsoft's Web site, `http://www.microsoft.com`, since any late-breaking technologies, as well as help information, free programs and controls, and other important information, can often be found there.

Having said that, the following section is a list and description of each of the major keywords in HTML and what they are used for.

The Title

The title tags are used inside an HTML document to indicate what the document is for and what it describes. Titles are commonly used to catalog Web pages, much like the titles of books are used as references on the library shelf. The title of a page normally shows up in the title bar of your browser when that page is active. The title tags are `<TITLE>` and `</TITLE>`.

The title is always placed inside the head section. An example of a title in action is

```
<HTML>
<HEAD>
<TITLE>What You Need to Know About Gardening</TITLE>
</HEAD>
<BODY>
… body code
</BODY>
</HTML>
```

Note that the contents in between the opening and closing tags of the title are used to specify that any text within those tags is part of the title. The tags do not need to be on separate lines,

3

nor do any of the tags shown. When you choose a title, you need to be brief, yet descriptive enough so that those browsing through the Web know what your Web page will provide them.

Headings

Headings are used to divide up sections of text on a Web page. You can use headings in much the same way they are used in this book—that is, to subdivide information into manageable parts for your user. Consider the Web page code shown in Listing 3.1, for example. This program, named, `headers.htm`, is located on the CD-ROM that accompanies this book.

Listing 3.1. A Web page using headers.

```
<HTML>
<HTML>
<HEAD>
<TITLE>Gardening Tips</TITLE>
</HEAD>
<BODY>
<H1>
<A HREF="http://www.mcp.com"><IMG  ALIGN=CENTER SRC="../shared/jpg/samsnet.jpg"_
        BORDER=2></A>
<EM>Gardening Tips</EM></h1>

<HR>

<H2>Soil Types</H2>
    <H3>Sandy Loam</H3>
    <H3>Loamy Sand</H3>
    <H3>Humus Soil</H3>
<H2>What to Plant</H2>
    <H3>Vegetables</H3>
    <H3>Fruits</H3>

<HR>

<center>
from <em>Teach Yourself VBScript in 21 Days</em> by
<A HREF="../shared/keith.htm">Keith Brophy</A> and
<A HREF="../shared/tim.htm">Tim Koets</A><br>
Return to <a href="..\default.htm">Content Overview</A><br>
Copyright 1996 by SamsNet<br>
</center>

</BODY>

</HTML>
```

 The browser ignores the leading spaces in the listing for each of the headings—they are there simply to make the listing more readable. Notice that each heading tag has a number inside it—<H1>, <H2>, and so on. Each additional heading is one level "deeper" than the one before it. This controls the rendering of the titles, with <H1> rendered as a larger heading than <H2>. Like all aspects of HTML, the use and ordering of the heading tags is a stylistic decision made by the Web page author. There is nothing to prevent you from using several consecutive <H1> headings, for example. This Web page is shown in Figure 3.1.

Figure 3.1.

A Web page using headers.

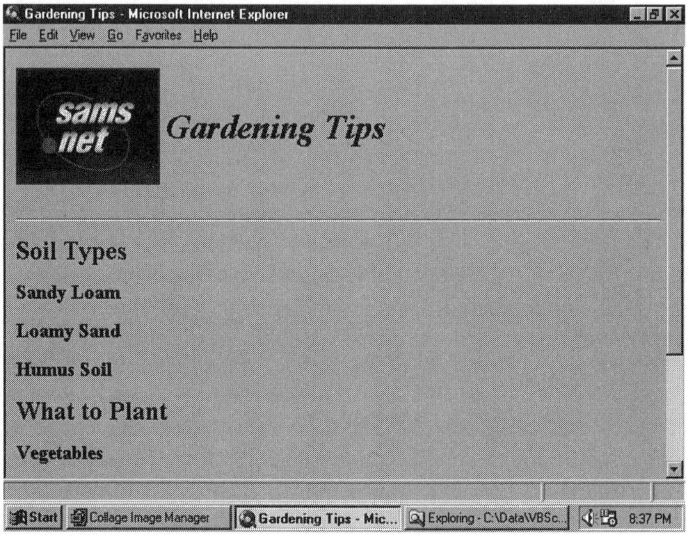

![Screenshot of Gardening Tips in Microsoft Internet Explorer showing the sams net logo, "Gardening Tips" heading, and headers for Soil Types, Sandy Loam, Loamy Sand, Humus Soil, What to Plant, and Vegetables]

You can add as many comments as you want, but be sure to close them off with the appropriate tags.

The Center Tag

The center tag is used to center something on the screen. If, for example, you wanted to center a sentence on the Web page, you would simply enter

```
<CENTER>I am centered.</CENTER>
```

You would probably also want to put some space above and below this sentence, which you can do using the paragraph tag discussed in the next section.

Paragraphs

Another useful tag in an HTML document is the paragraph tag. This tag doesn't require a closing tag. The paragraph tag is used to indicate paragraphs because most browsers will place extra space between them. The paragraph tag is simply

```
<P>
```

Consider the Web page in Listing 3.1. Then, make it more useful by adding some paragraphs, as shown in Listing 3.2. This Web page, named `paragrph.htm`, is also on the CD-ROM that comes with the book. (See Figure 3.2.)

Listing 3.2. A Web page using paragraphs and headers.

```
<HTML>

<HEAD>
<TITLE>Gardening Tips</TITLE>
</HEAD>
<BODY>
<H1>
<A HREF="http://www.mcp.com"><IMG  ALIGN=MIDDLE
SRC="../shared/jpg/samsnet.jpg" BORDER=2></A>
<EM>Gardening Tips</EM></h1>

<HR>

<H2>Soil Types</H2>

    <H3>Sandy Loam</H3>
    <H3>Loamy Sand</H3>
    <H3>Humus Soil</H3>

<H2>What to Plant</H2>

    <H3>Vegetables</H3>

<P>The type of vegetable you want to plant in your garden depends
a great deal on where in the country you live and what the average
type of weather is in the spring, summer and fall. Most gardens
include vegetables such as beans, corn, peas, and squash.
<P>The choice of vegetables is up to you. Consult with a grower or
store that supplies gardening supplies or seed for more information
about what grows best in your area.

    <H3>Fruits</H3>


<HR>

<center>
from <em>Teach Yourself VBScript in 21 Days</em> by
<A HREF="../shared/keith.htm">Keith Brophy</A> and
<A HREF="../shared/tim.htm">Tim Koets</A><br>
Return to Content <a href="..\default.htm">Overview</A><br>
Copyright 1996 by SamsNet<br>
</center>

</BODY>

</HTML>
```

ANALYSIS Note in Figure 3.2 that the two paragraphs inserted into the HTML document are indeed separated by a small amount of space. Also notice that it doesn't matter how pretty you make the text in your HTML document source code appear. The browser does its own formatting of the document. The browser ignores carriage returns in the document—all it sees or cares about are text and the tags it needs to recognize what to display.

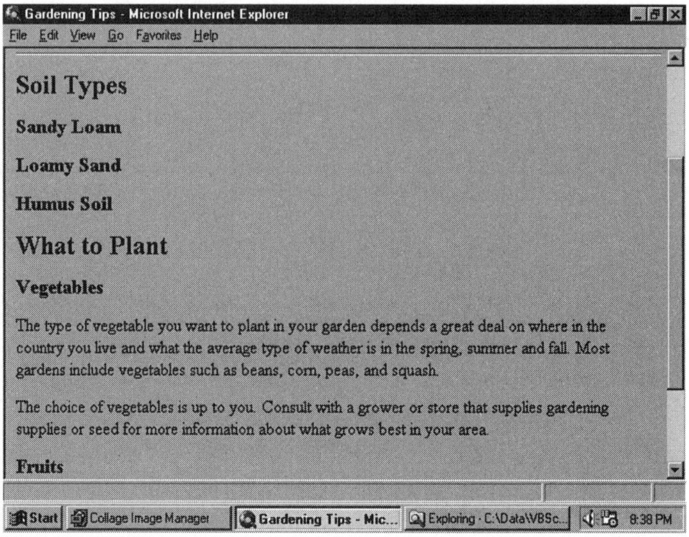

Figure 3.2.

A Web page using paragraphs and headers.

Comments

The comments tag is used to place comments in the document. Comments are often used for notes the designer wants to place in the document, such as who wrote the Web page and when. Comment tags are a bit different from the other tags. The opening comment tag looks like this:

```
<!--
```

The closing tag looks like this:

```
-->
```

Therefore, a comment would look like this:

```
<!-- This is a comment -->
```

While comment tags are necessary and very convenient for adding comments to a Web page, they are very important when writing VBScript code. This is because when you write VBScript code inside a Web page, you can't be sure the browser used to view the Web page will support VBScript. You may write and test your Web page using Internet Explorer 3.0, but once you make that page available on the Internet, you have no way of predicting the avenues users may take to view it. A user may view your "World's Greatest VBScript-Boosted Page" with the Acme, Inc., browser, which was produced in 1995 before VBScript even existed. Although you hope this pool of users would be small, there will definitely be some out there, and when they stumble across your Web pages, you don't want them to see ugly, confusing results. Therefore, you need to find a way to tell non-VBScript browsers to ignore any VBScript code if they cannot recognize it. The comment tags are used for that very purpose. You will see how this is done in the section "Placing a Script Within an HTML Document."

Scripts

Finally, you must understand the use of the script tag when working with VBScript. The script tag looks like this:

```
<SCRIPT>
```

It is closed using this:

```
</SCRIPT>
```

Unlike the other tags you have seen so far, however, the opening script tag requires an argument—namely, the language of the script. This is the tag used to embed VBScript code within an HTML document. For VBScript code, the tags are used as follows:

```
<SCRIPT LANGUAGE="VBScript">
...your VBScript code goes here
</SCRIPT>
```

The language parameter should be specified as "VBScript", including the quotation marks. Early beta versions of Internet Explorer used "VBS" and did not require the quotation marks, but later betas and the final release require the parameter as specified above. If you are using another scripting language, such as Java, you would enter an indicator such as "JScript" rather than "VBScript" in the language argument when you write the opening script tag. When the browser encounters a script tag, it checks to see what language the script has been written in. Then the browser checks whether an interpreter is available that can read the script code. If so, the interpreter takes over from there. If not, the script tag is ignored, and HTML moves on its merry way to the next line of code after the script tag.

There are a variety of other tags you can use in an HTML document. Some of these tags are introduced in later lessons because they are important in working with VBScript. Others are not directly applicable to VBScript but are useful to know anyway. Again, you may want to read Lemay's *Teach Yourself Web Publishing with HTML 3.2, Professional Reference Edition* for more information on how to use HTML in building Web pages. Now that you have all the pieces of the puzzle you need, let's put them together to give you the overall picture of how to place VBScript code in your Web pages.

Placing a Script Within an HTML Document

To place a script inside an HTML document, you should use the script and comment tags together. As previously mentioned, the comment tags are important just in case a browser that reads the Web page and does not support VBScript is used. You will see an example of the impact in a moment.

The following is the syntax for placing VBScript code inside an HTML document. This code can be placed anywhere within the framework of your HTML document:

```
<SCRIPT LANGUAGE="VBScript">
<!--
     … your VBScript code
     … goes here …
-->
</SCRIPT>
```

Notice that the comment tag appears immediately after the script tag. This comment tag appears here so that if the browser doesn't recognize the script, it will ignore the script tag and treat anything that follows as regular HTML text. The comment tags are used to prevent the browser from displaying the script code just in case it is a browser that doesn't recognize VBScript. The VBScript interpreter will not process the comment tags because when the browser finds an HTML comment, it does not bother to pass the comment on to the VBScript interpreter. As a result, you don't need to worry about VBScript not being able to figure out why the HTML comment tags are in there.

Internet Explorer will let you place VBScript code anywhere inside your HTML document. In practice, however, it is best to place your VBScript code at the very end of the body section in your HTML document. Without this convention problems can occur in certain situations. For example, you can reference controls in VBScript code when a page loads. If this code is placed before the lines where the controls themselves are included on the page, the code may not recognize the controls, at least with beta Internet Explorer 3.0 software. Also, you can place VBScript code within control definitions themselves. If you use this technique within the body of the HTML document, VBScript must also reside in the body of the document. Placing the script code at the end of the body section is, therefore, the safest place for it.

Listing 3.3 shows an example of a Web page that contains VBScript code placed at the end of the body section of the document. This Web page, named usingvbs.htm, is on the CD-ROM that comes with the book.

Listing 3.3. A Web page using VBScript code.

```
<HTML>
<HEAD>
<TITLE>VBScript Test Page</TITLE>
</HEAD>

<BODY>

<H1>
<A HREF="http://www.mcp.com"><IMG  ALIGN=MIDDLE
SRC="../shared/jpg/samsnet.jpg" BORDER=2></A>
<EM>VBScript Test Page</EM></H1>

<HR>

<CENTER><INPUT TYPE=BUTTON LANGUAGE="VBScript" VALUE="Test" NAME="TestButton">_
</CENTER>

<HR>

<center>
from <em>Teach Yourself VBScript in 21 Days</em> by
<A HREF="../shared/keith.htm">Keith Brophy</A> and
<A HREF="../shared/tim.htm">Tim Koets</A><br>
Return to <a href="..\default.htm">Content Overview</A><br>
Copyright 1996 by SamsNet<br>
</center>

<SCRIPT LANGUAGE="VBScript">
<!--
     Sub TestButton_OnClick()
         MsgBox "You just clicked the Test button."
     End Sub
-->
</SCRIPT>

</BODY>

</HTML>
```

This Web page is shown in Figure 3.3.

ANALYSIS   As you can see, the Web page includes a button that, when clicked on by the user, results in a message box being displayed (the message box is also shown in Figure 3.3). You will begin learning the details of this Web page tomorrow. The code used to create the Web page shown in Figure 3.3 works fine because the browser recognizes VBScript. If the browser didn't, the comments between the script tags would prevent the code from being displayed in the Web page.

Figure 3.3.

An example of a Web page using VBScript.

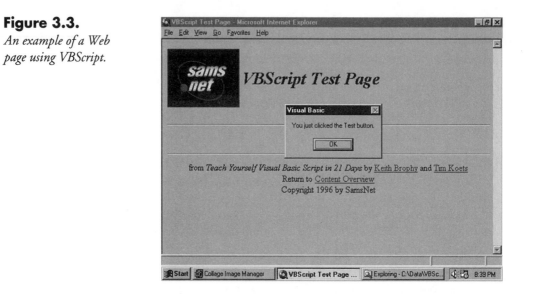

To see what would happen if you didn't use those comment tags, and then used a browser that was not VBScript aware, look at the Web page named nocomnts.htm, shown in Listing 3.4.

Listing 3.4. A Web page using VBScript code and no comment tags for the script.

```
<HTML>
<HEAD>
<TITLE>VBScript Test Page</TITLE>
</HEAD>

<BODY>

<H1>
<A HREF="http://www.mcp.com"><IMG  ALIGN=MIDDLE
SRC="../shared/jpg/samsnet.jpg" BORDER=2></A>
<EM>VBScript Test Page </EM></H1>

<HR>

<H2> No Comment Markers! </H2>

<CENTER><INPUT TYPE=BUTTON LANGUAGE="VBScript" VALUE="Test" NAME="TestButton">_
</CENTER>

<HR>

<center>
from <em>Teach Yourself VBScript in 21 Days</em> by
<A HREF="../shared/keith.htm">Keith Brophy</A> and
```

```
<A HREF="../shared/tim.htm">Tim Koets</A><br>
Return to <a href="..\default.htm">Content Overview</A><br>
Copyright 1996 by SamsNet<br>
</center>

<SCRIPT LANGUAGE="VBScript">
        Sub TestButton_OnClick()
              MsgBox "You just clicked the Test button."
        End Sub
</SCRIPT>

</BODY>

</HTML>
```

Rather than using the Internet Explorer, which supports VBScript, observe the Web page using Mosaic, which at the time of this printing did not support VBScript. The Web page is shown in Figure 3.4.

Figure 3.4.

An example of VBScript code with no comment tags.

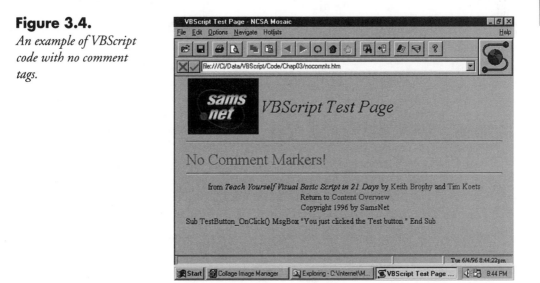

ANALYSIS Notice that, in this case, all the VBScript code is printed in the Web page—a very undesirable result! That is why it's so important to use the comment tags whenever you write VBScript code within a Web page. That's all there is to it!

One more thing you should know about writing VBScript code: If you want to break up a very large code statement that runs off the right side of your text editor, you can use the continuation character to break up the flow. An example of this is shown in Listing 3.5.

Listing 3.5. Using the continuation character.

```
<HTML>
<HEAD>
<TITLE>VBScript Test Page</TITLE>
<H1>Test Web Page</H1>
</HEAD>
<BODY>
<CENTER><INPUT TYPE=BUTTON VALUE="Test" NAME="TestButton"></CENTER>

<SCRIPT LANGUAGE="VBScript">
<!--
        Sub TestButton_OnClick()
            MsgBox "The total number is " & GetResult( 1, 2, 3, 4, 5,_
                                        6, 7, 8, 9, 10 )
        End Sub

        Function GetResult(a, b, c, d, e, f, g, h, i, j)
        ' This function adds up all the paramaters and returns the grand total
                GetResult = a + b + c / d * e + f * 2 _
                        + h/i + j
        End Function
-->
</SCRIPT>

</BODY>

</HTML>
```

ANALYSIS   Don't worry if you don't understand all the details of the code in Listing 3.5. It uses a function call, which is described in later lessons. You should take note of a couple details, however. In the code in Listing 3.5, you can see that the continuation character is used to break up the flow of text in two places where the line of code would otherwise be so long that it wouldn't fit on a page. You will see examples of the continuation character used throughout the rest of the book.

Another commonly used character is the single quote, which can be seen at the start of the first line after the function call declaration. This single quote character designates a VBScript comment. Everything that follows on that line will be ignored by the VBScript interpreter, and is just for documentation purposes for the programmer's benefit. Earlier in the lesson, the HTML comment indicator `<!-- -->` is discussed. It is important to understand the distinction between these comment indicators. Everything within an HTML comment is either ignored by HTML or passed off to the VBScript interpreter if the comment appears between the script tags that denote the start and end of VBScript code. The VBScript interpreter comment indicator will cause the remainder of the lines sent to the VBScript interpreter to be ignored, while the others will be processed by VBScript.

So the structure you see in Listing 3.5 contains many fundamental elements of the script. The script tags, the HTML comment tags, the VBScript line continuation characters, comments, and code structure are common to most of your VBScript programs. As you can see, the basic structure of a VBScript program is fairly straightforward and easy to implement. The remaining lessons deal with how to fill in the rest of the pieces.

Summary

Not only are a wide variety of browsers available for World Wide Web users, but a growing number of controls, applications, and other tools are becoming available for use as well. Today you have seen that VBScript can be supported in any or all of these tools, controls, and applications. All that is needed is for the designers of these tools to include with their product the VBScript run-time interpreter. Having done so, these tools will be able to recognize Web pages that use VBScript. But VBScript isn't restricted to the Web. Developers can take advantage of the technology in any circumstance, even in intranet environments where a company, for example, runs its own, self-contained intranet in its organization. In any of these cases, VBScript can be supported as long as the run-time interpreter is recognized by the browser, control, application, or tool in question.

Today's lesson begins by recognizing that the widest use of VBScript, at least at the outset, will be in working with Web browsers. Web browsers that support or might potentially support VBScript in the future are discussed. Keep in mind, of course, that the browsers are constantly changing, and since this book was written, many more than were listed in this lesson are probably supported. The browsers that support VBScript are expected to do so across various platforms, including Windows, Macintosh, and UNIX systems.

But the use of VBScript is not limited to commercial browsers. Many control vendors also offer OCXs that allow programmers to integrate the Internet into their applications. If those controls support VBScript, then any application that incorporates those controls to link to the Web will be able to recognize it. In addition to controls, tools such as the Internet Information Server and ActiveVRML also expect to contain support for VBScript.

Having presented many of the cases in which VBScript can be supported, the lesson focuses on how VBScript is used in the browser. This book concentrates on the browser because that is the most common place VBScript is used. Keep in mind, however, that no matter where you plan to use VBScript, this book will teach you what you need to know to be able to write useful VBScript programs for any environment.

The lesson gives a brief overview of the structure of an HTML document, including the keywords most commonly used to present output to the user. This is followed by a detailed explanation of how to use those keywords to put VBScript code in place within an HTML document. Special attention is paid to showing you how to safely include VBScript so that browsers that do not recognize VBScript will not display the source code all over the screen. The lesson shows an example of this, and shows the way to prevent this from happening.

Now that you've read today's lesson, you're ready to start learning the VBScript language. You learned about the World Wide Web and the Internet in general on Day 1, "Introducing

VBScript and the World Wide Web," as well as how VBScript fits into the picture. Then, on Day 2, you learned a bit more about VBScript itself and what you can do with it. You even saw some examples of Web pages using VBScript. In today's lesson you have seen some of the other places VBScript can be used. You saw how VBScript is used in the browser and how you embed VBScript code within it. On Day 4, "Creating Variables in VBScript," you will learn about a fundamental building block of any VBScript program—the variable. Congratulations! You're ready to become a VBScript programmer.

Q&A

Q How do I know which browsers currently support VBScript?

A The best way to find out is to go to the home page of the Internet site where you got the browser. You might also want to check the Microsoft page to see if it provides a list of the tools that support VBScript. Other Web sites with VBScript information may also eventually provide lists. Refer to Appendix B, "Information Resources," for further information.

Q If my Web page is used on a browser that doesn't recognize VBScript, what will happen?

A As long as you place comment tags around your code, the browser won't show the VBScript code on the screen, and the user will see no sign of it. However, the functionality of your Web page will obviously be severely limited, but it depends on how you designed the page. If your Web page revolves around VBScript, it simply won't work. If the user can still see what he or she needs to see without VBScript, you may be okay. In any case, you may want to let the users know up front that the Web page uses VBScript so that if their browsers don't support it, they will know why the page isn't working correctly. One good way you can do this is to include the logo of the browser that your page does work with, such as Internet Explorer, on your page to clue users in to your targeted browser. Such logo programs typically have guidelines, and you should review them before incorporating the browser logo into your page. At the time of this writing, information on Microsoft's Internet Explorer logo program was available under http://www.microsoft.com/ie. Fortunately, as VBScript gains popularity, more and more browsers will support it and the problem of users encountering your pages with browsers that do not support VBScript is likely to diminish.

Q I thought I wouldn't have to learn any HTML if I can learn VBScript instead. Is that true?

A Well, your use of VBScript means that perhaps you won't have to resort to HTML as much, but you'll still need to know some elementary HTML to make your Web page appealing. VBScript can be used to interact with controls on the Web page, but it doesn't replace the basic HTML needed to produce the content of your page. Furthermore, you have to need to know about HTML just to get the VBScript code on the Web page itself. So yes, you do need to know some HTML, but you may not need to be an expert. As always, the more you know, the better off you are. As you work through this book, you will be exposed to enough HTML that you should be able to pick up a starting level of information. Still, if you want a thorough understanding, you should read a book that covers all the fundamentals of HTML programming.

Workshop

To get the most out of programming with VBScript, now would be a good time to pick up a good reference on HTML. You may want to consider a good HTML programming book such as Lemay's *Teach Yourself Web Publishing with HTML 3.2, Professional Reference Edition* or, perhaps, you might simply want to take a look at many of the examples available on the Web. You may also want to take a look at the current HTML specifications out on the Web. Microsoft had an HTML specification available at the time of this book's writing reachable by navigating pages under http://www.microsoft.ie. W3C had very good HTML information available at http://www.w3.org/pub/WWW/MarkUp/Activity.html. No matter how you do it, become somewhat familiar with HTML now if you're not already—it will make learning VBScript much more enjoyable.

Quiz

NOTE | Refer to Appendix C, "Answers to Quiz Questions," for the answers to these questions.

1. What is needed for any browser, control, or other software to recognize a Web page that has VBScript within it?
2. What other software is out there besides browsers that can use VBScript?
3. Write a simple HTML document that contains a script tag for VBScript. You needn't write any VBScript code. All you should write are the container tags needed to make it happen.

Day **4**

Creating Variables in VBScript

If you've worked through the first three days, you should have a pretty good feel for what VBScript is and how it's used in a Web page to enhance its capabilities. Today begins a series of lessons that will teach you how to write VBScript code. Today, I will teach you how to create and use variables. Variables are necessary to create useful code with VBScript. You will learn how a variable is created, what can be stored within it, and how long a variable can remain in existence once you've created it. Variables are a fundamental part of any programming language, and this lesson will teach you everything you need to know about them.

I begin by explaining to you what a variable is, and then I show you how to create one. You will also learn what a variable can store, as well as how long a variable remains in existence. Then you will work with collections of variables, called *arrays*, which will round out your exposure to variables in VBScript. After today, you will be well versed in this fundamental concept, and you'll be ready to begin exploring more of the fundamentals of this exciting, new language.

What Is a Variable?

When users interact with computers, they usually get to some point where the computer asks them for information. That information is stored or manipulated by the computer in some way. Suppose, for example, that you want to keep a record of whether a user has clicked a button on your Web page. To keep track of this, you need to be able to store the indicator in the computer's memory so that whenever you want to see if the user has clicked on the button, you can simply check the indicator. Perhaps you want to store the number of times the user has clicked the button. In that case, you would want to store a value in memory. In any case, you need a "container" in which to store information. Programmers commonly call these containers *variables*.

NEW TERM A *variable* is a virtual container in the computer's memory that's used to hold information. In concept, it is much the same as a notepad. You can jot down information on the page of a notepad and return to that specific page later to remember what you wrote or modify the information. A computer program can store information in a variable and then access that information later by referring to the variable's name.

If you've ever done any programming using a language such as Visual Basic, Fortran, C, or C++, or if you've ever taken an algebra or a math class in school, you should already be somewhat familiar with variables. In most programming languages, when you create a variable, you have to tell the computer what kind of information you are going to store in it. Because some computer languages aren't very smart or don't want to risk making the wrong assumptions for you, they need to know exactly what kind of information you'd like to store. It's not enough to say, "I don't know...I just want to put stuff in this variable!" Usually, you have to say, "I want to store numbers in this variable," or "I want to store text." This means that you usually have to know ahead of time what you're going to store when you write the program. If you want to use a variable to store a person's age, for instance, you would probably first create a variable that stores numbers.

Fortunately, VBScript is very flexible about the type of information you can store. What's even better, the language is "smart" enough to let you store in the variable almost anything you want without telling it the kind of information ahead of time. There are, of course, limits to what and how much you can store (you can't store the Library of Congress in a variable because you'd run out of space), but VBScript is capable of letting you store a variety of types of information. When you create a variable in VBScript, you can assign to it numbers with or without decimal points, text, dates and times, and even objects such as ActiveX controls, which are discussed on Day 10, "An Introduction to Objects and ActiveX Controls," and Day 11, "More ActiveX Controls."

NEW TERM An *object*, in the context used in this book, is an entity that provides specialized function to a program or Web page. You can easily manipulate object behavior by setting well-defined characteristics of the object called *properties*. You can also cause the object to take specific actions by calling to action specific object orders called *methods*. By using an object's properties and methods, you can benefit from all the capabilities an object provides without having to worry about the internal rules of how the object itself works.

How Do I Create a Variable?

When you create a variable, you have to give it a name. That way, when you need to find out what's contained in the variable, you use its name to let the computer know which variable you are referring to. You have two ways to create a variable. The first way, called the *explicit method*, is where you use the Dim keyword to tell VBScript you are about to create a variable. You then follow this keyword with the name of the variable. If, for example, you want to create a variable called Quantity, you would enter

```
Dim Quantity
```

and the variable will then exist. It's that simple! If you want to create more than one variable, you can put several on the same line and separate them by commas, such as

```
Dim X, Y, Z
```

The second way to create a variable is called the *implicit method*. In this case, you don't need to use the Dim statement to create a variable. You can just start using it in your code and VBScript creates it automatically. If, for example, you want to store the quantity of an item the user is ordering, you can simply enter

```
Quantity = 10
```

using the implicit method. You don't have to create the variable explicitly using a Dim statement.

If you take no special steps, you can freely intermix the implicit and explicit methods of declaring variables. When you want to, you can choose to set aside a named storage space before you use it by giving it a name in advance through the Dim statement. On the other hand, you can also just rely on the fact that when you refer to something by name in a statement and space hasn't yet been reserved for storing that variable, it will be created for you on-the-fly.

This method of intermixing implicit and explicit declarations can lead to programs that are confusing to follow, to say the least. Fortunately, VBScript gives you a way to force a consistent explicit declaration approach. To make the explicit method a requirement and prevent the implicit allocation of names, you must place the command

```
Option Explicit
```

in the first line of the first code in your HTML document, as shown in the following segment:

4

```
<SCRIPT LANGUAGE="VBScript">
<!--
Option Explicit
[the rest of your code]
-->
</SCRIPT>
```

NOTE

At the time of this printing, VBScript was still in beta form, as was Internet Explorer 3.0. With the beta software, Option Explicit was not yet fully implemented and had to be placed in the first line next to the HTML comment tag to be included without errors. The beta implementation of Option Explicit did not always explicitly force variable declaration as specified.

It is expected that this will be fully implemented in the final release of Internet Explorer 3.0. You may find further updates on implementation status by visiting Microsoft's Web site at www.micosoft.com/vbscript, the Macmillan Computer Publishing site at www.mcp.com (look for the book title under Sams.net), or the author's update site at www.doubleblaze.com/vbs21day). In the samples in the book, the Option Explicit expression is placed next to the comment tag to prevent errors.

The Option Explicit statement therefore makes explicit declarations a requirement, and you will have to define every variable with a declaration such as Dim. With Option Explicit, if you haven't defined the variable before you use it, you can't use it! This means you need to enter the command

```
Dim Quantity
```

before you enter

```
Quantity = 10
```

In the explicit method, if you assign Quantity with a value of 10 before creating it, you will get an error.

You might be wondering why you'd use the explicit method when you can just start using variables. This is certainly more convenient while you are writing the code—that is, until you spell a variable wrong. What will happen? VBScript will go ahead and create another variable based on your misspelling, and you will not get the correct result. Consider, for example, the following code segment:

```
<SCRIPT LANGUAGE="VBScript">
<!--
Quantity = 2
Quantity = Quantity + 3
-->
</SCRIPT>
```

You would expect the result to be 5, right? And it would be. Suppose you misspelled Quantity in the second line of code:

```
<SCRIPT LANGUAGE="VBScript">
<!--
Quantity = 2
Quantity = Quantite + 3
-->
</SCRIPT>
```

In this case, the variable Quantite would be created on-the-fly, and because it's first created, it would have a value of 0. The result variable Quantity, then, would wind up being 3, not 5. If, on the other hand, you were using the explicit method of creating variables, you would enter the code as

```
<SCRIPT LANGUAGE="VBScript">
<!--  Option Explicit
Quantity = 2
Quantity = Quantity + 3
-->
</SCRIPT>
```

which would give you a run-time error if you spelled Quantity wrong because you had not declared it first. The run-time error that results from using Option Explicit typically makes it very clear that there is a problem and leads you right away to correcting the error. On the other hand, if you didn't use Option Explicit and therefore didn't receive the run-time error, you have a much more subtle problem. You might not even notice the incorrect result, and even if you did, it would be more difficult to immediately target the source of the problem.

The other reasons that the explicit method is better are discussed later today. Almost any seasoned programmer would recommend that you use the explicit method exclusively.

When you create a variable, you must think of a name for the variable. In most cases, the name you assign to the variable makes it easy for you to recall what the variable is used for. For example, a variable named Age is much easier to recognize than a variable named X.

VBScript lets you be quite creative when you name variables, but you can't name them just anything; you have to follow a few naming rules. The first rule is that the name must begin with a letter. A variable name of 1ToMany, for example, is not allowed. Second, the variable name cannot contain a period or space. A variable named Customer Name is illegal and will produce an error. You can't use a period either because a period is used to reference properties of objects (which will be discussed on Day 10). Third, the length of a variable name cannot exceed 255 characters. Anyone adventurous enough to supply 255 characters or more to name a variable is living life a bit on the wild side anyway! You should keep the size of your variables down to a meaningful, but acceptable, level, or else your fingers are bound to get very sore.

What Can Variables Contain?

VBScript is a new product, but it is a language derived from its parent product, Microsoft Visual Basic. VBScript is essentially a subset of Visual Basic. When you create variables in Visual Basic, you have the opportunity to specify what type of data you want to store in a variable. If, for example, you want to store integers in a variable, you can declare the variable as an integer variable using the *integer* data type. As a result, if you try to store anything other than an integer in the variable, Visual Basic either converts the data automatically into integer format or tells you the assignment cannot be made. If you can be specific about the type of data you are storing, your code has the potential to be less error prone because you make fewer mistakes when assigning data to variables. On the other hand, it is advantageous not to worry about restricting a variable to specific types of data. Visual Basic also gives you the choice of creating variables where it doesn't matter what kind of data you want to store. This special type of variable is called a *variant.*

NEW TERM   A *variant* is a type of variable that can store a wide variety of data types. In many programming languages, variables can only contain a specific predeclared type of information, such as integers or strings. Variants are not restricted to one type of data (such as integers, for example). You could assign an integer value to a variant in one statement and then replace that with a string value in a subsequent statement.

VBScript uses the variant as the basis for variables you create. The variant is used most often to store numbers and strings, but it can store a variety of other types of data. These data types are often called *subtypes* because the variant can represent them all internally. VBScript keeps track of these subtypes on its own; you usually just store whatever you want in the variable. VBScript matches the data to the best subtype and behaves accordingly. You can also override VBScript's decision of what subtype to use—you'll learn more about that later.

To better understand what the variant actually is, you should understand all the other data types that the variant can represent. These data types are taken from VBScript's parent, Visual Basic. By learning about these data types, you will begin to see how the variant works and what you can and cannot store in a VBScript variable. Here is a list of all the subtypes that the variant uses to represent the data you store in a variable:

☐ Boolean
☐ Byte

- [ ] Integer
- [ ] Long
- [ ] Single
- [ ] Double
- [ ] Date (time)
- [ ] String
- [ ] Object
- [ ] Error
- [ ] Empty
- [ ] Null

When considering how data is stored in a variable, think of a closet full of shoe boxes. Every type of shoe has a certain type of box that can store the shoe. In addition to the boxes that store specific types of shoes, other larger, generic-looking boxes are on hand. These generic boxes can be used to store any of the different types of shoes. The shoe boxes that store specific types of shoes represent the subtypes, whereas the boxes that can store any kind of shoe represent the variant. The variant is a "fit-all" data type that any of the "shoes," or subtypes, can fit into.

All of the subtypes mentioned previously are summarized in the following sections so you can see what type of data can be stored in VBScript variables.

Boolean

You can set the Boolean data type to either True or False, which are represented by -1 and 0, respectively, in VBScript. This subtype is useful when working with variables where you want to determine or set a condition.

Byte

The byte data type can store an integer value between 0 and 255. It is used to preserve binary data and store simple data that doesn't need to exceed this range.

Integer

The integer data type is a number that cannot contain a decimal point. Integers can range from -32,768 to +32,767. The integer is one of the most common subtypes because programmers often create variables that fit the integer best. Variables used for counting, for example, are represented internally as integers. Because a great many quantities can be expressed without a decimal point and the number itself can fit within the specified range of the integer, VBScript often chooses this subtype.

Long

Variables of the long data type are also integers, but they have a much higher range, -2,147,483,648 to 2,147,683,647 to be exact. Because this data type is also an integer, you cannot use decimal points with it. Long integers are also quite common and are usually used in cases where the range of the number exceeds the smaller range of the integer. In some cases, however, the range might even exceed that of the long. Perhaps a decimal point is needed in the number. In that case, you must use the single or double data types.

Single

The single subtype represents *floating-point,* or decimal, values, which means that numbers represented by this subtype include decimal points. The range jumps to a whopping $-1.4E^{-45}$ to $-3.4E^{38}$ for negative numbers and $1.4E^{-45}$ to $3.4E^{38}$ for positive numbers (these numbers are expressed in *scientific notation*).

NEW TERM   *Scientific notation* is a way to represent very small or very large numbers. A number is expressed as $x.xxE^{yyy}$ where $x.xx$ is a number and yyy represents how many places to shift the decimal point over in the number. If yyy is positive, move the decimal to the right. If yyy is negative, move the decimal to the left. Thus, the expression $3.45E^{02}$ becomes 345 and $2.34E^{-03}$ becomes 0.00234.

Double

Double is another floating-point data type, but this one has an even larger range than the single data type. The range for the double is $-4.9E^{-324}$ to $-1.8E^{308}$ for negative numbers and $4.9E^{-324}$ to $1.8E^{308}$ for positive numbers.

Date (Time)

The date subtype is often used because it places the date in a predefined format that other functions in VBScript can act on. If, for example, you have a date variable named HireDate and you want to know what year is in the date, you can simply use the function Year(HireDate) to find it. HireDate is represented by the date subtype so that the function can retrieve the year from the variable.

String

The string data type is used to store alphanumeric data—that is, numbers, letters, and symbols. The string is another one of the most commonly used subtypes that VBScript uses to represent a variable.

Object

The object data type is a subtype used to reference OLE automation objects within a VBScript application or another application. OLE automation is a technique Microsoft created that enables one application to share information and control with another. This concept will be explored further on Day 12, "Advanced Objects: ActiveX, Java, and ActiveVRML."

Error

The error subtype is used for error handling and debugging purposes. Day 17, "Exterminating Bugs from Your Script," discusses this subject.

Empty

The empty subtype is used for variables that have been created but not yet assigned any data. Numeric variables are assigned 0 and string variables are assigned " " in this uninitialized condition.

Null

The null subtype refers to variables that have been set to contain no data. Unlike the empty subtype, the programmer must specifically set a variable to null. Later in this lesson, I show you examples using the null subtype.

In many languages, you can allocate a variable to accept a specific type of data—say, integer data. As stated earlier, you cannot directly create a variable in VBScript that "knows" ahead of time it will contain just integer data. Instead, you can create a variable that can take on integer values along with any of the other subtypes listed previously. How is this possible? As mentioned earlier, VBScript does this for you automatically. Suppose, for example, that you declare a variable in VBScript as

```
Dim Item
```

Then, suppose that you set the variable Item equal to an integer value:

```
Item = 23
```

VBScript stores the value 23 in the Item variable as an integer. If, on the other hand, you were to set Item with a string, as

```
Item = "Tacoma, Washington"
```

the text you place in the variable Item gets stored internally as a string. What's great about the variant is that you don't have to worry about placing the wrong type of data in a variable. In Visual Basic 4.0, for example, you can declare an integer value with the statement

```
Dim Distance as Integer
```

You could enter a distance in miles easily by using the statement

```
Distance = 6
```

Suppose, however, that you have a distance of 6.5 miles that you want to enter. If you enter the statement

```
Distance = 6.5
```

Visual Basic 4.0 will store the distance as 7. This happens because you told Visual Basic that the variable was based on the integer data type, which cannot store decimal points. As a result, Visual Basic 4.0 obediently stores it as an integer by rounding the value, in this case, up to an even 7 miles. This problem is automatically solved for you in VBScript, where you simply enter the declaration

```
Dim Distance
```

and then set the distance using

```
Distance = 6.5
```

or

```
Distance = 6
```

or even

```
Distance = "6 Miles"
```

It doesn't really matter what you set the Distance variable to. Because the variant data type is used, VBScript automatically converts the data into the best possible subtype internally. The first assignment is converted into a single-precision value, the second to an integer, and the third to a string. As you can see, the variant gives you complete flexibility in entering data because you aren't limited by predeclared data types. Furthermore, the variant can automatically convert data from one type to another. If, for example, you have two variables assigned as

```
Distance = 6.75
Units = " feet"
```

you can put the two variables together into a third variable using

```
Result = Distance & Units
```

which makes `Result` equal to the string `6.75 feet`. (Day 5, "Putting Operators to Work in VBScript," discusses working with strings in more detail.) Now suppose you were using Visual Basic 4.0. If the `Distance` variable were defined using the single data type and `Units` were defined as a string, the command

```
Results = Distance & Units
```

would result in a `Type Mismatch` error. This simply means that Visual Basic 4.0 isn't able to add a string to a number. It can add strings to strings and numbers to numbers, but not strings to numbers. Visual Basic 4.0 doesn't automatically add a string to a number because the two are incompatible. When using variants, however, VBScript makes some assumptions for you. On its own, it determines that when you're adding a number to a string, you're going to get a string result. Because the variant can take on any of the data types, it simply stores the result in the variable as a string result.

Determining the Type of Data in a Variable

Because the variants choose the best way to represent data, you usually don't need to be concerned with what subtype is used to store data in a variable. Sometimes, however, you might want to inquire of the subtype being used or perhaps change it from one data type to another.

If, for example, you set a variable equal to a decimal value, VBScript will assign the double subtype to that variable. It would not choose the integer subtype because even though an integer would take less memory than a double, the integer would chop off the decimal and would not be the most accurate representation of the number. Why doesn't VBScript choose the single subtype rather than the double? VBScript chooses the double subtype because the double data type can more accurately represent the value than the single data type. Because the double data type uses more memory and you might not need the extra accuracy that the double data type gives you, you might want to override this decision and use the single data type instead. To begin with, you need a way to determine the variable's subtype. Then you need a way to change it.

Using VarType

In order to inquire about the subtype of a variable, you need to use the VarType function. This function takes one argument: the variable name. The function then returns an integer value that corresponds to the type of data storage VBScript is using for that variable. Table 4.1 shows you the return values for each data type.

Table 4.1. VarType **return types.**

Internal Representation	Value
Empty	0
Null	1
Integer	2
Long	3
Single	4
Double	5
Currency*	6
Date/time	7
String	8
OLE automation object	9
Error	10
Boolean	11
Variant**	12
Non-OLE automation object	13
Byte	17
Array**	8192

* The currency data type is not supported in VBScript, but a space is reserved for it in the ordering for consistency with Visual Basic 4.0.

**The return type 8192 is used to represent arrays. In VBScript, you can only create an array of variants. If you have an array of variants, the return type would be 8192 + 12 = 8204. Arrays of other data types are not supported in VBScript, but the array is treated in this manner for consistency with Visual Basic 4.0 (where an array of integers would evaluate to 8192 + 12, for example).

Recall the earlier example that defined a variable called Distance. The example first sets the value of Distance to 6, an integer. Consider the code in Listing 4.1, which belongs to the vartype.htm Web page that can be found on this book's CD-ROM. Notice the return values each time the VarType function is called.

Listing 4.1. Determining the internal data type of a variant.

```
Sub cmdTest_OnClick()

    Dim Result
    Dim Distance

    Distance = 6
    Result = VarType(Distance)          ' Result returns 2 (integer)
    MsgBox "The subtype for the variable representing 6 is " & Result

    Distance = 65535
    Result = VarType(Distance)          ' Result returns 3 (long)
    MsgBox "The subtype for the variable representing 65535 is " & Result

    Distance = 6/95
    Result = VarType(Distance)          ' Result returns 4 (single)
    MsgBox "The subtype for the variable representing 6/95 is " & Result

    Distance = 6.5
    Result = VarType(Distance)          ' Result returns 5 (double)
    MsgBox "The subtype for the variable representing 6.5 is " & Result

    Distance = "6"
    Result = VarType(Distance)          ' Result returns 8 (string)
    MsgBox "The subtype for the variable representing ""6"" is " & Result

End Sub
```

ANALYSIS As you can see, the internal representation of the variable changes as the variable is assigned new data. By using the VarType function, you can find out the variable's internal data type, or subtype. In each case, the message box displays the data being stored and the subtype of the variant variable being used to store the information.

The MsgBox statement simply displays a window with the specified message to the user, like the one shown in Figure 4.1.

Figure 4.1.

A message notifying the user of a problem.

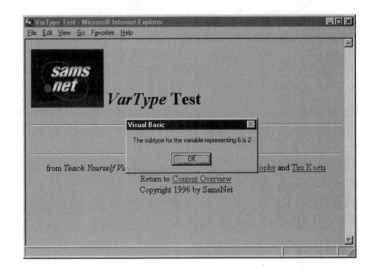

TIP

Message boxes are useful for presenting information to the user that he or she needs to see immediately. The MsgBox function requires at least one argument: the string that is contained inside the message box. Day 14, "Working with Documents and User Interface Functions," covers the MsgBox function in detail.

In addition to the VarType function, VBScript provides several other functions that return True or False based on the function and the data type of the argument passed to it. The following is a list of those functions:

- ☐ IsDate
- ☐ IsEmpty
- ☐ IsNull
- ☐ IsNumeric
- ☐ IsObject

These functions are often more convenient to use than the VarType function if you're looking for a specific data type that is listed in one of these functions. The following sections contain a brief explanation of each of the functions.

IsDate

The IsDate function requires the variable as an argument and returns the True value if the variable is a date. This function is often used to make sure the user has entered a valid date. For example, you might want to check the string a user has entered in a text box to see if the string is a valid date. The code in Listing 4.2, taken from the CD-ROM Web page isdate.htm, shows an example of one way you might use this function.

Listing 4.2. Using the IsDate function.

```
Sub cmdTest_OnClick()

    Dim TestDate

    TestDate = "4/1/96"

    If IsDate(TestDate) = True Then
         MsgBox TestDate & " is a valid date", 0, "Date Test"
    Else
         MsgBox TestDate & " is not a valid date.", 0, "Date Test"
    End If

    TestDate = "4/45/96"

    If IsDate(TestDate) = True Then
         MsgBox TestDate & " is a valid date", 0, "Date Test"
    Else
         MsgBox TestDate & " is not a valid date.", 0, "Date Test"
    End If

    TestDate = "Not a date"

    If IsDate(TestDate) = True Then
         MsgBox TestDate & " is a valid date", 0, "Date Test"
    Else
         MsgBox TestDate & " is not a valid date.", 0, "Date Test"
    End If
```

ANALYSIS This example creates a variable to store the start date. First, the code stores a valid date in the variable, and the IsDate function checks to see if the date is indeed valid. The IsDate function returns True, and a message box appears, telling the user that the expression is a valid date. This case is shown in Figure 4.2.

Next, the program places an invalid date of "4/45/96" in the variable. Because April doesn't have 45 days, the date is not valid, and the function returns False. The user is told that the date is invalid. Finally, the code stores the variable with an ordinary string that is not a date, and the test is conducted once more. In this case, the variable does not contain data representing a date, and the function again returns False. The value -1 is VBScript's internal value for the True condition, and 0 is the internal value for False. However, you can refer to True and False rather than the corresponding internal values in your programs. VBScript provides these expressions for you through a special type of keyword constant. The constant is True for -1, the true condition, and False for 0, the false condition. You can use true and false to represent -1 and 0 to make your code more readable. General-purpose constants are discussed later today.

Figure 4.2.

The IsDate *function in action, showing a valid date.*

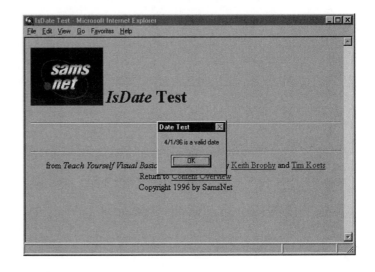

 TIP

A date must fall within acceptable limits to be valid, and you must use one of several predetermined formats for the date to be acceptable, such as 7/4/96, 7-4-96, July 4, 1996, and so on. The expression 7496, for example, would not be in an acceptable format for a date. When you assign a date in quotes, such as "7/6/62", this assigns it as a string variant in valid date format. If you want it to be represented internally directly as a date variant, you can instead assign it using the date # delimiter as #7/6/62#.

IsNumeric

The IsNumeric function returns True if the variable is storing a number and False otherwise. Again, this function is often useful to make sure the user has entered a number. If the user has entered something other than a valid number, you can use this function to check for that condition. The example shown in Listing 4.3, isnumeric.htm, illustrates the use of IsNumeric.

Listing 4.3. Using the IsNumeric function.

```
Sub cmdTest_OnClick()

    Dim Value

    Value = 23

    If IsNumeric(Value) = True Then
        MsgBox Value & " is a number."
    Else
        MsgBox Value & " is not a number."
    End If

    Value = "Twenty-Three"

    If IsNumeric(Value) = True Then
        MsgBox Value & " is a number."
    Else
        MsgBox Value & " is not a number."
    End If

End Sub
```

ANALYSIS   In this example, the first value is indeed a number. The second case shows the variable assigned a string. Strings that spell out numbers are just that—strings. They are not interpreted as numeric values. As a result, the second test returns False.

IsEmpty

IsEmpty determines if a variable has never been assigned any values. It might be useful to use this function to see if a variable has never been used in your code. If a variable has never been used, IsEmpty returns True. The example shown in Listing 4.4, isempty.htm on the CD-ROM, demonstrates the use of this function.

Listing 4.4. Using the IsEmpty function.

```
Sub cmdTest_OnClick()

    Dim Value

    If IsEmpty(Value) = True Then
        MsgBox "The variable is empty."
    Else
        MsgBox "The variable contains data."
    End If
```

continues

Listing 4.4. continued

```
Value = 23

If IsEmpty(Value) = True Then
    MsgBox "The variable is empty."
Else
    MsgBox "The variable contains data."
End If

End Sub
```

ANALYSIS In the first test, the IsEmpty function will return True because the variable has been created but not yet used. Because it hasn't been used yet, the variable is empty. Once the variable is assigned a value, the function will return False because the variable will have data assigned to it. To take a variable that has already been assigned data and wipe it from existence, you can enter the command

variable_name = Nothing

where *variable_name* is the name of the variable. The Nothing literal not only deletes the contents of the container, but it also eliminates the container entirely. If, after setting a variable equal to Nothing, you apply IsEmpty to the variable, the function will return True.

IsNull

Another useful condition to check is whether a variable is set to a Null value. If the Null literal has been assigned to a variable, IsNull returns True. Null empties the contents of a variable container, but it does not wipe out the container like the Nothing literal does. The example in Listing 4.5, isnull.htm on the CD-ROM, shows a useful example of this function.

Listing 4.5. Using the IsNull function.

```
Sub cmdTest_OnClick()

    Dim TestString

    If IsEmpty(TestString) = True Then
        MsgBox "The variable is empty."
    Else
        MsgBox "The variable is not empty."
    End If

    If IsNull(TestString) = True Then
        MsgBox "The variable is Null."
    Else
        MsgBox "The variable is not Null."
    End If
```

```
    TestString = "This is a test."

    If IsEmpty(TestString) = True Then
        MsgBox "The variable is empty."
    Else
        MsgBox "The variable is not empty."
    End If

    If IsNull(TestString) = True Then
        MsgBox "The variable is Null."
    Else
        MsgBox "The variable is not Null."
    End If

    TestString = Null

    If IsEmpty(TestString) = True Then
        MsgBox "The variable is empty."
    Else
        MsgBox "The variable is not empty."
    End If

    If IsNull(TestString) = True Then
        MsgBox "The variable is Null."
    Else
        MsgBox "The variable is not Null."
    End If

End Sub
```

ANALYSIS In this example, the variable TestString is first created. The first check is to see whether the variable is empty. Because nothing has been stored in it yet, the condition returns True, and the user sees the message box explaining that the variable is empty. Likewise, it has not been assigned a Null value at this point, so the message indicates that the variable is not Null.

Then the variable is assigned a string. The next check is to see whether the variable is empty by calling the IsEmpty function. Because the variable has been assigned data, it is not empty, and the IsEmpty function returns False. Furthermore, because the variable has been assigned a string, it is not Null either.

Finally, the string is set to Null. Even though the string has been set to Null, it is not empty, so IsEmpty returns False again. This time, the string is Null, so the IsNull function returns True.

These functions are useful in determining whether a variable has been loaded with data. The program can then make a decision based on whether a variable contains data. You will see how to do this on Day 6, "Controlling the Flow of VBScript Code."

IsObject

You use the IsObject function to see if a variable has been set to reference an object. A variable can be assigned to refer to an object with a statement such as

```
Set myVariable = document.MyForm
```

The line of code refers to document.myform. This specifies a user input form called myform contained on the current-page document. This form object is then assigned to the variable myVariable. Then subsequent statements can use the variable IsObject to verify that the variable myVariable does indeed refer to an object, as opposed to, for example, an integer or a string. You will learn more about object concepts on Days 8 through 10, beginning with "Intrinsic HTML Form Controls" on Day 8.

Changing the Type of Data in a Variable

Consider once again the example of assigning a decimal value to the Distance variable. Suppose that when you assign Distance a value of 6.5, you don't want it to take on the double data type because the single data type is faster and uses less memory. As a result, you might want to change the internal representation of the data type. You can use the set of functions shown in Table 4.2 to convert variables from one internal representation to another.

Table 4.2. Variant internal representation conversion functions.

Variant	Description
CBool	Converts data to the Boolean type
CByte	Converts data to the byte type
CDate	Converts data to the date type
CDbl	Converts data to the double type
CInt	Converts data to the integer type
CLng	Converts data to the long type
CSng	Converts data to the single type
CStr	Converts data to the string type

Suppose, for example, the user enters a value with a decimal point, but you want VBScript to convert the value to an integer instead. When the user enters the decimal value, VBScript will automatically assign the value to the double data type. You need to explicitly tell VBScript to convert the value to an integer so you use the CInt function. The example shown in Listing 4.6, called cint.htm on the CD-ROM that accompanies the book, shows you how you could use this function to accomplish that goal.

Listing 4.6. Using `CInt` to make sure a value is an integer.

```
Sub cmdTest_OnClick()

Dim Result

Result = 5.2

MsgBox "You have entered a floating-point value of " & Result

Value = CInt(Result)

MsgBox "Your floating-point value has been converted to an integer_
        value of " & Result

End Sub
```

ANALYSIS In this example, the variable named `Result` is stored with a value—in this case, `5.2`. (Obviously, in anything other than a sample program, you'd probably obtain the result from a calculation or user input, but for simplicity, the value is assigned directly here.) The `CInt` function then converts the value to an integer, and the result is stored in the variable. The result displayed from the first message box is `You have entered a floating-point value of 5.2`. The second message box, as you probably anticipated, displays `Your floating-point value has been converted to an integer value of 5`, as shown in Figure 4.3.

Figure 4.3.

The `CInt` *function in action, converting a floating-point number to an integer number.*

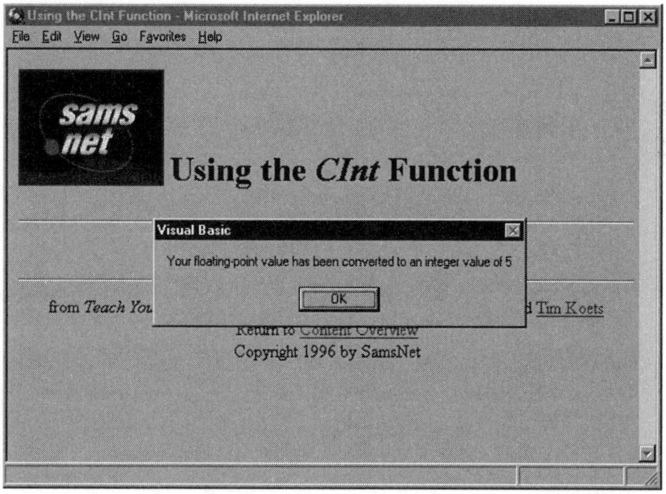

In this sample program, the result isn't used any further. In a more realistic program, the new result would typically be used elsewhere in VBScript code or it would be presented to the user.

Each of the related conversion functions is described briefly in the sections that follow. You will see numerous examples of these functions throughout the book.

CBool

The CBool function takes a variable and converts its subtype into the Boolean data type. Boolean values can be either True or False. Any number except zero is automatically converted to True, and zero is always converted to False. You cannot pass a string as an argument to this function. If you do, you'll get a run-time error.

CByte

The CByte function takes a variable and converts its subtype into the byte data type. In order for this function to work, the value to be converted must be a number in the acceptable range for a byte—between 0 and 255. If the number falls outside this range, a run-time error results. In addition, you cannot use strings as arguments for this function.

CDate

The CDate function takes a variable and converts its subtype into a date data type. The argument must be a string in an acceptable format for dates. If it's not, a run-time error results.

CInt

The CInt function takes a variable and converts its internal subtype into the integer format. It requires a number for its argument, and it rounds the value to the closest integer representation. If the number falls outside the range of the integer data type, a run-time error results.

CLng

The CLng function takes a variable and converts its internal subtype into the long integer format. It requires a number for its argument, and it rounds the value to the closest integer representation. If the number falls outside the range of the long data type, a run-time error results.

CSng

The CSng function takes a variable and converts the internal subtype into the single data type. The variable cannot be a string; it must be a number. Furthermore, the number must fall within the range of the single data type.

CDbl

The CDbl function takes a variable and converts the internal subtype into the double data type. The variable cannot be a string; it must be a number. In addition, the number must fall within the range of the double data type.

CStr

The CStr function converts the subtype of a variable into the string data type. The function can take any argument, whether it's a number or even a string, and convert it automatically to a string. This function is useful when you need to create a string that contains a number and insert that number into the string.

Working with Constants

Sometimes in writing code, you will want to refer to values that never change. The values for True and False, for example, are always -1 and 0, respectively. Values that never change usually have some special meaning, such as defining True and False. These values that never change are called *constants*. The constants True and False are sometimes referred to as *implicit* constants because you do not need to do anything to reference their constant names. They are immediately available in any code you write.

NEW TERM A *constant* is a variable within a program that never changes in value. Users can create their own constants by initializing variables accordingly and then not changing their value. VBScript defines the special True and False constants, as well.

Throughout this lesson, you have seen the True and False constants in action. Keep in mind that it is illegal to change the value of one of VBScript's intrinsic constants. Therefore, the statement

```
False = 10
```

would result in an error because VBScript has already defined False to be 0. VBScript won't let you change a constant even though you can change a variable.

Unfortunately, you cannot create true constants with VBScript in the sense that the language will still allow you to change the value of any constant variable you define. Many languages have ways to declare a constant so that you cannot alter its value anywhere in the program. VBScript does not offer this level of strictly enforced true constant declaration. You can *simulate* a constant, however, by following two rules:

4

☐ When you create the simulated constant, name the constant with uppercase letters if the constant represents a value unique to your program. If the constant is a special value expected by VBScript, prefix the constant name with the letters vb. This naming convention is not required, but it will help you distinguish the constant from all the other variables.

☐ After you assign the initial value to the variable, don't change the variable. VBScript will not enforce this for you, so you'll have to make sure you don't change the value of a simulated constant in your code.

If you wanted to create, for instance, a constant that contains your company name so you can use it throughout your code, you can use the following statements to define the constant:

```
Dim COMPANY
COMPANY = "Acme Enterprises"
```

Then use the variable throughout your code, never assigning the variable COMPANY to any other value. This convention will make it easier to work with and recognize simulated constants.

Special constants you supply to VBScript functions, methods, and statements should be prefixed with vb, as previously mentioned. Table 4.3 shows these constants and the values you should assign to them.

Table 4.3. A sampler of VBScript constants.

Constant	Value	Meaning
vbOKOnly	0	MsgBox buttons desired
vbOKCancel	1	MsgBox buttons desired
vbAbortRetryIgnore	2	MsgBox buttons desired
vbYesNoCancel	3	MsgBox buttons desired
vbYesNo	4	MsgBox buttons desired
vbRetryCancel	5	MsgBox buttons desired
vbCritical	16	MsgBox icon desired
vbQuestion	32	MsgBox icon desired
vbExclamation	48	MsgBox icon desired
vbInformation	64	MsgBox icon desired
vbDefaultButton1	0	MsgBox default button desired
vbDefaultButton2	256	MsgBox default button desired
vbDefaultButton3	512	MsgBox default button desired

Constant	Value	Meaning
vbOK	1	Return code: selected MsgBox button
vbCancel	2	Return code: selected MsgBox button
vbAbort	3	Return code: selected MsgBox button
vbRetry	4	Return code: selected MsgBox button
vbIgnore	5	Return code: selected MsgBox button
vbYes	6	Return code: selected MsgBox button
vbNo	7	Return code: selected MsgBox button
vbCrLf	chr(13) & chr(10)	Causes line break in text

These constants can be defined in your VBScript code and used when needed. For example, suppose you want to use the vbCrLf constant in your program to break up your text. You could enter the code as follows:

```
Dim vbCrLf : vbCrLf = chr(13) & chr(10)   ' Causes line break in text
Dim svResponse

svResponse = "The password is less than twelve characters.  " & vbCrLf & _
             "Please enter the password again."
```

In this case, the first line of code declares and defines the constant (note the vb prefix). Then, another variable is declared and stored with the string shown above. Because the constant vbCrLf is used by VBScript to break a line of text and is not a "homemade" constant, the vb prefix is used rather than uppercase letters.

NOTE

A complete listing of the values shown in Table 4.3 is presented on the CD-ROM that accompanies the book. The file constant.txt, which is located in Code\Shared\Tools, contains the declarations and assignments of each of these constants. You can then simply copy and paste the constants you want to use into your Web page. One of the advantages of using the vb naming convention for your constants—in addition to improved maintainability—is that it will make your code more compatible with standard Visual Basic for Applications code, if you ever need to move code between environments.

You'll learn more about constants on Day 13, "VBScript Standards and Conventions." For more useful conventions, refer to Day 13.

The Scope and Lifetime of a Variable

With VBScript you can create variables that are shared throughout your code, or you can create variables that are used only with code blocks called *procedures*. A procedure is a block of code that accomplishes a specific goal. For example, you might have a procedure that calculates the total cost of an item. Perhaps you have a procedure that is executed when the user clicks a command button. VBScript has three types of procedures: subroutines, functions, and events. Each of these will be defined and discussed on Day 7, "Building a Home for Your Code." For now, just think of a procedure as a body of code that gets executed for some reason. This section discusses a procedure that gets executed whenever the user clicks a button.

> **NEW TERM** A *procedure* is a body of code that is called from within VBScript to be executed.

When a variable is created, you can either use it within a specific procedure or share it among all the procedures in the script. The availability a variable has within its environment is referred to as the *scope* of a variable. Variables in VBScript can have two different kinds of scope. When a variable is declared inside a procedure, it has *local scope* and can be referenced only while that procedure is executed. Local-scope variables are often called *procedure-level* variables because they exist only in procedures. When you declare a variable in a procedure, it automatically has local scope, which means only the code within that procedure can access or change the value of that variable. You might want to share a variable among more than one procedure. If you declare a variable outside a procedure, it automatically has *script-level* scope and is available to all the procedures in your script.

> **NEW TERM** *Scope* refers to where within a script, such as a local procedure or globally across the script, a given variable is available for use based on the declaration.

Variables not only have a scope, but they also exist for different amounts of time depending on their scope. This property of a variable is often referred to as its *lifetime*. Script-level variables are created outside of any procedures using the `Dim` keyword. They exist from the time the variable is declared until the time the script is finished running. Listing 4.7 shows an example of a script-level variable. This Web page, named `scrptlvl.htm`, is on the CD-ROM that accompanies the book.

Listing 4.7. Using script-level variables.

```
<HTML>

<TITLE>Using Script-Level Variables</TITLE>

<H1><A HREF="http://www.mcp.com"><IMG  ALIGN=BOTTOM
SRC="../shared/jpg/samsnet.jpg" BORDER=2></A>
Using Script-Level Variables</H1>
```

```
<BODY>

<HR>

<CENTER><INPUT TYPE=BUTTON VALUE="Click Me" NAME="cmdTest"></CENTER>

<HR>

<center>
from <em>Teach Yourself VBScript in 21 Days</em> by
<A HREF="../shared/info/keith.htm">Keith Brophy</A> and
<A HREF="../shared/info/tim.htm">Tim Koets</A><br>
Return to <a href="..\default.htm">Content Overview</A><br>
Copyright 1996 by SamsNet<br>
</center>

<SCRIPT LANGUAGE="VBScript">
<!-- Option Explicit

   Dim Counter

   Sub cmdTest_OnClick()
      SetCaption
      cmdTest.Value = Counter
   End Sub

   Sub SetCaption()
      Counter = Counter + 1
   End Sub

-->
</SCRIPT>

</BODY>

</HTML>
```

4

NOTE

The code in Listing 4.7 makes use of the following HTML button control definition:

```
<INPUT TYPE=BUTTON VALUE="Click Me" NAME="cmdTest">
```

HTML form controls are one of several types of controls you can place on a Web page and manipulate using VBScript. These controls will be discussed in detail on Day 8. In this example, all you need to know about the button declaration is that it results in the display of a button on the form. This internal name of the button, which is visible to the VBScript application, is cmdTest. VBScript can assign or retrieve values from this button by referencing its caption with a statement like the following:

```
Variable1 = cmdTest.Value
```

When the user clicks the button, the browser informs VBScript that an OnClick event has occurred for that given button. VBScript will begin the routine cmdTest_OnClick if that procedure exists.

ANALYSIS In Listing 4.7, the variable, which is called Counter, is declared outside all the procedures in the script. As a result, any of the procedures within the script can use it. When the user clicks the cmdTest button in the Web page, the browser must handle the OnClick event that occurs. The procedure cmdTest_OnClick is called because it is associated with the button by virtue of its name. The first action of this procedure is to call SetCaption. The SetCaption procedure increments the counter variable by 1 and ends. Then the procedure that called SetCaption continues by setting the text on the command button equal to Counter. This, in effect, increments the number on the command button each time it is clicked, as shown in Figure 4.4.

Figure 4.4.

Script-level variables are used here to increment a value that appears on the button on the Web page.

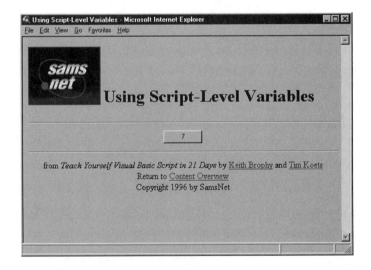

Because the variable is shared among all the procedures in the script, SetCaption doesn't need to be told the value of Counter; it can simply look for it itself.

What would happen if the variable were moved inside the calling procedure rather than outside, as is the case in the Web page incorvar.htm on the CD-ROM, shown in Listing 4.8?

Listing 4.8. Using procedure-level variables incorrectly.

```
<SCRIPT LANGUAGE="VBScript">
<!-- Option Explicit

   Sub cmdTest_OnClick()
      Dim Counter
      SetCaption
      cmdTest.Value = Counter
   End Sub

   Sub SetCaption()
      Counter = Counter + 1
   End Sub
-->
</SCRIPT>
```

 ANALYSIS Because of the `Option Explicit` command at the beginning of the script, running this code would result in an error! The `Counter` variable has been moved from outside the procedures into the `cmdTest_OnClick` procedure, so it is only available to that procedure. The `SetCaption` procedure no longer has access to the variable, so it would have to declare `Counter` before it could use it. Because `Option Explicit` is being used, VBScript does not recognize the variable without an explicit declaration, and an error results.

NOTE At the time of this printing, VBScript and Microsoft Internet Explorer 3.0 were still in beta form. As a consequence, the code in Listing 4.8 will not result in an error when run. In the discussion that follows, the text assumes that an error will occur in the final release of these products when the `Option Explicit` expression will be supported.

Listing 4.9, `inappvar.htm`, shows the fix for this error condition.

Listing 4.9. Using procedure-level variables inappropriately.

```
<SCRIPT LANGUAGE="VBScript">
<!-- Option Explicit

   Sub cmdTest_OnClick()
      Dim Counter
      SetCaption
      cmdTest.Value = Counter
   End Sub
```

continues

Listing 4.9. continued

```
Sub SetCaption()
    Dim Counter
    Counter = Counter + 1
End Sub

<--
</SCRIPT>
```

ANALYSIS Now the code will run, but it still won't work right. Because each procedure has its own copy of the variable, they can't share with each other. When the `SetCaption` procedure is called, it creates the `Counter` variable and sets it equal to 1. Then, when the calling function resumes, it uses its own copy of `Counter`, which has never been set. The result is that nothing at all is displayed in the command button when it is clicked, as can be seen in Figure 4.5.

Figure 4.5.

Here, a procedure-level variable is used and results in an unintended loss of data—the caption of the button is empty!

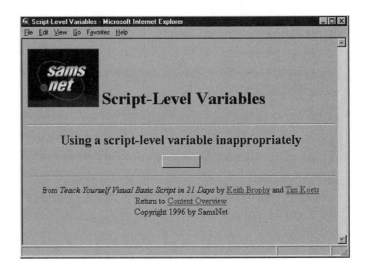

Sometimes, you might want to use two different copies of a variable. Consider Listing 4.10, `dim.htm`, for example.

Listing 4.10. Creating procedure-level variables with `Dim`.

```
<HTML>

<TITLE>Script-Level Variables</TITLE>

<H1>
<A HREF="http://www.mcp.com"><IMG  ALIGN=BOTTOM
SRC="../shared/jpg/samsnet.jpg" BORDER=2></A>
```

```
Script-Level Variables
</H1>

<BODY>

<HR>

<CENTER><H2>Using a script-level variable properly</H2>
<INPUT TYPE=BUTTON VALUE="Go!" NAME="GoButton">
<INPUT TYPE=BUTTON VALUE="You haven't clicked on Go yet!"
NAME="TestButton"></CENTER>

<HR>

<center>
from <em>Teach Yourself VBScript in 21 Days</em> by
<A HREF="../shared/info/keith.htm">Keith Brophy</A> and
<A HREF="../shared/info/tim.htm">Tim Koets</A><br>
Return to <a href="..\default.htm">Content Overview</A><br>
Copyright 1996 by SamsNet<br>
</center>

<SCRIPT LANGUAGE="VBScript">
<!-- Option Explicit

    Dim Action

    Sub GoButton_OnClick()
       Action = 1
    End Sub

    Sub TestButton_OnClick()
       If Action = 1 Then
          SetCaptionA
       Else
          SetCaptionB
       End If
    End Sub

    Sub SetCaptionA()
       Dim MyString
       MyString = "You've clicked on Go!"
       TestButton.Value = MyString
    End Sub

    Sub SetCaptionB()
       Dim MyString
       MyString = "You haven't clicked on Go yet!"
       TestButton.Value = MyString
    End Sub

-->
</SCRIPT>

</BODY>

</HTML>
```

4

ANALYSIS In this example, you have two command buttons on a Web page, as shown in Figure 4.6.

Figure 4.6.

The initial state of the `dim.htm` *Web page.*

When the first command button, called `GoButton`, is clicked, a procedure runs that sets a script-level variable called `Action` equal to 1. When the second button, `TestButton`, is clicked, a procedure runs that checks the value of `Action` and calls either `SetCaptionA` or `SetCaptionB`, depending on the value of `Action`. Figure 4.7 shows what happens after the user clicks the `GoButton` command button.

Figure 4.7.

The `dim.htm` *Web page after the user has clicked on the Go! command button.*

Both `SetCaptionA` and `SetCaptionB` create their own local copies of `MyString` and set the caption of `TestButton` with their respective strings. Both strings have the same name, but they are separate copies. As soon as each procedure ends, its own copy of `MyString` is destroyed.

You have seen that the lifetime of a script-level variable is equal to the entire life of the Web page. On the other hand, when you declare a procedure-level variable using `Dim`, the variable exists only while the procedure is run. Once the procedure ends, the variable is destroyed.

You should know one more thing about variables. Suppose you create a script-level variable called `MyVariable`, and then you create a procedure-level variable with the same name, as shown in Listing 4.11! This Web page is named `dupvar.htm` and, like the others, is on the CD-ROM that comes with this book.

Listing 4.11. Creating duplicate variables at different scopes.

```
<HTML>

<TITLE>Variable Scope</TITLE>

<H1><A HREF="http://www.mcp.com"><IMG  ALIGN=BOTTOM
SRC="../shared/jpg/samsnet.jpg" BORDER=2></A>
Variable Scope</H1>

<BODY>

<HR>

<CENTER><H2>Creating duplicate variables with different scopes</H2>
<INPUT TYPE=BUTTON VALUE="Click Me" NAME="cmdTest"></CENTER>

<HR>

<center>
from <em>Teach Yourself VBScript in 21 Days</em> by
<A HREF="../shared/info/keith.htm">Keith Brophy</A> and
<A HREF="../shared/info/tim.htm">Tim Koets</A><br>
Return to <a href="..\default.htm">Content Overview</A><br>
Copyright 1996 by SamsNet<br>
</center>

<SCRIPT LANGUAGE="VBScript">
<!-- Option Explicit

   Dim MyVariable

   Sub cmdTest_OnClick()
      Dim MyVariable
      MyVariable = MyVariable + 1
      cmdTest.Value = MyVariable
   End Sub
```

continues

Listing 4.11. continued

```
-->
</SCRIPT>

</BODY>

</HTML>
```

ANALYSIS If you create duplicate variables, VBScript will create two copies and use only the procedure-level variable in the procedure. It will not use the script-level variable. In Listing 4.11, two copies of MyVariable are created. Unfortunately for this programmer, the copy that gets used inside the procedure is not the one he would like to see used. If he removes the second Dim MyVariable that is inside the procedure, the code will increment the value every time the button is clicked. As it is now, MyVariable will be created locally every time the procedure is executed and will always be equal to 1, as shown in Figure 4.8.

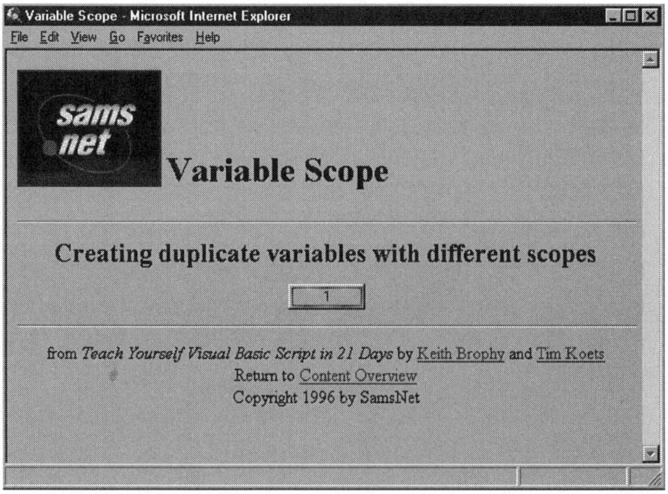

Figure 4.8.

The dupvar.htm *Web page with a button caption always set to* 1.

VBScript uses the variable with the smallest scope whenever there are duplicates. This might seem confusing, and it is. The best way to avoid this situation is to make sure you never give variables in your program the same name unless they are procedure-level variables residing in two separate procedures, as in the example in Listing 4.10.

Working with Arrays

So far today, you've learned what a variable is, how to create one, and what you can store inside one. You might be wondering if there is some easy way to group variables together in a set. For example, you may have a Web page that requests many of the same things—such as a list of screen coordinates—and you want to store those coordinates together. Rather than create ten separate variables, you can instead create one variable that holds all ten pieces of data. This type of container is called an *array*.

NEW TERM   An *array* is a type of variable that ties together a series of data items and places them in a single variable.

Arrays are useful when you're storing sets of similar data because they often make it easier to manipulate the data together. If you wanted to print out a list of ten coordinates, you would have to execute ten print statements to handle each one. Besides, how can you be sure you have ten? What if you have only six at the moment? How can your code handle this kind of situation where you really don't know ahead of time how many pieces of information you have? Here is where the array comes to the rescue!

The beauty of an array is that it enables you to store and use a series of data using one variable name and an *index* to distinguish the individual items. By using an index, you can often make your code simpler and more efficient so that it's easier for you to put a script together and change it later. With VBScript, the elements inside your array can hold any kind of data. The elements don't have to be all integers or all strings, for example. The array can hold a combination of data types.

Creating Arrays

You create arrays using the same keyword you use when creating variables—the Dim keyword. An array created with the Dim keyword exists as long as the procedure does and is destroyed once the procedure ends. If you create the array in the main script, outside the procedure, the values will persist as long as the page is loaded. You can create two types of arrays using VBScript: *fixed* arrays and *dynamic* arrays. Fixed arrays have a specific number of elements in them, whereas dynamic arrays can vary in the number of elements depending on how many are stored in the array. Both types of arrays are useful, and both have advantages and disadvantages.

Fixed-Length Arrays

You can create fixed-length arrays using the following syntax:

```
Dim Array_Name(count - 1)
```

where `Array_Name` is the name of the array and *count* is an integer value representing the number of containers you want the array to contain. The statement

```
Dim Names(19)
```

creates an array called `Names` that consists of 20 containers, often called *elements*. You can store 20 different names in this array of data called `Names`. Consider the shoe box analogy discussed earlier in this lesson. Creating an array is like having 20 shoe boxes, all the same size, that you can store shoes in. Rather than naming each box separately, you can give them all the same name and refer to them using an index, such as `ShoeBox(1)`, `ShoeBox(2)`, `Shoebox(3)`, and so on.

The index of the array always starts at `0` and ends at `count` `-1`. In the case of the `Names` array, the number of containers, or elements, in the array ranges from `Names(0)` to `Names(19)` for a total of 20 elements. To see how this works, look at the code in Listing 4.12. The complete Web page that executes this code is on the CD-ROM with the title `index.htm`. This simple code listing sets every element of the `Names` array equal to the string `"Unknown"`. This is similar to putting the same type of shoe in every shoe box in your closet.

Listing 4.12. Working with the index of an array.

```
Dim Names(19)
Dim i

For i = 0 to 19
    Names(i) = "Unknown"
Next
```

ANALYSIS This code listing uses a *loop* to set each element. Essentially, the program treats the variable i like a counter and keeps incrementing it by 1 all the way from `0` to `19`. The `Names(i) = "Unknown"` code statement is executed 20 times, and each time the i value is different. Day 6 covers loops in depth.

It's important to remember that the first container in your array has an index of `0`, not `1`. In this example, the first element in the array is `Names(0)`, not `Names(1)`. If you forget this and start with `Names(1)`, you'll only be able to use 19 of the containers, not 20.

Dynamic Arrays

The second type of array you can create is the dynamic array. The benefit of a dynamic array is that if you don't know how large the array will be when you write the code, you can create code that sets or changes the size while the VBScript code is running. A dynamic array is created in the same way as a fixed array, but you don't put any bounds in the declaration. As a result, your statement becomes

```
Dim Names()
```

Eventually, you need to tell VBScript how many elements the array will contain. You can do this with the `ReDim` function. `ReDim` tells VBScript to "re-dimension" the array to however many elements you specify. `ReDim` takes dimensions the same way `Dim` can. The syntax is

```
ReDim Array_Name(Count - 1)
```

So, if you enter

```
ReDim Names(9)
```

you will create an array that has room to store ten elements. This way, you can set the size of the array while the code is running rather than when you write the code. This can be useful when the user gets to decide how many names he will enter. For example, he might type the number of names he's going to give you into a text control. In that case, you could use code like what's shown in Listing 4.13. This Web page is called `dynamic.htm` and is on the CD-ROM that comes with the book.

Listing 4.13. Working with a dynamic array.

```
Dim Names()
Dim i
Dim Count

Count = txtCount.Value

ReDim Names(Count - 1)

For i = 0 to Count - 1
   Names(i) = "Unknown"
Next

MsgBox "The Names array has just been dimensioned to " & _
       Count & " elements and set with the string ""Unknown""."
```

ANALYSIS In this case, the number of elements is set using the variable `Count` instead of some fixed number. This code isn't very safe, of course, because the user might not enter a valid number, or for that matter, he might type in something strange like the name of his dog. In Day 17, you will see how to handle those kinds of situations by making your scripts as "dummy proof" as possible.

Suppose that you dimension an array in your code, and later on, you need to increase the size of the array. No problem, right? You just use `ReDim` again and increase the number of elements in the array. That will certainly work, but the entire array will be erased in the process. This is like adding more shoe boxes to your closet by taking out all the shoe boxes, emptying them, and putting the total number you want back in empty. Do not despair; VBScript contains a keyword called `Preserve` that comes to the rescue.

The `Preserve` keyword is very important when using `ReDim`. Suppose, for example, that you create a dynamic array, specifying its storage space by using `ReDim`, fill it with data, and then later decide to make it larger so you can fill it with more information without losing your original data. (See Listing 4.14.) The Web page is saved on the CD-ROM as `nopresrv.htm`.

Listing 4.14. Resizing a dynamic array without `Preserve`.

```
Dim Names()
Dim i
Dim Count

Count = txtCount.Text

ReDim Names(Count -1)

For i = 0 to Count - 1
    Names(i) = "Unknown"
Next

ReDim Names( Count + 49)

For i = Count to Count + 49
    Names(i) = "Extra Names"
Next
MsgBox "The Names array has just been dimensioned to " & Count & _
       " elements and redimensioned with an additional 50 elements."
```

ANALYSIS In this example the programmer has declared an array of size `Count` and then resized the array to `50` plus the original size. (You probably noticed that `49` is used instead of `50` in the `ReDim` statement. Keep in mind that because the array index starts at `0` rather than `1`, you set the size to be the desired `Count - 1`.) The problem is that without the `Preserve` keyword after the `ReDim` statement, the first `Count` elements are erased.

Now consider the code in Listing 4.15. This listing is based on the Web page titled `preserve.htm` located on the CD-ROM that accompanies the book.

Listing 4.15. Resizing a dynamic array with the use of `Preserve`.

```
Dim Names()
Dim i
Dim Count

Count = txtCount.Text

ReDim Names(Count-1)
```

```
For i = 0 to Count - 1
    Names(i) = "Unknown"
Next

ReDim Preserve Names(Count + 49)

For i = Count to Count + 49
    Names(i) = "Extra Names"
Next
MsgBox "The Names array has just been dimensioned to " & Count & _
       " elements and redimensioned with an additional 50 elements. _
       All items retain their original values."
```

ANALYSIS If you use `Preserve` after the second `ReDim` statement, as shown in Listing 4.15, VBScript will still retain the first `Count` elements. This is like adding shoe boxes to a closet without emptying the boxes already in the closet.

If you want to erase whatever is in the array when you resize it, leave off the `Preserve` keyword. If you want to keep what you've got, make sure to include it when you re-dimension an array.

You can use the `ReDim` statement again and again in your procedure. Suppose you want to change the size of the array twice in the procedure. You might have a Web page where the user enters two sets of names for a couple sports teams. You could have code similar to the Web page `redim.htm`, whose VBScript code is shown in Listing 4.16.

Listing 4.16. Working with a dynamic array and `ReDim`.

```
Sub cmdTest_OnClick()

    Dim Names()
    Dim i
    Dim Green_Count
    Dim Red_Count

    ' Initialize the values
    Green_Count = 0
    Red_Count = 0

    Green_Count = txtGreenCount.Value

    ReDim Names(Green_Count - 1)

    For i = 0 to Green_Count - 1
        Names(i) = "Green Team Player"
    Next

    Red_Count = txtRedCount.Value

    ReDim Preserve Names(Green_Count + Red_Count - 1)
```

continues

Listing 4.16. continued

```
        For i = Green_Count to Green_Count + Red_Count - 1
            Names(i) = "Red Team Player"
        Next

        MsgBox Green_Count & " Green team members and " & Red_Count & _
                            " Red Team members have been created."

End Sub
```

ANALYSIS   As you can see, ReDim is used here (along with Preserve) to dimension the array the first time and then later to make it larger.

Determining the Size of the Array

In the course of working with arrays, you might want to find out how large an array is. VBScript provides you with a function called UBound, which gives you the information you need. UBound tells you how many boxes of shoes you have set aside in the closet. This function returns an integer value and requires one argument—the array:

```
size = UBound(array_name)
```

where *size* is a variable that will contain the bound value of the array and *array_name* is the name of the array. To see how you can take advantage of these functions, compare Listing 4.17 to the Web page named ubound.htm, whose VBScript code is shown in Listing 4.17.

Listing 4.17. Using UBound on a fixed-length array.

```
Dim Names(19)
Dim i

For i = 0 to UBound(Names)
    Names(i) = "Unknown"
Next
MsgBox "The upper bound of the Names() array is " & UBound(Names)
```

ANALYSIS   In this example, you use UBound(Names) instead of 19. This might seem trivial, but what happens if you want to change the size of your array from 20 elements to 40? You would not only have to change the declaration of the array, but you'd also have to find every place in your code where you reference the size of the array and change the values. By using the bounding function, you only have to make one change, which makes your code easier to maintain.

Multi-Dimensional Arrays

The arrays you have seen so far today have had only one dimension. Using the shoe box analogy, it's like having a closet full of shoe boxes. Suppose that you not only want to put your shoes on shelves, but you also want to put your work shoes on one specific shelf, your dress shoes on another, and so on. If you did that, each shoe box "address" would first refer to the shelf and then to the particular box on that shelf.

When writing VBScript code, you might want to create an array in a similar way. You can do this by creating an array with more than one *dimension*, making it a *multi-dimensional array*. With VBScript, you can define up to 60 dimensions for a single array. How could this be useful? Suppose that you have a grid like a spreadsheet on your Web page, and you want to give the user the ability to enter data in each cell. You could keep track of the grid using a two-dimensional array by declaring the array as

```
Grid(rows - 1, columns - 1)
```

where *rows* is the number of rows on the spreadsheet and *columns* is the number of columns. If you wanted to obtain the value stored in row two, column three, you could use the statement

```
Value = Grid(3 - 1, 2 - 1)
```

to obtain the information. Notice that you have to decrease the index by 1 because the index starts with 0. Also, when you use the ReDim statement to re-dimension a multi-dimensional array, you can change the limit of any of the dimensions, but you cannot change the number of dimensions. For example, if you have declared the array

```
Dim Grid()
```

and you dimension the array as

```
ReDim Grid(10, 30)
```

you can execute another ReDim statement like

```
ReDim Grid(5, 100)
```

but you cannot add another dimension:

```
ReDim Grid(5, 10, 20)
```

The first ReDim statement you enter in a procedure sets the number of the dimensions of the array. After that, you cannot change the number of dimensions; you can change only the number of elements for that dimension.

Changing the Contents of the Array

One final word about arrays: You can clear the contents of an array entirely by using the `Erase` function. This function takes one parameter, the name of the array. If you want to erase an array out of memory, simply enter

```
Erase Array_Name
```

Not only will this erase the array's contents, but with dynamic arrays (those declared with `ReDim`), it will also free the memory that was used by the array. Because variables and large arrays in particular can take a lot of memory, it is wise to use the `Erase` statement whenever you're finished with an array in a procedure.

Summary

Today, you got the information you need to create and use variables within your VBScript code. It is one of several key lessons that get you up to speed on the basics of VBScript. If you've used Visual Basic or some other programming language, parts of this lesson might seem quite elementary to you. It is important, however, to get a survey of variable use in VBScript because each language has a different way of approaching variable creation and use.

Today's lesson begins by giving a definition of what a variable actually is—a container in which to store information. Then you saw how easy it is to create a variable by simply entering `Dim` followed by the name of the variable in your code. This lesson also describes all the various kinds of data you can place in a variable.

You have seen how VBScript figures out what kind of data you have stored in a variable. This is important because you sometimes need to know what VBScript thinks you have stored just in case you want to change its mind. You have learned about a series of functions you can use, if necessary, to ask VBScript about the internal representation of a variable. In this way, you can make sure the user has entered data correctly, or you can decide how to handle data based on how it is being stored. You then saw a group of functions that convert the internal data representation from one type to another. This is often useful when you want to change the format of the data in order to manipulate it with other variables.

Today's lesson also discusses the scope and lifetime of variables, pointing out that you can use `Dim` to create a procedure-level variable whose contents are erased once a procedure ends or you can declare a variable outside a procedure, making it a script-level variable that all the procedures can share within a script. That way, a variable can exist no matter what code the VBScript procedure is executing.

Having discussed simple variables, the lesson concludes by discussing arrays. Arrays are useful, powerful, and time-saving. You have seen how to create both a fixed-size array and a dynamic array. You have also seen how to re-dimension a dynamic array and preserve the contents of the array while doing so, how to create arrays of more than one dimension, and how you might use such arrays.

You've made it through the first day that teaches you how to write VBScript code! As you learn more about VBScript and its capabilities, all the concepts you are learning now will not only start to make more sense, but you will also begin to use VBScript in increasingly more powerful ways. A few days from now you'll be well along your way, developing powerful and fun Web pages. You can't get there without first learning the fundamentals, and this is the first lesson where you do just that. In tomorrow's lesson, you will learn how to put variables to use with operators. Day 5 is also when you will learn how to use arithmetic with your variables, compare one variable to another, set the contents of variables, and work with strings. Then, on Day 6, you will learn how to control the flow of your code and create procedures. Day 7 gets into more details on procedures, and on Days 8 and 9, you'll learn about the intrinsic HTML controls. Then, when you reach Day 10, you'll be ready to learn the powerful ActiveX controls.

Q&A

4

Q Why doesn't VBScript support all the other data types that Visual Basic supports?

A I can't speak for Microsoft, but they probably dropped the other data types to keep the language simple. A likely goal for the VBScript design team was to make the language as flexible, easy to learn, and safe to use as possible. The variant type is definitely the easiest to use, and it reduces the size and complexity of the VBScript run-time interpreter. This makes VBScript faster and more efficient at what it does.

Q Why would I ever need to figure out the subtype of a variable?

A Usually, you won't have to worry about variable subtypes. On occasion, however, you may need to inquire as to a variables subtype so you can convert it into another format or carry out a certain action depending on the variable. For example, you may want to execute code differently if the user enters None in a text box versus a value.

Q Arrays look pretty complicated. Will I ever need to use them?

A They might seem complicated to you now, but you will see as you work through this book that not only are they easy to use, but they can also save you a great deal of extra code and make your program a lot easier to write and understand later.

Workshop

Today you saw a Web page that makes use of simple variables. Take one of the code examples in this lesson and create your own Web page. Once you've got it running, create several variables and assign data to them. Practice displaying the contents of those variables on the Web page using MsgBox and the form button control I have discussed.

Quiz

NOTE

Refer to Appendix C, "Answers to Quiz Questions," for the answers to these questions.

1. What data type are VBScript variables based on? Can you remember the data types you can store inside a variable?

2. Write the code required within a procedure to create a variable for storing your name with VBScript code. Assign your name to that variable.

3. Assume you have a variable called Age that contains an age provided by the user. Write the code that ensures that the user has entered a number as her age. If the user hasn't entered a number, tell her she needs to enter her age correctly.

Day **5**

Putting Operators to Work in VBScript

On Day 4, "Creating Variables in VBScript," you learned how to create and use variables. It is important for you to master this skill because variables are fundamental in almost all aspects of VBScript programming. Now that you've seen how to create variables, you need to know how to use *operators* to make those variables do useful work for you. Operators are given that name because they *operate* on the variables associated with them. For example, the addition operator (+) is one of the operators you can use in VBScript. The addition operator is applied to operate on one or more variables—in this case, to add the variables together.

NEW TERM   An *operator* is a symbol applied to data values (such as variables) that causes the computer to carry out a specific operation on that data (for example, multiplication, subtraction).

Today you will learn each of the VBScript operators and see some examples of how to use them. If you've used Visual Basic or some other programming language in the past, much of what's contained in today's lesson will be a review for you. Still, you need to know how VBScript differs from the languages you've used before, so in either case, this lesson is important to you. After introducing the principals of fundamental operators, I also discuss string operators—particularly the rules about how to append strings together.

Today's lesson, together with yesterday's coverage of variables and the rest of the lessons in this first week, will give you a solid foundation for getting started with VBScript.

Working with Operators

As you begin to write VBScript code, you will use operators so much that their use will become natural to you. In this section, you will learn about each of the operators available to you in VBScript, as well as how you might go about using them.

Arithmetic Operators

The first major class of operators is *arithmetic operators*. Arithmetic operators enable you to perform simple arithmetic on one or more variables. Most of these operators will be familiar to you because you have been exposed to them in everyday life. Few people will be surprised to find, for example, that the + operator performs addition! Some operators, however, might be new to you. In any case, you need to understand how to apply these operators to variables and literals in VBScript code, and today's lesson will teach you how.

NEW TERM   *Arithmetic operators* are a class of operators specifically intended to perform arithmetic on the corresponding data.

NOTE   Just a reminder: The term *literal* means "take the data literally." For example, the following message box statement prints the contents of variable VarA:

```
msgbox "My favorite number is " & VarA
```

The next message box prints the literal 100. This means it will directly reference the number 100 without using a variable:

```
msgbox "My favorite number is " & 100
```

The second message box used the literal data representation, which was directly coded into the statement, rather than a variable. Such data is called literal data. Operators can essentially work on any type of data, whether it is literal data or the intrinsic constants and variables introduced yesterday. Because most of the time you'll use variables with the operators, I use the term *variables* for the sake of simplicity when I refer to what operators work on. (The more formal computer science term for what operators work on is *operands*.)

Addition (+)

The first arithmetic operator is the addition operator. You already used this operator yesterday and probably intuitively understood its purpose because it is so commonly used and easy to understand. The addition operator is used to add values, whether they are stored in variables, constants, or literal numbers. You also use the + operator to concatenate strings, but for now, just focus on its ability to add numbers—I'll discuss string concatenation later today.

You can add variables, numbers, and constants in a variety of combinations with the addition operator. For example, you can use the addition operator to add two numbers together and assign them to a variable:

```
Orders = 2 + 3
```

You can also add a number to a variable and assign it to another variable:

```
Result = Quantity + 15
```

You can even add a constant to a variable and store the result in another:

```
BoxType = vbYesNo + vbQuestion
```

You can add as many numbers, variables, and constants as you want:

```
Guests = Mine + 5 + His + 8 + Hers
```

In life, people are always adding things together. You add the tip to your meal cost over lunch; you add up your W2 forms at tax time. You add the number of bills you have to pay this month. You add numbers all the time. Likewise, when you're writing code, you use addition all the time. The addition operator can be used for a variety of purposes.

Consider the simple example in Listing 5.1. In this case, the user wants some way-out, radical t-shirts from your Way-Out, Radical T-Shirt Shop. The user must enter into the Web page the total number of shirts he or she wants of each color you offer. You can calculate the total number of shirts the user wants by simply adding the number of each color. That way, the

5

program can determine how many shirts the user wants so that the script can put together a cost.

Listing 5.1. Using the addition operator to calculate the number of shirts to order.

```
<HTML>

<TITLE>The Way-Out, Radical T-Shirt Shop</TITLE>

<H1><A HREF="http://www.mcp.com"><IMG  ALIGN=BOTTOM
SRC="../shared/jpg/samsnet.jpg" BORDER=2></A>
T-Shirt Order Form</H1>

<BODY>

<HR>

<CENTER>

<PRE>    Red Shirts     <INPUT NAME="txtRed" SIZE=5></PRE>
<PRE>    Green Shirts   <INPUT NAME="txtGreen" SIZE=5></PRE>
<PRE>    Blue Shirts    <INPUT NAME="txtBlue" SIZE=5></PRE></CENTER>

<CENTER><INPUT TYPE=BUTTON VALUE="Order!" NAME="cmdOrder"></CENTER>

<HR>

<center>
from <em>Teach Yourself VBScript in 21 Days</em> by <A HREF="_
../shared/info/keith.htm">Keith Brophy</A> and
<A HREF="../shared/info/tim.htm">Tim Koets</A><br>
Return to <a href="..\default.htm">Content Overview</A><br>
Copyright 1996 by SamsNet<br>
</center>

<SCRIPT LANGUAGE="VBScript">
<!-- Option Explicit

    Sub cmdOrder_OnClick()

        Dim Quantity_Ordered

        Dim Red
        Dim Green
        Dim Blue

        Red = CInt(txtRed.Value)
        Green = CInt(txtGreen.Value)
        Blue = CInt(txtBlue.Value)
```

```
        Quantity_Ordered = Red + Green + Blue

        MsgBox "You have submitted a request to order " & _
                Quantity_Ordered & " shirts!"

      End Sub

    -->
    </SCRIPT>

    </BODY>

    </HTML>
```

This example offers three colors to the user. Figure 5.1 shows the Web page, named tshirt.htm on the CD-ROM that accompanies this book.

Figure 5.1.

Web page for ordering t-shirts.

5

ANALYSIS As you can see from the figure, the Web page has three text boxes into which the user can enter how many shirts he or she wants to order. Then, the user simply clicks the Order! button to place the order. In this case, as shown in Figure 5.1, a message box appears, indicating the number of shirts the user has ordered.

Listing 5.1 shows the entire HTML document so you can see how the text box controls and button are placed on the Web page. Don't worry about the details of how this is done because these controls, along with many others, will be discussed on Day 10, "An Introduction to Objects and ActiveX Controls." In the procedure cmdOrder_OnClick, the number of shirts in red, green, and blue are taken from the text boxes where the user entered those numbers. The

`CInt` function converts each of those values into integers rather than strings. After that, they are added together using

```
Quantity = Red + Green + Blue
```

and stored in the variable `Quantity_Ordered`. Finally, a message box tells the user how many shirts he has ordered.

This example shows you one way to use the addition operator. You will see many more examples of its use throughout this book.

Subtraction (-)

The subtraction operator should also be very familiar to you. This operator works the same way the addition operator does except that it subtracts one or more numbers rather than add them. Otherwise, the syntax is the same. You can subtract two numbers and assign the result to a variable:

```
Result = 100 - 37
```

You can also use variables:

```
Result = 100 - Count
```

You can also subtract more than two values:

```
Result = 100 - Count - Extras
```

You can combine addition and subtraction in the same code statement:

```
Result = May + June - July
```

To see how you might use the subtraction operator, consider the example in Listing 5.2. It's the same Web page shown in Listing 5.1, but you're adding more capabilities to it as you go. Suppose that you're running a special this month where the customer automatically gets one shirt free, regardless of how many he orders. A pretty generous offer, but hey—you're a generous person! The Web page is named `discount.htm` on the CD-ROM that comes with the book.

Listing 5.2. Using the subtraction operator to calculate the number of shirts the user will have to pay for.

```
Sub cmdOrder_OnClick()

    Dim Quantity_Ordered
    Dim Quantity_Charged
```

```
    Dim Red
    Dim Green
    Dim Blue

    Red = CInt(txtRed.Value)
    Green = CInt(txtGreen.Value)
    Blue = CInt(txtBlue.Value)

    Quantity_Ordered = Red + Green + Blue
    Quantity_Charged = Quantity_Ordered - 1

    MsgBox "You have submitted a request to order " & _
        Quantity_Ordered & " shirts!"

    MsgBox "You will be charged for " & Quantity_Charged & _
 " shirts, because you get one shirt for free! "

End Sub
```

ANALYSIS This code segment creates another variable called Quantity_Charged because the quantity charged will be one shirt less than the quantity ordered. You calculate the quantity charged by subtracting one shirt off the quantity ordered. The code in Listing 5.2 performs that subtraction and tells the user how many shirts he or she will actually be charged for. Figure 5.2 shows the message box that tells the user how many shirts he or she must ultimately pay for.

Figure 5.2.

Web page for ordering t-shirts at a discount.

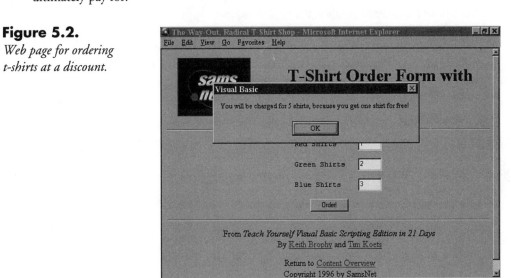

5

NOTE

You might have noticed that Listing 5.2 uses two separate message boxes to provide feedback to the user. Other, more elegant ways to provide user feedback will be covered in subsequent lessons. For now, using a message box in our examples for each piece of feedback to the user helps keeps things simple!

Multiplication (*)

Addition and subtraction are important, but you also need to be able to multiply values together. In most computer languages, the * symbol is used to indicate multiplication, not the x symbol. You might be able to use x on paper, but to the computer, x is a variable, not a multiplication symbol. If you enter the command

```
Result = 3 x 2
```

the interpreter will give you a syntax error. Rather, you should enter the command

```
Result = 3 * 2
```

to be correct. Consider the shirt business example. You have the total number of shirts the customer has ordered as well as the total number of shirts the customer is going to be charged for. Now, figure out the cost. You're charging a meager sum of $20 per shirt. In order to determine the cost, multiply the number of shirts the customer has to pay for by the cost per shirt. Listing 5.3, taken from the Web page cost.htm on the CD-ROM, performs that multiplication.

Listing 5.3. Using the multiplication operator to calculate the cost of the shirt order.

```
Sub cmdOrder_OnClick()

    Dim Quantity_Ordered
    Dim Quantity_Charged

    Dim Cost
    Dim Tax

    Dim Red
    Dim Green
    Dim Blue
```

```
Red = CInt(txtRed.Value)
Green = CInt(txtGreen.Value)
Blue = CInt(txtBlue.Value)

Quantity_Ordered = Red + Green + Blue
Quantity_Charged = Quantity_Ordered - 1

Cost = Quantity_Charged * 20

Tax = Cost * 0.06

Cost = Cost + Tax

MsgBox "You have submitted a request to order " & _
       Quantity_Ordered & " shirts!"

MsgBox "You will be charged for " & Quantity_Charged & _
       " shirts, because you get one shirt for free! "

MsgBox "The cost for the shirts is $" & Cost & "."

End Sub
```

ANALYSIS As for our customer, he or she now has the cost of the shirt, as shown in Figure 5.3.

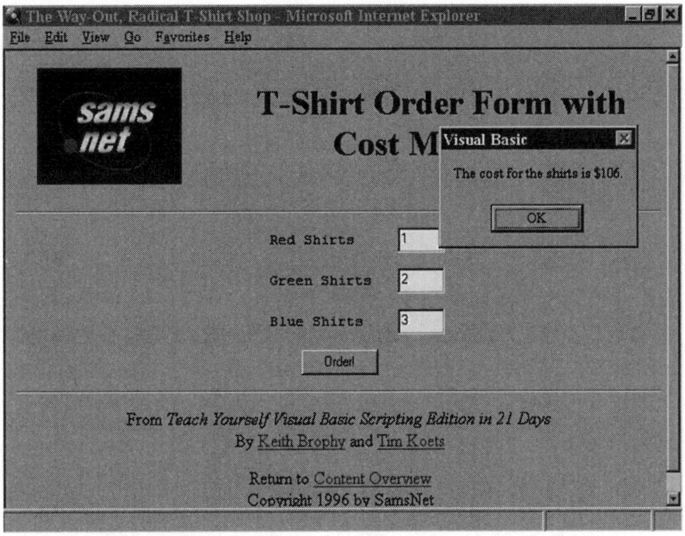

Figure 5.3.

Web page for ordering t-shirts with an added cost calculation.

5

A six percent sales tax is also added to the cost to make the local tax-collecting municipality happy. Now, you can present the customer with the total cost for the shirt. As you can see, not only is the multiplication operator useful, but it is often necessary to calculate useful information. You will see it used throughout the rest of the book.

Division (/ and \)

The division operator is the last of the four commonly used arithmetic operators. Among the common arithmetic operators, division is the most complicated arithmetic operation a computer performs. This shouldn't surprise you if you remember learning long division in grade school math class. VBScript has two types of division operators. The first operator handles numbers with decimal points. Usually referred to as the *floating-point* division operator, it's represented by the / symbol in code listings. If you are relatively new to programming, you might be wondering at this point if you can use a more familiar symbol for the same purpose. The answer is no; you cannot use the familiar ÷ symbol in computer speak—you must instead use the / symbol for floating-point division. The floating-point division operator is designed to divide values with decimal points, but it can also divide numbers without decimals. The syntax for division is the same as any of the other operators presented so far:

```
c = a / b
```

This code divides the variable b into a and puts the result into the variable c. Similarly, you could use numbers and perform a division such as

```
c = a / 2
```

which, in this case, divides the variable a in half. If the variable a were set to some valid numeric value, say 3, the result stored in c would be 1.5.

From time to time, you might want to divide integer values or perform a division without a decimal point in the result. Suppose, for example, that it's bonus time at the Way-Out, Radical T-Shirt Company, and you'd like to divide the profits to distribute equally among all your employees. Suppose your bonus money amounts to $1,204 and you have 16 employees. If you divide the bonus money by the number of employees you have, you get the result

```
1204 / 16 = 75.25
```

Rather than hand out a bunch of quarters, you would like to give them paper money without the change. If you were to drop the decimal point off 75.25, you could just give everybody an even 75 dollars. This is one case where integer division comes in handy.

The integer division operator essentially tells VBScript to return a non-decimal result. When considered in terms of the variant subtypes discussed on Day 4, the result will be either a long or integer subtype, depending on how large the resulting number is. In either case, the answer returned from the division will have no decimal representation. Although VBScript accomplishes this by treating each part of the division as an integer, you can picture the result as the normal floating-point result with any decimal points in the number rounded off. A calculation that would yield 14.75 with floating-point division becomes 15 with integer division. Similarly, a floating-point division that produces 14.25 would provide a result of 14 with integer division.

NOTE

> You can also apply your own rounding techniques to any floating-point number. These are covered on Day 16, "Extending Your Web Pages with Dates and Advanced Math."

Integer division is performed the same way floating-point division is, but the operator is different. Rather than use a forward slash (/), you use a backward slash (\). The following code shows the syntax:

```
Result = a \ b
```

Returning to the t-shirt example, if you coded the bonus calculation in your script as

```
c = 1204 / 16
```

you would end up with the value of 75.25 stored in variable c. On the other hand, if you coded the calculation as

```
c = 1204 \ 16
```

you would be left with the desired result of 75 in variable c because integer division would have occurred.

It is important to realize that integer division turns your result into an integer by rounding the original values of the operands to integers to calculate the results. For example, consider the result of the following calculation:

```
c = 4 \ 1.9
```

The value of variable c after this statement executes will be 2. VBScript processes this calculation after an internal rounding of the operands. The expression VBScript will act upon in this case is not c = 4 \ 1.9 or c = 4 \ 1. Rather, it rounds the operands to perform the calculation of c = 4 \ 2, which equals 2.

5

As mentioned earlier, division is one of the more complex arithmetic operators. You need to be aware of one condition that will always cause an error when dividing two numbers—dividing by zero:

```
2 / 0
```

This statement results in an error in VBScript. Most people know that it is impossible to divide by zero in the system of real numbers, and most programmers would never intentionally design code that divides by zero. Often, they simply fail to prevent it from happening or overlook cases where it could occur.

> **NOTE**
>
> The error caused by the divide-by-zero calculation would cause VBScript to return a run-time error. See Day 17, "Exterminating Bugs from Your Script," for a detailed discussion of such errors.

Consider the program in Listing 5.4, named speed.htm on the CD-ROM that comes with this book. This example shows a little application that calculates speed for a car or a runner. The user inputs the total distance traveled (in miles) as well as the amount of time it took to travel that distance (in hours). The program then calculates the speed in miles per hour by dividing the number of miles by the number of hours.

Listing 5.4. Speed calculation program that doesn't check for a divide-by-zero condition.

```
Sub cmdCalculate_OnClick()

    Dim Distance
    Dim TravelTime
    Dim Speed

    Distance = CInt(txtDistance.Value)
    TravelTime = CInt(txtTime.Value)

    Speed = Distance / TravelTime

    txtSpeed.Value = Speed

End Sub
```

ANALYSIS This code segment takes the distance and time from two text boxes, puts those values into variables, divides them, and places the result in another text box, as shown in Figure 5.4.

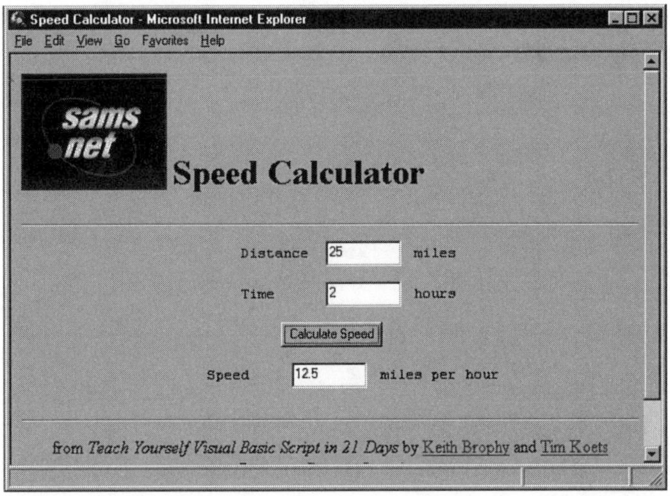

Figure 5.4.

This Web page calculates the speed by dividing the distance traveled by the time to travel that distance.

The program works fine as long as the user doesn't enter zero for the time. If she does, the program aborts with an ugly `Divide by zero` run-time error, as shown in Figure 5.5.

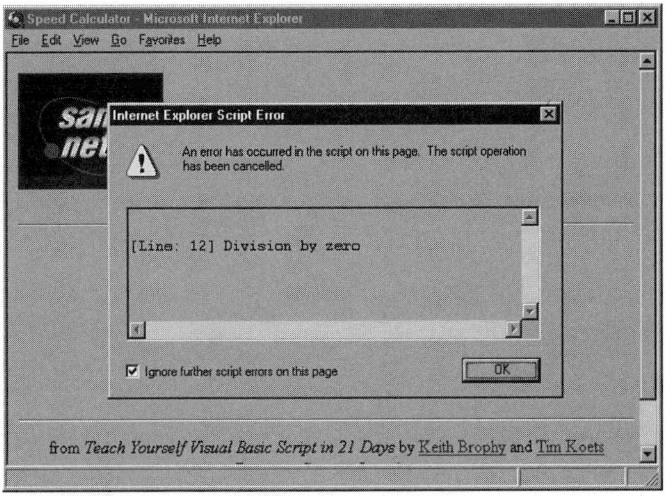

Figure 5.5.

The speed program crashes if the user enters a time of 0!

One of the best ways to prevent divide-by-zero conditions is to perform simple checks in the code to block them. Listing 5.5, based on the Web page enhspeed.htm, shows a revised version of the speed calculator program.

5

Listing 5.5. Speed calculation program that checks for a divide-by zero condition.

```
Sub cmdCalculate_OnClick()

    Dim Distance
    Dim TravelTime
    Dim Speed

    Distance = CInt(txtDistance.Value)
    TravelTime = CInt(txtTime.Value)

    If TravelTime = 0 Then
        MsgBox "The speed cannot be calculated because the time is zero. _
                Please enter a valid time."
    Else
        Speed = Distance / TravelTime
        txtSpeed.Value = Speed
    End If

End Sub
```

If the user enters zero for the time, a message alerts the user that the speed cannot be calculated because the time to travel any distance cannot be zero. This case is shown in Figure 5.6.

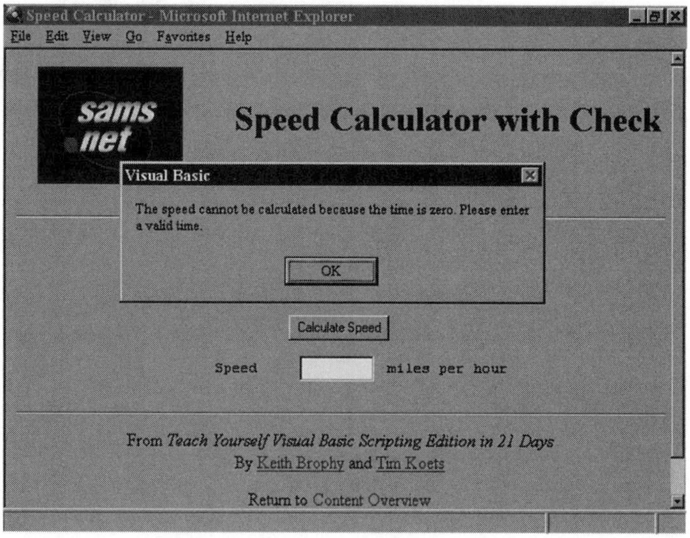

Figure 5.6.

The speed calculator has been enhanced to avoid a divide-by-zero error.

This is one technique you can use to prevent a divide-by-zero error and in a wider sense, to make your programs more error free. Other useful techniques are presented on Day 17.

Exponents (^)

The exponent operator calculates a result based on the following formula:

```
result = number ^ exponent
```

The expression

```
Result = 2 ^ 3
```

evaluates to 8 because 2 * 2 * 2 = 8. The exponent function, which is available on most scientific and business calculators, is often used in formulas relating to science, engineering, and accounting. This function is one of several more advanced functions that will be addressed further in Day 16.

Modulo Arithmetic (Mod)

The Mod function is another powerful arithmetic operator. Essentially, the Mod function returns the remainder after dividing one number into another. The syntax for the function is

```
Result = a Mod b
```

Consider what happens when you divide 2 into 5. The value 2 divides evenly into 5 twice with a remainder of 1. If you've ever performed long division, the expression would look like this:

As you can see, the remainder is indeed 1. The Mod operator returns the remainder. In the expression

```
Result = 5 Mod 2
```

the return variable Result is equal to 1. The usefulness of this function will be explored further on Day 16. For now, just keep in mind that this is another arithmetic operator.

Negation (-)

The last of the arithmetic operators is the negation operator. Simply put, this operator changes the sign of a value contained in a variable or creates a negative number. For instance, the expression

```
Result = -2 * 3
```

results in assigning the value -6 to the variable Result. Likewise, the following lines of code produce the same result as the preceding line of code:

```
a = 2
b = 3
Result = -a * b
```

Notice that you can assign the negation operator to either a variable or a literal number. The negation operator is commonly used when you want to create a negative number or treat a positive number like a negative number.

Arithmetic Operator Precedence

Now that you have seen all the arithmetic operators that VBScript has to offer, you might be wondering how all the operators behave when put together in a single line of code. For instance, is the following line of code

```
2 * 3 + 6 / 2
```

equal to 9 or 6? When you combine arithmetic operators in an expression, you need to know the order of *precedence* of the operators. That is, what operations will the computer execute first as it moves from left to right across the expression? Table 5.1 summarizes the order of precedence for the arithmetic operators.

Table 5.1. Arithmetic operator precedence.

Order	Operation
1	Exponents (^)
2	Negation (-)
3	Multiplication (*) and division (/ and \)
4	Modulo arithmetic (Mod)
5	Addition (+) and subtraction (-)
6	String concatenation (&)

Notice that multiplication and division are on the same level of precedence. In this case, multiplication and division are executed in left-to-right order when it's their turn in the order of precedence. The expression

```
2 * 3 + 6 / 2
```

has three arithmetic operators: multiplication, addition, and division. As you can see in this table, multiplication is the first operation performed in the expression as you move from left to right. Both multiplication and division have the same order of precedence, so they are handled on a first-come, first-served basis. Because the multiplication is first, it gets executed first. As a result, the first operation in the expression is 2 * 3, which equals 6. This reduces the expression to

```
6 + 6 / 2
```

That leaves an addition operator and a division operator in the expression. Using Table 5.1, you can see that division has a higher order of precedence than addition does, so the division is handled next. The expression 6 / 2 equals 3, so the expression now becomes

```
6 + 3
```

Because only one operator remains, the choice is obvious—the result equals 9. VBScript follows this process of ordering an expression of multiple operators every time. When you are writing code, you must keep this order in mind.

One good way to maintain the order of expressions when writing and maintaining code is to designate subexpressions in parentheses. You can use parentheses freely in expressions, and they ensure that the subexpression will be fully evaluated first before it is evaluated as part of the larger expression. For example, you could write

```
c = 2 * 3 + 6 / 2
```

and c would evaluate to 9, as figured previously. You could also code the same expression as

```
c = (2 * 3) + 6 / 2
```

or

```
c = 2 * 3 + (6 / 2)
```

or even

```
c = (2 * 3) + (6 / 2)
```

and the results would still be the same: 9. However, with these statements, particularly the last one, the expression is much easier for a programmer to read and understand.

When using the parentheses approach, you must be aware of how subexpressions are evaluated. If you coded the statement as

```
c = (2 * 3 + 6) / 2
```

you get a result of 12 / 2 = 6 stored in c. The subexpression always gets evaluated first, which in turn affects the results of the overall expression. Because the human mind can digest information more easily by breaking it down into smaller pieces, subexpressions will make your code easier to follow and probably less error prone as well.

5

Comparison Operators

The first set of operators VBScript provides are arithmetic operators. This section discusses the second type: *comparison operators.* As the name implies, you use comparison operators to compare one or more variables, numbers, constants, or a combination of the three. VBScript has many different types of comparison operators, and each checks for a different comparison condition.

Equality (=)

You use the equality operator to see if a variable, constant, or number is equal to another. It's common to mistake the equality operator for the assignment operator, which is also represented by an equal sign. You use the *assignment* operator to set a variable equal to another variable, number, string, constant, or other data entity. For example, the statement

```
a = b
```

assigns the value contained in b to the variable a.

The equality operator, on the other hand, is used to test whether one value is equal to another. The syntax for the equality operator looks similar to that for the assignment operator:

```
a = b
```

where *a* and *b* can be variables, constants, or numbers. It is the context in which you use the expression that determines whether it is treated as an assignment or an equality check. Equality is always used in the context of checking a condition. For example, a statement such as:

```
if a = b then
```

is an example of the equality operator because it is a conditional check. As a rule of thumb, you can assume that if a = b appears in a statement by itself, it is an assignment statement. If you see a = b as part of any other expression, it is used in the equality context.

If a does indeed equal b, the expression is true; otherwise, it is false. We have already been using the equality operator a great deal in the book so far. Refer to Listing 5.5, where you see the following section of code:

```
If TravelTime = 0 Then
    MsgBox "The speed cannot be calculated because the time is zero.
  Please enter a valid time."
Else
    Speed = Distance / TravelTime
    txtSpeed.Value = Speed
End If
```

This example uses the equality operator to see if the variable TravelTime is equal to 0. If it is, a set of instructions are executed, and if not, another set is similarly executed. You can also use the equality operator to check whether a variable is equal to a constant or even some other variable. You will see the equality operator used extensively throughout the book and in virtually any program. Likewise, you will also see the = symbol used as an assignment operator, where it actually assigns data to a variable. These are two of the most common operations in programming.

Inequality (<>)

Another important comparison operator is the inequality operator. You use this operator to test whether a variable is not equal to another variable or some data element. The syntax for the inequality operator is

```
a <> b
```

where a and b are variables, constants, strings, or numbers. Again, the expression returns True if the condition is indeed true and False if it isn't. For example, you could have taken the following code

```
If TravelTime = 0 Then
    MsgBox "The speed cannot be calculated because the time is zero.
  Please enter a valid time."
Else
    Speed = Distance / TravelTime
    txtSpeed.Value = Speed
End If
```

and made the following change, using the inequality operator rather than the equality operator, with the same results:

```
If TravelTime <> 0 Then
    Speed = Distance / TravelTime
    txtSpeed.Value = Speed
Else
    MsgBox "The speed cannot be calculated because the time is zero.
  Please enter a valid time."
End If
```

Sometimes, the inequality operator is more convenient and sensible to use than the equality operator. You will see such cases throughout the rest of the book.

Less Than and Greater Than (> and <)

You might have a condition where you don't care whether a variable is equal to another, but you do want to know whether it is greater than or less than another variable, number, or constant. In such a case, you need the greater-than and less-than operators. The syntax for

these two operators is

a > *b*

and

a < *b*

where *a* and *b* are variables, constants, numbers, or strings, and the result is True if the expression is true. Otherwise, the expression returns False. For an example of its use, consider the following code:

```
If TravelTime > 0 Then
    Speed = Distance / TravelTime
    txtSpeed.Value = Speed
Else If TravelTime < 0 Then
    MsgBox "You cannot enter a negative value for the time!"
Else If TravelTime = 0 Then
    MsgBox "The time must be greater than zero!"
End If
```

Here, you see the greater-than, less-than, and equality operators all in use. If the variable TravelTime is greater than zero, a speed can be calculated, but if TravelTime is less than zero or equal to zero, the user must be notified—any such value would not be valid.

You could write the same code in another way if you carefully think about the conditions being satisfied. If a travel time is not greater than zero and not less than zero, you know it must be zero. Even without checking for this value, you can tell that is the only possibility left! You could therefore rewrite the code as

```
If TravelTime > 0 Then
    Speed = Distance / TravelTime
    txtSpeed.Value = Speed
Else If TravelTime < 0 Then
    MsgBox "You cannot enter a negative value for the time!"
Else
    MsgBox "The time must be greater than zero!"
End If
```

This code works just as well as the previous code. The first method was used to emphasize the purpose of the equality expression. The first method is also a better approach in some respects, because with the conditions explicitly named, the purpose of each branch of the code is more clearly defined and easier to read and debug. Code that is clearer is usually also easier to maintain and less subject to bugs.

Less Than or Equal To and Greater Than or Equal To (>= and <=)

Sometimes, you also might want to see whether a variable is greater than *or equal to* some other variable, constant, or number. Perhaps you want to know if it is *less than or equal to* the entity. Then, you can combine operators to use the less-than-or-equal and greater-than-or-equal operators, <= and >=. The syntax for these operators is

```
a >= b
```

and

```
a <= b
```

The expression returns True or False, depending on whether the expression is true. Suppose you take the code shown in the previous section and change it to

```
If TravelTime > 0 Then
    Speed = Distance / TravelTime
    txtSpeed.Value = Speed
Else If TravelTime <= 0 Then
    MsgBox "You cannot enter a negative value or zero for the time!"
End If
```

This code combines the conditions of a zero time and a negative time into one simple check. Because both cases are invalid, it makes the code simpler to perform one check. It is more useful to the user to know whether a zero or a negative value was entered, but because both are invalid, you might not consider that very important. In any case, these conditional checks can tell you whether a condition is True.

Again in this example, you could write the code to simply use an else as the last condition because you know if a time isn't greater than zero, it must be less than or equal to zero. However, as in the earlier example, the explicit approach helps illustrate the use of the <= operator and also makes clearer code.

Object Equivalence (Is)

The last comparison operator is designed for objects, which are discussed in more detail on Days 8, "Intrinsic HTML Form Controls," through 11, "More ActiveX Controls." For now, consider an object such as a command button that you can place on a Web page. The syntax of the Is operator is

```
result = object_reference1 Is object_reference2
```

where *object_reference1* and *object_reference2* are references to objects and *result* is either True or False, depending on whether the statement is true.

This operator does not compare one object to another, nor does it compare values. This special operator simply checks to see if the two object references in the expression refer to the same object. Suppose, for example, you have included a command button in your script you have defined as TestButton. You have another variable, myObject, that is set to reference different objects at different points in your program. Assume that a statement has been carried out that assigns the variable myObject to reference this button, such as

```
Set myObject = TestButton
```

If the script later carries out the expression

```
result = myObject Is TestButton
```

it will return the True in the variable result because TestButton is indeed the same object as that referred to by myObject. If, on the other hand, you were to enter

```
result = myObject Is SomeOtherTestButton
```

result would be False because the two objects are not the same.

As you can see from this discussion, there are some special rules for dealing with objects. You must use the Set statement to assign an object's value. And you cannot directly compare two objects with an equal statement, such as

```
if myObject = TestButton   ' illegal syntax
```

The sample page objcomp.htm on the CD-ROM that comes with this book illustrates some of these concepts. You'll learn the nuances of objects in the days ahead. For now, it is just important to realize that among the full range of operators covered today, the Is operator is available for object equivalence checks.

Comparison Operator Precedence

Unlike arithmetic operators, comparison operators do not have a specific order of precedence. They are simply executed as they are found from left to right across an expression. When VBScript encounters an expression such as

```
If 3 > 5 < 10 Then
```

VBScript will evaluate the conditions in the order they appear from left to right. In this case, the part of the expression that comes first, 3 > 5, is evaluated first as False. False in VBScript is equivalent to 0, so the expression becomes

```
If 0 < 10 Then
```

Because 10 is greater than 0, the expression is True. As a result, the entire expression is True and whatever code follows this if-then expression will be executed. Conditional expressions will be discussed more fully on Day 6, "Controlling the Flow of VBScript Code."

Logical Operators

The last category of operators in VBScript is *logical operators*. The logical operators might require a more significant amount of understanding to appreciate. In some cases, the way you use logical operators seems to run counter to your intuitive thinking. If you've ever taken a course in logic, you have first-hand experience with this. Because logical operators are such an important part of VBScript, it's important to gain a good understanding, starting with the basics, so that you can use them effectively.

Logical operators use the binary number system to represent information. The part of the binary number system used in this lesson is very simple: Expressions evaluate to True or False, respectively. The logical operators discussed in this section are designed for binary numbers, not decimal numbers. The binary number system counts in units of two rather than ten, so it's quite different from the decimal system. It is beyond the scope of this book to explore all the details of the binary number system. If you are interested in learning more about the binary system, you can refer to any introductory computer science principles textbook. If you are not familiar with binary numbers, simply remember that True and False are the only values used with logical operators. A logical expression, such as

```
5 > 3
```

is a true statement and would return True if evaluated. If you inspect the value of True, you would see that it contains the true indicator of -1. It turns out that -1 is a convenient way to represent True internally in the binary system upon which your computer and VBScript are based. If you need to convince yourself that this is really the representation, you can try a quick test within a Web page script. Simply insert code like the following:

```
<SCRIPT LANGUAGE="VBScript">
' True condition, this will display "True"
msgbox (3 = 3)
' VBScript integer representation of True condition, this will display "-1"
msgbox cint(3 = 3)
' False condition, this will display "False"
msgbox (3 = 2)
' VBScript integer representation of False condition, this will display "0"
msgbox cint(3 = 2)
</SCRIPT>
```

As soon as your page is loaded, this script code will be launched. You will see a series of four message boxes. The first two expressions, based on (3 = 3), are true statements, of course. The first message box displays the VBScript text indicator of a true condition, True. The second message box uses the cint function to obtain the integer equivalent of this condition, which shows up as -1. Similarly, the next two statements display False and 0 because the condition (3 = 2) is false. You can always use the intrinsic VBScript constant True to represent

5

the true condition. Likewise, you can always use the intrinsic constant `False` to represent the false condition. If you were to display the integer value of the constants, you would see that they are similarly associated with `-1` and `0`, respectively. With that understanding of how Visual Basic handles true and false conditions, take a look at the suite of logical operators.

Negation (`Not`)

The first operator is called the *negation* operator. This operator has the following syntax:

```
result = Not expression
```

Table 5.2 shows the `result` variable in relation to `expression`.

Table 5.2. Negation (`Not`) results.

If *expression* is...	then *result* is...
True	False
False	True
Null	Null

If you enter the expression

```
a = Not 1 > 2
```

where the expression is `1 > 2`, the result is stored in the variable a. The value stored in variable a will be `True`. The expression `1 > 2` is false because 1 is not greater than 2. `Not` simply flips a false over to true or a true over to false. Because the expression is false, the `Not` operator makes the result true. As a result, the VBScript value for true, `True` or `-1`, will be stored in variable a. If the expression is null, the `Not` operator will return a null when applied to the expression.

Where might you use the `Not` operator? It is often used when working with if-then conditionals. Consider, for instance, the following code segment:

```
If GetZip(City, State, Zip) = vbFalse Then
     MsgBox "The zip code could not be determined."
Else
     MsgBox "The zip code is " & Zip
End If
```

This simple example calls the function `GetZip`. The arguments for this function are the city, state, and zip code. The function returns a Boolean value that indicates whether the function has succeeded. This return variable is often called a *return code*. The function loads the variable `Zip` with the zip code and returns `True` if it is successful. If the function fails, it returns vbFalse. The function could fail, for example, if an invalid state or city was passed as an argument to the function.

The conditional statement checks the return code. If it is true, the function has succeeded and the code proceeds to show the user the zip code. You could use the Not operator instead, in which case the code would look like this:

```
If Not GetZip(City, State, Zip) Then
     MsgBox "The zip code could not be determined."
Else
     MsgBox "The zip code is " & Zip
End If
```

The only difference is that you use the Not operator instead of the equality operator. In some cases, this makes the code easier to read. In other cases, such as the following:

```
GetZipFailure = Not GetZip(City, State, Zip)
```

the Not operator is necessary. If GetZipFailure is a variable that contains the failure status of the call, Not is the most convenient way to map the return value of the function to the variable. More uses for this operator will become apparent as you see more code examples.

Conjunction (And)

The conjunction operator compares two or more variables in some type of test. The syntax for the conjunction operator is

```
result = expression1 And expression2
```

Table 5.3 shows the *result* variable in relation to *expression1* and *expression2*.

Table 5.3. Conjunction (And) results.

If *expression1* is...	and *expression2* is...	then *result* is...
True	True	True
True	False	False
False	True	False
False	False	False

In order to obtain True in the *result* variable, both *expression1* and *expression2* must be true. You often use this operator to make sure two or more conditions are true before performing some action. Suppose you have a Web page for making airline reservations. You have several functions in your code: one to get the customer's name and address, one for the origination point, one for the destination, and one for the day he wants to travel. In order to book the reservation, each function must succeed. If any of them fail, the reservation cannot be made. The following statement is an example of what could appear in a VBScript code segment:

```
OkayToReserve = _
GetCustomer(Name, Address, Phone) And _
GetDepartureCity(DepartCity) And _
GetDestinationCity(DestinationCity) And _
GetTravelDate(TravelDate)
```

If the function that gets the destination city from the customer, for example, does not succeed for whatever reason, your program will not accept the reservation.

This example is simple, but you get the point. Each of these functions must return True. If any one of them fails, the variable OkayToReserve will be false. You can then make a simple check to determine whether to make the reservation:

```
If OkayToReserve = True Then MakeReservation( Name, Address, Phone, _
DepartCity, DestinationCity, TravelDate )
```

You can use the conjunction operator for a lot of other purposes. As you progress through the book, you will see more examples of its use.

NOTE

> VBScript lets you take a shortcut when referencing true in a condition. You don't have to explicitly compare the condition to true. If you have no comparison, it assumes you are checking the true condition. The following statement is functionally equivalent to the previous example without using the True constant:
>
> ```
> If OkayToReserve Then MakeReservation( Name, Address, Phone, _
> DepartCity, DestinationCity, TravelDate )
> ```

Disjunction (Or)

Another frequently used logical operator is the *disjunction* operator. This operator has the same syntax as the conjunction operator:

```
result = expression1 Or expression2
```

Table 5.4 shows the result variable in relation to expression1 and expression2.

Table 5.4. Disjunction (Or) results.

If *expression1* is...	and *expression2* is...	then *result* is...
True	True	True
True	False	True
False	True	True
False	False	False

This operator behaves quite a bit differently from the conjunction operator! In this case, any of the expressions can be true for the result to be true. The result is false only if all the expressions are false. You typically use this operator when you have to make a decision where any of a number of activities could occur, but only one must occur for the operation to proceed. Suppose you want to call a function on your Web page that processes an order for flowers. If you have five varieties of flowers, the customer could order one or more types. You simply want to see if any of them are on order. All it takes to process an order is a request for one type. The following code segment would handle this for you:

```
If Order1 Or Order2 Or Order3 Or Order4 Or Order5 Then
    OrderFlowers()
End If
```

In this case, five variables exist that are true or false, depending on whether the user wants to order flowers of that type. If the user wants to order flowers of any type, the script calls the OrderFlowers function. That function can then determine the specifics of the flower order.

Exclusion (Xor)

The exclusion operator is another in the family of logical operators that you can use to make decisions based on the contents of one or more expressions. It checks whether one and only one condition is exclusively true. The syntax of the exclusion operator is

result = *expression1* Xor *expression2*

Table 5.5 shows the *result* variable in relation to *expression1* and *expression2*.

Table 5.5. Exclusion (Xor) results.

If *expression1* is...	and *expression2* is...	then *result* is...
True	True	False
True	False	True
False	True	True
False	False	False

If you compare Table 5.5 to 5.4, you'll see that these operators differ in only one way. With the Or operator, if either or both expressions are true, the result is true. With the exclusion operator, however, if all the expressions in the statement are the same—that is, all true or false—the result is false. Only when they are different is the result true.

Logical Equivalence (Eqv) and Implication (Imp)

The remaining two logical operators are Eqv and Imp. The equivalence operator checks whether two expressions are bitwise equivalent to each other. The syntax is

```
result = expression1 Eqv expression2
```

The Imp operator performs a logical implication on two expressions. The syntax for that operation is

```
result = expression1 Imp expression2
```

If you're a very experienced programmer, you know what Imp and Eqv do, and you're probably glad to see them in the VBScript repertoire. However, if you're a beginner, you might be thinking at this moment, "What on earth is bitwise equivalence and logical implication?"

Like all the logical operators covered here, the Imp and Eqv comparisons are performed on a bit-by-bit basis and the results are set on a bit-by-bit basis. For the other operators, the functionality it provides and the expected results are intuitively obvious. For Imp and Eqv, the results are less intuitive. Of course, any expression is ultimately represented in bits on a computer, and to understand these operators, you must think in terms of these bits. Picture a comparison on two numbers, analyzing them each bit-by-bit and setting the result expression bit-by-bit according to the rules in Tables 5.6 and 5.7.

Table 5.6. Equivalence (Eqv) results.

If expression1 is...	and expression2 is...	then result is...
True	True	True
True	False	False
False	True	False
False	False	True

Table 5.7. Implication (Imp) results.

If *expression1* is...	and *expression2* is...	then *result* is...
True	True	True
True	False	False
False	True	True
False	False	True

Most types of programs use these operations infrequently, so they are typically the realm of advanced programmers. I do not outline them here in detail. You can refer to any computer science text for more details on the binary numbering system and bitwise operations to gain a full appreciation of how to use Imp and Eqv. It is important to realize that the language does provide the capability to carry such operations in case you sometime need to analyze data at this level.

Logical Operator Precedence

Like arithmetic operators, logical operators have an order of preference, shown in Table 5.8.

Table 5.8. Logical operator precedence.

Order	Operation
1	Negation (Not)
2	Conjunction (And)
3	Disjunction (Or)
4	Exclusion (Xor)
5	Equivalence (Eqv)
6	Implication (Imp)

Any type of operator is evaluated from left to right in an expression. For an example of logical operator precedence, consider the following code statement:

```
If a Xor b And c Or d Then
```

For this example, suppose a is true, b is false, c is false, and d is false. Moving from left to right, you have the operators Xor, And, and Or. Because And gets first precedence, the expression b And c is evaluated first. The result of False And False is False. As a result, the expression becomes

```
If a Xor False or d Then
```

Now, moving from left to right, the two operators are `Xor` and `Or`. `Or` is next in the line of precedence, so the next expression up for evaluation is `False Or d`. Because `d` is false, `False Or False` equals `False`. The expression becomes

```
If a Xor False Then
```

Now, `Xor` is the only operator left. Because `a` is true, `True Xor False` is `True`. As a result, the expression reduces to

```
If True Then
```

which means the code that follows the if-then statement will be executed. It is very important to understand the order of precedence when you have more than one expression connected together in a single statement. Make sure you walk through your code and know what it's doing before you turn your attention from this kind of code statement.

Working with Strings

One special operator does not fit in any of the other classes. This operator, called the *string concatenation* operator, is represented by the & symbol. You have already seen strings at work on Day 4, and you will learn more about them in this section. For complete coverage of how strings work, Day 15, "Extending Your Web Pages with Strings," describes all the essentials of string creation, manipulation, and use. We also cover the string concatenation operator here so that you learn all the operators in the VBScript suite.

String Concatenation (&)

You use the string concatenation operator to merge two strings together. If, for example, one variable holds the string

```
First_Name = "Buddy"
```

and the second holds the string

```
Last_Name = "Bird"
```

to form a complete name, you would want to concatenate these two strings together. You could accomplish this with the concatenation operator. The syntax for this operator is

```
result = string1 & string2 & ... & stringn
```

Note that you can concatenate any number of strings on the same line of code. If you want to concatenate the first and last names, your first instinct would be to enter

```
Name = First_Name & Last_Name
```

5

Oops! If you check the name, you find that the string becomes `"BuddyBird"`. You need to insert a space. No problem—you can simply add the space string right into the expression:

```
Name = First_Name & " " & Last_Name
```

Note that you can concatenate strings contained in variables as well as literal strings in one, single expression. Now, if you check the `Name` variable, the stored result should be

```
"Buddy Bird"
```

String Concatenation Using the + Operator

You should know one more thing about string concatenation. As you begin to see examples of VBScript code on the Internet, you might from time to time see strings concatenated using the + operator rather than the & operator. For example, you can build a name with this code:

```
Name = First_Name + " " + Last_Name
```

This statement would correctly build the string "Buddy Bird" for you. Although you can indeed use the addition operator to concatenate strings, you're not always guaranteed a correct result because the addition operator is designed for numeric values. It can handle strings, but when strings are mixed with numbers, VBScript can get into an ambiguous state, not knowing exactly how you want to concatenate the values. If, for example, one of the expressions is a number and the other is a string, the + operator gives you an error:

```
Dim a, b, c
a = 10
b = " Apples"
c = a + b
MsgBox c
```

When VBScript encounters the expression c = a + b, a type mismatch error will result. You're trying to add a number and a string that cannot be translated into a number. Instead, you should use

```
Dim a, b, c
a = 10
b = " Apples"
c = a & b
MsgBox c
```

and you will store "10 Apples" in the variable c. Table 5.9 shows you the rules for whether the + operator concatenates or adds, depending on the subtype of the variable or variables in question.

5

Table 5.9. String concatenation rules using the + operator.

Condition	Rule	Example

Both expressions are numeric	Add	`10 + 2`
		`15.6 + 3`
		`-6.2 + 18`

Both expressions are strings	Concatenate	`"Ten" + " Apples"` `"Going " + "shopping"`
One expression is numeric and the other is a string that can be converted to a number	Add	`10 + " 110"` `100 + " 25 "`
One expression is numeric and the other is a string that cannot be converted to a number	Error!	`10 + " Apples"` `100 + " Dalmatians"`

Notice that you must enclose literal numbers in quotes if you want to treat them as strings when you concatenate them to other strings. Because this is not very convenient and requires extra thought, it's safer and better to use the & operator whenever you're concatenating strings. This helps reduce potential errors in your code—always a wise decision.

You can do a great deal more with strings in VBScript. On Day 15, you will learn even more about strings, along with many supporting functions that let you handle strings in flexible, powerful ways. Until then, I'll just show you string concatenation and save the more advanced concepts for later.

Operator Precedence

Now you have seen all the operators VBScript has to offer. For each type of operator—arithmetic, comparison, and logical—you have seen the order of precedence. What happens when operators from different categories are all combined in the same statement? What is executed first?

VBScript first attends to the arithmetic operators, followed by the string concatenation operator, the comparison operators, and the logical operators, as summarized in Table 5.10.

Table 5.10. Operator precedence summary.

Order	Operation
Arithmetic	
1	Exponents (^)
2	Negation (-)
3	Multiplication (*), division (/ and \)
4	Modulo arithmetic (Mod)
5	Addition (+), subtraction (-)
6	String concatenation (&)
Comparison	
1	Equality (=)
2	Inequality (<>)
3	Less than (<)
4	Greater than (>)
5	Less than or equal to (<=)
6	Greater than or equal to (>=)
7	Object equivalence (Is)
Logical	
1	Negation (Not)
2	Conjunction (And)
3	Disjunction (Or)
4	Exclusion (Xor)
5	Logical equivalence (Eqv)
6	Implication (Imp)

When an expression has more than one operation, each part of that expression is evaluated in this order from left to right across the expression.

If you want to force VBScript to target a specific part of a code statement, you can use parentheses as discussed earlier today. For example, suppose you have the statement

```
x = 6 * 5 / 2 - 5 + r
```

in your code. In normal circumstances, the variable x would be expressed as

```
x = 10 + r
```

where the expressions would be evaluated in the following order:

```
x = 6 * 5 / 2 - 5 + r
  =    30 / 2 - 5 + r
  =        15 - 5 + r
  =            10 + r
x = 10 + r
```

If r is 5, the answer is

```
x = 10 + 5
x = 15
```

Suppose you wanted to treat the expression 5 + r as a single entity. You would simply put parentheses around 5 + r:

```
x = 6 *  5 / 2 - ( 5 + r )
```

which would result in the following order:

```
x = 6 * 5 / 2 - ( 5 + r )
  =    30 / 2 - ( 5 + r )
  =        15 - ( 5 + r )
  =
x = 15 - ( 5 + r )
```

If r is 5, the answer is

```
x = 15 - ( 5 + 5 )
x = 15 - 10
x = 5
```

The difference in results is due to the parentheses around part of the expression, which can have a dramatic impact on the results. For another example, suppose you had to calculate the sales tax on a customer's order where you had the cost of two items. Call the cost of the first item x and the cost of the second item y, and say the sales tax is 6 percent of the total cost. You could write this expression as

```
tax = x + y * 0.06
```

but it would be incorrect. If you follow the order of precedence, y * 0.06 would be evaluated, and the result would be added to x. This is not what you want. Rather, you first want x and y to be added and then multiplied by 0.06. The order of precedence is getting in your way, preventing you from obtaining a correct result. In this case, you have to force VBScript to do the addition first and then the multiplication. To do this, you simply enter the expression as

```
tax = (x + y) * 0.06
```

which will give you the correct result. Because the expression x + y is in parentheses, VBScript will evaluate it first and then multiply the total cost by the sales tax. The order of precedence is a very important part of handling expressions.

Summary

Today's lesson presents you with the entire suite of VBScript operators. Operators are the workhorses for variables; they put variables to work by making decisions and changing their contents. A fundamental knowledge of operators is necessary in understanding VBScript from top to bottom.

Operators fit into three separate categories: arithmetic operators, comparison operators, and logical operators. Each of these categories has a special use in a VBScript program. Today you have learned about all the operators in these three categories and saw examples of how to use each of the operators in your programs. You have also seen how operators can work together to accomplish a result. Operators are executed in a specific order when they are combined. Programmers must take this order into account when they write code. Today's lesson clearly lays out this order of precedence so that you know what to expect when using the operators presented today.

Today you have been introduced to concepts that will be addressed more thoroughly in upcoming days. As you venture deeper into the realm of VBScript programming, each day will build on the previous. Carefully consider the quiz questions because they will help prepare you for the exciting lessons to come.

Q&A

Q What are operators?

A Operators are symbols used in VBScript that perform some specific task. Operators come in three varieties: arithmetic, comparison, and logical. Arithmetic operators handle math operations such as addition and multiplication. Comparison operators help in comparing one variable to another. Logical operators are used in making decisions based on expressions that are either true or false.

Q What do operators operate on?

A Operators can operate on variables, literal numbers, constants, or entire expressions.

Q Why are operators important?

A Operators are important to programmers because they are used to make decisions, assign data to variables, and control the flow of programs.

5

Q   Are some operators more important than others?

**A   VBScript ranks the operators in a specific order, called the order of prece-
dence. The order of precedence helps determine how a code statement is
executed when it has more than one operator.**

Workshop

Design a Web page that asks the user for a series of values. Store those values in variables and
write code that exercises every one of the operators discussed today. Which ones are you the
most familiar with? Which ones do you anticipate using the most in your Web pages?

Quiz

NOTE   Refer to Appendix C, "Answers to Quiz Questions," for the answers to
these questions.

1.   Write a program that converts feet to inches. Hint: There are 12 inches in a
foot.

2.   Write a program that sells concert tickets to your customers. Get from the
customer her name, how many tickets she wants, and whether or not she
wants front-row tickets. Use the following formula in calculating the cost:
Ticket cost equals $20.00 plus $4.00 for front row tickets plus a 3% commission. Add 8% sales tax to the total cost of the ticket plus the commission.

3.   Determine the result of the following expressions using the order-of-
precedence rules:

   a.   `5 * 9 - 3 ^ 2`

   b.   `(72 - 3) / 3 Mod 3`

   c.   `7 + 2 - 5 * 2`

   d.   `True Or False And True`

   e.   `False Or Not True`

Week 1

Day 6

Controlling the Flow of VBScript Code

For the past two days, you've learned how to use variables and operators to assist you in creating VBScript programs. Both variables and operators are fundamental building blocks you need to understand to write useful code. Today, you will learn how to control the flow of your programs. This subject is very important when you want your programs to make on-the-spot decisions or execute differently based on what the user wants to do.

Today's lesson will introduce you to all the ways you can construct and control the order in which your code is executed. You will learn all the VBScript *control structures* and see several examples of how they can be applied. You will also learn which structures are more applicable and more useful under which situations. You'll learn not only *how* to control the flow of code, but also how *best* to do so.

Once you've learned how to control the flow of code within a procedure, you'll see how you can control the flow of code within the entire application. On Day 7, "Building a Home for Your Code," you will learn how to create procedures that house entire sections of code. The path of your application can flow into and out of procedures like a thread of cotton flows through a fabric. Once you've learned the useful information in today's lesson, your abilities as a VBScript programmer will bound forward to the point where you can build real-world applications from start to finish.

Why Control the Flow of Code?

Before you begin learning how to control the flow of your code, you might be wondering why you should do so in the first place. What is the "flow of code" anyway? To get this answer, you need to step back for a moment and take a look at the big picture.

Stripped of all the complex software languages and the big technical words used to describe application development, a computer program is really quite simple. A program is simply a list of instructions that a computer executes. Although we tend to give computers a lot of credit, a computer is actually quite stupid. It can only do exactly what you tell it to do; it has only a limited subset of the capabilities of the human mind without many important traits, such as the ability to draw inferences, use intuition, or use emotion to help make decisions. We humans don't fully understand these phenomena ourselves, and because a computer is a man-made machine, our computers certainly don't understand them either.

When a computer executes a list of instructions, it executes them one at a time in the order it is told. Depending on the type of computer and the language of the program, some computers can jump around a list of instructions if told to do so. For example, the computer might be told to execute instructions in the following order:

```
a
b
c
d
e
f
g
```

Perhaps it is told to execute them in an order like this:

```
a
b
f
g
c
d
e
```

That same computer might even be able to execute a series of instructions over and over again:

```
a
b
c
d
e
d
e
```

```
d
e
f
g
```

As you can see, each of these three paths through the code is different. The computer doesn't care what order of instructions it is given. You, on the other hand, might care a great deal. For the most part, you, the programmer, dictate the order instructions are executed on a computer. At times, you might want to execute the same instructions over again. Suppose, for instance, you have to ask the user for a set of data again because he didn't enter the data correctly the first time.

Other times, you might need to make a decision in your program to execute one line of code under one condition and another line of code in some other condition. For instance, you might need to calculate the sales tax of an item differently if the user enters California instead of Michigan as his state.

In both cases, depending on the user, your code can execute in a different order each time. As you can see, it is very important, if not fundamental, that you have this capability in your programs. That's why knowing how to control the flow of your code is important.

Using Control Structures to Make Decisions

With that brief explanation in mind, how do you control how your code executes? Fortunately, VBScript gives you a variety of ways to direct the flow of your code. The mechanisms used to accomplish this in VBScript are called *control structures.* They are called structures because you construct your code around them, much like you build and finish a house around its structure. Control structures are like the wood beams and boards in your house that all of your rooms are built upon. You can use each control structure to make your code travel in different ways, depending on how you want the decision to be made. In this section, you will learn about the two control structures used in VBScript to make decisions. Later, you will see the structures used to make code repeat based on criteria you specify.

NEW TERM A *control structure* is a combination of keywords in code used to make a decision that alters the flow of code the computer executes.

6

If…Then

The first control structure you should know about is If…Then. The syntax for this control structure is given as

```
If condition = True Then
    ... the code that executes if the condition is satisfied
End If
```

where *condition* is some test you want to apply to the conditional structure. If the condition is true, the code within the If and End If statements is executed. If the condition is not true, the code within these statements is skipped over and does not get executed.

NOTE

Rather than using this expression:

```
If condition = True
```

you can simply use this expression:

```
If condition Then
```

instead. VBScript automatically checks to see if the condition is true if you don't explicitly say so. Similarly, if you wanted to check to see if an expression were false, you could check to see if the condition is equal to false:

```
If condition = False
```

or you could have VBScript check the not true condition:

```
If Not condition
```

just to check to see if be required to use False. This convention may be used interchangeably throughout the book.

How might this work? Suppose you have a Boolean variable named ShowDetails. This variable is set to True at some point in your code if the user wants to see the specific details of a tax calculation your code has made in figuring out your user's taxes. You could set up a simple conditional statement that gives the user the help he or she needs by entering

```
If ShowDetails = True Then
    ...code that shows the details of the calculation to the user
End If
```

This way, if the user doesn't want to see the details and the variable hasn't been set previously, the code in between the two statements is ignored. The *condition* expression is typically some test, such as whether one variable is equal to another or whether a variable equals a certain value. The condition always comes out either True or False, but the conditional structure only executes the code within it if the condition is True. When using an If…Then structure, make sure your condition is expressed properly. The code contained within the expression

```
If 5 = 5 Then
    ...some code that executes if the condition is true
End If
```

will always get executed because 5 always equals 5. Likewise, the code within the expression

```
If 5 = 10 Then
    ...some code that executes if the condition is true
End If
```

will never get executed because 5 never equals 10. These decision structures are pointless because the decision never changes. When you enter the condition for an If…Then control structure, you should always make the condition one that could either be True or False.

Listing 6.1 shows a working example of VBScript code that uses the If…Then conditional. This Web page, named ifthen.htm, is also on the CD-ROM that accompanies the book.

Listing 6.1. A Web page that uses the If…Then control structure.

```
<HTML>

<HEAD>
<TITLE>Brophy & Koets' Teach Yourself VBScript - If-Then Sample</TITLE>
</HEAD>

<BODY>

<H1><A HREF="http://www.mcp.com"><IMG  ALIGN=BOTTOM
SRC="../shared/jpg/samsnet.jpg" BORDER=2></A>
<EM>Using the If-Then Statement</EM></H1>

<HR>

<P>Enter your age and click on the "Evaluate" button.  Visual Basic
Script will use the If-Then conditional to show a message depending on
the age you enter.

<PRE>
I am <INPUT NAME="txtAge" SIZE=10 > years old.    --
<INPUT TYPE="BUTTON" VALUE="Evaluate" SIZE=30 NAME="cmdEvaluate">
</PRE>

<HR>

<center>
from <em>Teach Yourself VBScript in 21 Days</em> by
<A HREF="../shared/info/keith.htm">Keith Brophy</A> and
<A HREF="../shared/info/tim.htm">Tim Koets</A><br>
Return to <a href="..\default.htm">Content Overview</A><br>
Copyright 1996 by SamsNet<br>
</center>

<SCRIPT LANGUAGE="VBScript">
```

6

continues

Listing 6.1. continued

```
<!--  Option Explicit

  Sub cmdEvaluate_OnClick()

   Dim Age

  Age = CInt(txtAge.Value)

   If Age <= 0 or Age > 120 Then
    MsgBox "Either you're not born yet or you're getting _
      too old for this stuff!"
   Else
      MsgBox "You are " & Age & " years old."
   End If

  End Sub

-->
</SCRIPT>

</BODY>
</HTML>
```

ANALYSIS This listing is for a Web page that takes as an input the user's age. When the user clicks the Test button, the conditional statement checks to see whether the user's age is valid. If the person enters zero, a negative number, or a value greater than 120, he is either the world's oldest VBScript user or he has made a mistake in entering his age, and a message box appears on the screen telling him so. Figure 6.1 shows the Web page.

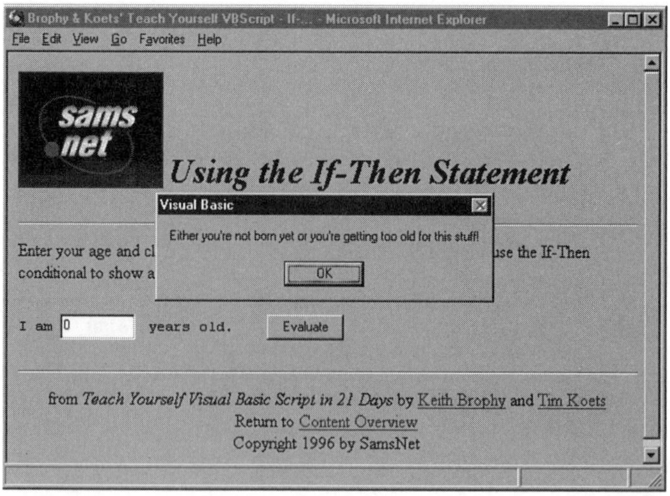

Figure 6.1.

A simple Web page with an If...Then *conditional structure.*

Notice that the condition takes advantage of the logical Or operator that you learned about on Day 5, "Putting Operators to Work in VBScript." If you don't remember how the Or operator works, you might want to take a look back at Day 5 to refresh your memory.

If...Then...Else

Now you know how to make a simple decision in VBScript. The If...Then structure is quite useful, but it has one limitation. Oftentimes, when people make decisions, they want to do one thing if a condition is true; otherwise, they want to do something different. For example, you may have imagined a simple decision structure in your mind that if Cardboard Burger World is open, you will go there to eat. Otherwise, you will go home and cook your own meal. You're certain to carry out either one of the two options because you're hungry, it's time for dinner, and hey—you deserve it after an afternoon of programming.

Apply this decision process to some code. Assume you had a variable that was previously set to indicate the state of whether Cardboard Burger World is open or closed based on the time a script is run. You want to have your code check this variable and put up a message box to let you know whether you can hit Cardboard Burger World. In this case, you wouldn't want to use the logic

```
If CardboardBurgerWorldOpen = True Then
    Msgbox "Go To CardboardBurgerWorld!"
End If
```

because that leaves out the alternative. You could use two statements:

```
If CardboardBurgerWorldOpen = True Then
    Msgbox "Go To CardboardBurgerWorld!"
End If
If CardboardBurgerWorldOpen = False Then
    Msgbox "Go Home and Cook!"
End If
```

but wouldn't it be nice if you didn't have to repeat the test where you check the negative instead of positive condition? This seems somewhat cumbersome. Fortunately, you have another control structure available to you in VBScript that makes this process easier. The control structure, called If...Then...Else, is represented as

```
If condition = True Then
    ...this is the code that executes if the condition is satisfied
Else
    ...this is the code that executes if the condition is not satisfied
End If
```

You could enter the expression you've formed in your mind as you drive toward Cardboard Burger World as

```
If CardboardBurgerWorld = True Then
    Msgbox "Go To CardboardBurgerWorld!"
```

6

```
Else
    Msgbox "Go Home and Cook!"
End If
```

This is certainly much simpler to understand, and it's equally helpful when writing your programs. Suppose your Web page gives the user the option of whether he wants the results of a calorie and fat counting Web page in calories or grams of fat. If you had a Boolean variable that was set to True if the user wanted the food item calculated in calories, you could use the expression

```
If Calories = True Then
    ...show the user the food in calories
Else
    ...show the user the food in fat grams
End If
```

where Calories is the variable that determines whether the user wants the result in calories. Notice that if the user doesn't want the result in calories, the only other case is fat grams.

What if you had a few other cases you wanted to test? You're in luck: You can do as many tests as you want by simply placing more ElseIf statements between the first If statement and the End If statement. The syntax of such a structure looks like this:

```
If condition1 = True Then
    ...the code that executes for condition1
ElseIf condition2 = True Then
    ...the code that executes for condition2
ElseIf condition3 = True Then
    ...the code that executes for condition3
End If
```

where you can have as many ElseIf statements as you want. Suppose that the same user wants to view the results of food intake in calories, fat grams, or total percentage of USRDA fat intake for the day. If you had the variables Calories, Fat_Grams, and Fat_Percent in your code, you could use the following expression to fill in the appropriate code to show the results to the user as well:

```
If Calories = True Then
    ...code to show the user the food in calories
ElseIf Fat_Grams = True Then
    ...code to show the user the food in fat grams
Else
    ...code to show the user the food in percentage fat intake
End If
```

A few comments are in order about this conditional structure. Notice that only one of the conditions can be true. If you want to execute code for more than one of these conditions, you cannot use this control structure. In other words, this structure can only execute one of the conditions. Once it finds the first condition in the list that is true, it executes the code off that branch and ignores all the rest. Even if Calories was equal to true and Fat_Grams was also equal to True, only the first true condition—in this case, the calories—would get executed. For most kinds of problems, you want to make sure that only one of your conditions is true or else they are all false. That is the second important point to consider. You don't have to include the last `Else` in your statement. You could just as easily have entered

```
If Calories = True Then
    ...show the user the food in calories
ElseIf Fat_Grams = True Then
    ...show the user the food in fat grams
End If
```

This would work fine as long as either `Calories` or `Fat_Grams` were equal to true. What if the user didn't specify which one and both variables were set to false? In that case, neither would get executed and the user wouldn't see anything. You have to be careful how you use these structures. If the logic of your problems demands that at least some action take place for a given condition, either make sure one of the two variables is set to true before you perform these tests, or be sure to provide an `Else` conditional at the end. The `Else` at the end will get executed if none of the other conditions is true. The `Else` condition acts as a fallback position just in case none of the other conditions is true. This might be valuable to you in cases where you want to make sure something happens in the conditional structure. After all, when you write code, it's best to take all possibilities into consideration; you never know when a pesky bug might enter or some unforeseen condition might take place, and you wouldn't want it to mess up your code.

Figure 6.2 shows a simple example of the `If...Then...Else` control structure. Here, you see a Web page that asks you for your age, just like the first example. Only this time, rather than perform one check, this Web page tests a variety of conditions and responds differently to each one.

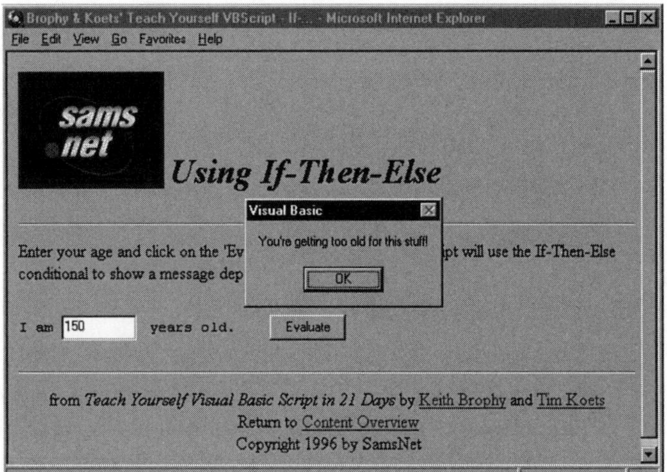

Figure 6.2.

A simple Web page with an `If...Then...Else` *conditional structure.*

Listing 6.2 shows the code for this Web page, named `iftelse.htm`, which is also on the CD-ROM.

Listing 6.2. A Web page that uses the If...Then...Else control structure.

```
<SCRIPT LANGUAGE="VBScript">
<!-- Option Explicit

  Sub cmdTest_OnClick()

    Dim Age

    Age = CInt(txtAge.Value)

    If Age = 0 Then
       MsgBox "Welcome to the human race!"
    ElseIf Age < 0 Then
       MsgBox "We hate to say this, but you have to grow up _
          a bit before you start using VBScript!"
    ElseIf Age > 0 and Age < 10 Then
       MsgBox "If you're bold enough, you must be old enough."
    ElseIf Age > 120 Then
       MsgBox "You're getting too old for this stuff!"
    Else
       MsgBox "You're at the perfect age to get started!"
    End If

  End Sub

-->
</SCRIPT>
```

ANALYSIS   In this case, you see that you can do more specific checks for various age groups and even provide an `Else` clause for the default case. You couldn't do that using `If...Then` statements unless you want to write a lot of excess code.

The `If...Then` and `If...Then...Else` control structures give you the ability to control the flow of your code based on decisions made within your code. These two structures are very important and are used throughout the book. Now look at the other structures available for your use.

Select Case

In the previous section, you saw how to use the `If...Then` and `If...Then...Else` conditional structures. In Listing 6.2 you saw an example in which five tests were made within this structure. In this case and cases where you have to perform a large number of tests on the same expression, you can instead use the `Select` statement. The `Select` statement often makes your code easier to read and interpret than would a long list of Else and Else If statements. The Select Case structure is defined as follows:

```
Select Case test_expression
    Case expression-1
        ...this is the code that executes if expression-1 matches test_expression
    Case expression-2
        ...this is the code that executes if expression-2 matches test_expression
    Case expression-3
        ...this is the code that executes if expression-3 matches test_expression
        .
        .
        .
    Case Else n
        ...this is the code that executes if expression-n matches test_expression
End Select
```

expression-1, expression-2, and expression-3 are one or more expressions that must match test_expression in order for the code below each Case statement to execute. As you can see, the same condition is evaluated throughout the structure. Only one case is executed when VBScript travels through. If more than one case matches, only the first one is executed. If none of the cases match, the code underneath the Case Else section is executed. The Case Else section is optional. However, VBScript won't do anything if none of the cases match.

Consider an example in which you want to print a message to the user based on what state the user lives in. The code may look like this:

```
Select Case State
    Case "Michigan"
            Message = "Michigan is a wonderful state to visit if you enjoy_
                        fresh-water lakes."
        Case "Virginia"
          Message = "Visit the Commonwealth for a wide variety of historical _
                    landmarks and beautiful mountain-scapes."
      Case "Arizona"
        Message = "Arizona is a wonderful getaway for those who love heat with low
_                       humidity"
        Case "Colorado"
        Message = "Colorado is almost unsurpassed for its majestic mountains and _ rivers."
    Case Else
        Message = "No specific information is available about this state."
End Select
```

There may be times when you have more than one expression in which you would like the same code to be executed. For example, you might want to provide the same message for Michigan and Minnesota. Rather than entering the code as this:

```
Select Case State
  Case "Michigan"
        Message = "A wonderful state to visit if you enjoy fresh-water lakes."
```

```
    Case "Minnesota"
        Message = "A wonderful state to visit if you enjoy fresh-water lakes."
    Case "Virginia"
        Message = "A wide variety of historical landmarks and beautiful mountains_
            make this a terrific state to live."
    Case "Arizona"
        Message = "A wonderful getaway for those who love heat with low humidity."
    Case "Colorado"
        Message = "Virtually unsurpassed for its majestic mountains and rivers."
  Case Else
    Message = "No specific information is available about this state."
End Select
```

which requires you to duplicate code, you can instead combine the two cases together as shown:

```
Select Case State
    Case "Michigan"
    Case "Minnesota"
        Message = "A wonderful state to visit if you enjoy fresh-water lakes."
    Case "Virginia"
    Message = "A wide variety of historical landmarks and beautiful mountains_
            make this a terrific state to live."
    Case "Arizona"
        Message = "A wonderful getaway for those who love heat with low humidity."
    Case "Colorado"
        Message = "Virtually unsurpassed for its majestic mountains and rivers."
    Case Else
        Message = "No specific information is available about this state."
End Select
```

To see an example of the Select Case structure in action, consider an example in which the user wishes to find out where the closest car dealership is in her state based on her area code. The example shown in Figure 6.3 shows the Web page to carry this out.

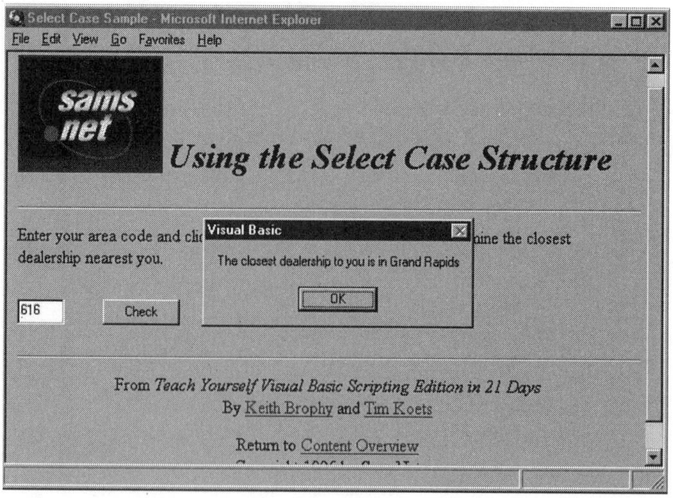

Figure 6.3.

A simple Web page that uses the Select Case *structure.*

The code for this Web page, named `select.htm`, is shown in Listing 6.3.

Listing 6.3. A Web page that uses the `Select` control structure.

```
<HTML>

<HEAD>
<TITLE>Select Case Sample</TITLE>
</HEAD>

<BODY>

<H1><A  HREF="http://www.mcp.com"><IMG    ALIGN=BOTTOM
SRC="../shared/jpg/samsnet.jpg" BORDER=2></A>
<EM>Using the Select Case Structure</EM></h1>

<HR>

<P>Enter your area code and click the 'Check' button.  VBScript will
determine the closest dealership nearest you.

<PRE>
<INPUT NAME="txtAreaCode" SIZE=5 >     <INPUT TYPE="BUTTON" VALUE="Check"
SIZE=30 NAME="cmdCheck">
</PRE>

<HR>

<center>
From <em>Teach Yourself VBScript in 21 Days</em><BR>
By <A HREF="../shared/info/keith.htm">Keith Brophy</A> and
<A HREF="../shared/info/tim.htm">Tim Koets</A><br>
<BR>
Return to <a href="back06.htm">Content Overview</A><br>
Copyright 1996 by SamsNet<br>
</center>

<SCRIPT LANGUAGE="VBScript">
<!-- Option Explicit

   Sub cmdCheck_OnClick()

      Dim AreaCode
      Dim DealerLocation

      ' Make sure user has supplied input
      if Not IsNumeric(txtAreaCode.Value) then
         msgbox "You must supply an area code!",0,"No area code given"
         exit sub
      end if

      AreaCode = CInt(txtAreaCode.Value)

   Select Case AreaCode
```

continues

6

Listing 6.3. continued

```
        Case 616
            DealerLocation = "Grand Rapids"

        Case 313
            DealerLocation = "Detroit"

        Case 517
    DealerLocation = "Lansing"

        Case 810
            DealerLocation = "Pontiac"

        Case 906
            DealerLocation = "Marquette"

        Case Else
            DealerLocation = "unknown"

    End Select

    MsgBox "The closest dealership to you is in " & DealerLocation

  End Sub

-->
</SCRIPT>

</BODY>

</HTML>
```

ANALYSIS   As you can see in Listing 6.3, the area code is first obtained from the user. A check is made to ensure that an area code has been supplied. Then, the `Select` structure performs various checks on the Michigan area codes to determine the closest city within that area code in which a dealership resides. If the user enters an unknown area code, the response string `"unknown"` is provided as a default.

It is generally a good idea to provide a default selection in the `Select Case` structure because it never hurts to expect the unexpected. Also keep in mind that you can nest `Select Case` structures if you wish, provided the correct syntax of `Select Case` and `End Select` are maintained.

NOTE   A `Case` can consist of a range of values separated by commas. For example, this statement matches for the area codes 616 or 517:

```
Select Case AreaCode
case 616, 517
DealerLocation = "Lower Michigan"
```

The `Case` statements can only work on discrete values (distinct values as opposed to symbolic values such as variables or conditional statements). You cannot provide conditional checks within a case statement. For example, this syntax is not legal:

```
Select Case MyVar
Case MyVar > 10 and MyVar < 25
```

In cases such as this, you must often rely on multiple checks with the `If…Then…ElseIf` if the `Select Case` structure can't be constructed to handle the expected range of values.

Using Control Structures to Make Code Repeat

On occasion, you will need to write code that repeats some set of statements. Oftentimes, this will occur when you need to perform some calculation over and over or when you have to apply the same calculations or processing to more than one variable, such as changing the values in an array. This section shows you all the control structures you can use in VBScript to control code in your program that repeats.

For…Next

The first structure is often referred to as the `For…Next` *loop*. The syntax for this structure is

```
For counter = start to finish
    ...code that gets repeated
Next
```

where `counter` is a variable used for counting purposes that begins at the number specified by the `start` variable and counts up by one, each time executing the code within the structure, until it reaches `finish`. Usually, `counter` is incremented by one each time through the loop, although you can change the value of the increment. I'll show you how to do this in a moment, but first, check out the `For…Next` loop in action.

Suppose you have an array called `Salaries` that contains 30 elements, and you want to set all these elements to a value of 30,000. One way to do this is to enter the code

```
Salaries(0) = 30000
Salaries(1) = 30000
Salaries(2) = 30000
  .
  .
  .
Salaries(29) = 30000
```

If you did it this way, you would have to enter thirty lines of code. Rather than go through all that work, however, you have a much easier way. In this case, you're repeating the same operation thirty times, but each time, you're assigning the value to a different element in the array. Instead, try entering the following code:

```
For i = 0 to 29
    Salaries(i) = 30000
Next
```

You've reduced the code to three lines. Quite a savings! What does VBScript do when it encounters this loop? The first thing it does is assign the counter variable, i, with the start value, or 0. Then, it executes the statement within the loop. In this case, the statement within the loop makes use of the counter variable. Because the first time inside the loop i has a value of 0, the statement

```
Salaries(0) = 30000
```

is effectively executed because i = 0. After that, VBScript executes the Next statement, which sends it back to the top where i is incremented. The counter variable then becomes 1 rather than 0. Once VBScript increments the counter variable, it checks to see if the counter variable is greater than the finish value, in this case, 29. Because i = 1 and the finish value is 29, i is still within range, so the loop continues. This time, the statement inside the loop effectively becomes

```
Salaries(1) = 30000
```

Then, the loop repeats, and i gets incremented to 3, and because 3 is less than or equal to 29, the process continues. In fact, the code inside the loop will be executed again and again until i equals 30. Once i is incremented beyond the finish value, the loop will end, and VBScript will advance past the Next statement. The end result is that every element of the array Salaries from element 0 to element 29 will be set with the value 30000.

The For…Next loop is quite flexible because you can tell VBScript how much you want the counter variable to be incremented each time through the loop. You can also decrement the counter rather than increment it. How do you do this? The counter is incremented by a value of 1 each time through the loop unless you specify otherwise. You can do so through the use of the Step keyword like this:

```
For counter = start to finish Step increment
    ...code that gets repeated
Next
```

where *increment* is a variable or value that tells the loop how much to increment the counter each time through the loop. As before, the moment *counter* falls outside the range of *start* and *finish,* the loop will stop. Suppose you wanted to set every third salary at 30,000 rather than every one of the salaries. You could write the loop as

```
For i = 0 to 29 Step 3
  Salaries(i) = 30000
Next
```

Here, i will equal 0, 3, 6, 9, 12, and so on, right up to 27. Each time through the loop, i gets incremented by 3. When i is set to 30, it exceeds the range of the loop and the loop stops. This loop effectively executes the following statements

```
Salaries(0) = 30000
Salaries(3) = 30000
Salaries(6) = 30000
Salaries(9) = 30000
Salaries(12) = 30000
Salaries(15) = 30000
Salaries(18) = 30000
Salaries(21) = 30000
Salaries(24) = 30000
Salaries(27) = 30000
```

If you wanted to move down the array from 29 to 0 rather than up from 0 to 29, you could have written the loop like this:

```
For i = 29 to 0 Step -3
   Salaries(i) = 30000
Next
```

Before you see an example of the For…Next structure, you need to keep in mind a few important rules. VBScript is fully dependent on you to tell it how many times you want to execute the loop. As you read earlier today, computers do exactly as they're told, even if they're told to do something that doesn't make any sense. If you tell VBScript to execute a loop forever, it will go off happily in that direction—that is, until you stop the program from running, the computer runs out of memory, or some kind of an error occurs. How could this happen? Consider the following code loop:

```
For i = 1 to 10 Step 0
   Salaries(i) = 30000
Next
```

Because the increment value is set to 0, the counter variable will never change, and the loop will spin its wheels forever. This is often called an *infinite loop.* You might be thinking to yourself, "I'd never be crazy enough to write something like that." Of course not, but you could do it by accident or have a loop like this:

```
For i = 1 to 10 Step Change
  Salaries(i) = 30000
Next
```

where Change somehow fails to get set in your code and takes on the value of 0. The point is that accidents do happen when you're writing code. Even the most expert programmer can fall prey to such a simple error.

One comforting thought about infinite loops is that most browsers will detect that no activity is happening in a script when an infinite loop is taking place. Internet Explorer puts up a message box stating, "This page contains a script which is taking an unusually long time to finish. To end this script now, click Cancel." This enables the user to interrupt a page in an infinite loop and get on with using the browser. Regardless, infinite loops are evil, and you obviously don't want your users to find them within your Web pages.

When you construct loops, make sure they always have the correct range and they're counting in the right direction. You should never, for example, write a loop like this:

```
For i = 1 to -5
    Salaries(i) = 30000
Next
```

This loop wouldn't work because the counter variable i cannot move from 1 to -5 in positive increments. VBScript checks the starting and ending values to determine whether it can get there using the step value. In this case, VBScript knows it cannot get from 1 to -5 with a step value of 1. As a result, the loop never executes. You can avoid all these problems if you follow these simple rules:

- ☐ When you use a positive step value, make sure the *finish* value is greater than the *start* value, or the loop won't execute at all.

    ```
    For i = 10 to 1 Step 2        Incorrect
    ```

    ```
    For i = 1 to 10 Step 2        Correct
    ```

- ☐ When you use a negative step value, make sure the *start* value is greater than the *finish* value, or the loop won't execute at all.

    ```
    For i = 1 to 10 Step -1       Incorrect
    ```

    ```
    For i = 10 to 1 Step -1       Correct
    ```

- ☐ Never use a step value of zero. In this case, VBScript will enter an infinite loop, and your program might run indefinitely.

    ```
    For i = 1 to 10 Step 0        Incorrect
    ```

    ```
    For i = 1 to 10 Step 3        Correct
    ```

If you make sure your code follows these simple rules, you'll avoid all the trouble I've discussed.

If you ever want to break out of a loop, such as when an error occurs, you can use the Exit For statement. Usually, you break out of a loop because of a problem or some exception. Consider Listing 6.4.

Listing 6.4. Exiting a For...Next loop.

```
For I = 1 to 10
    Response = MsgBox("Would you like to continue adding _
            the salaries?", vbYesNo)
    If Response = vbYes Then
        Result = Result + Salaries(I)
Else
    Exit For
End If
Next
```

ANALYSIS In this case, as long as the user keeps clicking the Yes button when asked, the loop will continue through to completion. If the user clicks No for any reason, however, the loop will stop prematurely.

Take a look at a sample Web page that uses the For...Next loop. Figure 6.4 shows the Web page named golfavg.htm, which is on the CD-ROM.

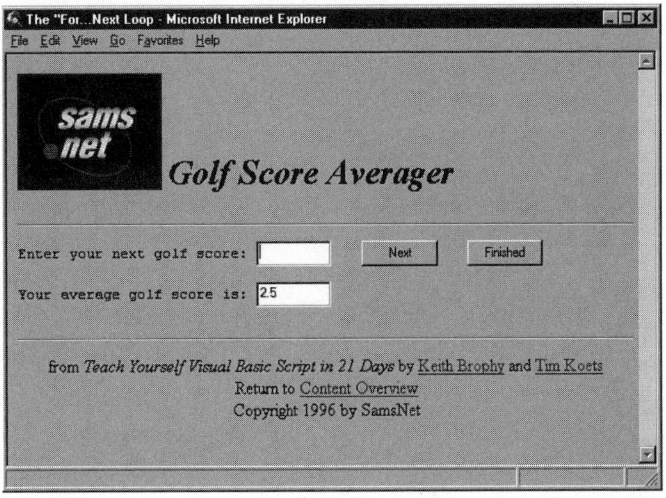

Figure 6.4.

A Web page that uses the For...Next structure.

As you can see from the figure, you can use the Web page to calculate a golfer's average score. The page consists of two text fields: the first to enter the scores and the second to display the average. The Web page also contains two command buttons labeled Next and Finished. The user can enter up to ten scores, clicking on Next to log each successive score. Then, when the user has entered all the scores, he simply clicks the Finished button and the average is calculated. Listing 6.5 shows the code for this Web page.

Listing 6.5. Using the For...Next statement in a Web page.

```
<SCRIPT LANGUAGE="VBScript">
<!-- Option Explicit

    Dim Count
    Dim Scores(10)

    Count = 0

    Sub cmdNext_OnClick()

        Dim Score
        Dim i

        Score = CSng(txtScore.Value)

        If Count > 9 Then
            MsgBox "You can only enter up to 10 scores.  Click the Finished _
                    button to calculate the average."
        Else
            Scores(Count) = Score
            Count = Count + 1
            txtScore.Value = ""
        End If

    End Sub

    Sub cmdFinished_OnClick()

        Dim Average
        Dim Sum
        Dim i

        For i = 0 to Count-1
            Sum = Sum + Scores(i)
        Next

        Average = Sum / Count
        txtAverage.Value = Average

        Count = 0

    End Sub

-->
</SCRIPT>
```

 ANALYSIS   As you can see, the example creates a script-level array so that both procedures can access the array of scores. The count, which stores the number of values the user actually entered, is also script level in scope because the procedure that does the averaging needs to know how many valid values have been entered. Armed with this information, the procedure enters a For...Next loop where the counter, i, ranges from 0 to Count - 1 to cover the number of values the user has entered. The loop adds up all the scores, which are divided after the loop to obtain the average score.

Notice that if the user never enters a score and just clicks the Finished button without entering data, the loop would take the form

```
For i = 0 to -1
    Sum = Sum + Scores(i)
Next
```

In this case, the loop would never execute. More dangerous, however, is the fact that the variable Count would have a value of zero, and when the average was taken using the expression

```
Average = Sum / Count
```

the Sum and Count would both be 0. This would result in a run-time, divide-by-zero error. To prevent this, you might want check for this condition and alert the user if he entered no data. Listing 6.6 shows a revised version of the program that makes sure this error could never occur.

Listing 6.6. Using the For...Next statement in a Web page with additional error-checking to prevent a divide-by-zero error.

```
<SCRIPT LANGUAGE="VBScript">
<!-- Option Explicit

    Dim Count
    Dim Scores(10)

    Count = 0

    Sub cmdNext_OnClick()

        Dim Score
        Dim i

        Score = CSng(txtScore.Value)

        If Count > 9 Then
            MsgBox "You can only enter up to 10 scores.  Click the Finished _
                    button to calculate the average."
    Else
        Scores(Count) = Score
            Count = Count + 1
            txtScore.Value = ""
    End If
```

6

continues

Listing 6.6. continued

```
End Sub

Sub cmdFinished_OnClick()

Dim Average
   Dim Sum
   Dim i

   If Count = 0 Then
      MsgBox "You must enter some scores before they can be averaged."
      Exit Sub
   End If


   For i = 0 to Count-1
       Sum = Sum + Scores(i)
   Next

   Average = Sum / Count
   txtAverage.Value = Average

   Count = 0

End Sub

-->
</SCRIPT>
```

You will learn more about error checking and debugging your programs on Day 17, "Exterminating Bugs from Your Script."

Do...Loop

The next conditional structure discussed in this lesson is the powerful Do...Loop structure. This section discusses each of the four variations of the Do...Loop that you can use.

Do While...Loop

The first loop structure you can use is the Do While...Loop structure. The basic syntax for this structure is

```
Do While condition
   ...code within the loop goes here
Loop
```

where the condition is either true or false. As long as the condition is true, the code within the loop gets executed. Once the condition becomes false, the loop stops and the code after the loop is executed. The only way for the program to break out of the loop is if the condition becomes false or if an Exit Do statement is encountered somewhere inside the loop. Consider the following example shown in Listing 6.7.

Listing 6.7. Using the Do While…Loop conditional structure.

```
Again = True
DoubleIt = 1

' Keep doubling the number as long as the user desires
Do While Again = True

    ' Show current results and prompt to see if we should continue

        If MsgBox("Current total is " & DoubleIt & ". Double it again ?", _
            vbYesNo) = vbYes Then
            DoubleIt = DoubleIt * 2
Else
            Again = False
        End If

Loop
```

In this example, the first line of code sets the variable that gets tested in the loop equal to true. The second line sets the variable that gets doubled in the code equal to one. Setting the loop variable equal to true allows the loop to get off and running because the third line says, "If Again is true, enter the loop." Because the variable has just been set to true, the loop begins. The first statement in the loop displays the result to the user. Because nothing has been doubled yet, the result is one—the initial value of the DoubleIt variable.

When the results are displayed, the user is asked if he wants to continue. If he chooses to go forward, the variable DoubleIt is multiplied by two. When the program hits the Loop instruction, it will return to the top of the loop and once again check to see if the condition is set to true. Because the condition has not changed, the loop executes again. It will continue to execute until the user chooses not to continue. Once that happens, the variable Again is set to False. Now, when Loop is reached, the code swings back up to the top of the loop and evaluates the condition once more. This time, the condition is false, so the loop does not execute again. The code moves on beyond the loop.

You can see an example of the Do While…Loop in action in a slightly revised golf average example. Here, the user once again enters golf scores to average them, but this time, things are handled a bit differently. Figure 6.5 shows the Web page, which is stored as golfdwlp.htm.

6

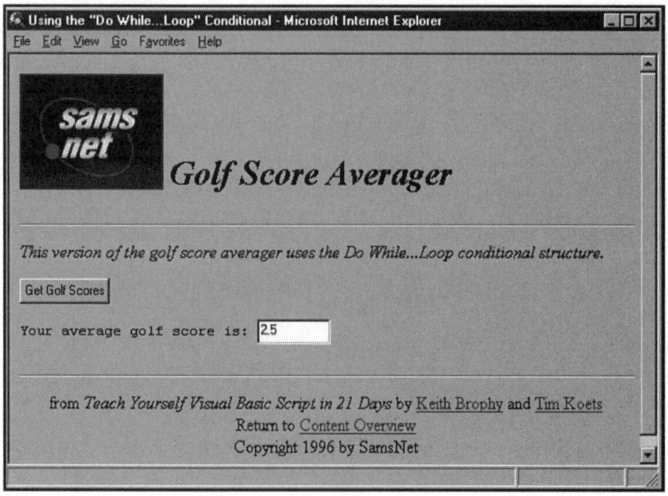

Figure 6.5.

A Web page that uses the
`Do While...Loop`
structure.

In this example, the user simply clicks the Get Golf Scores button, which proceeds to ask the user for a score using a special function called `InputBox`. We discuss this function in detail on Day 14, "Working with Documents and User Interface Functions." For now, just think of this function as a box where you put in a message for the user and out comes whatever he's entered in the box. If the user doesn't enter anything at all when the input box appears on the screen, the function returns an empty string, or `""`. The page shown in Figure 6.5 is asking the user for golf scores. Listing 6.8 shows the code that accomplishes this.

Listing 6.8. A Web page that uses the `Do While...Loop` structure.

```
<SCRIPT LANGUAGE="VBScript">
<!-- Option Explicit

Sub cmdGetScores_OnClick()

  Dim Count
  Dim Scores(10)
    Dim Score
    Dim Average
    Dim Sum
    Dim i

    Score = 0

  Do While Score <> "" And Count < 10
      Score = InputBox("Enter the next golf score _
                        (Press Return to quit): ")
    If Score <> "" Then
        Count = Count + 1
```

```
        Scores(Count-1) = CSng(Score)
      End If
    Loop

    For i = 0 to Count-1
      Sum = Sum + Scores(i)
    Next

  Average = Sum / Count

  txtAverage.Value = Average

  Count = 0

End Sub

-->
</SCRIPT>
```

ANALYSIS As you can see, the loop in this listing continues to ask the user for scores until the user doesn't enter anything or he's reached the ten score limit. At that point, the loop condition is no longer true and the average is calculated and displayed to the user. Notice that the score must be set to 0 before the loop begins, otherwise the expression

```
Score <> ""
```

would be false and the loop would never execute. In the next section, you will see a way to implement the program without that extra line of code.

The best way to exit from a Do…Loop is to make the condition false as you did in the previous listing. Sometimes, however, you might have to exit a function due to an error or some other factor that must pull you out of a loop. In that case, you can use the Exit Do statement, and VBScript will take you to the next statement below the loop.

Do…Loop While

In the Do While…Loop construct example shown previously, the condition that determined whether you stayed in the loop was a variable that had to be true. Notice that the code in Listing 6.5 first checks the conditional test before it enters the loop. You had better be sure to set the condition variable to true outside the loop before it starts. Otherwise, you have no way of making sure the variable Again was set to true before the loop began. If it had never been set or were set to False, the code inside the loop would never get executed.

6

Sometimes, it is more desirable to put the conditional test at the bottom of the loop rather than the top. You can accomplish this using the Do…Loop While structure. This control structure takes the form

```
Do
    ...code within the loop goes here
Loop While condition
```

As you can see, the only difference is that the condition is tested after the code inside the loop is executed. What difference does this make? Only this: The loop always executes at least one time because it doesn't test for the condition until after it's gone through the loop once. Then, at the end, it performs the test. If you want your loop to execute at least once regardless of the condition (the condition isn't even considered the first time through the loop), this is the structure to use. If you don't even want the loop to execute unless the condition is true first, use the Do While…Loop structure.

Listing 6.9 shows an example using the Do…Loop While structure.

Listing 6.9. Using the Do…Loop While conditional structure.

```
DoubleIt = 1

' Keep doubling the number as long as the user desires
Do
        '  Show current results and prompt to see if we should continue
    If MsgBox("Current total is " & DoubleIt & ". Double it again ?", _
        vbYesNo) = vbYes Then
  DoubleIt = DoubleIt * 2
     Again = True
Else
     Again = False
    End If

Loop While Again = True
```

ANALYSIS Notice that you have to make sure that the test variable Again gets set one way or the other within the loop. In this case, you can be sure the user will move through the loop at least once. The code is a bit easier to read and understand. In some cases, you might have other conditions where you want to execute the loop at least once and then decide to execute it again. In other cases, you will want to do the test before running anything within the loop. It depends on the application, but both control structures are available for your use.

Consider once more the golf score Web page. In the last section, you used Do While…Loop to accomplish the task. Listing 6.10 points out that you can write the code a bit better using Do…Loop While. The revised Web page called golfdwlp.htm is on the CD-ROM that accompanies the book.

Listing 6.10. A Web page that uses the `Do…Loop While` structure.

```
<SCRIPT LANGUAGE="VBScript">
<!-- Option Explicit

    Sub cmdGetScores_OnClick()

    Dim Scores(10)
    Dim Score
        Dim Average
        Dim Sum
        Dim i

        Do
            Score = InputBox("Enter the next golf score _
                              (Press Return to quit): ")
            If Score <> "" Then
                Count = Count + 1
                Scores(Count-1) = CSng(Score)
            End If
        Loop While Score <> "" And Count < 10

        For i = 0 to Count-1
            Sum = Sum + Scores(i)
        Next

        Average = Sum / Count

        txtAverage.Value = Average

    Count = 0

  End Sub

-->
</SCRIPT>
```

ANALYSIS Here, you guarantee the user will be asked for at least one score, and you don't have to worry about making sure the variable is equal to zero before you enter the loop. The `Do…Loop While` appears to be the better choice.

Do Until…Loop

The third type of `Do…Loop` is the `Do Until…Loop` structure. This is very similar to the `Do While…Loop` except that rather than perform the operations within the loop *while* the condition is true, it executes the operations inside the loop *until* the condition is true. If you think about this slight twist of logic for a moment, this will make some sense to you. To help, I'll use a familiar real-life analogy.

6

Suppose that your father wants you to clean out the garage until he cuts the grass. Using your logical, programming model of reality, you take this to mean that the only time you have to clean out the garage is until he gets outside and starts up the mower. Once he starts cutting the grass, you're outta there. You breathe a big sigh of relief when he walks out to the shed to start cutting the grass. Just before you escape out the back for the baseball diamond, however, your mother notices you. To your horror, she tells you that she wants you to clean out the garage while your father cuts the grass. Before, you only had to clean the garage until your dad started mowing the lawn. Now, you've got to slave away in the garage until he's done! What a life!

Besides the fact that you've got to do more work, can you see the difference? When you're constructing loops, you can set up the same kind of decision-making process. The Do Until...Loop structure takes the form

```
Do Until condition
    ...code within the loop goes here
Loop
```

where the code within the loop will only get executed until the condition becomes true. As long as the condition is false, the code in the loop will continue to be executed. Consider the result display implementation in Listing 6.8. What would that implementation look like using Do Until...Loop instead of Do While...Loop? Listing 6.11 provides the answer.

Listing 6.11. Using the Do Until...Loop conditional structure.

```
Again = True
DoubleIt = 1

' Keep doubling the number as long as the user desires
Do Until Again = False
    ' Show current results and prompt to see if we should continue
    If MsgBox("Current total is " & DoubleIt & ". Double it again ?", _
            vbYesNo) = vbYes Then
  DoubleIt = DoubleIt * 2
Else
      Again = False
    End If

Loop
```

 As you can see from the listing, rather than execute the loop while Again is true, this loop executes until Again is false. Because the logic has changed, you must change the test of Again from true to false to make the loop equivalent to the previous one.

You can also use the familiar golf score Web page to illustrate this loop structure. Listing 6.12 shows the revised Web page, which is also on the CD-ROM as golfdulp.htm.

Listing 6.12. A Web page that uses the Do Until...Loop structure.

```
<SCRIPT LANGUAGE="VBScript">
<!-- Option Explicit

    Sub cmdGetScores_OnClick()

        Dim Count
        Dim Scores(10)
        Dim Score
        Dim Average
        Dim Sum
        Dim i

        Score = 0

        Do Until Score = "" Or Count > 9
            Score = InputBox("Enter the next golf score _
                             (Press Return to quit): ")
            If Score <> "" Then
                Count = Count + 1
                Scores(Count-1) = CSng(Score)
            End If
        Loop

        For i = 0 to Count-1
            Sum = Sum + Scores(i)
        Next

        Average = Sum / Count

        txtAverage.Value = Average

        Count = 0

    End Sub

-->
</SCRIPT>
```

ANALYSIS Here, the logic of the loop changes a bit. Rather than loop while the scores are coming in, the program loops until the scores stop coming in. Also notice that you have to make sure Score equals zero before the loop starts because you check for its value before the code inside the loop begins.

Do...Loop Until

If you want to defer the decision in the loop to the end, you can use the Do...Loop Until structure. This takes on the form

```
Do
    ...code within the loop goes here
Loop Until condition
```

In this case, you're certain that VBScript will go through the loop at least one time, and the test takes place after that first iteration through the loop. From that point on, until the condition becomes true, the loop will continue to execute.

Take a look at the golf score Web page once again. As before, the code would read a bit better if you put the condition at the end of the loop rather than the beginning. Listing 6.13 shows how that is accomplished with the code named golfdulp.htm.

Listing 6.13. A Web page that uses the Do…Loop Until structure.

```
<SCRIPT LANGUAGE="VBScript">
<!-- Option Explicit

 Sub cmdGetScores_OnClick()

      Dim Count
      Dim Scores(10)
      Dim Score
      Dim Average
      Dim Sum
      Dim i

      Do
         Score = InputBox("Enter the next golf score (Press Return to quit): ")
         If Score <> "" Then
            Count = Count + 1
            Scores(Count-1) = CSng(Score)
         End If
      Loop Until Score = "" Or Count > 9

      For i = 0 to Count-1
         Sum = Sum + Scores(i)
      Next

      Average = Sum / Count

    txtAverage.Value = Average

    Count = 0

 End Sub

-->
</SCRIPT>
```

6

ANALYSIS   Of all the possible loop structures examined today, this one is probably the best for the golf score Web page. It accomplishes the task, yet it's easy to read and understand. As you see, any of the control structures in this section could work with this page. How do you know which is best to choose? The next section provides some good pointers.

You need to remember one more thing about Do…Loop conditional structures. In any of the Do…Loop structures, you can always force VBScript to exit the loop by using the statement Exit Do from within the loop itself. This is often useful for error conditions or special cases where the normal condition is insufficient for breaking out of the loop.

Putting It All Together

Now that you've seen all the decision structures at your command, you know that you have quite a wide variety of choices. You might be wondering at this point, "How do I know which control structure to use?" Oftentimes, you can structure your code where you can choose from one or more of the techniques explained today. I can't provide a specific set of rules to follow for every case. Often, it just boils down to using the structure that expresses what you want to do the most clearly. The If…Then…Else structure is fairly intuitive and straightforward. Still, you might want to keep the following points in mind:

☐ Do you want to take a single action based on a decision, or do you want to take more than one possible action based on a decision?

If you only have one action to consider, the If…Then structure is best for you. If, however, you have several tests to do and actions to match each, you might want to use a series of If…Then…ElseIf statements. Often, it helps to write a flowchart or a graph of what you want the program to do under what circumstances.

NOTE

> If you've used Visual Basic 4.0 or Visual Basic for Applications, you might be familiar with the SELECT statement, another powerful construct for evaluating a series of conditions. This is not supported in VBScript. Refer to Day 20, "Porting Between Visual Basic and VBScript," for more details on language differences.

6

☐ Sometimes, you might wonder whether you should use the For…Next control structure. Ask yourself the following question: Do you want the code in your loop to execute a certain number of times based on a counter that can be adjusted each time through the loop?

If so, and this is often the case, use the For…Next loop. If, for instance, you have to set a series of elements within an array or perhaps perform some calculation a certain number of times, the For…Next loop is the structure to use. If you can't find a connection between a counter, start value, and stop value for repeating the code in your conditional, you might have to consider a Do…Loop.

You might hesitate when deciding what type of Do…Loop to use for the case in question. You should keep the following tips in mind when making your decision:

☐ Do you want the code within your loop to always execute at least once?

 If so, you should use either the Do…Loop Until or Do…Loop While structures.

☐ Do you want to execute the code in the loop until something happens or while something is happening?

 If you want to loop through code until something happens, such as setting a variable or completing some procedure successfully, you should use the Do…Loop Until or Do Until…Loop structures. Any time you want to repeat the code in your loop while some condition is true or while something is happening, the Do…Loop While or Do While…Loop structures are probably best.

Take some time to think of the right looping approach. At the same time, realize that there is often no one best approach. Even experienced programmers might each choose different looping constructs to solve the same problem.

Summary

Today you have gotten a comprehensive overview of the various control structures you can use in a VBScript program. A control structure is a set of code statements you can use to enable blocks of code to repeat or to execute or not execute based on decisions made in those statements. You have seen many examples of each control structure available in VBScript. With your knowledge of variables, operators, and control structures, you are becoming an increasingly competent and knowledgeable VBScript programmer.

Control structures are at the heart of VBScript programming. Having read today's lesson, you should understand how they work and be quite comfortable using them. As you will see, the examples throughout this book use them extensively. A program almost always has to make a lot of decisions. Today's lesson has provided you with the information and strategies you need to get the most out of directing and controlling code flow within a procedure.

Q&A

Q Why are there so many Do…Loop structures available? They all seem so similar.

A Yes, they are quite similar, but each is slightly different. Believe it or not, you will undoubtedly find yourself using almost all of them at one point or another. When you're writing your code to get it just the way you want it, the last thing you want to worry about is whether or not there is a control structure available that gets the job done. By being familiar with them all, you've got all the bases covered.

Q Why is the use of `Exit Do` or `Exit For` statements within loops discouraged?

A These statements are acceptable for specific conditions, but they often make code less readable, which makes it difficult for others who look at your code to know what's really going on. If you make sure the only way out of a loop is to not satisfy the loop's condition, it's much easier to follow your code. Often, breaking out of a loop by force with an exit statement is a sign of a poorly constructed loop with a condition that does not meet your goals. Take a look at the loop structure and condition again to make sure you're not leaving something out.

Q How can I avoid creating loops that never stop?

A Loops that never stop place your code in what's called an *infinite loop*. Infinite loops obviously prevent subsequent portions of your program from ever being reached. The best way to avoid them is to make sure you know how and when the condition that keeps your code looping finally ends and your loop stops. Try to think of cases where your loop might never exit, and if you can find them, try to prevent them by not getting into the loop in the first place or making your condition more broad so that you can get out of the loop in additional ways. For example, consider the following loop code:

```
Do While Stop = False
    Name = InputBox("Enter a name:")
    If GetAddress(Name) = False Then
        Stop = True
    End If
Loop
```

In this case, it is possible that the user might not want to enter any more names. The way this loop is set up, it will continue until it finds a name whose address it cannot match. That's fine, but what if the user is done entering names? There's no way to break out of the loop. The solution is to set up another loop condition that takes this into account:

```
Do While Stop = False or NoName = True
    Name = InputBox("Enter a name:")
    If Name = "" Then
        NoName = True
    End If
    If GetAddress(Name) = False Then
        Stop = True
    End If
Loop
```

Now, the program can break out of the loop if the user hasn't supplied a name or if the address of the name the user entered cannot be found.

6

Workshop

Create a Web page that uses at least three of the control structures you've learned about today. Focus on the If...Then, For...Next, and Do While...Loop structures, but feel free to change or add new structures as needed.

Quiz

NOTE   Refer to Appendix C, "Answers to Quiz Questions," for the answers to these questions.

1. List three control structures you've seen today and a brief description of what each of them does. Provide a simple example of their use.

2. Write a simple program that asks the user for the year in which she was born. Use a control structure to inform the user if the year she's entered is invalid. Use the InputBox function to get the year from the user. InputBox hasn't been covered in detail yet, but you can use it in the same manner it was used in the example earlier today.

3. Now, include another control structure that keeps asking her for the year until she's entered the right one.

Day 7

Building a Home for Your Code

On this, the last day of the first week, you will learn one more fundamental concept: how VBScript code is organized. VBScript, like most other languages, stores code in what we call *procedures*. As you will see, you can design procedures in different ways for different purposes. Procedures are containers for groups of code that accomplish specific tasks. Procedures can call and be called by other procedures, giving the programmer a great deal of flexibility. Today, you will learn how to create and use procedures, as well as the benefits of using them.

NEW TERM A *procedure* is a grouping of code statements that can be called by an associated name to accomplish a specific task or purpose in a program. Once a procedure is defined, it can be called from different locations in the program as needed.

Procedures come in two varieties: *subroutines* and *functions*. Each have special characteristics that set them apart, and today's lesson considers both subroutines and functions individually. Having been introduced to subroutines and functions, you will learn about a type of procedure called an *event*. Events respond to user-initiated activities, such as clicking a button. Another type of procedure, called a *method,* performs a specific task of an object. You will learn how all these procedures work together as well as where you should place them in an HTML document.

Subroutines

The first type of procedure I will discuss is the *subroutine.* A subroutine is a container that holds a series of VBScript statements. Suppose you'd like to create a block of code that accomplishes some specific task. Maybe you need to accomplish that task in various places throughout your code. All you need to do is create, or declare, the subroutine in your script. Once you've declared the subroutine, you can call it anywhere within your code. When your program *calls* a subroutine, the flow of the code is temporarily diverted to the statements within the subroutine. Once the subroutine has finished executing, control returns to the code that called the subroutine and execution picks up from there.

NEW TERM A *subroutine* is a block of code that can be called from anywhere in a program to accomplish a specific task. Subroutines can accept starting data through subroutine declaration variables called parameters. However, subroutines do not automatically return result code or an argument to the caller.

Declaring a Subroutine

You declare subroutines using the Sub keyword and end them using the End Sub statement. The structure of a subroutine is

```
Sub Subroutine_Name(argument1, argument2, ..., argumentn)
   ...code within the subroutine
End Sub
```

where *Subroutine_Name* is the name of the subroutine and *argument1* through *argumentn* are optional *arguments,* often called parameters, that you can pass to the subroutine. If you choose not to pass any arguments to the subroutine, the parentheses are optional, as you will see in a moment.

NEW TERM An *argument* or a *parameter* is a variable that a procedure requires in order to execute. In VBScript, arguments must be supplied in the order specified by the procedure.

The name of a subroutine should adequately describe what the subroutine is for. Make the name as descriptive as you can, and name the subroutine in plain English rather than in some cryptic abbreviations only you understand and might even forget a week later. You must name subroutines using the same rules as variables; letters and numbers are fine as long as the first character is not a number, and you cannot use symbols. If you enter an invalid name for a subroutine, the VBScript run-time interpreter will alert you of the problem when you attempt to try your script. The following are some valid subroutine names:

```
WelcomeTheUser
PrintInvoice
Meters2Yards
```

The following are some unacceptable subroutine names:

```
User.Welcome
2Printer
Miles*1.609
```

If you want, a subroutine can require that the code statement that calls that subroutine provide one or more *arguments* or variables that the subroutine can work with. Any time you need preexisting data to perform the task within the subroutine, arguments are very helpful. For example, the following subroutine accepts an argument to be used in the subroutine as a message to be displayed to the user:

```
Sub ShowMessage(CurrentMessage)
   MsgBox CurrentMessage, vbOkOnly, "Important Message"
End Sub
```

In this case, `CurrentMessage` is the argument, and it is treated like any other variable in the subroutine. It is treated exactly as if it had been declared with a `Dim` statement with one very important difference. The `CurrentMessage` argument variable starts out pre-initialized with a value that was supplied by the code that called this subroutine. When you declare a procedure and specify that it will receive arguments, you can specify how it interacts with those argument variables. You can either give the subroutine a copy of a value supplied as an argument, or you can refer it to the actual variable that the caller is using. If you give the subroutine a *copy* of the variable, the subroutine can then make changes to its own copy without changing the original. If, on the other hand, the subroutine simply references the variable owned by the caller, it cannot change the variable—it doesn't own it. I'll discuss this in more detail later in today's lesson.

NOTE
> At the time this book was being written, VBScript was in the beta Internet Explorer and did not support the `ByRef` parameter familiar to many Visual Basic programmers, but it might be supported in the future. See the discussion later in this lesson for further details.

Often, a subroutine might not require any arguments, and you can drop the parentheses. Suppose you have a subroutine that simply displays information to the user. In that case, the subroutine doesn't need any arguments, as in the following case:

```
Sub ShowAboutMessage
   MsgBox "This Web page was designed by the WebWizard."
End Sub
```

7

In this case, you can see that the code lists no arguments, so it does not require the parentheses. On the other hand, if you declared a procedure using one or more arguments, you'd use the parentheses:

```
Sub ShowAboutMessage(Message)
    MsgBox Message
End Sub
```

Calling a Subroutine

Now that you've learned how to create a subroutine, how do you call one? You can call a subroutine throughout the rest of the application once you've declared and created it. You can call subroutines by using the Call keyword or just entering the name of the subroutine on a line of code. For example, to call a subroutine called ShowMessage, you could enter

```
ShowMessage "This is the message."
```

You could also use the Call keyword and enter

```
Call ShowMessage("This is the message.")
```

Notice that in the first method, you do not place parentheses around the arguments of the subroutine. On the other hand, if you use Call, you must enclose the arguments in parentheses. This is simply a convention that VBScript requires. What if a subroutine has no arguments? To call the subroutine ShowAboutMessage, you could enter

```
ShowAboutMessage
```

or

```
Call ShowAboutMessage()
```

or you could use

```
Call ShowAboutMessage
```

The first method simply lists the name of the subroutine. The second method uses Call but doesn't require parentheses because the subroutine has no arguments. Whether you use the parentheses when you call or declare a subroutine with no arguments is a personal preference about writing code. When you call a subroutine without the Call statement, it can be more difficult to figure out the difference between a subroutine and a variable in your code, especially if your code is lengthy. Although the choice is up to you, it is generally recommended that you always use the Call statement when calling subroutines for the sake of readability.

Exiting a Subroutine

The code within your subroutine will execute until one of two things happens. First, the subroutine might get down to the last line, the `End Sub` line, which terminates the subroutine and passes the baton back to the caller. This statement can appear only once at the end of the subroutine declaration. The second possibility is that VBScript could execute the following code statement:

```
Exit Sub
```

when placed inside the subroutine. You might use this statement if you need to provide more than one exit point for the subroutine. However, you shouldn't need to use this very often if your subroutine is constructed properly. Consider the following subroutine:

```
Sub ConvertFeetToInches
   Feet = InputBox("How many feet are there?")
   If Feet < 0 Then
      Exit Sub
   Else
      MsgBox "This equals " & Feet * 12 & " inches."
   End If
End Sub
```

This subroutine contains an `Exit Sub` statement, which could be avoided by changing the subroutine to

```
Sub ConvertFeetToInches
   Feet = InputBox "How many feet are there?")
   If Feet >= 0 Then
      MsgBox "This equals " & Feet * 12 & " inches."
   End If
End Sub
```

Here, the `If…Then` conditional structure was rewritten to avoid the need for the `Exit Sub` statement. In this case, the subroutine could be changed to avoid `Exit Sub`. Keep in mind, however, that you may occasionally need to use `Exit Sub` to exit a subroutine, particularly when handling errors.

> **NOTE** For more information on how to handle errors, refer to Day 17, "Exterminating Bugs from Your Script."

Functions

The second type of procedure is called a *function*. Like a subroutine, a function also holds a series of VBScript statements. The only difference is that a function actually returns a value to the code statement that called it.

NEW TERM   A *function* is a block of code that can be called from anywhere in a program to accomplish a specific task. Functions can accept parameters and can also return a result code to the caller.

You've seen in earlier lessons how you can fill a variable with a value supplied on the right side of an assignment statement:

```
ZipCode = 49428
```

In the same manner, you can fill a variable with a value supplied by a function you define:

```
ZipCode = GetZipCode("Jenison")
```

As with the subroutine, the flow of code is redirected to the function while the code within the function executes. Once the function has finished executing, control returns back to the code that called the function, the value from the function is assigned to the calling code, and execution picks up from there.

Declaring a Function

To declare a function, use the Function keyword instead of the Sub keyword. You end functions using the End Function statement. The structure of a function is

```
Function Function_Name(argument1, argument2, …, argumentn)
    ...code within the function
End Sub
```

where Function_Name is the name of the function and argument1 through argumentn are optional arguments you can pass to the function. As with the subroutine, the parentheses are not required if no arguments are passed to the function.

As before, make sure the name of the function adequately describes what the function does. The same naming conventions that apply to the subroutine also apply to the function. Also, arguments are passed to the function the same way they are passed to a subroutine. For example, if you had a function named GetMiles with an argument variable used to pass the number of kilometers into the function, your declaration would look like this:

```
Function GetMiles(Kilometers)
    GetMiles = Kilometers * 1.609
End Function
```

In this example, the function returns the number of miles. Notice that it looks like the programmer has accidentally used the same variable name as the function in storing the number of miles. In reality, there's nothing accidental about this. In order to pass a value back from a function, you must set a special function "variable" that is named after the function. VBScript automatically knows that your intention is to pass the value back to the caller, not to create a temporary variable within the function. If you don't set this "variable" in your program, the result will be a zero or an empty string. It's very important, therefore, that you make sure your function returns some valid value. This value should be assigned to the function name itself within the block of code that makes up the function.

It's very easy to get busy coding within a function, creating variables as you need them, and forget to store the result in the return "variable" for the function. For example, you might have a function like what's shown in Listing 7.1.

Listing 7.1. A function that doesn't return a result.

```
Function GetAge
    Dim Age
    Dim Valid
    Do
        Age = InputBox "Please enter your age ( 5 - 120, please): "
        If Age >= 5 and Age <= 120 Then
            Valid = vbTrue
        Else
            MsgBox "The age you have entered is invalid. Please enter it again."
        End If
    Loop While Valid = vbFalse
End Function
```

ANALYSIS   This function contains a loop that asks the user for his age and continues to ask the user until the age falls within the correct range. Once it does, the condition of the control structure is no longer met and the loop completes. The programmer was so happy she got the function working that she forgot one thing—to pass the age back to the caller! One very important line at the end was omitted.

The function in Listing 7.1 should be written as shown in Listing 7.2.

Listing 7.2. The same function, but now it does return a result.

```
Function GetAge
    Dim Age
    Dim Valid
    Do
        Age = InputBox "Please enter your age ( 5 - 120 ): "
        If Age >= 5 and Age <= 120 Then
            Valid = vbTrue
        Else
            MsgBox "The age you have entered is invalid. Please enter it again."
        End If
    Loop While Valid = vbFalse
    GetAge = Age
End Function
```

7

ANALYSIS Here, you can see that the programmer set the function variable equal to the variable Age declared inside the function. Then the programmer assigned that variable to the function, effectively returning it to the caller.

The programmer could have also written the function without the temporary age variable, as shown in Listing 7.3.

Listing 7.3. The same function without a temporary variable that stores the return result.

```
Function GetAge
    Dim Valid
    Do
        GetAge = InputBox "Please enter your age ( 5 - 120 ): "
        If GetAge >= 5 and GetAge <= 120 Then
            Valid = vbTrue
        Else
            MsgBox "The age you have entered is invalid. Please enter it again."
        End If
    Loop While Valid = vbFalse
End Function
```

Even though this implementation would work just fine, it's a good programming practice to use a temporary variable and then make the assignment at the end. This is useful in part because it's easier to read the code. The reader can make better sense of your code when every variable is declared and the function uses no variables that do not have declarations. Because the function "variable" has no formal declaration and could potentially be set in several different code branches within the function, it might confuse the surveyor of your code if your code is lengthy.

Another important point to keep in mind is that when you write a function that uses arguments, you must not declare variables with the same name as the arguments using the Dim statement. When you specify arguments in a function, those arguments are automatically declared as variables in the function, but they are set to whatever was supplied when the procedure is called. If you try to declare them again, you will get an error because they're already in use in the function. For instance, this function would result in an error:

```
Function ConvertToSeconds(OrigHours, OrigMinutes, OrigSeconds)
    Dim OrigSeconds
    OrigSeconds = OrigHours * 3600 + OrigMinutes * 60 + OrigSeconds
    ConvertToSeconds = OrigSeconds
End Function
```

The function would be incorrect because the variable OrigSeconds is already part of the argument list. Rather, you could assign the result directly to the function output variable or use some other variable:

```
Function ConvertToSeconds(OrigHours, OrigMinutes, OrigSeconds)
   Dim Total
   Total = OrigHours * 3600 + OrigMinutes * 60 + OrigSeconds
   ConvertToSeconds = Total
End Function
```

Calling a Function

Now that you've seen how to declare a function, you need to know how to call it. The benefit of using a function is that you can pass back a piece of data to the caller. The subroutine does not enable you to do this because it does not return anything. You will see a way to change variables in the calling code with a subroutine later today, but the function is a better way to get data back and forth. To call a function, you simply use the syntax

```
return_variable = function_name(argument1, argument2, …, argumentn)
```

Notice that in this case, the syntax is quite a bit different from the subroutine. Here, you can assign the function to a variable (or another expression that can be updated with a value, such as a property, which will be covered in later lessons), or you needn't assign it to anything. Also, the parentheses are optional. Even if you pass arguments to the function, the parentheses are not required. To those who use Visual Basic, this is quite a change from the familiar parentheses it requires when working with functions.

For an example of its use, suppose you have a function called GetAge. To use the GetAge function, you could enter the statement

```
UserAge = GetAge()
```

or

```
UserAge = GetAge
```

Notice that this function doesn't need any arguments, and the result is assigned to a variable named UserAge. The following function requires three arguments—hours, minutes, and seconds—and returns the number of seconds:

```
Function GetSeconds(Hrs, Min, Sec)
   GetSeconds = Hrs * 3600 + Min * 60 + Sec
End Function
```

NOTE   The terms *arguments* and *parameters* are usually used synonymously.

7

You could then call this function using a statement like

```
NumSeconds = GetSeconds(2, 34, 25)
```

or

```
NumSeconds = GetSeconds 2, 34, 25
```

where the total number of seconds is returned to the variable NumSeconds.

NOTE

> Make sure you never create variables that have the same name as keywords already used by VBScript. These keywords are called *reserved words* and include terms such as Date, Minute, Second, Time, and so on. For a complete list of reserved words, refer to Appendix A, "VBScript Syntax Quick Reference."

The statement

```
Call GetSeconds(2, 34, 25)
```

would also be valid, but it wouldn't be very useful because you're not retrieving the number of seconds from the function! This simply calls a function as if it were a subroutine, without handling the return value. You can also utilize a function within an expression, such as

```
MsgBox "There are " & GetSeconds(2, 34, 25) & _
" seconds in the time you have entered."
```

In this case, you must use parentheses around your arguments. You don't need to assign a variable to the return of the function because the return value is automatically used within the statement. Although this is certainly legal, it is not always the best programming practice. If you want to use the result of the function more than once, you must store the result in a variable. Otherwise, you will have to call the function again and waste the computer's resources in doing the calculation all over again. Likewise, storing the value in a variable to avoid repeated calls makes the code more readable and maintainable.

Exiting a Function

To exit a function, you use the same method as when you exit a subroutine, namely the End Function statement. This statement can only appear once at the end of the function declaration. You have seen this statement used in the functions discussed so far. You can also use the statement Exit Function to break out of a function just like you used the Exit Sub statement to exit a subroutine. As before, it's better to exit a function naturally when your code reaches the final End Function statement than to use an Exit Function line of code to terminate the function in the middle of the statements. The code is simply easier to follow when you avoid such forced exit statements.

Passing Arguments into Procedures

Earlier today, you saw the two ways you can pass arguments into a procedure. The manner you use is determined by the way you declare the procedure. Based on that declaration, when a procedure is called, you either provide a copy of a variable to a procedure so that it has a local copy to modify if necessary, or you refer the procedure to the original variable itself. Either way, the variable owned by the caller cannot be modified by the procedure. If you refer the procedure to the original variable, you are in effect supplying the memory address of that variable to the procedure. However, VBScript hides the memory address details from you. From the programmer's perspective, you are simply providing the variable name to the procedure. But VBScript does not allow you to change the variable—the interpreter will trigger an error when the Web page loads if you try to do so.

NOTE

The current VBScript in the beta Internet Explorer does not support the `ByRef` parameter familiar to many Visual Basic programmers. In Visual Basic 4.0, for example, if you use a `ByRef` parameter, you can make changes to that variable within the subroutine that defined the parameter and the changes are reflected back to the variable supplied in that parameter position by the calling code. This is a capability that one might expect to be introduced in subsequent releases. You might wish to check the current documentation to ascertain the current implementation level if you are interested in this feature. You can refer to Microsoft's online VBScript documentation at `www.microsoft.com/vbscript` and look up `Sub` and `call` under the language reference search. Alternatively, you can check to see if there is an update sheet for this book at Macmillan's site (`www.mcp.com`) under Sams.net, or at the authors' site (`www.doubleblaze.com/vbs21day`).

To illustrate this concept, suppose your secretary wishes to use a letter you sent to a client as a template for creating another letter. You don't mind sharing the letter with her, but you must not allow the original to be changed in any way. You could make a copy of your letter and give it to her, after which she could mark it up if she wished and make changes to it. In this case, she would not change the original because it would be in your hands. Or you could simply show her the original and only allow her to examine it without changing it. In that case, she wouldn't get her own copy, but she could use the contents of the letter to make her own letter if she wished, as long as she didn't change the original.

Giving your secretary a copy of the letter can be likened to passing a variable into a procedure *by value*. You give the procedure a copy of the variable that is totally divorced from its original.

7

To do this, you simply place the keyword ByVal in front of the variable in the declaration of the procedure.

NEW TERM Passing *by value* means that a copy of the original value is given to the procedure. The procedure can change its own copy, but it won't affect the original owned by the caller.

To refer the procedure to the original without giving it a copy of the variable, you omit the ByVal keyword. This is the default case and is called passing a variable *by reference*. If you try to modify a variable passed to a procedure by reference, VBScript will give you an error message when the Web page loads into the browser. The procedure can read the contents of a variable passed in by reference, but it cannot change its contents because the procedure doesn't own the variable.

NEW TERM Passing *by reference* means that the procedure is allowed to read the variable owned by the caller. The procedure is not allowed to change the value of the variable because it is not the owner of that variable.

If you wish to pass variables into a procedure by value, you simply declare the procedure using the format

```
Sub Subroutine_Name(ByVal argument1, ByVal argument2, ... ByVal argumentn)
```

when creating a subroutine and

```
Function Function_Name(ByVal argument1, ByVal argument2, ... ByVal argumentn)
```

when creating a function. To pass variables by reference, you simply omit the ByVal keyword as shown here for a subroutine:

```
Sub Subroutine_Name(argument1, argument2, ... argumentn)
```

and here for a function:

```
Function Function_Name(argument1, argument2, ... argumentn)
```

As an example of passing a variable by value, consider the sample Web page shown in Figure 7.1.

This Web page is named byval.htm and is located on the CD-ROM that comes with the book. This Web page contains a text box where the user can enter a number. That number is then passed into a subroutine, which takes the value and doubles it, displaying it to the user. Then, when the subroutine has finished, the caller resumes by displaying the value of the variable it passed in. The code for this Web page is shown in Listing 7.4.

Figure 7.1.

A Web page that doubles a value entered by the user.

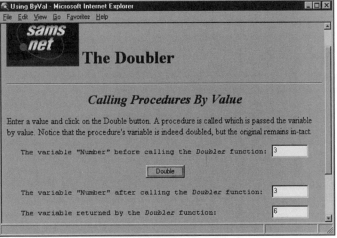

Listing 7.4. Passing variables to a procedure by value.

```
<SCRIPT LANGUAGE="VBScript">
<!-- Option Explicit

    Sub cmdDouble_OnClick()

        Dim Number
        Dim Doubled

        Number = txtBefore.Value
        Doubled = Doubler(Number)

        txtAfter.Value = Number
        txtNewValue.Value = Doubled

    End Sub

    Function Doubler(ByVal Number)
        Number = Number * 2
        Doubler = Number
    End Function

-->
</SCRIPT>
```

ANALYSIS   As you can see in Figure 7.1, the number remains unchanged after the `Doubler` function is called. The number returned by the function is indeed double that of the one passed to it. Since the calling subroutine passed the variable by value, the function could modify its own copy of the variable.

7

What would have happened if the variable had been passed by reference? Figure 7.2, which displays the Web page named badbyval.htm, shows the result.

Figure 7.2.

A Web page with a procedure that tries to modify a variable passed to it by reference.

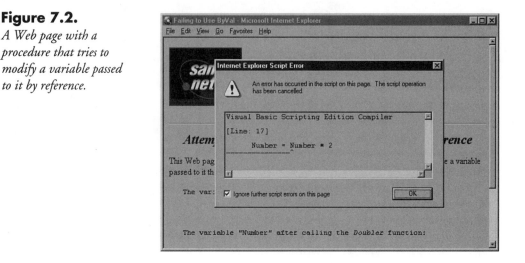

As you can see, an error results. Listing 7.5 shows the incorrect code.

Listing 7.5. Incorrectly trying to modify a variable passed by reference.

```
<SCRIPT LANGUAGE="VBScript">
<!-- Option Explicit

    Sub cmdTest_OnClick()

        Dim Number
        Dim Doubled

        Number = txtBefore.Value
        Doubled = Doubler(Number)

        txtAfter.Value = Number
        txtNewValue.Value = Doubled

    End Sub

    Function Doubler(Number)
    ' This code is incorrect for the sake of this example, as described above!
        Number = Number * 2
        Doubler = Number
    End Function

-->
</SCRIPT>
```

ANALYSIS As you can see, the function now gets the value by reference. When it tries to change the variable, VBScript flags the error that appears in Figure 7.2. It is your responsibility as a programmer to make sure you pass variables into procedures properly to avoid errors such as these.

Follow these rules of thumb to stay on safe ground:

☐ Never change a variable passed to a procedure by reference, or you will get an error. If you wish to change the variable within the procedure, pass it by value.

☐ Never expect to change a variable in the caller when passed to a procedure by value. You're only giving the procedure a copy of the variable, not the original.

You do not have to pass *every* variable into the procedure in the same way. You can pass some variables in by value and some by reference, as in the following example:

```
Function ConvertToMeters(ByVal Inches, Feet)
    Inches = Feet * 12 + Inches
    ConvertToMeters = Inches * 0.0254
End Function
```

Here, the variable Inches is passed in by value because the programmer designed the function to change the value of this variable. In order to accomplish this, he must declare the variable Inches by value so that the function gets its own copy and can modify it. The variable Feet, on the other hand, never gets changed, so it can be passed by reference.

Figure 7.3 shows a working implementation of this function in the Web page named meters.htm.

Figure 7.3.

The metric converter Web page using ByVal.

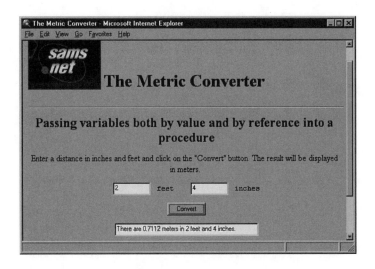

The code listing for this Web page is shown in Listing 7.6.

Listing 7.6. Passing variables to a procedure by value.

```
<HTML>

<HEAD>
<TITLE>The Metric Converter</TITLE>
</HEAD>

<BODY>

<H1><A HREF="http://www.mcp.com"><IMG  ALIGN=BOTTOM
SRC="../shared/jpg/samsnet.jpg" BORDER=2></A>
The Metric Converter</H1>

<HR>

<CENTER><H2>Passing variables both by value and by
reference into a procedure</H2>

<P>Enter a distance in inches and feet and click on the "Convert" button.
The result will be displayed in meters.

<PRE><INPUT NAME="txtFeet" SIZE=10 > feet
<INPUT NAME="txtInches" SIZE=10 > inches</PRE>
<P><INPUT TYPE="BUTTON" NAME="cmdConvert" VALUE="Convert">
<P><INPUT NAME="txtResult" SIZE=50 ></CENTER>

<HR>

<center>
from <em>Teach Yourself VBScript in 21 Days</em> by
<A HREF="../shared/keith.htm">Keith Brophy</A> and
<A HREF="../shared/tim.htm">Tim Koets</A><br>
Return to <a href="..\default.htm">Content Overview</A><br>
Copyright 1996 by SamsNet<br>
</center>

<SCRIPT LANGUAGE="VBScript">
<!-- Option Explicit

    Sub cmdConvert_OnClick()

      Dim Inches, Feet, Meters

      Inches = txtInches.Value
      Feet = txtFeet.Value

      Meters = ConvertToMeters(Inches, Feet)

      txtResult.Value = "There are " & Meters & " meters in " & Feet & _
                        " feet and " & Inches & " inches."

    End Sub
```

```
Function ConvertToMeters(ByVal Inches, Feet)

    Inches = Feet * 12 + Inches
    ConvertToMeters = Inches * 0.0254

End Function

-->
</SCRIPT>

</BODY>

</HTML>
```

ANALYSIS As you can see from Figure 7.2, the user simply enters the number of inches and feet in the text boxes shown and clicks on the Convert button. That calls the function ConvertToMeters, which converts the values into meters and returns the value, which is then displayed in the result text box on the Web page.

Because the variable Feet never gets changed, you do not have to worry about passing it by value. The variable Inches, on the other hand, does get changed because the function takes the number of feet and multiplies by 12 to convert to inches, adding that result to the original number of inches. In order to perform this operation, the function must have its own copy of the Inches variable, which is why it must be passed to the function by value.

You can, of course, decide to always pass variables into your procedures by value to avoid the possibility of introducing errors into your programs. This is fine, as long as you realize that the variables you modify will not change those found in the caller of the procedure. You also have to go through the extra work of placing a ByVal keyword in front of every variable of your function declarations. On the other hand, passing in values by reference is more efficient for the VBScript interpreter because it doesn't have to clone a copy of the variable for the procedure—it can simply refer the procedure to the variable instead.

Why Are Procedures Useful?

If you're new to programming, you might be wondering why procedures are useful in the first place. Now that you've seen how to use them, I'll discuss why they are so beneficial. There are three primary reasons: readability, maintainability, and correctness.

Procedures are useful any time you have a task that must be accomplished many times, perhaps in many places in your code, throughout your program. Suppose you request an order number from the user, and each time the number is entered, you want to make sure it's valid. One option is to write code that checks each time an order is entered as shown in Listing 7.7.

7

Listing 7.7. Code that should be placed in a function.

```
SpouseOrder = InputBox("What order would you like for your spouse?")
If SpouseOrder < 0 Then
   MsgBox "The order number is invalid."
End If
YourOrder = InputBox("What order would you like for yourself?")
If YourOrder < 0 Then
   MsgBox "The order number is invalid."
End If
ChildOrder = InputBox("What order would you like for your children?")
If ChildOrder < 0 Then
   MsgBox "The order number is invalid."
End If
```

 ANALYSIS   As you can see from this example, the same check is repeated three times in your code. This results in code that is not only more difficult to read, but also more difficult to maintain.

Rather than type the same code three times, wouldn't it make your code more readable if you created a function and placed the repeating code within that function? Suppose you call the function `VerifyOrderNumber` and place the common code in that function. Then, the code might look like that in Listing 7.8.

Listing 7.8. Using a function to improve the program.

```
Do
   SpouseOrder = InputBox("What order would you like for your spouse?")
Loop Until VerifyOrderNumber(SpouseOrder) = True

Do
   YourOrder = InputBox("What order would you like for yourself?")
Loop Until VerifyOrderNumber(YourOrder) = True

Do
   ChildOrder = InputBox("What order would you like for your children?")
Loop Until VerifyOrderNumber(YourOrder)

Function VerifyOrderNumber(OrderNumber)

   If OrderNumber < 0 Then
      MsgBox "The order number is invalid."
      VerifyOrderNumber = False
   Else
      VerifyOrderNumber = True
   End If

End Sub
```

ANALYSIS If the user enters values greater than zero, the function returns with a Boolean variable indicating the result is valid. Otherwise, the function returns the Boolean value for false, and the loop continues to prompt the user until an order number is entered, calling the function again each time through.

In this case, you have placed all the repeating code within a function so that the code within the function appears just once rather than several times throughout the program. Doing this has several advantages. First of all, it's a lot easier for the reader of the code. He can see what the code does in one word rather than having to wade through all the details. Furthermore, it cuts down on the size of the code listing. Perhaps most important, it makes the code more maintainable.

NOTE To keep the example simple, the amount of repeating code you save in this sample code is relatively small. Keep in mind that many blocks of code which are candidates for procedures could be many times larger. When these code blocks are moved to procedures, the advantages of "procedurized" code mentioned here become even greater. If you're an experienced computer programmer, you might realize that a computer has to do more work to call a procedure than to process statements that are simply in the flow of code without a procedure call. However, this extra amount of work is very slight in the context of your overall script and will typically have no visible effect on the speed of your script. In other words, "procedurizing" your code has a lot of advantages and virtually no disadvantages.

Suppose you realize that a valid order number not only should be greater than zero, but that it also must be less than 5000. If you wrote your program without the subroutine, as in Listing 7.8, you would have to look for every place in your program that asks for an order number and modify the code after it to include the additional check. Your code would look like that in Listing 7.9.

Listing 7.9. Code that is a pain to maintain because the repeatable code is not contained within a function.

```
SpouseOrder = InputBox("What order would you like to place for your spouse?")
If SpouseOrder < 0 and SpouseOrder >= 5000 Then
    MsgBox "The order number is invalid."
End If
YourOrder = InputBox("What order would you like to place for yourself?")
```

7

continues

Listing 7.9. continued

```
If YourOrder < 0 and YourOrder >= 5000 Then
   MsgBox "The order number is invalid."
End If
ChildOrder = InputBox("What order would you like to place for your children?")
If ChildOrder < 0 and ChildOrder >= 5000 Then
   MsgBox "The order number is invalid."
End If
```

ANALYSIS   In this case, you had to make three modifications to your program. You're fortunate because all the changes are in one place; in reality, they could spread all across the program! The better solution is to make the change in one place, as shown in Listing 7.10. Note that the calling code remains identical to the procedure-calling example shown earlier. It is only one statement in the body of the function itself that must change.

Listing 7.10. Using a function to improve the program.

```
Do
   SpouseOrder = InputBox("What order would you like for your spouse?")
Loop Until VerifyOrderNumber(SpouseOrder) = True

Do
   YourOrder = InputBox("What order would you like for yourself?")
Loop Until VerifyOrderNumber(YourOrder) = True

Do
   ChildOrder = InputBox("What order would you like for your children?")
Loop Until VerifyOrderNumber(YourOrder)
```

The function would be written in the following way:

```
Function VerifyOrderNumber(OrderNumber)

   If OrderNumber < 1 and OrderNumber >= 5000 Then
   MsgBox "The order number is invalid."
End If
MsgBox "The order number is invalid."
      VerifyOrderNumber = False
   Else
      VerifyOrderNumber = True
   End If

End Sub
```

ANALYSIS   Now, rather than make three changes, you simply have to make one. It doesn't matter how many times you call the function or where you make the calls in your code. Because all the functionality is wrapped up in one location, you only have to change that location itself.

Procedures help enhance a program in three ways. They make the program more readable because there is less code and the surveyor of the code isn't always forced to see the details of every part of the code. The program is also more maintainable because changing code in a function requires one change in only one place instead of many changes scattered throughout the application. Finally, your code is more correct because the likelihood of making a mistake when you're duplicating code across the application is greater than when you have the code in one place.

Clearly, the benefits of using procedures are numerous and important. Procedures are the foundation of a good program, and you will see them used throughout the rest of the applications in this book.

Event Procedures

Earlier this week you were exposed to procedures, although you may not have known it at the time. When you work with controls and other components, you frequently interface with them using *event procedures*. Event procedures are subroutines that are called automatically by the browser. They are different from regular subroutines in that regular subroutines must be called within the program by statements you write or else they are never used. An event procedure is called as a result of some action taken by the user or the system, such as the user clicking a command button or checking a box on a Web page or the system detecting that a predefined timer has expired.

NEW TERM An *event* is a subroutine called automatically by VBScript as a result of a user or system action. Subroutine and function calls must be manually specified by the programmer through normal calls in code, but event subroutines are called automatically as a result of what they represent. You just define a subroutine to be carried out when the user clicks on a particular button by means of a special name, for example. Then the button control object itself generates an OnClick event when it is clicked on, and VBScript responds to this event by calling the named subroutine associated with the event.

You don't have to worry about calling event procedures in your code because they are called automatically by the system and the browser, but you do need to create them if you want to write code that responds to these events. For instance, if you place a button on your Web page, you probably want your program to respond in some way when the user clicks it. If you construct an event procedure, you can write the code to do just that. If you fail to place the event subroutine in your code, however, your users can click the button all day long, and nothing will happen because there is no event procedure to process the click events.

The rules for creating and naming event procedures are more rigid and structured than regular procedure naming rules. First of all, the naming conventions for an event procedure are very specific. Except with some special cases discussed on Day 8, "Intrinsic HTML Form

7

Controls," you can't just name an event procedure anything you want. To name an event procedure, you must know two things: the name of the control, or component, and the name of the event you want to respond to. Suppose, for example, that you have a command button on your Web page labeled `TestButton`. As you will see on Day 8, buttons have an event called `OnClick` that you can write code for. This event occurs when the user clicks the button. To create an event procedure for this action, you must name your procedure

```
TestButton_OnClick
```

Notice that the name of the control comes first, followed by an underscore character, followed by the name of the event. You must spell everything correctly, or else VBScript will be unable to connect the event procedure to the button. The rule for assigning a name to a control or component is

```
Sub ControlName_EventName()
```

where `ControlName` is the name of the control and `EventName` is the name of the event corresponding to the control. In addition to what you'll learn on Day 8, you will also learn about intrinsic HTML controls and ActiveX controls on Day 9, "More Intrinsic HTML Form Controls," Day 10, "An Introduction to Objects and ActiveX Controls," and Day 11, "More ActiveX Controls." On those days, you will learn much more about event procedures and how to use them. For now, just keep in mind that event procedures are blocks of code grouped in subroutines within your scripts, just like those we have already discussed.

Method Procedures

You may have also heard of *method procedures*. Method procedures are like predefined procedures you can call, but they are provided by an object. You can't actually see the code for them, nor can you create them. Objects can have a set of methods that were created when the programmer designed the object.

NEW TERM A *method* is a procedure you can call that is associated with an object. Methods accomplish some specific task or service the object provides. Methods may or may not return values, depending on what they do.

For example, the error object, which you will learn more about on Day 17, has a method called `Source` that will return the error number of the error that has occurred. To invoke that method, you can simply call the method using the following convention:

```
object.method
```

where `object` is the name of the object and `method` is the name of the method. In this case, you could use

```
ErrSource = Err.Source
```

to get the error code for the error that has occurred. Methods are different from events, functions, or subroutines, however, because you cannot create them. They are an inherent part of an object that you can call.

Procedures, Subroutines, Functions, Events, and Methods!

Wow! What a collection of terms. It's easy to get confused in recognizing these terms, so think of them as shown in Figure 7.4.

Figure 7.4.

Sorting out procedures, subroutines, functions, events, and methods.

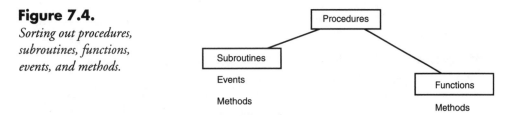

Procedures consist of subroutines and functions. Functions can return a value to the caller, and subroutines cannot. Events are special subroutines that are called automatically in response to the user triggering an event, such as clicking a button. Finally, methods are a special kind of procedure that can either be a function or a subroutine. That is, they could return a value or they might not. The only difference is that methods are part of an object. You can call a method in your code if you have access to an object, but you cannot create them or see the code that is executed behind them.

Where to Put Procedures

Finally, you need to understand where you can place procedures in your HTML document. On Day 3, "Extending the Power of Web Pages with VBScript," you learned about the general structure of an HTML document. You saw that, as a rule, you should put VBScript code in the <HEAD> section of an HTML document. You can place procedures within one script tag:

```
<SCRIPT LANGUAGE="VBScript">
<!--
    Sub GetMiles()
        ...code for subroutine
    End Sub
```

7

```
      Function CalculateTime(RunnerTime)
            ...code for function
      End Function
-->
</SCRIPT>
```

You can also place procedures in separate scripts:

```
<SCRIPT LANGUAGE="VBScript">
<!--
      Sub GetMiles()
            ...code for subroutine
      End Sub
-->
</SCRIPT>

<SCRIPT LANGUAGE="VBScript">
<!--
      Function CalculateTime(RunnerTime)
            ...code for function
      End Function
-->
</SCRIPT>
```

A good rule of thumb is to enter all the subroutines and functions first, making sure none is called before it is used. Also, it is much easier to put them as close together as possible, preferably all under the same script tag. That way, you have access to all of them at once and don't have to hunt through your Web page to find them.

Also, notice that not all VBScript code must be stored within a procedure. If you have code outside a procedure, such as the example shown below, keep in mind that this code is automatically executed in order from top to bottom when the browser first loads the Web page:

```
<SCRIPT LANGUAGE="VBScript">
<!-- Option Explicit

    Dim Miles_Ran
    Dim Total_Miles
    Dim Start_Time
    Call InitializeVariables

    Sub InitializeVariables
       Miles_Ran = 0
       Total_Miles = 0
       Start_Time = 0
    End Sub
-->
```

When the browser first loads the Web page, it's a good time to initialize variables, call procedures that set values to their default conditions, and so on. As a rule, it's usually better to place all such code in the same place so that you don't miss a line or two somewhere down the page. Likewise, it's a good idea to place your script, and all its startup code, at the bottom of your page prior to the </BODY> tag. This ensures that any objects your startup code references have already been defined in the page by the time the code is called as the page loads for the first time. If your code doesn't use any startup code executed as the page loads, this is not a necessary step, but still is a recommended convention for easy script viewing and maintainability.

Summary

Today you have learned how to create and use procedures in your VBScript programs. You can divide procedures into two types: subroutines and functions. Subroutines and functions both contain code that other parts of the application can call. You have seen that a function returns a value to the user when it's finished, whereas a subroutine does not. You have also discovered how to declare a function or subroutine and call it in other places throughout the application.

Both functions and subroutines can accept one or more arguments that they can use to perform their tasks. You can pass either a copy of the arguments or a reference to the actual values to a procedure. When passing variables by value, those variables can be changed because they are copies of the original. In the case of passing variables by reference, however, you can read but not change the variables, because the procedure does not "own" them. This implementation may change with future versions of VBScript. See the recommended update sites, described earlier in this lesson, for the latest information. You have learned how to pass variables into procedures using both ways and saw practical examples of both cases.

In studying how to construct procedures, you have discovered why they are so useful in the first place. You have learned that procedures help make your code more maintainable, more readable, and more prone to be free of errors. These are significant reasons to use procedures in your application wherever it is practical.

You have also been introduced to a special type of procedure called an *event procedure*. Event procedures are different from ordinary procedures in that they are called by the system and browser as a result of some activity initiated by the user or some other component on the Web page, such as a timer. Today's lesson briefly introduces event procedures, and next week you'll learn how and why you use them.

Today's lesson also discusses methods, which are special procedures contained within an object. You can call these procedures in your code by referencing them through the object. Although you can't modify a method or see the code, you can call it to accomplish a specific task within the object.

Finally, you have learned how and where to place procedures in your Web page. You can put the procedures all together within one script tag or spread them across multiple script tags.

7

To make your code more readable, you should place all your subroutines in the same script tag in one section. That way, you can debug and find procedures without hunting for them all over your page.

The purpose of today's lesson is to give you a practical grasp on how to create and use procedures. Throughout the rest of the book, we use procedures. Indeed, they have been used for quite some time, although you might not have recognized them. Today's lesson is the last of a series of lessons that presented you with the basics of VBScript programming. Next week you'll put the basics to work and have some fun writing some Web pages of your own.

Q&A

Q How many arguments can you give a procedure?

A At the time of this printing, VBScript was in beta form and you could pass up to 127 arguments to a procedure if you wanted. In reality, however, a good suggestion is that you not enter more than 10. The reason for this is that the more parameters you enter, the less readable and maintainable your procedures will be. If you find yourself passing more than ten parameters, you might want to redesign the procedure, possibly breaking it up into smaller pieces.

Q What happens if I forget to include an event procedure for a control on my Web page?

A Don't worry; nothing dangerous will happen on your Web page. The particular event that occurs in the control or component on the page simply won't find an event in your code to connect to and therefore will not perform any of your code statements. Of course, you should make sure event procedures exist for every control on your form where you want your code to respond. You will learn much more about this in next week's lessons.

Workshop

Create a Web page that uses VBScript code to ask the user for 10 values. All 10 values must be between 0 and 10. Get all 10 values from the user and make sure they are valid, but do not use any procedures in your code. Now, change the validation rule to accept values between 0 and 75 and test your Web page again. After you've done this, apply the same approach again, but this time, use procedures. By going through this exercise, you will begin to appreciate the value of using procedures in your code.

Quiz

Refer to Appendix C, "Answers to Quiz Questions," for the answers to these questions.

NOTE

1. What is the difference between a function and a subroutine?

2. Given the following code listing, what is the value of the variable A that is passed into the function after the function has been called successfully?

```
Sub cmdTest_OnClick()
    Dim A, B, C
    A = txtA.Value
    B = txtB.Value
    C = GetHypotenuse(A, B)
    MsgBox "The hypotenuse of the right triangle is " & C & " units."
End Sub

Function GetHypotenuse(ByVal A, ByVal B)
    A = A * A
    B = B * B
    If A + B >= 0 Then
        GetHypotenuse = Sqrt(A + B)
    Else
        GetHypotenuse = 0
    End If
End Function
```

3. The following code listing contains an error:

```
Sub cmdTest_OnClick()

    Dim Base_Cost
    Dim Total_Cost
    Dim Tax

    Tax = 5     ' Michigan sales tax (5%)

    Total_Cost = CalculateCost(Base_Cost, Tax)

    txtResult.Value = "The total cost is $" & Total_Cost

End Sub

Function CalculateCost(Cost, Tax)

    Tax = Tax / 100
```

7

```
    Cost = Cost + Tax * Cost

    CalculateCost = Cost

End Function
```

Find the error and fix the code listing so that it works properly.

In Review

This first week provided you with the context of what VBScript is and how you can use it to extend the capabilities of environments such as World Wide Web pages. You saw some basic examples of this and covered the fundamentals of how to build scripts yourself. Although you might not be a VBScript guru yet, you have reached the point where you can compose a fundamental script and understand the elements of it.

Where You Have Been

At the start of the week, you saw the overall picture of VBScript and the World Wide Web. That was followed by a good look at the specific purpose and capabilities of VBScript. Then, one-by-one, you learned about the specific fundamentals that you must master in order to use the language effectively. You saw how to use variables, operators, control structures, and procedures—all of which are the building blocks for the progressively more powerful scripts you will build in the days ahead.

8

9

10

11

12

13

14

At a Glance

With the background you gained in Week 1, you are ready to move on to some more advanced uses of the VBScript language. This week you will gain a fuller appreciation for the power and flexibility of VBScript, and you will pick up the skills needed to write programs that exploit this. This week includes a discussion of how you can make your scripts interact with other objects, controls, and components to easily expand their capabilities.

Where You Are Going

This week starts with at look at intrinsic HTML input controls. These controls can serve as the building blocks for sophisticated scripts that make truly interactive Web pages. You'll learn about the full range of controls, including the text box, radio button, check box, and others.

Next, the attention turns to how your scripts can integrate components—particularly ActiveX objects—through the HTML object declaration. After you have the background, you'll examine a variety of controls and then consider how VBScript interacts with some of the other types of components, such as ActiveVRML and Java applets. By this point, the scripts you are capable of tackling have become increasingly sophisticated, so we take a look at keeping the scripts manageable through the use of good standards and conventions strategies. Finally, you'll learn about user interface strategies to help you pull all these areas together. After having mastered this body of material during the week, you will be ready to tackle the advanced script subjects in the week to come.

Day 8

Intrinsic HTML Form Controls

Now that you've learned some of the important fundamentals of VBScript programming, it's time to see how you can put these skills and techniques to practical use. This is the first of several days this week that will teach you how to use *scripting elements*. Scripting elements reside within an HTML document. They include intrinsic HTML controls and objects that you can insert into HTML such as ActiveX controls. Controls and objects are entities you can place on a Web page to provide an interface to the user that enables him to interact with the page. You can also use them as the front ends to perform behind-the-scenes operations, such as submitting information to a program on a server.

NEW TERM *Scripting elements* reside within a Web page and include both intrinsic HTML controls and objects such as ActiveX Controls.

NEW TERM *Controls* and *objects* are elements you can include in a Web page that allow the user to interface with the page or perform some specific task from within the HTML document.

In today and tomorrow's lessons, you will be introduced to the first type of scripting element—intrinsic HTML controls. Then, in Days 10, "An Introduction to Objects and ActiveX Controls," 11, "More ActiveX Controls," and 12, "Advanced Objects: ActiveX, Java, and ActiveVRML," you will learn more about controls and objects, including ActiveX controls and OLE objects. Before we discuss scripting elements, however, you must first become familiar with HTML forms. This lesson begins by introducing you to HTML forms and discussing their importance. Then, you will learn about three intrinsic HTML controls—the button control, the text control, and the textarea control. In each case, you will learn how to create the control, place it on the form, and interact with it. Today's lesson gives you the basics of what you need to know to work with HTML controls and VBScript. Tomorrow, you will be presented with three more useful HTML controls: the radio button, the check box, and the select control.

The term *intrinsic* is included in the title of this lesson because the HTML language automatically supports intrinsic HTML controls; the controls are an inherent part of HTML. On Day 10, when you begin to explore ActiveX controls, you will see that ActiveX controls are not inherent to HTML and must be specifically inserted into an HTML document. Furthermore, ActiveX controls are designed for easy component integration into languages such as VBScript. Intrinsic HTML controls, on the other hand, have been around since before scripting languages such as VBScript and components such as ActiveX controls came to be. In their original form in HTML, intrinsic HTML controls were more commonly known as form input controls.

An Introduction to HTML Forms

As you can see by the title of this lesson, intrinsic HTML controls apply to HTML forms. It is necessary to understand what an HTML form is and what its capabilities are in order to appreciate the roles and capabilities of the intrinsic controls themselves. If you're unfamiliar with HTML forms, today's lesson will bring you up to speed.

A Web page can be represented in hierarchical fashion by representing the page as a window. This window contains, among many other entities, the document, which, in turn, contains the form. It is within the form that intrinsic HTML controls were originally designed to work. Forms serve as containers whose information can be sent across the Internet to the server that supplied the Web page to the client.

NEW TERM A *form* is a container into which controls and objects can be placed. The form can transmit the values of intrinsic controls back to the server for processing in response to selection of a submit button. Even if the controls in a form are not intended to gather data for a server, a form can still provide a convenient grouping of the controls it contains.

The form is particularly useful when data must be collected on a page and then submitted back to a server. An example of such a page would be one that collected survey data and then caused that data to be stored in a central database. You typically submit such data to a server using the HTML form submittal and CGI capabilities to launch a script on the server.

CGI stands for *Common Gateway Interface.* You can think of it as the protocol by which programs are launched on the server in response to interactions on a Web page. Forms gather input from the user to submit to the server. Before scripting languages such as VBScript, forms, coupled with the server application that processed the data they collected, were the primary method of giving a Web page any intelligence. That is, the gateway application on the server had to do the thinking for the Web page and the data had to be sent to the server first before it could act. The HTML form was the medium used to collect and exchange information between the Web page and the server.

NOTE

> If you're a Visual Basic 4.0 or VBA programmer, you are probably used to thinking of the form as the whole window your program is based upon. Now that you're in the Web page world, the terminology is different! A form is optional on a Web page, and even when present, it is typically just one part of the larger Web page that the user sees.

Now you see that HTML forms were really designed for Web pages as a means of collecting information from the user in various controls that can be placed on the form. These controls are the subject of the lessons today and tomorrow. An HTML form is an area of the Web page enclosed by the script tags <FORM> and </FORM>. When you use a form, the controls that appear to the user are usually placed within the form. Information they contain can be sent back to the server when the data is submitted. Keep in mind that you use the Common Gateway Interface, or CGI, with HTML to trigger programs on the server when needed. When using CGI to send data back and forth between the client and the server, the form is the container that houses all the information.

Although controls are intended to be placed within a form, they don't have to be. In all the examples so far in the book, we have been using simple controls such as the command button and text control. You have seen Web pages that use these controls, and not one example used an HTML form. You might be wondering, "If they are called HTML form controls, can they be used outside a form?" The answer is, "Yes." HTML enables you to use its intrinsic controls outside of form tags. The only catch is that CGI cannot pull data out of those controls; only the contents of a form can be submitted. Form declarations provide important CGI details such as how data is to be passed back to the server. As a result, the data contained in input controls cannot be sent to the server using CGI if the controls are defined outside of forms. Except for that restriction, your VBScript code can interact with intrinsic controls even outside of forms.

Often, you will create Web pages that simply "do their own thing" and have no need to send information back to a server. If you've got a Web page that doesn't need to use CGI to submit information to a server, then you don't need to place your controls in a form. It certainly is safer to do so, however, because some older browsers might not be able to present controls on a Web page unless they are contained within form tags. This is due to the fact that before scripting languages such as VBScript arrived on the scene, controls were always used within a form. Some browsers do not support them if they are outside the confines of a form. Of course, the older browsers that do not support non-form controls probably won't support your VBScript code either. Nevertheless, even if a user is using pages with an old browser, you'd still like as much of your program to show through as possible. In this and subsequent lessons, we will generally place controls within form tags for compatibility among various browsers.

How do HTML form controls work inside of a form? To understand this, look at the structure of a form. HTML forms are specified by the start tag <FORM> and end tag </FORM>. A form definition is part of the regular HTML body, not within your script tags. You must place all your form elements within these form tags, and you cannot nest a form within another. The opening tag of a form typically uses two attributes: METHOD and ACTION. These attributes are supplied as part of the definition of the behavior of a form. The METHOD attribute tells the browser the format of the data that will be presented to the server when the form is submitted. You can set METHOD to either GET or POST. Each of these commands sends the data to the server in a different format. If you don't specify the METHOD, the default is GET.

NOTE

Today's lesson provides background on CGI communication through forms to put the <FORM> declaration in perspective. It is important to understand what a form is to have a clear picture of intrinsic control definitions. However, it is not the intention here to provide a detailed understanding of all nuances of CGI or related aspects such as GET and POST methods because that is less directly related to VBScript. Refer to a book such as Sams.net Publishing's *HTML and CGI Unleashed* for more details in those areas. Some aspects of this topic will also be covered in slightly more detail on Day 19, "Dynamic Page Flow and Server Submittal."

The second attribute, ACTION, tells the browser how to find the script code where you send your data after a user's entry in the form is complete. In other words, it tells the browser where the server script is. You can set the ACTION attribute to the URL of the server script or you can use a relative path. In either case, you must have a CGI script on the server side to handle and process the data. The following tags specify a form where the data will be submitted to a specific Web server script:

```
<FORM METHOD="GET" ACTION="../cgi-bin/myscript">
</FORM>
```

This tag tells the browser to send the data to the Web server script that is referenced by the relative path of "../cgi-bin/myscript" and to use the "GET" method to send the data to that server. If you don't plan on submitting any data to a server but still want to use a form to contain your controls, you can just use the following statements:

```
<FORM>
</FORM>
```

Make sure all the controls you want to present to the user are within the form. These tags create a form that has no target server, so remember that you should not submit the data contained in the form (using the form's submit method described on Day 19)—it will have no place to go.

With an understanding of forms and the context that controls have with them, you can now focus attention on the controls themselves. You can use HTML form controls independently of CGI. Before scripting languages such as VBScript, submitting data to servers through CGI was very important in order to give your Web page even the simplest intelligence. Now that we have a sophisticated scripting language, however, this restriction can be overcome. Still, CGI is often vital and necessary to send data to a server, such as when ordering products, inquiring about information, and so on.

You will learn much more about communicating with Web servers next week on Day 19. For now, I'll defer that topic and discuss the controls themselves.

The Button Control

The first control I will explore is the *button*. We have been using buttons throughout the book because they are such an important part of a Web page. Buttons are commonly used to give the user the ability to execute VBScript code that performs some action indicated on the caption of the button. For example, you have seen Web pages used to calculate the pace of a runner. The Pace-Pal Web page used the Display Pace button to trigger some VBScript code that calculated the pace for the user and displayed it on the screen.

To create a button on a Web page, you need to use a special tag called an INPUT tag. The INPUT tag tells the browser you are about to create a control used to get input from the user. The button is just one type of control you can create using the INPUT tag. The actual input could come in the form of text, an indication of whether the user has checked the control, or a recognition of the control by clicking it. In any case, information is being exchanged with the user. The input tag takes at least two attributes: TYPE and NAME.

 TIP

> The <INPUT> tag is used to place intrinsic HTML controls on a Web page.

The TYPE attribute is very important because it tells the browser what type of control you want to create. You use the input tag to create text controls, radio button controls, and check boxes, just to name a few. Right now, because I'm discussing buttons, the TYPE attribute will be set equal to the keyword BUTTON. As you will see in this and the next lesson, other keywords are used for the other control types.

The second attribute that you must supply is the NAME attribute, which gives the control a name. Why would you want to name a control? To work with a control, you have to refer to it, and to do that, you must give it a unique name. The name can be any string as long as it starts with a letter. Make sure the names you assign to your controls are descriptive enough for you to easily tell them apart. There's nothing more frustrating than getting confused over what control is being referenced when you see some cryptic name in your code. The name should be clear and tell you what type of control it is. One recommended convention is to prefix the name of a button with the characters cmd, which stand for command button. This is borrowed from the Windows command button and lets you know the type of control you're dealing with. If you see the expression Test in your code, you might not be sure what type of control it is or even whether it is the name of a control. On the other hand, if you see cmdTest, you know right away that you're dealing with a button control.

NOTE

> You can use many more standards to help make your code clear, readable, and easy to maintain. It's hard to understand all the recommended standards until you've been exposed to the full VBScript language, so a detailed coverage of all standards is deferred until Day 13, "VBScript Standards and Conventions." In the meantime, I'll describe key standards as I discuss those topics, such as using cmd.

When you work with button controls, you want to set one more attribute—the VALUE attribute. The VALUE attribute sets the caption of the button. The caption tells the user why the button is there. Make sure the caption of your button is descriptive enough to let the user know what happens if he clicks it.

8

Here's a simple example of a line of HTML code that creates a button:

```
<INPUT TYPE="Button" NAME="cmdGetCost" VALUE="Get the Cost">
```

Here, the name of the control is `cmdGetCost` and the caption that will appear to the user on the Web page is "Get the Cost."

The size of a command button depends on the length of caption as well as the size of the font. The browser will automatically size the button based on the text you set in the `VALUE` attribute. The button surrounds the text, but the amount of real estate used to surround the button is beyond your control. The formatting is up to the browser, not HTML, in this case.

A command button appears in a Web page exactly where you put it, much like text or any other element you place within a Web page. For more information on HTML, you might want to refer to Lemay's *Teach Yourself Web Publishing with HTML 3.2 in 14 Days, Professional Reference Edition.* Otherwise, I'll assume you know how to format an HTML document sufficiently to place a command button where you want. Of course, you can look at the Web pages provided with this book to gain more insight, and you will also be taught more on how to do this on Day 14, "Working with Documents and User Interface Functions." Also keep in mind that buttons other than the submit button are not very useful in simple HTML because you can't use them to respond to the user. They do find usefulness, however, with the advent of VBScript. As you will see in a moment, it is very easy to write VBScript code to respond to the user clicking a button.

 TIP

> One commonly used strategy to position input controls such as buttons with a finer degree of detail is to place them within HTML tables. Refer to resources such as Lemay's *Teach Yourself Web Publishing with HTML 3.2 in 14 Days, Professional Reference Edition,* for more information on HTML table capabilities.

Listing 8.1 shows a simple example of a Web page that contains a button.

Listing 8.1. A simple Web page with an HTML button control.

```
<HTML>

<HEAD>
<TITLE>The Button Control</TITLE>
</HEAD>

<BODY>
<H1>
<A HREF="http://www.mcp.com"><IMG  ALIGN=MIDDLE
```

continues

Listing 8.1. continued

```
SRC="../shared/jpg/samsnet.jpg" BORDER=2 HSPACE=20></A>
<EM>The Button Control</EM></h1>
<HR>

<P>This Web page demonstrates how to place a simple button control on
a Web page.  If you click on the button, nothing happens yet, but the
next program will show the user a message box when they click on this
button.

<P>

<CENTER>
<INPUT TYPE="BUTTON" NAME="cmdBegin" VALUE="Click to Begin">
</CENTER>

<HR>

<center>
From <em>Teach Yourself VBScript in 21 Days</em><br>
by <A HREF="../shared/info/keith.htm">Keith Brophy</A> and
<A HREF="../shared/info/tim.htm">Tim Koets</A><br>
<br>
Return to <A href=Back08.htm>content overview</A><br>
Copyright 1996 by SamsNet<br>
</center>

<SCRIPT LANGUAGE="VBScript">
<!--
-->
</SCRIPT>

</BODY>

</HTML>
```

Figure 8.1 shows the corresponding Web page. The Web page with this simple button, named simpbtn.htm, is available on the CD-ROM that accompanies the book.

ANALYSIS The first thing you should notice is that this Web page contains start and end form tags. Within the form tags is the single input statement that specifies a button control within the form. The form script tags should always be a part of the body of the HTML document. You will also notice a set of VBScript tags in the head of the document. Right now, there is no code between the tags. As you learn more about the button control, you will place code there as needed.

That's pretty much all you must do to place a button on the screen. You cannot change the dimensions of the button manually, nor can you specify the color of the button or the text that appears in the button. All you can do is place the button in your Web page and give it a name and a caption. A button is pretty worthless, though, if you can't respond to it when the user clicks it. That's where VBScript comes in.

Figure 8.1.

A simple Web page with a button.

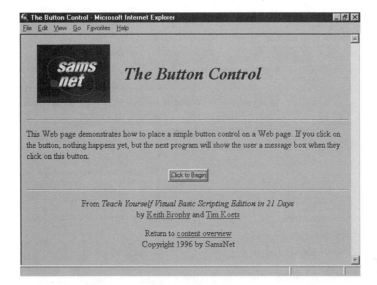

If you were merely using HTML, a button wouldn't do you much good. You wouldn't be able to respond to a button click. In HTML, the only button control the browser responds to is a control that is declared with the type SUBMIT. This places a special button on the form that, when clicked, submits the form within the Web page to the location specified in the ACTION attribute. You will learn more about this on Day 19 when you learn about CGI scripts and VBScript.

How do you go about connecting the button with VBScript code? Quite easily, in fact. On Day 7, "Building a Home for Your Code," you learned about a special procedure called an *event procedure.* You saw that event procedures are designed to respond to events initiated by the user, usually on controls. To get your VBScript code to respond to a button click, you have two options. First, you can use the *implicit* event procedure, which has the following format:

```
Sub ButtonName_OnClick()
    ...place your code here
End Sub
```

where *ButtonName* is the name of the button. You gave the button this name using the NAME property of the input tag when you created it. Consider Listing 8.2, which shows VBScript code that responds to the click of the button by showing the user a message box.

NOTE

In HTML terms, the NAME property of the input tag is an attribute. Because you will use it as a property of the control, the term property is used here.

Listing 8.2. A simple Web page with an HTML button control and VBScript code that responds to the user's click.

```
<HTML>

<HEAD>
<TITLE>The Button Control</TITLE>
</HEAD>

<BODY>
<H1>
<A HREF="http://www.mcp.com"><IMG  ALIGN=MIDDLE
SRC="../shared/jpg/samsnet.jpg" BORDER=2 HSPACE=20></A>
<EM>The Button Control</EM></h1>
<HR>

<CENTER><H2>Using the Implicit Event Procedure</H2></CENTER>

<P>This Web page demonstrates how to place a simple button control on
a Web page.  If you click on the button, you will see a message box appear.

<CENTER><INPUT TYPE="BUTTON" NAME="cmdBegin" VALUE="Click to Begin"

<HR>

<center>
From <em>Teach Yourself VBScript in 21 Days</em><br>
by <A HREF="../shared/info/keith.htm">Keith Brophy</A> and _
   <A HREF="../shared/info/tim.htm">Tim Koets</A><br>
<br>
Return to <A href=Back08.htm>content overview</A><br>
Copyright 1996 by SamsNet<br>
</center>

<SCRIPT LANGUAGE="VBScript">
<!-- Option Explicit

   Sub cmdBegin_OnClick()
      MsgBox "You have clicked on the command button. _
              I knew you couldn't resist!"


End Sub

-->
</SCRIPT>

</BODY>

</HTML>
```

Figure 8.2 shows the corresponding Web page after the user has clicked on the button. The Web page with this implicit button example, named implbtn.htm, is available on the CD-ROM that accompanies the book.

Figure 8.2.

Using a button and an implicit event procedure.

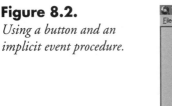

ANALYSIS As you can see, the implicit event procedure is named according to conventions. If you do not name the subroutine properly, it will not connect to the button and will never be called.

The other way of connecting a command button to code is through the *explicit* event procedure. Rather than create a procedure that uses the naming convention required using the implicit event procedure, in this case Sub *buttonname*.OnClick(), you can specify the subroutine you want to call, and it can be named anything you like. You do this by using a special attribute called ONCLICK when you create the button. All you need to do is set the ONCLICK attribute equal to the procedure you want to call when the user clicks the button. Then, you need to actually create the subroutine in your code. Consider the following declaration of a button.

```
<INPUT TYPE="Button" NAME="cmdGetCost" VALUE="Get the Cost"
LANGUAGE="VBScript" ONCLICK="GetCost">
```

In this example, the attribute ONCLICK executes VBScript code that calls the GetCost subroutine. Obviously, this subroutine must exist within the Web page. The benefit of this approach is that you don't need a unique event procedure for each event of a control. You can share a procedure among several controls if you like. Also note that you should set the LANGUAGE attribute to VBScript. If you don't, the browser may not be able to identify what scripting language you are using. It may, for example, assume that you are using JavaScript instead. Therefore, you should always set this attribute to make it clear to the browser what scripting language applies.

To see an example of this, consider the code in Listing 8.3. Here, you can see a Web page that uses this technique.

Listing 8.3. Using a button and an explicit event procedure.

```
<HTML>

<HEAD>
<TITLE>The Button Control</TITLE>
</HEAD>

<BODY>
<H1>
<A HREF="http://www.mcp.com"><IMG  ALIGN=MIDDLE
SRC="../shared/jpg/samsnet.jpg" BORDER=2 HSPACE=20></A>
<EM>The Button Control</EM></h1>
<HR>

<CENTER><H2>Using the Explicit Event Procedure</H2></CENTER>

<P>This Web page demonstrates how to use an explicit event procedure to
call the same procedure when you click on two different buttons. Click
on either button and the same procedure will be called.

<P><INPUT TYPE="BUTTON" NAME="cmdButton1" VALUE="Button One"
LANGUAGE="VBScript" ONCLICK="ShowMessage 1">
<P><INPUT TYPE="BUTTON" NAME="cmdButton2" VALUE="Button Two"
LANGUAGE="VBScript" ONCLICK="ShowMessage 2">

<HR>

<center>
From <em>Teach Yourself VBScript in 21 Days</em><br>
by <A HREF="../shared/info/keith.htm">Keith Brophy</A> and
<A HREF="../shared/info/tim.htm">Tim Koets</A><br>
<br>
Return to <A href=Back08.htm>content overview</A><br>
Copyright 1996 by SamsNet<br>
</center>


<SCRIPT LANGUAGE="VBScript">
<!-- Option Explicit

   Sub ShowMessage(ButtonValue)
      MsgBox "You have clicked on button #" & ButtonValue
   End Sub

-->
</SCRIPT>

</BODY></HTML>
```

Figure 8.3 shows this Web page, which is named exp1btn.htm. The Web page for this explicit button sample is also available on the CD-ROM that accompanies the book.

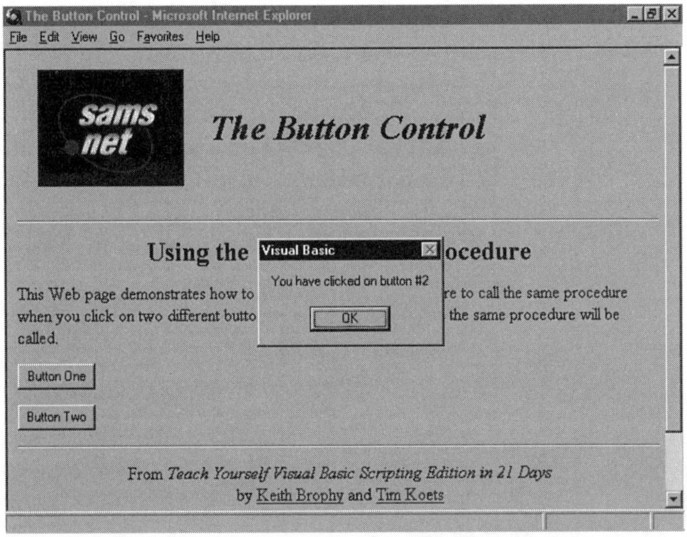

Figure 8.3.

A simple Web page with two buttons that both call the same event procedure explicitly.

ANALYSIS Now, either button will call the same procedure when the user clicks it. This can be useful when you want the same procedure to handle different controls on a form. Notice that in the ONCLICK attribute, a parameter is passed to the subroutine when the event procedure ShowMessage is called. This parameter tells the subroutine which button the user clicked. Although there is no way to pass the internal representation of the button object to the subroutine, you can pass any literal value that the subroutine can interpret. The subroutine can then look at the value of a string passed to it as a parameter, for example, and tell where it was called from. Using this approach, you can create very flexible procedures to respond to various controls that all call that same procedure. In this way, you can share data among controls and make your programs more flexible.

The ONCLICK attribute not only lets you indicate procedures to be activated when the event occurs, it also lets you create script code on the fly in the button definition. This is done by enclosing your code in single quotes immediately after the ONCLICK attribute. For example, if you wanted to pop up a message box for the user when he clicks a button without triggering a separate event procedure, you can simply use the following definition for the button:

```
<INPUT TYPE="BUTTON" NAME="cmdButton1" LANGUAGE="VBScript"
VALUE="Button One" ONCLICK='MsgBox "You just clicked on Button #1"' >
```

This technique is demonstrated in the Web page named onclick.htm on the CD-ROM that accompanies the book. This approach makes it very convenient to throw a bit of code here and there in response to controls, but beware! The more you scatter your code around in attributes of controls, the more difficult it will be to find and debug your code later. It is a good idea to keep your code within procedures and call those procedures using the ONCLICK attribute or use the implicit event procedure approach for your controls.

NOTE

> You can also specify code in the ONCLICK event by enclosing it in double quotes, but you need to be aware of a little trick if you have to use double quotes within the script statement. Simply specify two double quotes in a row in the inner statement, and they will be interpreted as one. For example, this doesn't work:
>
> ```
> <P><INPUT TYPE="BUTTON" NAME="cmdButton1"
> VALUE="Button One" LANGUAGE="VBScript"
> ONCLICK="MsgBox "You just clicked on Button #1"" >
> ```
>
> but this does work:
>
> ```
> <P><INPUT TYPE="BUTTON" NAME="cmdButton1"
> VALUE="Button One" LANGUAGE="VBScript"
> ONCLICK="MsgBox ""You just clicked on Button #1"" " >
> ```
>
> This same rule applies to all VBScript code inside or outside script procedures.

Another interesting feature of VBScript is the capability to create a special block of script code that responds to a control event without placing it within a procedure at all! This can be accomplished using the EVENT and FOR attributes in an opening script tag. The EVENT attribute is assigned a string indicating the event that the script is for, and the FOR attribute is assigned to the control that the script applies to. To write a script that presents a message box for the button cmdButton1, you could create the following script:

```
<SCRIPT LANGUAGE="VBScript" EVENT="ONCLICK" FOR="cmdButton1">
<!--
   MsgBox "You just clicked on button #1"
-->
</SCRIPT>
```

In this case, the entire script is for that specific event. You don't need to create a procedure because the entire script is devoted to the control and event you specify. Usually, any script statements between the <SCRIPT> and </SCRIPT> tags that are not enclosed in procedures are executed as soon as the page loads into the browser. If you use the EVENT attribute, however, this is not the case. The only time these statements of code are ever executed is when the event occurs. This can be a useful capability. You can declare several different scripts within the same page, and data declared in each script can be accessed by the other scripts. You could build a good event-handling approach by dedicating a separate script (enclosed in <SCRIPT> and </SCRIPT> tags) for each event instead of creating a separate procedure for each event. For purposes of clarity, using procedures within the same script might be easier. Then, all your information is in one place.

8

To see an example of this, consider the Web page `eventfor.htm` on the CD-ROM that accompanies this book. The Web page is shown in Figure 8.4.

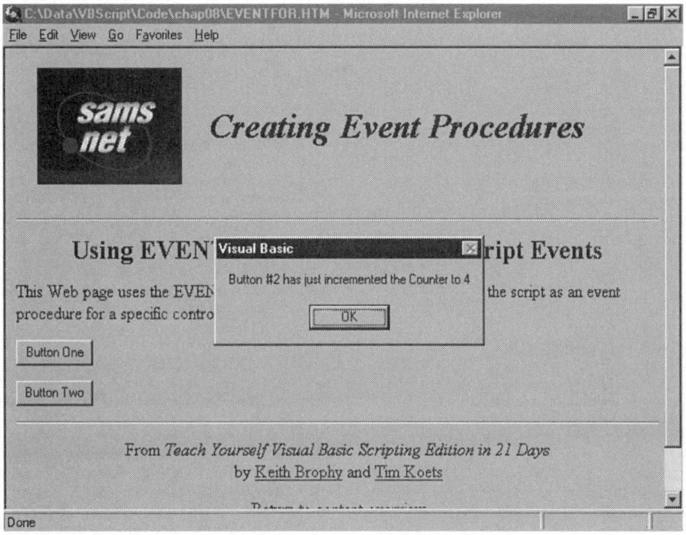

Figure 8.4.

A simple Web page with two buttons that increment a counter.

Listing 8.4 shows the code for the page.

Listing 8.4. Using the EVENT and FOR attributes of a script to trigger a control event.

```
<HTML>

<HEAD>
<TITLE>Creating Event Procedures</TITLE>
</HEAD>

<BODY>
<H1>
<A HREF="http://www.mcp.com"><IMG  ALIGN=MIDDLE
SRC="../shared/jpg/samsnet.jpg" BORDER=2 HSPACE=20></A>
<EM>Creating Event Procedures</EM></h1>
<HR>

<CENTER><H2>Using EVENT and FOR to Launch Script Events</H2></CENTER>

<P>This Web page uses the EVENT and FOR attributes of a script to
define the script as an event procedure for a specific control.

<P><INPUT TYPE="BUTTON" NAME="cmdButton1" VALUE="Button One">
<P><INPUT TYPE="BUTTON" NAME="cmdButton2" VALUE="Button Two">
```

continues

Listing 8.4. continued

```
<HR>

<center>
From <em>Teach Yourself VBScript in 21 Days</em><br>
by <A HREF="../shared/info/keith.htm">Keith Brophy</A> and
<A HREF="../shared/info/tim.htm">Tim Koets</A><br>
<br>
Return to <A href=Back08.htm>content overview</A><br>
Copyright 1996 by SamsNet<br>
</center>


<SCRIPT LANGUAGE="VBScript">
<!--
    Dim Counter
-->
</SCRIPT>

<SCRIPT LANGUAGE="VBScript" EVENT="ONCLICK" FOR="cmdButton1">
<!--
    Counter = Counter + 1
    MsgBox "Button #1 has just incremented the Counter to " & Counter
-->
</SCRIPT>

<SCRIPT LANGUAGE="VBScript" EVENT="ONCLICK" FOR="cmdButton2">
<!--
    Counter = Counter + 1
    MsgBox "Button #2 has just incremented the Counter to " & Counter
-->
</SCRIPT>

</BODY>

</HTML>
```

ANALYSIS This example has two command buttons on the Web page. Each button has its own associated OnClick event procedure that displays a message box on the screen. Each script has access to a script-level variable named Counter that each script increments. The message box for each button displays the value of the counter variable. This demonstrates the usefulness of the EVENT and FOR attributes in a script.

In the examples shown this far, the command button's OnClick event was executed automatically whenever the user clicked on the button. Suppose, however, that you want to place the focus on a command button in code rather than by user intervention. To do this, you need to execute a special instruction called a *method*. Methods are statements associated with objects and controls that cause some action to be carried out. You call a method associated with a control using the following syntax:

```
formname.controlname.methodname
```

where *formname* is the name of the form, *controlname* is the name of the control, and *methodname* is the name of the method. At the time this book went to print, you had to create and use the form in order to work with control methods.

NEW TERM A *method* is an instruction associated with a control that causes some activity to occur within the control. One way that methods are used in VBScript is to cause control events to occur from code rather than as the result of direct user interaction with the control.

In the case of the button, if you want to simulate the user's clicking on the button, you simply call

```
formname.buttonname.Click
```

where *formname* is the name of the form and *buttonname* is the name of the button control. Notice that you must create and use a form in order to use methods in VBScript. Consider the Web page named click.htm, which is shown in Figure 8.5.

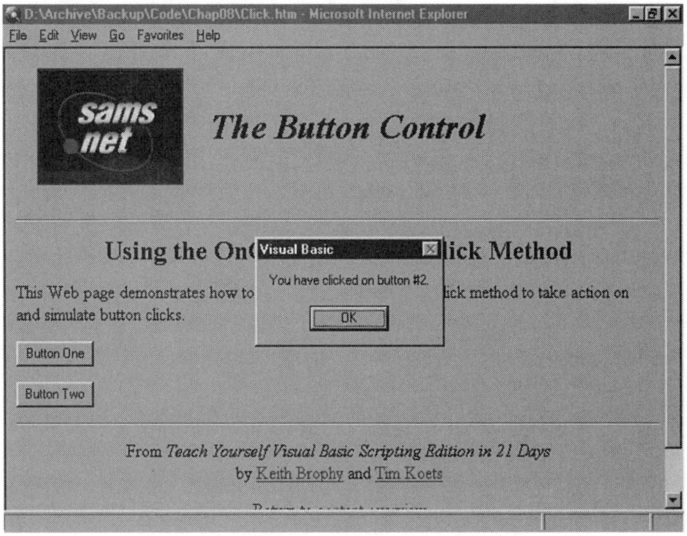

Figure 8.5.

A Web page that uses the Click method of a button.

The code for this Web page is shown in Listing 8.5.

Listing 8.5. Using the `Click` method of a button control.

```
<HTML>

<HEAD>
<TITLE>The Button Control</TITLE>
</HEAD>

<BODY>
<H1>
<A HREF="http://www.mcp.com"><IMG  ALIGN=MIDDLE
SRC="../shared/jpg/samsnet.jpg" BORDER=2 HSPACE=20></A>
<EM>The Button Control</EM></h1>
<HR>

<CENTER><H2>Using the OnClick event and Click Method</H2></CENTER>

<P>This Web page demonstrates how to use the OnClick event and Click method
to take action on and simulate button clicks.

<FORM NAME="MyForm">
<P><INPUT TYPE="BUTTON" NAME="cmdButton1" VALUE="Button One" >
<P><INPUT TYPE="BUTTON" NAME="cmdButton2" VALUE="Button Two" >
</FORM>

<HR>

<center>
From <em>Teach Yourself VBScript in 21 Days</em><br>
by <A HREF="../shared/info/keith.htm">Keith Brophy</A> and
<A HREF="../shared/info/tim.htm">Tim Koets</A><br>
<br>
Return to <A href=Back08.htm>content overview</A><br>
Copyright 1996 by SamsNet<br>
</center>

<SCRIPT LANGUAGE="VBScript">
<!-- Option Explicit

    Sub cmdButton1_OnClick()

        MsgBox "You have clicked on button #1."

    End Sub


    Sub cmdButton2_OnClick()

        MsgBox "You have clicked on button #2."

        MyForm.cmdButton1.Click

    End Sub
```

```
-->
</SCRIPT>

</BODY>

</HTML>
```

ANALYSIS This Web page consists of two buttons. If you click the first button, a message box pops up, telling you that you have clicked the first button. If you click the second button, a message box comes up, similarly saying you clicked the second button. But then, the code for the second command button executes the `Click` method of the first command button. That action simulates a button click of the first button. As a result, the first command button's click event is called, resulting in a second message box saying that you've clicked on the first button. In reality, you've only clicked the second button, but the code causes the click event of the first button to execute as well.

Before learning about the text control, you should be aware of new additional properties of the button control. You can use the `Form` property to figure out which form the button belongs to in your code. You can also use the `Enabled` property to enable and disable a button. This can be accomplished by setting `Enabled` to either `True` or `False`. There are additional methods and events available with the command button, and these will be discussed as additional controls are introduced. At the end of Day 9, you will see a table that shows each property, method, and event for all of the intrinsic HTML controls.

The Text Control

Another versatile and useful control in your HTML control toolkit is the text control. This control displays a simple region on the Web page into which the user can enter alphanumeric data such as numbers, strings, and so on. It's as easy to use a text control as it is the button control. The text control is another of the suite of HTML input controls and is commonly defined as follows:

```
<INPUT TYPE="TEXT" NAME="txtCost" SIZE="10">
```

Here, the TYPE attribute is set to "TEXT" rather than "BUTTON". By the way, "TEXT" is the default value of the attribute, so if you do not specify any TYPE with an input definition, you'll get a text control. Notice that you must also set the familiar NAME attribute. The typical convention when creating a text control is to prefix the name with txt. The rules for naming controls are the same no matter what the type.

The SIZE attribute is an optional attribute that enables you to specify the width of the text control in approximate characters. Due to differences in font representation, the resulting size of your text box will probably not be exactly that many characters wide on the page. If you omit the size, the browser determines a default size. Typically, you set the size equal to the maximum number of characters that you want the user to enter into the control. In a moment, you will see an example of how you can restrict the user to entering a specific number of characters as well.

The VALUE attribute is not included in the preceding example, but you can use it to assign initial text to the text box. If you want the text box to be filled with data when the Web page is loaded, you can specify it in the definition. Whatever you set for the VALUE attribute will appear in the text control when the page is loaded into the browser. It's easy to include a text control on a Web page. Listing 8.6 shows the code for a Web page that includes the text control.

Listing 8.6. Placing a simple text control on a Web page.

```
<HTML>

<HEAD>
<TITLE>The Text Control</TITLE>
</HEAD>

<BODY>
<H1>
<A HREF="http://www.mcp.com"><IMG  ALIGN=MIDDLE
SRC="../shared/jpg/samsnet.jpg" BORDER=2 HSPACE=20></A>
<EM>The Text Control</EM></h1>
<HR>

<P>This Web page demonstrates how to place a simple text control on a
Web page. Later, this Web page will be expanded to retrieve the value
of the text control that the user has entered.

<P>

<INPUT TYPE="TEXT" NAME="txtData">
<INPUT TYPE="BUTTON" NAME="cmdBegin" VALUE="Get Text Control Data"

<HR>

<center>
From <em>Teach Yourself VBScript in 21 Days</em><br>
by <A HREF="../shared/info/keith.htm">Keith Brophy</A> and
<A HREF="../shared/info/tim.htm">Tim Koets</A><br>
<br>
Return to <A href=Back08.htm>content overview</A><br>
Copyright 1996 by SamsNet<br>
</center>

<SCRIPT LANGUAGE="VBScript">
<!--
-->
</SCRIPT>

</BODY></HTML>
```

This simple text control specified the NAME but not the SIZE or VALUE. You accepted the default size and didn't supply an initial value. Figure 8.6 shows the page, which is named `simptxt.htm` on the CD-ROM that accompanies the book.

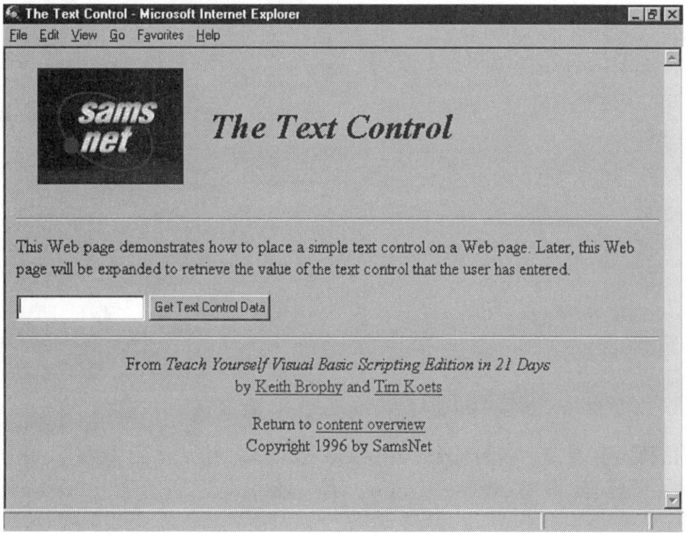

Figure 8.6.

A simple Web page with a text control.

The Text Control - Microsoft Internet Explorer

File   Edit   View   Go   Favorites   Help

sams net   *The Text Control*

This Web page demonstrates how to place a simple text control on a Web page. Later, this Web page will be expanded to retrieve the value of the text control that the user has entered.

[   ] [Get Text Control Data]

From *Teach Yourself Visual Basic Scripting Edition in 21 Days*
by Keith Brophy and Tim Koets

Return to content overview
Copyright 1996 by SamsNet

Unlike the button, the text control has no events you can connect to it. For example, you can click a button, which causes an event that can trigger code to execute. Currently, VBScript doesn't support events for the text control. Most often, all you need to be able to do is store and retrieve text from a text box, which you can accomplish using a special property of the text control called the VALUE property.

If you set the VALUE property equal to a literal string or variable that stores a literal, that string or value will be stored in the text control. Similarly, if you read the VALUE property from a text control, you will get the data that is stored in that text control. Figure 8.7 shows a simple example of this.

Here, the user is prompted to enter his or her age. The Web page loads the text control with a default value of 25. If the user clicks the button labeled Get Age, he will see a message box that echoes the age. Listing 8.7 shows the code for this Web page, which is named `impltxt.htm` on the CD-ROM.

Figure 8.7.

A Web page that gets the user's age through a text control.

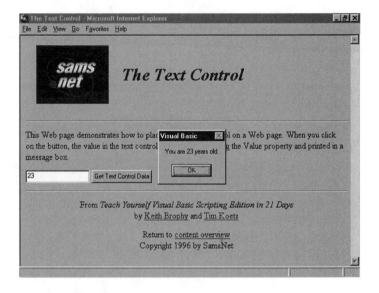

Listing 8.7. Getting a user's age from a text control and reporting it through a button using an explicit event procedure.

```
<HTML>

<HEAD>
<TITLE>The Text Control</TITLE>
</HEAD>

<BODY>
<H1>
<A HREF="http://www.mcp.com"><IMG  ALIGN=MIDDLE
SRC="../shared/jpg/samsnet.jpg" BORDER=2 HSPACE=20></A>
<EM>The Text Control</EM></h1>
<HR>

<P>This Web page demonstrates how to place a simple text control on a
Web page. When you click on the button, the value in the text control
will be retrieved using the Value property and printed in a message box.

<P>

<INPUT TYPE="TEXT" NAME="txtData">
<INPUT TYPE="BUTTON" NAME="cmdBegin" VALUE="Get Text Control Data">

<HR>

<center>
From <em>Teach Yourself VBScript in 21 Days</em><br>
by <A HREF="../shared/info/keith.htm">Keith Brophy</A> and
<A HREF="../shared/info/tim.htm">Tim Koets</A><br>
<br>
```

```
Return to <A href=Back08.htm>content overview</A><br>
Copyright 1996 by SamsNet<br>
</center>

<SCRIPT LANGUAGE="VBScript">
<!--

   Sub cmdBegin_OnClick()

       MsgBox "You are " & txtData.Value & " years old."

   End Sub

-->
</SCRIPT>

</BODY>
</HTML>
```

ANALYSIS Notice here how the text control's text is retrieved in the subroutine that responds to the button click. The data of the text control is read by accessing the VALUE property of the control. If you wanted to place the control within a form, you would first need to refer to the form. You could refer to the form and text box on it with the name `document.MyForm.txtData.Value`. This is obviously a fairly long and somewhat intimidating name! Fortunately, VBScript provides a shorthand method to reference the same control. To do this, you simply declare a variable, in this case called `form`, and set that variable using the `Set` keyword so that the variable refers to the form defined in the body of your HTML document. That form is referenced using the statement

`Set form = document.FormName`

where *FormName* is the name of the form you created in your HTML document using the FORM tag and NAME attribute for that form. Notice the use of the object named document. The document object represents the entire HTML document. A form is a specific part of the entire HTML document, and that's why the form is referred to as one of the properties of the document object. To refer to the form, you must first refer to the document and then to the document's form as shown. Once you've entered this command, you can then reference any control on the form using the following syntax:

`form.control.property`

With the `cmdResult_OnClick` subroutine, you must use

`form.txtData.Value`

to refer to the text of the text control you want if you place the controls within a form. You might be a bit unsure about documents and forms right now, but they will be covered in more detail on subsequent days. Day 14, "Working with Documents and User Interface

Functions," includes a further look at the document object, and Day 19 looks at using a form to submit data to the server. For now, just remember that you access a control through a form, and you access a form through a document. If you use the structure outlined previously, you will make the necessary connections in your code.

As you can see from Listing 8.7, the input controls we used were defined without enclosing them in a form. If you simply declare a text box control:

```
<INPUT TYPE="TEXT" NAME="txtSample">
```

you can then refer to the name `txtSample` anywhere in your script. For example, you could assign a new value to it:

```
txtSample.Value = "37"
```

You don't need to reference the document because it is automatically recognized as part of the document. Similarly, because the control is not a part of any form, you don't need to make a form reference. This is an easier way to define and reference controls. Keep in mind, however, the restrictions of defining intrinsic controls outside of forms that were discussed earlier. One such restriction present in the beta-level software is that you cannot use the methods of a control without first defining a form around the controls whose methods you wish to invoke.

The MAXLENGTH property is another attribute of the text control worth mentioning. This enables you to restrict the number of characters a user can enter in a text control. Why is this useful? Suppose you wanted the user to enter a five digit zip code; obviously, you wouldn't want him to enter six or seven characters! Suppose he had to enter his age. He wouldn't need more than three characters. Why allow him to type more than three? If he does so by accident, he will be pleasantly surprised that your Web page is smart enough to stop him from entering more than three characters. Simply set the MAXLENGTH attribute equal to the maximum number of characters you want to allow the user to enter.

To see how this works, consider the revised Web page that asks for the user's age. This time, the MAXLENGTH property is set to three so the user is restricted to that number of allowable characters. Listing 8.8 shows this "more text example," which is found on the CD-ROM under the name `moretxt.htm`.

Listing 8.8. Getting a user's age with a text control and reporting it through a button, restricting the age to three characters.

```
<HTML>
<HEAD>
<TITLE>The Text Control</TITLE>
</HEAD>
```

```
<BODY>
<H1>
<A HREF="http://www.mcp.com"><IMG  ALIGN=MIDDLE
SRC="../shared/jpg/samsnet.jpg" BORDER=2 HSPACE=20></A>
<EM>More on the Text Control</EM></h1>
<HR>

<P>This Web page demonstrates how to place a simple text control on a
Web page. Click on the button to retrieve the value of the text
control that the user has entered.
<P>

<FORM NAME="MyForm">
Enter your age: <INPUT TYPE="TEXT" NAME="txtData" SIZE="5" MAXLENGTH="3">
<INPUT TYPE="BUTTON" NAME="cmdResult" VALUE="Get Age">
</FORM>

<HR>

<center>
From <em>Teach Yourself VBScript in 21 Days</em><br>
by <A HREF="../shared/info/keith.htm">Keith Brophy</A> and
<A HREF="../shared/info/tim.htm">Tim Koets</A><br>
<br>
Return to <A href=Back08.htm>content overview</A><br>
Copyright 1996 by SamsNet<br>
</center>

<SCRIPT LANGUAGE="VBScript">
<!--
   Sub cmdResult_OnClick()
      Dim form
      Set form = document.MyForm
      MsgBox "You are " & form.txtData.Value & " years old!"
   End Sub
-->
</SCRIPT>

</BODY>

</HTML>
```

ANALYSIS Keep in mind that the MAXLENGTH attribute specifies how many characters you can enter. SIZE determines how big the control is in approximate character units. If you make MAXLENGTH larger than SIZE, you will only be able to enter text until you hit the right edge of the text control. For instance, if you make SIZE equal to 3 and MAXLENGTH equal to 30, you will run out of space before you have entered 30 characters. You might be able to squeeze in more than three characters, but your space restrictions will prevent you from entering them all.

Like the button control, the text control also has useful events and methods you can use. Two equally useful events are the OnFocus and OnBlur events. The OnFocus event occurs whenever a control, in this case the text control, receives focus. A control can receive focus in one of two ways—the user can press the Tab key to place focus on the control, or the developer can use the Focus method to put the control into focus using code (this was the case with the Click event using the Click method). When a control receives focus, a gray box typically silhouettes the control.

NEW TERM *Focus* is a term used to indicate a control on a Web page that has special recognition as being the control the user is interested in. When a control has focus, certain keys cause the control to react in some way. For example, pressing the Enter key when a button has focus simulates clicking on the button.

Consider the Web page named onfocus.htm, shown in Figure 8.8.

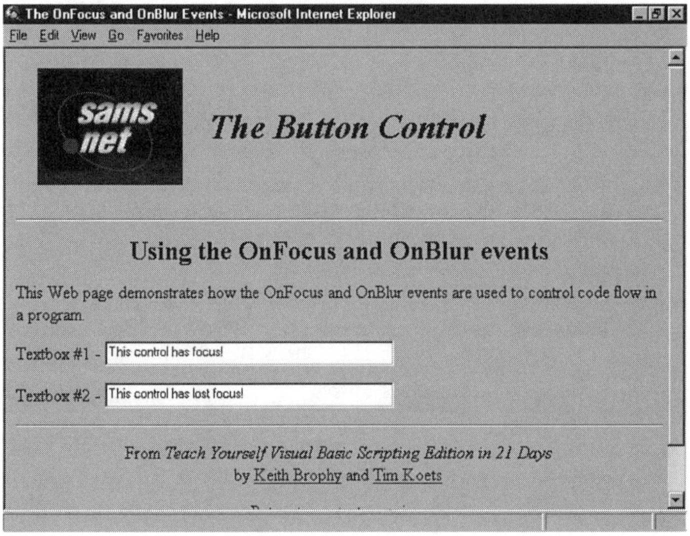

Figure 8.8.

A Web page that uses the OnFocus *event and* Focus *method of a text control.*

The OnFocus and OnBlur Events - Microsoft Internet Explorer
File Edit View Go Favorites Help

The Button Control

Using the OnFocus and OnBlur events

This Web page demonstrates how the OnFocus and OnBlur events are used to control code flow in a program.

Textbox #1 - This control has focus!

Textbox #2 - This control has lost focus!

From *Teach Yourself Visual Basic Scripting Edition in 21 Days* by Keith Brophy and Tim Koets

The code for this Web page is shown in Listing 8.9.

Listing 8.9. Using the Focus method and OnFocus event of a text control.

```
<HTML>

<HEAD>
<TITLE>The OnFocus and OnBlur Events</TITLE>
</HEAD>

<BODY>
<H1>
<A HREF="http://www.mcp.com"><IMG  ALIGN=MIDDLE
SRC="../shared/jpg/samsnet.jpg" BORDER=2 HSPACE=20></A>
```

8

```html
<EM>The Button Control</EM></h1>
<HR>

<CENTER><H2>Using the OnFocus and OnBlur events</H2></CENTER>

<P>This Web page demonstrates how the OnFocus and OnBlur events are
used to control code flow in a program.

<FORM NAME="MyForm">
<P>Textbox #1 - <INPUT TYPE="TEXT" SIZE="50" NAME="txtControl1" >
<P>Textbox #2 - <INPUT TYPE="TEXT" SIZE="50" NAME="txtControl2" >
</FORM>

<HR>

<center>
From <em>Teach Yourself VBScript in 21 Days</em><br>
by <A HREF="../shared/info/keith.htm">Keith Brophy</A> and _
    <A HREF="../shared/info/tim.htm">Tim Koets</A><br>
<br>
Return to <A href=Back08.htm>content overview</A><br>
Copyright 1996 by SamsNet<br>
</center>

<SCRIPT LANGUAGE="VBScript">
<!-- Option Explicit

    Sub txtControl1_OnFocus()

        Dim form
        Set form = document.MyForm

        form.txtControl1.Value = "This control has focus!"

    End Sub

    Sub txtControl1_OnBlur()

        Dim form
        Set form = document.MyForm

        form.txtControl1.Value = "This control has lost focus!"

    End Sub

    Sub txtControl2_OnFocus()

        Dim form
        Set form = document.MyForm

        form.txtControl2.Value = "This control has focus!"

    End Sub

    Sub txtControl2_OnBlur()
```

continues

Listing 8.9. continued

```
        Dim form
        Set form = document.MyForm

        form.txtControl2.Value = "This control has lost focus!"

    End Sub

-->
</SCRIPT>

</BODY>

</HTML>
```

ANALYSIS This Web page consists of two text controls. If you click one of the text controls, giving it focus, it indicates it has focus. The other button will not have focus. If you click the second button, the first will indicate that it has lost focus while the second has gained the focus. You can see by clicking both controls how the focus switches from one control to the other. The OnFocus and OnBlur events are being fired, respectively, as you alternate between the text controls.

The button control discussed in the previous section also supports the OnClick and OnFocus events, as well as the Focus method. As for the text control, in addition to supporting the OnFocus and OnBlur events, it also has events such as OnChange, which is executed whenever the contents of a text control change. The OnSel event is another event available to the programmer that gets executed whenever the user selects text within the control. The text control has more useful methods as well. You can use the Focus and Blur methods, which cause their respective events to execute, and you can also use the Select method, which automatically selects the text in the control and calls the OnSelect event. Finally, the text control has several useful properties you can use. The defaultValue property can be used to set a text control to some initial value when the Web page loads into the browser. The Enabled property can also be used to enable or disable the user from changing the contents of a text control. These capabilities were not present in early beta versions of Internet Explorer 3.0, but added in subsequent versions.

The text control is powerful, necessary, and useful to many Web pages. What if you don't want to restrict the users to entering just one line of text? What if you want them to be able to use a whole area of text, such as when they want to provide a description that spans several lines? In that case, you need another special control called a textarea control.

8

The Textarea Control

The textarea control is a special type of control for those who want to extend the power of a regular text control. Textarea controls, unlike regular text controls, can contain many lines of text. This is very useful when you want the user to enter more than one line of information. Depending on the browser, the user can use scroll bars to move across and down the textarea. Some browsers also wrap text when it reaches the end of a specific line.

The textarea control differs from regular text controls in that the textarea control has both a starting and ending tag. In the textarea start tag, you should specify at least three attributes: the NAME, ROWS, and COLS attributes. As with the other controls, the NAME attribute gives the control a name. The naming convention recommended for the textarea control is the prefix txa before the name of the control. If you wanted to call your control MailNote, you could use the convention txaMailNote to name the control.

ROWS specifies the height of the textarea, where the units are the number of rows of text displayed between the top and bottom of the area. COLS specifies the width of the textarea. Again, the units are characters. Keep in mind one important thing about the ROWS and COLS properties: They simply specify the size of the control, not how much text you can place within it. The behavior of the textarea control depends, in part, on the browser. Suppose you specify that ROWS equal 10, which means the textarea control will be ten lines high. Similarly, suppose you set the COLS attribute to 50, making the textarea control space 50 characters wide. All the browsers will give you the space on the screen you specify, but some browsers will not let you enter text beyond the right edge of a textarea control. Other browsers enable you to enter text beyond the right border by providing scroll bars to let you adjust the window to cover the area of text. Still other browsers automatically wrap the text to the next row when you've reached the right edge of the control on a given row. The formatting depends on the browser. Microsoft Internet Assistant provides scroll bars for both columns and rows so you can scroll through the text you have entered. Internet Assistant does not automatically wrap text to the next row, however, so you can enter as much text in a row as you like.

The following line is an example of the syntax of a textarea control:

```
<TEXTAREA NAME="txaMemo" ROWS="20" COLS="50"></TEXTAREA>
```

With the textarea control, you cannot use the VALUE property to initially place text in the textarea as the Web page loads in the browser. Instead, you must enclose in textarea tags any initial text that you want assigned when the page loads:

```
<TEXTAREA NAME="txaMemo" ROWS="20" COLS="50">This is my initial data!</TEXTAREA>
```

However, the program can use the VALUE property, as it did with the text control, to supply text to the textarea control or retrieve data from it.

Consider the sample Web page shown in Figure 8.9. This simple textarea Web page, called simptxa.htm, is on the CD-ROM that accompanies the book.

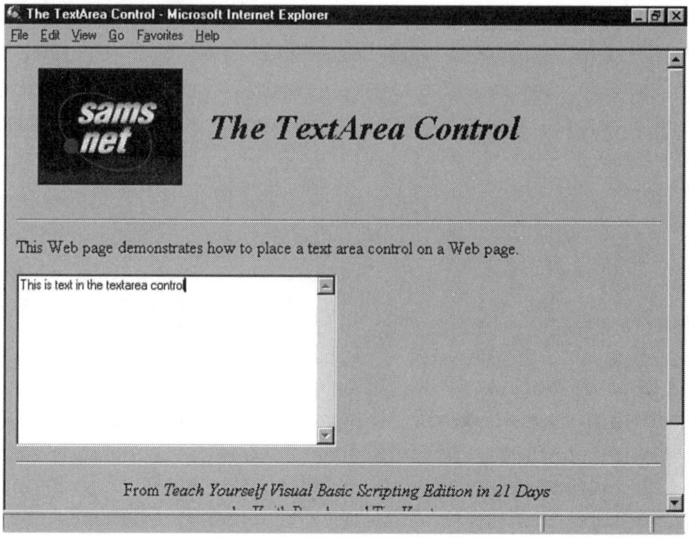

Figure 8.9.

A Web page that uses a textarea control.

As you can see, Internet Explorer provides scroll bars on the sides of the textarea so that you can navigate beyond the borders of the control. Listing 8.10 shows the code.

Listing 8.10. A simple Web page that uses a textarea control.

```
<HTML>

<HEAD>
<TITLE>The TextArea Control</TITLE>
</HEAD>

<BODY>
<H1>
<A HREF="http://www.mcp.com"><IMG  ALIGN=MIDDLE
SRC="../shared/jpg/samsnet.jpg" BORDER=2 HSPACE=20></A>
<EM>The TextArea Control</EM></h1>
<HR>

<P>This Web page demonstrates how to place a text area control
on a Web page.
<P>

<TEXTAREA NAME="txtData" ROWS="10" COLS="60"></TEXTAREA>

<HR>
```

```
<center>
From <em>Teach Yourself VBScript in 21 Days</em><br>
by <A HREF="../shared/info/keith.htm">Keith Brophy</A> and
<A HREF="../shared/info/tim.htm">Tim Koets</A><br>
<br>
Return to <A href=Back08.htm>content overview</A><br>
Copyright 1996 by SamsNet<br>
</center>

<SCRIPT LANGUAGE="VBScript">
<!--
-->

</BODY></HTML>
```

ANALYSIS The browser usually chooses a fixed font, such as Courier, although it depends on the browser. You can also change the font using the necessary HTML tags, if you want. Retrieving text to and from the text control is really quite simple. You simply use the VALUE property of the control as you did with the text control. As with the text control, VBScript does not associate any events with the textarea control. Common uses of the textarea control are cases where the user must enter more than one line of data, such as an address, list of information, a memo or mail to another user, and so on.

Listing 8.11 shows a simple example of retrieving text from a textarea control much like the example using the text control in Listing 8.7. This implicit textarea sample Web page, called `impltxa.htm`, is on the CD-ROM that accompanies this book.

Listing 8.11. A Web page that uses the textarea control to retrieve text.

```
<HTML>

<HEAD>
<TITLE>The TextArea Control</TITLE>
</HEAD>

<BODY>
<H1>
<A HREF="http://www.mcp.com"><IMG  ALIGN=MIDDLE
SRC="../shared/jpg/samsnet.jpg" BORDER=2 HSPACE=20></A>
<EM>The TextArea Control</EM></h1>
<HR>

<P>This Web page demonstrates how to place a simple text control on a Web
page. Click on the button to retrieve the value of the text control that
the user has entered.
<P>
```

continues

Listing 8.11. continued

```
<TEXTAREA NAME="txtMemo" ROWS="10" COLS="60"></TEXTAREA>
<INPUT TYPE="BUTTON" NAME="cmdShow" VALUE="Show the Text">

<HR>

<center>
From <em>Teach Yourself VBScript in 21 Days</em><br>
by <A HREF="../shared/info/keith.htm">Keith Brophy</A> and
<A HREF="../shared/info/tim.htm">Tim Koets</A><br>
<br>
Return to <A href=Back08.htm>content overview</A><br>
Copyright 1996 by SamsNet<br>
</center>

<SCRIPT LANGUAGE="VBScript">
<!--
    Sub cmdShow_OnClick()
        MsgBox "The text you have entered is: " & txtMemo.Value
    End Sub
-->
</SCRIPT>

</BODY></HTML>
```

 This Web page shows the text of the textarea control in a message box when the user clicks the Show the Text button. You can use this control together with the other two you have seen to help build a useful and effective Web page.

> **NOTE**
>
> You can also assign individual lines of text to the textarea programmatically. The sample program PPalErr5.htm, which you will see on Day 17, "Exterminating Bugs from Your Script," uses this advanced technique to generate a debug window on a Web page.

The textarea control, like the text control, also supports the defaultValue and Enabled properties; the Focus, Blur, and Select methods; and the onFocus, onBlur, onChange, and onSel events. A complete summary of each intrinsic control and the properties, events, and methods it supports is summarized in Day 9.

Putting It All Together

Now that you've seen each control and simple examples of how they work, consider them together in a simple example. Use the familiar example of entering an order—in this case, for concert tickets. This example uses the text control, the textarea control, and the button all together to retrieve data from the user. Figure 8.10 shows the Web page called tickets.htm.

Figure 8.10.

Web page to order
concert tickets.

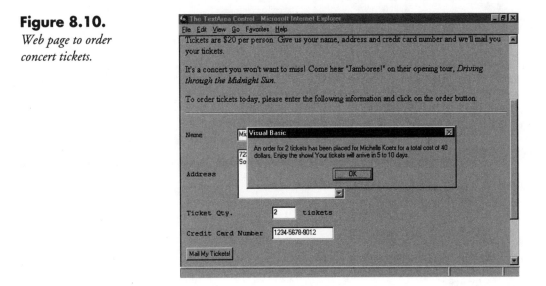

Listing 8.12 shows the source code for this Web page.

Listing 8.12. Source code for the Ticket Booth Web page.

```
<HTML>

<HEAD>
<TITLE>The TextArea Control</TITLE>
</HEAD>

<BODY>
<H1>
<A HREF="http://www.mcp.com"><IMG  ALIGN=MIDDLE
SRC="../shared/jpg/samsnet.jpg" BORDER=2 HSPACE=20></A>
<EM>The Ticket Booth</EM></h1>
<HR>

<P>Come see "Jamboree!" in concert July 4, 1996 at the Kick Stand in
Grand Rapids, Michigan. Tickets are $20 per person. Give us your name,
address and credit card number and we'll mail you your tickets.
```

continues

Listing 8.12. continued

```
<P>It's a concert you won't want to miss!  Come hear "Jamboree!" on
their opening tour, <EM>Driving through the Midnight Sun</EM>.

<P>To order tickets today, please enter the following information and
click on the order button.

<HR>

<FORM NAME="MyForm">
<PRE>Name          <INPUT TYPE="TEXT" NAME="txtName" SIZE="20"></PRE>
<PRE>Address       <TEXTAREA NAME="txaAddress" COLS="40"
ROWS="5"></TEXTAREA></PRE>
<P>
<PRE>Ticket Qty.          <INPUT TYPE="TEXT" NAME="txtTickets"
SIZE="5" MAXLENGTH="5"> tickets</PRE>
<PRE>Credit Card Number  <INPUT TYPE="TEXT" NAME="txtCard"
SIZE="19" MAXLENGTH="19"></PRE>
<P>
<INPUT TYPE="BUTTON" NAME="cmdOrder" VALUE="Mail My Tickets!">
</FORM>

<HR>

<center>
From <em>Teach Yourself VBScript in 21 Days</em><br>
by <A HREF="../shared/info/keith.htm">Keith Brophy</A> and
<A REF="../shared/info/tim.htm">Tim Koets</A><br>
<br>
Return to <A href=Back08.htm>content overview</A><br>
Copyright 1996 by SamsNet<br>
</center>

<SCRIPT LANGUAGE="VBScript">
<!-- Option Explicit

    Sub cmdOrder_OnClick()

        Dim form
        Dim Name
        Dim Address
        Dim CreditCard
        Dim Quantity
        Dim Cost

        Set form = document.MyForm

        If form.txtName.Value = "" Then
           MsgBox "You need to enter your name!"
        ElseIf form.txaAddress.Value = "" Then
           MsgBox "You need to enter your address!"
        ElseIf form.txtCard.Value = "" Then
           MsgBox "You need to enter your credit card number."
        ElseIf form.txtTickets.Value = "" Then
           MsgBox "You should order at least one ticket!"
```

```
    Else
        Name = form.txtName.Value
        Address = form.txaAddress.Value
        Quantity = form.txtTickets.Value
        CreditCard = form.txtCard.Value
        Cost = Quantity * 20

        MsgBox "An order for " & Quantity & " tickets has been placed _
                for " & Name & " for a total cost of " & Cost & " dollars. _
                Enjoy the show! Your tickets will arrive in 5 to 10 days."
    End If

  End Sub
-->
</SCRIPT>

</BODY></HTML>
```

ANALYSIS Notice that the textarea is used to enter the user's address, which could eventually be printed on a mailing label. You could submit the user's name to a server, along with the credit card number (in a secure fashion, of course) and the total cost. The credit card number is restricted to 19 spaces, which includes four sets of four numbers plus three spaces. The button control triggers a script.

The script also has some very simple validation code to make sure the user enters all the required information. This validation code could be much more sophisticated, but it serves its purpose here. You could add even more validation code and then trigger a special form method called Submit that would send the data to a CGI script program on the server, which would actually process the data. The message box that appears to the user could, in reality, be a Web page that the server sends back to the user with order information. To keep the code clear and simple, the actual submittal code was not included with this example. You will learn more about that process on Day 19.

Summary

Today's lesson presents you with three intrinsic HTML form controls: the button control, the text control, and the textarea control. Each of these controls, traditionally called form input controls, are defined by the HTML standard and usually used in conjunction with an HTML form. You have learned what an HTML form is, as well as how it is used, which helped better define what a "form control" is. Because these controls are intrinsic to HTML and browsers, they do no not need to be "registered" or "loaded" into the program as OLE and ActiveX controls and components do. You'll learn more about those on Day 10.

You have learned how to create button controls and place them on a Web page. Furthermore, you have learned how to hook up code in VBScript Web pages by using event procedures.

Today's lesson also presented the text and textarea controls, and you learned how define and place them on a Web page. Unlike the button, the text and textarea controls have no events that are recognized by VBScript. The user can simply use the VALUE property of these controls in VBScript to send and retrieve information to a text control.

For more information on HTML, refer to one of the resources mentioned today and in Appendix B, "Information Resources." Tomorrow, you will learn about some of the other popular HTML form controls. By then, you will have a good, working knowledge of all these controls. Once you've also learned ActiveX controls, you will be able to present very powerful Web pages to your users.

Q&A

Q What is the difference between ActiveX controls and HTML controls?

A The main difference between the two is that HTML controls are defined as part of the HTML language standard. ActiveX controls are extras that you can add to a Web page but are not part of HTML. The ActiveX control standard that was created by Microsoft can give the programmer more powerful and capable controls than what HTML controls provide. HTML controls provide many of the fundamental controls that you use every day such as the text control and the button. ActiveX controls add extra pizzazz to your Web pages by providing you services that take you beyond the conventional HTML controls such as fancy labels that can be displayed at an angle.

Q Why can't I have better control over the placement and size of the controls as I can in Visual Basic?

A The whole philosophy behind HTML is that it enables the browser to do the formatting for you. Any control based on HTML adheres strongly to that principle. For example, you cannot adjust the size of a button; the browser does it for you. You can set the length of the text control, and the textarea properties enable you to specify the dimensions of the control. However, you cannot specify X and Y coordinates for placing controls on a page. You must adhere to the HTML standards.

Q Are there any limits to the amount of text the user can enter in a textarea control?

A There is a limit, but it's pretty large. The current limit is approximately 65,000 characters. The user is not likely to enter that much information, however. If he wants to send information of that magnitude, a better approach might be to provide him with the capability to FTP a file directly to the server rather than work through a textarea control on a Web page.

Workshop

Create a Web page that uses each of the controls presented today. Make the goal of your Web page to get information from the user from various text fields. Do you find that text and textarea controls are adequate to get what you want from the user? What are the advantages of the text and textarea controls? What are their disadvantages?

Quiz

NOTE

Refer to Appendix C, "Answers to Quiz Questions," for the answers to these questions.

1. How is the textarea control different from the text control?

2. Write a Web page where the user must enter a list of products that he wants more information about from your company. Don't forget to give him a way to tell you he is finished entering the products and ready to get the information. Don't worry about supplying the piece of this page that communicates to the server; just provide the portion that collects the data.

Day 9

More Intrinsic HTML Form Controls

On Day 8, "Intrinsic HTML Form Controls," you saw some of the simple controls available for your use with VBScript. Today you will see the rest. The first two controls presented today are useful when you need to present a series of choices to the user of your Web page. The first control, called the *radio button,* enables the user to select one of several choices—but only one. The next control, called the *check box,* allows the user to select one or more choices—not just one. The last control presented in this lesson is called the *password control.* This control enables the user to enter text such as a password into a text box. The actual text the user enters appears as a series of asterisks. This feature serves to protect the user from someone who might look over her shoulder as she enters a password, credit card number, or other sensitive piece of information. You will see all these controls in action today, and rest assured, you're likely to use all of them sooner or later in the Web pages you develop.

The Radio Button Control

The first control discussed today is the *radio button.* The radio button control is useful when you want to present several choices to the user, but you only want the user to choose one of those choices. For example, you might want the user to specify whether he or she is male or female. You intend for the user to choose one or the other, but you certainly don't want him to choose both. The radio button control makes it easy to require the user to only choose one option. Take a look at how this works.

Figure 9.1 shows a Web page that uses radio button controls. This Web page, `radio.htm`, is available on the CD-ROM that comes with this book.

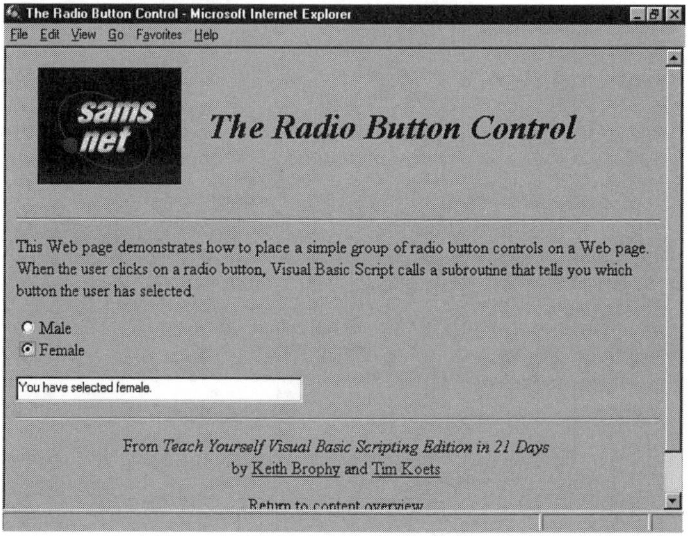

Figure 9.1.

A simple example that uses the radio button control.

In this example, the user must click the radio button designating his sex. Usually, one of the two values is selected as a default for the user; in this case, it's Male. If the user clicks Female, the Male button will automatically become lightened, or deselected, and the Female button will become darkened, or selected. Both buttons cannot be selected at the same time. Sometimes, you might have a list of choices where you don't mind if the user chooses more than one option. In that case, you would not use the radio button control. You'd instead use the check box control, which is discussed in the next section.

How do you put radio buttons on a Web page? The syntax is not difficult to understand. You need to use the HTML INPUT tag because this control accepts input from the user. The following line shows the syntax for the radio button:

```
<INPUT TYPE="RADIO" NAME="name" VALUE="value" LANGUAGE="VBScript"_
        ONCLICK="procedure">
```

The NAME parameter enables you to set the name of the radio button control. As you will see in a moment, if you want to create a group of radio button controls where only one can be selected, you must assign the same name to each of the controls in the group. VALUE is an optional parameter you can use if you embed the control in a form for submission to a Web server. It specifies a unique value for that particular control so that the server can recognize which button was clicked in a group of radio button controls. The ONCLICK parameter is another optional parameter that enables you to call a VBScript procedure when the button is clicked. But you need to make sure you also include the LANGUAGE attribute and set it to "VBScript" so that the browser knows the language embedded in the control definition. This is the way to interface VBScript with the radio button controls on your Web page. You can also include the CHECKED attribute in the list if you want the button to appear checked automatically when the Web page loads. To do this, you simply use the following syntax:

```
<INPUT TYPE="RADIO" NAME="name" VALUE="value" CHECKED LANGUAGE="VBScript"_
            ONCLICK="procedure">
```

Figure 9.1 shows a Web page with two radio buttons labeled Male and Female. These two buttons are grouped together because the programmer wants the user to select one button or the other, but not both. You need to put all the buttons in your list of choices in the same group. To do that, you simply give each button in the group the same name.

If you intend to submit the form to a Web server, you should also assign each of the buttons in the group a different value so the server can tell them apart. If your radio buttons are contained in a form and that form is submitted, the browser will submit the name of the radio button group within the form, as well as the value of the button that is currently selected in each group on the form. Because I'm not concerned with interacting with the server at this point, I'll omit the VALUE attribute from the radio button controls.

Listing 9.1 shows the code for the Web page in Figure 9.1 and illustrates how you put the buttons on the Web page.

Listing 9.1. Using radio button controls.

```
<HTML>

<HEAD>
<TITLE>The Radio Button Control</TITLE>
</HEAD>

<BODY>
<H1>
<A HREF="http://www.mcp.com"><IMG  ALIGN=MIDDLE
SRC="../shared/jpg/samsnet.jpg" BORDER=2 HSPACE=20></A>
<EM>The Radio Button Control</EM></h1>
<HR>
```

continues

Listing 9.1. continued

```
<P>This Web page demonstrates how to place a simple group of
radio button controls on a Web page.  When the user clicks on
a radio button, VBScript calls a subroutine that
tells you which button the user has selected.

<P>
<INPUT TYPE="RADIO" NAME="optGender" LANGUAGE="VBScript"
OnClick="SetGender('male')  "> Male<BR>
<INPUT TYPE="RADIO" NAME="optGender" LANGUAGE="VBScript"
OnClick="SetGender('female')"> Female<BR>
<P>
<INPUT NAME="txtResult" SIZE="50">

<HR>
<center>
From <em>Teach Yourself VBScript in 21 Days</em><br>
by <A HREF="../shared/info/keith.htm">Keith Brophy</A> and
<A HREF="../shared/info/tim.htm">Tim Koets</A><br>
<br>
Return to <A href=Back09.htm>content overview</A><br>
Copyright 1996 by SamsNet<br>
</center>

<SCRIPT LANGUAGE="VBScript">
<!--
   Sub SetGender(Gender)
      txtResult.Value = "You have selected " & Gender & "."
   End Sub

-->
</SCRIPT>

</BODY>
</HTML>
```

ANALYSIS   Notice in Listing 9.1 that both buttons have the same name, optGender. You can use the prefix opt to make the control more easily recognizable in your code. It's not required, but it does help make your code more readable.

NOTE   See Day 13, "VBScript Standards and Conventions," for more information on control naming conventions.

Both buttons call the same subroutine, SetGender, when clicked. Notice that each button passes a different parameter into the subroutine—in this case, the gender that the button represents. These arguments are simple strings, but they could just as easily be any other value. When the user clicks either button, the subroutine is called and the text control gets the appropriate sentence about which option the user selected.

Earlier in this section, you learned that you must place radio buttons in the same group to force the user to choose only one of several buttons. To accomplish this, each button control must have the same name. To see what would happen if you didn't follow this rule, take a look at the Web page shown in Figure 9.2. This Web page is also on the CD-ROM as `badradio.htm`.

Figure 9.2.

An example of two radio buttons not grouped together.

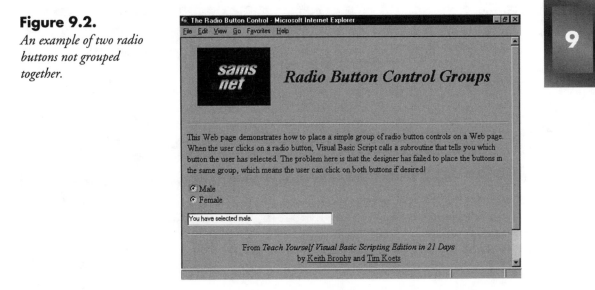

In this example, notice that the user has selected both the male and female radio buttons! Obviously, this is not what you intend in your program. What's the problem? You haven't placed the buttons in the same group. Placing them in the same group makes VBScript realize that only one button in the group can be selected at a time. When you select one, all the others in the group are deselected. In this case, you have effectively placed both buttons in their own groups, which means that the user can click on both. The section of incorrect code is shown here:

```
<INPUT TYPE="RADIO" NAME="optMale" LANGUAGE="VBScript"
OnClick="SetGender('male')  "> Male<BR>
<INPUT TYPE="RADIO" NAME="optFemale" LANGUAGE="VBScript"
OnClick="SetGender('female')"> Female<BR>
```

It's easy to make this mistake because each of the other controls except the radio button must have a unique name. With radio buttons, however, duplicate names are allowed and must be applied to properly group them.

What's the value of groups? Why can't all the buttons on a Web page behave like one big group? Sometimes you might want to put more than one group of radio button controls on a page. Suppose that you not only want the user to select his gender, but you also want him to indicate the age group he belongs to. In this case, you would have two groups of radio buttons to present to the user.

Figure 9.3 shows a Web page that accomplishes that task. The Web page is also on the CD-ROM as radiogrp.htm.

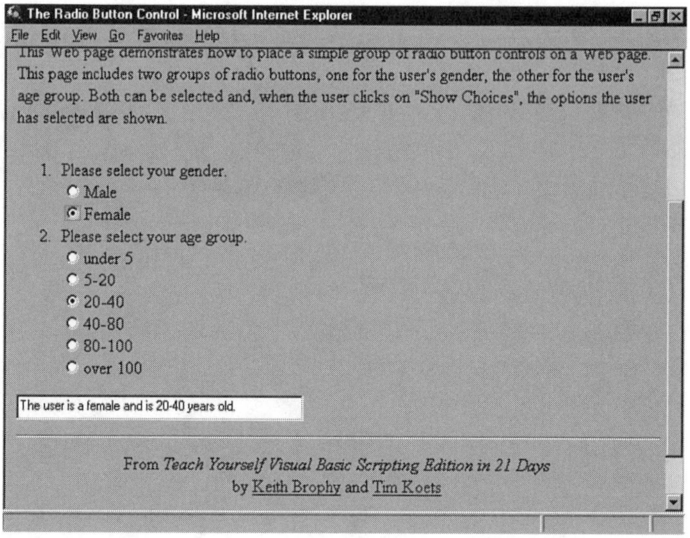

Figure 9.3.

An example using two radio button groups.

This Web page consists of two groups of radio buttons: one for the user's age and another for his gender. Whenever the user clicks a button, the appropriate script-level variable changes: one for age, the other for gender. The code in Listing 9.2 makes this more clear.

Listing 9.2. Using two radio button groups to set variables.

```
<HTML>

<HEAD>
<TITLE>The Radio Button Control</TITLE>
</HEAD>

<BODY>
<H1>
<A HREF="http://www.mcp.com"><IMG  ALIGN=MIDDLE
SRC="../shared/jpg/samsnet.jpg" BORDER=2 HSPACE=20></A>
<EM>Effectively Grouping Radio Button Controls</EM></h1>
<HR>

<P>This Web page demonstrates how to place a simple group of
radio button controls on a Web page.  This page includes two
groups of radio buttons, one for the user's gender, the other
```

for the user's age group. Both can be selected and, when the
user clicks on "Show Choices", the options the user has
selected are shown.

```
<P>

<OL>
<LI>Please select your gender.<BR>
<INPUT TYPE="RADIO" NAME="optGender" CHECKED
OnClick="SetGender('male'  )"> Male<BR>
<INPUT TYPE="RADIO" NAME="optGender"
OnClick="SetGender('female')"> Female<BR>

<LI>Please select your age group.<BR>
<INPUT TYPE="RADIO" NAME="optAge"
OnClick="SetAge('under 5' )"> under 5  <BR>
<INPUT TYPE="RADIO" NAME="optAge"
OnClick="SetAge('5-20'     )"> 5-20      <BR>
<INPUT TYPE="RADIO" NAME="optAge" CHECKED
OnClick="SetAge('20-40'    )"> 20-40     <BR>
<INPUT TYPE="RADIO" NAME="optAge"
OnClick="SetAge('40-80'    )"> 40-80     <BR>
<INPUT TYPE="RADIO" NAME="optAge"
OnClick="SetAge('80-100'   )"> 80-100    <BR>
<INPUT TYPE="RADIO" NAME="optAge"
OnClick="SetAge('over 100')"> over 100 <BR>
</OL>

<P><INPUT NAME="txtResult" SIZE="50"
VALUE="The user is a male and is 20-40 years old.">

<HR>
<center>
From <em>Teach Yourself VBScript in 21 Days</em><br>
by <A HREF="../shared/info/keith.htm">Keith Brophy</A> and
<A HREF="../shared/info/tim.htm">Tim Koets</A><br>
<br>
Return to <A href=Back09.htm>content overview</A><br>
Copyright 1996 by SamsNet<br>
</center>

<SCRIPT LANGUAGE="VBScript">
<!--
    Dim Age
    Dim Gender

    Gender = "male"
    Age = "20-40"

    Sub SetGender(NewGender)
        Gender = NewGender
        Call ShowStatus
    End Sub

    Sub SetAge(NewAge)
        Age = NewAge
```

9

continues

Listing 9.2. continued

```
        Call ShowStatus
    End Sub

    Sub ShowStatus()
        txtResult.Value = "The user is a " & Gender & " and is " &_
                          Age & " years old."
    End Sub


-->
</SCRIPT>

</BODY>

</HTML>
```

ANALYSIS This example defines two script-level variables titled Age and Gender. When the Web page first loads into memory, these two variables are initialized to their default values of 20-40 and Male, respectively. Two groups of radio buttons are defined on the Web page. In the first group, each button is labeled optGender. Notice that the first button has the CHECKED attribute specified in the tag and that, when clicked, it calls the procedure SetGender and passes it the string argument male. The SetGender function, when called, sets the script-level Gender variable equal to the string passed to it. This is how the user can change the gender. Likewise, the second button calls the same procedure and passes the string female to it. You could just as easily pass a numeric value to the procedure and, based on that value, change the gender variable. In other words, you have a great deal of flexibility in the ultimate implementation you decide to make.

The second group of buttons enables the user to specify his or her age group. Every button in this group is named optAge. Again, you must assign the same name to each of the radio buttons associated in the same group. The default value assigned to the script-level Age variable was 20-40, so the radio button that sets the age to 20-40 is checked as a default. When the user clicks any of these buttons, the procedure SetAge is called and the appropriate argument is passed to the procedure. As with the gender, the procedure sets the script-level variable Age to whatever argument was passed to the procedure.

Both SetAge and SetGender then call the procedure ShowStatus, which displays the values in the text control txtResults. Whenever the user clicks a button, the text control gives the user a printed description of his latest choices. To make the default choice appear when the Web page is loaded, set the VALUE attribute of the text control to display what would appear if the user clicked the buttons for the default choices.

It's fairly easy to use radio button controls. You simply group radio button controls together, assign the same name to them, and assign an OnClick procedure to each so you can set variables or perform actions in your code when the user clicks each of the buttons. You can assign each button a separate procedure or assign them all the same procedure, or you can assign some to separate procedures and others to the same. You don't need to set the VALUE attribute of the radio button control unless you are sending the data within a form to a Web server. Communicating with Web servers will be discussed in more detail on Day 21, "Security, Stability, and Distributed Source Control Issues." Again, you have a great deal of flexibility. Your only limitation is your own creativity in building a solution.

In addition to the properties and events already discussed, there are other properties that may be useful to you. You can figure out what form a radio button control belongs to by referencing the Form property. You can also set the Enabled property to True or False if you want to prevent the user from activating the control. The radio button also has Focus and Click methods to cause the browser to give a radio button focus or to simulate a mouse click of the control. Finally, the radio button control supports the OnClick and OnFocus events. You have already seen the OnClick event in action, and you can also establish an OnFocus event for each individual radio button in a group.

The Check Box Control

The next control discussed today is the *check box* control. Check boxes are similar to radio buttons, with two notable exceptions. The first is that a radio button is circular, whereas a check box is a square that, when checked, is marked with a checkmark or an ✕. The most significant difference between the two is that check boxes don't follow the "one selection only" rule. In other words, you use check boxes when you want the user to select one or more choices, not just one. Radio buttons, when grouped, only allow one selection of many possible choices. Check boxes, on the other hand, do not follow the same rule; you can check as many as you want without deselecting any of the others.

To see how this works, you will see the same type of application first introduced when in the discussion on radio button controls. The first radio button example allowed the user to select his or her gender. If Male was selected, Female was deselected, and vice versa. Only one choice of several was allowed. When working with check boxes, the user can select more than one at the same time. The gender choice would therefore not be appropriate for check boxes. What would be appropriate, however, is the list of choices the user can make on the Web page shown in Figure 9.4.

This Web page, named chkbox.htm, is on the CD-ROM that accompanies this book. As you can see, a checkmark appears in each box selected. Here, the user has clicked the Show Selections button to see the choices he selected. Notice that he can make more than one choice. In this case, radio buttons would not be appropriate because it's okay for the user to select more than one choice.

Listing 9.3 shows the source code for this Web page.

Figure 9.4.

*A simple example of
using check box controls.*

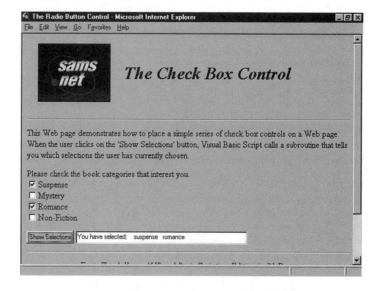

Listing 9.3. Using a set of check box controls to make selections.

```
<HTML>

<HEAD>
<TITLE>The Radio Button Control</TITLE>
</HEAD>

<BODY>
<H1>
<A HREF="http://www.mcp.com"><IMG  ALIGN=MIDDLE
SRC="../shared/jpg/samsnet.jpg" BORDER=2 HSPACE=20></A>
<EM>The Check Box Control</EM></h1>
<HR>

<P>This Web page demonstrates how to place a simple series of
check box controls on a Web page.  When the user clicks on the
'Show Selections' button, VBScript calls a subroutine that tells
you which selections the user has currently chosen.

<P>
Please check the book categories that interest you.<BR>
<INPUT TYPE="CHECKBOX" NAME="chkSuspense" > Suspense<BR>
<INPUT TYPE="CHECKBOX" NAME="chkMystery"  > Mystery<BR>
<INPUT TYPE="CHECKBOX" NAME="chkRomance"  > Romance<BR>
<INPUT TYPE="CHECKBOX" NAME="chkNFiction" > Non-Fiction<BR>
<P>
<INPUT TYPE="BUTTON" NAME="cmdResults" VALUE="Show Selections">
<INPUT NAME="txtResult" SIZE="60">

<HR>
<center>
```

```
From <em>Teach Yourself VBScript in 21 Days</em><br>
by <A HREF="../shared/info/keith.htm">Keith Brophy</A> and
<A HREF="../shared/info/tim.htm">Tim Koets</A><br>
<br>
Return to <A href=Back09.htm>content overview</A><br>
Copyright 1996 by SamsNet<br>
</center>

<SCRIPT LANGUAGE="VBScript">
<!--

   Sub cmdResults_OnClick()

      Dim Result

      Result = "You have selected:    "

      If chkSuspense.Checked Then
         Result = Result & " suspense   "
      End If

      If chkMystery.Checked Then
         Result = Result & " mystery    "
      End If

      If chkRomance.Checked Then
         Result = Result & " romance    "
      End If

      If chkNFiction.Checked Then
         Result = Result & " non-fiction    "
      End If

      txtResult.Value = Result

   End Sub

-->
</SCRIPT>

</BODY>
</HTML>
```

ANALYSIS When you look at Listing 9.3, you can see a series of four check box controls using the INPUT tag. The syntax for a check box control is

```
<INPUT TYPE="CHECKBOX" VALUE="value" NAME="name">
```

If you want the check box to appear checked initially, you can use the syntax

```
<INPUT TYPE="CHECKBOX" VALUE="value" NAME="name" CHECKED>
```

In both cases, *name* refers to the name of the particular check box control. You can prefix your check box controls with the chk convention to help distinguish the type of control when you

9

see it in your code. In the example shown in Listing 9.3, VBScript refers to a special property of the check box control called the Checked property. The Checked property does not exist for the radio button control, which is why the ONCLICK attribute is used to trap information about which radio buttons a user clicks. The check box control, however, has the useful Checked property to work with. It turns out that you can also use the ONCLICK attribute for the check box.

Consider a modified version of the Web page that was just presented. Figure 9.5 shows the new version. This Web page is named chkboxoc.htm on the CD-ROM that accompanies this book.

Figure 9.5.

Using the ONCLICK *attribute with check box controls.*

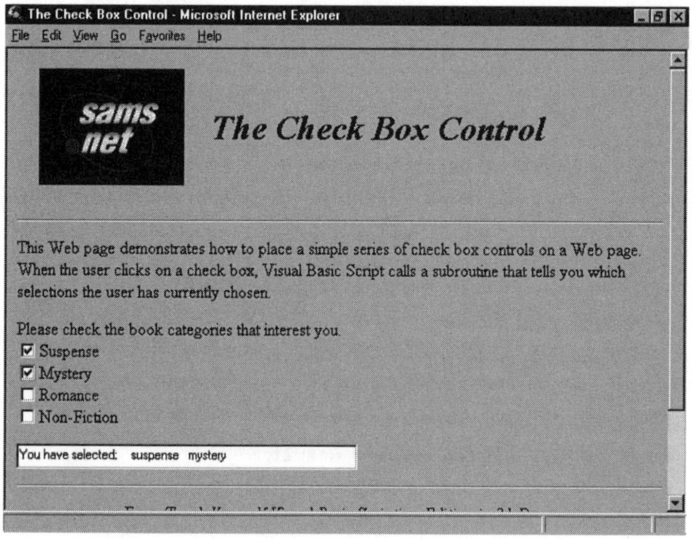

In other languages, such as Visual Basic 4.0, code can directly query a Checked property of the radio button just as it can for the check box. At the time of this writing, VBScript only enables you to look at a check box's Checked property. You cannot perform a similar query on the radio button's Checked property to see if it's on or off, as you might expect.

As you can see, this Web page has no Show Selections button. Otherwise, it appears the same. Look at Listing 9.4 to discover what else is different.

Listing 9.4. Using a set of check box controls and ONCLICK.

```
<HTML>

<HEAD>
<TITLE>The Check Box Control</TITLE>
</HEAD>

<BODY>
<H1>
<A HREF="http://www.mcp.com"><IMG  ALIGN=MIDDLE
SRC="../shared/jpg/samsnet.jpg" BORDER=2 HSPACE=20></A>
<EM>The Check Box Control</EM></h1>
<HR>

<P>This Web page demonstrates how to place a simple series of
check box controls on a Web page.  When the user clicks on a
check box, VBScript calls a subroutine that tells you which
selections the user has currently chosen.

<P>
Please check the book categories that interest you.<BR>
<INPUT TYPE="CHECKBOX" NAME="chkSuspense" LANGUAGE="VBScript"
ONCLICK="ShowResults" > Suspense<BR>
<INPUT TYPE="CHECKBOX" NAME="chkMystery"  LANGUAGE="VBScript"
ONCLICK="ShowResults" > Mystery<BR>
<INPUT TYPE="CHECKBOX" NAME="chkRomance"  LANGUAGE="VBScript"
ONCLICK="ShowResults" > Romance<BR>
<INPUT TYPE="CHECKBOX" NAME="chkNFiction" LANGUAGE="VBScript"
ONCLICK="ShowResults" > Non-Fiction<BR>
<P>
<INPUT NAME="txtResult" SIZE="60">

<HR>
<center>
From <em>Teach Yourself VBScript in 21 Days</em><br>
by <A HREF="../shared/info/keith.htm">Keith Brophy</A> and
<A HREF="../shared/info/tim.htm">Tim Koets</A><br>
<br>
Return to <A href=Back09.htm>content overview</A><br>
Copyright 1996 by SamsNet<br>
</center>

<SCRIPT LANGUAGE="VBScript">
<!--

    Sub ShowResults()

        Dim Result

        Result = "You have selected:    "

        If chkSuspense.Checked Then
            Result = Result & " suspense   "
        End If
```

continues

Listing 9.4. continued

```
        If chkMystery.Checked Then
            Result = Result & " mystery  "
        End If

        If chkRomance.Checked Then
            Result = Result & " romance  "
        End If

        If chkNFiction.Checked Then
            Result = Result & " non-fiction  "
        End If

        txtResult.Value = Result

    End Sub

-->
</SCRIPT>

</BODY>
</HTML>
```

ANALYSIS Notice that this example uses ONCLICK in the check box controls. No button appears in the code. Here, when the user clicks a check box, the subroutine ShowResults is automatically called. The subroutine ShowResults then checks the state of each check box and puts the string in the text box just like before. The only difference is that rather than click a button to see the changes, the user sees the updated text each time the check boxes are changed.

How could this be of value to you? You might need to catch changes made to check boxes right away in your code instead of waiting until some other time to check the controls. The ONCLICK attribute gives you the flexibility of going either way. Furthermore, the Checked property is helpful in VBScript because you can not only query the status of the check box, but you can also check and uncheck the check box manually in code by setting the value of Checked to True or False. Don't forget to include the LANGUAGE property when using ONCLICK. If you leave out LANGUAGE, the browser might not recognize the scripting language and may produce an error.

Neither of these examples uses the VALUE attribute of the check box because the Web page doesn't concern itself with submitting data to a server. However, if you do use a form and include check box controls inside the form, the browser sends each check box control to the server along with the value of that check box control. HTML will let you get away with giving check box controls the same name, but VBScript will not work properly if you try to reference the Checked property of a check box that has the same name as another. Which would it choose? It takes the first one it finds and ignores all the rest!

9

The moral of the story: Make sure you give each check box in your page a different name. With radio button controls, you need to give each control within the same group the same name. This tells the browser that the buttons are all grouped together. The downside to this is that you can't use anything like a Checked property because VBScript won't know which radio button you're referring to. As a result, HTML doesn't give radio button controls a Checked property. With the check box control, however, you don't need groups, so you don't need to use duplicate names. If you don't have to use duplicate names, VBScript can use the Checked property because it can distinguish between each check box control. The Checked property is supported with the check box control because it is practical to do so in this case.

The check box control, like the radio button control, also supports the Click and Focus methods, as well as the OnClick and OnFocus events. The check box control has an Enabled property that can be used to enable or disable the control to the user.

The Password Control

The next control discussed today is the *password* control. This control is almost identical to the text control with one exception. When the user enters text into the control, the actual text he is typing does not appear. Instead, a series of asterisks appears as he types. The advantage of this control is that nobody knows what the user is typing at the moment he enters the text into the control. You might have experience with such a control if you've ever run Windows on a computer network. When it's time to enter your password, you are presented with a box to enter it. When you do, you cannot see what you are typing. If anyone happens to be near you when you're typing it, he won't be able to see your password.

You might have also seen this technique used at your local ATM. Some ATMs show a series of asterisks on the screen when you enter your PIN. This tells you that the computer is accepting the digits you are entering even though you can't see them. That way, if the person next in line happens to be a bit too nosy, he won't be able to see what you've entered at the ATM.

How does the password control work? The syntax is the same as for the text control, except for the TYPE attribute. You can create a password control by entering

```
<INPUT TYPE="PASSWORD" NAME="control_name" SIZE="size"
VALUE="value" MAXLENGTH="max_length">
```

where the attributes SIZE, VALUE, and MAXLENGTH are optional. *control_name* is the name of the control, usually prefixed with the string pwd for easy identification as a password in your code. You can set the SIZE attribute to any size, equal to a width approximately equal to the number of characters you can enter across the control. The VALUE attribute is another optional parameter that gives you the capability to store text in the control by default when the Web page loads into the browser.

`MAXLENGTH` enables you to restrict the number of characters the user enters in the box. This is often useful with the password control. When the user must enter a password or credit card number, you can restrict these entities to a maximum size. For example, you might require a password to be greater than 5 characters but no more than 10. In this case, you can set the `MAXLENGTH` attribute equal to 10 to make sure the user doesn't exceed the 10-character limit. You cannot enforce a minimum length here when you're creating the control, but you can use VBScript to enforce it. You'll see an example of this in a moment.

To see the password control in action, check out a simple Web page that asks the user for a password. The password must be no fewer than 5 characters and no greater than 10. Figure 9.6 shows the Web page named `password.htm`.

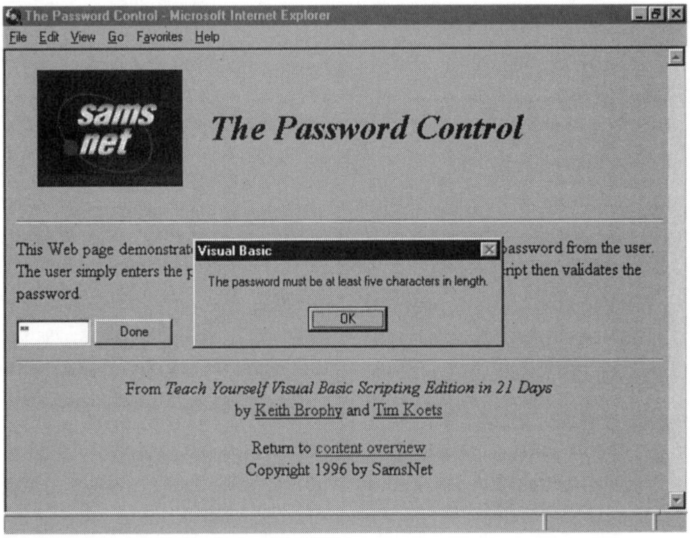

The Password Control - Microsoft Internet Explorer
File Edit View Go Favorites Help
sams net
The Password Control
This Web page demonstrat
The user simply enters the
password.
password from the user.
ript then validates the
Visual Basic
The password must be at least five characters in length.
OK
Done
From Teach Yourself Visual Basic Scripting Edition in 21 Days
by Keith Brophy and Tim Koets
Return to content overview
Copyright 1996 by SamsNet

Figure 9.6.
A simple Web page using the password control.

Listing 9.5 shows the code for this Web page. VBScript is used to validate the password.

Listing 9.5. Source code for the password control Web page.

```
<HTML>

<HEAD>
<TITLE>The Password Control</TITLE>
</HEAD>

<BODY>
<H1>
<A HREF="http://www.mcp.com"><IMG  ALIGN=MIDDLE
SRC="../shared/jpg/samsnet.jpg" BORDER=2 HSPACE=20></A>
<EM>The Password Control</EM></H1>
<HR>
```

```
<P>This Web page demonstrates how to use the password control to
accept a password from the user.  The user simply enters the
password and clicks on the "Done" button. VBScript then validates
the password.
<P>

<INPUT TYPE="PASSWORD" NAME="txtPassword" SIZE="10"
MAXLENGTH="10" MASK="X">
<INPUT TYPE="BUTTON" NAME="cmdDone" VALUE="Done">

<HR>
<center>
From <em>Teach Yourself VBScript in 21 Days</em><br>
by <A HREF="../shared/info/keith.htm">Keith Brophy</A> and
<A HREF="../shared/info/tim.htm">Tim Koets</A><br>
<br>
Return to <A href=Back09.htm>content overview</A><br>
Copyright 1996 by SamsNet<br>
</center>

<SCRIPT LANGUAGE="VBScript">
<!--
   Sub cmdDone_OnClick()

      Dim Password
      Password = txtPassword.Value

      If Len(Password) < 5 Then
         MsgBox "The password must be at least five_
                 characters in length."
         txtPassword.Value = ""
      End If

   End Sub
-->
</SCRIPT>

</BODY>
</HTML>
```

ANALYSIS This example uses the MAXLENGTH attribute to restrict the user to 10 characters. As Figure 9.6 shows, the user's password is hidden behind a series of asterisks. The Web page and VBScript know what's hidden behind those asterisks, but the user or any onlookers do not.

When the user clicks the Done button, the event subroutine for that button executes. The contents of the control are assigned to a variable. Then, the script uses a special function called Len to ascertain the length of the string the user has entered. If the length is less then five, the user hasn't entered a valid password and he is notified accordingly. The script deletes the text in the box, and the user must start over. Otherwise, you could submit the password to a server, for example, to see if it is valid.

The password control is very useful to mask characters on the Web page, but beware. When you submit the password to a server, the password is not secure. It is presented to the server in regular text, which means that anyone can intercept the password and read it. The masking effect of the password control is only a visual aid when the user is entering text on the Web page. In light of such risks, developers are paying more and more attention to security on the Web. As security mechanisms are implemented, data on the Web will become increasingly secure. You will learn more about WWW security issues on Day 21.

Intrinsic HTML Form Controls at a Glance

You have seen in today's and yesterday's lessons many of the intrinsic HTML controls you can use in your Web pages. As this book went to print, some of the controls were not implemented yet and others were implemented, but not fully in the current beta. Table 9.1 represents, to the best of the authors' knowledge, a complete list of all the intrinsic HTML controls, including their properties, methods, and events. Check Microsoft's Web site at `www.microsoft.com/intdev` for the latest status.

Table 9.1. Intrinsic HTML controls.

Control	Events	Methods	Properties	Description
Button	OnClick, OnFocus	Click, Focus	Form, Name, Value, Enabled	A standard HTML control that the user can click on to cause some activity or activities to take place.
Reset	OnClick, OnFocus	Click, Focus	Form, Name, Value, Enabled	A button that resets the Web page to the values it had when it was first loaded into the browser.
Submit	OnClick, OnFocus	Click, Focus	Form, Name, Value, Enabled	A button that submits the contents of an HTML form to a Web server.
Check box	OnClick, OnFocus	Click, Focus	Form, Name, Value, Checked, Enabled	Presents a check box the user can either check on or off. A check box control is used to allow the user to select one or more choices from a list.

Control	Events	Methods	Properties	Description
Radio	OnClick, OnFocus	Click, Focus	Form, Name, Value, Checked, Enabled	Presents a circular button the user can click on or off. Radio controls are used to allow the user to select one choice from a list of possible choices.
Combo	OnClick, OnFocus	Click, Focus, RemoveItem, AddItem, Clear	Form, Name, Value, Checked, Enabled, ListCount, List, ListIndex, MultiSelect	Presents a list of choices to the user. Any selection can be chosen in the list, and more than one may be chosen if desired.
Text	OnFocus, OnBlur	Focus, Blur, Select	Form, Name, Value, DefaultValue, Enabled	Presents the user with a single-line box of variable width into which the user can enter text and text can be placed by a scripting program.
TextArea	OnFocus, OnBlur	Focus, Blur, Select	Form, Name, Value, DefaultValue, Enabled	Presents the user with a multiple-line box of variable width into which the user can enter text and into which text can be placed by a scripting program.
Select	OnFocus, OnBlur, OnChange	Focus, Blur	Name, Length, Options, SelectedIndex	Presents a list from which the user can select one of several items.
Hidden	(None)	(None)	Name, Value	Essentially an invisible text control that allows the user to store values within a Web page in these "holding areas" without being seen by the user.

9

NOTE   The controls presented in Table 9.1 were obtained from the ActiveX SDK help located at `www.microsoft.com/intdev`. Additional details are also available for each of these controls, including their properties, methods, and events, when you download the ActiveX SDK, and its accompanying documentation.

To see a simple example of each control presented on a Web page, see Figure 9.7.

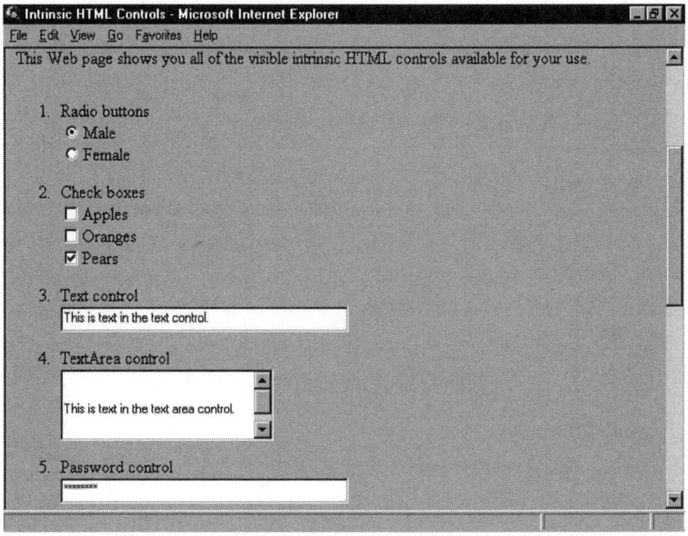

Figure 9.7.

A Web page that shows all the intrinsic HTML controls.

This Web page is named `controls.htm` and is on the CD-ROM with the rest of the sample programs in this lesson. Some of the controls, such as the combo control, were not discussed in detail today simply because they were not fully implemented in VBScript, which was in beta at the time of this printing.

Summary

Today's lesson presents you with detailed descriptions of three more intrinsic HTML form controls that you can use along with VBScript to produce useful and powerful Web pages. The remaining HTML controls are also presented and displayed at the end of the lesson. The first two controls are quite similar in that they enable the designer to present a series of choices to the user. The radio button control, which was covered first, presents the user with a series of choices where he can select only one choice at any given time. A circular button appears over the choice, and the moment one choice is selected, the other is deselected. You have learned how to create a group of radio buttons that present the user with a list of choices, and you also learned how to connect those controls to VBScript.

The next control covered today is the check box control. Like the radio button, this control also presents the user with a list of choices. In this case, however, the user can make more than one choice from the list. A square with an × inside appears when the user makes a selection. You have also learned how to place this control on a form as well as how to integrate it into VBScript.

Finally, you have learned about the password control. The password control enables the user to enter text but hides the characters on the screen so that nobody can see what the user is typing. Although the password control does not ensure security if the password is transmitted over the Internet, it does prevent onlookers from seeing what the user enters.

Over the next two days, you will learn about ActiveX controls. ActiveX controls extend the power of the Web by providing controls that are even more functional and powerful than the intrinsic HTML controls you have studied for the past two days. Intrinsic controls are commonly used in almost every Web page because they are the "staple" diet of all Web programmers.

Q&A

Q Are all the intrinsic HTML controls supported in VBScript?

A No, not all the controls are supported. For example, at the time this book was written, the HTML select and combo box controls were not supported in VBScript. Intrinsic HTML controls that are not supported by VBScript are probably provided in the ActiveX control suite, which you will learn about over the next two days. You should check the latest VBScript documentation to see which controls are supported and which are not.

Q Do ActiveX controls supplement or replace HTML controls?

A Intrinsic HTML controls and ActiveX controls complement each other. For instance, one of the ActiveX controls you can use is the label control, as you will see tomorrow. The label enables you to rotate text and present it to the user in a variety of ways. Such functionality is not available in the HTML control set. On the other hand, the text control is a standard control that a separate ActiveX does not duplicate; it's available as part of the HTML control set. Therefore, you can use both types of controls together to present your Web page to the user.

Q **How does the user know the difference between radio buttons and check box controls?**

A The user probably recognizes the difference between these two types of controls based on experience with them in other software, but you can't necessarily make that assumption. It will be helpful to the user if you add text above a list of choices that makes his responsibilities as clear as possible. Statements such as "Please select one of the following choices" and "Select all the choices that apply" help the user figure out what he or she needs to do next.

Workshop

Now that you've been exposed to all the intrinsic HTML controls that work with VBScript, write a Web page for ordering software. The Web page should retrieve the user's name and address; the type of computer she uses from a list of choices; whether she prefers 5.25" disks, 3.5" disks, or a CD-ROM; and several sentences on what she does for a living in a text area on the screen. Utilize all of the controls you've learned about over the last two days:

- ☐ The text control
- ☐ The textarea control
- ☐ The button control
- ☐ The radio button control
- ☐ The check box control
- ☐ The password control

When you're finished, place form tags around all the controls and add a submit button so that you could submit the data to a server. (Day 21 covers this side of the picture in more detail.)

Quiz

NOTE Refer to Appendix C, "Answers to Quiz Questions," for the answers to these questions.

1. What is the primary difference between a radio button and a check box control?
2. List all the intrinsic HTML controls supported by VBScript and the reasons you might use them.

3. Write a simple program that converts length from feet, inches, or yards to meters. The page should have one text control for the unit to be converted, followed by a series of radio buttons that the user can choose. The units in these radio buttons should be feet, inches, and yards. The page should also include a button to launch the conversion, followed by a text control that presents the result. Use the following rules for performing the conversions:

If user chooses feet, multiply the value by 0.3048 to obtain the result in meters.

If the user chooses inches, multiply the value by 0.00254 to obtain the result in meters.

If the user chooses yards, multiply the value by 0.9144 to obtain the result in meters.

9

Day 10

An Introduction to Objects and ActiveX Controls

Yesterday you looked at some of the intrinsic controls you can manipulate from your VBScript code. If you've been a Web page author for a while, you probably recognized the intrinsic control types; the check box, text box, radio button, and other controls have been supported in HTML all along. Traditionally, they collected input to pass back to the server, but with the advent of VBScript, you can control them directly. What if you want to offer some level of interaction not supported by those intrinsic controls? Some very powerful alternatives exist. The emerging HTML object extension opens the possibilities to incorporating virtually any object into your pages, and VBScript provides a means to control those objects. As a result, the possible ways to expand the bounds of your Web pages are virtually unlimited. However, one of the easiest, most powerful ways to extend those bounds is through a type of object introduced by Microsoft as part of their Internet strategy called ActiveX controls.

Using objects in general, and ActiveX controls in particular, is central to the art of VBScript programming if you plan to develop scripts of any level of sophistication. A clear view of these fundamental building blocks lays the foundation for more elegant and advanced programming. Today's lesson provides that view by first providing some overall background, context, and definition for what an object is. Then, you'll learn about the particulars of ActiveX controls. Many ActiveX controls exist, but today's lesson examines one particular control to highlight the approach for integrating an ActiveX control into your program. That control is the label control, one of the most commonly used ActiveX controls. Subsequent lessons then build on this starting point by introducing more ActiveX controls and the code necessary to create scripts that incorporate them.

Objects

You might find that you want to incorporate more visual pizzazz into your Web pages than you can by strictly using core HTML constructs. Perhaps you want to add some advanced multimedia capabilities to your Web page. The technology to support what you need to do exists if you could just graft it into your page. You might have a special programming function that you'd like to perform that is hard or impossible to program in VBScript. It might be available in some form of usable component that you can purchase from someone else, if only you could integrate it into your script. You just need to know how to add the relevant files and references to your page. The HTML element that enables you do this is the *object*. Objects let you incorporate components into your Web page. Generally speaking, if you incorporate a component into your page, you can incorporate it into your script as well.

Why Objects Are Needed

Over the last two days, you have looked at some ways to integrate added functionality into your pages and scripts with input controls. These are very similar to objects, but with a key difference: They are a native part of the HTML language. The browser/VBScript environment (under Microsoft Internet Explorer) inherently knows about them. The rules for handling these intrinsic controls are preprogrammed into the browser. You can reference intrinsic controls directly from your code as long as you have defined them with the <INPUT> tags discussed on previous days.

Objects, including the external ActiveX controls, are a slightly different beast. Consider the case of controls, which provide visual and programmatic extensions to your pages and scripts. Any developer with adequate knowledge can provide such a control. Because in theory you can have thousands of controls from thousands of providers, it is impossible for the browser to have support preprogrammed for all of them. These controls are packaged in separate files and defined to the operating system through systemwide classes. Some means is necessary to tell the browser and script the location, calling conventions, and characteristics for these components.

Object Definition

The HTML language provides the means to make the object definitions. At the time this book was published, the procedure for inserting objects was still in draft form but had gained widespread support. You can expect leading edge browsers to follow this model or a close derivative. To indicate to a browser that you want to insert an object, the first step in HTML source code starts, as you probably expect, with a tag. The tag to use to indicate an object is one that even makes perfect intuitive sense: <OBJECT>!

You might need to insert objects for a wide range of purposes other than what ActiveX controls fulfill. A Web page can consist of many types of elements, including images, controls, Java applets, video, audio, and embedded compound documents, as well as other new forms of media that might yet spring into existence. As the World Wide Web Consortium (W3C) assessed these needs, it realized that a hodgepodge of different approaches for incorporating different media, each with its own tag, was not ideal. Instead, a well-defined <OBJECT> methodology provides a general solution that you can use for all objects to be incorporated into a page. The discussion that follows pertains to incorporating any object into a Web page. The examples later today will look specifically at how an <OBJECT> definition is used with ActiveX controls. However, keep in mind that <OBJECT> provides the generic framework for integrating any type of object. Later, we will examine its use for other types of objects as well.

NOTE

> The World Wide Web Consortium defines Web standards. If you want more information on the W3C working draft for "Inserting Objects into HTML," you can find it at http://www.w3.org/pub/WWW/TR/WD-object.html. You can find a list of W3C working drafts at http://www.w3.org/pub/WWW/TR.

Use of the <OBJECT> tag is best understood by looking at some simple examples. The label control is a good place to start. This control is one of a new generation of ActiveX controls that will be discussed shortly. For now, you just need to understand a couple of high-level details about this control to understand how it is treated as an object. The label control enables you to define, through appropriate statements in an object declaration, a string of text characters that can appear anywhere on a page. So far it sounds like a heading, but there are a few differences. One difference is that the label text can be positioned at an angle, so it can appear diagonally across a page. Another is that the label, like most objects, can be modified by a VBScript program even after a page has been initially generated. Figure 10.1 shows a page that uses a label control. The label is the diagonal text on the left of the page.

Figure 10.1.

A page with an object— the ActiveX label control

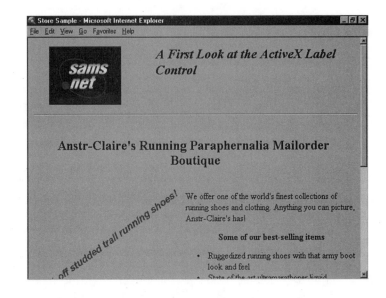

If you looked at the HTML source file for this page, you would see that the control is included by using the <OBJECT> tag. The <OBJECT> tag uses the relevant attributes and settings for the label control. Listing 10.1 shows the format for this object definition used to include the label control on the Web page.

Listing 10.1. The object declaration for an ActiveX label control.

```
<OBJECT
classid="clsid:99B42120-6EC7-11CF-A6C7-00AA00A47DD2"

    id=lblAd
    width=240
    height=240
    align=left
    hspace=5
    vspace=5
>
<param name="angle" value="45" >
<param name="alignment" value="2" >
<param name="BackStyle" value="0" >
<param name="caption" value="50% off studded trail running shoes!">
<param name="FontName" value="Arial">
<param name="FontSize" value="20">
<param name="FontBold" value="1">
```

```
<param name="FontItalic" value="1">
<param name="ForeColor" value="255">
</OBJECT>
```

Object Attributes

The object tag is similar to the standard HTML <BODY> tag format in many respects. It has both a start tag <OBJECT> and an end tag </OBJECT>. Within the start tag, you can define additional attributes that further describe characteristics common to all objects. In other words, all the lines shown in Listing 10.1 following the <OBJECT portion of the tag but preceding the next > are attributes. These attributes, which are specifically defined by the HTML draft standard for objects, describe standard object characteristics to the browser.

You can specify many different attributes for an object. Only some may be pertinent to any specific type of object. For example, the specific type of object defined in Listing 10.1 is an ActiveX control. That object's declaration uses attributes that pertain to an ActiveX control object. Table 10.1 summarizes the full list of attributes for all types of objects.

10

Table 10.1. Object tag attributes.

Tag	Description
ALIGN*	Where the object should be placed—current text line, distinct unit, or aligned left, right, or center.
BORDER	The width of the visible border around the object.
CLASSID*	Class identifier or URL that identifies the implementation of an object.
CODEBASE	Additional URL to supplement the CLASSID URL. This can be used, for example, to locate the control on the network if it can't be located as already existing on the system from the CLASSID.
CODETYPE	The Internet Media Type of the code that is referred to by the CLASSID attribute. This provides further information about the type of entity this is, such as an OLE Automation

continues

Table 10.1. continued

Tag	Description
	object. With ActiveX controls, the CLASSID itself is sufficient for the browser to verify the type of entity, and CODETYPE is not required.
DATA	URL that indicates an object's data, such as the GIF file for an image object.
DECLARE	Indicates the object should be declared but not instantiated.
HEIGHT*	The height of the object picture.
HSPACE*	The horizontal margin around the object picture.
ID*	Defines a documentwide identifier.
ISMAP	Signifies that the object is defined within a hypertext link, and static image mouse clicks should be sent to the server.
NAME	When DECLARE is not in effect, this tag signifies that the object's NAME attribute and associated data should be sent to the server along with other form fields in response to the submit process.
SHAPES	Signifies that the object contains anchors with shape-associated hypertext links.
STANDBY	A short text string the browser can show while loading the data and object implementation.
TYPE	The Internet Media Type for the data that is referred to by the DATA attribute.
USEMAP	The URL for a client-size static image imagemap.
VSPACE*	The vertical margin around the object picture.
WIDTH*	The width of the object picture.

* The attributes that apply most directly to ActiveX controls.

Table 10.1 presents all the object attributes that are part of the current draft standard so that you can appreciate the full range of object declaration capabilities. As shown in the example in Listing 10.1, you will probably only use a subset of these attributes when you define ActiveX controls. The following sections describe in greater detail the key attributes that apply most directly to ActiveX controls.

The Object's CLASSID Attribute

The CLASSID is an essential part of any ActiveX object declaration. It identifies the implementation of an object to the browser. In other words, it provides the browser with a path to the code behind an object. It describes what kind of class an object belongs to and thereby identifies the code that defines its behavior. The CLASSID indicates, for example, whether this is a label object that should look and behave like a label or a graph object that should look and behave like a graph. The information supplied for CLASSID with the current beta Internet Explorer 3.0 and Windows 95 implementation consists of class registration information contained in the system registration database. The browser uses this to locate the relevant file on the system.

10

In the early beta versions of Internet Explorer, this class registration information consists of a cryptic-looking string of digits that corresponds to information in the registration database. The registration database, in turn, knows the location of the library file (with an OCX extension in Windows) that provides the code for this class. In later versions of the Internet Explorer, this will probably evolve to a more easily understood program ID such as r (for example, ="PROGID:Internet.Label.1") rather than the corresponding number reference in the previous example (clsid:{99B42120-6EC7-11CF-A6C7-00AA00A47DD2}).

Another characteristic of CLASSID in the very early beta versions of Internet Explorer was that the CLASSID was enclosed within curly brackets. This syntax, however, did not conform with the draft standard for objects. As a result, later versions of the Internet Explorer eliminated support for a CLASSID definition that used curly brackets. This is pointed out just in case you ever come across a page written for the early beta-level browser. The current-level Internet Explorer will give you warning messages when you're loading the page if object definitions with the old syntax are encountered.

According to the object attribute specification, you can also identify the base location of an object in terms of a URL (uniform resource locater) through the CODEBASE attribute. This means an object can potentially be specified as a file available on the Web. This opens the door to some of the most exciting possibilities with using object components. You can access and download controls across the Web with pages that use them.

If a control doesn't exist on your system (which the browser verifies using CLASSID), the CODEBASE URL is used, if present, to retrieve the component from wherever it resides. In the early beta versions of Internet Explorer, you had to provide ActiveX access for your system by downloading and installing a specific ActiveX control kit. With the beta that was out at the time of this printing, CODEBASE seems to be fully implemented. If you don't have a control that a page uses and CODEBASE points to Microsoft's Web repository, for example, the control is automatically downloaded. The browser does provide you with a dialog to notify you and give you the option to suppress the download, depending on the security option settings of the browser.

It is a good assumption that later distributions of the browser will directly install at least some of the Microsoft-supplied ActiveX controls along with the browser when you install the browser on a system. Ultimately, an Internet model of ActiveX distribution will probably evolve based on the URL attributes of an object. Today's lesson focuses on controls rather than issues of component distribution and assumes the controls are already available on your system and registered in your system registry. Control distribution issues are addressed in more detail on Day 19, "Dynamic Page Flow and Server Submittal."

NOTE

The ActiveX control kit was available for download at the time this was written from www.microsoft.com/intdev. Search for ActiveX control. You should ensure the ActiveX controls are available on your system in order to use the examples that appear throughout this book. Not all the samples make use of the CODEBASE property, so the automatic retrieval won't take place in every case. If you have the controls downloaded ahead of time (whether through an explicit download or perhaps through installing later versions of Internet Explorer), you'll be all set.

The Object's ID Attribute

The ID of an object defines the identifier of the element. This is the name that you must use to refer to this specific instance of the object anytime it is referenced within the page. Why would you need to refer to an object? The most likely place is within your VBScript code itself. If your code interacts with the object at all, you need a name to use when you refer to that object. Suppose you wrote a program that changed the color of a label when a user clicked a button (a sample you will see later today). The name you would use in the code statement that manipulates the label control is the name that is specified by the ID attribute. An ID attribute must start with a letter and can be followed by letters, digits, and - (hyphen) and . (period) characters. (Note, however, that although you can define an ID to contain a . and - in the object declaration, you will run into problems if you attempt to reference a name with these characters from your VBScript code. For that reason, you can consider the set of legal characters for the ID for practical purposes to be letters and digits.) Lb1Ad is the ID of the control used in the object declaration in Listing 10.1.

The Object's WIDTH and HEIGHT Attributes

The WIDTH and HEIGHT attributes together specify the size of the object when it is drawn on the Web page. If an object area's true dimensions differ from those indicated by WIDTH and HEIGHT, the visible picture for the object will be stretched to match the specified size. Some browsers use this information for additional purposes. The Internet Explorer, for example, also uses these dimensions to draw an appropriately sized placeholder for the object's picture representation as the object is being loaded. These attributes are specified in pixels by default but can also be described in terms of screen percentage, such as

```
height=50%
```

In Listing 10.1, the width of the area containing the label is constrained by the <OBJECT> attributes to be 240×240 pixels. If caption text was supplied for the label in a font size that did not fit within this area, that text would be truncated to fit.

The Object's ALIGN Attribute

The ALIGN attribute designates where to position the object. Based on the current draft standard, the ALIGN attribute can take any of the following values:

Value	Description
BASELINE	The object's bottom is vertically aligned with the current font's bottom.
CENTER	The object appears centered between the left and right margins.
LEFT	The object appears down the current left margin.
MIDDLE	The object's middle is vertically aligned with font's baseline.
RIGHT	The object appears down the current right margin.
TEXTMIDDLE	The object's middle is vertically aligned halfway between the baseline and the current font height.
TEXTBOTTOM	The object's bottom is vertically aligned with the current font's bottom.
TEXTTOP	The object's top is vertically aligned with the current font's top.

The Object's VSPACE and HSPACE Attributes

The VSPACE and HSPACE attributes combine to designate the margins for the object's picture representation. VSPACE indicates the vertical margins, and HSPACE indicates the horizontal margins. An HSPACE of 5 and a VSPACE of 5, for example, would indicate that the browser should provide a margin of 5 pixels around the object picture. These attributes are specified in pixels by default but can also be described in terms of screen percentage, such as

```
HSpace=2%
```

Syntax for Specifying an Attribute

Now that you have a feel for what attributes are, you should keep in mind the syntax that you can and cannot use when specifying them. The label example shown in Listing 10.1 references attribute values without any quotation marks:

```
id = Label1
```

If you've studied the source code for many Web pages, you might notice that some pages reference attribute values with quotation marks:

```
id = "Label1"
```

Either of these approaches is legal. You can omit the quotation marks if an attribute value consists only of the characters a to z, A to Z, 0 to 9, the hyphen, and the period. Another rule will probably cheer Windows users and sadden UNIX diehards. Attributes are entirely case insensitive. That means that

```
id = Label1
```

is the same as

```
id = LABEL1
```

to any browser—at least, any browser that adheres to the standards!

Visual Representation of Objects

As mentioned earlier, you will need only some of the many legal object attributes when defining an ActiveX control—specifically, the CLASSID, ID, WIDTH, HEIGHT, ALIGN, HSPACE, and VSPACE attributes. Notice that four of these attributes pertain to the way an object is rendered on the page. The majority of controls have a visible representation that appears on the page. For example, the label control displays text to the user and is clearly visible on the page. However, some controls do not show up on the page but simply perform a task at the request of code with no visible representation of the control for the user to see.

A timer control falls in this category. Code you write can use this control for timing purposes, but the user of your Web page doesn't see a visible sign of the timer control except through whatever interface your program presents. For an object such as this control, even the WIDTH, HEIGHT, HSPACE, and VSPACE attributes are not relevant. Therefore, they do not need to be specified. This will be illustrated more fully in the ActiveX control examples that you see over the next two days.

NOTE

Many programming environments for software that runs under graphical operating systems now provide sophisticated visual tools to incorporate components into programs. Often, you can just drag and drop a component icon onto a program interface to add the component to your program. Fortunately, at the time of this writing, such tools are starting to appear in some forms. Microsoft has an ActiveX control insertion utility that moves object tag text for a control to the clipboard for easy text insertion. Microsoft's ActiveX Control Pad editor (discussed in detail on Day 18, "Advanced User Interface and Browser Object Techniques") has a built-in capability to do the same type of insertions and represents controls visually in the left margin of the editor. Both of these tools are currently free on the Microsoft Web site (under www.microsoft.com/intdev). More tools will likely evolve as well. Short of having a snazzy tool, the only way to add objects is to insert the lines of code of the object declaration right into your source file. Tools will evolve with time, and the state of the art seems to change from month to month. Check online resources and industry periodicals to find out the current state of the art when you read this. You can also refer to the book's tips and pointers page on the Web documented in Appendix B, "Information Resources," which lists some late-breaking findings.

10

Object Parameters

If you've used HTML to build Web pages, the attributes of the object tag are probably somewhat familiar to you. The attributes are common to other tags such as <BODY> and <IMG> as well as <OBJECT>. Another aspect of the object tag that is unique to it, however, is the <PARAM> tag. <PARAM> specifies object parameters within an object definition. An object parameter is a characteristic of an object that is defined by the object itself, rather than the HTML standards. If you have experience with Visual Basic or an object-oriented programming language, you can picture a parameter as a property of the object. For that reason,

<PARAM> parameters are often referred to interchangeably as properties or parameters, and you will find the property terminology used throughout the rest of this book. The <PARAM> list of an object is essentially its property sheet. It defines a list of property characteristics and the initial settings for those characteristics. The properties provided and the way these properties are utilized by an object is object dependent. In the case of ActiveX controls, it depends completely on the way the control was written. Typically, the properties of a control are well documented and describe the way in which various property settings affect the appearance or behavior of the control.

<PARAM> is therefore a tag that is a part of an object definition; it is embedded between the <OBJECT> and </OBJECT> tags. <PARAM> requires no ending tag and carries with it just two main attributes: NAME and VALUE. NAME is used to designate the name of a property, and VALUE determines its initial value. If you refer to Listing 10.1, you can see that the label ActiveX control object definition defines a font name property:

```
<param name="FontName" value="Arial">
```

TIP

> An object's <PARAM> tags perform essentially the same function as do properties within Visual Basic 4.0.

The FontName property is a property of the label control that determines the font used to display the label's caption. The FontName property is specified a parameter rather than an attribute in the object definition because it is object specific rather than generic to all objects. Odds are that many objects will have no use for such a property; an image or audio file doesn't need a font specification, for example. In general, think of object attributes as standard instructions to the browser on how to deal with a generic object. Object parameters are object-specific properties that deal with characteristics unique to that object or similar objects.

You first assign object properties when authoring a page to create the initial state of an object. You also will probably reference many properties in your scripts to control the behavior and characteristics of an object. You can reference a specific property in your code by designating the ID of the object, a period to indicate that what follows is a property, and then the specific property. For example, to print a message box containing the caption property of the label object (which is defined in Listing 10.1), you would use the following statement:

```
msgbox lblAd.Caption
```

When you reference the name of the object and property in a statement, the corresponding value is returned. When the object and property indicator appear on the left side of an assignment statement, such as

```
"lblAd.Caption = "Sales Off"
```

the object's property value changes to the new value indicated in the assignment. This capability to set and retrieve the value of object properties provides a powerful means to interact with controls within your scripts. You can write code to inspect and control any aspect of the controls you incorporate in your programs.

ActiveX Technology

ActiveX is a technology standard that was introduced by Microsoft in March 1996. It defines a standard approach for implementing controls that can be easily integrated into applications, including Web pages. ActiveX grew out of the very successful Visual Basic–related component technologies and strategies that preceded it. These included controls called VBXs, which were used by the early versions of Visual Basic, and controls called OCXs, used by Visual Basic 4.0 and most other Windows programming languages. OCXs provided component integration based on Microsoft's OLE (object linking and embedding) technology. OLE is a sophisticated, complex family of standards, which in a general sense deal with communication between applications, registration, and storage issues.

VBXs and OCXs provided the capability to quickly and easily expand the function of a program to Visual Basic and other rapid application development languages. You simply had to insert a component into your program to add function, and then you could programmatically drive that component to perform work. As a result, you could easily expand the power of your programs by taking advantage of communication and control with what were essentially code libraries provided by other companies. If you wanted to add a calendar to your program, you could simply add a calendar control you purchased from a third-party provider, and—presto!—you had a fully programmable calendar with a complete user interface built into your program.

This is a powerful programming model. It was a natural to apply it to Web page programming with the maturation of scripting languages such as VBScript. There was only one problem. The steady evolution of controls in the Windows environment was at a state where the technology was rather bloated and platform specific. OCX controls carried with them the considerable overhead involved in communicating according to the OLE protocols. OLE support was not available in many other environments. A good Internet-targeted control needed the potential for downloading across the network to accompany a Web page that used

10

it. That would require small controls with a light footprint. Likewise, you'd need controls that could efficiently operate in a variety of operating environments to craft a page that could be used anywhere.

Microsoft provided further control standard guidelines that encompassed the old OCX technologies as well as went beyond it. This technology was named ActiveX, as part of a broader ActiveX strategy to revolutionize many aspects of Windows for the Internet era ahead. It is important to realize that traditional OCX controls are now ActiveX controls under the umbrella of the new ActiveX control term. This terminology does reflect a powerful capability, for it means that you have literally thousands of controls you could potentially incorporate into your Web pages.

Actually, the ActiveX controls are just one part of a broader ActiveX technology strategy. This technology centers on the concept of treating applications as well as traditional Web pages as active documents hosted in an all-encompassing shell. The shell becomes the next generation browser that can essentially host all interactions with the computer. The core of the strategy then, at least on the Windows environment, is that the operating system and browser become one. Web pages, as well as everything else, become "active." The browser user of the future will be able to shift from applications to Web pages without detecting much difference between documents and applications rather than interact with the traditional static Web page content of the recent past. In this new vision, everything—document and application—has full-scale active capabilities. The label control discussed today makes use of this ActiveX technology. They provide a means to make pages active. These controls enable you to incorporate client-side smarts into Web pages. ActiveX controls are just one type of object that you can insert into a Web page. They are also one of the most common types of objects that you will handle in your scripts because the controls provide one of the easiest ways to extend the power and function of your programs.

ActiveX Control Overview

ActiveX controls come from three main areas of origination. The first is Microsoft itself. Microsoft has provided many free-of-charge ActiveX controls already, and you can expect more to be available to help foster growth of their Internet and operating system environments. The second source of controls is third-party vendors. Many companies will produce ActiveX controls that can perform specific tasks and sell these controls through various avenues. It is typically cheaper to purchase a control than to expend the labor to write the same code yourself, so a steady market for controls exists.

The third source for controls is you (or your company) yourself. Why would you write an ActiveX control? Suppose you want to integrate some type of functionality into your program but cannot locate a control on the market that serves the purpose. The prospect of writing it yourself so that you can write the control once and then use it from many different VBScript programs might start to sound appealing. You can write ActiveX controls in a variety of languages that are not as restricted as VBScript. ActiveX controls also often can offer significant performance advantages. They also provide a very good package for reusable code if you want to share some functions with many different scripts. For all these reasons, many developers will probably produce their own ActiveX controls at times, as well as use those provided by Microsoft and third-party vendors.

One of the reasons that considerable discussion is focused here on ActiveX controls is that much of your ability to use VBScript to produce impressive, active Web pages will depend directly on your ability to incorporate these controls. VBScript is to a large extent the glue that holds your program together. By using this glue, you can quickly incorporate components according to your needs and build a powerful application engine.

It is important to be clear on some fundamentals of using controls to employ them effectively. These fundamentals include the use of control properties, methods, and events. The same property/method/event model that applies to the intrinsic controls discussed on Day 8, "Intrinsic HTML Form Controls," and Day 9, "More Intrinsic HTML Form Controls," applies to ActiveX controls as well. The primary difference is that intrinsic HTML controls have a more limited number of events, properties, and methods than do most ActiveX controls declared through object declarations. You set and get control-related characteristic values through assignment statements, referencing control properties by referring to the object and designating the relevant property after a period (.).

When you define properties within the <OBJECT> tag, you are supplying startup values for that object to use. If you choose not to define a particular property because you don't feel you will need to reference it, you can simply leave it off the <PARAM> list. The control will use its own defaults for any properties not supplied.

The following sample line of code shows a VBScript statement that changes the value of the label control caption property. The name of the control, lblAd, was designated when the object was declared earlier in the HTML source through the <OBJECT id="lblAd" > attribute. Caption was designated as a property within this object declaration by the <PARAM NAME="Caption"> parameter. This example assigns a new string to the caption property of the label object. This statement could appear within any block of script code; for example, it could execute in response to a button click. As soon as the script code containing this statement finishes, the new caption is displayed for the label:

```
lblAd.caption = "This is a new caption!"
```

NOTE   If you're familiar with Visual Basic 4.0 or VBA, you might be accustomed to using the with statement to refer to properties. This statement is not supported in VBScript.

In addition to manipulating object properties, you can also use object methods in your code. When you use an object's method, you are essentially calling prepackaged function or subroutine calls from the object. In the following example, the lblAd control's AboutBox method is called to display an AboutBox associated with that control. The AboutBox method is an intrinsically defined method or function built into the control. You do not have to explicitly define such methods in your Web page <OBJECT> declaration. You get access to all the methods of an object simply by including the <OBJECT> tag:

```
' Show the about box for this control
lblAd.AboutBox
```

As you can see, you can weave a lot of programming around controls. You can set properties of ActiveX controls and call methods that trigger code performed in the control. You've covered all the bases except one. What if the user interacts with the control on the Web page, or the control reaches a certain state you want your code to react to? How can you write code that reacts in such a situation? These types of situations are called events. ActiveX controls provide the same solution for handling events that you saw covered on previous days in the discussion of intrinsic controls. Events are predefined conditions of the control with which you can associated code. When the condition occurs in the control, your code is triggered.

Consider again the label control. A predefined event for the label control is the Click event. If the user clicks a label, the control's Click event handler subroutine is performed, if the script has one defined. The block of code in Listing 10.2 is the event-handling code for the Click event of the label shown in Figure 10.1.

Listing 10.2. The Click event for the label control.

```
<SCRIPT LANGUAGE="VBSCRIPT">
<!--
    sub lblAd_Click
        msgbox "Our studded trail shoes are especially well-suited " & _
               " for running over glaciers or through muck-covered " & _
               " streams with nary a slip!",0,"A Steal at $49.00!"
    end sub
-->
</SCRIPT>
```

It is the name of the lblAd_Click subroutine that associates this code with the label's Click event. The first part of the subroutine name, lblAd, associates it with the ID of the ActiveX control object. The underscore (_) is the notation that indicates an event definition may follow. Then, because the Click that follows is the name of a predefined label event, the code in subroutine lblAd_Click will be performed whenever that specific label is clicked. You can see the result in Figure 10.2. Whenever the user clicks the label advertising the 50 percent off sale, the message box shown in the figure pops up to provide more details to the user.

Figure 10.2.

A message box is displayed in response to clicking the label.

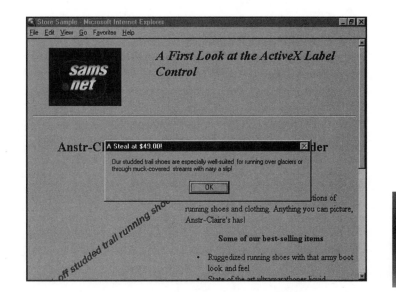

VBScript provides another alternative method for defining event procedures as well. You can explicitly define an event procedure for a block of script code through the script tag. You simply specify the event that the script code is to handle in the tag through the EVENT parameter and indicate the ID of the control the event code is associated with through the FOR parameter. The example in Listing 10.3 performs exactly the same event handling as the example shown in Listing 10.2. If you use this approach, the event handling code is specified in the main code in the script rather than within a procedure. A script associated with an explicit event only gets executed when the event occurs, but the main code within that script body is executed at the time of the event.

Listing 10.3. Another way to define the `Click` event for the label control.

```
<SCRIPT LANGUAGE="VBSCRIPT" EVENT="Click" FOR="lblAd">
<--
    msgbox "Our studded trail shoes are especially well-suited " & _
            " for running over glaciers or through muck-covered " & _
            " streams with nary a slip!",0,"A Steal at $49.00!"
-->
</SCRIPT>
```

A natural question arises if you're thinking about controls for the first time. How do you know which properties, methods, and events you can use for any given control? You might wish you could add your own properties to the label control, extending its functions in the ways you want. Maybe you can think of some really nice code you could write if only a control supported a certain type of event. Wishing won't do you any good, however. Because you're using prepackaged code by using the control, the properties, methods, and events are already defined. It's a strictly defined set. You can only reference properties in your code or <PARAM> tags if they have been supported within the designated control. Likewise, you can't call methods unless they are supported within the control. The only event code that ever will get triggered is code for the events that the control directly supports.

NOTE

> You can always write your own ActiveX control if you can't find one that meets your needs. Writing an ActiveX control is not a task for beginners. On the other hand, you don't have to be a guru to tackle the task either, as long as you know a language such as C++ that supports creation of ActiveX controls. The next version of Visual Basic Enterprise Edition will probably let you create controls from the Visual Basic language, making the task even approachable for many more programmers.

Your choice of control interaction is clearly defined by the control. When you incorporate a control, one of your first tasks should be to round up the documentation for it, whether it's online or on the Net. Thoroughly read up on all the supported properties, methods, and events. This will serve as your guide for incorporating that control into your scripts and writing code around it. You can't read the control developer's mind to understand what he was thinking when he constructed the control. You could perhaps determine how a control behaves through lengthy experimentation. Good documentation provides a much faster path, however. In that respect, well-documented controls with plenty of examples of how their properties and methods should be used are a very important part of component integration.

Now with the definition of objects and ActiveX controls in perspective, you can began to put specific ActiveX controls to work. The rest of the day, I'll focus further on the label control. This control is one of the simpler, yet most frequently used, controls. Once you follow the examples of integrating the label control into VBScript, you will have mastered one of the fundamental skills of creating active Web pages—incorporating objects to make your pages more powerful.

Some of the other core ActiveX controls provided by Microsoft to extend the function of your Web pages and scripts will be illustrated in the pages ahead. Day 11, "More ActiveX Controls," will cover some more control usage in detail; examples with the new item control and the timer control will illustrate these points. Other controls will be used in samples throughout the upcoming days. Bear in mind that although the controls you will see are some of the most commonly used controls, many other ActiveX controls are also available to extend the function of your scripts in other ways. Table 10.2 lists the Microsoft ActiveX controls covered.

Table 10.2. The Microsoft ActiveX controls examples in this book.

Control	Description	Lesson
Label	Displays a label on a page	Day 10
New Item	Displays a new item indicator until a given date	Day 11
Timer	Used for timing events	Day 11
Chart	Produces a variety of charts	Day 12
Preload	Loads graphics in advance	Day 18
Layout	Provides 2-D item placement	Day 18

10

The Label Control

You've seen examples of the label control already today. The brief glimpse provided in Figure 10.1 showed one important distinguishing trait of most controls: They typically enable you to perform more than you could with just the HTML language. The first sample with the label control shows that it can display text at an angle. If you restricted your authoring efforts to present-day HTML, you would not be able to position text in this manner; boring old horizontal positioning would be your only alternative. Of course, you could incorporate a graphic that displays an image of angled text. An image, however, would not give you the rich ability to make your page more interactive that the label control provides. You saw the first taste of this in Figure 10.2; the label can provide a response when it's clicked (assuming that you write the code to do this).

Properties, Methods, and Events Supported by the Label

The label has many ways to make your pages alive. You must have a full awareness of all the properties, events, and methods of the label control to use it effectively.

Properties

The purpose of the label control is to display text. The text can be displayed with a lot of different characteristics—color, an angled alignment, the font of your choice, bold text, and more. As you have seen, you define properties of the label in the object declaration as shown in Listing 10.4.

Listing 10.4. Object declaration for a label with parameters.

```
<OBJECT
    classid="clsid:99B42120-6EC7-11CF-A6C7-00AA00A47DD2"
    id=lblSample
    width=125
    height=125
    align=left
    hspace=20
    vspace=0
>
<param name="angle" value="65" >
<param name="alignment" value="3" >
<param name="BackStyle" value="0" >
<param name="caption" value="Master the Label!">
<param name="FontName" value="Arial">
<param name="FontSize" value="17">
<param name="FontBold" value="1">
<param name="FontItalic" value="0">
<param name="FontUnderline" value="0">
<param name="FontStrikeout" value="0">
<param name="ForeColor" value="0">
</OBJECT>
```

Properties specified in the object declaration are simply initial properties. You do not have to specify every single property here. If you don't specify a property, it will simply assume a default value. These properties determine how the label will appear when it is first drawn on the page at the initial page load. After that point, the script code can control properties in response to user interaction. Table 10.3 lists all the properties for the label.

Table 10.3. Label properties.

Property	Description
Caption	The text that is to be displayed
Angle	The degree at which to display the text, in counter-clockwise degrees
Alignment	The manner in which text is aligned in the control
	0: left aligned

Property	Description
	1: right aligned
	2: centered
	3: top aligned
	4: bottom aligned
BackStyle	Background appearance of label
	0: transparent; you see the page underneath the label
	1: opaque; you see the label background and not the page beneath it
FontName	Name of a TrueType font
FontSize	The size of the font
FontItalic	0: no italicized font
	1: font will be italicized
FontBold	0: no bold font
	1: font will be bold
FontUnderline	0: no underline under font
	1: font will be underlined
FontStrikeout	0: no strikeout through font
	1: font will have strikeout (line through middle of characters)
ForeColor	The color of the label text

10

NOTE

If you have used other visual programming environments, you probably have used properties of controls to dynamically control the positioning of the control. At the time of this writing, this level of positioning is supported only if you use the Layout Control to facilitate positioning, as described on Day 18. Control is not supported. In other words, you cannot modify a top and a left property of a label from your program to move the location of the label on the page. A label control is placed on the page in the order in which it is defined within that page. If you use the layout control, you can carry out such manipulations.

> The properties, events, and methods presented in this book are intended to show you the capabilities of a control. This book does not necessarily present every possible setting supported. Check the Microsoft Web site documentation or use a control tool like those described earlier today to verify the complete set of available properties, methods, and events.

A Note on Handling Angles

Because a circle has 360 degrees, an angle can be defined in degrees from -360 to 360. An angle of 0 degrees indicates a label that reads straight out to the right, along what is a conceptual X-origin line. An angle of 90 degrees indicates a label that reads straight up. When you specify an angle as a negative number, it is displayed in terms of a clockwise rather than counterclockwise angle from the origin. An angle of -30 degrees, for example, will be displayed the same as an angle of 330 degrees.

360 degrees indicates a complete rotation around the origin. You can even specify an angle greater than 360 degrees or less than -360 degrees. In angular terms, this means that one or more complete rotations are made around the axis before the angle rotation. The angle is displayed in terms of the remainder angle after multiples of 360 degrees are subtracted (called the modulo value). In other words, 390 degrees is displayed as a 30 degree angle (because the 360 rotation is removed).

When you assign a value to the label angle property, any values under -360 or over 360 are stored as the corresponding modulo angle between -360 and 360. For example, if you assign 390 degrees to a label's angle property and then use a message box statement to inspect the value of the property, you will see that VBScript has stored the equivalent 30 degree representation for the angle. Likewise, if you have an angle of 350 in the angle property and add 20 to it, you will end up with an angle of 10 degrees in the angle property.

A Note on Handling Colors

Most of the properties are either fairly self-explanatory or best understood through simple trials. However, one property that does require a bit more explanation is ForeColor. This property determines the color of the label text. Similar properties are used in many other controls. You must specify the ForeColor in numeric terms. The number you supply represents the color mix based on the amount of blue, green, and red that go into that color. The amount of each color component can range from 0 to 255. If you know hexadecimal (base 16) arithmetic, you realize that this is exactly the range of values you can represent in two hexadecimal digits (which takes up a byte in a computer). Therefore, each color

10

component can be represented in terms of two hexadecimal digits, and they can be combined to make a grand total that represents the entire mix.

Consider a color that is all blue with no green or red:

Blue component = 255 = hexadecimal &FF

Green component = 0 = hexadecimal &00

Red component = 0 = hexadecimal &00

Combined blue/green/red representation in hex = &FF0000

Combined blue/green/red representation converted to decimal = 16711680

To set the color of a label to blue, you would use a statement like the following:

```
lblAd.ForeColor = 16711680
```

Alternatively, you could use hexadecimal notation to achieve the same effect:

```
lblAd.FforeColor = &FF0000
```

NOTE

An & is used to signify the start of a hex number in VBScript and many other languages as well. &FF means a hexadecimal FF, which equals 255 in decimal notation. You can refer to a basic computer math book if you want more details on converting between hexadecimal and decimal systems.

In either case, you'd end up with a blue label. The same values you use to specify the ForeColor within your code statements can also be used in the object declaration when you specify the ForeColor parameter.

It can be a tedious, error-prone matter to designate color values for properties. It's a challenge to figure out which values to use, and when you type in a long cryptic-looking number, there's always a chance you'll transpose digits. It is easier to type in colors in terms of hex digits using the &H prefix than to type decimal digits. Because the hex digits are easy to view in terms of the separate byte components, you can more easily picture the color mix. Even this approach is still somewhat cryptic and error prone, though. Fortunately, constants come to your rescue. At the time of this writing, there were not yet any intrinsic color constants for script statements. The intrinsic constants you can use with HTML work for the object <PARAM> attributes but do not work within VBScript. You can define your own variable values and treat them as constants, however. You can simply supply color constants for your favorite colors at the beginning of your script code, as shown in Listing 10.5.

Listing 10.5. Setting up color constants at the start of a script.

```
<SCRIPT LANGUAGE="VBSCRIPT">
<!--
   dim BLUE, GREEN, YELLOW, RED, BLACK

   ' Assign these global values once, then use as constants
   BLUE = &HFF0000   ' Blue = 255, Green = 0, Red = 0
   GREEN = &HFF00  ' Blue = 0, Green = 255, Red = 0
   YELLOW = &HFFFF  ' Blue = 0, Green = 255, Red = 255
   RED = &HFF   ' Blue = 0, Green = 0, Red = 255
   BLACK = &H00   ' Blue = 0, Green = 0, Red = 0
```

Events and Methods

Properties alone are often not enough to do all you must do with a control. When you want to cause the control to execute specific actions or respond to specific actions it generates, you must turn to events and methods. The label control has only two of relevance:

> Event: `Click` is triggered when the user clicks on the label.

> Method: `AboutBox` is a method you call from your script code to display the label's About box.

As you saw in Listing 10.3, whenever the user clicks the label, any script code associated with the `Click` event subroutine is executed. All you have to do to define a `Click` event subroutine in your code is start the name with the name of the control object and after an underscore, conclude it with the name of the event, `Click`.

The `About` method is common to many controls but is used less frequently. This method displays an About box with information about the label control when you call it from your code.

The Label-Tweaker Sample: Putting Properties to Work

If all you could do with the label control is set its properties in the object declaration and govern how the control first appears, it might have little value to you. The page really starts to seem alive and responsive, however, when your code manipulates the control after the page is loaded and your user interacts with it. The application pictured in Figure 10.3 demonstrates this potential.

10

Figure 10.3.

The Label-Tweaker sample.

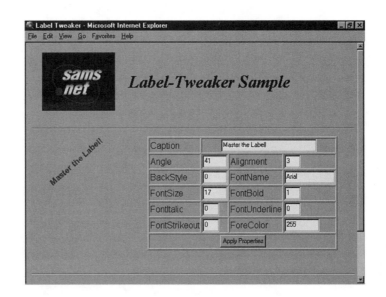

This application is called the Label Tweaker. *Tweak* is an old programming expression that refers to slightly modifying a program to observe the results. The Label Tweaker enables you to tweak one property value at a time and see firsthand the changes that result in the label control. You simply specify the property in a text box input control and then click the Apply Properties button. All property values are reassigned, and the label control appearance is modified accordingly. Listing 10.6 shows the object declaration that defines the initial appearance of the label.

Listing 10.6. The object declaration for the Label-Tweaker label.

```
<OBJECT
    classid="clsid:99B42120-6EC7-11CF-A6C7-00AA00A47DD2"
    id=lblSample
    width=125
    height=125
    align=left
    hspace=20
    vspace=0
>
<param name="angle" value="65" >
<param name="alignment" value="3" >
<param name="BackStyle" value="0" >
<param name="caption" value="Master the Label!">
<param name="FontName" value="Arial">
<param name="FontSize" value="17">
<param name="FontBold" value="1">
<param name="FontItalic" value="0">
```

continues

Listing 10.6. continued

```
<param name="FontUnderline" value="0">
<param name="FontStrikeout" value="0">
<param name="ForeColor" value="0">
</OBJECT>
```

NOTE The Label-Tweaker sample program is available on the CD-ROM that comes with this book in file Lbltwkr.htm.

An input form collects the desired property values from the user. After the user selects the command button to assign properties, the values stored on the input form are assigned to the label properties. Figure 10.4 shows the result of specifying new values and selecting the command button.

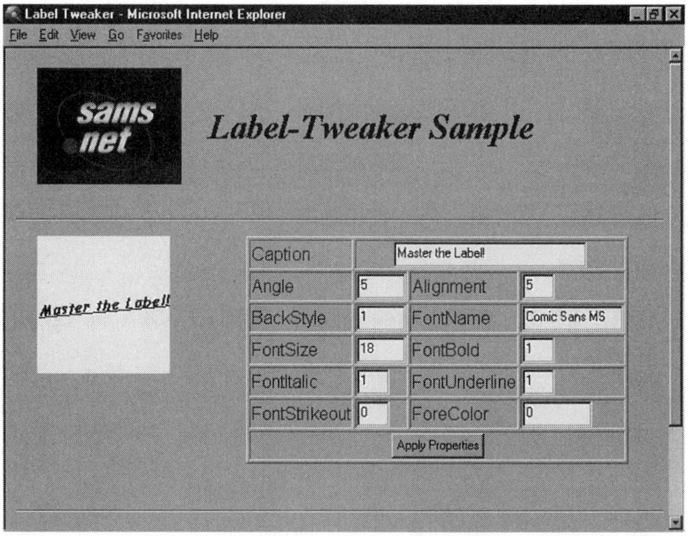

Figure 10.4.

Label Tweaker after user-supplied values have been assigned to label properties.

Listing 10.7 shows the code that modifies the label properties when the user presses the command button. Each property value is simply transferred from the text box where it was specified to the control property itself by the assignment statement.

Listing 10.7. Code that modifies label properties.

```
Sub cmdApply_OnClick
    'This routine is called when the user clicks the apply button.
    ' It applies the property values specified on the form to
    ' the label control.

    dim frmCurrent

    set frmCurrent = document.frmProperties

    lblSample.caption = frmCurrent.txtCaption.Value
    lblSample.angle = frmCurrent.txtAngle.Value
    lblSample.alignment = frmCurrent.txtAlignment.Value
    lblSample.BackStyle = frmCurrent.txtBackStyle.Value
    lblSample.FontName = frmCurrent.txtFontName.Value
    lblSample.FontSize = frmCurrent.txtFontSize.Value
    lblSample.FontBold = frmCurrent.txtFontBold.Value
    lblSample.FontItalic = frmCurrent.txtFontItalic.Value
    lblSample.FontUnderline = frmCurrent.txtFontUnderline.Value
    lblSample.FontStrikeout = frmCurrent.txtFontStrikeout.Value
    lblSample.ForeColor = frmCurrent.txtForeColor.Value

    end sub
```

The Set statement simply enables you to use a variable name in place of the longer document and form descriptor that designates the form used to collect input. Set fills the variable with the data that follows, which in this case is the form object. In subsequent references to form data, you can use just the variable rather than the lengthier document designator. This is just a convenient form of shorthand often used with document definitions.

Using a Control's Properties When the Page Loads

This subroutine modifies the label and causes its appearance to change on the page. Because the subroutine references object properties, the script containing this subroutine had to appear after the object definition. One more aspect of this program helps it to convey the state of the control properties to the user. It starts out with a display of all the current label control properties. This could have been accomplished simply by setting the initial value attribute of the input text controls to a value that matched the object declaration. In that case, however, every time the object declaration changed, the input text control value would have to change, too. Instead, the program automatically determines the state of the label control on startup. This is accomplished through the code shown in Listing 10.8.

Listing 10.8. Startup code that captures initial label control property settings.

```
<SCRIPT>
<!--
'-----------------------------

    ' Startup Code

    'This block of code is executed when the page is generated, since
    '   it appears in the main body of the script rather than in a subroutine.

    'Display the initial property settings of the label control
    Call ShowStartingProperties


    ' End of Startup Code
    '----------------

    Sub ShowStartingProperties

      dim frmCurrent

      set frmCurrent = document.frmProperties
      frmCurrent.txtCaption.Value = lblSample.caption
      frmCurrent.txtAngle.Value = lblSample.angle
      frmCurrent.txtAlignment.Value = lblSample.alignment
      frmCurrent.txtBackStyle.Value = lblSample.BackStyle
      frmCurrent.txtFontName.Value = lblSample.FontName
      frmCurrent.txtFontSize.Value = lblSample.FontSize
      frmCurrent.txtFontBold.Value = lblSample.FontBold
      frmCurrent.txtFontItalic.Value = lblSample.FontItalic
      frmCurrent.txtFontUnderline.Value = lblSample.FontUnderline
      frmCurrent.txtFontStrikeout.Value = lblSample.FontStrikeout
      frmCurrent.txtForeColor.Value = lblSample.ForeColor
    end sub

-->
</SCRIPT>
```

All the input text controls are filled with the label control property values when the program starts. This ensures that the display of properties is in sync with the actual state of the control. This block of code is located after the object and form declaration. Because it is called at startup (the main script code is not in a procedure), it needs to follow these declarations to reference them.

Change Properties Through the Click Event

The sample program also uses the label Click event to modify properties. When the label is clicked, the code in Listing 10.9 is executed. This code modifies the label's angle and shows the change in the input text control.

Listing 10.9. Modifying the label angle through the `Click` event.

```
Sub lblSample_Click
    ' This routine is called when the label is clicked.
    '    It will alter the angle of the label by 5 degrees.

    ' Advance the angle
    lblSample.angle = lblSample.angle + 5

    ' Reflect the current setting back in the property display
    document.frmProperties.txtAngle.Value = lblSample.angle

    end sub
```

Experimenting with the Script

At this point, two things will probably help you to understand the program well. The first is to study the source code carefully. The second is to spend time modifying each and every property value through the program interface and observe the changes that occur when you click Apply Properties. Also, click the label itself and cause the `Click` event to occur. You might find that you get new ideas about possible ways to use this control for your own scripts as you observe the properties changing and cause those changes firsthand.

When Painting Updates Occur On-screen

You can note a couple interesting things about controls and VBScript with this sample program. The first is that updates to the page caused by your script code don't take effect until all code has completed. If your first statement changes the caption of a label and then 50 more statements follow, your user won't see the update on-screen until after the 51st statement has been completed and the block of code has been completely executed. VBScript subroutines are processed in their entirety before screen updates take place.

NOTE If you've worked with Visual Basic 4.0 or Visual Basic for Applications, you might be accustomed to using the `DoEvents` statement that gives other parts of your code a turn at executing their processing and in some cases, affects screen paint strategies. This statement is not available in VBScript.

When a Page Is Reinitialized

Another issue of concern or curiosity to most programmers is the point in time that a page and the code in it is initialized. When a page is first loaded, it is rendered onscreen, and any object declarations and startup code (within a script statement but not inside procedures) are executed. What happens if a Web page user advances to another page and then returns to return to the original page? Label Tweaker can demonstrate that no reinitialization takes place on the return.

To verify this, first load some other Web page in the browser. Then start Label Tweaker and observe the initial appearance of the label. Change the color and the angle of the label and click the Apply Properties button to make these changes take effect. Then select the previous page tool button to back up to the previous page you viewed. From there, select the advance page tool button and return to Label Tweaker. If the page was reloaded and reinitialized, you would see it back in its original startup state at this point. The property values you established in the object definition would be in effect. Instead, you will see the same appearance that changed after you selected Apply Properties.

You can select the browser refresh option with View | Refresh to cause a reload in Internet Explorer. When you do, the change in appearance confirms that only at this point has the page been reloaded and the label reinitialized. This is an important point of script programming. Your script programs retain their state once the page is loaded, even as the user moves between other pages and tasks. When you modify a control, its properties remain in the modified state on that page until the page is reloaded.

The Tutorial Sample: A Highly Interactive Script

So far, you've seen the label control used in ways that might not be exactly what you'll need in your own scripts. The first example with the store ad wasn't very interactive. The second sample program, Label Tweaker, was more for experimenting than for any true-to-life purpose you're likely to need for your own scripts. Now it's time to see how you can use the label control to create a highly interactive Web page.

A tutorial program called the VBScript ActiveX Tutorial demonstrates how you can use the label control to give your users a high degree of feedback during their interaction with your scripts. Figure 10.5 shows the initial appearance of the page built around this script program.

Figure 10.5.

The VBScript ActiveX Tutorial Program.

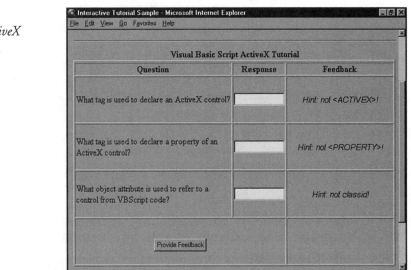

A series of questions is displayed on the screen using standard HTML. Next to each question is a standard input text control to collect the answer. To the right of that is a column of hints, displayed with the label control. All question-related information is also presented within a HTML table to help neatly align the columns of information.

NOTE

The tutorial program is available on the CD-ROM in the file `interact.htm`.

When the user interacts with this program, she enters her response in the corresponding text box for each question and then presses the Provide Feedback command button. This command button triggers code that evaluates each answer. If an answer is correct, a green label displays Correct! If an answer is incorrect, a red label provides the correct answer. To provide a high degree of visual cue feedback, a correct answer changes the angle of the feedback label to point slightly upward with a jaunty air. If an answer is incorrect, the feedback label angle changes to droop slightly downward. A label at the bottom of the feedback area shows the total number of correct answers. Figure 10.6 shows the result from entirely incorrect responses. Compare that to Figure 10.7, which shows the results when every question is answered correctly.

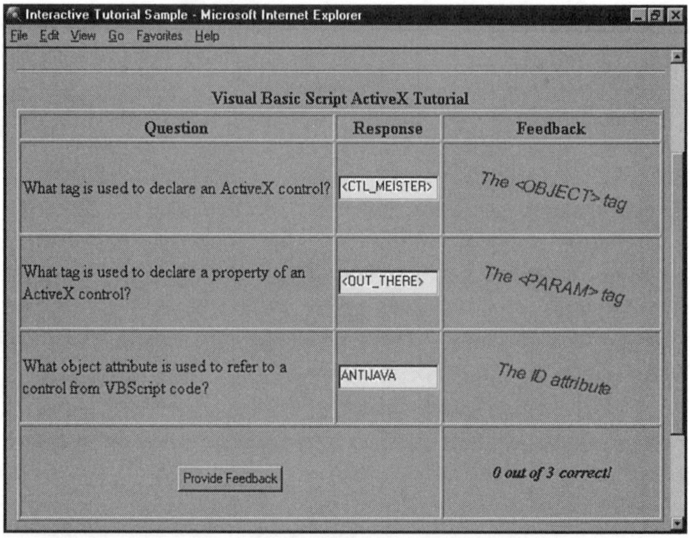
Interactive Tutorial Sample - Microsoft Internet Explorer
File Edit View Go Favorites Help
Visual Basic Script ActiveX Tutorial
Question
Response
Feedback
What tag is used to declare an ActiveX control?
<CTL_MEISTER>
The <OBJECT> tag
What tag is used to declare a property of an ActiveX control?
<OUT_THERE>
The <PARAM> tag
What object attribute is used to refer to a control from VBScript code?
ANTIJAVA
The ID attribute
Provide Feedback
0 out of 3 correct!

Figure 10.6.
Results feedback for wrong answers.

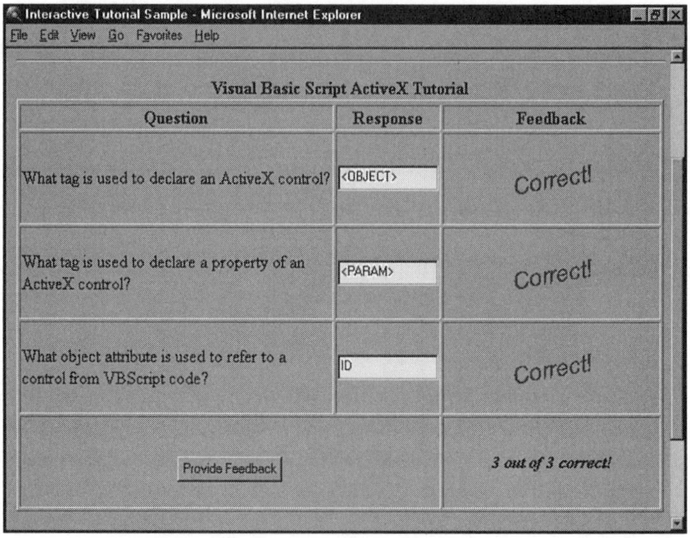
Interactive Tutorial Sample - Microsoft Internet Explorer
File Edit View Go Favorites Help
Visual Basic Script ActiveX Tutorial
Question
Response
Feedback
What tag is used to declare an ActiveX control?
<OBJECT>
Correct!
What tag is used to declare a property of an ActiveX control?
<PARAM>
Correct!
What object attribute is used to refer to a control from VBScript code?
ID
Correct!
Provide Feedback
3 out of 3 correct!

Figure 10.7.
Results feedback for correct answers.

The degree to which the feedback of this program impresses you probably depends on your background. If you're coming to VBScript from a traditional programming background, you might think, "This interactivity is very much like what I can already do with a Windows program." If you're approaching VBScript from a heavy Web page development background, you might be thinking, "This really lets me do a lot more than I ever could before in my Web pages." Both of these perspectives are accurate. VBScript integrates controls and provides programmability much like its parent product Visual Basic has for some time in the Windows environment. VBScript now extends this power to the Web page.

Listing 10.10 shows the code that assesses the answers to the tutorial questions and provide the feedback. A comparison is performed on each text box answer. For the sake of the example, the comparison has been kept very simple. In an actual tutorial, you would probably perform much more extensive comparisons, converting the response to uppercase, checking for close variations on the correct answer, and so on. With this sample program, if an exact match occurs on the answer, it is considered a correct response.

Listing 10.10. Providing feedback based on responses.

```
<SCRIPT LANGUAGE="VBSCRIPT">
<!--

    Sub cmdFeedback_OnClick
    'This routine is called when the user clicks the feedback button.

        dim Correct

        Correct = 0

        ' Change all feedback labels to italic rather than bold
        lblFeedback1.fontbold = 0
        lblFeedback1.fontitalic = 1
        lblFeedback2.fontbold = 0
        lblFeedback2.fontitalic = 1
        lblFeedback3.fontbold = 0
        lblFeedback3.fontitalic = 1


        ' Assess Question 1
        if txtQuestion1.Value = "<OBJECT>" then
            ' Correct response
            Correct = Correct + 1
            lblFeedback1.angle = "10"
            lblFeedback1.fontsize = "24"
            lblFeedback1.caption = "Correct!"
            lblFeedback1.ForeColor = "65280"
        else
            ' Incorrect response
            lblFeedback1.angle = "350"
            lblFeedback1.caption = "The <OBJECT> tag"
            lblFeedback1.ForeColor = "255"
        end if

        ' Assess Question 2
        if txtQuestion2.Value = "<PARAM>" then
            ' Correct response
            Correct = Correct + 1
            lblFeedback2.angle = "10"
            lblFeedback2.fontsize = "24"
```

continues

Listing 10.10. continued

```
                    lblFeedback2.caption = "Correct!"
                    lblFeedback2.ForeColor = "65280"
            else
                ' Incorrect response
                    lblFeedback2.angle = "350"
                    lblFeedback2.caption = "The <PARAM> tag"
                    lblFeedback2.ForeColor = "255"
            end if

            ' Assess Question 3
            if txtQuestion3.Value = "ID" then
                ' Correct response
                Correct = Correct + 1
                    lblFeedback3.angle = "10"
                    lblFeedback3.fontsize = "24"
                    lblFeedback3.caption = "Correct!"
                    lblFeedback3.ForeColor = "65280"
            else
                ' Incorrect response
                    lblFeedback3.angle = "350"
                    lblFeedback3.caption = "The ID attribute"
                    lblFeedback3.ForeColor = "255"
            end if

            ' Show the results
            lblResults.caption = cstr(Correct) & " out of 3 correct!"

    end sub
-->
</SCRIPT>
```

Once a correct response occurs, the label angle, caption, font size, and ForeColor are all adjusted accordingly. Likewise, if an answer is incorrect, the angle, caption, and ForeColor are adjusted for incorrect response feedback. The lblResults label that is updated in the last line of the script illustrates a particularly useful technique. You can make a response appear to materialize for your user just when you want it to. The lblResults label does not initially appear to the user because the following parameter is used to declare the starting object caption:

```
<param name="caption" value="">
```

When you want a caption to appear, you simply assign one in your code, and presto! The user sees text where there was none before. This program makes use of many labels—four to be exact—to provide a dynamic page that updates with user feedback. In the old Web programming model, you probably would have provided such function with at least two separate Web pages, one of them custom-generated by a CGI script on the server. The simple addition of the label control and VBScript enable you to integrate all this feedback into one relatively simple page.

> **NOTE**
>
> A rather interesting behavior occurs with the label control if you don't include any parameter tag for the caption in your object declaration. When the label is drawn on screen, it will appear with the caption "Default!" You can still assign values to properties even if they are not declared with the parameter tag in an object declaration. You can change the caption at some point in your program if you start with this default caption. However, if you don't want to generate a caption until some interaction with your program occurs, you would prefer that your user see nothing for the label rather than the confusing "Default" on screen. Setting the parameter equal to the empty string, as defined previously, solves this problem.

10

Summary

Today's lesson provided an introduction to objects and ActiveX controls. An object is a component to be integrated into the page. An ActiveX control is one specific kind of object. A draft standard that details how an object should be defined within a Web page was outlined in detail. The <OBJECT> tag declares the object, along with standard attributes that define a generic object. In addition, the <PARAM> tag defines properties uniquely provided by the specific object that has been declared.

The ActiveX control technology evolved from the concepts of older Visual Basic VBX controls and the more recent OCX controls based on Microsoft's object linking and embedding (OLE) standards and technology. The ActiveX control encompasses OCX controls, which can be utilized in Web pages through VBScript.

The lesson then examines the ActiveX label control in detail, outlining the properties, methods, and events of the control. With the label control, you can fully control the appearance of a label placed on a Web page. This includes control of the color, the font, and even the angle of the text. The lesson provides several examples, including a program that allows experimentation with changing the various label properties and a tutorial that demonstrates the high degree of user feedback that the pages that integrate this control can provide.

Q&A

Q **Which object attribute provides a name for the object that your code will use to reference the object?**

A The ID attribute designates a name for the object.

Q **Are ActiveX controls available from sources other than Microsoft?**

A Yes, you can purchase ActiveX controls from other vendors or even write them yourself if you have adequate expertise and tools.

Q **Can a label be blank initially so the user doesn't see it until some later point in the script?**

A Yes, just supply an empty caption by providing two double quotes with nothing between them for the caption parameter declaration of the object. The tutorial program used this technique. Keep in mind that you must supply an empty string. If you omit the caption parameter all together, the word "default" is supplied as the starting caption.

Q **Does a label control have any useful events?**

A Yes, you can use the Click event to provide code that is executed when a label is clicked.

Workshop

Take a Web page that you have previously developed and add a label control somewhere within it. Experiment with various properties, such as different colors and angles. Add several input command buttons, and write code associated with each button to provide a different angle and color scheme for the label when you click it. Assess your previously developed Web pages and see if you can design one where a dynamically updated label would provide valuable feedback to the user, instead of just providing a jazzier look.

Quiz

NOTE

Refer to Appendix C, "Answers to Quiz Questions," for the answers to these questions.

10

1. Given the object declaration below, write code to change the caption of this object to "Kenny Jasper" whenever it is clicked:

```
<OBJECT
    classid="clsid:{99B42120-6EC7-11CF-A6C7-00AA00A47DD2}"
    id=lblTester
    width=125
    height=125
    align=left
    hspace=20
    vspace=0
>
<param name="angle" value="65" >
<param name="alignment" value="3" >
<param name="BackStyle" value="0" >
<param name="caption" value="Master the Label!">
<param name="FontName" value="Arial">
<param name="FontSize" value="17">
<param name="FontBold" value="1">
<param name="FontItalic" value="0">
<param name="FontUnderline" value="0">
<param name="FontStrikeout" value="0">
<param name="ForeColor" value="0">
</OBJECT>
```

2. Use the label control declared in the previous question for this question as well. Write an If statement that will change the caption of the label to Brooke only if the current angle of the label is between 20 and 40 degrees inclusive. If the caption change is not made, increase the angle by 10 degrees. (Don't worry about which subroutine the If statement should go in.)

10

Day 11

More ActiveX Controls

Yesterday you had the opportunity to get acquainted with perhaps the most simple of the ActiveX controls, the label control. You know what an ActiveX control is all about. Now it's time to expand your ActiveX control repertoire. The purpose of this lesson is to move you from the realm of a one-control developer to a jack-of-all-trades control expert. The best way to reach the point where you have the confidence and background knowledge to use any control is to see a variety of controls at work. This lesson will achieve that by introducing two more very important controls: the new item control and the timer control.

By learning about these controls, you will gain exposure to a wider variety of control properties and events representative of a broader range of controls. You will also see further examples of applying controls to specific solutions through the sample programs. Additional controls will be introduced after today throughout the rest of the book, but in the context of specific solution areas. By the time you have digested the nuts and bolts of today's controls, you will have enough general control background to easily apply similar control integration techniques to other controls you will later encounter.

The New Item Control

The new item control is one of the new generation of ActiveX controls that seems to have been introduced specifically to solve a common Web page problem. Often on Web pages, new material is highlighted with a graphic or a new indicator to let the user know that a certain piece of content was recently added. For example, if a computer book store lists its stock of books on a Web page, it might have a brightly colored "new" graphic after any book titles that were added to the list in the last week or so. Users visiting the page are more likely to take a look at the title if their attention is drawn to the fact that the item is a recent addition.

Suppose you have a page that documents the behavior of VBScript, and you add an additional hypertext link to some important notes. If you have a lot of information grouped on the page, even your frequent visitors might overlook a specific piece of new material unless you call their attention to the fact that it is a new piece of information. Similarly, consider the case of an ice cream shop advertising its flavors. Highlighting any new flavors from a lengthy list would not only ensure that users are aware of the new introductions—but it would probably also help those flavors to sell.

All these cases demonstrate a need to draw the users' attention to the new items. The typical way to do that is through a splashy new graphic that makes a piece of material stand out on the page as new content. Figure 11.1 shows the page for an ice cream store that uses such a graphic to point out a new flavor. When you view the page with this graphic, you have a clear impression in your mind afterward of what the new flavor is.

Figure 11.1.

A page that uses the new item control to highlight new information.

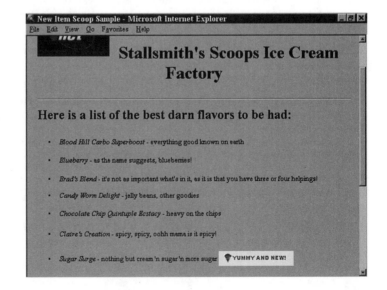

The use of such graphics is not hard to implement, even without controls. You simply add the graphic to your page. It does present some maintenance nightmares, however. You have to make sure that you change the page with the new item as soon as the item is no longer new. If you have a lot of pages, all with new items, you have a lot of maintenance to perform. You have a lot to track and a fair amount of pressure. What if things are busy and you don't have time to perform this low-priority maintenance, or what if your webmaster goes on vacation for a couple weeks? Then you are left with "stale" new items. Nothing turns users off faster than to see something flagged as new day after day. It leaves the same impression as the appliance store that has a big "going out of business sale of the century" sign in its window week after week. Eventually, you begin to tune out the sign and question the credibility of the sign poster.

Maintaining new item indicators is often a low-priority, tedious but important, high-visibility task. As with most such tasks, it is a natural choice for a more automated solution. The new item control provides such a solution. You can position it anywhere on a page just as you would an image, but most often you position it after new material on a page. When you add the new item's object declaration to a page, you associate an image file with it. The control will then display this image, which is typically a "new" graphic, on the page.

The real power of this control is that you can also associate a date with it. The image will only be displayed until the given date. After that, it will no longer show up on the page at all. You can have 100 new items on 100 different pages. Perhaps all of them should be deactivated on a given week, but the webmaster is off on a sabbatical to Katmandu when that week comes. Everyone else who could fill in is in the middle of meeting a busy deadline. Nobody has time to go back and remove the new indicator graphics from the pages. If you've used the new item control, it doesn't matter! The new item indicators stop appearing automatically on the designated date. As a matter of fact, you never have to remove the new item indicators from those pages if you don't want to. The new item controls have, in effect, activated a conditional display for you. They will never again display the graphic as long as the date of that condition is past.

Object Definition

The first step in using this feature in your page is to add the appropriate object declaration for it. The ice cream page new item shown in Figure 11.1 was actually generated by a new item control. Listing 11.1 shows the declaration for that control.

Listing 11.1. New item control declaration for a new flavor on the ice cream page.

```
<OBJECT
id=newCone4
classid="clsid:642B65C0-7374-11CF-A3A9-00A0C9034920"
width=0
height=0
align=middle
>
<PARAM NAME="date" value="5/22/1999">
<param name="image" value="yum.bmp">
</OBJECT><BR>
```

Attributes

Some pieces of this definition probably look quite familiar from yesterday. Each object control declaration supports the same attributes. That is one of the advantages of a well-defined object standard; once you've learned to handle one object, the same knowledge applies to integrating other objects as well. The ID attribute is the familiar identification label. The name you assign here will be what you use within your code if you reference this control. classid indicates the name or number that this class of control has within your system registry. This tells the browser its family of controls and therefore provides the path to its implementation. With ActiveX controls, the browser can determine the type from the classid information, so that information is not specified here.

The width and height attributes tell the browser how much space to make for the graphic on the page. Because the attributes are 0 here, the browser decides how much space to use based on the size of the graphic. As a matter of fact, as long as these attributes are less than the size of the graphic, and even if they are omitted from the attribute list altogether, the browser will use however much space it needs for the graphic. If the attributes specify an area larger than the size of the graphic, however, that much extra space is used on your page and will show up as a blank area. The align attribute is also the same one discussed yesterday and simply aligns the image with the middle of the preceding text area.

Properties

Now that I've addressed the object attributes, it is time to turn your attention to the properties of the control that are defined through the parameter tag. The properties are typically more relevant to the programmer because it is these elements that you can adjust from your program. The new item control has two such properties: image and date.

The image property provides the image to be displayed. This is defined in terms of a URL address of a location on the World Wide Web or a local filename for the file that contains the image. This image can have any of the standard graphics formats a normal image has. Although this image typically displays a "new" indicator graphic, this is not a requirement. The image can be anything you assign it—a bright logo that says "new," a graphic of a setting sun, or even a picture of your dog playing Frisbee. Regardless of the content, it is simply an image that will be displayed until the desired date is reached. If you don't specify any image or you designate an image file that is not present, the new item control will render its own default image for you. That image is a standard "new" indicator, as shown in Figure 11.2. You cannot access the image property within your script with the present new item control. You can only specify it within your object declaration, and then you cannot change or read it within your script program.

Figure 11.2.

A page that uses the new item control with the default "new" image.

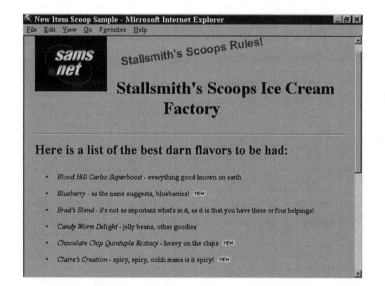

The date property specifies the "expiration" date; once this date is reached, the control ensures that the image is no longer displayed. This date must be specified in standard date format such as 10/1/96. Your script program can both read and write to this property.

Methods and Events

Many controls have methods and events that you can use. Other controls do not. The new item control falls into the second category. The control does its work without providing any major methods for you to call or generating events that you can respond to. The new item control does support one minor undocumented method, the AboutBox method. If you have a statement in your program that triggers the AboutBox, such as newControl.AboutBox, an About box displays and shows information about the control. This is typically used to provide control integration information but is not something you are likely to rely on heavily in your programs. An example of a typical About box is shown later today when I describe the next control.

Setting Properties for the New Item Control

Now you know a little about what the new item control can do. As a matter of fact, you might be thinking, "Where's the programming?" You bought a programming book, but here you are, reading about a control that doesn't seem to have much to do with programming. You plop it in your page, and it's ready to go. It might seem that there isn't much opportunity to write scripts that use this control. You saw just a couple properties, only one of which you can change. You can specify all the standard property values to control the display through an object declaration. Without any real methods or events for your program to interact with, this is basically a pretty simple control that you can integrate just with an object declaration.

Nevertheless, you can still interact with this control within your programs in a very dynamic fashion, as you will soon see. This is precisely why I highlight this control here—to illustrate that even though a control might not give you a lot to work with in terms of properties, methods, or events, you can still accomplish a great deal with it from VBScript. A newcomer to VBScript might read the new item control definition and determine that it's not really a programmable control. With a little thought and creativity, however, it can be.

Before looking at a sample solution that uses the new item control, first consider how its properties are modified. I provide a new item control property tweaker program for this purpose. Remember from yesterday that the term *tweak* is often used to mean experiment or slightly change. That is exactly what the new item tweaker control lets you do—experiment with the date property, the one and only property of this control that you can change. Figure 11.3 shows the new item property tweaker Web page. I'll explain the new item tweaker program by examining a series of key code blocks. You might want to skim over the structure of the entire Web page and its embedded script first to help you understand the overall context of the various code examples you will see.

NOTE

You can find the new item tweaker program on the CD-ROM with the name newtweak.htm.

Figure 11.3.

The new item property tweaker program.

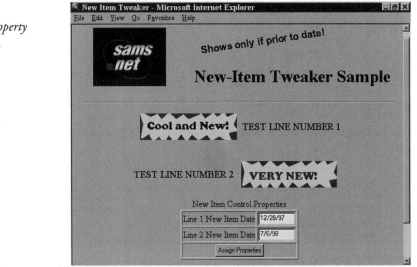

The new item tweaker uses two new item controls—one after each of the two large lines of text that appear at the top of the page. Notice that each new item control displays a different image, which illustrates that you can use any image with a new item control on the same page. Typically, you will use the same new indicator for every new item for consistency, but this is not required by the control.

At the bottom of the page is a property box that enables you to respecify the date property for each of these controls. When you click the Assign Properties button, the values you supply are immediately applied to the control. When you first load the program, the dates you see are those that have been assigned to the new item controls through their object declarations. These dates are retrieved and assigned to the date text boxes with code that reads the date property as the page is loaded. Listing 11.2 shows this code.

Listing 11.2. Reading the new item date property to display the initial date setting.

```
<SCRIPT LANGUAGE="VBSCRIPT">
<!--

    '    ----------------------------------------------------
    '    STARTUP Code: these statements are carried out on page load.
    '    Retrieve initial values from the new item controls
    '      to display them in the textbox at startup
         txtLine1.value = newSample1.date
         txtLine2.value = newSample2.date
```

continues

Listing 11.2. continued

```
¡    - - - - - - - - - - - - - - - - - - - - - - - - - - - - - - - - - - - - - - - - - - - - - - - - - - - - -

... more subroutines here

-->
</SCRIPT>
```

ANALYSIS   The date is accessed by simply referencing the date property of the new item controls and assigning that to the text box. In the sample code, the two new item controls are named newSample1 and newSample2, and the text boxes are named txtLine1 and txtLine2.

The object declarations for the new item controls precede the script in the HTML file and have the format shown in Listing 11.3.

Listing 11.3. Object declaration for new item control in the new item tweaker program.

```
<OBJECT
id=newSample1

classid="clsid:642B65C0-7374-11CF-A3A9-00A0C9034920"
width=200
height=100
hspace=10
vspace=5
align=middle
>
<PARAM NAME="date" value="12/28/1996">
<param name="image" value="cool.bmp">
</OBJECT>
```

ANALYSIS   You can see from the object declaration that the designated date for the newSample1 new item control is December 28, 1996. Until that time, the graphic cool.bmp will be displayed. Once that date is reached, the graphic will no longer be displayed. The starting page shown in Figure 11.3 demonstrates that this is working correctly. The cool.bmp graphic does indeed appear because the suppression date had not yet been reached at the time the program was run. The date retrieved from the newSample1 data property and displayed in the property box at the bottom of the page corresponds to the initial object date. The other new item control graphic also appears because the suppression date for that object is set to July 6, 1998.

Now it's time to experiment with changing the date. Assume that you provide new dates of April 10, 1996 and March 6, 1996 in the new property input text boxes. Then, click the Assign Property button to execute the new assignments. The new assignments are made to the new item control by assigning the new values to the date property of each control. Listing 11.4 shows the code.

Listing 11.4. Code to assign new date properties.

```
sub cmdAssign_OnClick
    ' update the New Item control properties when button clicked
        newSample1.date = txtLine1.value
        newSample2.date = txtLine2.value
    end sub
```

ANALYSIS The code is again quite straightforward. Text box control values are assigned to new item control date properties. As soon as this script completes, the controls immediately update and display the result on the current Web page. Figure 11.4 shows that result.

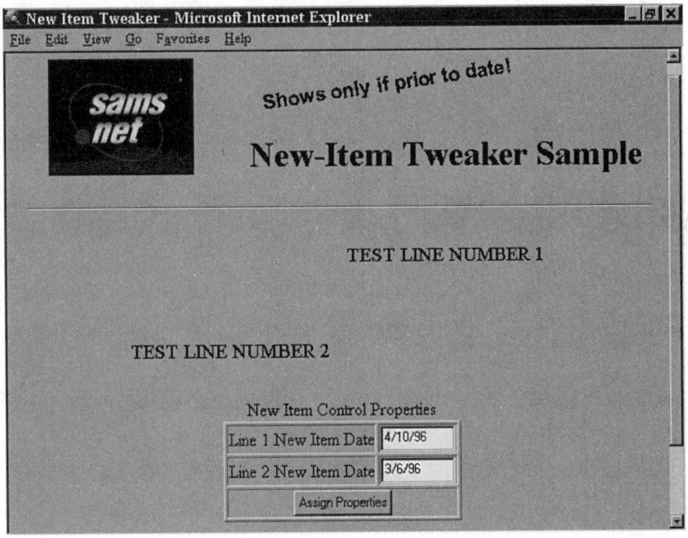

Figure 11.4.

The new item property tweaker program with dates changed to be prior to today.

As you can see, the graphics no longer appear. The control detects that the date to start suppressing the graphics has already been reached based on its current date property and therefore does not display the associated image.

The new item tweaker program demonstrates that a new item control does dynamically react to dates modified through VBScript. Next, you can use it to gain some insights into valid date formats. Another test that you can perform with the new item tweaker program is assigning a date in the year 2000. For example, specify 5/4/00 as a new property value. You might expect that the new item image would be displayed after you click Assign Properties because the suppression date is some time off. Surprise! The image does not appear as expected but is suppressed immediately (at least in the beta incarnation of VBScript). This demonstrates that the new item control, at least in its beta incarnation, does not support dates for the year 2000 and beyond. This is behavior you can likely expect future versions of the control to fix.

Now, try a test relating to the internal storage format of the control. Use the property modification area at the bottom of the page again to specify a date of April 10 1996. Notice that this date is in a different format from those specified before. Next, click the Apply Properties button. The date assignment takes place…or does it? What do you think is stored in the new item control's date property now?

There is a way to find out. If you click the label at the very top of the screen, which has the caption "Shows only if prior to date," the script executes code that displays the current date setting of the new item control in a message box. If you take this action to inspect the current date, you get the result shown in Figure 11.5.

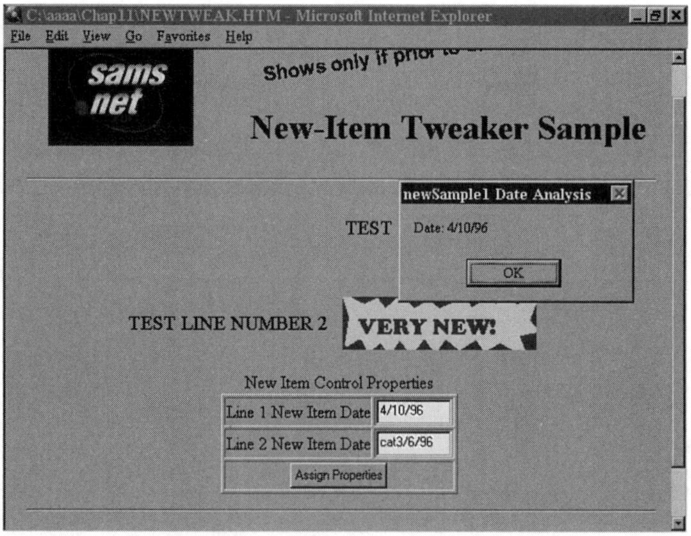

Figure 11.5.

Feedback from the new item property tweaker program when you enter a legal date of April 10 1996.

As you can see, the date supplied as April 10 1996 was treated as a legal date. It was converted and stored internally in the control as 4/10/96. Now, see what happens if you assign a date that is more clearly illegal, say cat3/6/96. Enter that into the lower property text box and click Assign Property. Once again, click the label at the top of the page to inspect the current value stored in the control. Will you see a valid date there? Figure 11.6 shows the result of the inspection.

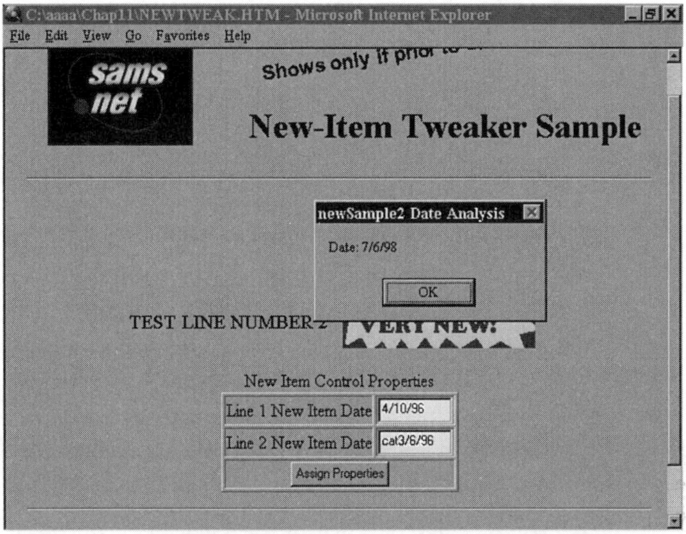

Figure 11.6.

*Feedback from the new
item property tweaker
program when you enter
an invalid date of*
`cat3/6/96.`

The result shows that a new date was not assigned, but the old date remains.

It is helpful to understand what happens after you assign a property to a control, as you have
seen from the previous examples. It is easy to make an inspection with a few lines of code that
evaluate the property when the label is clicked. Listing 11.5 shows the code executed for this
evaluation when you click the label.

Listing 11.5. Code to inspect a variable.

```
sub lblInfo_Click
' display date info when label clicked
    Msgbox AnalyzeDate(newSample1.date),0,"newSample1 Date Analysis"
    Msgbox AnalyzeDate(newSample2.date),0,"newSample2 Date Analysis"
end sub

function AnalyzeDate(CurDate)
'--- This subroutine is called to analyze the date format
    dim svDate, svTemp

    ' See if format is legal
    if isDate(CurDate) then
        svDate = "Date: " & CurDate
    else
        ' Illegal format, store detailed analysis
        svDate = "Date not in legal format."
        svDate = svDate & " Vartype is " & vartype(CurDate)
        svDate = svDate & ". Length= " & len(CurDate)
        if len(CurDate) > 20 then
```

continues

Listing 11.5. continued

```
            svDate = svDate & ".  Too long to display."
        else
            svDate = svDate & ".  Contents: " & CurDate
        end if
    end if

    ' Return value
    AnalyzeDate = svDate

end function
```

ANALYSIS This code calls a function, `AnalyzeDate`, that analyzes each control. That function makes a check to see if the new item control date property is a valid date. If it's not, the code performs more checks to see what type of data representation is stored in the control and to view its size if it's a string.

This analysis code shows that the beta new item control, at the time of this writing, stored everything correctly. Only valid dates could be stored. In very early alpha versions of this control, a large string of meaningless data would be stored when an invalid date format was provided to the control. This is no longer a problem, but the process of investigating it is pointed out to emphasize the kind of groundwork you often must do when integrating controls into your applications. You have to check them out and understand them first! If you want to inspect the behavior of later versions of this control or any other control to figure out how it is behaving and write your code accordingly, you have an easy means at your disposal. You can simply use the new item tweaker or a program like it to fully understand the behavior of the control. You will find over time that your own experimentation scripts are probably as informative to you in shaping your control approach as any manuals you might find or advice you might receive from others.

Looking at the new item control has highlighted another important point: Always keep in mind that it is very important to have a full understanding of any control you integrate. Oftentimes, the easiest and most comprehensive way to gain that understanding is to use test scripts such as the new item tweaker.

Dynamically Adjusting Program Feedback with the New Item Control

You've now had the rundown on the capabilities of the new item control and seen how to explore those capabilities with a test program. Now it's time to take a look at a more real-life application. Refer to today's first figure, Figure 11.1. This figure shows a page for a fictitious ice cream store that offers a variety of flavors of ice cream for sale. Its market niche is the wacky flavors it creates. Successful business for this ice cream store depends heavily on marketing these flavors. As a result, it is very important for this business to drum up interest in any new flavors it creates.

This is the purpose of the new item control you see in Figure 11.1. The webmaster for the ice cream store (who gets paid in consumables) has to ensure that every new flavor added to the page has a new item control after it so that the new flavor is initially highlighted. However, the ice cream store doesn't want to highlight the flavors too long. If it did, it would risk having its page visitors start to believe none of the information was that current and end up ignoring any new indicator. It sets the expiration date of the new item controls to expire after one week from the time of introduction. After that point, the new item image is automatically suppressed, and the flavors are no longer highlighted.

This bothers the webmaster, though. He knows that a lot of page visitors only stop in every few months. When they visit, one of their prime areas of concern is what flavors have been introduced since their last visit. The webmaster knows he could build a fancy CGI script with a database on the server to let visitors request update lists, but he doesn't even have access to a server. The ice cream parlor's pages are hosted on a gigantic mega-provider service that doesn't let its customers write any server-side control.

Fortunately, it occurs to the webmaster that he doesn't need a server! With some clever scripting, he can easily build a date-oriented search approach right around the very same new item control that is already being used. The approach consists of using the new item controls as an index of when the flavor was introduced. Then, if the user supplies the date when he last visited the page, the code can examine the new item date properties and determine which flavors should be flagged as new flavors for the user. For the flavors that should be highlighted, the script can simply reassign the image suppression date to be some point in the future. Then, the graphic will be displayed.

What does it take to make this happen? First of all, you must have a standard input text box at the bottom of the page. In addition, you need a button the user can click to indicate he wants a date search to take place. Then, you need some code to examine each flavor-associated new item control whenever the user specifies that the search should occur. Listing 11.6 shows that code.

Listing 11.6. Code that displays new item controls for all the flavors that have been added after the user's last visit.

```
<SCRIPT LANGUAGE="VBSCRIPT">
<!--

    dim datOrigCone1, datOrigCone2, datOrigCone3, datOrigCone4
```

continues

Listing 11.6. continued

```
'---   Startup code carried out when page loads --
' Store the original dates of New Item controls for each flavor.
'   These are used to restore to original settings later.
datOrigCone1 = newCone1.date
datOrigCone2 = newCone2.date
datOrigCone3 = newCone3.date
datOrigCone4 = newCone4.date
'-----------------------------------------------

sub cmd96_Onclick
' Highlight all new items if they are for a flavor that was
'    introduced after the user's last visit. We can determine when
'    a flavor was introduced by looking at the date of the New Items.


Dim datLastVisit, datFlavorIntro

 ' Make sure a date has been provided
 if len(txtLastVisit.Value) = 0 then
 msgbox "Please enter date of last visit!",0,"Missing Date"
    exit sub
 end if

 ' Use the date specified to see if flavors have changed since
 datLastVisit = txtLastVisit.Value

 ' Check to see if we should force item 1 to display by shifting date
 datFlavorIntro = newCone1.date
 if cdate(datLastVisit) < cdate(datOrigCone1) then
     ' They haven't seen this flavor, so extend the corresponding
     '   new items display range to encompass today
     newCone1.date = "12/31/99"
 else
     ' This flavor isn't new to user, use original flavor date
     newCone1.date = datOrigCone1
 end if

 ' Check to see if we should force item 2 to display by shifting date
 datFlavorIntro = newCone2.date
 if cdate(datLastVisit) < cdate(datOrigCone2) then
     ' They haven't seen this flavor, so extend the corresponding
     '   new items display range to encompass today
     newCone2.date = "12/31/99"
 else
     ' This flavor isn't new to user, use original flavor date
     newCone2.date = datOrigCone2
 end if

'... Similar checks take place for all other new items
```

NOTE

> The Web page containing this script is available on the CD-ROM that comes with this book in the file newscoop.htm.

ANALYSIS Notice that in Figure 11.1 only one flavor was highlighted as new. Suppose you go down to the last visit prompt, specify that you haven't visited the page since April 7, 1996, and then click the highlight button. Now you will see two flavors highlighted—all the flavors that are new for you. You can see this result in Figure 11.7.

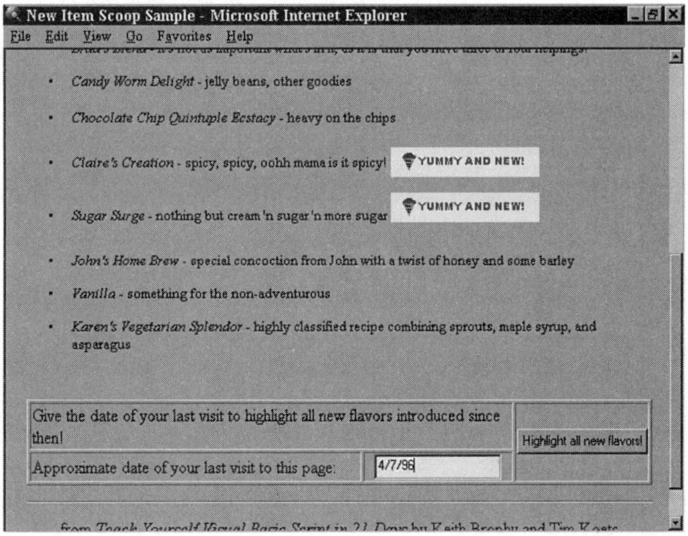

Figure 11.7.

The Scoops page when the user enters a last visit date of 4/7/96.

Assume your ice cream-swilling buddy comes over and notices you have the page up. She remembers she last visited the site around the spring of 1995, and she's very curious about what they have added since. You specify her last visit date and reselect the highlight button. Now, four flavors are highlighted on the page, as shown in Figure 11.8.

The ice cream Web page can do a lot for the user. Of course, it shows all the flavors available, which is easily accomplished through standard HTML. It also indicates which flavors are new as of today, which happens through the new item control simply by virtue of the object. No code is required yet. Then, it also lets the users perform a historical search and highlights all new flavors introduced after the date they specify. It does this without requiring any interaction with a server. All the search capabilities take place locally through VBScript and a creative use of the new item control property. This example shows that you can't always judge the power of a control by the size of a property and event list. The new item control doesn't give you much to work with, but when coupled with the power of VBScript, it can still present to the user a seemingly smart Web page.

Figure 11.8.

*The Scoops page when
the user enters a last visit
date of* 5/22/95.

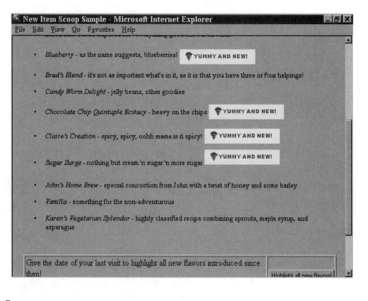

Timer Control

So far, you've seen controls that are visually oriented. The label control and the new item control both communicate visual information to the user. Our scripts can control to some extent this visual communication through the control properties. Ultimately, the power of those controls is in the picture they paint on the page. Now to round out your picture of the range of capabilities of ActiveX controls, it's time to consider a different type of control. This is the type of control that is not visually oriented. It never appears on the screen.

Pages are certainly a visual medium. What good is a control that you can never see? The power lies in the fact that your scripts can make use of a nonvisual control. Code can use a nonvisual control to help make decisions, display other elements, perform calculations, and so on. The specific control in this nonvisual category that I tackle next is the timer control. As its name implies, this control is used for timing purposes. However, the concept of interacting with a control the user can't see through your code will apply to many other controls as well. For now, I focus specifically on what the timer control can do for you.

You can assign the timer control some specified period of time and turn it on from code or from its initial object declaration. Once turned on, the timer starts a timed countdown, but the countdown is out of sight and out of mind as far as your script and Web page interaction are concerned. The timer is out there dutifully counting down, but you don't see any signs of it—that is, until the entire time period has elapsed and the countdown reaches zero. When that happens, a timer-related event occurs. If you have associated code with this event, the code is executed at that point. Once your code completes, the timer starts the countdown over again, if you didn't write code to explicitly turn it off.

You can picture the timer control as somewhat like a kitchen timer. Assume you ask your child to set the timer for 10 minutes and to call you when the timer buzzes. (Your child is playing the role of the timer control.) You settle down on the couch for a quick chance to study the patterns on the ceiling. Just as you're dozing off—er, rather, mastering the layout of the patterns—you are rudely shaken. A shout in your ear informs you that the timer went off. (The timer event has occurred.) At this point, you lean forward on the couch, look around to make sure the house isn't on fire, and then slump back down. (You have just performed actions in response to the timer event.) Your child has been through this many times before and knows just what to do. She troops back into the kitchen and sets the timer for another 10 minutes. The scene will be repeated over and over until one of two circumstances prevails. Either you finally get up and leave (and the program is terminated), or one time when the child wakes you at the regular 10-minute interval, you inform her that she doesn't need to set the timer again because you intend to be studying the ceiling patterns for some time to come. (You've just turned off the timer control.)

An analogy can only take you so far, and so it is with the timer control. An important consideration to keep in mind is that the user of the Web page never sees a timer control. It has no visual representation. It does have a code representation: an object declaration, an event procedure you can define, properties you can set, and methods you can invoke.

The timer control is not intended to be something the user sees; it is a building block for your scripts. There isn't only one reason to use a timer. You might have many different reasons to build a timer control into your script. Any action that should occur after a precisely specified interval is fair game for implementing with a timer and the code you can associate with a timer expiration. Perhaps you want a program to make a label on your Web page periodically change color and catch the user's attention. Maybe you want to refresh a Web page at regular intervals with a new advertising slogan. Maybe you're a Lamaze instructor and you want to write a program that guides couples through timed relaxation and breathing exercises. The possibilities are endless. All you need is a timer control, its object declaration, and some basic knowledge about its properties and main timer event.

Object Declaration

The object declaration for the timer control looks somewhat similar to the other types of controls covered so far. You can see a timer control object declaration in Listing 11.7.

Listing 11.7. The object declaration for a timer control.

```
<!------------- Timer object definition  ---------->
<OBJECT
classid="clsid:59CCB4A0-727D-11CF-AC36-00AA00A47DD2"
CODEBASE="http://www.microsoft.com/ie/download/activex/_
          ietimer.ocx#version=4,70,0,1086"
id=timer1
>
<param name="Interval" value="5000">
<param name="enabled" value="0">
</OBJECT>
```

ANALYSIS This declaration has only a couple differences from other object declarations. As with all controls, classid indicates the type of control it is and provides the browser's path to the implementation behind the control. The classid in the preceding code is therefore specific to the timer class of control. The ID serves the same purpose as in the other examples; it lets you define the name that you will use when you refer to the timer in your code. The timer does not have many of the attributes you've seen in other object declarations that relate to appearance. Because you won't see the timer on-screen, you don't have to specify those attributes. Some of the appearance attributes do have an effect if you choose to use them, oddly enough. The declaration in Listing 11.8 creates a large blank space on your page, reserved for the timer. The best approach for attributes is to use them only if you need them and go with a minimal declaration like that in Listing 11.7. The CODEBASE attribute was also used here to point to a master source for this control. This would allow the browser to automatically retrieve it if it was needed and not currently on the system. You can use CODEBASE with any control definitions. Base the decision on whether you want your pages to automatically trigger such downloads for your page user.

Listing 11.8. A timer declaration with width and height attributes, which makes blank space on the page.

```
<!------------- Timer object definition  ---------->
<OBJECT
classid="clsid:59CCB4A0-727D-11CF-AC36-00AA00A47DD2"

id=timer1
width=1000
height=1000
>
<param name="Interval" value="5000">
<param name="enabled" value="0">
</OBJECT>
```

Properties

The more interesting part of the timer control declaration is the properties declared through the parameter statements in Listing 11.7. The two main properties for the timer control are enabled and interval. enabled determines whether the timer is turned off or on. If enabled is set to -1, which represents a true value in VBScript, the timer is in an enabled state. In other words, the timer is turned on and it's counting down the given time period. When the specified time period has gone by, the timer event procedure will be called if one exists. If enabled is set to 0, on the other hand, the timer is turned off. In this disabled state, no timer countdown occurs, and the timer event procedure will not be called.

The interval property specifies how much time must elapse between turning on the timer and calling the associated event procedure, if any. The interval property is so named because it defines the interval between timer events. This value must be specified in terms of milliseconds. A second has 1000 milliseconds, so to set the timer for 5 seconds, you would set the interval property to 5000.

The greatest amount of time that you can set for the timer interval property is about 64K seconds, or 65534 milliseconds. If you need to time a duration that lasts longer than 65 seconds, you have to write code that uses the shorter timer expiration event repeatedly to gauge when some longer period of time has elapsed. If the interval value is set to 0 or less, it essentially disables the timer. No timer events will occur. Note that the interval property does not change as the timer counts down. The timer keeps track of its countdown progress internally, and the interval property itself always indicates the last interval that was requested.

Event

The timer event occurs whenever the timer is turned on and the specified timeout interval has expired. If you have defined a timer event procedure in your code, that event procedure is called when the timeout interval expires. The approach for defining control-related events was discussed in detail on Day 10, "An Introduction to Objects and ActiveX Controls." The key to remember is that you must couple the name of the control, as specified by the ID attribute, with the control's predefined event name. With the timer control, the predefined event name for an interval expiration is simply Timer. To define a timer event for a control named Timer1 then, you would supply a subroutine such as that shown in Listing 11.9.

Listing 11.9. A subroutine to handle the time event for a timer control named Timer1.

```
<SCRIPT LANGUAGE="VBSCRIPT">
<!--

    '--- Startup code carried out when page loads --
    ' Display the initial settings of the timer control
    txtEnabled.Value = timer1.enabled
    txtInterval.Value = timer1.interval
    '-----------------------------------------------

    sub timer1_timer
    '--- Timer event carried out whenever the timer goes off

        ' Show the message box if user requested it
        if txtMessageBox.value = 1 then
            MsgBox "The timer has expired!",0,"Message"
            txtMessageBox.value = 0
        end if

        ' Shift label up or down each time
        if lblEvent.angle = 0 then
            ' Move it up
            lblEvent.angle = lblEvent.angle + 5
            lblEvent2.angle = lblEvent2.angle - 5
        else
            lblEvent.angle = 0
            lblEvent2.angle = 0
        end if

        ' Move the old current event info to the prior info area
        lblEvent2.caption = lblEvent.caption

        ' Show the current time in the timer
        lblEvent.caption = "Timer went off at " & now

        ' Update the total number of events
        lblTotalEvents.caption = lblTotalEvents.caption + 1

    end sub
```

ANALYSIS The timer's time event is the code in subroutine Timer1_Time. It is important to be clear on one point in particular when you use timer events. When a timer event occurs, your event code gets executed. If you do not turn off the timer by changing its Enabled property, it will immediately start another countdown, using the same TimeOut interval that was previously specified. In this manner, the timer will keep running and triggering the event procedure indefinitely until the browser is no longer loaded with that page or until some area of code sets the Enabled property to 0.

You are not required to have a timer event procedure. Of course, it does you little good to use a timer if you do not have an event procedure to go with it. You can't perform useful work with a timer unless you have a means to know when the timer has expired. The only way to tell is to supply code in the event procedure.

You can have more than one timer. Each timer typically has its own event procedure. The Enabled and Interval properties can be different on each timer. Multiple timers on one page are usually completely independent. Assume you want to have one label that changes colors every second and another label that switches its angle every fifth of a second. You could implement this with one timer by having the timer interval occur every 200 milliseconds and writing code that handles both cases. Of course, label color should only change once every second, so you'd have to include code to make sure that happens only on every fifth event. However, it is often easier to use two separate controls in such a case. One control can trigger an event every 200 milliseconds to move the first label, and the other control can trigger an event every second to update the color of the second label. This makes for much cleaner code.

You should keep in mind some special code considerations with a timer that are not as relevant to other controls. Once you load a page with a timer and enable it, what happens if you switch to another page, or for that matter, another program? Suppose a timer event occurs every second, and each time it occurs, a counter variable is incremented. If you switch to a previous page in the browser or a different program such as a word processor, the timer event will continue to be triggered under Windows 95. When you come back to your timer page after leaving it for 12 seconds, the timer would have been incremented 12 times. This behavior might vary based on the operating system and environment because it has to do both with an operating system's multitasking capabilities and the browser and VBScript run-time implementation.

Methods

The timer control has only one method—the AboutBox method. You call this method from your code by referencing the control name, a period, and the method within a code statement:

```
Timer1.AboutBox
```

When this statement is executed, a box with information about the timer control is displayed. This is probably not an activity that the user of your Web page will need on a frequent basis. However, the need to support such a method is significant in the World Wide Web model because users will start to use more and more controls that come along for the ride with the Web pages they pull up. People will begin to pay more attention to where a control comes from and what it is. The AboutBox method lets you determine this information and provides an easy way for you to give the user access to this information. An example of the AboutBox for the timer control will appear in the sample program that follows.

Setting Properties for the Timer Control

The first step to using the timer control is having a firm understanding of its properties. I provide a handy timer tweaker program for this purpose. It will enable you to execute a series of property modifications on the timer so that you can observe the effects. In addition, this script will log all timer events that occur by displaying them right on the page. This makes it easy for you to see how properties and the time event relate. Figure 11.9 shows a picture of the timer tweaker page. At this point, the page has just loaded, and no timer events have occurred yet.

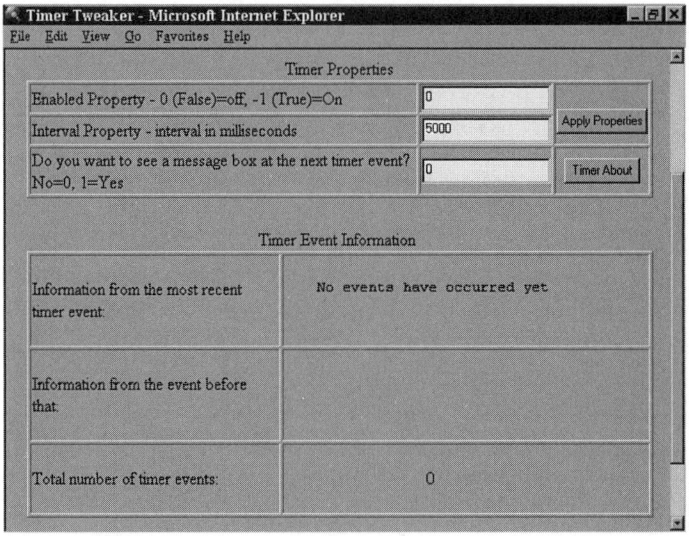

Figure 11.9.

The timer tweaker program before any events have occurred.

Timer Tweaker - Microsoft Internet Explorer

| File | Edit | View | Go | Favorites | Help |

Timer Properties

Enabled Property - 0 (False)=off, -1 (True)=On	0	
Interval Property - interval in milliseconds	5000	Apply Properties
Do you want to see a message box at the next timer event? No=0, 1=Yes	0	Timer About

Timer Event Information

Information from the most recent timer event:	No events have occurred yet
Information from the event before that:	
Total number of timer events:	0

As you can see from Figure 11.9, the timer is not turned on in its initial state, and the interval of time to use once it is activated is 5 seconds. Both of these settings were determined by the attribute values provided in the timer object declaration. This declaration was shown previously in Listing 11.7. The initial values that are displayed when the page loads are retrieved from the timer's `Enabled` and `interval` properties. You can see the code that extracts these properties and displays them on-screen in the first several lines of Listing 11.9.

NOTE

The timer tweaker program described here is available in the file `timetwk.htm` on the CD-ROM.

11

You can start the timer tweaker timer by changing the Enabled Property text box to -1 and clicking Apply Properties. If you watch the event log area of the page, you will see that the label begins to update with news of events. Every 5 seconds, the event occurs and the label is updated. Old event information is shifted to the secondary label. In addition, the labels' angles are shifted so that the user has a clear visual sign that timer event activity is occurring.

Refer to Listing 11.9 to see the code that performs these updates. The code associated with the procedure timer1_timer will be executed every time 5 seconds goes by. Because the timer1_timer subroutine has no code that turns off the timer, it immediately restarts the countdown and keeps repeating this periodic event trigger. Figure 11.10 shows the program after nine events have occurred. If you carefully examine the information that is displayed in the event information labels in this figure, you can see that the timed events are occurring every 5 seconds as expected.

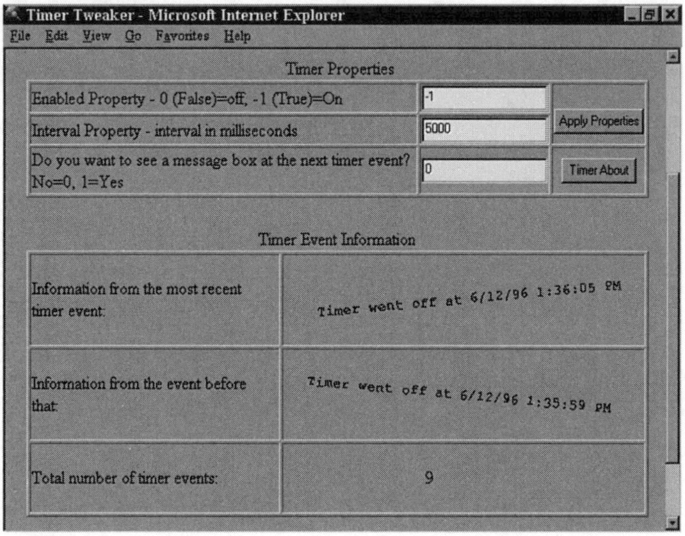

Figure 11.10.

The timer tweaker program after nine events have occurred.

To stop the timer from triggering the timer event procedure, you can simply supply a 0 to the Enabled text box. When you click the Apply Properties command button, the Enabled property of the timer is updated accordingly, and the countdown will come to a halt. Listing 11.10 shows the code that is executed after you click the Apply Properties command button.

Listing 11.10. A subroutine that assigns the properties of the timer.

```
sub cmdApply_OnClick
    Timer1.Enabled = txtEnabled.value
    Timer1.Interval = txtInterval.value
end sub
```

 ANALYSIS Now assume that the timer tweaker program is modified by the user again. He sets `Enabled` to `1` and `interval` to an interval of **2000**. Then, he clicks the Apply Properties button. At this point, the timer will trigger the event procedure at 2-second intervals. Figure 11.11 shows the display on the page after this interaction. The label readouts show that the period between events now is 2 seconds.

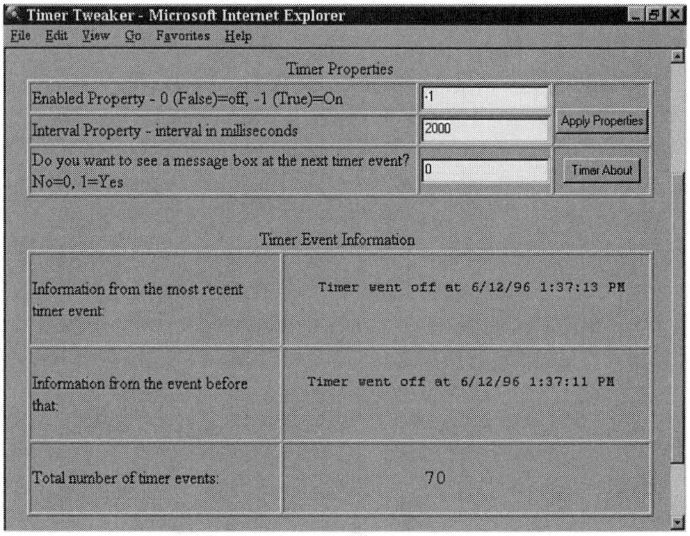

Figure 11.11.

The timer tweaker program with the interval *set to 2 seconds.*

Timer Tweaker - Microsoft Internet Explorer
File Edit View Go Favorites Help

Timer Properties

Enabled Property - 0 (False)=off, -1 (True)=On	-1	
Interval Property - interval in milliseconds	2000	Apply Properties
Do you want to see a message box at the next timer event? No=0, 1=Yes	0	Timer About

Timer Event Information

Information from the most recent timer event:	Timer went off at 6/12/96 1:37:13 PM
Information from the event before that:	Timer went off at 6/12/96 1:37:11 PM
Total number of timer events:	70

NOTE It is possible under some operating system circumstances to have timer events occur at some period slightly off the interval you specified. The timer interval is quite reliable on a multitasking system such as Windows 95 but can be affected by severe performance demands if a significant amount of other activity is occurring on the system. Likewise, the precision can vary between operating systems. Generally speaking, the timer is reliable for non-timing-critical purposes. If you were writing what's known as a real-time program where guaranteed response at the millisecond level is critical, such as a program that controls a low-level device, then the timing reliability might be less than ideal. You probably wouldn't be writing such software using VBScript because it's not a language targeted for that kind of work.

The timer tweaker program has another option available. You can specify that you want to see a message box when the next event occurs. If you set this option on, the timer's time event generates a message box. Listing 11.9 shows the code for this action under the comment Show the message box. You can see an example of the message box that is generated in Figure 11.12. The most interesting use of this in testing the timer event is demonstrating how the timer continues even after you move to other Web pages. Turn on the message box generation through the page, and then move back to another page. Note that the message boxes continue to be generated even when the timer tweaker page is not the current page. The timer still counts down, and the event procedure is still triggered when appropriate.

Figure 11.12.

The timer tweaker program with the message box generated on each event.

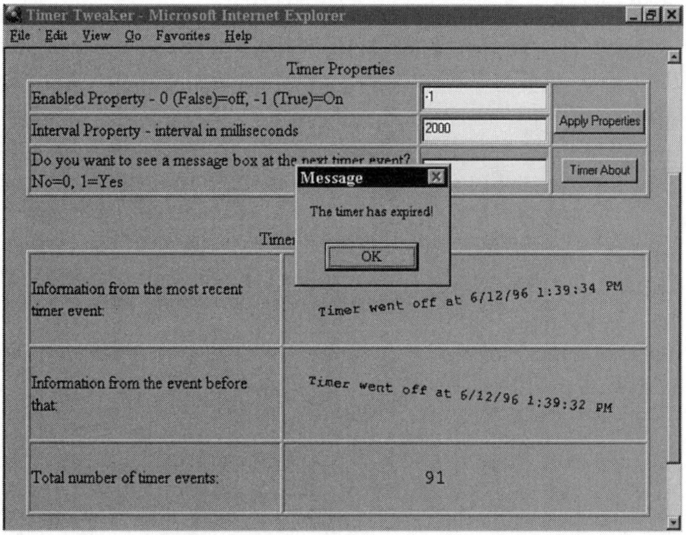

You can also use the timer tweaker program to observe what happens when you assign an invalid value to the interval property. First, set the interval property to 5000 milliseconds if it's not already there. Then use the property assignment area to try to assign an invalid property value of "goofy" to the interval property and click the button to perform the assignment. Inspect the current property value after this bad assignment is attempted by clicking the Timer About button. That button displays, in addition to the About box, a message box that shows the timer's current property state. You can see the code in Listing 11.11.

Listing 11.11. Code to show the current timer property state, as well as the About box.

```
sub cmdAbout_OnClick
        msgbox "Current Enabled property is " & Timer1.Enabled & _
            " and Interval property is " & Timer1.Interval, 0, _
            "Property Inspection"

        ' Display the timer's About info
        Timer1.AboutBox
    end sub
```

ANALYSIS   You will see that the interval value is still 5000 milliseconds. The timer control is smart enough to ignore bad data and still retain its prior valid setting. I mentioned earlier that the maximum value the interval property can take is 65534 milliseconds. Try to set it to 70000 milliseconds and inspect the value again. You will see it once again remains at 5000 milliseconds. If you try to assign a value that is larger than the maximum, the timer control doesn't set itself to the legal maximum. Instead, it remains set at the original value. Finally, set the value to 65534 milliseconds. Inspect the value to see if it was retained. You will see, as shown in Figure 11.13, that you have succeeded in setting the timer for 65 seconds.

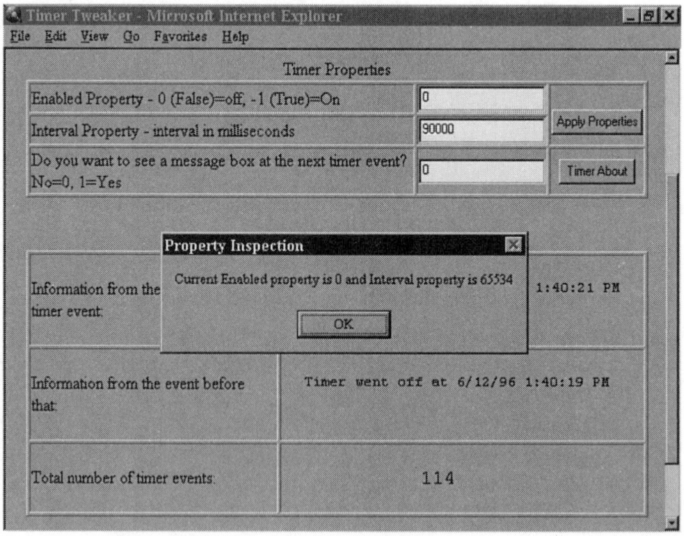

Figure 11.13.

The timer tweaker program showing maximum interval *setting of* 65534.

The code that is executed when you click the Timer About button has one other aspect that bears consideration—the use of the AboutBox method itself. The last line of code in Listing 11.11 calls the AboutBox method for the timer control. This simply causes the control itself to display a message box with information about its name and version number. You can see this About box in Figure 11.14. The version number information can come in handy if you run into problems, both for you and the user who uses your Web page. Where it is practical, it is a good idea to make this information available; perhaps you can associate it with a label click for a label discretely placed at the bottom of the page that reads "Version information for controls used with this page."

Figure 11.14.

The timer tweaker program About option.

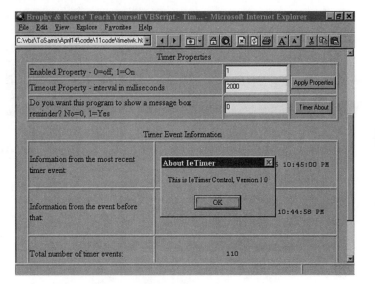

Providing Dynamic Feedback in Your Web Page with the Timer Control

Now that you've mastered the timer properties, it's time to see an example of how you can provide to your user interactive programs based on the timer. The Heart Timer program shown in Figure 11.15 provides this type of feedback.

The Web page directs the user to measure his pulse for 60 seconds and provides a timer to make this as easy as possible. The program lets the user initiate the start of a timer. Listing 11.12 shows the code that starts the timer.

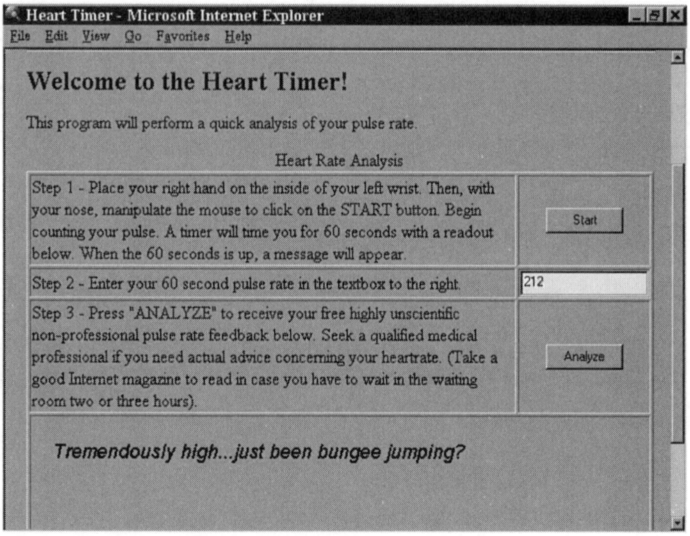

Figure 11.15.

*The Heart Timer
program after dynamic
timer feedback.*

Heart Timer - Microsoft Internet Explorer

File   Edit   View   Go   Favorites   Help

Welcome to the Heart Timer!

This program will perform a quick analysis of your pulse rate.

Heart Rate Analysis

Step 1 - Place your right hand on the inside of your left wrist. Then, with your nose, manipulate the mouse to click on the START button. Begin counting your pulse. A timer will time you for 60 seconds with a readout below. When the 60 seconds is up, a message will appear. | Start |

Step 2 - Enter your 60 second pulse rate in the textbox to the right. | 212 |

Step 3 - Press "ANALYZE" to receive your free highly unscientific non-professional pulse rate feedback below. Seek a qualified medical professional if you need actual advice concerning your heartrate. (Take a good Internet magazine to read in case you have to wait in the waiting room two or three hours). | Analyze |

Tremendously high...just been bungee jumping?

Listing 11.12. Starting the timer at the user's direction.

```
sub cmdStart_OnClick
      ' Set the label to the starting state to count the seconds
      lblFeedback.fontsize = 20
      lblFeedback.forecolor = &HFF
      lblFeedback.caption = 0
      ' Start the timer
      Timer1.Enabled = 1
   end sub
```

ANALYSIS   Once the timer starts, it's very important to provide dynamic feedback to the user. Not too many users will be content to stare at a Web page for some timed period if they have no visual feedback that the timing is underway. The timer's time event provides an easy way to give that feedback. The program needs to measure a period of 60 seconds, but a goal is also to provide progress feedback to the user every second during that 60 seconds. The original `timeout` interval of the timer was set to 1000 milliseconds rather than 60000 milliseconds in the object declaration.

At the end of each second, the timer time event is called, and a counter is incremented to keep track of how many seconds have elapsed. Each time the event is called, the current number of seconds is displayed at the bottom of the page in the feedback area in a large colored font. The user sees a steadily advancing counter every second as he continues to take his pulse. He knows exactly how much time remains. When 60 seconds are up, the program informs the user that his pulse measurement is complete and turns off the timer. Listing 11.13 shows the code that accomplishes this.

Listing 11.13. The time event that displays continuously updating user feedback.

```
sub timer1_timer
    '--- Timer event carried out whenever the timer goes off
    ' Keep track of how many seconds have gone by
    lblFeedback.caption = lblFeedback.caption + 1

    ' if 60 seconds have elapsed the user should have a pulse
    '     count, so stop timer
    if lblFeedback.caption = 60 then
        Timer1.Enabled = 0
        msgbox "60 seconds have gone by. Please enter the total "_
        " number of heartbeats counted!",0,_
        "Time up for counting 60 second resting pulse!"
    end if

end sub
```

ANALYSIS Once the timing is complete, the user can enter the number of pulses he counted and click the Analyze button to see what that means. Note that the output from the Analyze button appears in the same label as the second-by-second feedback. Usually, the timer will be complete before the final feedback appears there. If not, the timer data would wipe out the final feedback data because the timer data is written every second. As a result, you must take one more safeguard in this kind of program. Because the user might get impatient and click Analyze even as the timer count is progressing, the code for the Analyze button immediately turns off the timer as a precaution. This ensures that the final feedback, if requested before the 60 seconds is completed, will not be overwritten. Listing 11.14 shows the code that accomplishes this.

Listing 11.14. Disabling the timer before presenting final feedback.

```
sub cmdPulse_OnClick

    ' Ensure that timer is turned off
    Timer1.Enabled = 0

    ' Set label font back to normal size and color for feedback
    lblFeedback.fontsize = 20
    lblFeedback.forecolor = &H00


    ' Provide feedback based on heartrate
    if IsNumeric(txtPulse.Value) = 0 then
        lblFeedback.Caption = "You have no heart!"
    elseif txtPulse.Value < 40 then
```

continues

Listing 11.14. continued

```
            lblFeedback.Caption = _
                "Very slow heartbeat. You need to get out more!"
        elseif txtPulse.Value < 60 then
            lblFeedback.Caption =  "Good heartbeat - Healthy as a horse!"
        elseif txtPulse.Value < 90 then
            lblFeedback.Caption =  "Average heartbeat, nothing to fret about"
        elseif txtPulse.Value < 110 then
            lblFeedback.Caption =  "Somewhat on the high side...been exercising?"
        elseif txtpulse.Value < 140 then
            lblFeedback.Caption =  "Quite high, may want to seek medical advice"
        elseif txtpulse.Value < 180 then
            lblFeedback.Caption = _
                "Very high resting pulse...better get it down!"
        else ' Over 179
            lblFeedback.Caption = "Tremendously high...just been bungee jumping?"
        end if

    end sub
```

As you can see, with a little attention to detail, you can easily build code around the timer control to give your Web pages a high degree of timed interaction and feedback.

Other ActiveX Controls

There are many ActiveX controls available today. Vendors across the world have custom ActiveX controls on the market that you can purchase. Microsoft shares its standard ActiveX controls for free. So far this book has considered only some of the Microsoft ActiveX controls. Availability of types of controls may increase in the future. Even today there are plenty of free Microsoft controls to choose from in building your solutions. One of the ones that hasn't been discussed yet is the Microsoft gradient control. This control lets you blend a range of colors for striking visual effects. Another Microsoft control is the stock ticker control. This can display a continuous ticker tape–type summary of data from a file or other URL resource in the expected format. If the data resource is continually refreshed, the stock ticker tape control will display a constantly updating stream of data. Even if the data file does not change, the stock ticker tape will display a continuous scrolling of the same data. The image control is one that is very likely to be a part of most VBScript Web page solutions. It offers the image presentation capabilities of the <IMAGE> tag and more. With it you can hide an image control, for example. There are many more controls, properties, and methods than can be documented here.

Keep in mind that you can integrate any control with VBScript. The first step in getting familiar with a control should be to refer to its documentation. Review all the properties, methods, and events for a control. For the Microsoft standard controls, this information is on the Microsoft Web site at www.microsoft.com/intdev under the active control topic. When you encounter a new control that you are considering integrating with your VBScript code, pay particular attention to the events it supports. These can help highlight the ways you can use the control as part of your Web page solution. A sample page, MoreCtl.htm, is included on the CD-ROM to illustrate some of the additional Microsoft ActiveX controls. It's a good place to start looking when you're thinking about expanding your control repertoire.

Summary

Today's lesson builds on the information in Day 10 to provide more details on how to effectively deploy ActiveX controls in your VBScript Web pages. The focus is on two specific controls, but the intent is largely to show the overall control integration approach you can use with VBScript. The two controls used to illustrate this approach are the new item control and the timer control.

The new item control displays a preset graphic image on the screen until the specified suppression date is reached. When that day arrives, the graphic no longer appears on the page. Today you have learned about the advantages of learning about a control and integrating it through a property experimentation program. You have produced a rather sophisticated dynamic inventory feedback program around the very simple new item control. This illustrates that even a simple control can be put to very powerful uses if it's applied creatively.

The timer control is a control that has no visual representation on-screen. Like other similar controls, it is provided as a construct that you can build scripts around, rather than as a visual component the Web page user will see. The timer event makes it possible to execute a block of code at specified intervals. Through code, you can control the length of the intervals and whether it responds repeatedly or only once. An example shows how the timer control can provide dynamic feedback to users during timed events.

Today's lesson is important for two reasons. The specific controls it covers are very useful. You might find yourself incorporating them into a lot of your Web page scripts now that you are well versed in their capabilities. Additionally, you now have a very well-grounded exposure to controls in general. You know what it means to use a control; you can declare it, experiment with it to understand its capabilities, and integrate it into your code. The heart of VBScript is really its capability to merge powerful components into a page. You now have unlocked the door to this capability and can proceed through the days to come with this key firmly in hand.

Q&A

Q Are you limited to one new item control or timer control on a page?

A No, as today's examples demonstrate, you can have multiple instances of these controls. Just declare each with its own object declaration.

Q Is there a click event for the timer control?

A No, there is only a time event for the timer control, which is called when the timer is turned on and the set interval expires.

Q Do I have to use a standard graphic with the new item control to indicate new Web page content? Can I change this through code?

A No. You should keep an eye to the approach commonly used on the Web, which is the new indicator in blazed yellow. However, you can use any indicator you choose. The new item control lets you provide your own graphic. In some cases, it enhances your Web pages to use a more customized graphic, such as in the ice cream store example with its ice-cream-cone-based new logo. You cannot change the graphic through code as your script runs. You must set it ahead of time in the object declaration.

Workshop

Today you saw a Web page that provided timer-based feedback while a user took his pulse. Can you think of other Web pages that might benefit by incorporating a timer as part of the page? You could present a series of test preparation pages that provide sample questions with recommended times for completion and then provide the answers. Try to implement a few pages with such an approach. Note that you can implement the time limit, provide the time limit notification, and even check the answer on a page and give feedback by using local client code. No server code is required.

Quiz

NOTE

Refer to Appendix C, "Answers to Quiz Questions," for the answers to these questions.

1. Write an event procedure for a timer named MyTimer. Assume that this timer has an initial timeout interval of 2 seconds. Make this procedure shorten the timer interval to 1 second the first time it is called, one-half second the second time it is called, and finally turn off the timer the third time it is called. You could use several possible solutions for this.

2. Assume you have a new item control named MyItem, and it is currently displaying the new item graphic. You want to force this graphic to not be displayed in your code. Show the one code statement you can use to do this. There are many right answers, but the concept is the same in all of them.

11

Day 12

Advanced Objects: ActiveX, Java, and ActiveVRML

Now you've seen a broad spectrum of ActiveX controls. You have learned the fundamentals, and you've seen the overall approach to integrating these controls. It is time to apply the base of knowledge you've gained so far to some advanced concepts. Today's lesson takes a look at integrating some more advanced objects, including objects other than just ActiveX controls. Strategies for designing effective ActiveX documents around these objects are considered as well.

The first control discussed is the chart control for generating graphs. This is another ActiveX control from Microsoft, but it makes use of some types of features that you haven't encountered yet with the other controls. For example, you can associate much larger quantities of data with this object than the other controls because you must provide the data to be graphed to it. The control also offers many more properties than those considered so far. You can assign a variety of properties to make the data representation take on many different forms. This control makes it easy to graph data from your scripts right before your users' eyes.

Next, the discussion turns to integrating non-ActiveX controls. I discuss issues pertaining to integrating Java applets. Java, a widely used programming language that originated from Sun Microsystems, Inc., is largely targeted for World Wide Web–related applications. A wide variety of Java applets or mini-applications suitable for embedding in a Web page are available, and the number is sure to grow steadily higher. Incorporating such objects can enable you to greatly extend the power of your Web pages, just as incorporating ActiveX controls does. Fortunately, you can incorporate Java applets in much the same manner that you incorporate ActiveX controls. This approach is discussed in some detail so that you know your options when considering such an integration.

The third area addressed today is ActiveVRML objects. VRML, Virtual Reality Modeling Language, pertains to the support of animations, three-dimensional images, and related technologies. With VRML, for example, you can present the user with a three-dimensional ski slope to navigate right on-screen. ActiveVRML is a VRML standard put forth by Microsoft. An ActiveVRML viewer control is available from Microsoft so that you can view VRML within a page. As you probably expect from its mention here, the good news is that you can manipulate this control from VBScript. As a result, you have control over ActiveVRML from your code. I explore the related approaches for integrating this technology.

Finally, today's lesson will present an overview of control download technologies and issues. By the end of today, your scripting horizons will have broadened considerably. You will understand advanced issues of VBScript object integration. The strength of VBScript as an ultimate Web page glue tool for incorporating the power of all types of objects into your page will be clearly in focus.

Working with Objects

Before you consider more advanced concepts, there are just a few more object fundamentals to get straight. Object definitions can encompass several different types of entities that are not, strictly speaking, part of the Visual Basic syntax, but that can be controlled by VBScript code with appropriate references. One example of such entities is the intrinsic form controls and forms themselves. Another example is ActiveX controls and Java applets that can be included in the HTML source through the use of the object tag. In addition, many more objects—such as the intrinsic input controls—are automatically provided by the host browser environment and can be accessed. These include objects such as the page's document, location, and window objects. These are discussed in further detail on Day 18, "Advanced User Interface and Browser Object Techniques."

It is important to realize that these objects are not a part of the VBScript definition. Rather, they are part of the host environment (such as Internet Explorer) that incorporates Visual Basic. Or they are separate controls such as ActiveX objects that the host environment lets you incorporate. Objects provide a set of characteristics you can control; they are called properties. They also provide calls that result in a specific action; they are called methods. And objects can make it possible for code to be associated with certain conditions that are triggered by an object such as a mouse click. So an object in the general VBScript sense is an entity that can be controlled through properties and methods and reacted to through events. You deal only with the well-defined interface and do not have visibility into the code of the object itself.

VBScript itself only has one object that is inherent in the VBScript engine, or the core language definition of VBScript. That is the `err` object, which is discussed on Day 17, "Exterminating Bugs from Your Script."

NOTE

The term *object* is used in several slightly different contexts. HTML has an object tag that is used to explicitly define certain types of objects. On the other hand, many more entities that can be thought of as objects are automatically exposed by the Internet Explorer environment. In the discussion that follows, it is important to realize that an object is any such entity you incorporate into your pages, including those automatically exposed. The object-handling techniques are not limited to just controls defined through the HTML object tag.

You should also keep in mind that objects are specific to the environment that VBScript is hosted in. The core language of VBScript will be the same from environment to environment. However, the objects exposed by the host environment (such as the intrinsic controls or document object of a Web page) might not be the same in every environment that hosts VBScript. You can probably expect a fairly high degree of conformance of available objects between different browsers. Microsoft Internet Explorer's set of objects exposed to scripts (called the Script Object Model) is very similar to the set that Netscape exposes to JavaScript. Other browsers that incorporate VBScript would likely model their approach on many of the same objects.

12

A much bigger difference in available objects will be evident in non-browser environments that host VBScript as a script language. Suppose you use a file-management application that hosts VBScript as its scripting language. Many of the exposed objects that you are accustomed to using in VBScript code for the browser might not be available to VBScript code in the file-management application environment. For instance, the browser provides a window object with a navigate method you can use to advance to new pages. This probably wouldn't make sense in the context of a file-management application and wouldn't be provided as an object for scripts to use there. Although VBScript keywords and language usage would remain constant between the browser and file-management application, the objects that VBScript can use will differ between environments.

So what does all this mean to your code? There are some rules for dealing with objects in VBScript. VBScript needs an indicator that the data it is dealing with should be handled as an object. You provide this indicator through the set statement. The following is a set statement that assigns an intrinsic text box control to a variable:

```
Set myVar = txtcontrol
```

This assigns the object to the variable. You can check to see if a variable currently contains an object with an IsObject keyword, as discussed on Day 4, "Creating Variables in VBScript." For example, to see if myVar does indeed contain an object, you could use this check:

```
If ISObject(myVar)then
```

You can also check to see if two object references pertain to the same object. However, the = statement cannot be used for the comparison as you might expect. Once again, rules apply to guide VBScript in dealing with this special data type. The way to compare two object references is with the IS keyword, as discussed on Day 5, "Putting Operators to Work in VBScript." For example, if you need to see if myVar is currently referencing a command button called CMDSubmit, you can use this check:

```
If myVaris CMDSubmit then
```

This expression will evaluate to True if both of the references are to the same object entity.

Since an object is treated as just another data type that the variant variable can store, there is much you can do in code with objects. For example, you could define a procedure that checks to see if a certain string is supplied in a text box. The procedure could have a parameter for the text box control to be evaluated:

```
Function CheckTextControl(txtCurrentTextbox)
```

This subroutine could then be called with many different text box controls as parameters. For example, you could make this call to check the txtName text box that contains a user's name:

```
RC = CheckTextControl(txtName)
```

And you could make this call to have the same check carried out on the txtCompany text box control that contains a company name:

```
RC = CheckTextControl(txtCompany)
```

An object, then, is really just another data type that can be handled by variant variables. You will find that your code becomes much more powerful if you take advantage of this fact. VBScript provides all the necessary capabilities to handle objects. Then the host environment, such as a browser or the components that you tell the host environment to integrate (such as ActiveX controls), provides the object entities that VBScript can work with. The specific objects exposed by the Internet Explorer host environment will be addressed in much more detail on Day 18. The rest of today will be devoted to incorporating ActiveX control objects.

The ActiveX Chart Control

The chart control can really pack a punch when it comes to making an impressive, dynamic Web page. It is quite interesting from a VBScript programming standpoint because it enables you to supply rather extensive amounts of data dynamically through your script. The chart control can produce a variety of graphs in response to its property settings. It graphs data that you can initially supply through property values. Then, after the initial load, the graph can be regenerated in response to data changes through the script.

The first step to mastering this control is to understand the range of properties it provides. There are many properties for the control. Some of the main ones are summarized in Table 12.1. You can refer to Microsoft's Web site or use one of the control insertion/inspection tools described on Day 10, "An Introduction to Objects and ActiveX Controls," to see the full list of properties.

12

Table 12.1. Chart control properties.

Property	Description
ChartType	Specifies the chart type such as pie or bar chart.
ColorScheme	Region fill color set to use, ranges from 0 to 2.
Columns	The number of data series columns.
ColumnIndex	Indicates the current column index pertaining to the DataItem property.
DataItem	Indicates one specific data value, indexed by current RowIndex and ColumnIndex settings.
HorizontalGrid	Shows horizontal grids.
Rows	The number of data series rows.
RowIndex	Indicates the current row index pertaining to the DataItem property.
RowNames	Names displayed under each data row.
Scale	Percent scale factor for display purposes.
VerticalGrid	Shows vertical grids.

A brief explanation of the properties follows. Because the graph is a visual control, the best way to understand the capabilities of the properties is by simply experimenting and observing the results. A sample application, charter.htm, is available on the CD-ROM for this purpose.

The first property that you must understand to use the graph control is ChartType. This affects the type of graph that will be displayed, such as a pie graph or bar graph. There are 20 different types available, which gives you lots of graphing options! Some of the most commonly used types appear in Table 12.2.

Table 12.2. Chart types.

Chart Type	Value
Simple Pie	0
Pie with wedge out	1
Simple Point Chart	2
Stacked Point Chart	3
Full Point Chart	4
Simple Line Chart	5
Stacked Line Chart	6

Chart Type	Value
Full Line Chart	7
Simple Area Chart	8
Stacked Area Chart	9
Full Area Chart	10
Simple Column Chart	11
Stacked Column Chart	12
Full Column Chart	13
Simple Bar Chart	14
Stacked Bar Chart	15
Full Bar Chart	16
HLC Stock Chart	17
HLC Stock Chart WSJ	18
OHLC Stock Chart	19
OHLC Stock Chart WSJ	20

The `ColorScheme` property enables the user to specify a color scheme for the graphed data. `Rows` and `Columns` specify the number of rows and columns in the graph. The `VerticalGrid` and `HorizontalGrid` properties can be set to 1 to enable the display of grid lines on the graph.

The three remaining properties, `ColumnIndex`, `RowIndex`, and `DataItem`, are all related to specifying a new data value for a data point on the graph. Data is initially specified in the object declaration as a series of rows and columns, as shown in the ActiveX chart control object declaration in Listing 12.1.

12

Listing 12.1. ActiveX chart control object declaration.

```
<!--------------- Chart Object ---------------------->
<OBJECT
CLASSID="CLSID:FC25B780-75BE-11CF-8B01-444553540000"
id=chtData
width=500
height=200
align=center
hspace=20
vspace=20
>
<param name="ChartStyle" value="0">
<param name="ChartType" value="2">
<param name="hgridStyle" value="1">
```

continues

Listing 12.1. continued

```
<param name="vgridStyle" value="0">
<param name="colorscheme" value="0">
<param name="rows" value="3">
<param name="columns" value="4">
<param name="RowNames" value="Week1 Week2 Week3">
<param name="data[0][0]" value="60">   <!-- Mike's Mileage for Week 1 -->
<param name="data[0][1]" value="70">   <!-- Karen's Mileage for Week 1 -->
<param name="data[0][2]" value="60">   <!-- John's Mileage for Week 1 -->
<param name="data[0][3]" value="80">   <!-- Brad's Mileage for Week 2 -->
<param name="data[1][0]" value="10">   <!-- Mike's Mileage for Week 2 -->
<param name="data[1][1]" value="70">   <!-- Karen's Mileage for Week 2 -->
<param name="data[1][2]" value="40">   <!-- John's Mileage for Week 3 -->
<param name="data[1][3]" value="80">   <!-- Brad's Mileage for Week 3 -->
<param name="data[2][0]" value="70">   <!-- Mike's Mileage for Week 3 -->
<param name="data[2][1]" value="80">   <!-- Karen's Mileage for Week 4 -->
<param name="data[2][2]" value="70">   <!-- John's Mileage for Week 4 -->
<param name="data[2][3]" value="90">   <!-- Brad's Mileage for Week 4 -->
</object>
```

ANALYSIS The object attributes are the same as those of the other ActiveX controls we have covered. The properties are specific to the chart control, as outlined in Table 12.1, and you set them through the parameter definitions. You can also use these parameter definitions to supply the individual piece of data to be associated with each row and column data point on the graph. This technique is used in Listing 12.1. The data point at row 2, column 2 will be displayed as the value 90 on the graph that is generated when the page loads.

If you wanted to have a script reassign a value as the user interacts with the page, you would indicate the value to change through the ColumnIndex and RowIndex properties. Then you would supply the new value in the DataItem property. That would change the value at the data point indicated by the current ColumnIndex and RowIndex property values. Listing 12.2 shows an example of this technique.

Listing 12.2. Reassigning the data point in row 2, column 2 through code.

```
chtData.RowIndex = 2
chtData.ColumnIndex = 2
chtData.DataItem = 50
```

This capability to reset data as the script is running enables you to generate dynamic graphs in response to changing conditions or new user input. It's not just data that you can change. You can change the graph color, style, and even the number of rows or columns! Any assignments made in a script are performed as soon as that block of code is done executing.

Figure 12.1 shows a sample application to illustrate the code used to change the graph dynamically. It provides the weekly training mileage information for four runners for three weeks. The graph shows the miles trained on the vertical y axis and number of weeks on the horizontal x axis.

Figure 12.1.

The training mileage graph Web page.

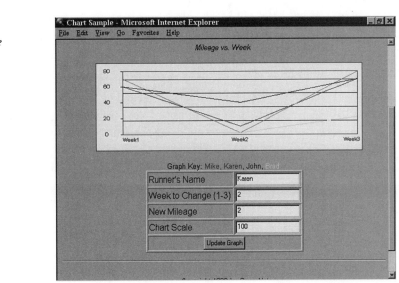

Because the graph object supports multiple columns of data, all four runners can be represented on the same graph at once. A line type graph is used to present the data as well as the data trends. Input areas let the user enter replacement data to be immediately graphed. For example, maybe a user notices that Karen's mileage is inordinately low and wants to correct it. He can then supply the runner's name and the week that should be changed in the input field. The name and week essentially define the row and column for the data point. The user can also provide the new data, as well as a graph style indicator. Then, he selects the command button to perform the updates. Listing 12.3 shows the code that is executed in response to clicking the button. The source code for this sample is available on the CD-ROM in file charter.htm.

Listing 12.3. Graph update script.

```
<script language="VBScript">
<!-- Option Explicit

sub cmdApply_OnClick
' Update the graph
```

continues

Listing 12.3. continued

```
dim intRunner ' current runner
dim intRow ' row translated from week

' Determine which runner was specified
if txtName.value = "Karen" then
    intRunner = 1
elseif txtName.value = "John" then
    intRunner = 2
elseif txtName.value = "Brad" then
    intRunner = 3
elseif txtName.value = "Mike" then
    intRunner = 0
else
    msgbox "That runner is not known.",0,"Unfamiliar runner"
end if

' Data array starts at index 0
intRow = txtWeek.Value - 1

' Update the graph
chtData.RowIndex = intRow

chtData.ColumnIndex = intRunner

chtData.DataItem = txtMiles.Value

chtData.Scale = txtChartStyle.Value

end sub
-->
</script>
```

ANALYSIS　User input is converted from name to column index, and then the changes are applied. The results will show up to the user immediately. This sample illustrates modification of one data point, but your script could just as easily modify a series of 1000 points by coupling loop control code with the same technique.

The chart is a visually oriented control that scripts can heavily customize. However, it is not a control that the user can directly interact with unless you build special code around it. Even though the chart control has many properties to control its appearance, it has no events to go with it. Likewise, the chart control has only one property—the AboutBox property, which provides version information about the control. Although you might write a lot of code for the chart control, it will be code that modifies the appearance of a chart through properties. It won't be code that gets executed based on chart events or takes advantage of chart method calls (other than AboutBox).

As you can see, you don't have to access a lot of events and methods to be able to heavily customize the display of a control and interact with the user through the control. The chart control has many different graphical representations it can assume. It's a good idea to be

12

familiar with the formats listed in the ChartType property, so when a graphing need does arise, this control can provide a quick, easy-to-implement solution.

Integrating Java Applets

So far you've seen a lot of examples of how to integrate ActiveX controls. Now, the discussion turns to integrating some very important non-ActiveX types of objects, including one of the most famous citizens of the Internet technology world. Anyone who has followed the Internet very closely has probably heard of Java. Java, which originated from Sun Microsystems, Inc., is a language with many facets. Due to the tremendous growth in interest in this language, Sun now has an entire business unit, JavaSoft, which is focused on Java issues. Java is a language used for creating programs on the World Wide Web as well as intranet solutions.

NOTE A wealth of information about Java is available on the World Wide Web. A good place to start is the official Java page from Sun Microsystems at http://java.sun.com.

The Java language is particularly well-suited for the Web because it is platform independent. A Java applet downloaded from a server, with appropriate run-time support in a browser, could run on an Apple Macintosh, UNIX workstation, or IBM PC. Java is an object-oriented language with many elements in common with the C++ language. However, it does not provide memory pointers for the programmer. This avoids the memory referencing problems they can introduce. As a result, Java facilitates the creation of stable, safe applications. You can think of Java as existing in three main forms: JavaScript code, Java applets, and Java applications.

You can use the JavaScript form of this language for embedding code into a page and controlling interaction on the page. The concept is similar to that of VBScript, although the language and integration capabilities differ. Java applets are programs created in Java that are then generated in a platform-neutral byte code format. These bytes are not specific to a UNIX workstation, a PC, or an Apple Macintosh but remain in a general, predefined form that cannot be directly executed by a computer. How does an applet ever run? You can download a Java applet with a page as a separate file, and then a browser can launch that Java applet through a piece of software called a run-time interpreter. This run-time interpreter translates the generic byte codes of the applet file into specific actions executed by the computer. The third form of Java is a Java application. A Java application is like a standard application. It is generated in the byte format understood by a computer type. It can then run directly on computers of that type with no additional translation.

12

NOTE

> After the preceding discussion, you might be wondering if JavaScript and VBScript give you two different ways to do the same thing. The answer is that, to a large extent, they do, although there are some very significant differences between the languages as well. VBScript is viewed by many to be a far easier language to use because of the relatively straightforward Visual Basic syntax. Although the syntax and overall approach of these languages is quite different, they both can be used to produce dynamic Web pages.

By this point, you might be thinking, "Okay, all this stuff about Java is fine, but if I wanted to know about JavaScript, I'd be reading a JavaScript book instead of a VBScript book!" The payoff for VBScript programmers is in the Java applet arena. Think of it: A lot of files full of function in platform-neutral format are sitting around, waiting to be integrated into Web pages. JavaScript isn't of much interest because you can just use VBScript instead. Java applications might not be of direct interest because you don't want to deliver a platform-specific application to your users; you want to provide them with a smart Web page. The payoff sits squarely in the Java applet domain. VBScript lets you take advantage of all the Java applets out there right from your script. There are lots of Java applets today, and you can bet that there will be more and more coming in the future.

You can integrate the applets into your programs and directly use their capabilities from your script. Sound familiar? In many respects, it's very much like the ActiveX object integration model. There are some important differences, such as the events that ActiveX provides, but there are also a lot of similarities. You incorporate a Java applet through an object definition. You provide a name for it that you will reference from your code. You interact with it through the properties and methods that it has defined. An applet can show up on the page as a visible component that the user sees and interacts with, but it doesn't have to. It can also do its job relatively out of sight. A Java applet, like an ActiveX control, can be included in a page even if a script doesn't reference it. It will still appear on the page and provide whatever inherent capabilities it has. Your script can become the glue that enables you to drive the Java applet in response to user input and make the page smarter, more active, and more dynamic through its capabilities.

Listing 12.4 shows a sample of a Java applet object declaration. The discussion that follows outlines the probable implementation of Java applets. As this book went to print, this support is not yet in the Internet Explorer beta so final details may change. This applet provides an estimate of the time needed to develop a simple Web page based on the lines of HTML and the lines of code planned. Your script will be able to reference this Java applet object by the name `jvaEstimator` because that is the name assigned through the `ID` attribute. The `java:` portion of the `CLASSID` attribute indicates to the browser that this is a Java applet. ActiveX

12

controls, by contrast, start with a clsid: prefix to indicate they are an entity that you can reference by standard system class IDs. The remainder of the CLASSID attribute indicates the class name of the Java applet, which is estimator.process.

NOTE

Don't get confused by the two levels of class IDs used here! An object has a CLASSID attribute that specifies the class or type of object it is. Then, some objects, such as ActiveX controls, define this further in terms of clsid:classname to provide a reference to a system-wide class for that control. Other objects, such as Java, define it further in terms of an application-type indicator and the class that application supports, as in java:app.class. All approaches have the same purpose—to provide an ultimate pointer to the object methods and properties available.

Listing 12.4. An object declaration for a Java applet.

```
<OBJECT
       ID="jvaEstimator"
       CLASSID="java:estimator.process"
       CODETYPE="application/java-vm"
       CODEBASE="http://www.mcp.com/pathinfo/"
       HEIGHT=100
       WIDTH=100
     >
Get a 20th century browser, buddy!
</OBJECT>
```

ANALYSIS The CODETYPE attribute in Listing 12.4 identifies the general type of the object defined. This is a similar but much more general piece of information than the CLASSID, which defines specifics of what the object is and the class to use to reference it further. One of the uses of the CODETYPE attribute is that the browser can see what the supported type is and then determine whether that type is supported by the client's browser and installed support software before it attempts to download the object. If a script referenced a Java applet but the user's browser and extensions didn't support Java, the object would not be downloaded. Instead, the message that precedes the end of the object declaration, Get a 20th century browser, buddy!, would be displayed on the page. This is commonly called an "apology message." It provides more information for those users whose browsers are not up to speed with the technology of your page. (Of course, you should use your own more subtle version of an apology for real pages.) CODETYPE is an optional attribute. What would happen if CODETYPE was not included in the declaration? The applet file would be downloaded even though it could not be used by the current page.

12

The next attribute is CODEBASE. You can use this to specify the URL where the Java applet is located. If the applet was at the same location as the page itself, the optional CODEBASE could be omitted, and the applet would still be located correctly. HEIGHT and WIDTH specify the visible area where the object is displayed. You could also use the ALIGN attribute discussed on Day 10 to control alignment. The Estimator applet, for example, might display the resulting estimate itself in its applet area. You would then want to control the size and alignment of this area on the page. On the other hand, the applet could also be written to simply store the resulting estimate in an applet property for your script to retrieve. If that were the case, no visible display of the applet would be needed.

> **NOTE**
>
> At the time of this writing, this method of declaring Java applets as objects was likely but not yet reflected through official Microsoft documentation. If you want to verify the implementation at the time you read this, you can refer to the Microsoft VBScript object information page at http://www.microsoft.com/vbscript/us/vbstutor/vbsobjs.htm. Most aspects of this implementation are also documented as part of the W3C standard committee working draft at http://www.w3.org/pub/WWW/TR/WD-object.html.

Listing 12.5 shows another declaration for this applet without some of the optional attributes. Because CODEBASE is not supplied, the Java applet will be located in the base directory of the page itself. No CODETYPE attribute means that the applet will be downloaded for all users of the page, even if they have an old browser and it won't work for them. Because this applet will have no visible interface that it directly supports, no WIDTH and HEIGHT are defined.

Listing 12.5. An object declaration for a Java applet without optional attributes and with parameters.

```
<OBJECT
    ID="jvaEstimator"
    CLASSID="java:estimator.process"
>
    <PARAM NAME="LinesHTML" VALUE="300">
    <PARAM NAME="LinesScript" VALUE="200">
</OBJECT>
```

ANALYSIS The declaration in Listing 12.5 also uses something that should look familiar from the ActiveX controls: the parameter tag. You use the parameter tag <PARAM> to supply initial values for properties of the Java applet. Properties are referenced through the NAME field, and the starting value is supplied by the VALUE field. In the preceding example, LinesHTML and

LinesScript are both properties defined in the applet itself. The <PARAM> statements load those properties with the specified default values when the page is loaded. The Estimator applet also makes use of several more properties. However, if this page doesn't need to supply custom default values, they do not need to be initialized as the page loads, and therefore you don't need to specify them at the beginning of the code. You can still reference and modify all the properties from the VBScript code that uses the applet, even if they're not specified in the initial object declaration.

As you can see, the declaration approach is very much like that used for other controls. Using a Java applet object from code is even more similar. Listing 12.6 shows code that uses the applet. This code is executed in response to a user click on a command button defined on the page. The code assigns the values supplied by a user in text boxes on the page to the properties of the applet. Then, a Calculate method is called to calculate the estimate itself, which results in the assignment of the correct estimate to the applet's EstimatedTime property. The script then displays this estimate to the user by referencing the property in a message box call.

Listing 12.6. Using a Java applet from VBScript.

```
<SCRIPT LANGUAGE="VBScript">
<!--
    sub cmdEstimate_OnClick
      '  This routine is called when the user clicks Calc button on the page
       'Assign applet properties from user supplied values in page's textboxes
       '  If no user input is supplied, default property values used
       if len(txtUserDistance.Value) > 0 then
           jvaEstimator.LinesHTML = txtUserDistance.Value
       end if
       if len(txtUserTime.Value) > 0 then
           jvaEstimator.LinesScript = txtUserTime.Value
       end if

       ' Use the applet to calculate the estimate, then display the results
       jvaEstimator.Calculate
       msgbox "The estimated time for this job is " & jvaEstimator.EstimatedTime
end sub
```

12

The ActiveVRML Viewer Object

ActiveVRML is a fascinating technology laden with potential. ActiveVRML is the control of 3-D animations, multimedia, and virtual reality type applications. You can integrate ActiveVRML with VBScript. The information that follows is not intended to show you all the details of how to use ActiveVRML. That will require further study of your own if you want to pursue it. It is quite a broad area that justifies a book in its own right. The information that follows will show you one more side of the VBScript component integration model.

> **NOTE**
>
> ActiveVRML is certainly worth learning and learning well if you have an interest in it or see applications for your Web page. Refer to http://www.microsoft.com/intdev/avr.

ActiveVRML instructions are based on the Active Virtual Reality Modeling Language. The approach of this language is script-like in many aspects, and it's sometimes referred to as ActiveVRML script language. However, ActiveVRML is different from VBScript. ActiveVRML scripts deal with the ActiveVRML content itself. You can use an ActiveVRML viewer control to view the ActiveVRML contents on a page. VBScript can control this viewer control. The events and methods of the viewer control essentially provide a communications conduit between VBScript and the ActiveVRML script that controls the ActiveVRML display contents. The viewer control provides just one method and one event that you use to shuffle information between the two. To effectively integrate the ActiveVRML viewer in your VBScript, you need a fair amount of familiarity with ActiveVRML itself. The viewer is integrated much like other components you have seen before. Listing 12.7 shows the familiar object declaration.

Listing 12.7. Declaring the ActiveVRML viewer control object.

```
<OBJECT
CLASSID="CLSID:389C2960-3640-11CF-9294-00AA00B8A733"
ID="avViewer"
WIDTH=50
HEIGHT=50>
<PARAM NAME="DataPath" VALUE="http://www.address.yours/its_location/avr_
                              yourfile.avr">
<PARAM NAME="Expression" VALUE="myImage">
<PARAM NAME="Border" VALUE=False>
<PARAM NAME="Frozen" VALUE=True>
</OBJECT>
```

ANALYSIS   The attributes of the object probably look familiar at this point. The use of CLASSID, width, and height is the same as for other objects. However, the parameter properties are unique to this control. Datapath indicates the URL of the file. Expression is the ActiveVRML expression that the viewer will display. Border specifies whether a border will appear around the viewer control. Frozen indicates whether script-level changes to the properties will cause the viewer display to be refreshed.

The ActiveVRML viewer provides one key method and one key event, but they are very powerful. Just the one method enables you to trigger a wide variety of actions. The single event allows you to respond to a wide variety of events from within the ActiveVRML. This

12

is because additional information is passed in parameters for both the event and the method. The method shown in Listing 12.8 is used to trigger action in the viewer control.

Listing 12.8. Triggering a method for the ActiveVRML control.

```
<script Language="VBScript">
<!--
    sub cmdTest_OnClick
        AVViewer.FireImportedEvent 50, 40
    end sub
--!> </script>
```

ANALYSIS   In this case, `FireImportedEvent` generates the event for the ActiveVRML script to receive. It supplies the user-defined event ID of 50 and an additional parameter of 40. This technique demonstrates the interaction possible with ActiveVRML.

Receiving events uses an approach that is similar to that used for triggering a method. Listing 12.9 shows code that handles an event from the viewer control.

Listing 12.9. A script event handler for the ActiveVRML viewer control.

```
<script for="AVViewer" event="ActiveVRMLEvent(EventId, Param)"_
                        Language="VBScript">
<!--
    ' Respond to event from viewer control
    MsgBox "Event in viewer control occurred, it is Id=" & _
        EventId & "  Param=" & Param, 0, "Event Notification"
--!>
</script>
```

ANALYSIS   The `ActiveVRMLEvent` that is generated by the ActiveVRML script can be caught and handled by VBScript with an event handler such as that shown in Listing 12.9. You could also use the subroutine declaration syntax

```
sub AvViewer_ActiveVRMLEvent (EventId, Param)
```

within a script to catch this event. When this event occurs, the `EventId` parameter will indicate the event identification supplied by the ActiveVRML script. The parameter supplied could be empty, a string, or a number, depending on what the ActiveVRML script supplied when it generated the event.

You've had a taste of integrating ActiveVRML into your scripts through the ActiveVRML viewer. ActiveVRML is an area that takes some study to master, and the preceding discussion is not intended to be sufficient for you to churn out your own 3-D virtual Web pages. For

12

that, you will also need to master the ActiveVRML concepts and script language. However, you have seen how this object, like the others before it, follows the same set of integration principles. Declare the object with an object declaration, and then reference its properties and methods and respond to its events. The viewer takes a somewhat special approach to the method, supplying a general-purpose method that you can use to communicate a variety of user-defined events back to the ActiveVRML script. Likewise, the viewer generates just one generic event for VBScript to respond to. By inspecting the parameters that are supplied with that event, the VBScript code can determine full details of the information supplied from the ActiveVRML script. You can see that VBScript once again serves as a kind of nerve center for the page. It is a capable glue for pulling all the pieces together into a comprehensive Web page and providing script-level control of those pieces.

Component Downloading Issues

There are some important issues to consider beyond just declaring objects and referencing them from code. What happens when a user downloads a page that utilizes a dozen of the latest and greatest objects on the scene? She might have some of the controls present on her system, or maybe she has none of them present. Should the page notify the user? Fail to work? Carry out the download across the Internet?

The ideal solution, and the solution now in place, is to supply the user with the component. To get the most productivity out of the Web, the user should be able to wade between pages and links counting on the fact that the pages are usable. The ideal situation for the user is that when she needs a capability from an object, she's transparently provided with that capability through the object download.

It turns out that this approach has quite a few complications. One is download time. It can take a while to download a lot of controls across the network. Another issue is installation. Many objects such as ActiveX controls require some installation for system registration and other aspects in addition to just merely downloading the file. Still another issue is control. If a company sells a control, they don't want copies of it to bounce willy-nilly across the Internet free of charge. Perhaps the most important issue is security. Because of its importance, it is addressed in detail on Day 21, "Security, Stability, and Distributed Source Control Issues." Component certification, the capability to track components through unique signatures, and browser capabilities to allow or prevent downloads are all ways of addressing different sides of the issue.

Currently, the state of browser support for object download varies based on the browser and the version, but the early framework is largely in place. In the discussion of Java applets earlier today, you saw that a download location for the applet can be specified through the object's CODEBASE attribute, and if that's not provided, the applet can be retrieved from the same path as the page. According to the current draft W3C standard, this would apply to any object. Microsoft early beta plans and implementation go even a step beyond this. Specific guidelines have been formulated to describe how downloading ActiveX controls can be addressed by browser writers and component creators. This includes specific download Application Program Interface calls, component packaging guidelines, and areas of component storage and cache. Some interesting issues addressed as part of this approach include providing the release number of objects as part of the URL and providing a configuration file to control installation for a group of files that can be processed by download service software.

These issues are all at various stages of draft proposal and evolution. As they are resolved, the low-level technical details will probably most directly affect browser writers and component creators more than they will affect VBScript writers. The high-level end results will affect you and the distribution of the scripts you write. You must be aware that these issues exist because they do affect the ability of users to take advantage of your object-based scripts. Soon the technology will be at the point where any leading browser will magically provide users with everything they need to interact with a page. The leading browsers are largely there already. But still, VBScript writers will have to keep an eye toward these evolving standards and the capabilities of the browsers the users view their pages with.

Summary

Today you have learned about the ActiveX chart control. This is more complex than some of the other ActiveX controls examined on earlier days in the sense that you can assign sets of data to it. The control then renders a graph based on this information. You can change the properties of the chart control from a script just as you can for any other control. You can even change the graphed data and graph type itself from a script. When such changes occur, the graph updates as soon as the code completes. The chart control makes it possible to dynamically produce charts based on changing user data as the user interacts with a page.

Another way to extend the power of Web pages is through Java applets. Java applets are written in the Java language and distributed as files of byte code. This byte code can then be interpreted by browsers on a variety of platforms to execute the applications. You can include Java applets in a Web page through the object declaration. The best news is that VBScript can use them! The techniques for controlling a Java applet from code are much the same as those for controlling ActiveX control objects. The applet is referenced by an ID attribute that is declared as part of the object declaration. Its properties and methods can be called directly from the code.

An additional control that offers another type of capability to your scripts is the ActiveVRML viewer control. This object lets you control the display of ActiveVRML sessions, which can display 3-D displays including animations and multimedia. A fairly high degree of integration is possible with the capabilities offered by this control.

12

Finally, this lesson discusses the issue of downloading objects on demand. Objects that are embedded in Web pages are downloaded across the network when a page requires them. This requires that the object is present on the network and correctly specified in the page object declaration. It is also a capability not present in older browsers. The security implications are addressed on Day 21. This distribution model makes it even easier to share dynamic pages rich in functionality across your company or across the world.

Q&A

Q **Can you reference Java applets, ActiveX controls, and ActiveVRML control objects all from the same script, or are you restricted to just one type of object per page?**

A There is no restriction. The script can reference any object definition on the page, and all types can be present on the same page.

Q **Suppose you have a page where you want to calculate and present the result of the average wage and standard deviation wage of five workers. You could write this in VBScript, but you also hear that there is a large ActiveX math control available, as well as a Java applet that does wage calculations. Is there an obvious choice as to the best way to proceed?**

A Not necessarily. There are tradeoffs in choosing any of the options. If you use VBScript, you have to write the calculation yourself. On the other hand, if you use the objects, you're taking advantage of code that has already been written (and debugged!) by others. It could be quicker to integrate the object. On the other hand, if you use an object, the user will have to wait for an additional file to download if it must be downloaded across the network.

Q **Does an object have to be present in advance on the user's computer for him to make use of a page that requires it?**

A No. Objects that have URLs defined as part of their location or objects that are in the same path as the home page will be downloaded when needed. However, depending on browser settings, the user will be warned when these downloads take place.

NOTE

Downloading components on demand is a maturing technology. If you have an early browser—for example, the beta version of Internet Explorer 3.0—this capability might not yet be supported.

12

Workshop

Create a Web page that utilizes the ActiveX chart object and scripting. The graph should come up by default with a graph of the hours of sleep and the hours of computer time you've had over the last seven days. Provide two command buttons. The first button should update the graph to display your ideal data if you could choose any amount of computer time. The second button should present the actual data that is also used for the default presentation.

Quiz

NOTE Refer to Appendix C, "Answers to Quiz Questions," for the answers to these questions.

1. Show the object declaration you would need to use to declare a Java applet that you can access by the name `jvaGifts` in your script. This applet suggests birthday gifts when supplied with user demographics. The applet has a class name of `Birthday.Logs`. Assign a default value of `200` to the applet's `MaxSpend` property in the declaration. Assume the applet is located at the fictitious path given in `http://www.mcp.com/javastuff` and that this is different from the location of the page that uses the applet.

2. Show the code statement that you could use within a script procedure to change the `MaxSpend` property to `$300`.

12

Day 13

VBScript Standards and Conventions

On the preceding days, you learned how to write scripts. You have even learned how to use controls and programming techniques to create very powerful active pages through VBScript. However, you have not yet seen one of the most important aspects of producing good scripts. The quality of your scripts is directly influenced by the standards and conventions you apply when creating them. Today's lesson focuses on standards and conventions you can apply to your script development. You can improve maintainability, ease the debug process, and design and implement your code in a more organized fashion with good standards. All you have to do is apply a standard, consistent approach to the way you design your code.

This standard approach applies to everything from the way you name your variables to the type of comments you place in your code. It is possible to write functioning scripts without worrying about standards at all. You don't have to use standards for your scripts to work. As a matter of fact, the VBScript interpreter and browser that process your scripts don't care at all about standards. Standards are purely a human convenience for the sake of the programmer. Those standards and conventions, however, are a convenience that often enables you to produce better programs. Today's lesson will tell you everything you need to know to use standards and conventions to improve your own code and make it more maintainable.

Advantages of Standards and Conventions

Using standards and conventions has many dividends. Some are obvious and some are subtle, but they all add up to better scripts and saved time in the long run.

Code Maintenance Advantage

Most scripts that you create will have to be maintained. Software needs tend to evolve over time. A Web page that suffices today is a likely candidate to be improved in the future. The code that goes along with it will probably evolve to support added capabilities. For this reason, any script you write should be viewed as a piece of code that might need revisiting in the future. You can improve future maintainability by writing code with good standards today.

Perhaps the most recognized motivation for applying good standards is that standards make code much easier to maintain. Suppose another programmer has to work with your programs in the future. It will be much easier for her to dive in, understand, and work with your code if you have used a consistent naming, commenting, and structuring approach on all the code she must examine. This advantage holds true not only for someone else who might look at your code, but also for you. If you write a script today and then return to it a year from now to make a minor change, you will make that change much more quickly and safely if your code was written with standards you use all the time. If it was, you won't have to spend as much time refamiliarizing yourself with the standards, or lack thereof, in your year-old program. Good procedure names, variable names, and comments will bring you up to speed quickly when you must update code you wrote a while ago.

This better understanding of your code, in turn, helps you make a safer fix. You are more likely to introduce a bug if you are not completely clear on what the code is doing. Returning to code that was written with a good set of standards and conventions maximizes the chance that you will have a clear understanding of it.

Improved Team Communication

The benefits of standards and conventions become even greater if code will be shared between programmers. When this is the case, the task of understanding code becomes even greater, and the potential for misunderstanding somebody else's work is increased many times over.

Different programmers have different styles and ways of approaching problems. Without a common approach, you can spend a great deal of effort simply trying to decipher what another programmer was thinking when he wrote a certain piece of code. Scripts written to standards provide these answers up front. If all the programmers exchanging code are all using the same standards, it is much easier to trade code because good standards make your code easier to read. If you have other programmers in your company with whom you will be sharing code, using identical standards guarantees quick and efficient communication of script logic and approaches.

Easier Debugging

Few would dispute the claim that code written with clear and consistent standards is easier to maintain. Standards provide another very important advantage that is often overlooked. Code that is clear also makes debugging programs much easier. When you are testing your program and something doesn't work right, think about the steps you'll probably follow to get to the bottom of the problem. You will need to review variables, trace through procedures, and take an overall look at what your code is doing. Good variable names, script structure, and comments certainly help with all those activities.

Faster, More Effective Code Implementation

Good standards pay off in program development in another, closely related, way. When you apply standards as you write your scripts, you will find that the scripts become easier to write. Because you are using a consistent approach for naming variables, objects, and procedures and you are commenting throughout the script, you will spend less time agonizing over these minor details. Instead, you will be able to immediately apply a standard approach without devoting thought to how to address those areas. As your scripts begin to shape up before your eyes, the clear documentation based on a standard approach helps you expand and flush out the scripts. A clear, well-understood foundation is easier to build on. Standards provide you with this clear foundation for your programs.

The Dangers of Not Using Standards

Using standards and conventions has many advantages. The advantages apply when you're creating your scripts and bring future paybacks when you're maintaining the scripts. Because standards provide benefits even at the time a script is created, it seems obvious that you should follow standards and conventions right from the start. Unfortunately, this is often not the case in software development. Many times, inexperienced developers perceive that it is quicker to plunge into writing a program without paying heed to standards. They omit comments for the sake of rapid coding and give no thought to descriptive procedure names to save slivers of time. They take similar shortcuts in all areas. The intentions are usually good when this happens; the programmer usually plans to go back and apply good comments and procedure names and other standards after the program is working. The typical reasoning is that the program is in too much flux to spend the time on standards initially, but the programmer can add comments and other cleanup after the fact once the program logic is firm.

Don't fall into this trap! Most programmers who intend to go back and clean up their code and make it consistent and standardized somehow never seem to find the time to do so. Perhaps more importantly with such an approach, you don't realize any of the benefits of standards as you create and debug your initial code. Using standards often forces you to stop and think about what your code is doing as you review procedures, variables, and comments. As a result, using standards from the ground up helps lead you to more logical thinking. If you cut the standards initially, you also cut these advantages.

Standards to Use

Once you've decided to use standards, you need to settle on a set of standards and conventions that you feel comfortable with and stick to them. It won't do you much good to use one set of standards today and then switch to a different style of standards next week and then choose a different approach the week after that. This defeats the very purpose of standards in the first place. The consistency that standards provide requires that you use the same standards from one project to another. The advantages of standards are even greater as code is shared between programmers. If programmers use the same standards, they stand to benefit more when scripts are shared.

Worldwide Standards?

VBScript provides a unique twist on the share code model, too. One of the interesting aspects of VBScript is that source code for programs is now shared across the world as never before. Any Web page that uses VBScript essentially delivers the script source code to the user as a part of the page. If that user happens to be interested in VBScript, he can easily view the source of your scripts. Likewise, you can view the source of any other scripts on the World Wide Web.

Sharing and understanding one another's code applies not just across your own programs or your company, but also across the world. Given this tremendous source code sharing potential, you might expect that there would be one worldwide standard for scripts—and there is, in a way. Microsoft provides standard and convention guidelines for VBScript, which are documented on the World Wide Web.

NOTE At the time of this writing, Microsoft's standards and conventions were documented as a part of its online VBScript documentation at `http://www.microsoft.com/vbscript`.

No universal law, however, requires every programmer to follow the Microsoft standards. The Microsoft standards are very good, but not all scripts will be created exactly to those standards. Other programmers might have their own extensions to the standards that they feel make their programs even more maintainable. In some cases, developers might not want the worldwide users of their pages to view their scripts at all. Their goal might be to ease maintenance at their own company and discourage unsolicited code lifting from their own scripts. The motivations for such a programmer to follow a single set of worldwide script conventions would be small. In other cases, a development team might decide that they just wanted to apply a subset of Microsoft standards, coupled with some of their own. Some companies might need a great many company-specific standards if their large projects are shared among many programmers and have some unique characteristics.

Adopting Standards That Are Right for You and Your Company

For all the reasons cited previously, you will probably find that the scripts you encounter on the World Wide Web take a variety of similar but slightly different standard and convention formats. Today's lesson provides one set of standards and conventions. It would be nice to say that the standards provided in this book, which are derived largely from the Microsoft standards, are the right set of standards and conventions to follow. It would be even greater if this book served as the universal set of standards and conventions that every VBScript programmer on the face of the earth was forced to adhere to! However, doing so would not be the right approach.

The standards and conventions you should apply to your projects are those that make sense in the context of your work. You should carefully consider the standards presented here, the standards online from Microsoft, and the standard styles you see in Web pages that use VBScript across the Internet. Put some thought into deciding on the set of standards you will use because it is a decision you will live with for quite a while. Perhaps your company has some special information that should appear in the comments for every procedure, such as the department and lead programmer responsible for producing that procedure. Perhaps you need to have variable names in a certain format to be consistent with an approach dictated by a Department of Defense contract. With many special cases, you might need to derive your own smorgasbord of standards from the base model.

13

If you don't have any such reasons, you can happily apply the following standards and conventions without modification. The closer you can follow the recommended industry-standard approach, the better. Once you settle on a set of standards and conventions, make sure it is consistent throughout your company and stick to it! With this approach, you will make standards and conventions work for you to improve your programs in efficiency, rather than work against you as simply a set of regulations you must follow.

Variables

You now have some background on standards and conventions and why they are important. It is time to consider the standards themselves. The first area of focus is variables, perhaps the most important place to apply standards because variables form the backbone of most programs. You will probably use a lot of them throughout your code. If you don't use variables correctly, the results can be devastating. Likewise, if you must maintain and modify code, it is essential that you understand what the variables do. As a result, the variable standards are aimed at clearly communicating the purpose and intent of variables.

Descriptive Variable Names

One of the easiest ways to make the use of a variable clear is to give it a meaningful name. Consider the following variable declaration:

```
Dim nm
```

This line declares a variable with the name nm. From this declaration, it is impossible to tell the purpose of the variable. The programmer could be using nm as an abbreviation for name, number, or the population of New Mexico. If you are maintaining this code listing and you see this variable declaration, what will go through your mind? You'll likely cogitate on the meaning of nm, making a few mental guesses. You will have to spend some time deciphering the code to figure out the true purpose of this variable. Suppose, on the other hand, that it had been declared in the following way:

```
Dim number
```

This declaration tells you a lot more. You can tell after reading the declaration that this variable will contain a number as opposed to a name, the population of New Mexico, or anything else. However, even this variable declaration could be improved. You can tell from the name that the variable declares a location in memory to contain a number, but you don't know what type of number.

If the variable name was expanded to include an adjective that describes the purpose of the number, you'd know much more about its context. Then you could tell even more about the variable at a quick glance when maintaining the source code. The following declaration communicates even more information about the purpose of the variable:

```
Dim Student_Number
```

This illustrates one important convention for naming variables: Make sure your variable names are descriptive. Include an adjective to make your variables readable in an adjective-noun format when appropriate. If it's been a while since your last English class and you're thrown by the adjective-noun rule, just remember that your variable names should clearly describe the purpose of the variable. In most cases, you can best do this by joining more than one word.

Mixed-Case Variable Names

Hand-in-hand with the convention of descriptive variable names comes another important guideline. Use mixed-case variable names to help make them more readable. Start each piece of the variable name with a capital letter. This naming approach makes it much easier to visually browse through your code when writing, debugging, or otherwise maintaining it.

This rule is easily illustrated through an example. Suppose that you have several variables, each of which is used to keep track of the number of students in a different grade. If you don't use mixed case but instead provide declarations, as shown in Listing 13.1, you can see it is rather hard to decipher the purpose of the variables. The words tend to run together, which not only affects the readability of those variables but also dilutes the overall clarity of the program as a whole.

Listing 13.1. An example of variable declarations not using mixed case.

```
Dim freshmanclassstudenttotal
Dim sophomoreclassstudenttotal
Dim juniorclassstudenttotal
Dim seniorclassstudenttotal
Dim totalhighschoolpopulation

If freshmanclassstudenttotal > 200 then
    msgbox "Insufficient seating for " & freshmanclassstudenttotal & _
    " students."
End if
```

ANALYSIS It's not easy to see the meaning of these variables at a glance. They don't stand out when you view the source code. If you use mixed case and start each word with a capital letter, on the other hand, the meaning becomes much clearer, as shown in Listing 13.2.

13

Listing 13.2. Variable declarations using mixed case.

```
Dim FreshmanClassStudentTotal
Dim SophomoreClassStudentTotal
Dim JuniorClassStudentTotal
Dim SeniorClassStudentTotal
Dim TotalHighSchoolPopulation

If FreshmanClassStudentTotal > 200 then
     msgbox "Insufficient seating for " & FreshmanClassStudentTotal & _
     " students."
End if
```

ANALYSIS The variable names in these examples are rather long to help highlight the point of how non-mixed-case names tend to run together. These are not bad names, but they could be better. Generally speaking, overly long names can impede readability and clarity by overwhelming the reader with too much information, just as overly short names sacrifice clarity because they're not descriptive.

Variable names should be long enough to convey their intended meaning without being too wordy. Consider Listing 13.3 and compare it to Listing 13.1 and Listing 13.2 for clarity.

Listing 13.3. Variable declarations with moderate length names.

```
Dim FreshmanTotal
Dim SophomoreTotal
Dim JuniorTotal
Dim SeniorTotal
Dim HighSchoolTotal

If FreshmanTotal > 200 then
     msgbox "Insufficient seating for " & FreshmanTotal & " students."
End If
```

ANALYSIS You can see that these variables are much easier to read and interpret because they are shorter in length.

Variable Name Prefix

You've seen how to make a variable name convey more information. Even a descriptive name, however, doesn't tell you everything about a variable. For example, you can't tell if HighSchoolTotal refers to an integer total or if it could also contain a string. The programmer who uses this variable name might have included logic so that this variable is set to the string Unknown under certain conditions. You cannot tell the intended data representation of this variable just by looking at the name.

You can convey this information as part of the name. Many standards for other languages use a name prefix to provide data type information. Assume, for example, that the variable HighSchoolTotal should contain an integer only and was declared as type integer in another language. According to typical rules, it would be preceded by a lowercase int prefix.

A glance at the name intHighSchoolTotal tells you that the variable contains a student number that is also represented within the program as an integer. This type of naming convention fits somewhat better in other languages than it does in VBScript. Most other languages let you specifically designate the type of a variable. When you declare a variable with the Dim statement in Visual Basic 4.0, for example, you can specify in the same declaration whether it will contain integer, long, string, or some other type of data. With such a strongly typed language, it becomes very important to make sure your variables are used only for data of that type.

VBScript uses a somewhat different approach to variables, as you saw on Day 4, "Creating Variables in VBScript." All VBScript variables are defined automatically to have the type variant. A variant variable determines the type of data representation based on which assignments have been made to that variable. Even if you use int at the start of a variable name, there is no guarantee that the variable will be used only for integer data. You have to ensure the variable is used in that manner when you write the program. Suppose you named a variable to start with int, indicating it is an integer, to make the name more descriptive. Then you assigned string data to the variable at some point in your program. You would have made matters more confusing than if you had used no prefix at all. A glance at the variable name would tell you that it was set aside for only integer data. However, if you made a mistake and used it for integer and string data but proceeded with the assumption that only integer data was contained there, the task of debugging or maintaining your programs could become more time-consuming and difficult.

For this reason, a modified version of the standard prefix variable name approach is often the best for VBScript. This convention places a data-specific type of prefix such as int at the front of integer variables or str at the front of string variables only if the variables will be used just for that purpose. In addition, when the programmer uses such a prefix naming convention, she must make a special effort to see that no other type of data is assigned to the variable when creating the program. This is relatively easy because if the variable name starts with int, the programmer has a clear indication that integer should be the only type of legal data assigned.

However, the majority of VBScript variables might contain more than one data type representation at different points when the program is running. A variable such as HighSchoolTotal, for instance, might initially contain the string Unknown but at some later point in the program take the result of a calculation and contain an integer value. In this case, that variable can take both an integer and a string representation. It would be misleading to prefix it with either int or str.

13

Generally speaking, if you use good design and planning, you will know when you declare a variable what data type it will hold. In some cases, you might not know ahead of time all the forms of data a variant variable will eventually assume when you make the variable declaration. At other times, you might intentionally plan on a variant storing more than one type of data during the execution of the script. In either case, you can indicate this multifaceted role of the variable by designating the prefix for the variable name to be a v. This prefix tells readers of the program that the variable will handle multiple types of data by the specific intention of the programmer (rather than by accident). The declaration for `HighSchoolTotal` would be

```
Dim vHighSchoolTotal
```

When you see this variable or others like it in your program that start with the v prefix, you know that the programmer is explicitly indicating that the variable is not necessarily restricted to just one type. If you see a variable name that starts with `int` or `str`, however, you know those variables are expected to be restricted to just those types and that the program logic depends on that. The prefix table in Table 13.1 shows prefixes for all the various types you might want to designate.

Table 13.1. Variable name prefixes.

Prefix	Variable Subtype	Example
bln	Boolean use of variant variable	blnClassFull
byt	Byte use of variant variable	bytDownloadedData
dtm	Date or Time use of variant variable	dtmFirstSchoolDay98
dbl	Double use of variant variable	dblPiValue
err	Error use of variant variable	errStudentRegistration
int	Integer use of variant variable	intFreshmanTotal
lng	Long use of variant variable	lngMichiganPopulation
obj	Object use of variant variable	objArtClass
sng	Single use of variant variable	sngGradePointAverage
str	String use of variant variable	strTeacherLastName
v	Variant	vClassGrade

When you use these prefixes as an everyday standard, you will find that they enable you to follow your code and the intended use of its variables much more easily. For example, consider the declarations in Listing 13.4. If this was code that you had written a year ago, could you tell from the declaration how you are using the variables in your program?

Listing 13.4. An example of variable declarations without a subtype prefix.

```
Dim StudentGrade
Dim TotalGraduates
Dim GraduationDate
```

It's not easy to tell the intent from these declarations. Suppose you examine the code and find the comparison of a date value to the string Unknown. Was that date variable intended to ever contain a string, or is this an error? You don't know the programmer's intention. Now assess whether you can tell the intent from the declarations in Listing 13.5.

Listing 13.5. Variables with a subtype declaration.

```
Dim vStudentGrade
Dim intTotalGraduates
Dim vGraduationDate


' ... Lines of code that update the variables would appear here

If vStudentGrade <> 'I' and vStudentGrade <> 0 then
    intTotalGraduates = intTotalGraduates + 1
    If vGraduationDate <> "unknown" then
        msgbox "you are still on schedule to graduate in " & vGraduationDate
End If
```

ANALYSIS   From just the declarations in Listing 13.4, you can't easily tell whether StudentGrade will contain just number grades or strings as well. It turns out that this variable contains both numeric grades and letters such as an I for incomplete. The variable declaration in Listing 13.5 makes this dual purpose clear because the variable name starts with a v.

Likewise, the data representation of TotalGraduates is not clear in Listing 13.4. Although you might assume from the name of the variable that it would be a number, you can't tell if the programmer has utilized a scheme where descriptive strings are assigned to the variable as well or whether the code keeps track of fractions of students. The more explicit intTotalGraduates variable name used in the subsequent listing lets you know that the programmer is using this variable only to store integer data.

Finally, the GraduationDate variable in Listing 13.4 doesn't tell you much about its intended representation. From the name, you might guess that it stores only date values. If you made this assumption, you would be wrong. Listing 13.5 shows this variable declared with the variant prefix, vGraduationDate. Because the variable name starts with v, you can tell that the programmer intends for the variable to use more than one type of data representation.

13

As the code statements show, `vGraduationDate` stores the text string of `Unknown` when the graduation date is not clear and contains the normal graduation date when it is known.

The second set of declarations gives you a much quicker overview of how the variables are used. Of course, variable declarations should be accompanied by good comments describing the intended purpose as well, but a prefix is a good start for documenting and clarifying the way variables are used within a script. The variable name prefixes should be a part of any good VBScript standard. It is important to keep in mind, however, that just using a prefix doesn't mean that the code is guaranteed to use the variable in only that fashion. This will only happen when the naming convention is coupled with the programmer's vigilance. However, the informational benefit from the prefix standard is well worth the effort.

Scope Prefix

The *scope prefix* is one more special type of variable prefix. If you declare a variable right at the beginning of your script without placing it in a procedure, you can reference that variable anywhere within your script. It is said to have global, or script-level, scope. It is important to realize which variables are script-wide scope variables when you write your code. Generally speaking, it is a good idea to keep as many of your variables at the procedure level as possible and only use global variables for information that's important to share between procedures. Likewise, when you assign information to a global variable to share it with other procedures, you want to take special care that you do not wipe out previously existing values or set a global variable to a value not expected by other procedures.

In general, you should use a special level of awareness when coding with global variables. Most programmers apply this caution intuitively, but it is much easier to do if you have a clear indication of what your global variables are when you are changing your code. The scope prefix solves this problem. Any variables that are global in scope are preceded by s_. You can see this at work in Listing 13.6.

Listing 13.6. A code segment that uses a global variable.

```
Dim vStudentGrade
Dim vGraduationDate

' ... Lines of code that update the variables would appear here


If vStudentGrade <> 'I' and vStudentGrade <> 0 then
    s_iTotalGraduates = s_iTotalGraduates+1
    If vGraduationDate <> "unknown" then
        mfgbox "you are still on schedule to graduate in " & vGraduationDate
End If
```

ANALYSIS Take a look at Listing 13.5, which does not use the global variable prefix. At first glance, this code does not quickly tell you whether the variables used are local to the procedure or global. You can always back up to the start of the procedure and look for Dim statements to figure this out; however, this can be time-consuming, especially if the procedures are large. Now take a look at Listing 13.6. Because the scope prefix was used here, it is very easy to tell at a glance whether a variable is global. If s_ does not precede the variable name, the variable is local. If s_ does precede the variable name, the variable is clearly global in scope.

NOTE

In VBScript, any variable that is declared outside of a procedure has script-level, or global, scope. Any code can access and modify this type of variable anywhere within the page. This includes the same script where it was defined or other scripts if more than one script is included in the page. It also includes any VBScript code embedded in a control tag. For example, in the input line

```
<input type="button" value="Yes" name="cmdYes" onclick="msgbox_
s_Var1">
```

the value of s_Var1 would be displayed correctly even though that variable is referenced outside of the script that defined it.

Script-level variables should always start with the s_ prefix. This indicates a variable can be referenced anywhere on the page. Variables cannot be shared between different pages. The only other type of scope a variable can have is procedure level. The absence of a scope prefix indicates a procedure-level variable.

You can see in this example that s_iTotalGraduates is a global variable. Because of the script-level scope naming convention, you know that it is declared in a manner such as the following:

```
<script language="vbscript">
<!--
Dim s_iTotalGraduates
```

A scope prefix is easy to declare and will really improve the clarity of your script programs if they grow in size beyond the trivial level. As with the data subtype prefixes, there is nothing magical about scope-level prefixes. A programmer could use a prefix incorrectly. You might use the scope prefix on a local variable, which would be quite misleading when programs are reviewed with the assumption that s_ indicates global variables. Just like before, you must have an awareness about applying this prefix correctly along with your standards and conventions. If you have that awareness, these prefixes work well, and you should use them routinely.

13

Comments

Good comments are perhaps the most important part of script standards and conventions. They also pose one of the biggest challenges in defining standards. The questions of what constitutes a good comment and what level of comments is ideal can be quite subjective. Good comments depend largely on the situation. If you do a good job structuring your code and providing descriptive variable names and procedure names, this should decrease somewhat the number of comments it takes for the reader to get up to speed with your program. Likewise, if you make good use of prefixes, the reviewer of your code, whether it's a fellow programmer or you yourself some months down the road, will have a greater amount of insight into variables. In some respects, the need for comments is decreased when you follow standards in other areas of code, but some comments are still essential.

A comment that accompanies a variable and describes the purpose of the variable can be a great help to those struggling to understand a program. The comment delimiter as you have seen throughout the examples so far is the single quotation character ('). You can use this to set off entire lines. All text that follows this symbol on a line is treated strictly as a comment and not acted upon by the VBScript run-time interpreter.

You can also put a comment at the end of a statement line. After a Dim statement, for example, you can have on the same line a ' followed by comments that describe that variable. You should follow this convention for all but the simplest of variables. If the purpose of the variable is glaringly clear from the variable name and the code where it is used, you can bypass the variable comment. For example, if you have a variable used in a For...Loop index declared at the top of a procedure and that procedure has only five lines of code, it will be fairly obvious to the readers of your code the purpose of that variable. This assumes you have given the variable a descriptive name as well.

For any variable that does not have such a clear and simple application, some descriptive text should appear after it to elaborate on its purpose. If a variable is central to an entire algorithm and has some special use or if you should assign only certain values to it, then it might be appropriate to precede the variable Dim statement with several lines of comments that elaborate on its use. If you have several related variables and the reader should understand the relationship of all of the variables when reviewing any of them, those variable declarations should be grouped together. The entire group should be preceded by a comment that describes any important relationships. Look at the following code and determine what you can tell about these variables:

```
Dim s_intAcademicAdvisingCode

Dim s_strStudentID
Dim s_strStudentLastName
Dim s_strStudentBuilding
Dim s_strStudentLocker
```

ANALYSIS As you can see, even though the variable names are descriptive, you can't tell a lot about what these variables do in the program. Without good standards, you would have to dig through the code to determine how it uses the variables.

Now look at how some good comments can provide this information even before you dig into the following code:

```
' code used to reflect current academic advising status
'   0 = status is undetermined at this time
'   1 = student needs academic advising
'   2 = academic advising requirements fulfilled
Dim s_intAcademicAdvisingCode

'Student id is assigned by a function which returns an encrypted result based
'   on the student's last name, building, and locker. If any of these elements
'   have not been assigned then the student id cannot be generated for the
student.
Dim s_strStudentID 'the id number for the student returned by function GetID
Dim s_strStudentLastName 'the last name the student is registered under
Dim s_strStudentBuilding 'the name of building which contains the student's home
room
Dim s_strStudentLocker 'the student's locker number
```

ANALYSIS You can see that the information in the second segment is much more descriptive than that of the first. A glance at this listing provides fairly complete details on how these variables will be used in the program and what they are intended for. Notice that strStudentLocker is pretty fully described by its name alone. The comments to the right of the Dim statement don't add that much description. This is one area where you could leave out the comments. Other than that, the comments shown here enhance the program maintainability considerably. A good comment strategy such as this should be the backbone of your standards and conventions.

Constants

Constants are symbolic names for values that never change within your code. For example, if the sales tax were 4 percent, you could represent that in a constant and your code would base its calculation on the symbolic name SALES_TAX rather than the number .04. If you used the constant throughout your program and the sales tax changed at some point in the future, you would only have to modify the one line of code that declares the constant. All the other lines that reference the constant could remain unchanged.

Most languages provide direct support for such constants. VBScript provides no such support, as you saw on Day 4. If you want to use a constant, you must use a variable to represent it. You declare the variable through a regular Dim statement and then assign the value of that variable once in the startup area of your script. Thereafter, you can refer to the constant value. If you are treating it as a constant, you should never modify the value.

13

Most languages do not enable you to change the value of a constant. With VBScript, you can change the value because a constant is really just a variable. When you use a variable-based constant in VBScript, you are simply using a variable that you make sure not to change to provide yourself with a simulated constant. Most languages use the convention of all capitals to make a constant value distinct in the code. What about VBScript? You already have a nice set of variable conventions that don't have any provisions for constants, but you can easily extend the variable conventions discussed so far to encompass constants. If you're going to use a variable as a constant, you should declare it in all uppercase letters. This signifies to the reader of the source code that it is a value that you intend to never change within the program.

Common convention in other languages is that constants usually do not have type or scope prefixes. However, there is no reason not to add this to the VBScript convention you use. Prefixes can provide valuable information, even with constants. Listing 13.7 shows an example of a global constant.

Listing 13.7. An example of a global constant declaration.

```
<script language="VBScript">
<!--
    Dim s_sngSALES_TAX ' CONSTANT Sales Tax Rate
    Dim s_sngCOUNTRY_A_CONVERSION_RATE ' CONSTANT for the conversion rate for
                                       '    country A to be applied to the dollar

    ' Set up values for variable constants which should not be changed anywhere
    s_sngSALES_TAX = 0.04  'CONSTANT initialization
    s_sngCOUNTRY_A_CONVERSION_RATE = 1.56   'CONSTANT initialization
```

The sng prefix tells you that this constant contains a single data subtype representation rather than an integer. It becomes a very easy matter to understand where a constant is and what it represents if you declare your constants in this manner. Consider the following code:

```
vCurrentSale = iItemPrice * s_sngSALES_TAX
vConvertedDollars = intCurrentDollars *s_COUNTRY_A_CONVERSION_RATE
```

ANALYSIS If you follow the constant conventions recommended here, the use of constants will jump out at you as it does in the previous code segment. Several things are clear at a glance in this code. It uses constants that are global in scope. You even know the type of the constants. This type of consistent approach to using constants will make maintaining your code much easier for the same reasons that the variable convention pays off.

A Convention for Intrinsic Constants

Some necessary constant values are dictated by the VBScript language itself. For example, a certain value is expected for the second parameter of the VBScript MsgBox function to cause it to display yes/no buttons. A different value is expected to cause it to display OK. For example, you can use vbYesNo to request a message box with yes and no buttons, as detailed on Day 14, "Working with Documents and User Interface Functions." The Visual Basic 4.0 language automatically defines these values as a special kind of constant called an intrinsic constant. No declarations are needed to use these constants. The constants start with a vb prefix to indicate they are values expected by Visual Basic, such as vbOkOnly.

VBScript does not provide such automatically defined intrinsic constants in the current beta version. However, you can declare your own intrinsic constants as needed by using variable declarations, as shown on Day 14. For this type of constant, it is recommended that you use the same vb prefix naming convention used by Visual Basic 4.0. When you reference intrinsic constants in code, you should use the approach defined by Microsoft for the intrinsic constants. Intrinsic constants start with a lowercase vb and then use mixed case for the remainder of the name. For intrinsic constants, the vb prefix indicates that this is a Visual Basic intrinsic constant, and the mixed case improves readability.

This serves a couple purposes. It helps you distinguish which constant values are required by the language (vb prefix names) versus which constant values are defined by you for your own constant purposes (all-uppercase constant names). Also, if VBScript does add support for automatically defined intrinsic vb constants in the future, you can simply remove your declaration statements and your code will already take advantage of the expected names. And if you ever need to port code between VBScript and VBA or Visual Basic, the porting will go more smoothly if you have used the same constant names supported in those other environments. A file of such vb constant declarations is available on the CD-ROM that accompanies this book under \shared\tools\constants.txt. These declarations are compatible with the values required by the VBScript language and use the same names as the automatically defined constants of Visual Basic 4.0, so you can be assured of maximum future compatibility. You can double-click on this file to bring it up in Notepad or another text editor, and then copy and paste the declarations you need into your VBScript code.

Objects

Now you have seen details about standards and conventions for referencing variables. Other elements that your code will frequently reference are objects. Day 10, "An Introduction to Objects and ActiveX Controls," looks at how to insert objects such as controls into your Web page and then reference those from your code. That lesson describes how you can name an object through its ID attribute. The name that you specify as the ID is the name you use in code when referring to the object. You have also seen many different types of ActiveX control objects, including text boxes, timers, new item controls, and many, many more. On Day 18, "Advanced User Interface and Browser Object Techniques," you will find out about many more host environment objects automatically defined by the browser. What if you use many of these objects on one page? How do you keep them straight in your code statements? The answer, of course, is more conventions!

13

The good news is that the approach for objects is very similar to that of variables. Descriptive names are essential. In many cases, it might be helpful to use two words to describe an object; one is the descriptor and one is the noun. You don't need to indicate whether an object is global in scope because every object declared through the object tag is global by definition. Likewise, all the automatically declared browser objects you will learn about on Day 18 are global in scope. As a result, you don't need to worry about the s_ prefix. You do need to worry about an object type prefix. Objects come in a variety of types, and you indicate that an entity is an object and the kind of object it is through the prefix. Table 13.2 shows the prefixes you can use for some of the more commonly encountered objects.

Table 13.2. ActiveX control object prefixes.

Prefix	Control Object Type	Example
chk	Check box	chkOrderPlaced
cht	Chart or graph	chtStockPrices
cmd	Command button	cmdPlaceOrder
lbl	Label	lblHeartRateFeedback
obj	Generic Object	objWindowDocument
opt	Radio button (also called option button)	optSmallSize
pre	Preload	preCompanyLogo
tmr	Timer	tmrPulseRateMeasurementDuration
txt	Text box	txtShoeSize

These prefixes provide descriptive, meaningful names for your objects. You should give the objects descriptive names that are combined with their prefixes. Notice that the names for some objects, such as the command button object, should be descriptive of an action, as in cmdCalculate. Other objects that contain user-supplied information but are not directly associated with an action, such as a text box control, should have descriptive names similar to those of variables, as in txtShoeSize. You should make your own customized object-naming convention list a part of your standards because this is one part of your standards in particular that is likely to evolve. Over time, more and more controls of various types will probably become part of your programming repertoire as more controls become available. You will want to expand your standards to make sure to include standard prefixes for any controls you purchase in the future for your development.

Table 13.2 includes the subhead "Prefix," but the definitions include those for intrinsic HTML elements that are automatically defined, such as text box and check box controls, in addition to those that you explicitly define with the objects tag. These are a special type of object, and conceptually, your code treats them the same.

The `obj` tag is a generic tag that can be used to refer to any object. There is a virtually unlimited number of types of objects that you may encounter. Each new control created by vendors is a new kind of object. You may find that if you try to come up with a new meaningful prefix for each control you use, your code soon becomes filled with variable prefixes that confuse and befuddle you rather than serve the intended purpose of clarifying your code! For that reason, it is a good strategy to prefix the many objects under the spectrum that aren't addressed in Table 13.2 as `obj`. If you couple that with a meaningful name, then at a glance you can tell everything you need to know about the identifier. You know from the prefix that it's an object, and you know what kind of object from the remainder of the name. This can encompass ActiveX controls; browser objects such as windows, documents, frames, and the navigator; Java applets; and more. On the other hand, if you use one specific type of object frequently, it may warrant designating a standard prefix for it to help it stand out in your code. Remember, the overall goal is that you want prefix payback without prefix clutter!

Good naming conventions for objects are just as important as—and in some instances, more important than—naming conventions in other areas. This is because you can declare objects in many different places throughout a script. Keeping them straight can become a bit of a maintenance challenge as your Web pages grow larger. If you use good naming conventions, you have immediate feedback about exactly which types of objects the code is using and whether they are implicit or explicitly declared. Consider the following line where neither prefixes nor descriptive names are used in referring to an object:

```
feedback="normal"
```

This statement doesn't tell you too much without additional digging. A little dose of conventions makes it more descriptive even without looking further into the source code:

```
lblHeartRateFeedback.caption="normal"
```

This line tells you that a label object is used and provides more details on the type of information displayed in that label. Just the application of standard naming conventions to this statement is enough to tell you that the line fills a label with heart rate feedback. The modified statement also illustrates that object names, just like variable names, use a mixture of uppercase and lowercase for clarity and reading. The appropriate use of conventions in referencing objects can contribute a lot to the clarity of your overall script.

Procedure Declarations

By now you've seen many illustrations of how clear documentation and a consistent approach pay off. These same benefits hold true for procedure declarations as well. Several different areas of procedure conventions are important.

13

Descriptive Names for Procedures

Once again, descriptive names are the first step to a good, consistent approach. Because procedures carry out some action, the descriptive names have a slightly different focus. Procedure names should begin with an action word. If you saw a code statement that made a call to a procedure named GPA, it might not mean that much to you. Even if you realized that GPA stands for grade point average, you don't know whether this procedure displays a student's grade point average or prompts them for it or performs some other activity.

A better name for the procedure can make its intent very clear. It is no surprise that a procedure named CalculateGPA calculates a student's grade point average. This is one of the standard areas that you should never bypass. If a procedure does not start with an action word, the description name is generally not adequate. Procedure names, like variable names, should appear in mixed case to improve readability of the word components that make up the name.

Prefixes for Procedures

Prefixes indicating data subtypes of return codes are not generally used for procedures, although in some cases, this could add further clarity. Declaring functions with the appropriate prefix of the type of data that they are to return makes those function names even more descriptive. Because a programmer commonly refers to function description comments when reviewing function call statements, good comments usually suffice.

Procedure Comments

A procedure declaration should have a comment line that summarizes in one brief sentence the purpose of that procedure. There should also be a comment line that describes any arguments whose purpose is not immediately obvious from the arguments' names. Then you should have a line that specifically describes return values from the function if this is a function type procedure. It is important to document the return value for error conditions as well as normal conditions when appropriate. Following these comment lines should appear another descriptive block of comments for procedures that are of substantial size or complexity. The description area explains in detail the logic or algorithm of the procedure.

When writing these comments, the programmer should keep in mind that the reader of the comments will already know VBScript. You should make this assumption when writing comments to avoid unnecessarily over-commenting or adding comments of little value. For example, you don't need to describe the manner in which a For...Next loop works just because a For...Next loop appears within the algorithm. You have to make some basic assumptions about the programming level of the reader; otherwise, you would end up writing a book like this with each program!

13

Although the intrinsic VBScript syntax is a well-defined, finite topic that you can expect the comment reader to understand, control usage is not. There is no limit in sight to the number of controls that might evolve, and you shouldn't assume that your comment reader is aware of anything other than the basic ActiveX controls such as those covered in this book. Although it is a good hunch to assume that your reader knows VBScript, it is not a safe hunch to assume that your reader knows the usage of every control that your code references. If your code uses an ActiveX control, the reader of your comments and code might not be familiar with that control's functionality, properties, or methods. For that matter, if you are making a change to your script a year after it was written, you might not remember the characteristics of a control if it is one you don't use very frequently.

For this reason, it is appropriate to document in your comments any special uses of a control within the script. Descriptive comments are perhaps more subjective than any other standards area. A brief, well-done description can save time over the code maintenance life of a script. However, a poorly thought-out description or a few lines of description that you provide just for the sake of complying with a standard are often of little value. The best standard for the description area is to provide a description that illuminates the reader's understanding of the source code where necessary and appropriate.

Good Procedure Conventions in Action

Following good standards is a combination of using descriptive variable and procedure names and using comments. A script with very good names and a few appropriately placed comments by key declarations can be much more maintainable than a script with poor names and many lines of poorly composed comments. The best standard for procedures is to use descriptive names and start them with an action word in every case. Always include at least a one-line comment with the procedure declaration that briefly describes what it does. If the procedure has arguments or returns a value, include lines that outline that. Then include additional lines that describe the purpose, if needed. If you follow these guidelines, readers of your code will have a good feel for the capabilities of a procedure just by glancing at the top of a procedure declaration. They can dig deeper into the code when needed, but they won't be forced to dig through and decipher a procedure when they simply want to get a feel for what it does.

Listing 13.8 shows a good procedure declaration.

Listing 13.8. A procedure declaration that conforms to standards.

```
Function CalculateGPA(intGrade1,intCredits1,intGrade2,intCredits2)
'Purpose: Calculates grade point average for a two class-load term based on
'    the student's grade and credit hours for each of the classes
```

continues

Listing 13.8. continued

```
'Arguments:
'    intGrade1,intGrade2 - integer grades for class 1 and class 2 of
'        the student. These will be 4 for A, 3 for B, 2 for C, 1 for D, 0 for E
'    intCredits1, intCredits2 - the number of credit hours for each of the
classes,
'        ranging from 1 to 3 hours
'Returns: student's grade point average in single subtype ranging from 0 to 4
'Description:
'    Calculates the grade point average based on the average grade earned per
'    credit hour. Each class's grade is weighted by the number of credit hours
'    for that class to derive an overall average GPA for the student.
```

Within Your Code

You've seen how to use good conventions for variable names, constants, objects, and procedures. All that's left is the code itself! Most of the steps you can take to write good, maintainable, consistent code have already been described in terms of the other areas. Comments are critical. The same guidelines for procedure comments apply to code in general. Brief comments should accompany any block of code whose purpose is not obvious by the syntax and variable names. Again, the purpose of your comments should not be to explain VBScript. It should be to explain the nature of the problem, the reasoning and algorithms of the code, and the use of any unconventional controls.

There is no set guideline that works in every case for the number of comments required to describe your code statements. Generally, a comment for every line is overkill; but with complex code, this might be appropriate. The best approach is to use a brief comment for a group of statements that serve a common purpose. The placement of comments can help make your code more or less readable, too. Code statements are generally not as readable if comments appear at the end of a statement line. Comments nestled among code statements tend to stand out much better when they appear on a line of their own.

Using white space is another technique that can improve the readability of your code. Using white space simply means inserting a blank line in your code to separate one conceptual block of code from another. This makes each related group of statements stand out more as a separate entity. Some standard recommendations downplay white space for the sake of keeping the overall lines in a Web page as small as possible. It's true that each line of white space increases the overall number of bytes in the script, but the additional overhead from good use of white space is negligible. The maintainability advantages of good white space far outweigh the disadvantages.

Another technique to make code more readable is using proper indentation. We've used indentation throughout the samples in this book. Good indentation consists of spacing over statements that are logically subservient to a high-level statement. For example, in an If…Then

13

conditional, the statements inside the conditional are only performed if the condition is true. Indenting those statements four additional spaces makes it clear that the If statement always gets evaluated and the indented statements only get executed in certain conditions. Typically, you use four spaces for each level of indentation. Comments that follow a procedure declaration are usually indented one space from the procedure name.

You should also write VBScript syntax keywords consistently. The standard approach is to used mixed case. If…Then is more readable than if…then. The purpose of standards is to enhance the clarity and readability of code. You can use development tools for this purpose as well. Some commercial code editors can, with some effort on the part of the user, be custom configured to highlight VBScript keywords in a given color, and with time you can expect more and more VBScript-targeted tools to emerge in this category. Tools such as Microsoft's Control Pad Editor, described in Day 2, "The Essence of VBScript," also can lead to better code through features like the VBScript Wizard, which provides some automatic code generation. Such tools go a step beyond standards because it's not an action you can control in the way you write programs. However, it is important to realize that to some extent, standards and code viewing and generation tools are aimed at the same purpose—making the maintenance of code easier and more efficient.

NOTE

You can find more details on some of the tools in this category at www.doubleblaze.com as they emerge.

A good standard approach for your code statements like that described here is essential. This area in particular pays off when you're writing programs for the first time as well as when they're maintained in the future. If the program is easy to read, it will be easier to spot bugs and improve your logic as you write and work with the code. If the program is hard to read, it will tend to mask bugs and obscure your logic as you compose the program. Notice the code in Listing 13.9.

Listing 13.9. An example of code that was not written according to standards.

```
if intQuantity < 5 then
msgbox "additional $10 shipping charge will be applied for low volume order"
intOrderSurcharges=intOrderSurcharges+10
end if
if blnPromotionalOrder <> vbTrue then
msgbox "$20 handling fee will be applied"
intCharges=intCharges+20
end if
intTotalPrice = intCostOfOrder + intCharges
intTotalCost = intTotalCost * sngYEN_CONVERSION_FACTOR
```

You can see from the preceding code segment that it takes a little bit of strain and digging to understand what the code does. Now take a look at the readability when a good dose of standards has been applied in Listing 13.10.

Listing 13.10. Code that has been written with good adherence to standards.

```
'calculate the low volume order surcharge if needed
If intQuantity < 5 Then
    msgbox "additional $10 shipping charge will be applied for low volume order"
    intOrderSurcharges = intOrderSurcharges + 10
End If

'Add the standard handling fee unless it is a promotional order
If blnPromotionalOrder <> vbTrue Then
    msbbox "$20 handling fee will be applied"
    intCharges = intCharges + 20
End If

'Now calculate total price in yen using item cost computed earlier plus sur-
charges
intTotalPrice = intCostOfOrder + intCharges
intTotalCost = intTotalCost * sngYEN_CONVERSION_FACTOR
```

ANALYSIS You can see that it is much easier to read the second segment than it is to read the first. Unless you have a real penchant for puzzling other programmers as well as yourself, the second approach is clearly the recommended one.

Script Structure

A few guidelines pertain to overall script structure. An overview comment should appear at the start of the script. After the script tag <SCRIPT>, an HTML comment should appear on the next line. The use of the HTML comment indicator was discussed on Day 3, "Extending the Power of Web Pages with VBScript." This tag (<!--) should start a script so that browsers that don't support VBScript will treat the whole VBScript as a comment and not display it on screen. The corresponding ending tag (-->) then appears at the end of your script to terminate this comment behavior for browsers that do not support VBScript. Immediately after the comment tag at the start of the script should come an overview comment that states the overall purpose and goals of the script. It might seem to you that the goals of the script would be obvious, but if your page is large, it might not be immediately obvious to a reader who is trying to sift through the entire page. Code can be associated with many different aspects of a page and more than one script can appear in a page, so it is important to describe exactly what purpose a specific script serves.

13

Generally, your code should appear at the bottom of your page right before the </BODY> end-of-body tag. There are several advantages to this approach. This makes it very easy to locate all the code in a page. And there are some situations, particularly dealing with VBScript code intended to run as the page loads, in which the code must appear after the objects it references. Placing code at the bottom of the script frees you from any such concerns.

You can insert multiple scripts in your Web page. When possible, you should use one script rather than multiple script sections throughout the page. Using multiple scripts makes it that much harder to understand and maintain the code. In most cases, there is no reason not to combine multiple scripts into one script. One of the reasons that multiple scripts are sometimes used is that you can set up scripts to handle specific events, as in the line that follows:

```
<SCRIPT Language="VBScript" event=OnClick FOR=cmdButtonName>
```

This dedicates the entire script to that event, as was described on Day 7, "Building a Home for Your Code." If you have more than one event to catch, you'll need more than one script with this approach. However, you can easily convert such an event to a subroutine within one main script. The same event that is handled in a separate script can be converted to a subroutine that is named as follows:

```
<SCRIPT LANGUAGE="VBScript">
Sub_cmdButton_OnClick
```

The name assigned to the subroutine will cause it to be called as the event handler for the OnClick event of the button cmdButton. Using this approach, you can group all your event procedures in one script. A quiz solution at the end of today's lesson illustrates this approach.

You can also associate code with other input controls themselves, right on the input control definition line. This technique was addressed on Day 8, "Intrinsic HTML Form Controls." This line calls a message box right from the input control tag:

```
<INPUT TYPE="Button" NAME="cmdMyButton" LANGUAGE="VBScript"_
   OnClick="msgbox 'VB Rules': msgbox 'And it is fun!'">
```

Similarly, this line calls code directly from the body tag:

```
<BODY LANGUAGE="VBScript" OnLoad="msgbox 'VB Rules': msgbox_
   'And it is fun!'">
```

In general, avoid the temptation to blend code directly with input control definitions or other elements like this. The more you can group code together in one consolidated script block, the easier your maintenance will be. The code in the input control example above with the input button could be replaced by a subroutine named cmdMyButton_OnClick in the main script body, and the input tag could simply read

```
<INPUT TYPE="Button" NAME="cmdMyButton">
```

13

The code in the body tag example could simply be moved to the main script and placed at the start of the script, before the procedure definitions. Then it would get called at the end of the page load and the body statement could simply read

```
<BODY>
```

In both of these cases, you avoid tangling up code with your HTML statements, spread across your page. Instead, you consolidate the code into one well-defined place in your page—the script section. You've laid the groundwork for pages that are much easier to understand, debug, and modify in the future.

Startup code itself warrants some special consideration. Any code in your script that is not in a procedure is executed when it is sequentially encountered as the page loads. As a result, it is very important to know what and where this startup code is. Typically, you should include it right at the start of the script, explicitly commented with a line that says Startup code. But rather than have a large block of startup code, it is better practice to just have one statement that calls a StartUp subroutine you define. The name can be anything you define, but it is important to use the same name consistently across your pages for easiest maintenance, and StartUp is recommended for consistency across the industry (or at least across the pages of readers of this book!). This StartUp subroutine then becomes the well-known place for any page initialization code, consistent from page to page and project to project.

A previous example from today illustrates that you can associated startup code directly in the body tag. This opens the door to the possibility of calling the StartUp subroutine there, with a statement such as

```
<BODY LANGUAGE="VBScript" OnLoad="StartUp">
```

This works as well, but in some respects, it is a much less maintainable approach. If your startup code is clearly designated at the top of your script section, it is perfectly clear when you look at the code what startup code gets executed. If you use the practice of triggering your startup code from the body tag, on the other hand, a reader could review the script statements and never realize that some routine there had special startup characteristics. So the <BODY OnLoad=> approach to indicating a starting procedure can be slightly less clear. If you do use that approach, make sure to use ample comments in the script to indicate the startup behavior caused by the body tag.

NOTE

It is interesting to compare the behavior of a StartUp subroutine called from the <BODY OnLoad=> tag versus a StartUp routine defined at the top of a script appearing immediately prior to the end of the document's closing </BODY> tag. If you use both of these methods in the same script, you will find that the <BODY OnLoad=> subroutine gets triggered first, followed by the subroutine defined in the script at the end of the document. When you consider that a page is processed sequentially on load, this makes intuitive sense.

Concerns

You have heard a lot of reasons for using standards and conventions. If you've talked to many other programmers or thought much about these issues, you might also have some concerns about the disadvantages of adherence to standards and conventions. Several concerns often come up in relation to standards.

Myth: The Overhead Penalty Outweighs the Advantages of Standards

One of these concerns is quite unique to the nature of VBScript—whether you should avoid using white space and plenty of comments because it makes the Web page size larger. Most programming languages are compiled into a final executable and the end user pays no price for size of the source code. However, in the case of VBScript used with Web pages, the end user is affected. If you put many hundreds of lines of comment into the script on a Web page, the end user will have to download a Web page that is many hundreds of lines larger.

Should this make you avoid comments? The answer is no. The advantages of writing good code through comments far outweigh the disadvantages of this overhead penalty. The extra download time caused by including additional bytes of the script to download will usually be negligible and not something your user will perceive. It would take many lines of comments to add up to the several kilobytes of data that would be necessary to introduce a noticeable wait even on systems connected by the slowest of means. On the other hand, you don't want to turn the comments for your scripts into gargantuan guides to every aspect of a project.

You should keep in mind the download overhead factor and avoid the temptation to add unnecessary fluff or extensive documentation to scripts. If you feel that a lot of documentation is needed to supplement a script, it might be better addressed in a separate design document you could maintain elsewhere. Many projects use a design document approach to document overall goals for a project. Then the developers proceed to build the specific programs or scripts, including only comments relative to that specific script in the script itself. This is a good approach for larger projects and can cut down on extensive comments within the scripts without sacrificing the advantages of documentation.

13

Myth: Standards Slow Me Down

Another common concern about standards and conventions is that it takes more time to write code when you must worry about making it adhere to standards. This argument is based on a shortsighted view. If you put careful thought into following a good set of standards and conventions and carefully documenting your code through good comments and procedure and variable names, it might indeed take you longer to type in the keystrokes of your program. When this time penalty is compared to the significant maintenance, debug, and even design time benefits that result from good documentation, the truth becomes clear. Carefully adhering to standards and conventions saves time over the long run.

Trying to bypass standards and conventions is a lot like trying to speed up your vacation trip by skipping the visit to the gas station. You'll get on the road more quickly, but you're more likely to run into delay before you reach your final destination when you run out of gas. A good way to make sure that the time taken to comply with standards is productive is to keep in mind that the purpose of your standards and conventions is to increase efficiency overall. If one of your standards seems particularly troubling and time-consuming, you should examine it with respect to your overall standards. If you don't see the benefit of a certain standard, don't use it, but carefully weigh the pros and cons before making such a decision.

The Non-Myth: Standards Constrain Me!

Finally, perhaps the most common concern about standards is that they require discipline on the part of the developer and can make the developer feel constrained. This is no myth but is the cold hard truth, and it is true for good reason. Discipline and constraint is not always a bad thing. Producing software is a creative art, but it is also a logical science. It is something that affects other people and sometimes businesses and their bottom line. Although it might be more fun to program free-form with no thought for the future, it is not the best programming practice.

Paying the price of a slightly more disciplined and constrained approach is well worth the effort. This is especially true because the benefits of following standards and conventions don't mean any loss of creativity or flexibility in design. You just exercise your creativity under more controlled circumstances. The graffiti artist who plies his trade by recklessly defacing buildings has no more claim on creativity than the professional artist who sketches within the borders of a notepad. The professional artist simply has more foresight. The benefits are there for the taking for whoever is wise enough to apply them.

Summary

Today's lesson discusses many aspects of standards and conventions and points out the advantages to using standards and conventions. Code that conforms to a common set of conventions will be easier to maintain, easier to debug, and even easier to write. Often, the act of writing good code as you go along leads you to clearer organization and structure. One of the challenges for getting started with standards and conventions is deciding exactly which standards to use. A good general recommendation is to follow the Microsoft guidelines as closely as possible, extending them where you feel it is necessary for the sake of your project. Today's lesson presents a detailed set of such guidelines.

The lesson first introduces the standards for variables. One important aspect of declaring variables is giving them meaningful, descriptive names with an adjective as part of the name, where appropriate. You should name variables in mixed case to enhance readability. You should also use prefixes with variables, where appropriate, to indicate the intended data subtype representation of the variable. However, this technique is a bit harder to apply in VBScript than in other languages because VBScript is not a strongly typed language. As a result, an important part of the standard approach for VBScript is to use the v prefix to indicate a variable is a variant with a subtype that might change representation. You should use a scope prefix that consists of s_ to indicate global variables that can be referenced from any procedure.

Comments can help a great deal in highlighting the purpose of variables. You can use comments at the end of a variable declaration on the same line as the Dim statement. You can also use them to describe a group of related variables. Such related variables should be grouped together, and any relationships between the variables should be described in the declaration comments. Such comments are provided in a line or group of lines preceding the variables.

Today's lesson also examines constants. VBScript constants are really variables but can still be indicated separately by using uppercase letters for the constant names. Intrinsic VBScript constants are not defined by the user and will always be preceded by a vb. Object names should be similar to variable names. You should use mixed case for readability. You should also use descriptive prefixes to indicate the type of the object. For example, an intrinsic text box control would have a name that starts with txt. An ActiveX control object such as a timer would have a name that starts with tmr. In this manner, the type of object is easily apparent from looking at the source code.

It's also important to provide a standard approach in procedure declarations. Like variable and object names, procedure names should be descriptive. However, procedure names should start with an action type word to indicate the action performed when the procedure is called. It is important to use comments in a procedure declaration, including at least one line that briefly describes what the procedure does. If it's appropriate, you should provide additional lines describing arguments and return codes. If the procedure is not trivial, you can provide additional lines of description in the procedure comment area at the top of the procedure. In any comments, it is safe to assume that the reader knows VBScript. Comments should elaborate on aspects of algorithm, logic, or infrequently used control aspects.

13

The guidelines for code statements are much the same as those for procedures. You should use good comments, which can refer to groups of statements where appropriate. You should also use indentation and blank lines to set apart code statements and make them clearly readable where needed. Show VBScript keywords in mixed case. Some utilities can also help with the maintainability of code by highlighting keywords in certain colors.

Finally, today's lesson addresses some concerns about following standards and conventions. It is true that to a certain extent, adhering to the conventions listed here can result in larger Web pages. The source code for your scripts will grow larger through the comments and as a result, so will your Web pages. However, in most cases, this additional overhead is very insignificant. It's also true that following conventions might take a little more time in the short run to initially write your programs. This time is more than saved by the improvements in development, debugging, and code maintenance that come about through the use of the conventions. It's also true that using conventions makes you or some of the programmers you work with feel constrained. This is another price that is worth paying if you care about efficient software development and developing the best program possible.

The benefits of standards and conventions are clear and overwhelming in the software industry. Good style and use of conventions pays off in many ways. For example, the use of good, descriptive variable names and procedure names often makes the code very readable in itself and lessens the need for many lines of comments. A more readable program can end up producing many benefits. Code can be easier to debug, maintain, and even originally design. As a result, the end product you provide on the Web for the user of your Web pages and scripts is better.

Q&A

Q **If you will be the only one using your scripts, is there any advantage to using standards and conventions?**

A Yes, there certainly is. Adhering to standards and conventions can help you even at the initial script development time. It forces you to think through and document your code, procedures, and variables to a greater degree. This can lead to better design and implementation. It can be a great help in debugging when you must traverse through your code to track down problems. If you have to return to your code in the future, you'll have a much easier time if it has been written to standards and conventions. It is amazing how quickly a developer can forget programs that he has written a few months back!

Q **Which procedure name is better for a procedure that converts inches to centimeters? Is it `inchtoc` or `ConvertInchesToCm`? Is it better to have a shorter name to save keystrokes?**

A `ConvertInchesToCm` is a much better procedure name. It is far more descriptive and therefore will be easier to maintain. The few extra bytes this name will cost you will probably not have any noticeable impact on your end user if your script is an average size.

Q **Suppose you have a text box that collects an age from the user. Is `objAge` a good name for that text box?**

A No, it is not. If you glance at the name of that object, the type of the object is not apparent. A better name would be `txtAge`. Then, it is clear that the object is type text.

Workshop

View the sample scripts from Microsoft on the World Wide Web. Take a look at their standards and conventions. (You can find all this information at `http://www.microsoft.com/vbscript`.) Document your own standards and conventions based on what you see there, what you've read today, and what you feel is appropriate. Document an approach that is good for you and your workplace. In what areas do you deviate from Microsoft and this book? Do you think the industry standard approach will be similar?

Quiz

NOTE   Refer to Appendix C, "Answers to Quiz Questions," for the answers to these questions.

1. Observe the following program. Its purpose is to accept an age and present one message if the age indicates that the user is in Generation X. Otherwise, it will present a different message. If the age is invalid or hasn't been supplied yet, the user should receive appropriate feedback. Take the following segment and change the variable names and indentation to make it more readable.

```
nm = info.value
If IsNumeric(nm) then
if nm < x then
msgbox "Dude, prepare to surf!"
else
msgbox "Welcome - Prepare to enter our Web page"
End if
Elsif nm = "unknown" then
msgbox="you must supply an age to proceed"
Else
msgbox "please supply a valid age"
End if
```

13

2. Take the following two scripts and merge them into one script:

```
<script Language="VBScript" FOR="lblFeedback" event=click>
msgbox "Feedback label has been clicked"
</script>

...html definitions appear here...

<script Language="VBS" FOR=cmdCalculate"event=OnClick>
msgbox "Button has been clicked"
</script>
```

Day 14

Working with Documents and User Interface Functions

A key goal of VBScript is to enable you to make your documents come alive. With VBScript, your documents are no longer just another pretty document for the user to stare at. Instead, your document becomes an interactive application. It responds to the user's requests, obtains information from the user, and carries out processing at his request. By now you know a lot of what it takes to make a document come alive. You've seen how to put together a script that interacts with component objects on the Web page. Examples of integrating intrinsic controls, ActiveX objects, and Java applets have appeared on previous days, along with techniques for wrapping code around them to let your scripts interact with them. But you haven't yet seen all the details of how to make the page itself be responsive above and beyond the components placed on it.

The details of scripting responsive, interactive Web pages is the topic today. Some specific techniques allow you to interact with the user right from your code, without going through an integrated component. You have already seen a simple form of one of these inherent capabilities, the message box function MsgBox. Now you will learn how to use MsgBox to its fullest and see a similar function supported by Internet Explorer that you can make use of, called Alert. Also presented in detail is the InputBox function, which offers even more interaction possibilities than the message box. Finally, the document object that represents the page itself is addressed. You can control generation of that document page through code as well as through the standard HTML statements behind it.

The most exciting aspect of these capabilities is that they allow you to perform advanced interaction with the user. If you come from other graphical programming environments, you may have felt constrained by VBScript so far. If you're used to writing programs that display an additional form or window for each piece of user interaction, the one-page model central to VBScript has probably left you wondering "How do I easily give my user dynamic feedback, prompt him for the next piece of information, or generate a different form based on changing conditions?" The user interface approaches addressed here give you much of the answer. Today's lesson highlights how to implement interaction without going through integrated components. Even if you know about the message box and input box from Visual Basic or another background, don't bypass this chapter entirely. The fundamental functions are introduced first, but a detailed look at the document.write method and dynamically generating HTML follows. This culminates in an example at the end of the lesson that shows how message box capabilities and document.write can be combined to provide a user-customizable page at load time. Then the remaining pieces of the picture are wrapped up on Day 18, "Advanced User Interface and Browser Object Techniques," as the tradeoffs of user interaction across single or multiple pages are discussed.

Giving the User the Message Through Message Boxes

Sometimes, particularly in a programming language, simple is beautiful. An easy-to-use programming function or element is less likely to cause you bugs, which saves you time, effort, and the pain of banging your head on the monitor in frustration. Simple means good, clear, maintainable code. The message box function is just that—good and simple!

You have seen examples of the message box in earlier chapters. For example, you can insert a statement in your code that displays a small window with the message Break time! with just 20 characters of typing:

```
MsgBox "Break time!"
```

When this code statement is carried out, a window containing this message pops up in the middle of the screen. Not only does the user see this message in a nice little window, but that window even comes with a handy acknowledgment button. The window hangs around until the user clicks on the button to make it go away.

VBScript offers another way to send a message to your user: You can use the Alert function. This function was first used in the JavaScript language. It actually isn't a part of the VBScript language, but is a function supported by the Internet Explorer host environment. Because you have access to this type of host functions (covered in more detail on Day 18), you can use Alert. Like MsgBox, Alert displays the text in a message window and provides a button that must be selected to acknowledge the message. The windows generated by Alert and MsgBox are shown in Figure 14.1.

Figure 14.1.

The Alert *and* MsgBox *message windows.*

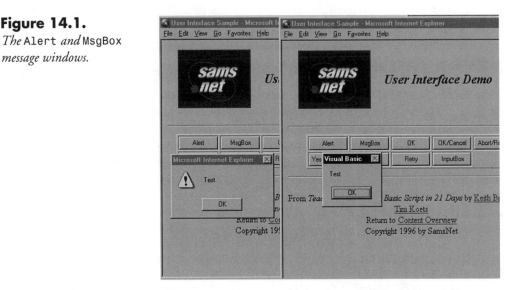

One obvious difference between these two functions is shown in Figure 14.1. Alert places a title at the top of the window that says Microsoft Internet Explorer and uses the ! icon; MsgBox provides the default title Visual Basic and does not show an icon.

Line Separation

The MsgBox function allows extensive customization of the information it presents. The first parameter to this function, as you have seen, provides the message that is displayed to the user. If you want this message to be provided as more than one line when the message is presented, you simply separate each desired line with the VBScript intrinsic constant vbCrLf. For example, the following sample displays "Line1", "Line2", and "Line3", each on a separate line within the message box:

```
Dim vbCrLf : vbCrLf = Chr(13) & Chr(10)
MsgBox "Line1" & vbCrLf & "Line2" & vbCrLf & "Line3"
```

In addition to using vbCrLf to force a line separation, you could also use just Chr(13) or Chr(13) & Chr(10). These are all different ways of telling VBScript to separate a line. VBScript knows to separate a line if it sees a carriage return character or a line feed character, represented by these constants and ASCII character codes. These invisible characters don't show up on the screen, but they do convey formatting information.

You may be wondering why you have so many choices about how to request a line separation. It used to be that for a particular operating system you had to supply exactly the right characters from a language to control line separation. For example, you had to use the command Chr(13) on some systems, and Chr(13) & Chr(10) on other types of systems. VBScript is smart enough to relieve you of this burden. If it gets any of these characters, it knows you want to separate a line. It won't be picky.

NOTE

> Alert offers capabilities similar to MsgBox in the line separation area. The rest of this section focuses specifically on the MsgBox function, since it is used for a wider variety of situations than Alert.

Buttons and Titles

Figure 14.1 shows a plain-looking message box that provides a minimum amount of interaction. First, let's consider the issue of interaction. The user could choose to click on OK, or he could choose to click on OK. There are no other choices! The purpose of forcing the user to select OK is to ensure that he has read the message presented. The OK button, in this case, is simply an acknowledgment button.

There are ways to use MsgBox to get much more information from the user than simply an acknowledgment. The second parameter of the function is used to specify message box attributes. One attribute that can be specified is the type of button choices that the message box can provide to the user. Consequently, this affects the type of return code information that is provided back to your code.

Several types of button choice attributes may be designated. Each attribute can be specified by a specific integer number. To make working with these attributes easier and make code that uses them more maintainable, a file is provided on the CD-ROM to define them. The file is constant.txt in the shared\tools directory. The needed declaration lines can be copied and pasted to your own script. The constant names, values, and purposes are summarized in Table 14.1. Normally you will refer to these attributes by constant name only, and will not have to use the value.

Table 14.1. VBScript button constants.

Constant Name	Value	Purpose
vbOK	0	Show only OK button
vbOkCancel	1	Show OK and Cancel buttons
vbAbortRetryIgnore	2	Show Abort, Retry, and Ignore buttons
vbYesNoCancel	3	Show Yes, No, and Cancel buttons
vbYesNo	4	Show Yes and No buttons
vbRetryCancel	5	Show Retry and Cancel buttons

The message box shown in Figure 14.1 has the OK button. This button is provided by default if you do not supply a second parameter to designate the button attribute. A message that presents just an OK button is typically used to present information to the user and have him acknowledge that the information has been read.

You can use button attribute constants to request different combinations of buttons as well. All the available combinations are documented in Table 14.1. Most of these combinations give the user the opportunity to provide more feedback to the script than just a simple acknowledgment. The vbYesNoCancel constant, for example, provides three choices for the user. The script can then interpret which button the user selected and perform further processing based on that response.

The approach to interpreting the user's response from a script is considered next. But first, consider the cosmetic aspects of the message box. An example of a vbYesNoCancel message box appears in Figure 14.2.

The line of code that produced this message box is

```
rc = MsgBox( "rc = MsgBox ""Text""", vbYesNoCancel + vbExclamation, _
        ""Title"" ", vbYesNoCancel + vbExclamation, "vbYesNoCancel")
```

14

Figure 14.2.

A message box with Yes, No, and Cancel buttons.

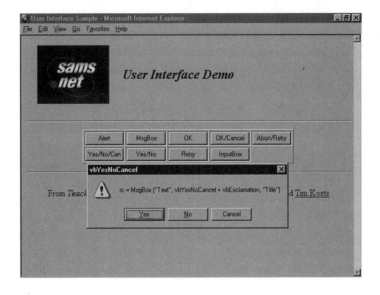

NOTE

When you want a quote to be displayed within a string, use two consecutive quotes. Only one will appear in your string, and the string will not be terminated by the occurrence of the double quotes. This is the technique used in the code example, which prints out a message box that has quotes as part of the message string. Because a double quote (represented by two double quotes) needs to be printed at the end of the main string (closed by a double quote), you see three double quotes at the end.

The preceding is a complicated-looking line of code at first glance, but that is largely because the message that is provided in the first parameter contains sample syntax for a message box. For the sake of clarity, assume you wanted to use the same type of message box to display the question Do you use VBScript?. The call to generate that question with Yes, No, and Cancel buttons would be

```
rc = MsgBox( "Do you use VBScript?", vbYesNoCancel + vbExclamation, "My Title")
```

Consider this call a piece at a time. First of all, rc is the variable that is used here to receive the return code from the function call. This variable will be filled with a number that indicates the user's button choice. Then consider the three parameters to the MsgBox function. The first parameter is simply the message or question that you want to display. Turn your attention next to the third parameter (an easier one!). That parameter indicates the title that is displayed on the caption area of the message box. If no third parameter is supplied, `Visual Basic` will show up as the default title.

Finally, consider the second parameter. The values you supply here are codes that determine the attributes of the message box. Table 14.1 lists the attribute constant values you can use for certain combinations of buttons. The intrinsic constant `vbYesNoCancel` is used in the preceding sample to cause the Yes, No, and Cancel buttons to appear. When buttons are requested, the message box automatically takes care of generating them and returning a predefined number for that specific button through the function's return code. So the `vbYesNoCancel` constant in the second parameter causes generation of a window with three specific buttons, and each button will cause a specific documented number to be generated when it is clicked.

But that's not the whole story of the second parameter. The second parameter has two pieces joined by a plus sign. The button indicator code is on the left side. What's that on the right side? It's a value that indicates the icon to display with the message box. These values are represented by a VBScript intrinsic value declarations in `shared\tools\constant.txt` on the CD-ROM. Just like the button value, they can be one of the entries in Table 14.2.

Table 14.2. VBScript message box icon values.

Constant Name	Value	Purpose
vbCritical	16	Show an X, used for a critical error
vbQuestion	32	Show a question mark, used for a question
vbExclamation	48	Show an exclamation point, used for a warning
vbInformation	64	Show an I, used for an informational message

The attribute parameter can be used to convey two pieces of information to the message box function. This simply requires adding the button attribute and icon attribute value together. For example, the `vbOKCancel` value is 1 and the `vbCritical` icon value is 16. Normally you would request this combination of attributes with a statement like this:

```
MsgBox "Testing", vbOKCancel + vbCritical, "My Title"
```

But you could achieve the same result with this statement:

```
MsgBox "Testing", 17, "My Title"
```

The first approach is recommended because it makes for more readable, more maintainable code. But both work just the same. Even the combined number uniquely identifies both attributes because command button values are 5 and less, and icon values are 16 and higher.

14

All you really have to know to use these effectively, however, is that you can combine both values into this one parameter.

Look again at Figure 14.2 to see an example of the exclamation point icon. This was produced, along with the Yes, No, and Cancel buttons, by this line of code:

```
rc = MsgBox( "rc = MsgBox ""Text""", vbYesNoCancel + vbExclamation, ""Title""", _
    vbYesNoCancel + vbExclamation, "vbYesNoCancel")
```

Figure 14.3 shows an example of the information icon on a message box.

Figure 14.3.

A message box with the information icon.

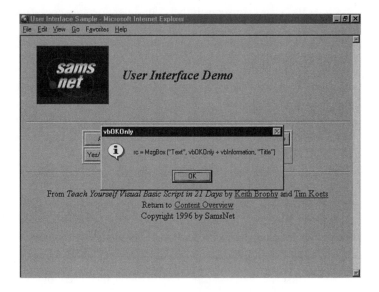

This message box has only the OK button. It was generated by the following statement:

```
rc = MsgBox( "rc = MsgBox ""Text""", vbOKOnly + vbInformation, _
    ""Title"" ",vbOKonly + vbInformation, "vbOKOnly")
```

The value of the vbOKOnly constant is 0. Therefore, this code would work exactly the same if the following statement were used:

```
rc = MsgBox( "rc = MsgBox ""Text""", vbInformation, ""Title"" ", vbInformation, _
    "vbOKOnly")
```

Figure 14.4 shows a message box that uses the question mark icon, along with Yes and No buttons. That message box was generated by the following statement:

```
rc = MsgBox( "rc = MsgBox ""Text""", vbYesNo + vbQuestion, ""Title"" ", _
    vbYesNo + vbQuestion, "vbYesNo")
```

Figure 14.4.

A message box with a question mark icon and Yes and No buttons.

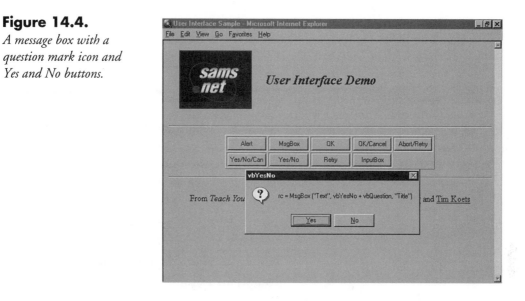

Figure 14.5 rounds out the list of icon types. This figure shows an example of the critical error icon, combined with the OK and Cancel buttons. It was produced by this line of code:

```
rc = MsgBox( "rc = MsgBox ""Text"", vbOKCancel + vbCritical, ""Title"" ", _
    vbOKCancel + vbCritical, "vbOKCancel")
```

Figure 14.5.

A message box with a critical error icon and OK and Cancel buttons.

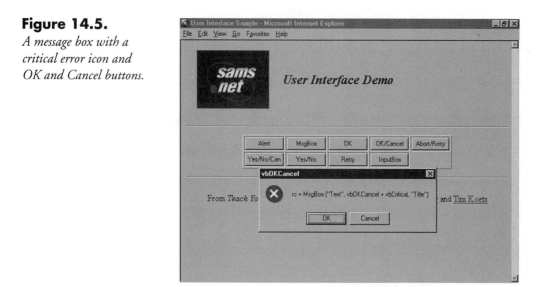

14

The choice of which icon to use in which situation should be based on the criteria that the icon names imply. Informational feedback that is not an error condition should use the information icon. If you are asking the user a direct question, use a question mark icon. Less severe errors are typically presented with the exclamation point icon. Very severe errors that can bring a script to a halt or invalidate results would warrant the use of the critical error icon.

Each of the code statements in the icon type illustrates the use of a variable to capture the MsgBox return code. When this function is used, it sends a return value back to the statement it was called from. This return code can be assigned to a variable of any name, although the convention of rc for return code is often used. The return code will indicate which button the user selected. This value will be one of the ones shown in Table 14.3.

Table 14.3. VBScript button response values.

Constant Name	Value	Purpose
vbOK	1	Returned by MsgBox if OK is selected
vbCancel	2	Returned by MsgBox if Cancel is selected
vbAbort	3	Returned by MsgBox if Abort is selected
vbRetry	4	Returned by MsgBox if Retry is selected
vbIgnore	5	Returned by MsgBox if Ignore is selected
vbYes	6	Returned by MsgBox if Yes is selected
vbNo	7	Returned by MsgBox if No is selected

If you have used programs in a Windows environment, you probably know one very important aspect of the message box window: It is modal. This means that when a message box is presented to the user, he must respond to it before he can interact further with that Web page. This is great news from a script programming standpoint. When a script puts up a message box, you know that by the time the next code statement is carried out, the user will have already provided a response to that message. This gives you a high degree of control over the interaction. You know the user has to respond when you offer a message, and you know that in the statement after the message you have a record of the user's response.

Your script can take further action based on the return code. An example of code that evaluates the return code from MsgBox is shown in Listing 14.1.

Listing 14.1. Evaluating the return code from MsgBox.

```
Sub cmdYesNoCan_OnClick
    dim strFeedback ' Feedback string
    dim rc ' return code from message box call
```

14

```
rc = MsgBox( "rc = MsgBox ""Text"", vbYesNoCancel + vbExclamation, _
    ""Title""", _
        vbYesNoCancel + vbExclamation, "vbYesNoCancel")

strFeedback = "Response was " & rc & "." & vbCrLf
if rc = vbYes then
    strFeedback = strFeedback & _
    "This is equal to vbYes and indicates Yes was clicked."
elseif rc = vbNo then
    strFeedback = strFeedback & _
    "This is equal to vbNo and indicates No was clicked."
elseif rc = vbCancel then
    strFeedback = strFeedback & _
    "This is equal to vbCancel, indicates Cancel clicked."
else
    strFeedback = strFeedback & _
    "This is not equal to any expected constant."
end if

msgbox strFeedback, vbOKOnly, "vbYesNoCancel Return Code"
end sub
```

ANALYSIS The message box is generated by the third line of this code. Since the `vbYesNoCancel` attribute value is specified, the message box will have only three buttons—the Yes button, the No button, and the Cancel button. Therefore, these are the *only* possible buttons the user can interact with. As a result, the only possible values that can result from this call to the `MsgBox` function are `vbYes`, `vbNo`, and `vbCancel`. The code in the last half of the listing compares the return code to each of these possible values to build the final result string.

The message box provides yet another interaction choice to the user. You can specify a help file name and help file context in a fourth and fifth parameter to the function. The help file indicates a file with help information that corresponds to the message. The help file context identifies a specific topic within that help file to be displayed. If help file information is provided, a help button will also appear on the message box. Display of the help file will only occur if the user clicks on the help button or selects the F1 key. Help information is typically used to provide more details on an error message for the user.

Now you have been exposed to all the parameters of the message box. The only parameter that must be specified is the message parameter. The rest are optional. They are summarized here for your reference:

```
ResultVariable = MsgBox(prompt_string, optional_button_and_icon_values,
optional_title, optional_helpfile, optional_context)
```

Why might you want to get a user response through a message box? Perhaps your script detects invalid input and needs to know whether the user wants to respecify it or ignore it. Or maybe you need to ask a series of yes-and-no questions to determine how to carry out a calculation for a user. Or, if a calculation ends up taking many loops, you might want to

14

present the user with a choice to continue or cancel the operation. In situations like these, feedback from the user can be crucial to the operation of your script. If you had to get this feedback by interacting with form controls every time, your pages would look intimidating to the user. They might contain prompt fields that are rarely used, and the user's interaction task would be much more complex. Instead of a window popping up before the user's eyes in the middle of the screen, the user would have to locate the equivalent field. For all these reasons, message boxes can play a very important role in your script user interface design.

NOTE

This discussion focuses on using `MsgBox` as a function. `MsgBox` can also be used as a subroutine call. The difference in that case is that a subroutine call does not return a value. Simply call it as a statement rather than treating it as a function and capturing its value in a return code if you don't care about the return code. Here's an example:

```
MsgBox "rc = MsgBox ""Text"", vbOKCancel + vbCritical,_
    ""Title""",vbOKCancel + vbCritical, "vbOKCancel"
```

This statement will not provide a value back. `InputBox`, which is considered next, can also be called as a function or a call. The function-based approach is considered here. It is the more common and powerful approach because you can take action base on the return codes.

Input Boxes

Message boxes can greatly extend the power of your scripts. You can provide feedback to the user without having to run it through the Web page. You can get responses from the user that the script can act on, all in a separate window that the user must interact with before proceeding. The message box model works great for collecting responses unless you want more feedback than simply yes, no, cancel, abort, retry, or ignore. But in the case of certain data on a form, you might need more information from the user before submitting the data. The information you need might be additional string information such as alternative supplier information. Ideally, you want to collect this information in a supplemental window to your page for the same reasons that message boxes are handy. If you had to provide additional input fields for just a few special cases, your page could be quite messy. It might be hard to highlight the appropriate fields for the user, and it would be difficult to ensure that all the information has been provided as you proceed through a sequence of steps. Fortunately, the message box has a close cousin that can come to the rescue in cases like this. The input box function `InputBox` provides a separate modal window much like the message box. It can present a prompt message to the user and collect an input string that is returned back to the script.

An example of an input box appears in Figure 14.6. Unlike the message box, the input box has no icon that is displayed. It also does not provide any control over the buttons that appear. OK and Cancel buttons appear on every input box.

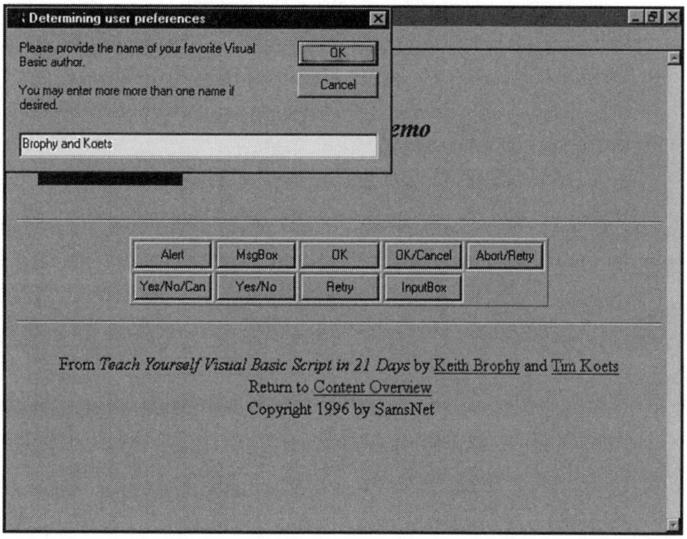

Figure 14.6.

The input box prompting for user input.

The input box gives you control over the most important aspects. Namely, you can retrieve text from it. The code that generated the input box in Figure 14.6 is shown in Listing 14.2.

Listing 14.2. The `InputBox` function call.

```
Sub cmdInputBox_OnClick
    dim strFeedback ' Feedback string
    dim rc ' return code from message box call
    rc = InputBox( _
        "Please provide the name of your favorite Visual Basic author." & _
        vbCrLf & vbCrLf & _
        "You may enter more more than one name if desired." , _
        "Determining user preferences", "Brophy and Koets", 0, 0)

    strFeedback = "Response was " & rc & "." & vbCrLf
    if rc = "" then
        strFeedback = strFeedback & _
        "The user did not care to provide a response."
    elseif rc = "Brophy and Koets" then
        strFeedback = strFeedback & "The user used the default response."
    else
        strFeedback = strFeedback & _
```

continues

14

Listing 14.2. continued

```
        "The free thinking user supplied their own response."
    end if

    msgbox strFeedback, vbOKOnly, "InputBox User Response"
end sub
```

ANALYSIS The InputBox function statement appears in the fourth statement of the listing. This is the function call format:

```
ResultVar = InputBox(prompt_message, optional_title,
optional_default_response, optional_x_position,
optional_y_position, optional_helpfile,
optional_helpfile_context )
```

The first parameter is the prompt message. This is the message displayed in the input box window that prompts the user for his response. As you can see in Figure 14.6, the prompt for the sample is spread over more than one line. The vbCrLf declaration discussed earlier today can serve as a line separator for input box prompts, just as it can for message box prompts. The prompt must be supplied, but the rest of the parameters are optional.

The next parameter is the title of the window, which is displayed in the top caption area. If a title is not supplied, Visual Basic will appear in its place.

The third parameter is the default response. This response will show up in the text input area that is supplied for user input when the input box is generated. In the input box shown in Figure 14.6, Brophy and Koets was supplied as the default response. The default response is a response that the user is likely to provide. If he wants to go with the default, he can simply select the OK key and doesn't have to type in any text. To provide a specific response, the user simply types the desired response, then selects OK. The new input will automatically replace the highlighted default, and no backspacing or deletion is necessary.

The fourth and fifth parameters control the placement of the input box in x and y coordinates from the top of the screen. In the sample, the X and Y were specified to be 0, so the input box appeared at the top-left corner of the screen. If no values are supplied, the input box appears centered horizontally on the screen and a third of the way down. It is interesting to note that you cannot control the message box placement, but you can control the placement of the input box. You might want to control placement of an input box if you ask the user for information relating to what he has on the Web page in front of him. In that case, you don't want to obscure the user's view of the page any more than you have to in case he wants to rely on information on the page while deciding on his input.

The sixth and seventh parameters of the InputBox function call are for help file and help file context information. The help file support for InputBox is the same as that for the message box.

The manner of retrieving the user response for an InputBox call is also similar to that of MsgBox. After the user enters a string into the input area and clicks OK, that user-supplied value is returned. In the case of the example in Listing 14.2, the return value is assigned to the return code variable rc. From that point on, you can do anything with the variable that you would do with any string. The options are many, including comparing it, reassigning it, or searching it for a substring. If the user just selects OK without providing his own input, the default string will be returned. If there is no default, if the user deletes the text and presses OK, or if the user selects the Cancel button at any point, a zero-length string of " " will be returned. The code in Listing 14.2 illustrates how to check the return code to determine if a new string was provided, if the default string was used, or if a cancel occurred.

The InputBox function can extend the capabilities of your scripts very easily. The function is easy to use and integrate. Many languages provide similar functions. With traditional non–Web page applications, it might be considered bad form to rely too heavily on this function. A series of more detailed windows, or of good data collection on one dynamic window, often provides easier and better interaction for the user. However, in the scripted Web page model you are dealing with, your options are limited. It's not as easy to make the entire page dynamic since you often must share it with static HTML-generated text, and you can't provide the user with a series of windows controlled from one main script. Often, the closest you can come is with controlled use of InputBox. This technique allows your scripts to make a page one step closer to an application and one step further away from being just a static display of information. At the end of this chapter a detailed example built on a flow of input boxes is provided. But first, consider one more interesting way to provide information to the user.

Documents

So far you've seen examples of many different ways to extend and control a Web page through your scripts. Integrated components such as input controls and ActiveX controls that can be manipulated through scripts were addressed on Day 10, "An Introduction to Objects and ActiveX Controls," and Day 11, "More ActiveX Controls." There are also capabilities for feedback that are intrinsic to VBScript such as the message box and input box functions examined today. But one area has not yet been approached. That is the Web page document itself and the HTML code on which it is based.

The document Object and the form Object

On earlier days, including Day 9, "More Intrinsic HTML Form Controls," you saw that a form is referenced with respect to the intrinsic document object. Suppose you have definitions like those in Listing 14.3.

14

Listing 14.3. An HTML definition to include a form on the page.

```
<FORM NAME="MyForm">
<INPUT NAME="txtAge">
<INPUT NAME="txtLastName">
</FORM>
```

A special means of designating these entities is needed if you want to reference that form and the text input controls on it through VBScript code. You must describe the controls in terms of the form object they are associated with, and the form object in terms of the page's document. To display the value of the input control in a message box, you would use code like the following:

```
MsgBox document.MyForm.txtLastName
```

document represents the page itself, and HTML forms are a part of that page. You don't have to worry too much about the document object in this context, other than to realize it is a part of the name you must use to reference a form control. There is even a VBScript shortcut to get you past using document in the reference every time. Just define a variable that refers to the document, as in the following:

```
Set frmCurrent = document.MyForm
```

Then, in subsequent references to the txtLastName control you don't even have to include the document object:

```
MsgBox frmCurrent.txtLastName
```

The document.write Method

document can do a lot more than just give you a means to reference a form. To understand the additional capabilities, it helps to first consider what a document is and how it is generated. The Web page document is rendered by the browser based on the HTML instructions for the browser. The HTML tags are read in and interpreted when the page is loaded, and then are not processed again by the browser unless the document is reloaded by the user. Script options to control the document by generating HTML source code for the page are therefore limited. The only window of opportunity for a Web page script to affect the HTML behind a document is when the page is initially loaded.

Fortunately, an intrinsic document object is available for this purpose. document represents the page itself and has a write method that can be applied to the page. The document.write method can be used from code to write HTML statements to that page. Any valid HTML statement can be generated to the page by document.write. This method can be used to write to the page at load time if it is carried out by direct VBScript startup code when a page loads.

The only way to have code launched as a page loads is to associate it with a script tag, but not within a specific procedure. The script in Listing 14.4, for example, would generate a heading that says Thanks for joining us at <current date and time>! as the page is loaded. The write method in the nonprocedure area of the code, shown in Listing 14.4, accomplishes this.

Listing 14.4. Using the `document.write` method as a page loads.

```
<HTML>
<HEAD>
<TITLE>Brophy & Koets' Teach Yourself VBScript - Document.Write Sample</TITLE>
</HEAD>
<BODY>
<H1>Weclome to this Web Page!</H1>
<SCRIPT LANGUAGE=VBS>
        document.write "<H2>Thanks for joining us at " & now & "!<H2>"

</SCRIPT>
<p>This is a pretty short but cool web page. Notice it displays the time!
</BODY>
```

ANALYSIS A page is rendered in sequential order of tags. That means the final result of the page in Listing 14.4 is a page in the browser that shows the title Welcome to this Web Page!, followed by the line Thanks for joining us..., followed by This is a pretty short but cool web page.... The resulting Web page is shown in Figure 14.7. If you moved the document.write statement to precede the <H1> tag, the Thanks for joining us... line would be at the top of the page.

Figure 14.7.
A Web page partially generated by document.write.

The HTML Body ONLOAD Event Procedure and Restrictions on Using document.write

If document.write appeared within an event procedure as a command button, the statement would cause an error when the user selected that button. This is because document.write cannot be called after page loading when the content drawing is complete. document.write can be used to build content but not to change it. The same is true with calls associated with the body tag ONLOAD attribute. You can specify a block of code that is called when your page loads by adding the appropriate language and ONLOAD attributes to the normal HTML body tag of your main script. For example, this statement specifies that a VBScript subroutine named Your_VBS_Subroutine will be called after the page is loaded:

```
<BODY lang=VBS ONLOAD="Your_VBS_Subroutine">
```

Then at some point in your HTML page, you must have defined the procedure Your_VBS_Subroutine between <SCRIPT LANGUAGE="VBS"> and </SCRIPT> tags. Any code in the procedure will get carried out as startup code, but it cannot use document.write.

Using document.write from VBScript at Page Load Time

The code in Listing 14.4 uses document.write successfully. That is because document.write is used within direct VBScript startup code. Direct VBScript startup code statements are those statements that are between the <SCRIPT> tags but *not* contained in a routine. This code is carried out whenever it is sequentially encountered as the page is loaded. document.write statements work in this context, and the resulting strings are just inserted after any preceding page content but before any page content lines not yet carried out.

On the other hand, a procedure that is designated by the ONLOAD event in the body tag is not called until after the page has been rendered. The whole page, including any direct VBScript startup code, will be sequentially drawn before this event is called. When the ONLOAD procedure finally gets its chance, it is too late to change the content of the page. document.write calls will fail at this point.

So document.write calls can be used only in nonprocedure direct VBScript startup code because that is the only code carried out during the code definition phase. However, code cannot interact with a control during this time unless the definition in the page source code has sequentially preceded the code block. You can think of this in terms of the phases shown in Figure 14.8. There is a loading phase during which page source code is processed sequentially. HTML code is processed on the page in the order in which it is encountered. Any VBScript code encountered in the sequential flow will be carried out at this time as well, if it is not contained in procedures. This code can render HTML through `document.write`. However, this code cannot reference a control which has a definition further down in the page of source code because that definition is not yet in effect.

Figure 14.8.

The VBScript event time line.

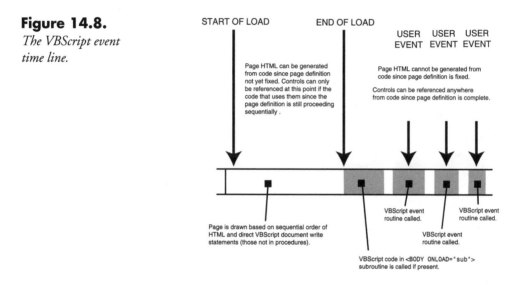

The `ONLOAD` event occurs when the page generation is completed. If an `ONLOAD` event has been defined through the body tag, it will be carried out at this point. `document.write` can no longer be utilized because the page rendering is complete. However, because all control definitions are also complete, a control can be referenced regardless of the sequential relationship in the source code between the code and the control.

After the completion of the `ONLOAD` event, the page is presented to the user. As the user interacts and causes events to occur, the associated event procedures will be carried out if they have been defined in script. The event code cannot use `document.write` because page rendering is complete. But because page definitions are complete, the event code can reference a control from anywhere. Listing 14.5 shows code with comments on each phase.

14

Listing 14.5. VBScript code for page rendering, on the load event, and at a user-initiated event.

```
<HTML>
<HEAD>
<TITLE>Brophy & Koets' Teach Yourself VBScript - Phase Sample</TITLE>
<SCRIPT LANGUAGE=VBS>
<!--
sub MyOnLoad
' This procedure is called at load due to BODY ONLOAD attribute.

    ' Document.write cannot occur after page is rendered
    msgbox "MyOnLoad procedure cannot use " & _
      document.write since page is already rendered!"

    ' Control can be modified even though its definition follows this code
    '       since page definition complete.
    cmdTest.Value = "MyOnLoad"
    msgbox "MyOnLoad procedure has modified control value."

end sub
-->
</SCRIPT>
</HEAD>

<!-- Use tag attribute to specify that a
VBScript procedure is carried out when page is loaded-->
<BODY LANGUAGE="VBS" ONLOAD="MyOnLoad">
<H1>Weclome to this Web Page!</H1>
<SCRIPT LANGUAGE=VBS>
<!--

' This is startup code. Since it is not in a procedure it is
' carried out when browser encounters it during page rendering.
document.write "<H2>Thanks for joining us at " & now & "!<H2>"
msgbox "Startup code has modified HTML content with document.write."

' Control cannot be modified since sequential page definition complete
'       still in progress and control not encountered yet.
msgbox "Startup code cannot modify control value since " & _
    " definition not in effect yet."


sub cmdTest_OnClick
' This event code is only processed when user clicks on cmdTest
'   button after page is loaded

    ' Document.write cannot occur after page is rendered
    msgbox "cmdTest_OnClick cannot use document.write since " & _
      " page is already rendered!"

    ' Control can be modified even though its definition follows this code
    '     since page definition complete.
    cmdTest.Value = "cmdTest"
    msgbox "cmdTest_OnClick procedure has modified control value."
```

```
end sub
-->
</SCRIPT>
<p>This is a pretty short but cool web page.

<INPUT TYPE="Button" VALUE="Initial" NAME="cmdTest">

</BODY>
</HTML>
```

ANALYSIS The code shown in Listing 14.5 is stored on the CD-ROM in file `Phase.HTM`. There is a block of code for each specific phase of the page life. The nonprocedure code is carried out as the page is rendered. The `ONLOAD` event occurs after the page loads. Then the event code is carried out in response to the user-initiated event. The comments in the listing indicate the legal actions at each phase. They reinforce the points made earlier—`document.write` can only be used as the page is rendered, and control definitions can only be used universally after the page is rendered.

Why Should You Use `document.write`?

The question of when to use `document.write` should now be quite clear. It can only be used in startup code. The remaining question is why `document.write` would be used at all. After all, `document.write` generates HTML statements when the script is run, but they can only be added as the page is loaded. If you needed additional HTML statements, why not just put them in the original page of source code in the first place?

Generally speaking, you will want to put your HTML directly in the page to begin with. If you know what the starting view of the page should be and no load time factors should influence the page's appearance, you have no need for `document.write`. On the other hand, there are several reasons you might wish to add HTML to a page through code as it is loaded.

The first reason is illustrated in Listing 14.4. With `document.write` you can easily insert a date, time, day of week, or other information into the page. Perhaps you want the date at the top of a page that serves as a report. You don't want to have to write server-side page generation code to do this because you can place pages on your provider's server but cannot place CGI scripts there. You'd use `document.write` to insert the date on each page as it is loaded, as shown in Listing 14.4. The smarts to carry out this dynamic customization are embedded right in the page itself rather than in a server application.

Another reason you may wish to use `document.write` is that in some cases it may be easier to generate information on a page through a code loop than to write out all the HTML statements directly. Suppose you wanted to create a page that listed multiples of 17 between

14

0 and 100,000. Perhaps this is to provide a check sheet or counter sheet for inventory control, where the shipments will occur in lots of 17. It would take an enormous amount of time to create this page by typing it; you'd have to type more than 5000 numbers. But with `document.write`, you just type a few lines of code (see Listing 14.6).

Listing 14.6. Using a code loop and `document.write` to avoid typing in many lines of code.

```
<HTML>
<HEAD>
<TITLE>Brophy & Koets' Teach Yourself VBScript
 - Inventory Count Sheet Sample</TITLE>
<SCRIPT LANGUAGE=VBS>
<!--

' This is startup code. Since it is not in
' a procedure it is carried out when browser encounters it during page render-
ing.
document.write "<H2>Counter sheet for inventory on " & now & "<H2>"
dim lngLoopCount

do while  lngLoopCount < 100000
    document.write "<p>Lot Number " & loop
    lngLoopCount = lngLoopCount + 17
loop
-->
</SCRIPT>
</BODY>
</HTML>
```

ANALYSIS   The startup code in Listing 14.6 has the same end result as if you wrote the page with all 5000+ lines. Unless you are specifically seeking finger exercise, the `document.write` approach is clearly desirable! As an added bonus, the page based on the VBScript `document.write` approach will be quicker to download from the server since it contains fewer lines of code.

So any page that could make use of a loop to generate repeated patterns of tags and content is a candidate for a `document.write` approach. Likewise, pages that display the results of repeated calculations, such as a trig table, can lend themselves to this approach. Such pages are not the norm, but if you create enough, you are likely to come across such a candidate eventually.

The final type of page to consider for a `document.write` approach is one where you give the user the choice of page presentation as the page loads. You can do this with the message box or input statements covered earlier. This can make for a very user-customizable page without requiring any server code.

For example, assume you want to supply a kid's activity planner. You want to provide slightly different customization and feedback, depending on whether the user wants to activities to cost money. However, you believe the basic design of the pages is similar enough that you want to just implement this solution on one page. That way, you'll just have one page to store and maintain for the future.

You could involve the server to help produce a custom page, but in this case, it is unnecessary. Server code takes more debugging, requires server script creation access, and will mean more network traffic for your user. On the other hand, VBScript code allows all customization to be embedded right in your page. In other words, you craft your own script customization.

For the kid's activity planner example, the first step of customization is to find out if the user wants to spend money on the activities. You use a message box in the script startup code to prompt the user for his response as soon as the page starts to load. This code is shown in Listing 14.7.

Listing 14.7. Find out the user preferences as the page loads.

```
<HTML>
<HEAD>
<TITLE>Brophy & Koets' Teach Yourself VBScript - Dynamic Page Sample</TITLE>
</HEAD>
<BODY>
<SCRIPT LANGUAGE=VBS>

    dim rc             ' Stores return code value
    dim Spender        ' True if user says they don't mind spending money
    rc = msgbox("Are you willing to spend some bucks if needed?", _
        vbYesNo + vbQuestion,"Setting up the Kid's Rainy Day Activity Planner")
    if rc = vbYes then

      ' Show Big Spender Page
      Spender = vbTrue

      document.write "<H2><A HREF=""http://www.mcp.com"">"
      document.write _
        ""<IMG  ALIGN=BOTTOM SRC=""../shared/jpg/samsnet.jpg"" BORDER=2></A>"
      document.write _
        "<EM>Kid's Activity Planner for the Big Spender</EM></h2>"
      document.write "<HR>"
      document.write "<p>Activities that cost, but keep them happy!"
      document.write "<UL>"
      document.write _
        "<LI>Let them go on a shopping spree in the local toy store."
      document.write "<LI>Take them to a movie."
      document.write "<LI>Buy them a new bike, but let them put it together."
      document.write "</UL>"
    else
      ' Show Cheapskate Page
      Spender = vbFalse
```

14

continues

Listing 14.7. continued

```
        document.write "<H2><A HREF=""http://www.mcp.com"">"
        document.write _
          "<IMG  ALIGN=BOTTOM SRC=""../shared/jpg/samsnet.jpg"" BORDER=2></A>"
        document.write "<EM>Kid's Activity Planner on a Budget</EM></h2>"
        document.write "<HR>"
        document.write "<p>Activities that won't cost you a dime!"
        document.write "<UL>"
        document.write "<LI>Send them to the neighbors to play."
        document.write "<LI>Tell them you lost your wallet in the backyard " & _
            " and half of the money in it is theirs if they find it for you."
        document.write "<LI>Show them how to play Solitaire on the computer."
        document.write "</UL>"
    end if
</SCRIPT>
</BODY>
</HTML>
```

ANALYSIS The block of code in Listing 14.7 will be carried out as the page starts to load because it is not contained in a procedure. The code's first action will be to ask the user via a message box if he wants to spend money. This message box is shown in Figure 14.9.

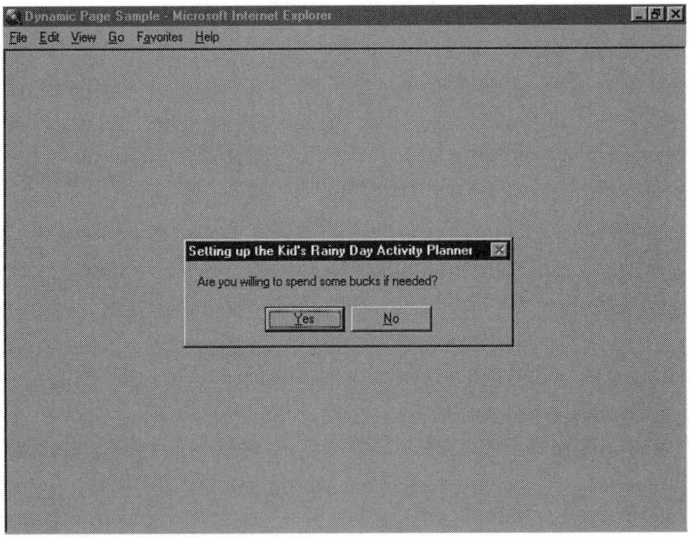

Figure 14.9.

Prompting for user preferences at page load time.

The return code with the user's response to the message box is evaluated next. If the return code indicates that the user wants to spend money, one set of HTML tags is generated with `document.write` with content directed at those users who are willing to spend money. Otherwise, `document.write` generates a different set of HTML tags targeted at the cheapskate crowd.

14

You have a user-customized page! But if this were all that was involved, you might as well have just created two separate pages in the first place. However, assume there is still more information that you want to show on every page, regardless of the user's attitude toward money. An additional list of generic activities is provided in either case, along with a helper button. This common HTML can be generated just once, following the customized section. The portion of the page that generates this generic information is regular HTML (with no script needed) and is shown in Listing 14.8.

Listing 14.8. `Planner.htm` generic information.

```
<HR>

<p>Here are some more ideas to consider:
<UL>
<LI>Play duck-duck-goose. Have a rule that the goosed must go
around the circle <EM>300</EM> times before sitting.
<LI>Ask the kids to draw a picture of the universe.
<LI>Provide a box of toothpicks and have them figure out the dimensions
of each room of the house in terms of the toothpicks.
</UL>

<HR>
<FORM NAME="frmAdvice">
<p>Chester the cat, an expert on kids, can
provide more suggestions based on an analysis
of your situation. Select <em>Advice from Chester</em> if you'd like his help.
<br>
<br>
<center>
<INPUT TYPE=BUTTON VALUE="Advice from Chester" SIZE=30 NAME="ChestersAdvice">
</center>
</FORM>
```

NOTE
Source code for this page, called `Planner.htm`, is available on the CD-ROM.

ANALYSIS The fact that this block appears only once in Listing 14.8 highlights the first clear benefit of the customized page. VBScript lets you generate multiple lead-in sections for the same page. You have just one Web page to maintain and update. The advantages of this approach may seem slight, since just a couple pages would be required to implement a traditional solution with this specific example. But if you amplify the situation to consider the case of many customizations and lines of generic code that follow, the avoided redundant pages become greater incentive for using this technique.

14

After the user indicates his preference regarding spending money on activities, a page like the one shown in Figure 14.10 is displayed. If the user had indicated he didn't want to spend money, he would have been presented with the same page, but with a different customization, which is shown in Figure 14.11.

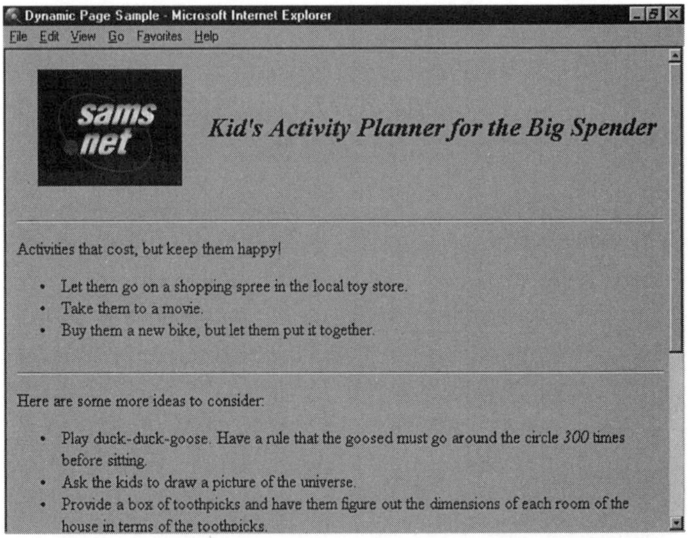

Figure 14.10.

The page customized for big spenders.

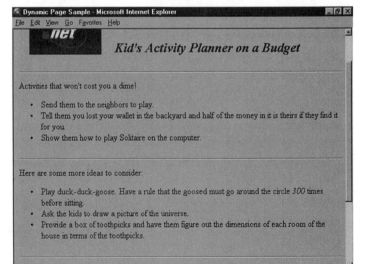

Figure 14.11.

The same page customized for cheapskates.

The dynamic interaction offered by this page can go even further. At the bottom of the page is a button the user can select if he wants even more ideas that are derived in a question and answer session. The code behind this button will provide a series of questions to the user through message boxes and input boxes. Based on the user's responses, a highly customized activity recommendation will be produced. The final recommendation will be displayed to the user through an input box (as shown in the sample). It also could have been displayed directly on the page through other means, such as a label, a text box, or another control.

This sample program shows a highly interactive page that is customized based on user preferences when it is loaded. Then, in response to a request for further information, the user can access a detailed set of questions designed to glean more information from the user. After the user supplies the answers, an additional recommendation can be provided based on this information. All this is done with the same page and controlled by easily maintained code within that page.

There is a lot more you can do with the document object. You can write information after a page is loaded. You simply use document.close to make your changes take effect after a document.write. This will cause the page to be generated again, but will wipe out your old contents! Intrinsic browser objects like the document object will be discussed in more detail on Day 18.

Summary

Today's lesson looks at how you can make dynamic documents through intrinsic functions of VBScript and the document object rather than through separate components of the page. The message box function MsgBox provides feedback to the user in a message window. The message remains for the user until it is acknowledged. The Alert function serves the same purpose, but places the title Alert at the top of the window. Parameters of the MsgBox function control the message, title, icon, and buttons displayed. This function can even be used to solicit a response from the user. If more than one button has been requested, the function returns an indication of which button was selected.

The MsgBox function goes a long way toward creating interactive pages without integrating components, but a closely related function goes even further: the InputBox function. The InputBox function works like the message box function in many respects. Parameters control a prompt message and title. In addition, parameters can indicate where the input window should be positioned onscreen. The most important distinguishing characteristic of InputBox, however, is that it uses the prompt message to prompt the user for an input string. That input string is then returned to your script.

14

There is yet another way to communicate from scripts without integrating components. This is through the intrinsic document object and its document.write property. Your scripts can generate their own HTML statements on the page. For example, a script can tell the browser to place the title Heading 2 at the top of the page; you simply enclose the text Heading 2 in <H2> and </H2> tags. Or a script can generate an ordered list. Essentially, anything that can be done through HTML tags can be generated by your script directly to the document. However, the document.write method can only be carried out at form load time. The page is generated sequentially, so if any normal HTML tags appear in the HTML file prior to the script that references document.write, those tags will precede the ones generated by the script.

Some ideas of where you can use document.write are discussed in today's lesson. These include a look at the VBScript event time line. VBScript startup code is the only place you can use document.write. An additional approach for defining code carried out as the page loads through the use of the <BODY> tag and ONLOAD attribute is provided, but document.write cannot be used from this event or from normal control events. The reasons for this are outlined, as are considerations of accessing controls in each of these different phases of code execution. One or more document.writes can be used at any time if they are followed by a document.close, but that will result in the replacement of the old contents of your page by whatever you wrote.

After providing a discussion of dynamic interaction and document generation, this lesson provides an example that uses the techniques discussed. A Web page with dynamically generated content based on a user's response to a prompt during the page load operation is illustrated. This page also has the capability to initiate an extensive series of questions for user response, and can display new results at the end of the series of questions.

All this interaction takes place on the same Web page, with no server intervention required. You can use VBScript in this manner to easily make truly interactive Web pages. As the lesson shows, VBScript is not only the glue that lets you control the components in your pages, it is also the framework for user interaction.

Q&A

Q Can you use document.write to modify a Web page in response to the user clicking on an intrinsic command button or label control?

A No. document.write can only be used at page load time. Since Click events on controls can occur only after the page is loaded, document.write will not work in that event code.

Q **How can you supply a default response for the user when you use the `InputBox` function to prompt for input?**

A The optional third parameter of `InputBox` supplies the default value:

```
Response = InputBox ("What gift would you like to select " & _
     " for that lovely couple Marco and Terri for their wedding?", _
       "Please select a gift", "Gold-plated electric banjo")
```

The user will see `Gold-plated electric banjo` in the input area as soon as `InputBox` is displayed. He can press Enter to accept this response or type over it with his own response.

Workshop

Generally, there is more than one approach for providing user feedback. Determining which approach is best is a subjective matter. For example, suppose you want to write a Web page that lets the user provide three bowling scores. Then, when the user clicks on a Calculate button, your Web page provides the average.

If the user enters a score greater than 300 for one game, you need to provide an error message. After all, 300 is the highest score possible, so your user either made a mistake or is trying to fib to the program! You could provide the error feedback in several different ways. Your script could pop up a message box calling the user's attention to the error. Or it could display the error message in a label that had been previously blank on the Web page. Or the script could generate the error right to the label or text box where the final average would normally appear.

Implement three different Web pages for the bowling average score program. Make the pages identical *except* for the error feedback. Then interact with all three pages, forcing the error. Decide which method you think provides the best user feedback. Although you can always find an opinionated programmer to tell you his way is the only way, there is no universal programmer's rule that dictates which approach you must use in such cases. Most pages implement the message box approach because it easily catches the user's attention, demands a response that ensures the user has seen it, and is easy to implement. Do you agree this is the best approach after trying all three methods?

Quiz

NOTE

Refer to Appendix C, "Answers to Quiz Questions," for the answers to these questions.

14

1. Provide code that asks the user if he wants to see extra hints when a page is loaded. If the user responds affirmatively, have the code write the heading Extra Hints at the top of the page.

2. Use your answer to the first quiz question as the basis for this solution. Take that code and modify it so that Extra Hints appears between the question and answer sections (between the two <BR> lines) when the user responds affirmatively to the prompt.

3. If you supply Yes, No, and Cancel buttons on a message box, one of the buttons will be highlighted and the user can select it by pressing Enter (or the space bar, in Windows 95). Show the code that will highlight the No button, which is the middle of the three buttons that appear on the message box. Use anything for the message and title content.

In Review

The first week of this book took you through some basic language fundamentals. That laid the groundwork for the second week, in which you started to see how VBScript can tie together a variety of components to make more active pages. You saw a variety of entities and objects that you can control through VBScript, including HTML form controls, ActiveX controls, Java applets, and ActiveVRML. Of course, you need a well-crafted approach to smoothly integrate such components. To help you along the way, we exposed you to some helpful guidelines and user interface techniques. Taken as a whole, the techniques covered in this second week bring you to the point where you can put together real, productive, active pages. You can do this by taking advantage of a wealth of integrated components, as well as writing your own VBScript code.

Where You Have Been

The week started with a look at intrinsic HTML form controls on Day 8. Day 9 addressed more HTML form controls. Then, Day 10 switched to a slightly different type of component, the object. It focused on perhaps the most important type of object to the VBScript programmer, the ActiveX control. On Day 11, you learned about more ActiveX controls. Day 12 addressed advanced object issues, including more sophisticated ActiveX controls, Java applet objects, and the ActiveVRML viewer object. Component download issues were also addressed here. Day 13 switched tracks slightly by focusing on an area very important to good component integration—VBScript standards and conventions. Finally, the week ended with a look at working with the document object of a page and user interface functions on Day 14. After making it through this week of material, you are past the raw novice stage and have the abilities, with practice, to produce professional-caliber scripts. You still need more tricks, techniques, and even fundamental issues to round out your knowledge, which is the topic of Week 3.

At a Glance

By now you have a very good background for creating your own VBScript code. You have a well-grounded understanding of the basic language elements and component integration, the core of scripting, but there are still some important weapons missing from your arsenal. You need advanced functions and techniques that can help you develop scripts even more quickly with more flexibility. Advanced functions in string handling, math, dates, and other areas will round out your knowledge of the VBScript syntax. In addition, there are some important strategic areas where a keen understanding of various approaches will lead to better scripts of your own. This is true in a wide variety of areas, including finding bugs, advanced user interface techniques, validation and server techniques, porting code, and security. By the end of this third week, you will have knowledge of all the VBScript fundamentals. In addition, you will be aware of the many advanced strategical techniques and will understand the key ancillary issues that go along with this language.

Where You Are Going

The week starts with a look at advanced string functions on Day 15. Working with math and dates will be introduced on Day 16. Day 17 will take a look at exterminating bugs from your script, and Day 18 will show you how to use advanced user interface techniques in your script. Dynamic page flow and server submittal strategies will be covered on Day 19. Day 20 will discuss porting between Visual Basic and VBScript. Finally, key security and server considerations will be addressed on Day 21.

Day **15**

Extending Your Web Pages with Strings

You've seen a lot of the capabilities of VBScript in the lessons you've covered so far. The VBScript syntax provides you with the elements needed to piece together programs. You can use it to put together program logic with variables, operators, control structures, and procedures. You can greatly extend the power of the language by incorporating components into your programs, but the language of VBScript itself is quite powerful. A lot of advanced functions are part of the VBScript language.

These functions are built into VBScript, just as keywords such as If-Then, Sub, MsgBox, and Dim are. You can't *see* the source code for these functions because they are an inherent part of VBScript. No special declarations are needed to make use of these. They stand ready to be used from anywhere within your script. This potpourri of functions includes date-handling procedures, string-handling procedures, mathematical procedures, and more. Today's lesson focuses on the string-handling functions. The date and math functions are addressed on Day 16, "Extending Your Web Pages with Dates and Advanced Math."

String functions, in particular, are likely to be frequently used in Web page programming. Any page that collects data from the user to send to a server can use these functions to validate dates and string formats before sending the information on. This allows you to provide quicker, more responsive user feedback and minimize network traffic. If the situation warrants, the string functions, which are the topic of today's lesson, are easy to apply.

NOTE

> One sample Web page, containing a collection of scripts, demonstrates all the string functions in today's lesson. This page, `String.htm`, is available on the CD-ROM. The sample scripts referred to throughout this lesson can be found there.

Whenever you're preparing information for or receiving information from the user in your script, there is a good chance that you're dealing with a string of characters. VBScript provides many functions that make work easier. Knowing about these functions can save you a lot of time; not knowing about them can cost you a lot of time.

A vivid example of the value of knowing what the language provides in areas such as string handling occurred recently in a classroom situation. A student proudly called the teacher over and showed off a rather lengthy Visual Basic function he had written. The 30+ lines of code in his function, he explained, made use of ASCII character codes and the offsets between lowercase and uppercase letters. The end result was that the function could convert any lowercase string into the equivalent uppercase letter string. The student went on to hint that, if some extra credit could result, he might even be willing to share the algorithm with other students. As gently as possible, the instructor told the student that he had just invented a function that was already provided by Visual Basic! His several hours of work was wasted effort. All he had to do was use a standard part of the language to make use of the same uppercase conversion in his code.

Knowing the range of string functions' capabilities will save you from the same fate. Good data validation is central to Web pages of the future, and it depends on effectively evaluating strings. Therefore, strong string-handling skills are a must if you plan to be an effective VBScript developer. Fortunately, the string functions, like the date functions, are relatively easy to apply after you understand the capabilities they offer.

Asc **and** Chr

A string is made of a series of characters. Each individual character is represented internally in the computer by a unique numeric code called an *ASCII code*. A different ASCII code exists for every character in the alphabet, for uppercase and lowercase versions of the same letter, for every number, and for most of the symbols on your keyboard. Usually when you write programs, you aren't too concerned with these codes. There may be times, however, when you need to be. For example, maybe you have to provide a Web page that aids your users in typing ASCII codes into an electronic sign board. They need a way to take a character like *A* and get the equivalent numeric code, so they can type in that code. The Asc function provides this capability. Listing 15.1 shows code that uses the Asc function to display the ASCII code for *A*.

Listing 15.1. Asc **and** Chr **functions.**

```
<!-------- Asc and Chr ------------------------------------>
<INPUT TYPE=BUTTON VALUE="Asc/Chr"  NAME="cmdAsc">
<SCRIPT LANGUAGE="VBSCRIPT" FOR="cmdAsc" EVENT="onClick">
<!--
    msgbox "The character ""A"" ASCII code is " & Asc("A") & "." & chr(13) & _
          "The character for ASCII code 66 is " & chr(66) & ".",0,"Using Asc/Chr"
-->
</SCRIPT>
```

Situations also arise where the conversion must be done in the other direction. For example, perhaps you're inspecting the memory contents of a computer with some advanced debugging tool. In an area that you know is supposed to contain a string variable, you see that the first byte contains a 66. You need to know what character that represents so you can tell if the correct string is in memory. The Chr function can give you the answer. Chr takes the numeric value that you provide it and returns the corresponding character (refer to Listing 15.1). The ASCII code for the character *A* is displayed with the Asc function, and the character represented by the ASCII code 66 is displayed with the Chr function. The results are shown in Figure 15.1. The results show that the ASCII code for *A* is 65. Not surprisingly, then, the character represented by ASCII code 66 turns out to be a *B*.

One of the more common uses of the Chr function is to generate special characters that are not available on the keyboard. The character represented by the ASCII code 13, for example, is not one you can see. This character is called the carriage-return character. You can use this character in many places to force a line separation (for example, in the MsgBox function). If you include the ASCII character code 13 in the MsgBox text, more than one line will be displayed. The only problem is, how do you enter this character on your statement when you type in your program?

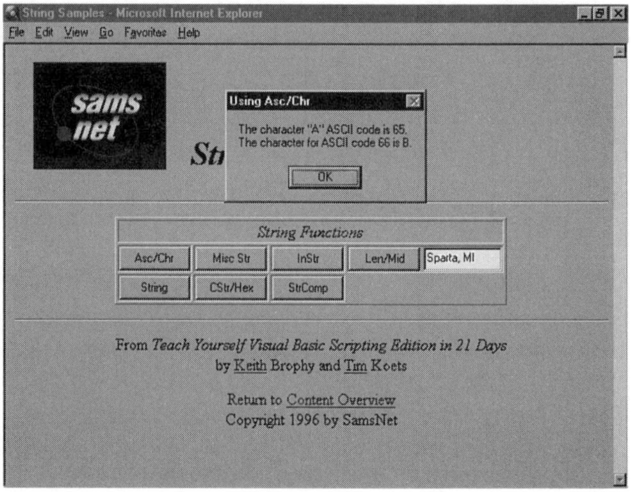

Figure 15.1.

Using the Asc *and* Chr *functions.*

If you've been looking carefully at the examples, you've seen the answer many times already. You just supply the character with Chr(13):

```
msgbox "This will be line1" & chr(13) & " and this will be line 2",0,"Title"
```

On Day 4, "Creating Variables in VBScript," you learned how you can declare a variable to serve the purpose of an intrinsic constant for commonly used values. The constant.txt file in the tools directory on the CD-ROM contains statements you can copy and paste to put these variables in your code. Then you'll have an easy-to-read variable to serve the same purpose because it is equated to Chr(13). That constant is vbCr and can be used as follows:

```
msgbox "This will be line1" & vbCr & " and this will be line 2",0,"Title"
```

You can also use the combined carriage-return and line-feed characters (Chr(13) & Chr(10)) to carry out line separations. The end result is the same. In either case, you are generating the special character from the ASCII code rather than from your keyboard. Asc and Chr give you the full flexibility to work at the ASCII code or character level, even if you can't see those characters.

NOTE

Functions similar to Asc and Chr work at the byte rather than the character level. AscB returns the first byte of a string. ChrB returns the byte that corresponds to an ASCII code rather than the character. For practical purposes, you are likely to work simply in characters. However, if you were making use of extended character sets, particularly foreign language string support where more than one byte might be used to represent a character, these functions may be necessary.

15

Miscellaneous Functions: Ucase, Lcase, LTrim, RTrim, Trim, Left, and Right

NOTE

> You may have noticed that the functions used in the samples start with a capital followed by lowercase letters. This is a good naming convention. VBScript itself, however, does not care about case. You can supply functions and keywords in capitals or lowercase letters. But for your own sake, try to use a consistent approach!

Seven functions in one little section may seem overwhelming, but like most of the string functions, they are easy to understand and apply, and these functions are all somewhat related. They all return a modified string based on an original string, and they are all frequently used in Web page data validation to verify correctly entered data before data is submitted back to the server. The case functions modify the case to upper- or lowercase. The trim functions trim off extra spaces, and the Left or Right functions return just the left or right portions of the original string. The best way to tackle them is to consider them one at a time.

Ucase and Lcase are a good place to start. These functions are commonly used in validation. Suppose, for example, that you have a page that requires the user to supply his department name. If the user is from the Engineering Department, you want to display a special message during validation to let him know that he has additional paperwork to fill out. Then you could put a check like this in your code:

```
if txtDepartment.Value = "Engineering" then ' provide special message
```

This may work fine for Fred, Ned, Ted, Jed, Holly, and Molly. But then Ed may come along and enter engineering, and Dolly may enter ENGINEERING. You could put the burden on the user and have your program fail to recognize Ed and Dolly as valid engineering users. However, placing perfect data entry expectations on the user is generally regarded as poor programming style. It would be especially so if Ed or Dolly happened to be your boss, and the Web page didn't give them the expected feedback. Don't saddle your users with a less than optimal solution when a very simple way to fix this problem is available. Convert the string you're examining to all uppercase letters, and compare it to a string with all uppercase letters:

```
if Ucase(txtDepartment.Value) = "ENGINEERING" then ' provide special message
```

Now it doesn't matter how the user enters Engineering. Your program will work correctly no matter how Ned, Ed, or Dolly enters his or her department name.

Ucase takes whatever string it is supplied and returns all uppercase characters. Of course, uppercase only works for letters, so digits and symbols are unaffected when passed to this function. Lcase works exactly the same, except it converts everything passed to it to lowercase. For example, the statement

```
msgbox lcase("Timmy Kenny JJ")
```

would result in the display of the message `timmy kenny jj`.

Another problem could still creep into your department check, and you could thank nonconformist users once again. Suppose Dolly unwittingly entered `Engineering`, and Ed in a wild-fingered frenzy entered `Engineering`. Would this input result in a `True` condition when the following statement is carried out?

```
if Ucase(txtDepartment.Value) = "ENGINEERING" then ' provide special message
```

Of course not! This conditional expression does an exact match on the word ENGINEERING, and the presence of the extra blanks causes the conditional to fail. Your bosses might not expect you to accept this input, but likely they'd be happy if you could. You can accept this input with virtually no added effort. The Trim function removes all extra blank spaces that precede or follow characters within the string. So this statement:

```
msgbox Trim("   Lisa Kayla Ryan   ")
```

would display a message box that said `Lisa Kayla Ryan` with no blanks in front of or behind it.

Trim has two closely related cousins, LTrim and RTrim. Although Trim does the work of both cousins, LTrim simply removes blanks from the left of a string, and RTrim just removes blanks at the end or right of a string. The statement

```
msgbox LTrim("   Lisa Kayla Ryan   ")
```

would display a message box that said `Lisa Kayla Ryan   `. The statement

```
msgbox RTrim("   Lisa Kayla Ryan   ")
```

would display a message box that said `   Lisa Kayla Ryan`. To fix your Web page department validation to make it *leading- and trailing-blank proof,* you'd supply this statement:

```
if Trim(Ucase(txtDepartment.Value)) = "ENGINEERING" then ' provide special
message
```

Now you have a check that can withstand an entry like `EnGinEeRinG`. However, never underestimate the ability of a Web page user to provide unexpected input. Dolly and Ed still provide one more twist. Suppose their organization refers to the Engineering Department on some documents as "Department of Engineering" and on other documents as "Engineering Dept." Most users simplify their department as "Engineering." But not Dolly and Ed. Dolly supplies Department of Engineering in the input area, and Ed enters Engineering Dept. Of course, users in the Engineering Department should know better. They are really trying to test your program, and you're ready for them. You simply apply two more functions in the VBScript bag of string tricks—Left and Right.

Left allows you to extract the leftmost characters from a string. You can extract as many as you specify. Right allows you to extract rightmost characters from a string, again as many as you specify. For example, this statement:

```
msgbox Left("Ginny Emma Ben",10)
```

would display a message box that said Ginny Emma. This statement:

```
msgbox Right("Ginny Emma Ben",8)
```

would display a message box that said Emma Ben.

Because you know that engineering has 11 letters in it, you can check both the first and the last 11 characters. If the first or last 11 characters contain "ENGINEERING," it can be considered a match. The check that accomplishes this is shown in Listing 15.2.

Listing 15.2. Full validation on a department check.

```
if (Left(Trim(Ucase(txtDepartment.Value)),11) = "ENGINEERING") or _
   (Right(Trim(Ucase(txtDepartment.Value)),11) = "ENGINEERING")   _
        then ' provide special message
```

A couple aspects of this check may make it even more robust than it first appears. If you ask Left or Right for more characters than are present in a string, the return value will simply be the number of characters that exist in the string. You're safe even if your user enters a string shorter than 11 characters. Your program will correctly detect that no match occurred, rather than blowing up with an error.

The order in which these functions are applied is also important. This statement:

```
msgbox Left(Trim("     Chester"),3)
```

displays the message Che, while this similar-looking statement:

```
msgbox Trim(Left("     Chester",3))
```

displays the message   .

Expressions are evaluated from the inner parentheses to the outer. In the department validation, evaluation occurs in the correct order. First, the user's input value is converted to uppercase. Then extra blanks are trimmed. Only then are the left or right characters extracted. With this approach, the validation will accept just about anything Dolly and Ed might throw at you. This even includes `EngINEEring dePT` and `Department of Cool EnginEERING`.

You can see the flexibility of these string functions. Listing 15.3 shows some sample code that further demonstrates the use of each of these functions. Figure 15.2 shows the results from running this test.

Listing 15.3. A demonstration of miscellaneous functions.

```
<!-------- Misc: Lcase, Ucase, LTrim, RTrim, Trim, Left, Right -------------->
<INPUT TYPE=BUTTON VALUE="Misc Str"  NAME="cmdCase">
<SCRIPT LANGUAGE="VBSCRIPT" FOR="cmdCase" EVENT="onClick">
<!--
    dim strFeedback
    dim CLUBNAME

    CLUBNAME = "Mutt"

    strFeedback = "Lcase/Ucase: " & CLUBNAME & " should appear as " & _
        lcase(CLUBNAME) & " when used to refer to a pooch, and as " & _
        ucase(CLUBNAME) & " when used as the acronym for the " & _
        "Michigan Ultra Trail Team." & vbCrLf & vbCrLf

    strFeedback = strFeedback & "LTrim applied to ""     mutt     "" is: ***" & _
        ltrim("     mutt     ") & "***" & vbCrLf
    strFeedback = strFeedback & "RTrim applied to ""     mutt     "" is: ***" & _
        rtrim("     mutt     ") & "***" & vbCrLf
    strFeedback = strFeedback & "Trim applied to ""     mutt     "" is: ***" & _
        trim("     mutt     ") & "***" & vbCrLf & vbCrLF

    strFeedback = strFeedback & "Left two characters of Mutt: " & _
        Left(CLUBNAME,2) & vbCrLf
    strFeedback = strFeedback & "Right two characters of Mutt: " & _
        Right(CLUBNAME,2) & vbCrLf
    msgbox strFeedback,0,"Using case, trim, left/right"
-->
</SCRIPT>.
```

The validation approaches offered by these string functions are powerful. They let your code stand up to some of Dolly and Ed's best stuff, but Dolly and Ed can still foil these checks. All it takes is an entry like `Cool Engineering Department` to cause the check to fail. Don't despair, though. There are some more string functions in the bag of tricks, and one in particular lets you address even this challenge.

Figure 15.2.

Using Lcase, Ucase, LTrim, RTrim, Trim, Left, *and* Right

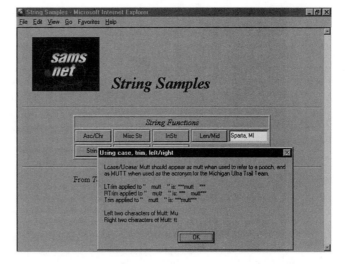

InStr

The InStr function checks for the presence of one string within another. If the desired string is present in the search string, the InStr function returns the position of that string. If the string can't be found, a 0 will be returned. For example, this statement:

```
msgbox InStr("Brad Mike Karen John Claire", "Mike")
```

will display 6. This result indicates that the desired string of Mike was found at the sixth character of the search string in the first argument.

This function is the perfect one to apply to the Engineering Department check. Because the function searches for the desired string anywhere in the search string, there is no need to trim the user input or extract just the left or right side of the user input. The check with InStr is therefore even more straightforward than its predecessor:

```
if Instr(Ucase(txtDepartment.Value), "ENGINEERING") > 0 _
    then ' provide special message
```

This one check will now correctly detect if engineering is supplied in any part of the input string. It will match for my Engineering dept , EnGINEERING department, or any other similar variation. Now you see how you can use string functions to make your Web page scripts sturdy enough to validate the input of even the Dollys and Eds of the world.

A couple more aspects of InStr are important to note. InStr normally starts searching for the desired text at the start of the search string, but it doesn't have to. You can direct it to start the search at any character. To do this, provide the search start character as the first argument to the function. For example, assume you want to see if the word Task appears anywhere other than in the first five characters, so you indicate that the search should begin at the sixth character. Then this search:

```
msgbox InStr(6, Ucase("Task List: re-org meeting; year-end report task"),"TASK")
```

would display 44. Notice that the search string had to be converted to uppercase with the Ucase function. Otherwise, the desired string TASK would not have matched task at the 44th position because the search is case sensitive. A way to carry out a non-case-sensitive search is to simply supply an additional parameter as the fourth parameter to InStr. By default, when this parameter is not presented, it is treated as if it has a 0 value, which means case-sensitive or only exact matches occur. If you supply a 1 for this parameter, matches will not be case sensitive. In other words, tAsK would show up as a match against TAsk. Then the search for task can be rewritten as

```
msgbox InStr(6, Ucase("Task List: re-org meeting; year-end report_
task"),"Task",1)
```

and it will still display the result 44.

Listing 15.4 shows another example of how case sensitivity can make a difference in a search. In the first conditional check, the word pear is not located in the string of food names. In the second conditional check, it is located. These results are shown in Figure 15.3. The only difference in the two checks is that the second check uses the option that's not case sensitive and the start character option. Whenever a value is supplied for the case option, the start character must be supplied as well.

Listing 15.4. An InStr search with and without case sensitivity.

```
<!--------- InStr ------------------------------------------->
<INPUT TYPE=BUTTON VALUE="InStr"  NAME="cmdInStr">
<SCRIPT LANGUAGE="VBSCRIPT" FOR="cmdInStr" EVENT="onClick">
<!--

    Dim strFoods, strFeedback

    strFoods = "banana orange apple pear"

    ' Check for exact case
    if InStr(strFoods,"PEAR") > 0 then
        strFeedback = "PEAR is in " & strFoods & vbCrLf
    else
        strFeedback = "PEAR is not in " & strFoods & vbCrLf
    end if

    ' Check regardless of case
    if InStr(1, strFoods,"PEAR", 1) > 0 then
```

15

```
        strFeedback = strFeedback & "PEAR is in " & _
        strFoods & " without case-sensitivity" & vbCrLf
    else
        strFeedback = strFeedback & "PEAR is not in " & _
        strFoods & " without case-sensitivity" & vbCrLf
    end if

    msgbox strFeedback,0, "Using Instr"

-->
</SCRIPT>
```

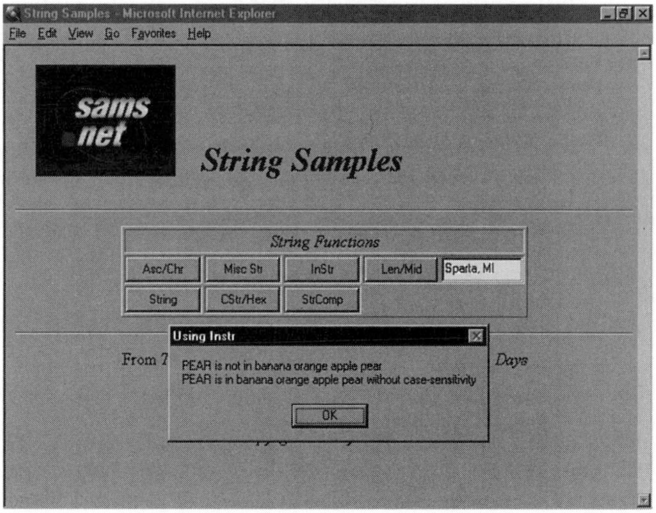

Figure 15.3.

An InStr *search with and without case sensitivity.*

If you carry out much string processing in your scripts, InStr will likely become a cornerstone of your string-handling strategy. When InStr is coupled with the capabilities of Len and Mid, which will be addressed next, you can extract strings as well as just locate them.

NOTE

You saw earlier that Asc and Chr have corresponding byte-oriented versions, AscB and ChrB. The same is true with InStr. An InStrB version of this function matches bytes rather than characters. This is useful for matching extended character sets typical of some foreign languages.

Len **and** Mid

The Len and Mid functions are two of the more frequently used string-handling procedures. Len returns the length of a string. For example, the following would display 26:

```
msgbox Len("abcdefghijklmnopqrstuvwxyz")
```

Blanks are included in the count, so the following would display 28:

```
msgbox Len("I ran with determination up Blood Hill")
```

The Len function is especially handy for validating input when you require some minimum number of characters. Perhaps you have a Web page that prompts for a student identification, for example. Assume that a student ID must be at least nine characters long. You could perform a validation check, such as

```
if len(txtID.value) < 9 then ' corrective action or message
```

The Len function is also one way to see if a variable has been assigned. Consider the code in Listing 15.5.

Listing 15.5. Checking Len on an unassigned string.

```
sub TestIt
    dim VarAge
    msgbox len(VarAge)
end sub
```

ANALYSIS This routine would result in a display of 0. Because the variable VarAge hasn't been assigned when the length is checked, it has no current length, and a length of 0 is returned.

Len is one function that is helpful in validation and is closely focused on the number of characters in a string. Mid, a similar function, allows you to retrieve a string or substring from another original string. The name Mid can be deceiving if you aren't used to BASIC. It sounds as if it implies that you can only take these substrings from the middle of the original string. However, you can take any portion of the original string, whether at the start, end, or anywhere in between.

The best way to appreciate Mid is to examine some examples. Consider the following:

```
msgbox Mid("Joe Jacko BigAl", 4, 5)
```

This statement will display Jacko in the message box. The first argument to this function is the source string that will be used to copy the substring from. The second argument is the character position where the substring copy is to start. The VBScript Mid function calls the first character in its sequence character 0. So it considers the first character of the string, J, to be at position 0, the second character o to be at position 1, the third character e to be at position 2, and so on. Therefore, position 4 actually indicates the fifth character over, which is J. Finally, the last argument specifies how many characters will be copied. In the preceding sample line, five characters are to be copied from the start of the substring. Five characters from and including the J at the fourth position encompass all of Jacko, so this is what shows up in the message box display.

Mid is often used in conjunction with InStr. InStr can locate where a key phrase or delimiter starts in a string, and then Mid can extract it. For example, if you had a field on your page that asked the user for a city and a state, the code in Listing 15.6 would parse out just the state value, assuming that the user entered a comma between the city and the state.

Listing 15.6. Using InStr and Mid together.

```
<!-------- Len/Mid  ------------------------------------->
<INPUT TYPE=BUTTON VALUE="Len/Mid"  NAME="cmdMid">
<INPUT NAME="txtLocation" VALUE="Sparta, MI" SIZE=12>
<SCRIPT LANGUAGE="VBSCRIPT" FOR="cmdMid" EVENT="onClick">
<!--

    Dim intPosition, intSize, strState
    ' Find the comma
    intPosition = InStr(txtLocation.Value,",")

    ' The purpose of this code is to transfer the state portion of the
    '   user-supplied location to a variable for later use in the program.
    if intPosition = 0 then
        msgbox "The location is not in the expected city, state format."
    Else
        ' Determine how long the state portion is based on where the
        '   city/state comma is and the overall length of the string
        intSize = len(txtLocation.Value) - intPosition

        ' Assign the state string to the variable
        strState = mid(txtLocation.Value, intPosition+1, intSize)

        ' Remove any leading or trailing spaces
        strState = Trim(strState)


    end if


  MsgBox """" & strState & """" extracted after comma in position " &_
 intPosition & " from source string """ & txtLocation.Value & """", 0,_
"State Parsing Using InStr/Len/Mid"

-->
</SCRIPT>
```

ANALYSIS The results from running this test are shown in Figure 15.4. When the user supplies a city and state, such as the default Sparta, Mi, the script will parse just the state portion and display it. This code is not likely to be the life of the party at your next computer science social. As far as algorithms go, it is quite straightforward, and that's exactly the beauty of it. You can easily implement sophisticated parsing and validation on any input on your Web pages. You don't have to build up your own library of procedures to support your string handling. They're already there, ready to use.

Figure 15.4.

The results of parsing the state from a user input field using InStr, Len, *and* Mid.

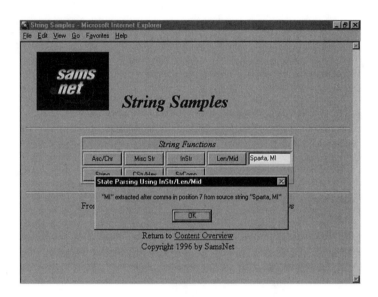

Mid and Len, coupled with InStr, let you get at any portion of a string. You can carry out sophisticated string extractions and parsing with these functions. There's no need to turn to another language on a Web page server to handle your advanced input parsing and validation. If you can picture what needs to be done with the string input on your pages, VBScript provides the function toolkit to accomplish it.

 NOTE The Len and Mid functions are also available as byte-oriented calls, when LenB and MidB are used.

Space **and** String

The Space and String functions are some of the simpler members of the string handling family, but they do come in handy on occasion. Suppose you are generating a message that you want to have preceded by 20 spaces. You could simply put them within double quotes:

```
msgbox "                    Visual Basic Rules!"
```

This is a bit cumbersome, however. An easier approach is to use the Space function to request a string consisting of the specified number of spaces:

```
msgbox Space(20) & "Visual Basic Rules!"
```

Space is somewhat like a specialized version of String. String also gives you repeated occurrences of a character, but you can request any character you want, whether it is a blank, an asterisk, or anything else. For example, the following displays a string with 20 leading blanks:

```
msgbox String(20, " ") & "Visual Basic Rules!"
```

but this:

```
msgbox String(20, "*")& "Visual Basic Rules!"
```

displays the string as

```
"********************Visual Basic Rules!"
```

Listing 15.7 shows sample code that generates two messages—one preceded by spaces and the other preceded by dashes. The spaces are generated with the Space function, and the dashes are generated by the String function. The results from this code can be seen in Figure 15.5. Note that although both lines are indented, they do not line up evenly since a proportional font was used. In other words, 20 spaces do not take up the same amount of screen space as 20 dashes.

Listing 15.7. Using Space and String to indent messages.

```
<!-------- Space/String ------------------------------------------->
<INPUT TYPE=BUTTON VALUE="String"  NAME="cmdString">
<SCRIPT LANGUAGE="VBSCRIPT" FOR="cmdString" EVENT="onClick">
<!--

    Dim strFeedback

    strFeedback = space(20) & "This line was indented with Space(20) " & vbCrLf
    strFeedback = strFeedback & string(20,"-") & _
        "This line was indented with String(20,""-"") " & vbCrLf

    msgbox strFeedback,0, "Using Space/String"

-->
</SCRIPT>
```

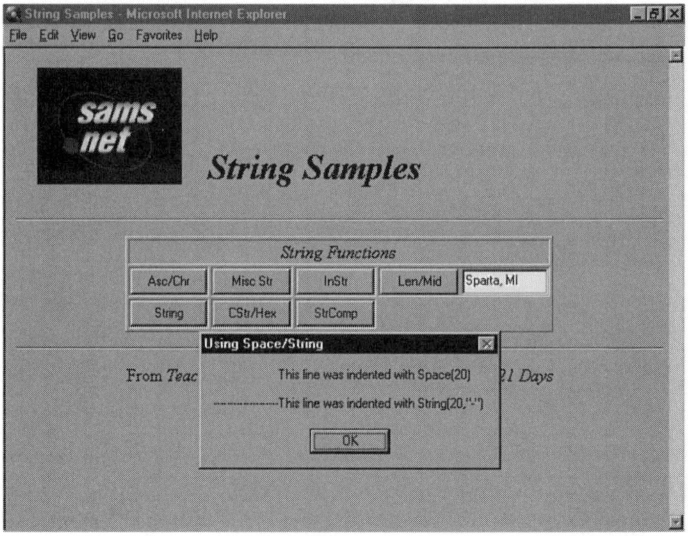

Figure 15.5.

Messages based on the Space *and* String *functions.*

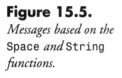

The Space and String functions are useful in many ways for string formatting. They let you easily generate strings that you want to display as part of your feedback, and they also let you easily carry out initializations. If you had a string that you needed to initially create to contain 1KB of 0 characters, for example, you could easily do it with a statement like this:

```
strVarA = String(1024,"0")
```

You can also supply an ASCII character code for the character that is to be assigned to the string. If you wanted to fill a string with carriage-return characters, you could use a statement like this:

```
strVarA = String(1024,13)
```

These functions are easy to apply. They can also be quite a convenience, considering that the alternative would be writing a code loop to carry out such an assignment.

Even More String Functions: IsEmpty, Cstr, Val, Hex, Oct, **and** StrComp

Many important string functions have been covered so far, but there are even more that you can put to work. These are summarized briefly here, either because they have already been introduced earlier in the text or because they are not likely to be used as frequently as some of the other string functions examined in today's lesson.

IsEmpty

You saw an earlier example of how you can check to see if data is in valid date format, with the IsDate function, before working with it. Likewise, you can use the IsEmpty function to determine whether a string is empty or uninitialized. As mentioned earlier, this gives you largely the same information as using the Len function to see if a string has a length of 0.

CStr

No separate IsString function exists, however. Why isn't there an IsString function? Everything can be converted to a string representation, regardless of its original data subtype. The function that converts values to strings is CStr, as discussed on Day 4. With CStr, you can take a number and assign the corresponding string to a variable with statements like this:

```
strVarA = CStr(3019.53)
```

This fills the variable strVarA with the string 3019.53. CStr automatically handles some advanced localization issues you could run into if you are marketing your software in other countries. Some countries separate decimal numbers with commas rather than the period used in the United States. CStr will automatically take this into account when producing a string for a number. Str will not. Therefore, unless you have some reason not to, it is wise to use CStr for your string conversions.

You now know how to convert a number to its string format. You may also have occasions when you need to go in the other direction—convert a string to its numeric data subtype representation. Several functions were covered on Day 4 that carry out these conversions. They include CDbl, CInt, CLng, and CSng. An example of a CInt assignment is

```
intVarA = CInt(strVarB)
```

Such statements take a valid string representation of a number, such as 155, and provide the corresponding numeric data representation.

Val

If a variant variable is used to store the result, it internally records the fact that its data is of a numeric subtype rather than a string subtype after such a conversion. As you saw earlier, this is important for certain types of calculations.

But these functions do not work as well when a number must be converted from a string that is not in perfect numeric format. Assume that the number that must be converted is stored as the string 155 pints. CInt and the other similar functions would not convert this successfully. The related function Val can come to your assistance here, but Val is not supported in the current beta version of VBScript! However, it is supported in Visual Basic, and some documentation seems to indicate that it might be a part of the final VBScript.

Val converts just the numeric portion of a string to its corresponding numeric representation. Val always returns a data subtype of a double number (a decimal point number that can contain very large or very small values). If you don't want the data in double format, you can easily convert it to the appropriate numeric type using the result of Val. Consider the following example. Assume that strVarB contains 155 pints of fine ale. You want to store this number of pints in an integer. An integer, of course, can't deal with additional verbiage such as "pints of fine ale." The Val function can filter these out for you. This statement would carry out your assignment:

```
intVarA = Cint(Val(strVarB))
```

Val can handle numbers in Hex and Octal format as well. Hex numbers start with a &H indicator, and octal numbers start with an &O indicator. Val only converts up to the first nonblank character it finds. Val will return a 0 if there are no numeric portions in the string that it can convert. Therefore, this statement:

```
msgbox Val("Pints - 155")
```

will display 0.

As you can see, Val can do a lot for you. It could also confuse you, or worse yet, allow confusion to creep into your programs, if you did not realize how its conversion rules work. But for certain situations, it can't be beat. When you know you will have string input that starts with numeric characters and is followed by non-numerics, Val provides a quick, easy-to-use conversion path to your code. As mentioned earlier, at the time of printing Val is not functional in VBScript. Check later versions or documentation for updates on future status.

Hex **and** Oct

Two other interesting string functions are Hex and Oct. They convert a decimal number to the string representation of its octal or hexadecimal number system equivalent. If you design calculators, these can come in handy; otherwise, you may not have frequent use for them. But every now and then computer problems require working at the hex or octal level for low-level debugging, and then these functions can be a tremendous aid.

Listing 15.8 shows additional examples of each of the functions just discussed, and Figure 15.6 shows the results of these tests. The best way to understand these functions is to study plenty of examples and experiment with them yourself. If you are familiar with these functions, you will find many situations where this knowledge saves you time in the future.

Listing 15.8. The examples of IsEmpty, CStr, Hex, and Oct.

```
<!-------- IsEmpty, Str, Cstr, Val  ------------------------------------->
<INPUT TYPE=BUTTON VALUE="Str/Val"  NAME="cmdVal">
<SCRIPT LANGUAGE="VBSCRIPT" FOR="cmdVal" EVENT="onClick">
<!--

    Dim strFeedback, strValue, intValue

    ' Check to see the initial status of variable
    if IsEmpty(intValue) then
        strFeedback = "intValue has not been assigned yet." & vbCrLf
    else
        strFeedback = "intValue contains : " & intValue & vbCrLf
    end if

    ' Assign a value to the variable
    intValue = 255

    ' Now check again to see the status of variable
    if IsEmpty(intValue) then
        strFeedback = strFeedback & "intValue still has not been " & _
        assigned yet."  & vbCrLf & vbCrLf
    else
        strFeedback = strFeedback & "intValue now contains : " &_
intValue & vbCrLf & vbCrLf
    end if

    ' Show the value from intValue using string conversion functions
    strValue = Cstr(intValue)
    strFeedback = strFeedback & "CStr of intValue is:""" & strValue &_
        """ Size=" & len(strValue) & vbCrLf

    ' Show the value in hex and octal
    strValue = Hex(intValue)
    strFeedback = strFeedback & "Hex of intValue is """ & strValue & _
        """" & vbCrLf
    strValue = Oct(intValue)
    strFeedback = strFeedback & "Oct of intValue is """ & strValue & """"

    MsgBox strFeedback, 0, "Using IsEmpty, Cstr, Hex, Oct"


-->
</SCRIPT>
```

Keep in mind when considering the conversion functions like CStr that in many cases you don't have to explicitly convert your data. If you are supplying data to be printed out in a message box, for example, the appropriate string representation of a variable will be used automatically. However, when the time comes that you do care about explicitly converting the data subtype of a variant variable, as discussed on Day 4, conversion functions like CStr can be invaluable aids.

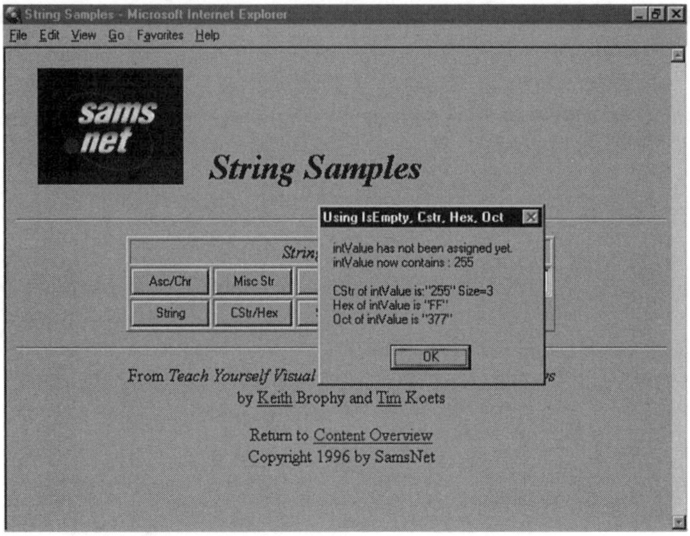

Figure 15.6.

The results of the IsEmpty, CStr, Hex, *and* Oct *tests.*

StrComp

The last string function to consider is StrComp. You have seen some examples in today's lesson of string comparisons. They have been carried out directly with the = comparison operator. For example, the following compares one string to another to see if they are exactly alike:

```
if txtDept = "Engineering" then
```

But what if you wanted to see which string came first in alphabetical order? A function called StrComp lets you easily accomplish this and more. If you provide two strings as arguments to StrComp, the function will provide back the values shown in Table 15.1.

Table 15.1. The StrComp return values.

Value	Condition Represented
-1	string1 < string2
0	string1 = string2
1	string1 > string2
Null	string1 or string2 is Null

An example of StrComp in shown in Listing 15.9. The corresponding results are shown in Figure 15.7. This code carries out two simple comparisons. In the first comparison, the first string argument precedes the second in alphabetical order. As you can see by the results, StrComp returns the value -1 on the comparison. In the second comparison, the second string precedes the first alphabetically. In this case, as the results show, StrComp returns the value 1.

Listing 15.9. The StrComp example.

```
<!-------- StrComp  -------------------------------------->
<INPUT TYPE=BUTTON VALUE="StrComp"  NAME="cmdStrComp">
<SCRIPT LANGUAGE="VBSCRIPT" FOR="cmdStrComp" EVENT="onClick">
<!--

    Dim strFeedback, intCompare, strValue1, strValue2

    ' Assign starting values
    strValue1 = "apple"
    strValue2 = "zebra"

    ' Compare the two strings
    intCompare = StrComp(strValue1, strValue2)

    ' Evaluate results of comparison
    if intCompare = -1 then
        strFeedback = "StrComp determined that " & strValue1 & " precedes " & _
            strValue2
    elseif intCompare = 0 then
        strFeedback = "StrComp determined that " & strValue1 & _
        " is the same as " & _
            strValue2
    elseif intCompare = 1 then
        strFeedback = "StrComp determined that " & strValue1 & " follows " & _
            strValue2
    elseif IsNull (intCompare) then
        strFeedback = "One of the arguments was null"
    end if

    strFeedback = strFeedback & vbCrLf


    ' Try another test
    strValue1 = "apple"
    strValue2 = "aardvark"

    ' Compare the two strings
    intCompare = StrComp(strValue1, strValue2)

    ' Evaluate results of comparison
    if intCompare = -1 then
        strFeedback = strFeedback & "StrComp determined that " & strValue1 & _
            " precedes " & strValue2
    elseif intCompare = 0 then
```

continues

Listing 15.9. continued

```
        strFeedback = strFeedback & "StrComp determined that " & strValue1 & _
            " is the same as " & strValue2
    elseif intCompare = 1 then
        strFeedback = strFeedback & "StrComp determined that " & strValue1 & _
            " follows " & strValue2
    elseif IsNull (intCompare) then
        strFeedback = strFeedback & "One of the arguments was null"
    end if

    MsgBox strFeedback, 0, "Using IsEmpty, Str, CStr, Val"

-->
</SCRIPT>
```

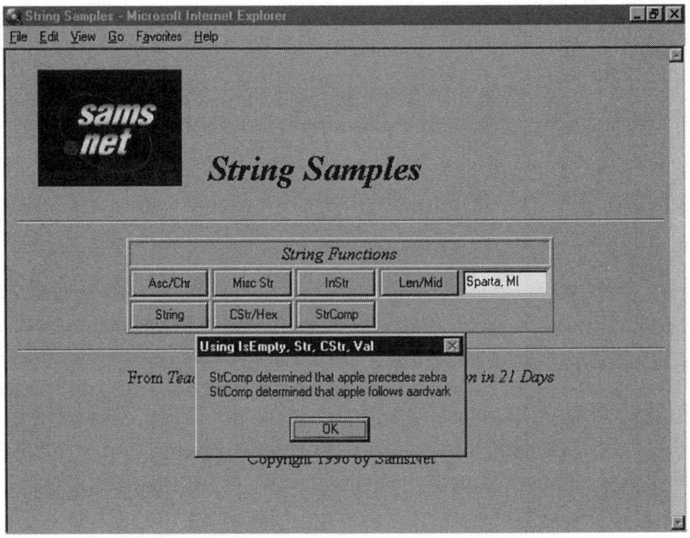

Figure 15.7.

The results from the
StrComp *example.*

Through code such as this example, you can use StrComp to carry out detailed comparisons of ordering and equivalence. But StrComp provides still another helpful capability. Earlier in this lesson you used Ucase to make a string uppercase before comparing it to an uppercase match string with =. If StrComp is used for the comparison, you can simply provide a third parameter to it to tell it to do a comparison that is not case sensitive. If this third parameter is other than 0, a comparison that is not case sensitive is used. If the parameter is 0 or is not present at all, then a case-sensitive comparison takes place. For example,

```
if StrComp("test","TEST") = 0 then
```

would not evaluate to True because the case of the strings is different. However,

```
if StrComp("test","TEST",1) = 0 then
```

would evaluate to True because case is not considered in that comparison.

StrComp provides you with powerful string evaluation capability. If your string processing needs are simple, you will likely find that a simple = comparison between two strings can serve your purpose. However, if you are doing advanced comparisons, such as alphabetical comparisons or comparisons in which you don't care about case matching, StrComp can save you a lot of coding.

Summary

When you construct a Web page and use script capabilities to make it active, you almost always need to deal with strings in one way or another. If the user supplies input through a text control, you receive it as a string. If you need to provide feedback through a message or label, you supply back a string. One of the most powerful capabilities of Web page programming is the potential to validate user input and provide meaningful feedback through a script without sending data back to the server. This requires the parsing and validating of strings. Working with strings is central to working with VBScript in many cases.

Today's lesson shows you the functions that VBScript provides for dealing with strings. Asc and Chr are used to deal with a character's ASCII code representation. Ucase and Lcase convert strings to uppercase and lowercase, respectively. LTrim, RTrim, and Trim are functions that return a string with leftmost, rightmost, or left and right blanks removed. Left and Right return a string that represents the requested number of leftmost or rightmost characters of the original string. InStr searches for a substring within a string. Len returns the length of a string. Mid can be used to return a substring from the specified position of a string. Space returns a string consisting of the requested number of blank spaces. String returns a string consisting of the requested number of designated characters. IsEmpty can be used to determine whether a string has been assigned or is still in an empty uninitialized state. Cstr converts a number to a string and also makes use of localization settings to use the decimal indicator of the current country localization setting. StrComp carries out string comparisons, including alphanumeric comparisons that are not case sensitive. This function returns indicators of the comparison results, including the less than, equivalent, greater than, or null status of the compared strings.

As you can see, a wide variety of functions are available for string handling. It is important to be familiar with all of them. While you may not use them all frequently, you might run into a situation that one of the functions is perfectly suited to handle. If you know about it, you will have an easy solution at your disposal.

Q&A

Q **If you wanted to write code to see how many characters a string contained, would you use `Len` or `InStr`?**

A `Len`. This function will return the number of characters in a string. `InStr`, on the other hand, searches for the occurrence of a substring within a string.

Q **What string would be assigned to the `VarA` variable from this line of code:**

`VarA = Lcase(Ucase(Ucase("bean sprout")))`

A `VarA` would contain the string `bean sprout`. Expressions are evaluated from inner to outer parentheses. Therefore, the last function applied to the string would be `Lcase`. This would convert the entire string to lowercase regardless of its current value.

Q **Assume that you know you have a string of the form `Cost=XXX` in a variable. You want to assign just the numeric cost factor, `XXX`, to another string. What function would you use to achieve this, `InStr` or `Mid`?**

A You would use `Mid` because it is the function you use to copy a substring from a given position in a string. `InStr`, on the other hand, locates a substring within a string and returns the character position. But in this problem, you already know the character position of the substring `XXX` and simply want to copy that substring to another variable.

Workshop

This lesson shows an example of parsing user input, or extracting pieces of information from larger strings that the user supplied. Think of examples in pages you work with where it might be helpful to parse user input to check its format. For example, consider whether you have any phone number fields on your Web pages. Think through and sketch out the algorithm that you would have to use to parse the area code of a phone number and to verify that it consists of three digits. You can assume that the area code is provided between parentheses, as in the format `(555)`.

Quiz

NOTE Refer to Appendix C, "Answers to Quiz Questions," for the answers to these questions.

1. Show the If conditional expression you could use to validate that a user had entered Accounting for the txtDepartment input control, regardless of case. Use StrComp to carry out this check.

2. Suppose you were working with a script for a library. A scriptwide variable string called s_strBorrower lists the last names of all the borrowers of a particular book. The s_strBorrower variable might look like Jones Smith Brophy Koets Kringle, for example. Assume that one person may have borrowed a book more than once. Write a code statement that will determine how many times Brown borrowed the book. Essentially, you have to determine how many times Brown is present in the string s_strBorrower.

Day **16**

Extending Your Web Pages with Dates and Advanced Math

Yesterday you saw how you can extend the capabilities of your Web pages by incorporating the advanced string handling built into VBScript. This is fine if you're parsing standard data, but there will be times when you want your scripts to do more. Perhaps you'll need to work with dates and provide future payment due information to your users. Maybe you'll need to provide a time estimate of when service for a certain type of car repair will be complete. Or maybe you'll need to generate random numbers on the page to implement an online slot machine. Who knows? Depending on what type of programming you are doing, the day might even come when you have to dust off the old trig books to provide an algorithm based on trigonometric principles.

You need to go beyond string functions in situations like these. You might think that you would have to provide your own layers of support functions in such cases, but VBScript has many useful functions you can turn to in cases like these. In today's lesson you will gain full knowledge of the additional functions VBScript provides you to work with. After today's lesson, you will have been exposed to nearly all the major functions that are part of the VBScript programming language. Some of the functions, particularly date handling, you may use frequently. Others, such as advanced math, may be of use only from time to time. But when you need them, they'll be there. Easy to use and broad in function, they are one of the elements of VBScript that make it possible to piece together quick, robust Web page solutions for almost any scenario.

NOTE

> One sample Web page containing a collection of scripts is used to demonstrate all the functions in today's lesson. This page, `AllFunc.htm`, is available on the CD-ROM. The sample scripts referred to throughout the lesson can be found there. A separate command button is used to launch individual tests that focus on specific functions and display test results in a message box.

Dates

Date information can be an important part of a script. Perhaps your script receives an order request date from a user and compares it to an expected shipment date to determine if the order can be met. Maybe it collects a date of employment from a user and ensures that the date range is valid before uploading it to the server. Or your script might figure out what day of the week an appointment falls on, based on the date for which it's scheduled, to determine if the user should be warned about busy Fridays. All these tasks would be fairly difficult to perform if a date was simply a string like `April 22, 1994` that you had to figure out how to analyze. Luckily, VBScript functions can come to your rescue. They provide you with a ready toolkit of functions for working with date and time information.

Working with Dates and Times

Many of the functions that follow can work with a date, a time, or a time and date. In VBScript, dates and times are often stored together. The date subtype is viewed as representing both a date and time in its own format.

Date, Time, and Now

Some of the easier functions to use are Date, Time, and Now. They simply tell you, through a character string, what the current date and time are. Date returns a string with the current date. Time returns a string with the current time. Now returns a string with the current date and time.

Date, Time, and Now lead to the same results. The difference is that while Date returns an individual date and Time returns an individual time, Now returns both the current date and time.

The Now function, on the other hand, provides both date and time information to the user, combined into one string. Listing 16.1 shows how to use Now to provide feedback to the user.

Listing 16.1. Displaying current date and time using the Now function.

```
<!-------- Now Sample ------------------------------------->
<INPUT TYPE=BUTTON VALUE="Now" SIZE=5 NAME="cmdNow">
<SCRIPT LANGUAGE="VBSCRIPT" FOR="cmdNow" EVENT="onClick">
<!--
    msgbox "Current date / time is " & now, 0, "Using now"

-->
</SCRIPT>
```

When the user clicks on this test command button, Now is displayed, as shown in Figure 16.1.

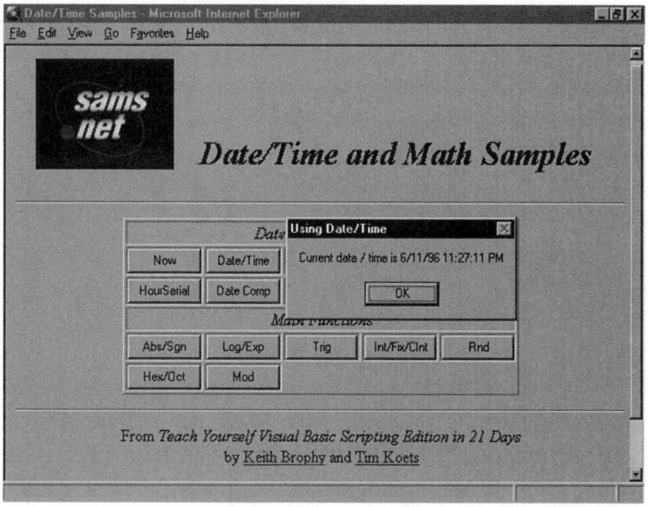

Figure 16.1.

Using the Now function to inspect the current time.

Listing 16.2 uses Date and Time to provide feedback to the user about the current time.

Listing 16.2. Displaying current date and time using the Date and Time functions.

```
<!-------- Date Sample --------------------------------------->
<INPUT TYPE=BUTTON VALUE="Date/Time" SIZE=5 NAME="cmdDateTime">
<SCRIPT LANGUAGE="VBSCRIPT" FOR="cmdDateTime" EVENT="onClick">
<!--
    msgbox "Current date / time is " & date & " " & time, _
           0, "Using date and time"

-->
</SCRIPT>
```

When the user clicks on the test command button, the date and time are displayed, as shown in Figure 16.2.

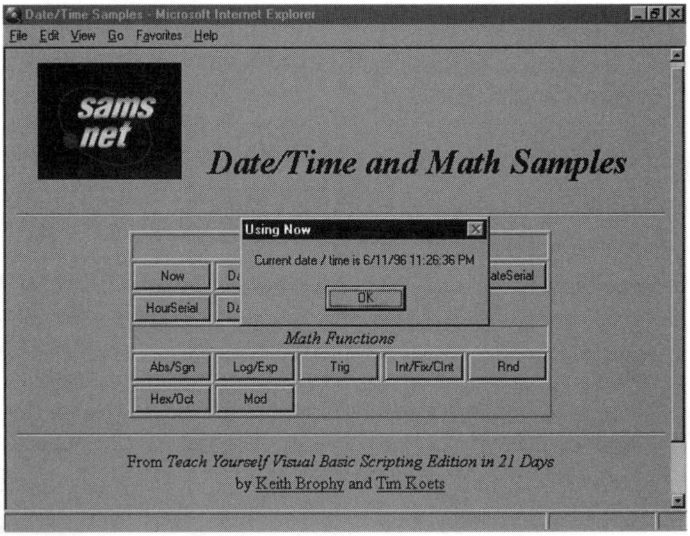

Figure 16.2.

Using the Date *and* Time *functions to inspect the current time.*

Year, Month, Day, Weekday, Hour, Minute, and Second

These functions allow you to easily work with pieces of a date and time string. If you need to use just the current hour figure to determine what type of data a program runs, you can easily parse out this information with the hour function. The same type of helpful function is available if you need to know what day of the week a certain date fell on. Use the Weekday function to get your answer. There is no need to write a detailed procedure to parse this information out of a date because it is already there.

Several such functions are provided for handling dates and extracting information. Year returns a number representing the current year, Month returns an integer representing the current month, Day returns an integer representing the current day number, and Weekday returns number 1–7 to represent Sunday through Saturday, respectively. All the functions take a date specification as an argument and return data about that date supplied as an argument. The date specification argument is typically one of your variant variables, but it could also be the function Now or anything else in date and time format. Listing 16.3 shows these functions in use.

16

Listing 16.3. Using Year/Month/Day/Weekday **to get detailed information about the current time.**

```
<!-------- Year/Month/Day/Weekday Sample ----------------------------->
<INPUT TYPE=BUTTON VALUE="Year/Month/Day" SIZE=5 NAME="cmdDay">
<SCRIPT LANGUAGE="VBSCRIPT" FOR="cmdDay" EVENT="onClick">
<!--
    dim dtmCurrent

    ' Start out with current time as value to use
    dtmCurrent = now

    msgbox "Current year is " & Year(dtmCurrent) & "; month is " &_
        month(dtmCurrent) & "; day is " & day(dtmCurrent) &_
        ": weekday is " & weekday(dtmCurrent), _
        0, "Using year/month/day/weekday"

-->
</SCRIPT>
```

The year/month/day/weekday date information appears, as shown in Figure 16.3, after the user clicks on the test button.

The time-based functions work much the same. Hour, Minute, and Second can derive this information from the time supplied as an argument. Listing 16.4 shows these functions in use.

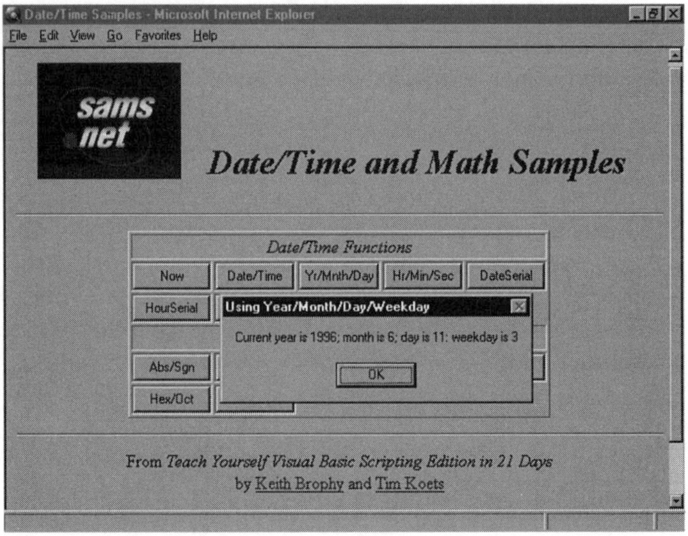

Figure 16.3.

Using the date informa-
tion functions to inspect
characteristics of the
current date.

Listing 16.4. Using the Hour/Minute/Second functions.

```
<!-------- Hour/Minute/Second Sample ------------------------------------->
<INPUT TYPE=BUTTON VALUE="Hour/Minute/Second Sample" SIZE=40 NAME="cmdHour">
<SCRIPT LANGUAGE="VBSCRIPT" FOR="cmdHour" EVENT="onClick">
<!--
    dim dtmCurrent

    ' Start out with current time as value to use
    dtmCurrent = now

    msgbox "Current hour is " & Hour(dtmCurrent) & "; minute is " &_
        minute(dtmCurrent) & "; second is " & second(dtmCurrent) _
        0, "Using hour/minute/second"
-->
</SCRIPT>
```

The hours/minutes/seconds information test appears, as shown in Figure 16.4, after the user clicks the test button. This code, like the other examples in this chapter, is easy to write because the functions are very straightforward to use.

DateSerial **and** TimeSerial

The serial functions give you an easy way to calculate future or past dates based on an offset from today's date. With these functions at your disposal, you can make these calculations in one line of code. Suppose that you've heard that a friend's baby is due in seven months and three weeks. The code in Listing 16.5 could tell you the exact date that equates to.

Figure 16.4.

Using the Hour/
Minute/Second
*information functions to
inspect characteristics of
the current time.*

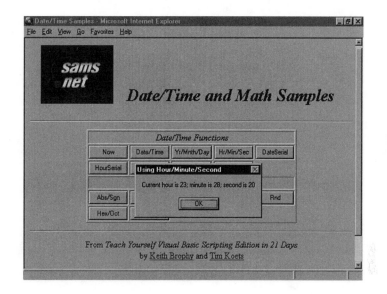

Listing 16.5. Using the DateSerial **function.**

```
<!-------- Date Serial Sample ------------------------------------------->
<INPUT TYPE=BUTTON VALUE="DateSerial"  NAME="cmdDateSerial">
<SCRIPT LANGUAGE="VBSCRIPT" FOR="cmdDateSerial" EVENT="onClick">
<!--
    dim dtmCurrent

    ' Show what the will be 7 months and 3 weeks from now
    dtmCurrent = DateSerial(year(now),month(now)+7,day(now)+21)
    msgbox "The date will be " & dtmCurrent
-->
</SCRIPT>
```

The resulting message box, shown in Figure 16.5, provides the date 12/11/96 (when this program was run on April 20) from the date offset supplied to DateSerial.

DateSerial is handy at constructing a date from the year, month, and day components. The DateSerial approach can be much easier to use than building a date string by piecing together substrings.

The TimeSerial function serves the same purpose, but for times rather than dates. Assume that you want your script to remind the user that he is to meet someone exactly 2 hours and 17 minutes from now. You could use a code like that shown in Listing 16.6.

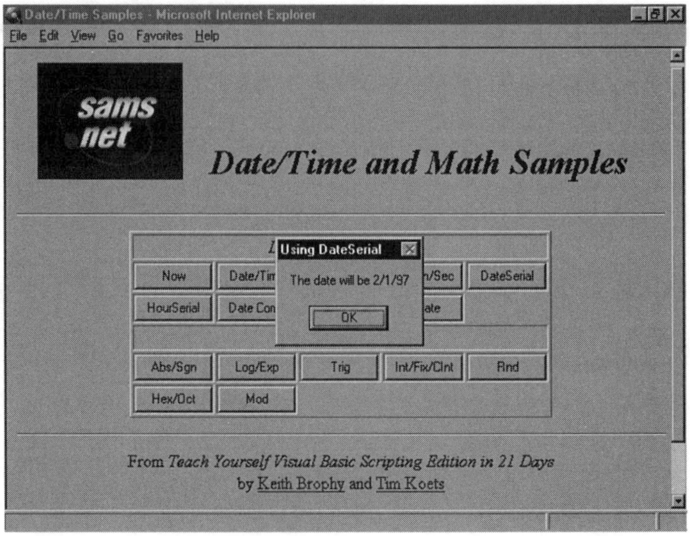

Figure 16.5.

Using the DateSerial *function to derive a future date.*

Listing 16.6. Using the TimeSerial function.

```
<!-------- Hour Serial Sample ------------------------------------------->
<INPUT TYPE=BUTTON VALUE="HourSerial"  NAME="cmdHour">
<SCRIPT LANGUAGE="VBSCRIPT" FOR="cmdHour" EVENT="onClick">
<!--
    dim dtmCurrent

    ' Start out with current time as value to use
    ' Show what the time will be in 2 hours and 17 minutes
    dtmCurrent = TimeSerial(Hour(Now)+2, Minute(Now)+17,0)

    msgbox "The time will be " & TimeValue(dtmCurrent)
-->
</SCRIPT>
```

If you run this program at 1:03 p.m., you will see a result of 3:20 p.m., as shown in Figure 16.6. The VBScript TimeValue function is used to return just the time portion of the date and time information stored in the variant variable. Try this code without the TimeValue conversion and you will see that you get back a meaningless date along with the expected time.

NOTE

These functions work well going in the forward direction, but may provide results slightly different from what you might expect when going backward in time. There are no other alternative functions. Just make sure to test these functions carefully and make sure you understand all aspects of their behavior if you will be using them in this manner.

Figure 16.6.

Using the TimeSerial *function to derive a future time.*

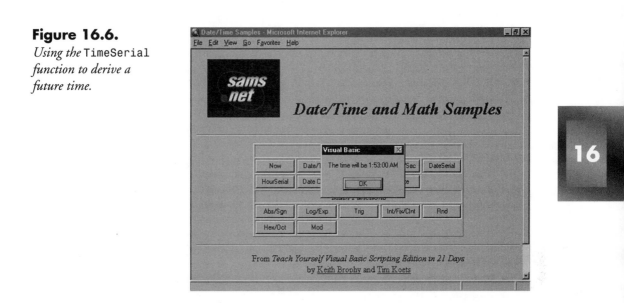

The TimeSerial function, like the DateSerial function, is convenient for building an hour variable based on the hour, minute, and second numerical components. Often it is easier to build a time based on numeric expressions than on strings if calculations are involved.

Date and Time Comparisons and
DateValue/TimeValue

If you do much with dates and times in your scripts, sooner or later you likely will want to compare two of them. Logical decisions can be made based on date and time comparisons. However, you have to keep a little trick in mind. The comparisons must be based on dates that are stored as date subtype variables, rather than based on string subtype variables.

Listing 16.7 can help illustrate this point. First, two different dates are assigned to variant variables. The variant variables regard the dates as string data at this point. Even though the dates are provided in a valid date format, the double quotes around them cause the VBScript run-time interpreter to assume that you want to work with string data. When the comparison is made, the two strings are compared based on, essentially, alphabetical order. The strings are ordered based on the ASCII characters. With this ordering, whichever year came first is irrelevant because the months are sufficient to separate to two strings. Therefore, the older date is regarded as the greater date.

Listing 16.7. Using the DateValue function.

```
<!-------- Date Comparison ------------------------------------------->
<INPUT TYPE=BUTTON VALUE="Date Compare"  NAME="cmdDateCompare">
<SCRIPT LANGUAGE="VBSCRIPT" FOR="cmdDateCompare" EVENT="onClick">
<!--

dim DateA, DateB, strFeedback1, strFeedback2

' These dates are assigned as strings
DateA = "1/5/96"
DateB = "5/5/95"

' See which string-format date is more recent
if DateA > DateB then
  strFeedback1 = "First try - DateA is greater."
else
  strFeedback1 = "First try - DateB is greater."
end if

' Now store these dates in date format rather than string format
DateA = DateValue(DateA)
DateB = DateValue(DateB)

' See which date-format date is more recent
if DateA > DateB then
  strFeedback2 = "Next try - DateA is greater."
else
  strFeedback2 = "Next try - DateB is greater."
end if

Msgbox strFeedback1 & " " & strFeedback2,0,"Using Comparisons and DateValue"
-->
</SCRIPT>
```

After this comparison, the DateValue function is used to convert the string subtype variables to date subtype variables. Now the variant variables both contain date format data. When the comparison is again made after this assignment, the results are completely different. VBScript can now tell it is working with two dates, and the conditional expression correctly evaluates the fact that the new date is greater than the old date. The feedback from running this test can be seen in Figure 16.7.

The very same comparison rules apply to time values. String-based times will be compared as strings. Times stored in date and time format through the TimeValue function will be correctly treated as times in comparisons. Listing 16.8 illustrates how a.m. and p.m. times can be compared with this technique.

Figure 16.7.

Date comparisons using `DateValue`.

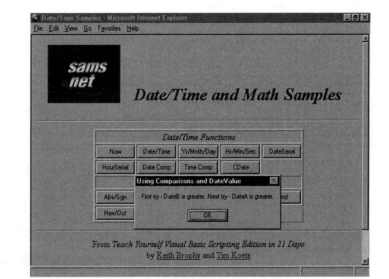

Listing 16.8. Using the `TimeValue` function.

```
<!-------- Time Comparison -------------------------------------->
<INPUT TYPE=BUTTON VALUE="Time Compare"  NAME="cmdTimeCompare">
<SCRIPT LANGUAGE="VBSCRIPT" FOR="cmdTimeCompare" EVENT="onClick">
<!--


dim TimeA, TimeB, strFeedback1, strFeedback2

' These times are assigned as strings
TimeA = "9:00 AM"
TimeB = "2:00 PM"

' See which string-format time is more recent
if TimeA > TimeB then
  strFeedback1 = "First try - TimeA is greater."
else
  strFeedback1 = "First try - TimeB is greater."
end if

' Now store these times in time format rather than string format
TimeA = TimeValue(TimeA)
TimeB = TimeValue(TimeB)

' See which date and time-format time is more recent
if TimeA > TimeB then
  strFeedback2 = "Next try - TimeA is greater."
else
  strFeedback2 = "Next try - TimeB is greater."
```

continues

Listing 16.8. continued

```
end if

Msgbox strFeedback1 & " " & strFeedback2,0,"Using Comparisons and TimeValue"
-->
</SCRIPT>
```

The result of running this script is shown in Figure 16.8.

Figure 16.8.

Time comparisons using
TimeValue.

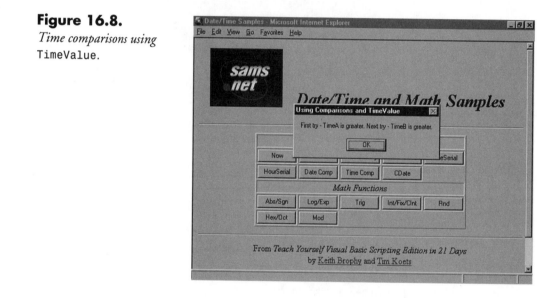

Understanding Date and Time Formats

So far you have seen some functions that work on dates, some that work on times, and some, such as Now, that work with both dates and times. You might be wondering how you tell VBScript to store a time as opposed to a date. The good news is that you don't have to. The VBScript date format is actually a date and time format. If there is pertinent time information, it gets stored as part of the date representation in a variable assignment. If you apply a date- or a time-based function to a variable, the function will work on the date or time portions of that variable as appropriate.

CDate **and** IsDate

Now that you have more insight into the date type, you can appreciate the role of yet another function, CDate. CDate converts an expression into a date and time. It can be used to assign a date string to a variant variable and cause that variable to represent the date with a date subtype. This may cause you to think, "Wait a minute! That's what DateValue does! Is this some conspiracy between Microsoft and authors to provide redundant functions to beef up the size of computer books!?"

A better explanation is available, however. CDate converts date *and* time format data to date and time representations. DateValue converts *only* to date representations, and TimeValue converts *only* to time representations. Suppose you provide the expression 12/28/62 5:00 AM as an argument to TimeValue, DateValue, and CDate, respectively. TimeValue will return 5:00 AM, and DateValue will return 12/28/62, but CDate will return the entire date and time of 12/28/62 5:00 AM.

Since CDate has this dual date and time capability, it can also handle some formats that would cause DateValue or TimeValue to generate errors. Consider the following example:

```
msgbox CDate(( 96 * 365) + 0.5)
```

This would generate the date December 7, 1995, 12 p.m.. Date calculations start with the year 1900 as a basis. Advancing 365 days 96 times moves you forward almost 96 years. The date ends a little shy of 1996 because leap years have 366 days. Then, the 0.5 gets translated into half a day, or 12 hours. Listing 16.9 shows several more uses of CDate.

Listing 16.9. Using CDate for date and time conversions.

```
<!-------- CDate Conversion ------------------------------------->
<INPUT TYPE=BUTTON VALUE="CDate"  NAME="cmdCDate">
<SCRIPT LANGUAGE="VBSCRIPT" FOR="cmdCDate" EVENT="onClick">
<!--
dim strFeedback, VarA, VarB

' CDate converts days to date
strFeedback = "(1) " & CDate(( 96 * 365) + 0.5) & vbCrLf & _
        "(2) " & CDate("12/7/95 12:00") & vbCrLf & _
        "(3) " &  CDate("Dec 7, 1995 12PM") & vbCrLf & vbCrLf

VarA = "Pig"
VarB = "Dec 28, 1962"

if IsDate(VarA) then
    strFeedback = strFeedback & "VarA is " & CDate(VarA) & vbCrLf
else
    strFeedback = strFeedback & "VarA cannot be converted!" & vbCrLf
end if

if IsDate(VarB) then
    strFeedback = strFeedback & "VarB is " & CDate(VarB)
else
```

continues

Listing 16.9. continued

```
      strFeedback = strFeedback & "VarB cannot be converted!"
end if

msgbox strFeedback, 0, "Using CDate"
-->
</SCRIPT>
```

The corresponding results appear in Figure 16.9. Notice that CDate accepts date expressions in a variety of formats in addition to the numeric day specification. Valid expressions include 12/7/95 12:00 and Dec 7, 1995 12PM. However, even CDate can be brought to its knees by invalid data. Suppose you tried a function call like this:

```
VarA = CDate("Pig")
```

This statement would cause an error. VBScript doesn't know how to map Pig to a valid date or time. This could present a bit of a problem in your scripts. How can you tell if something is in valid date and time format before you try to convert it? Fortunately, another function comes to the rescue. IsDate evaluates an expression and returns True if it can be converted to date format. Therefore, you can use code like that shown in Listing 16.9 to make sure an expression is in valid date and time format before you try to convert it.

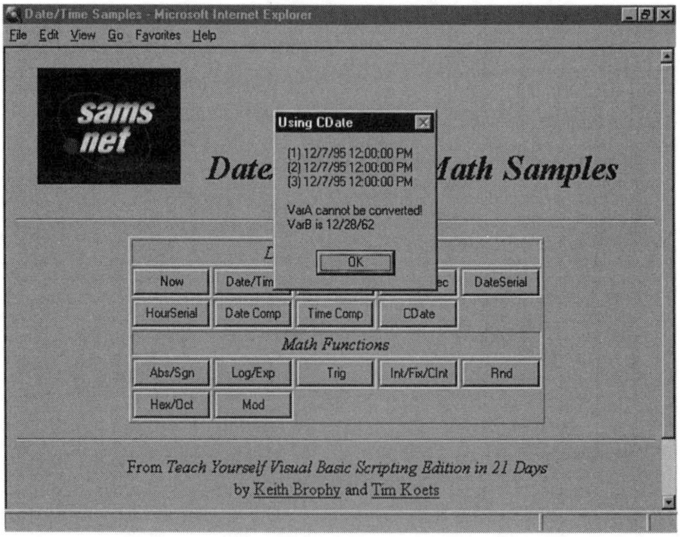

Figure 16.9.

Using CDate *to convert date and time expressions.*

16

There is one more trick to learn about date handling. How do you assign a time or date to a variable and ensure that the variant variable represents it internally as a date subtype rather than as string data? For example, this assignment just stores a string (that happens to be in valid date format) into varA:

```
varA = "7/6/62"
```

There is a symbol (#) for telling VBScript to treat a value as the date subtype when it stores it. This assignment would store date subtype information into varA:

```
varA = #7/6/62#
```

If you want to convince yourself that it works, you can write a test to display the subtype using the VBScript VarType function after each assignment.

It turns out that in most cases you can work in the string format with your dates and everything will be just fine. There are times when you may want to use #, however. For example, if you need to store a series of date values for calculations with DateSerial, the efficiency of your code will be improved by storing them as date subtype variants.

As you can see, a full range of functions supports date and time handling in your scripts. These functions make it easy to validate, compare, and calculate future dates and times. With them, the days of old when date and time information had to be sent to a server for evaluation are past. Your scripts can use these functions to take an active role in dealing with date and time information.

Math

Ask any computer science major to summarize his educational background, and it'll come to light that hidden in the dark recesses of his past is math. Plenty of math. Many students would claim that the reason for the emphasis on math in a computer science curriculum is faculty cruelty. But many of the computer programs written require some type of math to process user data and provide results. Many require extensive mathematical operations. The ability to carry out precise calculations is an integral part of programming.

It comes as no surprise then that an important part of any programming language is the mathematical capabilities it supports. These capabilities influence the type of programs that can be easily produced in a given language. VBScript is often thought of, like many scripting languages, as a lightweight scripting language with a focus on gluing together other components rather than language features themselves. Therefore, you may have expected that you would need to incorporate controls into your Web pages to carry out advanced mathematics. However, this isn't entirely true. VBScript provides a fairly rich set of mathematical capabilities. You can accomplish a lot in your Web pages by just using the math functions that are inherently supported in VBScript. These functions are described in the sections that follow.

What Does VBScript Let You Do with Math?

The answer to this question lies in the operators and variables supported by VBScript. VBScript has a full range of mathematical operators, as introduced on Day 5, "Putting Operators to Work in VBScript." Of course, the ability to carry out operations is of little value unless you have data to act on and have somewhere to store the intermediate and final results. That is where variables come into play. The type of variables used during mathematical operations has a direct impact on the results that can be produced. On Day 4, "Creating Variables in VBScript," you learned that the variant data type is the only type used for Visual Basic variables. This also significantly shapes the approach you can take to mathematically based problems in VBScript. Just as you can't really describe the taste of a good bowl of cereal by describing the flakes and not the milk, so it is with variables and operators. Neither of these issues can be considered in a vacuum. The function of the operators is related to the variable types they act on, and variable behavior is affected by the values assigned from operators. So let's take a look at operators and the variant variable in tandem and consider how they play together.

Abs **and** Sgn

If you work very much with numeric data, there is a good chance that sooner or later you will have to be concerned with the issue of the mathematical sign with a number. Suppose, for example, that you have a Web page that prompts the user to enter the amount he spent on a business trip. Because of your company travel policy, users are never given money ahead of time and can only receive a reimbursement later. Suppose that some users indicate the amount they spent as a negative number, and others enter it as a positive number. You need to write a script that totals the amount and adds it to some other figures. In this case, you want your script to ignore the sign the user has entered and treat the value as a positive one. The Abs function can do this. It will return the positive representation of the number passed to it as an argument. So the following statement would display 10 10:

```
msgbox Abs(-10) & " " Abs(10)
```

Signs are essentially discarded by this function.

The Sgn function has somewhat of an opposite role. This function determines the sign of a number. The function returns an integer that provides information about the sign through the return codes, documented in Table 16.1.

Table 16.1. Return codes from the `Sgn` function.

Return Code	Meaning
1	Number passed as parameter to `Sgn` is greater than 0
0	Number passed as parameter to `Sgn` equals 0
-1	Number passed as parameter to `Sgn` is less than 0

One way this function could be used is to provide feedback about input. In the case of the expense account form example, you could encourage your users to enter information in a consistent manner. If you found that a user had entered an expense as a negative value, code like that shown in Listing 16.10 could guide him.

Listing 16.10. Using `Sgn` to check the sign of user input.

```
if Sgn(Val(txtExpense.Value)) = -1 then
    MsgBox "Please provide expense amounts as positive values in the future. "
end if
```

Another example of `Sgn` and `Abs` is shown in Listing 16.11. In this case, the absolute value of a number is displayed, followed by the results of checking its sign. Because the number evaluated is -10, the absolute value becomes 10. The return code from the `Sgn` function is -1, indicating a negative number. The results are shown in Figure 16.11.

Listing 16.11. Using `Sgn` and `Abs`.

```
<!-------- Sgn and Abs ------------------------------------------->
<INPUT TYPE=BUTTON VALUE="Abs/Sgn"  NAME="cmdAbs">
<SCRIPT LANGUAGE="VBSCRIPT" FOR="cmdAbs" EVENT="onClick">
<!--
dim strFeedback, intResult, VarA

VarA = -10
strFeedback = "VarA is " & VarA & " and the absolute value of VarA is " & _
    Abs(VarA) & vbCrLf

intResult = sgn(VarA)
if intResult = 1 then
    strFeedback = strFeedback + "VarA is more than 0"
elseif intResult = 0 then
    strFeedback = strFeedback + "VarA is 0"
elseif intResult = -1 then
    strFeedback = strFeedback + "VarA is less than 0"
end if

msgbox strFeedback, 0, "Using Abs and Sgn"
-->
</SCRIPT>
```

Figure 16.10.

Using Sgn *and* Abs.

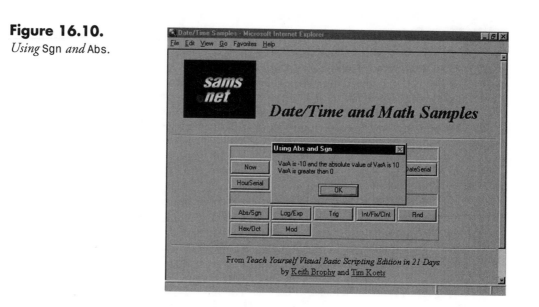

You could easily implement both the Sgn and Abs functions yourself if they were not provided for you. To carry out the interpretation provided by Sgn, you would simply need to check if a number is less than 0, equal to 0, or greater than 0. The Abs conversion can be achieved by just checking to see if a number is less than 0, and if so, multiplying by -1 to convert it to the corresponding positive number. Even though it's easy to write code that carries out the equivalent of these functions rather than use them, avoid this temptation. Using the functions provided brings several advantages. You know they work, and if you write your own functions, you might introduce silly coding errors. Just as importantly, the use of these functions provides a clear, standard approach in your code. It is easy to tell the intention of code that uses Sgn and Abs when reviewing and maintaining it.

The Logarithmic Functions—Log **and** Exp

The math functions examined so far today have been very straightforward in purpose. The next set may take a little more thought if your math books have gathered some dust over the years. VBScript provides support for dealing with natural logarithms and antilogarithms of numbers. The explanation that follows is simplified to convey the power of these functions. If you are in the dusty math book category and the time comes when you have to apply these functions in a script of your own, find a good math book to ensure that you are clear on the purpose.

Consider the number 1,000 in the context of base 10. Suppose you want to know how many times 10 must be multiplied by itself to produce 1,000. The answer, of course, is 3 ($10 \times 10 \times 10$). You can use the Log function to help derive this answer.

The Log function works in terms of *base e*. This natural logarithm has special properties, which are left to the math books to address. The base *e* constant behind these special properties is approximately 2.718282. Log works in terms of this base. When you supply the following expression you will get a result of approximately 1, based on the base value of 2.718282. Another way to think of this is that a single instance of the e constant (2.718282) yields a value of 2.718282:

```
Msgbox Log(2.718282)
```

When you supply the following expression, you will get a result of approximately 3. This result reflects the fact that e * e * e (or 3 instances of multiplying e by itself) is equivalent to 20.086:

```
Msgbox Log(20.086)
```

In other words, 20.086 is approximately equal to 2.71828×2.71828×2.71828.

If you're not a math jockey, at this point you may be thinking, "I may have to find out how many times 2 goes into a kilobyte from time to time, but I'm never gonna care about this *e* stuff!" The natural logarithm *is* useful for something other than academic exercises. One of the neat characteristics of the natural logarithm is that it can be used to derive logarithms in other bases.

Assume that you want to find out how many times you must multiply 2 by itself to get a kilobyte, or 1,024 bytes. The problem you are faced with is how to calculate a base-2 log for the number 1,024. VBScript doesn't allow you to do this directly. But you can calculate this, or any similar problem, by combining two base *e* Log function calls. Simply use this:

```
Msgbox "The problem Log 2 (1024) is equal to:" & Log(1024) / Log(2)
```

The result that is displayed from this call is 10. And sure enough, 1024= 2×2×2×2×2×2×2×2×2×2.

So the natural log Log functions provide you with the means to calculate a logarithm of any base. For a base n and number x, just use this formula:

```
Logn(x) = Log(x)/Log(n)
```

You don't have to resort to exotic math libraries or server-side processing if you have an algorithm that needs to use logarithms of any base. You can use the VBScript function now that you know the secret of how to apply it.

Log has a close cousin called Exp. This function is sometimes called the antilogarithm, and it returns *e* raised to the given power. For example, consider this statement:

```
Msgbox Exp(3)
```

This will display 20.086, which is approximately equal to 2.71828×2.71828×2.71828. In the earlier example, you saw that Log(20.086)=3, so you can see that these two functions are closely related.

Note that this is different from the exponent operator discussed on Day 5. In that lesson you saw how an expression like the following evaluates to 8 because 2×2×2= 8:

```
Result = 2 ^ 3
```

In the case of the ^ operator, the value to the left of the operator is raised to the given power. With Exp, *e* itself is raised to the power provided.

Another example of the use of Log and Exp appears in Listing 16.12. This example first demonstrates the use of the natural exponent base *e*. The first statement raises *e* to a power using the Exp function. The next statement computes the corresponding log in base *e*, providing the result of the first calculation as the argument to the Log function. The next statement shows how to raise a number with a regular base to the given exponent by simply using the standard ^ operator. Finally, the last statement calculates the corresponding log to base 10. To do so, the Log base *e* of the previous statement's result is divided by the Log base *e* of the desired base of the solution, 10.

The results from running this example can be seen in Figure 16.11. Once you understand what these functions are doing, they are as easy to understand and apply as the other math operators covered so far. The important thing is to be aware that they exist, so when opportunities arise to make use of them, you don't have to turn any further than VBScript.

Listing 16.12. Using Log and Exp.

```
<!-------- Log and Exp ------------------------------------------->
<INPUT TYPE=BUTTON VALUE="Log/Exp"  NAME="cmdExp">
<SCRIPT LANGUAGE="VBSCRIPT" FOR="cmdExp" EVENT="onClick">
<!--
dim strFeedback

strFeedback = "e * e * e * e = Exp(4) = " & Exp(4) & vbCrLf & vbCrLf

strFeedback = strFeedback & "Log base e of 54.598 = Log(54.598) = " &_
    Log(54.598) & vbCrLf & vbCrLf

strFeedback = strFeedback & "10 * 10 * 10 * 10 * 10 * 10 = 10 ^ 6 = " & _
    (10 ^ 6) & vbCrLf & vbCrLf

strFeedback = strFeedback & "Log base 10 of 1,000,000 = Log(1000000)/Log(10) &_
    = "Log(1000000)/Log(10)

msgbox strFeedback, 0, "Using Log and Exp"
-->
</SCRIPT>
```

16

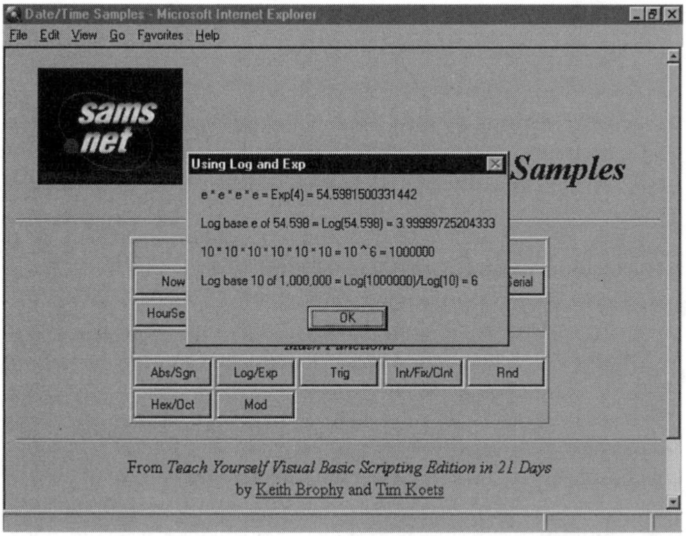

Figure 16.11.

Using Log *and* Exp.

16

The Square Root Function—Sqr

In the last section you learned about the use of the standard exponentiation operator ^ to raise a number of a given base to the specified power. For example, the following statement displays a 25, the result of 5×5:

```
Msgbox 5 ^ 2
```

A corresponding function, Sqr, returns the square root of a given number. Sqr is as straightforward as the exponentiation operator. For example, the following statement will display a result of 5, because 5×5=25:

```
Msgbox Sqr(25)
```

Likewise, the following statement will display a result of 3, since 3×3=9:

```
Msgbox Sqr(9)
```

The square root function returns data that is in the variant double subtype because the result can contain decimal data to a great degree of precision.

The Trig Functions—Sin, Cos, Tan, **and** Atn

Keep out the dusty math book for the next set of functions. The trigonometric functions in VBScript consist of Sin, Cos, Tan, and Atn. You likely either use trig functions quite frequently in your programming and already know what they are or never use them and have long since forgotten what a hypotenuse is. If you need to brush up on your trig, refer to a good math book. However, if you are not hypotenuse literate, there is something important to take from the discussion that follows. Realize that VBScript provides trig support. You can have local trig processing on your pages without resorting to a control. You may not be using trig today, but many types of programs do require it, and you could find yourself implementing a trig-related solution tomorrow. When that time comes, turn to `Sin`, `Cos`, `Tan`, and `Atn`.

The names of all these functions are relatively self-explanatory. They deal with the relationships of triangle angles and sides. `Sin` takes an angle as a parameter and returns the sine of an angle, as you might expect. The sine of the angle is the ratio of the side opposite the angle under consideration divided by the hypotenuse length. `Cos` takes an angle parameter and returns the ratio of the length of the side adjacent to the angle divided by the hypotenuse length. `Tan` returns the tangent of an angle. An angle is supplied as a parameter. Then the length of the side opposite the angle is divided by the length of the side adjacent to the angle to determine the ratio return value. `Atn` provides the arctangent for the given ratio. The number representing the ratio is supplied as a parameter. This ratio consists of the side opposite the angle divided by the side adjacent to the angle. The angle that corresponds to this ratio is returned.

Angles are traditionally represented in radians. However, when angles are used with these functions, they are represented in terms of radians. If you have a number in degrees you want to convert to radians, just multiply the degrees by 3.141593/180. If you want to convert radian results back to degrees, multiply the radians by 180/3.141593. The value `3.141593` is a special number in angular geometry called pi.

Now that you know the function names and how angles are represented, you can do anything you need with these angles. An example that demonstrates the use of these functions can be seen in Listing 16.13. The sine, cosine, and tangent of 45 degrees are all displayed by using the `Sin`, `Cos`, and `Tan` functions, respectively. To provide 45 degrees as an argument to the trig functions, the degrees to radians conversion factor is applied. Then, the arctangent of the ratio of two equivalent sides of a triangle is calculated. That result is returned in terms of radians by the `Atn` function. Therefore, it must be converted back to degrees using the radians to degrees conversion factor. The results from this sample program appear in Figure 16.12.

Listing 16.13. Using `Sin`, `Cos`, `Tan`, and `Atn`.

```
<!-------- Sin, Cos, Tan, Atn ------------------------------------->
<INPUT TYPE=BUTTON VALUE="Trig"  NAME="cmdTrig">
<SCRIPT LANGUAGE="VBSCRIPT" FOR="cmdTrig" EVENT="onClick">
<!--
dim strFeedback

strFeedback = "Sin of 45 degrees = " & Sin(45 * (3.141593/180)) & vbCrLf
strFeedback = strFeedback & "Cos of 45 degrees = " & _
```

```
     Cos(45 * (3.141593/180)) & vbCrLf
strFeedback = strFeedback & "Tan of 45 degrees = " & _
     Tan(45 * (3.141593/180)) & vbCrLf
strFeedback = strFeedback & "Atn of 1/1 ratio in degrees = " & _
     Atn(1) * (180/3.141593)

msgbox strFeedback, 0, "Using Sin, Cos, Tan, and Atn"
-->
</SCRIPT>
```

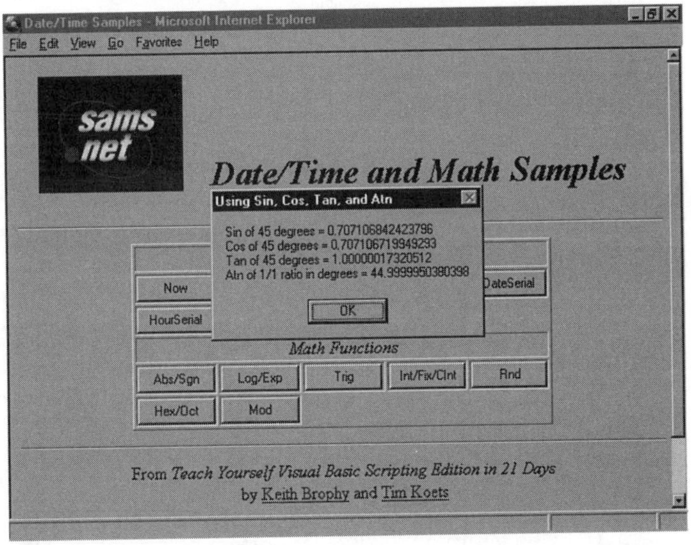

16

Figure 16.12.

Using Sin, Cos, Tan,
and Atn.

Extending the Power of VBScript Through the Log and Trig Functions

VBScript obviously is perfectly capable of performing basic trig and natural log functions. Of course, if you have some really math-intensive projects, you might wish you could get more from your scripts. Some day you may find yourself staring into space, dreamily thinking, "If only I could figure out an inverse hyperbolic tangent from VBScript…then I'd have it all." There's good news for when this day comes. It turns out that by using these functions as building blocks, you can carry out a whole host of additional functions. For example, you can code the inverse hyperbolic tangent as follows:

```
HyperArcTan = Log((1 + arg) / (1 - arg)) / 2
```

If you need the cosecant, you can get it with

```
CoSecant = 1 / Sin(X)
```

By building on the functions you already know, you can implement many more advanced functions. It is beyond the scope of this book to describe and illustrate all these advanced functions. If you find yourself in a situation that requires them, all you'll need is a good math book that lists the formulas and knowledge of the intrinsic functions described here to serve as the building blocks. Then your Web pages can come alive with advanced math that would warm the heart of your old math teacher, all without even leaving the confines of VBScript.

Rounding and the Integer Functions—`Fix` and `Int`

When you deal with numbers and produce results, you need to handle them in different ways. You will want to keep some results, such as the grade point average of a student, in decimal format. Other results, such as the total number of employees you need to hire to staff a factory based on average staffing history, you may need to round. After all, it could be hard to hire 20.7 workers if your company doesn't make use of part-time help. It's better just to hire 21 workers. Still other results may need to be truncated. If you are writing a program that provides billing estimates based on the number of days a patient stays at a hospital, but you only charge for full days, you might treat a total of 14.2 days or 14.9 days as simply 14 days.

VBScript provides the means to carry out all these tasks with the help of a couple easy-to-use functions. First of all, consider the case of truncating. Truncating a decimal point is essentially the same as returning the corresponding integer. The `Int` function serves this purpose by returning the integer portion of a number. This statement:

```
msgbox Int(14.9)
```

displays 14, as does this statement:

```
msgbox Int(14.2)
```

These statements would have worked exactly the same if the `Fix` function were used. `Fix` also truncates a number to display its integer representation. For example, the following statement would display 15:

```
msgbox Fix(15.7)
```

One difference between these two functions—and it is a subtle one related to rounding negative numbers—is that `Fix` truncates a negative number so that the value is greater, and `Int` produces the negative integer that is less than the value supplied. So the following would display -15:

```
msgbox Fix(-15.7)
```

But this statement would display -16 instead:

```
msgbox Int(-15.7)
```

If you need to round a number rather than truncate it, you can always build in the rounding yourself. If you add .5 to a decimal number and then take the integer value using Int, the result is to round it to the next higher integer if the number originally contained a decimal portion greater than .5. If VarA contains 1.7, the following statement will display the result 2.0:

```
msgbox Int(VarA + .5)
```

An easier and slightly different way to round is built into VBScript. The Cint function, which was discussed on Day 4, will round a number to the nearest integer. If decimal values are less than .5, the number is rounded down. If decimal values are greater than .5, the number is rounded up. If the decimal portion of a number is exactly equal to .5, then it is rounded to the nearest even number. For example, 7.5 would be rounded up to 8. Since 7.5 is between the two even numbers 6 and 8, 8 is the nearest even number and is selected as the rounding result. Likewise, 6.5, sandwiched between 6 and 8, would be rounded down to 6.

These functions have many potential applications in code. But it is critical to understand exactly what they are doing before making use of them. Listing 16.14 provides a series of examples to highlight the behavior of the functions.

Listing 16.14. Using `Int`, `Fix`, and `Cint` to truncate and round.

```
<!-------- Int, Fix, Cint  -------------------------------------->
<INPUT TYPE=BUTTON VALUE="Int/Fix/CInt"  NAME="cmdFix">
<SCRIPT LANGUAGE="VBSCRIPT" FOR="cmdFix" EVENT="onClick">
<!--
dim strFeedback, intResult, VarA

VarA = 14.5
strFeedback = "VarA = " & VarA & vbCrLf
strFeedback = strFeedback & "Int(VarA) = " & Int(VarA) & vbCrLf
strFeedback = strFeedback & "Fix(VarA) = " & Fix(VarA) & vbCrLf
strFeedback = strFeedback & "Cint(VarA) = " & Cint(VarA) & vbCrLf & vbCrLf

VarA = -6.5
strFeedback = strFeedback & "VarA = " & VarA  & vbCrLf
strFeedback = strFeedback & "Int(VarA) = " & Int(VarA) & vbCrLf
strFeedback = strFeedback & "Fix(VarA) = " & Fix(VarA) & vbCrLf
strFeedback = strFeedback & "Cint(VarA) = " & Cint(VarA) & vbCrLf & vbCrLf

VarA = -3.902
strFeedback = strFeedback & "VarA = " & VarA  & vbCrLf
strFeedback = strFeedback & "Int(VarA) = " & Int(VarA) & vbCrLf
```

continues

Listing 16.14. continued

```
strFeedback = strFeedback & "Fix(VarA) = " & Fix(VarA) & vbCrLf
strFeedback = strFeedback & "Cint(VarA) = " & Cint(VarA) & vbCrLf

msgbox strFeedback, 0, "Using Int, Fix, and CInt"
-->
</SCRIPT>
```

ANALYSIS The result from this series of tests appears in Figure 16.13. As you can see, in many cases Int, Fix, and Cint end up providing the same result. The differences between the functions are only apparent for certain types of arguments. It helps to think of these functions in terms of a number line. If you really want a number to be rounded, rather than truncated, you should use Cint. This moves you to the closest integer on the number line and chooses the closest even integer when the choice is a toss up. If you simply want to truncate the number and you always want to truncate to a lesser value, then Int is the way to go. This always advances you left on the number line to the previous integer. If you do have a special situation where you want to truncate, but you always truncate closer to 0, then use Fix. This function will always advance you to the next closest integer to 0, moving you left on the number line when you started with a positive number, and right on the number line when you started with a negative number.

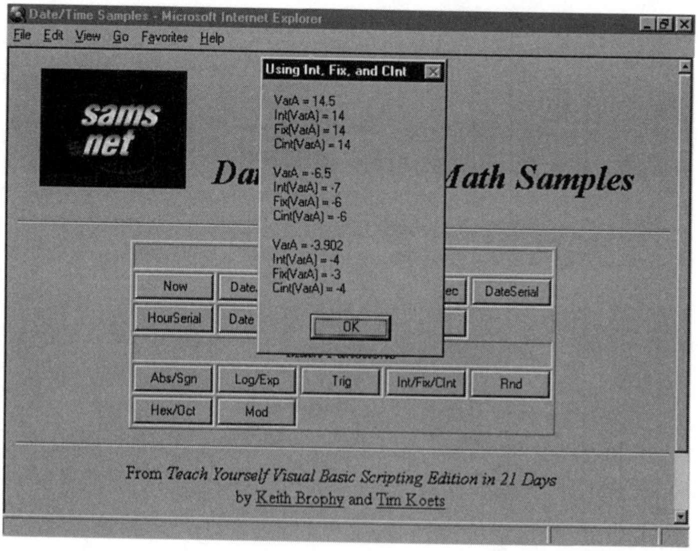

Figure 16.13.

Using Int, Fix, *and* Cint *to truncate and round.*

Randomize **and** Rnd

So far the discussion has focused on predictable results. But under some circumstances, you may want the behavior of your Web pages to appear random. Maybe you have a label that flashes different colors, and you want to generate those colors in a random pattern. Or perhaps you want to carry out a virtual roll of the dice each time a page is loaded, and provide the user with a different customized greeting based on the number that is generated. This would give your users a feeling of freshness. They'd feel like your pages were changing daily. Because many Web development guidelines emphasize variability as the key to keeping users coming back for repeat visits to a page, this is an especially important strategy.

It is hard to make computers perform randomly since they are essentially dumb devices that act consistently on whatever instructions are provided to them. (It is hard to remember that computers are consistent in the middle of an all-night bug-chasing session, but they are!) However, with the help of a function, Rnd, you can introduce an element of random behavior. Rnd returns a number from an internal random number sequence.

Rnd pulls numbers from the internal sequence in the same manner each time it is used. So if you had a script that made use of Rnd to display a series of random numbers, the series would look the same every time the program ran. This reduces the variability impact you would hope to achieve by using random numbers in the first place.

A statement can be used to avoid this effect, however. The Randomize statement initializes the internal sequence of numbers subsequently used by Rnd with a different sequence. The sequence used is based on the argument provided with Randomize, and is called a seed. If you do not provide this argument, then it is automatically based on a system timer. The timer value is likely to differ from one time to another when a script is run. Therefore, using Randomize with no argument prior to code that makes use of the related Rnd function is a common approach. The prior use of Randomize forces Rnd to generate a different sequence of random numbers from one time a script is run to the next.

The number returned by Rnd will vary from between greater than or equal to 0 up to less than but not equal to 1. The specific value returned depends on the random sequence in use. So the statement that follows returns a value that will never be less than 0 and never be equal to or greater than 1:

```
VarA = Rnd
```

This is somewhat of a problem if you want a random number outside this range. Suppose you're trying to simulate the role of a die. You want the code to generate a random integer between 1 and 6. If you multiply the result of Rnd by 6, you get a number that can range from 0 to 5.99999. If you add one to whatever the result, you have shifted your possible outcomes to range from 1 to 6.99999. Then, if you truncate the decimal portion of the number using the Int function, you have ensured that the result will be either 1, 2, 3, 4, 5, or 6. This statement appears as

```
VarA = Int(6 * Rnd + 1)
```

This approach to force random numbers to fall as integers within a given range can be represented more generically by the following formula:

```
Int((High_integer_desired - Low_integer_desired + 1) * Rnd + Low_integer_desired
```

You can see this formula at work in Listing 16.15. This sample program simulates the roll of six dice. The Random statement is used at the beginning of the script to ensure a different series of numbers will be provided each time the script is run. Then each specific role is generated by a call to the Rnd function. The formula listed earlier is used to massage the return value somewhere into the range of 1, 2, 3, 4, 5, or 6.

Listing 16.15. Using Rnd to simulate dice rolls.

```
<!-------- Rnd -------------------------------------->
<INPUT TYPE=BUTTON VALUE="Rnd"  NAME="cmdRnd">
<SCRIPT LANGUAGE="VBSCRIPT" FOR="cmdRnd" EVENT="onClick">
<!--
dim strFeedback, intCounter

Randomize

' Perform six rolls of the dice
for intCounter = 1 to 6
   strFeedback = strFeedback & "Roll " & intCounter & ": " & Int((6 * Rnd) + 1)
& chr(13)
next

msgbox strFeedback, 0, "Using Rnd to Simulate Dice Rolls"
-->
</SCRIPT>
```

ANALYSIS   The results from one trial of this script can be seen in Figure 16.14. Notice that two different rolls of six resulted. If you run this script again, you will get different results each time.

One way that Rnd is commonly used with Web pages, aside from rolling dice, is to produce random colors to liven up pages or make them appear fresh from one use to another. For example, you could have a code event associated with a timer control that is triggered every second. At each interval when it is called, that code could change the color of a label control that displayed a greeting. Listing 16.16 shows this type of code.

Figure 16.14.

Using Rnd *to simulate rolls of dice.*

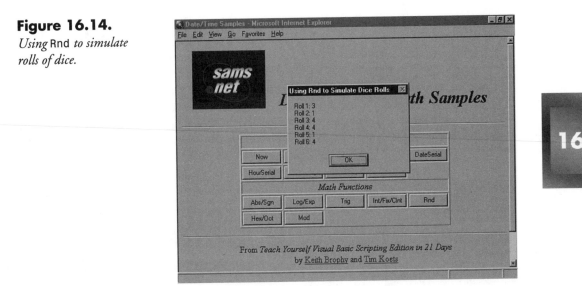

16

Listing 16.16. Code that randomly changes the color of a label.

```
sub timer_time
    lblGreeting.forecolor = rnd() * 16777216
end sub
```

The random number normally will fall between 0 and 1. Therefore, the standard range-producing formula is applied to the random number result. The formula forces the number to fall somewhere between 0 and 16777216, which is the highest color that can be represented. A color anywhere within this spectrum could appear.

The dice-rolling script and the code to produce random colors are just two of the many ways to use random numbers in your scripts. Random numbers have many other uses ranging from games, to lively screens, to random-sequence quizzes, to advertising blurbs. Two important aspects to remember when you work with random numbers are initializing the random-sequence seed number and converting the Rnd result. You initialize the random-sequence seed number by calling Randomize at the start of your script. This will ensure that you get a different series of numbers from one time the script is run to another. Also make sure that you convert the Rnd result to the desired range. You'll be able to welcome random behavior into your scripts on your own terms with this standard approach.

Working with Non-Decimal Systems—Hex and Oct

You may be able to go your entire programming career without ever having to worry about producing hexadecimal or octal numbers. Most math work tends to be our common base 10 system, rather than the base 16 hexadecimal system or base 8 octal system. On the other hand, you may not have this luxury if you work on scripts that are centered on math or computer software or hardware. If you do need to deal with hexadecimal or octal numbers, two handy VBScript functions are at your disposal. Hex returns a string containing the hexadecimal representation of the number passed as an argument. Oct returns a string containing the octal representation of the number.

You can see these functions in action in Listing 16.17. The corresponding results are shown in Figure 16.15.

Listing 16.17. Using Hex and Oct.

```
<!-------- Hex and Oct ------------------------------------->
<INPUT TYPE=BUTTON VALUE="Hex/Oct"  NAME="cmdHex">
<SCRIPT LANGUAGE="VBSCRIPT" FOR="cmdHex" EVENT="onClick">
<!--
dim strFeedback, VarA

VarA = 256

strFeedback = "VarA is " & VarA & vbCrLf
strFeedback = strFeedback & "Oct(VarA) is " & Oct(VarA) & vbCrLf
strFeedback = strFeedback & "Hex(VarA) is " & Hex(VarA) & vbCrLf

msgbox strFeedback, 0, "Using Hex and Oct"
-->
</SCRIPT>
```

ANALYSIS The first statement of the code assigns the value 256 to a variable. Then the variable is printed out in the default base 10 representation. 256 results, with the 2 signifying 2 units of 100, the 5 signifying 5 units of 10, and the 6 signifying 6 units of 1.

The next statement prints the base 8 octal representation of the number through the Oct function. The same value 256 is now represented by 400 octal. The 4 indicates 4 units of 64, with 0 units of 8, and 0 units of 1.

The final statement prints out the base 16 hexadecimal representation by using the Hex function. The value 256 is now represented as the number 100 hexadecimal. The 1 signifies 1 unit of 256, with 0 units of 16 and 0 units of 1.

The Hex and Oct functions give you the flexibility to easily handle the most common bases you're likely to run into. You don't need to build your own functions to convert from decimal to octal or hexadecimal. Simply apply these conversion functions, and your script has all the power and more of a hexadecimal/octal/decimal calculator.

Figure 16.15.

Using Hex *and* Oct.

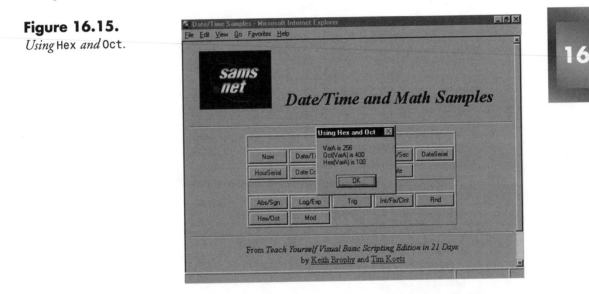

Representation and Storage of Hex and Octal Numbers

If you want to represent a hex number directly in your code, you can do it by preceding the hex number with &H. The following statement, for example, assigns 256 to a variable by setting it to the hex equivalent:

```
VarA = &H100
```

Likewise, &O can be used to represent an octal number. This statement also assigns 256 to a variable by setting it to the octal equivalent:

```
VarB = &O400
```

These variables just contain 256, with nothing special about it. The &O and &H representation of the data is just a convenient way to describe it to VBScript. However, since all numbers are stored internally in the computer as a series of bits, there is no internal notion of which base a number was assigned in. If you print out the values of the variables used in the preceding examples, you will see the default base 10 notation. For example, the following will print out 256 256:

```
MsgBox VarA & " " & VarB
```

On the other hand, you can present the data in hexadecimal format with the Hex function:

```
MsgBox Hex(VarA) & " " & Hex(VarB)
```

This prints out 100 100, which is the hexadecimal representation of 256.

The Mod **Operator**

So far the focus in today's lesson has been largely on functions. Operators were covered in detail on Day 5. One operator deserves some additional coverage, however. The Mod operator is commonly used in scripts by those who understand how to use it. Mod carries out what is termed as a *modulus* operation. It takes two numbers, divides them, and then returns the remainder as the result.

The example in Listing 16.18 takes the grand total of days, divides by 7 to determine how many full weeks were taken, and then uses the modulus to determine the remaining number of days beyond the last full week.

Listing 16.18. Using Mod to determine the number of weeks and days that have gone by.

```
Dim intWeeks
Dim intDays
intWeeks = s_intTotalDays \ 7
intDays = s_intTotalDays Mod 7
MsgBox "The total time is " & intWeeks & " weeks and " & intDays " days. "
```

ANALYSIS Mod is very handy for certain types of loop control as well. Suppose you have a loop that performs a lengthy series of calculations. This may keep the user waiting several minutes, so you want to provide occasional feedback on a regular basis after a given number of loops have been carried out. The code in Listing 16.19 shows one such approach. Figure 16.16 shows the corresponding results after the first period of loops.

This code carries out 1,000 loops, adding the value of every number between 1 and 1,000. After each 200 loops, a message box is provided to the user to let them know how far along the calculation is. (In a script intended for real use, you would not want to use a message box for the progress indictor since it requires user interaction. A label on the page would be better. But it makes for a nice clear example, so this approach is used here.) Now you could detect every 200th loop by checking to see if the counter variable intCounter is equal to 200, 400, 600, 800, or 1,000. This code is kind of cumbersome and not maintainable. If you modify the calculation to go up to 10,000 loops next week, just think of all the additional numbers the code would have to check. A much more elegant solution is shown in Listing 16.19.

Simply take the modulus of the current counter variable. If you divide by 200 and look at what's left over, you will only find a remainder of 0 once every 200 loops. Mod becomes the perfect means to monitor a loop and takes action at a given period. It is true that Mod will make your loop take longer to execute. After all, you're doing another division every time through the loop. However, this effect is normally not a big factor in user script speed. Also, in many situations, the advantages of this approach can outweigh such considerations.

Listing 16.19. Using Mod to provide periodic feedback in loops.

```
<!-------- Mod ---------------------------------------->
<INPUT TYPE=BUTTON VALUE="Mod"  NAME="cmdMod">
<SCRIPT LANGUAGE="VBSCRIPT" FOR="cmdMod" EVENT="onClick">
<!--
dim intCounter, lngTotal

for intCounter = 1 to 1000

    lngTotal = lngTotal + intCounter

    if (intCounter mod 200) = 0 then
        ' This only occurs after every 200 loops.
        '    Provide the user with a progress indicator at this point
        MsgBox "Have processed " & intCounter & " records.",0,"Progress_
                Indicator"
    end if
next

msgbox "Grand total is " & lngTotal, 0, "Using Mod"
-->
</SCRIPT>
```

Variable Representation of Numeric Data

The final area of focus in this lesson is simply a reminder of the functions available for data conversion that have already been covered. Day 4 looked at variable representation. You can use Cint, Cdbl, Clng, and Csng to convert expressions into a specific numeric data subtype of integer, double, long, and single, respectively. Also, insights from Day 15, "Extending Your Web Pages with Strings," help explain some of the considerations when converting numbers to strings and strings to numbers. Str and CStr can be used to convert numbers to strings Val, the function to convert in the opposite direction, is used to convert a string to a number of the double subtype. Coupled with the Cdbl, Csng, Clng, and Cint functions, you can control the data subtype of variables and expressions whenever needed.

16

Figure 16.16.

Using Mod.

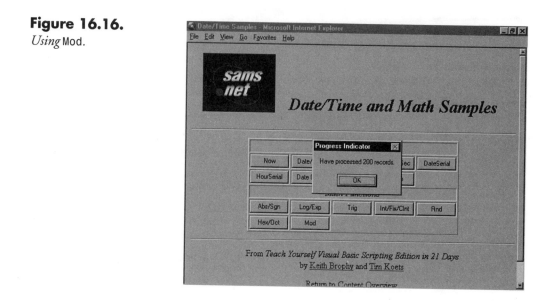

Summary

Today's lesson shows you a wide variety of advanced functions that are part of the VBScript language. The first functions are the date and time functions. Dates are represented internally in a variant variable with components for both the date and the time. For date and time information, you can use Date, Time, or Now to get information on the current date, time, or date and time setting. Many functions for working with date and time components are available. They include Year, Month, Day, Weekday, Hour, Minute, and Second. DateSerial and TimeSerial provide a means to build dates and times, including those in the future as offsets from the current date or time. The functions DateValue, TimeValue, CDate, and IsDate allow for easy conversion of strings to dates.

Many math functions can save you a lot of time in math-intensive scripts, just as many date functions are supported in VBScript to make date handling easier. Trigonometric functions allow you to carry out angular geometry calculations in your code. The logarithmic functions Exp and Log allow you to calculate exponents and logarithms based on the natural log base *e*. Perhaps more useful is the fact that if you know how to use Log, you can apply the formula to determine the logarithm of any number, regardless of base. Supported trig functions are Sin, Cos, Tan, and Atn. Many other commonly used trig values are not directly supported by VBScript, such as the inverse hyperbolic tangent. But by using the functions that are supported as building blocks, any of the more advanced functions can be easily supported directly in code.

Techniques for producing random numbers with `Randomize` and `Rnd` are provided in today's lesson. Some common uses of random numbers in Web pages are discussed. Rounding is examined. Approaches for truncating with `Int` and `Fix` and for rounding with `Cint` or self-produced functions are illustrated. Many other functions are considered, including `Abs`, which removes negative signs, and `Sgn`, which tells whether a sign is present. `Hex` and `Oct` are highlighted and a sample of those functions producing hex and octal numbers is provided.

16

Q&A

Q Is using the `Date` and `Time` functions and combining the results more accurate than using the `Now` function?

A No. Essentially these functions just provide different ways to access the same data. `Date` and `Time` are appropriate to use when you need to get at the individual date or time components. `Now` is appropriate to use when you need to reference the entire date and time format information.

Q What is the difference between `TimeValue` and `TimeSerial`? Can you use either to calculate what the time will be in 1 hour and 15 minutes?

A `TimeValue` converts a string to a time format. `TimeSerial` provides a time-format return code that is based on the hour, minute, and second parameters. `TimeSerial` accepts offsets to its hour, minute, and second parameters. Therefore, it provides a powerful ability to generate future dates based on the input provided to it.

Q What would happen if you used `Rnd` in a script but forgot to include `Randomize`?

A The same series of numbers would be used every time the script is run. `Randomize` is required to set the random number generator seed and ensure it is unique. If you don't use it, any random numbers generated will follow the same sequence from one run of the script to another.

Workshop

Earlier in this lesson you saw a partial example of displaying a label in varying colors, by using the `Random` and `Rnd` functions from within a timer event. Consider whether you have Web pages that would be more attractive to your users if your pages made use of a random factor to convey fresh information each time the page was visited. Perhaps you can generate a different greeting or tip based on a list of choices in your code and a random lookup. If you identify areas where you could benefit by a dose of random behavior, think about how much work it would likely take to do this.

Quiz

NOTE   Refer to Appendix C, "Answers to Quiz Questions," for the answers to these questions.

1. Write a script that displays a message only if the date previously stored in a global variable s_dtmEvent is chronologically later than the current time.

2. List the results that will be displayed for each of the following lines:

```
msgbox Int(-5.5)
msgbox Fix(-5.5)
msgbox Cint(-5.5)
```

3. Write code that determines how many players are left over if you divide up the number of players specified by s_TotalPlayers into bowling teams of nine bowlers each. Use Mod to accomplish this.

Day **17**

Exterminating Bugs from Your Script

If you have been a programmer for very long, you probably realize that writing programs is sometimes the easy part of software development. It's getting the bugs out that can be the real challenge! Judgment is needed to effectively sift through many hundreds or thousands of possible causes of a problem and hone in on a specific bug. At the same time, extreme amounts of logical, objective analysis must be applied to scientifically pinpoint the bug and prove its presence. The process of bug-hunting, therefore, often requires a special focus and concentration seldom encountered in other aspects of life. Likewise, hunting complex software bugs can cause a special frustration seldom encountered in other aspects of life! The good news is that a good set of problem-solving techniques and top-notch tools can make this process much easier. The not-so-good news is that top-notch tools do not come with VBScript. However, the tips and techniques suggested here go a long way toward minimizing debugging pitfalls.

VBScript Error Handling Support (or Lack Thereof!)

Unfortunately, VBScript offers little in the way of sophisticated debugging tools and error handling when your program is running. Most commercial language products, including Visual Basic 4.0, offer a development environment that is tremendously helpful when you're debugging programs. Later you'll learn more about those capabilities and what debug tools VBScript lacks, but first, let's examine what VBScript *does* provide.

Syntax Errors: Say What You Mean!

Errors come in a variety of shapes and sizes. The easiest types to picture and correct are simple typing or language usage errors in your Visual Basic code. For example, consider what would happen if you mistakenly typed this:

```
Dimwit C
```

instead of this:

```
Dim C
```

to declare a variable named C. Because the word Dimwit is not part of Visual Basic's language or syntax, the first statement can't be processed. This kind of error is commonly called a *syntax*, or *syntactical, error*.

Obviously, if you have a syntax error, your program is not going to work as intended. Fortunately, a program with a syntax error normally won't even run! Such stubborn behavior is fortunate because the sooner you find a problem, the better. You'd probably rather have your program go "on strike" immediately than have the problem pop up during a user's interaction with your script, or worse, give your user a bad result that he's not even aware of!

So how does a script go on strike? Suppose you have a statement like the following:

```
Dim c, c, c
```

This statement, too, contains a syntax error, but this error consists of an illegally duplicated definition rather than an incorrectly typed keyword. This statement is not legal according to the rules of VBScript because a variable name can only be used once; here, it has been defined three times in a row. When you attempt to load the page containing this program into the browser, you'll be greeted with the message shown in Figure 17.1.

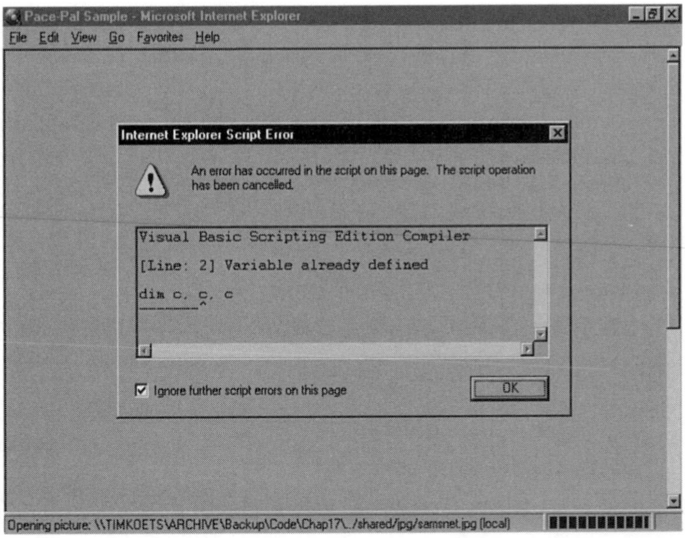

Figure 17.1.

A syntax-checking script error message.

This particular error was identified as soon as the page was loaded in the browser, but other syntax errors might not be caught until after the Web page is loaded. Suppose, for example, that a certain code statement is only carried out when a specific button is clicked. In the script event handler routine that is associated with that button, after a series of other calculations, you have a statement like this:

```
a = b / c
```

Assume that c is computed internally prior to the calculation, and c's value varies from one calculation to another. This statement may work perfectly well for the first several times the button is clicked. However, if the value of c ever turns out to be 0, this statement will fail. Because the computer is unable to divide by 0, VBScript will generate a message box similar to the one in Figure 17.1. This will bring your program to a screeching halt.

NOTE

When you are presented with the run-time error message from the Internet Explorer browser, you are given a check box option to suppress notification of future run-time errors. If you check this box, labeled Ignore, further script errors on this page, notification of future errors in other scripts on the page will be suppressed. Loading of the specific script that caused the problem will still be halted when errors occur.

These are just two examples of syntax errors that can be detected when VBScript tries to run your program. These various error conditions are called *run-time* errors. Hopefully, your user never sees any run-time errors. Ideally, you would write perfect, error-free code! However, given the complexity of programming, the odds of producing a perfect program are slim, so you must be able to thoroughly test your programs to remove all problems before you turn them over to your users. Also, you can take steps when writing your code to make it more robust if a run-time error should occur.

NOTE

> When a browser runs your VBScript code embedded in HTML, it does so by passing the VBScript statements to a separate component of software called the *VBScript Interpreter.* This interpreter checks and runs the VBScript code.

Unfortunately, there is no standard VBScript interactive development environment from Microsoft to make the debugging task easier. This makes the task of error-proofing your programs a considerable challenge. However, VBScript does provide some help in recovering from errors and pinning them down. You can write code that helps a program robustly continue after an error has occurred. The `On Error Resume Next` statement serves this purpose. After an error occurs, a convenient source of information, called the `err` object, is available for use in your code as well. With the `err` object, you can write program logic that prints out error information or takes a code path based on an analysis in code of what error has occurred. These techniques for dealing with run-time errors are detailed in the section "Effective Error Hunting" later in this lesson. But first, let's examine another category of error.

Semantic Errors: Mean What You Say!

By now you may be feeling a little more at ease, comforted by the idea that there is some support in the VBScript language to help you handle errors. Don't get too comforted, though! First, the VBScript support for run-time errors may help you handle them, but it won't prevent or eliminate them. Second, semantic errors can pose an even bigger problem than syntax errors. A *semantic* error is an error in meaning (that is, you fail to write the program to achieve the purpose you intend). For example, suppose you want to add a 4 percent sales tax to the cost of an item. You provide the following code statement:

```
total = orig_price + orig_price * 4
```

4 was used here in place of .04. The result is that this incorrect statement won't add 4 percent to your total sale, but it will add four times the cost of your item to your total sale! This is clearly an error. However, as far as the VBScript interpreter can tell, this statement is fine.

VBScript doesn't know what a sales tax rate is. It obediently carries out the calculation you give it.

With a semantic error, the problem rests squarely on your shoulders. VBScript is not able to automatically highlight these for you. Rather, after noticing an incorrect result, you must work backward until you hone in on the problem. Semantic problems do not directly cause run-time errors; they just lead to bad results. And while bad results may suggest that you have a problem, they won't tell you where it is. Often, you must trace through your program line by line, ensuring that each line is correct and produces valid results before proceeding to the next line.

Some languages offer support for this kind of tracing. In the case of VBScript, however, you must put together your own traces. Trace tactics that can be used to address semantic errors will be discussed in the next section, and you'll get a closer look at run-time error handling techniques that can be used to tackle syntax errors. For now, recognize that it is not too important that you know the textbook description of semantic versus syntactical errors. It *is* important, however, that you are aware of the techniques available for dealing with them. You should also realize that the most important tools for debugging—patience and persistence—are provided by *you*.

Effective Error Hunting

Now that you have a feel for the type of error support in VBScript, it's time to observe it in action. The Pace-Pal program, introduced briefly on Day 2, "The Essence of VBScript," serves as our first case study. Pace-Pal is the running pace calculation program shown in Figure 17.2. It is available in file `pace-pal.htm` on the CD-ROM. Like the other programs you've learned about in this book, this program consists of a standard HTML Web page with embedded VBScript. Pace-Pal allows the user to specify a distance in either miles or kilometers, and a time in minutes/seconds format (hours can also optionally be provided if you're willing to run that long!). With this information, a pace per mile can be calculated. For example, if you ran a 6.2-mile race (10k) in 37 minutes and 12 seconds and supplied that information to Pace-Pal, Pace-Pal would calculate that you averaged 6-minute miles.

Pace-Pal does its job very nicely when it has perfect, well-mannered, never-make-a-mistake users. It runs into problems, however, when faced with the more typical user who occasionally makes mistakes.

Specifically, Pace-Pal does a poor job of handling nonstandard input.

Pace-Pal can derive a 10k pace from a time of 37:12 faster than you can blink an eye. But if you accidentally type in 37:12AA rather than 37:12 for the time, disaster strikes. Pace-Pal's code is not constructed to deal with a time in such a format. The code doesn't check the data integrity. Instead, it tries to process the data, causing the VBScript interpreter to attempt the impossible with the current statement. The poor VBScript interpreter is left holding the bag, asked to carry out a statement that makes no sense and will lead to a wrong result! Needless to say, the interpreter balks, tossing up the famed run-time error window. A picture of the run-time error window generated when Pace-Pal attempts to process a time of 37:12AA is shown in Figure 17.3.

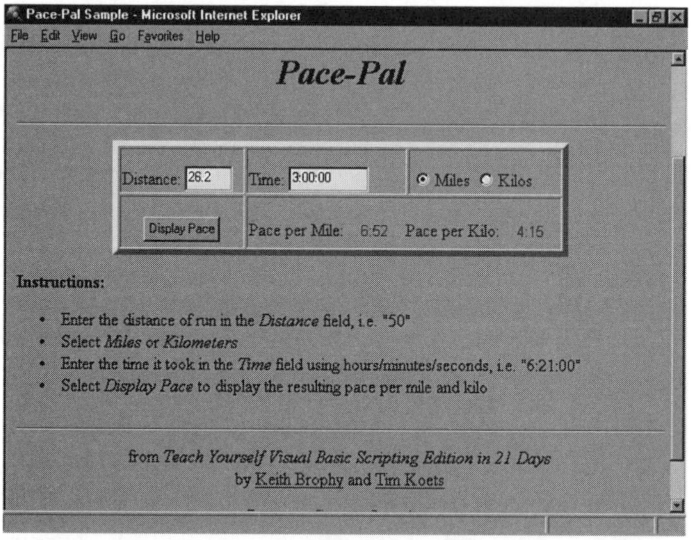

Figure 17.2.

The Pace-Pal program with bad input data.

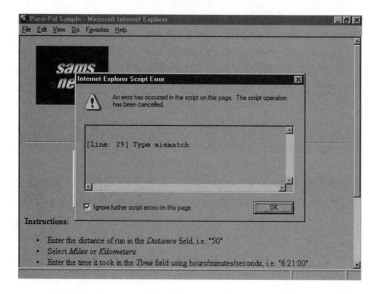

Figure 17.3.

A run-time error in the Pace-Pal program.

VBScript is nice enough to clue you in to the problem. The error message that is displayed tells you that the problem is related to an attempted type conversion that is illegal under the rules of VBScript. Unfortunately, VBScript doesn't tell you where this error occurred. And even worse, from the user's point of view, VBScript halts execution of the script since it has detected problems there. If you go back and specify good input and click the Pace button, nothing happens. Until the page is reloaded, VBScript will consider this a bad script and won't process any of it.

As you saw earlier in this lesson, VBScript does provide you with location details for some types of errors. In many cases, fundamental flaws in language definition can be detected and pointed out with line number information when a page is loaded. This was the case with the error shown in Figure 17.3. More subtle errors, or errors that only show up when there are certain data conditions, cannot be predetected. The 37:12AA bad-data-induced error falls into this category. Debugging then becomes considerably more complicated, because half the battle is simply determining which statements caused VBScript to balk.

For example, take a look at the code in Listing 17.1. This is just one section of the rather lengthy Pace-Pal program. Even after you've gotten a hint that the culprit statement lurks somewhere in this subset of the code, does it easily jump out at you?

NOTE

> The source file for the Pace-Pal program is contained on the CD-ROM under pace-pal.htm. The CD-ROM also contains a main viewer page, default.htm, that provides an overview for each day's material with an easy index to all programs. This is the recommended mode for viewing the pages discussed today.

Listing 17.1. An insect lives here—buggy code!

```
Function ConvertStringToTotalSeconds (ByVal sDuration)
'--------------------------------------------------------------------
' Takes HH:MM:SS format string and converts to total seconds

    Dim iPosition      'Position of ":" separator
    Dim vHours         ' Number of hours required
    Dim vMinutes       ' Number of minutes required
    Dim vSeconds       ' Number of seconds required

    'Start working from right of string, parsing seconds
    sMode = "Seconds"
```

continues

Listing 17.1. continued

```
    ' Get leftmost time component
    iPosition = InStr(sDuration, ":")
    if iPosition = 0 then
        ' no more time info, assume time info just in ss format
        vSeconds = sDuration
    else ' more time info is on string
        ' store first portion in hours for now, assume hh:mm:ss format
        vhours = left(sDuration,iPosition - 1)
        ' Parse string for further processing
        sDuration = right(sDuration, len(sDuration) - iPosition)

        ' Get middle time component
        iPosition = InStr(sDuration, ":")
        if iPosition = 0 then
            ' no more time info, must just be mm:ss format
            vMinutes = vHours
            vSeconds = sDuration
            vHours = 0

        else ' time info must be in hh:mm:ss format

            vminutes = left(sDuration,iPosition - 1)
            seconds = right(sDuration, len(sDuration) - iPosition)
        end if
    end if

    ' Represent all components in terms of seconds
    vHours = vHours * 3600
    vMinutes = vMinutes * 60

    ' Return total seconds value
    ConvertStringtoTotalSeconds = CInt(vHours) + _
        CInt(vMinutes) + CInt(vSeconds)

End Function ' ConvertStringtoTotalSeconds
```

As you can see even from this relatively straightforward example, isolating a bug by visually inspecting the code is an inexact process as well as being a slow, tedious way to solve problems. Fortunately, there are better, easier, more precise ways to hunt down the error.

The Brute Force MsgBox Approach

The debugging difficulty presented by Pace-Pal is that you can't tell where things start to run amok. As a matter of fact, "start" to run amok is rather misleading. Things really go amok all at once, with no gradual transition, because VBScript treats any run-time error as fatal! So the first step is to hone in on our error. Many languages come with development environments that help you easily monitor the flow of your program and pinpoint such errors. Unfortunately, VBScript does not.

However, if you've debugged in other environments, one obvious tool to pinpoint the rogue statement may come to mind—the MsgBox function. You learned about the MsgBox function on Day 14, "Working with Documents and User Interface Functions." When this function is encountered, the designated message will be displayed to the user, and the flow of your program halts until the user clicks on the message box button to acknowledge the message and proceed.

That means that the MsgBox function gives you a way to tell where your program's execution is. Therefore, it gives you a way to get insight into the exact location of a run-time error. Suppose you're chasing an error in your program. You insert the following statement in the middle of your program and re-run it:

```
MsgBox "I made it this far without my program choking!"
```

If your program displays that message when you re-run it, you have some additional insight into the error you're chasing. You know the run-time error was *not* caused by any statement preceding the MsgBox function call. The error lurks in some statement after that point in your code. For the next step, you could shift the MsgBox statement down a line and re-run the test. If that works, do it again. And again. And again. Until you hit the line that causes the run-time error.

Or you could take the tried-and-true "narrow it down one step at a time" approach. You put your MsgBox function halfway through your code and see if it is reached. If so, you know the problem must be in the last half of your code statements. Put it halfway through the remaining statements. If that test is successful, put it halfway through the new smaller remaining section of statements. And again. And again. Until you hit the run-time error. If the flow of code is not sequential, the process of isolating the problem is even tougher. For example, suppose that a line of code calls another routine that branches to one path of a Select Case statement, which in turn calls another routine as the result of an If condition. In such a case, determining where to put the message box traces in advance gets very difficult, not to mention complex!

If both of these approaches sound similarly tedious and time-consuming, that's because they are! You could save yourself a few test runs by starting right out with a MsgBox statement after each and every statement, each with a different message. For example, assume your program consists of these statements:

```
sub Test_OnClick
dim a, b, c
a = text1.text * 3
c = text2.text * 4
d = a + c
end sub
```

You could then modify it to get a `MsgBox`-based program flow trail:

```
sub Test_OnClick
dim a, b, c
MsgBox "Point 1"
a = text1.text * 3
MsgBox "Point 2"
c = text2.text * 4
MsgBox "Point 3"
d = a + c
MsgBox "Point 4"
end sub
```

If your program runs and then dies with a run-time error, the `MsgBox` statement that was the last to display on your screen will tell you right where the problem is. This method of tracking down the rogue statement does work, but it takes time to insert all the statements and then remove them after you finish debugging. There is nothing wrong with this approach if your program is small. If your program is large, however, there are better, sleeker, quicker ways to chase down the bug. You just have to reach deep into the VBScript bag of tricks and pull out another language construct: the `On Error Resume Next` statement.

Soothing the Wounds with the `On Error` Statement

It would be nice if a program could simply continue after it caused a run-time error. That way, at some later point in the script, you could use code statements to learn if the end of a procedure was successfully reached, or to print out the values of variables for you to inspect, or to show you the result of calculations. If only a program had the perseverance to forge on after it hit rough waters so you could retrieve this information, the debugging task would be easier.

There's another reason, too, that you might wish your program could survive a run-time error. Although VBScript is trying to save you from bad data or results when it produces a run-time error, there are cases where you might prefer to continue execution after the error occurs, even if it means living with bad results. For example, maybe your program calculates a runner's calories burned, the amount of shoe rubber rubbed off, and the fluid ounces of sweat produced based on distance as well as pace. If so, it could be quite annoying to your user to halt the whole program just because he entered one piece of information incorrectly.

A real-life situation can serve as an analogy, at least for parents, aunts, uncles, and babysitters. Assume you have asked a six-year-old to clean her toy-strewn room. After a little complaining, she tackles the task; meanwhile, you finally settle down in the armchair to read the latest issue of *The Visual Basic Programmer's Journal*. Just as you become immersed in an article, you hear little, rapid footsteps. "You can't be done already!" you exclaim.

In response, the youngster replies, "I can't clean anymore. My dolly box is at Grandma's!" The youngster's mind has just experienced the equivalent of a fatal run-time error. She's encountered a situation she does not know how to handle. She is letting you know that due to the perceived direness of the situation, the whole task must be aborted.

As she skips out the door to play, you shout after her in frustration, "Whoooaaa there! What about the stuffed monkey, box of crayons, 57 marbles, and your collection of paper doll clothes scattered all over?! You could've picked those up!"

Needless to say, in programming as well as room-cleaning, there are certainly times when this abandon-ship philosophy is not optimal. If you wish to perform additional debugging after the problem statement, or if you want to beef up your program, you need a way to override the abort at the first sign of trouble. Fortunately, VBScript gives you this override power. It comes in the form of the On Error Resume Next statement. This statement tells the VBScript Interpreter that, when an error is encountered, it should simply ignore it and continue on with the next statement. An example of this statement applied to the Pace-Pal problem procedure is shown in Listing 17.2.

17

Listing 17.2. Code made more robust with an On Error statement.

```
Function ConvertStringToTotalSeconds (ByVal sDuration)
'---------------------------------------------------------------------
' Takes HH:MM:SS format string and converts to total seconds

' When error occurs, continue with next statement rather
'     than halting program
  On Error Resume Next

    Dim iPosition      'Position of ":" separator
    Dim vHours         ' Number of hours required
    Dim vMinutes       ' Number of minutes required
  Dim vSeconds         ' Number of seconds required

On Error Resume Next
```

NOTE

> The modified Pace-Pal program with the change shown here is contained on the CD-ROM under ppalerr1.htm.

ANALYSIS When the On Error Resume Next statement is used, you don't get any scary messages of gloom and doom, and your program doesn't come to a screeching halt. Instead, the VBScript interpreter keeps on chugging with the next statement, leaving your user none the wiser. The results from running Pace-Pal with this modification are shown in Figure 17.4.

You'll note that the program manages to provide a final pace result, albeit an incorrect one, in the pace box. But it will work correctly on any valid input that is subsequently entered, even without reloading the page.

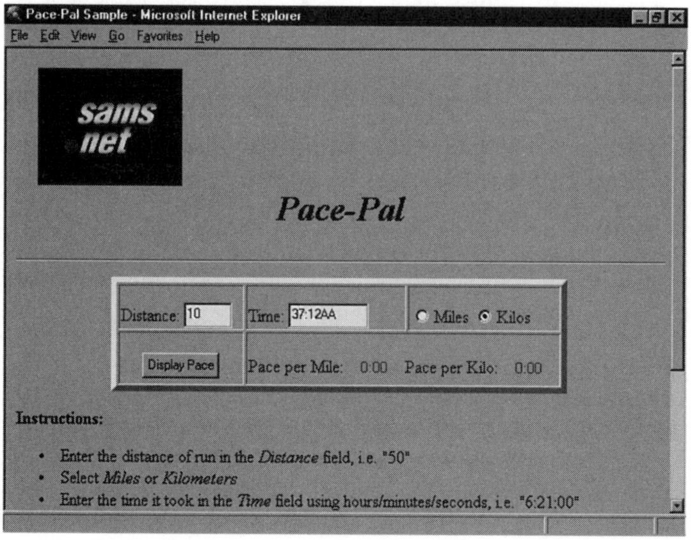

Figure 17.4.

The Pace-Pal program faced the bug and lived to tell about it!

Alas, all is not perfect; there is a problem with the On Error Resume Next approach. The room-cleaning analogy serves to illuminate this problem as well. Assume you are once again starting your young helper on a room-cleaning task, and this time you are determined to make the ground rules clear. You provide some specific direction: "Go clean your room. I don't care what happens, I want you to plug away until you've taken care of every last thing. If you run into problems, I don't want to hear about it!" The cleaning task seems to be going well, until you notice water seeping out from under the door. When you go to inspect, the grinning child, knee deep in water, points to a ruptured water pipe in the ceiling. Just as you start to ask, "Why didn't you tell me?" you realize the answer to your question: You asked her not to.

The On Error Resume Next statement gives you an analogous mechanism to ignore errors, as the Pace-Pal sample demonstrates. Unfortunately, when you use this statement, you run the risk that you won't find out about a program problem that you really do care about. For that matter, unless you know specifically what caused an error, it is rarely safe just to ignore it.

If you've used other languages with error handling, particularly VBA or Visual Basic 4.0, you may realize that most error handling systems provide even more error handling flow-control capabilities. In Visual Basic 4.0 or VBA, for example, you can use the On Error Goto statement to direct your program flow to a specific area of error handling code. For example, On Error

`Goto Shared_Error_Handling` would direct the program flow to one specific block of error-handling code labeled `Shared_Error_Handling` whenever an error occurs. This capability is *not* available in VBScript. The only thing you can do with the `On Error` statement is to tell it to `Resume next`. If an error occurs in a procedure while this statement is in effect, your program will simply move on to the next statement in the procedure. Once again, though, the VBScript language comes to our rescue. There is a way to use `On Error Resume Next` wisely. You must couple it with the power of the `err` object.

If You Object to Errors, Use the `err` Object!

If you combine `On Error Resume Next` with a special VBScript object called the `err` object, your program can not only survive run-time errors, it can even incorporate program logic that analyzes them after the fact. The `err` object is useful for two reasons—it can be a great help in debugging, and in some cases it can be a feature you want to incorporate into your final program to make it more robust. The `err` object analysis takes place to see what kind of problem, if any, has occurred within a body of code. You can display the problem error code and description after an error occurs, and still let your program continue on for further debugging after you display this information. You may even choose to directly build recovery techniques into your programs. If the `err` object tells you that data of the wrong type was used in a calculation, for example, you could prompt the user to re-enter the data.

The `err` object is an intrinsic VBScript object. That means you don't have to do any work to use it. No special declarations are required. You can simply reference it anywhere in your code and inspect the current error-related property values of this object. These properties provide several important pieces of information:

☐ Number—The numeric error code. This value is set by the VBScript interpreter when an error occurs. `0` represents no error, and any other number means an error has occurred. Each type of error has its own specific error code. Type conversion errors, for example, always generate an error code of `13`. Error codes can range from `1` to `65535` for VBScript.

☐ Description—A description of the error that corresponds to the error number. When `err.number` contains `13`, `err.description` will contain the corresponding `Type conversion` text description. Note that a description doesn't necessarily exist for every number.

☐ Source—Who caused the error. This would be, for example, the name of your VBScript project if the error was caused within VBScript, or the name of an OLE automation object if it was caused by an OLE automation component.

☐ Helpfile—The path and filename of a help file, if relevant, containing more details on the error.

17

☐ HelpContext—A help file context ID (topic index) that corresponds to the help file error information. The help file and context information can be used to make your program open a relevant help file containing further information on the error.

There are two methods for using the err object, which are explained more fully in the next section:

☐ Raise—Generates an error.

☐ Clear—Resets the contents of the error object.

Using the information from the err object, you can check whether an error occurred and then examine relevant information to aid you in debugging a detected error. It's easy to check whether an error has occurred. If err.number equals 0, no problems have been detected. Any other value represents an error code. If you do find an error code, the err.description field will provide the standard text description of the error. This message is the same one that would pop up on the run-time message error box when the program screeched to a halt if you weren't using On Error Resume Next to ignore the errors. You can even look at the originator of the error in the Source property. Most often, the source will be the name of your VBScript file itself if it was your VBScript code that caused the problem. In some cases, however, you may find that the error source is a component you have integrated, such as an ActiveX control. You can even get information on associated help files for errors, although this information is less likely to be of use to you in structuring your error recovery code. The code sequence in Listing 17.3 shows one example of how you might check to see if an error has occurred.

Listing 17.3. Checking the err object to see if an error has occurred.

```
sub Test_OnClick
On Error Resume Next
dim a
a = text1.text / text2.text
if err.number <> 0 then
    msgbox "Error : " & err.description & " from " & err.source
end if
```

ANALYSIS Code analysis of the err object like that shown in Listing 17.3 can also be applied to debug problems like the Pace-Pal situation. If On Error Resume Next is used to turn off run-time error reporting and aborting, you can look at the end of the suspect procedure to see if any errors occurred within it. If errors did occur, you can use the err object to print out full details. One important consideration with this approach, however, is that if more than one error has occurred within the procedure, you will see only information on the most recent error. Still, this is helpful when you simply want to know whether a block of code is error free. If an error occurred, you can add additional error checks and debug further to determine if there were multiple errors. Listing 17.4 shows an example of the Pace-Pal code with a check inserted at the end of a procedure.

Listing 17.4. Code with additional error diagnostics from the err object.

```
        vminutes = left(sDuration,iPosition - 1)
        seconds = right(sDuration, len(sDuration) - iPosition)
      end if
   end if

   ' Represent all components in terms of seconds
   vHours = vHours * 3600
   vMinutes = vMinutes * 60

   ' Return total seconds value
   ConvertStringtoTotalSeconds = CInt(vHours) + CInt(vMinutes) + _
                                 CInt(vSeconds)

   if err.number <> 0 then
      msgbox "Error #:" & err.number & " Description:" & err.description _
         & " Source:" & err.source, 0, "Error in ConvertStringtoTotalSeconds!"
   end if

End Function ' ConvertStringtoTotalSeconds
```

17

NOTE The source file for Pace-Pal with the change shown here is contained on the CD-ROM under `ppalerr2.htm`.

ANALYSIS Notice that this code will print out information *only* if the error occurred. If the error did not occur, the user will not be disturbed by error information. The results of this error check are shown in Figure 17.5. As the figure shows, the error check added to the Pace-Pal code does detect an error within the procedure. The cause is clearly identified as a type conversion error, and the source is pegged to be the script itself.

Bolstered by the err object checking, the Pace-Pal code is more robust and provides you with more insight. It is more robust because despite the error, the program still continues through its code path and produces results without aborting. In this case, a pace of 00:00 is presented as the result since there is not valid data to work with. You have more insight because you can be certain that an error has occurred in the ConvertStringtoTotalSeconds function. Additionally, you know precisely which error occurred within that function, and that error's source. Armed with this information, you can isolate the cause of the error using the following tracing techniques. But before tackling the isolation steps, it helps to fully understand the intricacies of these error-handling mechanisms. We'll turn next to a few more advanced details of the err object and the On Error Resume Next statement, followed by a look at more tracing techniques, before we return to the quest for our Pace-Pal bug.

Figure 17.5.

Information about the error.

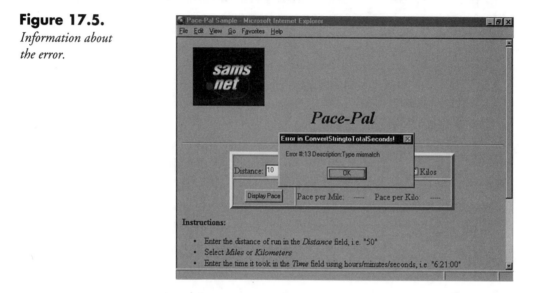

More on Error Handling with err **and** on error

The On Error Resume Next statement, also called an error handler, is a procedure-level statement. It only remains in effect within the procedure that contains the on error declaration. Imagine that a higher-level procedure that uses On Error Resume Next calls a lower-level procedure that does not use it. If an error occurs in the lower-level procedure, the flow of statements in that procedure halts immediately. VBScript prepares to alert the user of the error, but before doing so, it checks whether any higher-level procedures with an On Error Resume Next function were in the process of calling this lower-level procedure. If they were not, the error is treated as a normal run-time error, halting the program and displaying the run-time error to the user. However, if a higher-level procedure with an On Error Resume Next function were calling a lower-level procedure with no error handling, then when the lower-level procedure causes the error, it would be addressed by the higher-level procedure.

This is commonly called "raising the error." The VBScript interpreter, like many languages, raises an error to higher calling levels until it finds a procedure with error handling. If none is found, the script halts and the user is presented with the error results by the interpreter.

Once the error is passed to that higher-level procedure, that procedure's error handling `Resume Next` rule goes into effect. That procedure provides instructions to continue to the next statement when an error occurs, so execution picks up right after the call to the lower-level procedure that went awry.

You can't expect to analyze `err` object information within a procedure unless that procedure contains the `On Error Resume Next` statement. As long as this statement exists within the procedure, errors do not cause the procedure to be halted. If the VBScript interpreter finds that no higher-level procedure with an error handler that was calling the procedure caused the problem, the entire program will be halted. The bottom line is that if you want to use the `err` object to carry out any error analysis in a procedure, make sure an `On Error Resume Next` first appears within that procedure.

The `err` object itself has a couple more interesting capabilities you have not yet learned about—the `clear` and `raise` methods. The `raise` method generates an error. More precisely, it simulates an error. In other words, you can tell `raise` what kind of error you want to simulate. To simulate a certain type of conversion error, for example, you could use the statement

```
err.raise 13
```

to have VBScript respond in its normal fashion, just as if it had encountered an actual code statement that caused an error of error code type 13. Raising an error causes the program to behave exactly as if it had encountered a real error. If any procedure in the active lineup of calling and current procedures has an `On Error Resume Next` statement, the program will flow to the next applicable statement. In such a case, the `err` object will then contain the appropriate information for the error that was raised. For example, `err.number` will equal 13. On the other hand, if there is no `On Error Resume Next` in the active lineup of calling and current procedures, the program will treat the raised error as a regular run-time error, displaying a message to the user and terminating the program.

You may be thinking that it would take a pretty twisted programmer to purposely inject a simulated error into his code. There are some situations where such a tactic is warranted, however. (Naturally, the VBScript development team at Microsoft wouldn't have included this method if it could only be used for evil purposes!) One way you might use this method for good is to evaluate the `err` object within a procedure to determine the severity of potential problems. You may write code that inspects `err.number` to determine if the problem is a minor one that won't affect results, or a major one that presents critical problems to the program. In the event of a minor problem, you may decide to write code that continues on with the normal flow of statements in the current procedure.

For a major problem, however, it might be imprudent to continue with the program after the detection of an error. In that case, you might want the calling procedures at higher levels to address the error without going any further in the current routine. There is an easy way to redirect the program flow back to the error-handling code in the higher-level procedures. If those calling procedures have On Error Resume Next defined, you can simply raise the error with err.raise, and control will flow to the first higher-level calling procedure that has an active error handler.

To have full mastery of VBScript error handling, one more technique remains: the clear method. A little insight into the err object and the way it gets cleared is necessary to understand what clear does. The err object, as you have learned, keeps a record of information on the last error that occurred. When an error occurs, the appropriate information is loaded into the err object by the VBScript interpreter. If this information lingers forever, though, it can cause some headaches. If an error was set in err.number indefinitely, you would end up addressing the same error over and over.

For this reason, VBScript clears the err object whenever your flow of statements reaches the end of a subroutine or function that contains an On Error Resume Next, or whenever an On Error Resume Next statement itself is encountered. All fields are set to their initial state. Any err.number containing an error code resets to 0 (indicating no error). Using On Error Resume Next at the start of each procedure guarantees that old errors from previous procedures will no longer be stored in the err object. You get a clean slate.

This works fine if you just check the value of the err object once within each procedure. But what if you have multiple places within the same procedure where you check err.number? What if your code checks the value after each and every statement? Then, if the first statement causes an error, err.number will be set accordingly. If you check err.number immediately after that statement, you will correctly detect the error, such as a type conversion error. But all the subsequent statements within the same procedure that check err.number will still find the old type conversion error indicator for the error that was already analyzed, even if the most recent statement caused no error.

If you make use of err.number multiple times within a procedure, you'll want to ensure you're not reacting to leftover error data. Fortunately, VBScript provides a means to do this: the err.clear method. This method will reset all fields of the err object, and will assign err.number back to 0 to indicate no error. So when you want to make sure you are starting with a clean error slate, simply insert an err.clear into your code. Typically this is carried out right after an error is detected and addressed. Some caution must be exercised with this method, however. There is nothing to prevent you from clearing errors that have not yet been addressed. Make sure that you use err.clear only after checking err.number and carrying out any handling needed.

Many error-handling strategies can be built on On Error Resume Next and the err object. If you don't use On Error Resume Next at all, your run-time errors will show through to you (or your user) loud and clear! If you do use the On Error Resume Next statement, you risk inadvertently ignoring errors, unless you diligently check the status of the err object in every routine that uses On Error Resume Next. When you check error codes, you must remember that error codes may still be set from previous statements unless some action has occurred to clear them.

When writing your error-handling code for higher-level procedures that use On Error Resume Next, you must remember that errors can trickle up. This is true whether those errors are natural errors or "simulated" errors caused by err.raise. Errors that occur in lower-level procedures can trickle up into your higher-level procedure if lower levels do not use On Error Resume Next. That means you may need to insert statements that give you more details about an error to pinpoint the cause of it. Fortunately, further hand-crafted techniques are available to trace and understand your code. So next you'll learn about what tracing code is really all about.

Tracing Your Code

Tracing your code is the act of following the flow of statements as your program progresses. Usually, code is traced to isolate bugs and solve problems. You might also trace code simply to better understand the inner workings of a block of code. You already saw a rudimentary form of tracing earlier in the lesson—simply insert MsgBox function calls into the code, run your program, stand back, and watch where message boxes pop up. Since you know where you inserted the MsgBox calls, you can easily follow the progression of the code. There are, however, more powerful, elegant ways to trace code. Inserting and responding to a series of message boxes can be a cumbersome task. In addition, an important part of code tracing can consist of watching the values of variables in conjunction with tracking the flow of statements. Data values and knowledge of the last statement processed often must be viewed in tandem to understand the state of your program and its behavior. There are ways to achieve this type of tracing in VBScript. Before moving on to more sophisticated tracing methods in VBScript, however, let's consider the debug and tracing mechanisms of some other environments to put the VBScript capabilities in perspective.

Traditional Debug Environments Versus VBScript

When you get a browser that supports VBScript, you do not get a VBScript development environment along with it. You are left to your own devices to decide how to construct the segments of VBScript code you insert in your Web pages. You might build VBScript programs in an HTML-generation tool, Microsoft's ActiveX Control Pad editor, or you could generate them directly in a text editor. No matter how you're doing it, odds are it's not in a dedicated VBScript development environment with the full-fledged debug features of Visual Basic 4.0. Although such tools are expected to materialize over time, at this date they do not exist. By contrast, almost all high-end computer languages do have their own sophisticated development environment. Typically, a special editor is used for producing programs; the editor can sometimes help check syntax as you type the programs in. Also, these environments often include powerful debugging environments that assist with the task of tracing a program and isolating problems. The Visual Basic 4.0 environment, and VBA 5.0, offer a rich set of debug facilities. While you can't use these debug facilities directly with VBScript, you can apply some of the same concepts with the "build-it-yourself" trace techniques you'll learn about soon.

Visual Basic 4.0 Trace Capabilities

The Visual Basic 4.0 programmer has no excuse for not having keen insight into all areas of his source code. Visual Basic 4.0, the high-end member of the Visual Basic family, has powerful, easily controlled debugging facilities. For example, Visual Basic 4.0 allows you to stop the program at any location by simply selecting a line of source code in the program editor and pressing a function key to designate the line as a temporary "breakpoint." Upon hitting this breakpoint, the running program screeches to a halt, allowing you to spring into debugging action. You can inspect the value of variables in a special debugging window provided by the Visual Basic 4.0 design environment. You can even type more complex expressions in the window. This lets you evaluate any other statements that might help you understand the problem. You can use this window to inspect the current state of variables even as your program remains suspended. A view of the Visual Basic 4.0 development environment, with a suspended program that has reached a breakpoint, is shown in Figure 17.6.

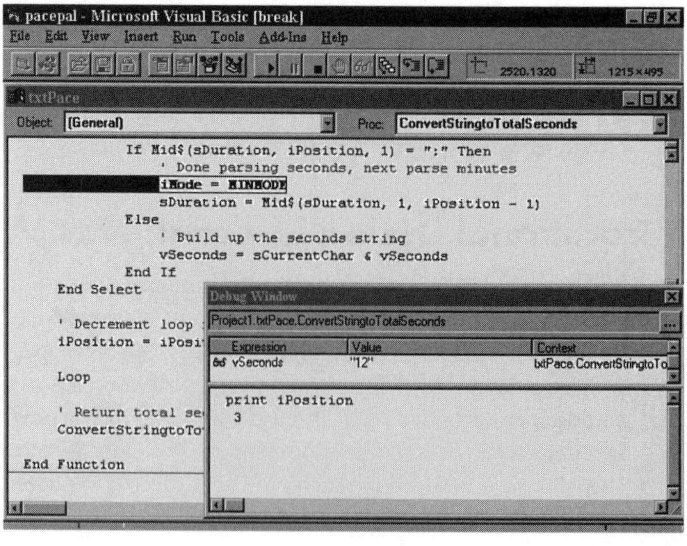

Figure 17.6.

The Visual Basic 4.0 debug environment.

Once you are done checking out the state of your suspended program, you can send it on its merry way, right where it left off. You can have it proceed one statement at a time, providing you with the opportunity to query its state line by line. You can also just let it continue until program completion or some other predefined breakpoint. You can even tell it to pick up at an entirely different program location than the one where it is stopped. And if you're even nosier about what is going on, you can make arrangements to automatically monitor the contents in your favorite variables as the program chugs along. As variable values change, the new values are automatically displayed in the debug window without stopping your program. You can even provide instructions for your program to stop and show you the last statement it carried out if a variable reaches a certain value.

By now your head is probably spinning from this dizzying array of debugging weapons, and you're wondering how many of them apply to VBScript. Unfortunately, the answer is that virtually none of these whiz-bang Visual Basic 4.0 debug features are available to you as you develop VBScript programs. There is no inherent means through the browser or standard text editor to place breakpoints on VBScript programs, to pop up a debug window, to make your program leap to a new location from a suspended state, or to automatically monitor the contents of variables.

On the other hand, there are several rays of encouragement to offset this lack of tools. One comforting thought for the long term is that as the language matures, tools will likely come. True, that doesn't help you for the short term, but even today's VBScript provides the foundation you need to build similar trace and monitoring capabilities right into your programs. It takes a little extra effort, but as you'll see in the sections that follow, the techniques are really quite easy to apply.

 NOTE

You can find further information on some VBScript development tools as they become available at www.doubleblaze.com. There are also many utilities available for various aspects of Web page authoring available at the Microsoft site under www.microsoft.com/intdev.

Secret Strategy for Visual Basic Programmers Who Are Debugging VBScript Code

If you happen to be one of the million plus Visual Basic 4.0 or VBA programmers, you have a secret weapon that you can use in developing VBScript code. Try writing the code in Visual Basic first, then move it to VBScript! You can take full advantage of the rich debugging capabilities of Visual Basic as you get the bugs out of your program. Then, once it is stable, you can move it to VBScript.

A note of caution, however: There's no such thing as a free lunch, and there's also no such thing as a free debugger (or at least so it seems). There are language differences between Visual Basic and VBScript. A program that works fine in Visual Basic 4.0 can be obstinate in VBScript. VBScript is a subset of Visual Basic for Applications, so much of what works in your Visual Basic application will not work in your script. Depending on your knowledge of the two languages, it can take some work to weed out the syntax differences as you move the code over from Visual Basic 4.0 to VBScript. Some of the language differences are subtle and may not be immediately obvious, even if you know both languages fairly well. Day 20, "Porting Between Visual Basic and VBScript," provides a detailed look at these differences. The bottom line is that if you use the "debug in Visual Basic first" approach, don't think you're home free after you get the program working there. Porting work may still lie ahead in moving the code to VBScript.

HTML Trace Capabilities

So it's clear that the king of the debugging realm is Visual Basic 4.0. To put our view of VBScript into perspective, it's worthwhile to consider the low end of the debugging spectrum—HTML itself. One thing HTML has going for it is a rich set of tools that can aid in quickly developing well-structured pages. But if you don't have one of those tools, or have a low-end tool, debugging HTML itself can be the cause of serious hair pulling and grimacing. Consider the HTML shown in Listing 17.5, and note the <A that marks the beginning of an anchor reference.

Listing 17.5. Normal HTML.

```
<H1><A HREF="http://www.mcp.com"><IMG  ALIGN=BOTTOM SRC="
/shared/jpg/samsnet.jpg" BORDER=2></A>
<EM>Pace-Pal Sample 3</EM></H1>
```

Suppose this markup language had been mistakenly entered with just one character different. Assume that the < was inadvertently omitted from in front of the A, as shown in Listing 17.6.

Listing 17.6. HTML missing a tag.

```
<H1>A HREF="http://www.mcp.com"><IMG  ALIGN=BOTTOM  SRC="
/shared/jpg/samsnet.jpg" BORDER=2></A>
<EM>Pace-Pal Sample 3</EM></H1>
```

ANALYSIS   The effects of such an omission are ugly indeed, as you can see in Figure 17.7. Not only are they ugly, but they result in a Web page that doesn't work as intended, with a nonfunctioning link. HTML has no run-time sequence of logic to step through to help pinpoint the error. Rather, it is just a markup or page-generation instruction set. In the absence of sophisticated authoring tools for HTML, you are stuck with the old visual inspection mode of debug. You must look at the page, visually scan it, and review each tag for proper syntax one by one.

Figure 17.7.

Pace-Pal with a missing tag.

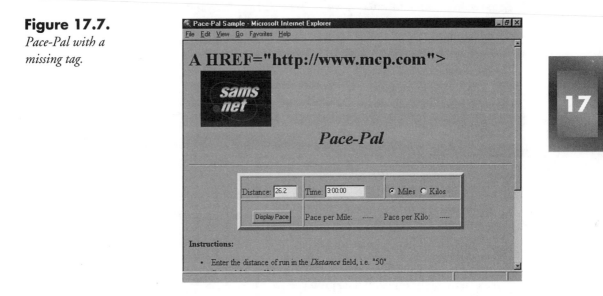

It is important to recognize that VBScript presents a whole different debug model than HTML, requiring a different mindset and approach. If you come from a Visual Basic background, this comes as no surprise. You simply have to downscale your debug support expectations from Visual Basic 4.0 for the VBScript environment and realize that you'll need to build with source code statements much of the trace capability that was automatically there in Visual Basic 4.0. On the other hand, if you come from an HTML background without extensive programming experience, it is important to recognize that the old visual inspection and trial and error methods that may serve you well in HTML debugging will not suffice in tracing through more sophisticated programmatic logic or syntax problems. In either case, the hand-crafted VBScript trace strategies that follow can serve as a fundamental, timesaving part of the debug process.

VBScript Trace Capabilities

Today's lesson has talked a lot about what VBScript can't do in terms of trace debugging. Now let's talk about what it can do. As you learned earlier in the lesson, a tried and true approach to following the flow of a program is to simply insert standard message boxes to help trace where your program is going. This works reliably and is easy to implement, but it does have some drawbacks. It takes some effort to insert the statements. Then, when you run the program, you must interact with every message box you insert, even if no error occurs. If you've inserted 150 message boxes to trace the flow of your program, it can be rather tedious to respond to each and every one! There is an easier way to get the same kind of tracing payback. First, for simplicity, let's consider the case of a trace with just one area of message box feedback.

The Message Box Trace Approach

There is an easy way to avoid responding to each and every message box in the course of tracing a program. This alternative method consists of combining two aspects of the VBScript language. We've already covered both halves of the equation; now we just need to join them. If you use On Error Resume Next in your program, you have seen that not only will your program survive any errors, you also have ready access to error information through the err object. This object tells you if an error has occurred. The message box gives you an easy way to display such status.

If you can be assured that you will see a message after an error occurs, there is no need to view the status of the program if no problems have been detected. You can make the message box trace more elegant by only displaying trace information if an error has actually occurred. You achieve this by placing a pair of message box statements around the suspected bad line of code. When that trace feedback is displayed, full details on the type of error can be provided. This technique is shown in the modified Pace-Pal code in Listing 17.7.

Listing 17.7. Tracing the flow with a message box statement.

```
'  .  .  . SAME CODE UP TO THIS POINT AS SHOWN IN PREVIOUS LISTINGS

        vMinutes = vHours
        vSeconds = sDuration
        vHours = 0
    else ' time info must be in hh:mm:ss format

        vminutes = left(sDuration,iPosition - 1)
        seconds = right(sDuration, len(sDuration) - iPosition)

    end if
```

17

Listing 17.7. continued

```
end if

' Represent all components in terms of seconds
vHours = vHours * 3600
vMinutes = vMinutes * 60

if err.number <> 0 then msgbox "An error is present prior"

' Return total seconds value
ConvertStringtoTotalSeconds = CInt(vHours) + _
  CInt(vMinutes) + CInt(vSeconds)
if err.number <> 0 then msgbox "An error is present here"
```

ANALYSIS An informative tracing message is generated when this script is run, as shown in Figure 17.8. Now to trace your program you no longer have to click on trace message boxes when everything is going okay. If you see a message box come up, you know it's coming from an area of your code that detected an error.

NOTE

The modified Pace-Pal program with the change shown here is contained on the CD-ROM under `ppalerr3.htm`.

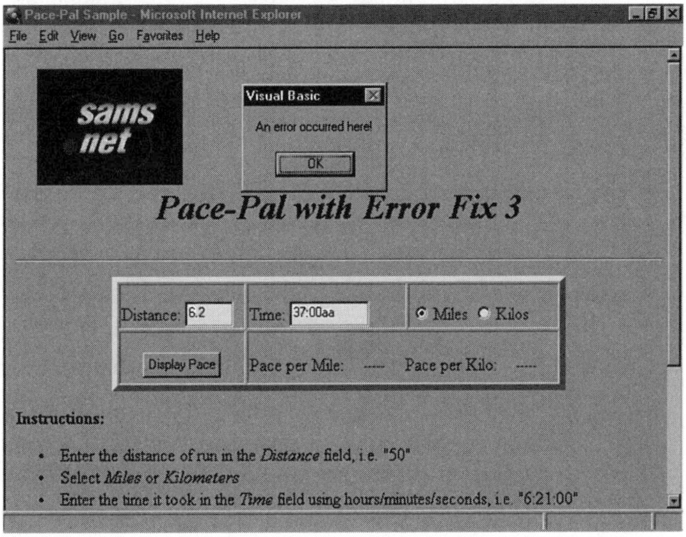

Figure 17.8.

Output from the message box trace.

More Tools to Make Debugging Easier

The example in the previous section shows the use of many trace statements in just one area of code. In some cases, you may find that inserting one or more trace statements and moving them around is an effective strategy. For example, if you have a 100-line script but suspect that the problem is somewhere in the first 5 lines, you might put the error check after line 5. If the trace indicates an error at this location, it simply means that the error occurred somewhere on or prior to that line. To prove exactly where within the first five lines the error occurs, your next step might be to move the trace statement so it comes right after line 4, and so on.

This type of trace statement movement is actually quite typical of debug efforts. A statement is moved in the HTML page editor, the browser is activated, and the page is reloaded to test the effect of the change. The same cycle is repeated as often as necessary. As a result, you may find that much of your debug time is spent in transition between your page editor and browser. It is worth noting that the mechanics of making such changes and testing them can consume a significant part of your debug time. Take careful stock of the tools you have available, and find a process that works well for you.

For example, one approach that works well in the Windows environment is to simply have the Notepad text editor loaded with your source file. You can specify View|Source from the beta Internet Explorer 3.0 menu to launch Notepad. Then you can use Notepad to modify your script and save it. Once you save the script, however, *don't* close Notepad. It doesn't hurt to leave it up and running. Simply activate the browser, and then reload your page to pick up the new modifications. You can do this in Internet Explorer by selecting the F5 function key. Once your modified page is loaded, you can test your script. When you find that more changes are needed, just shift back to the still-open Notepad and repeat the cycle. You avoid the time hit of reopening the editor with this method.

This Notepad scenario is outlined here not to emphasize how to best work with Notepad, but to stress that whatever your tool, you need to put some thought into how you are applying it. The idiosyncrasies of interacting with it will be multiplied many times over, since debugging, and particularly tracing, is a often a tedious, repetitive process. As more tools become available, choosing the right tool is likely to become more and more critical.

Because technology and toolsets are evolving on almost a daily basis, simply finding out about the right tools for debugging can be a challenge. The best way to get an up-to-date view of available tools for VBScript is to search the Web for current information. Appendix B, "Information Resources," summarizes many good places to visit to get the latest tool information.

The Message Box Saturation Trace Approach

Using a single pair of message box trace statements may be sufficient if you have a pretty good idea where your problem is. But if you have a really tough problem and want to make sure to cover all the bases, it may be just as easy to insert a trace after each statement. That way, you are virtually guaranteeing that you will pinpoint the exact statement that causes the problem.

When you take this approach, remember to clearly and uniquely identify each trace statement through the message box text. It would do you little good to add 200 trace statements to a program if they all said just Error has been detected!. If you ran the program and only Error has been detected! popped up on your screen, you'd have no idea which statement the message originated from!

The more descriptive the trace messages, the better. If you have messages spread across more than one procedure, it is helpful to identify the procedure name in the message. The idea is that when you see the message, it will quickly lead you to the corresponding location in the program. Listing 17.8 shows the Pace-Pal program with extensive trace messages added. Each is uniquely identified within the message text.

NOTE   The modified Pace-Pal program with the change shown here is contained on the CD-ROM under ppalerr4.htm.

Listing 17.8. Tracing the flow with many message box statements.

```
' . . . SAME CODE UP TO THIS POINT AS SHOWN IN PREVIOUS LISTINGS

        vMinutes = vHours
        if err.number <> 0 then msgbox _
            "Error occurred prior to Point A!"
        vSeconds = sDuration
        if err.number <> 0 then msgbox _
            "Error occurred prior to Point B!"
        vHours = 0
        if err.number <> 0 then msgbox _
            "Error occurred prior to Point C!"
    else ' time info must be in hh:mm:ss format

        vminutes = left(sDuration,iPosition - 1)
        if err.number <> 0 then msgbox _
            "Error occurred prior to Point D!"
        seconds = right(sDuration, len(sDuration) - iPosition)
        if err.number <> 0 then msgbox _
```

continues

Listing 17.8. continued

```
                "Error occurred prior to Point E!"
        end if
    end if

    ' Represent all components in terms of seconds
    vHours = vHours * 3600
    if err.number <> 0 then msgbox _
        "Error occurred prior to Point F!"
    vMinutes = vMinutes * 60
    if err.number <> 0 then msgbox _
        "Error occurred prior to Point G!"

    ' Return total seconds value
    ConvertStringtoTotalSeconds = CInt(vHours) + CInt(vMinutes) + _
                        CInt(vSeconds)
    if err.number <> 0 then msgbox "Error occurred prior to Point H!"

    if err.number <> 0 then
        msgbox "Error #:" & err.number & " Description:" & err.description _
            & " Source:" & err.source, 0, "Error in ConvertStringtoTotalSeconds!"
    end if

End Function ' ConvertStringtoTotalSeconds
```

ANALYSIS The message resulting from this modified code run with the same 37:12AA program input presented earlier is shown in Figure 17.9. From reading this trace message and looking at Listing 17.8, it should be clear exactly which statement caused the problem: the ConvertStringtoTotalSeconds = statement. If you had inserted just one trace statement at a time, it might have taken many debug iterations to come to this conclusion. Although you spend more time editing the code when you insert multiple trace statements, you can hone in on the specific problem statement after many fewer iterations.

The Message Box Variable Watch Approach

So you've located the statement that is causing the problem, but you don't know why the error is occurring or how to fix it. That often takes further debugging, typically requiring a look at the variable contents if variables are involved in the rogue statement. One way to get this information is to print out the contents of the variables and the variable subtypes located right before the problem statement. This technique is applied to the Pace-Pal program in Listing 17.9.

Figure 17.9.

Output from tracing with sequential message boxes.

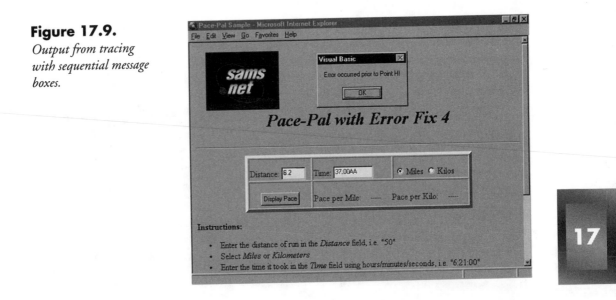

Listing 17.9. Tracing variable contents with message box statement.

```
' Return total seconds value

    msgbox "vHours = " & vHours & " with type = " _
        & vartype(vHours) & _
        "    vMinutes = " & vMinutes & " with type = " _
        & vartype(vMinutes) & _
        "    vSeconds = " & vSeconds & " with type = " _
        & vartype(vSeconds),0, "Var Dump"

    ConvertStringtoTotalSeconds = CInt(vHours) + _
        CInt(vMinutes) + CInt(vSeconds)

    if err <> 0 then
        msgbox "Error #:" & err.number & " Description:" & err.description _
            & " Source:" & err.source, 0, "Error in ConvertStringtoTotalSeconds!"
    end if

End Function  ' End of function ConvertStringtoTotalSeconds
```

ANALYSIS The results of this variable trace are shown in Figure 17.10. A full description of the variables is now available. One variable is empty, another has an integer value, and another contains string data. Even after viewing this information, confusion may remain over exactly what causes the error. There is yet one more step that can be taken to shed light on the problem.

Figure 17.10.
Output from the message box variable trace.

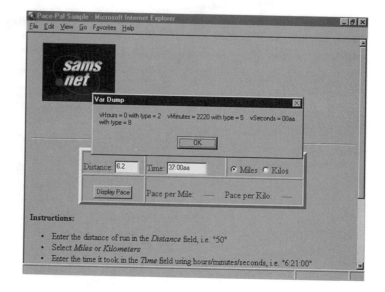

Breaking Apart Complex Statements to Uncover the Slimy Bug!

The problem has now been isolated to one statement, and the values and subtypes of the variables prior to that statement are known. In the problem statement, the Cint (convert to an integer) function is applied to both a variable that is empty and to a variable that contains a string. How can you see which of these is the problem conversion, or if both are to blame? The problem statement consists of multiple pieces or expressions, any of which might be the cause of the problem. Your next goal should be to isolate the problem to just one of these pieces. Therefore, the next step is to break it down into smaller pieces, and then apply the same trace techniques to those subpieces. Shown in Listing 17.10 is the modified Pace-Pal script with the problem statement decomposed into smaller pieces that can be individually traced.

Listing 17.10. The complex statement broken apart into multiple simpler statements.

```
Loop

' Temporary code to isolate problem to one statement

if err.Number <> 0 then msgbox "Error prior to debugA: " _
     & err.Description
debugA = Cint(vHours)
```

17

```
if err.Number <> 0 then msgbox "Error after debugA: " _
        & err.Description
debugB = Cint(vMinutes)
if err.Number <> 0 then msgbox "Error after debugB: " _
        & err.Description
debugC = CInt(vSeconds)
if err.Number <> 0 then msgbox "Error after debugC: " & _
        err.Description
ConvertStringtoTotalSeconds = debugA + debugB + debugC

' Return total seconds value
    ' ***Decomposed above for Debug ConvertStringtoTotalSeconds = _
' CInt(vHours) + CInt(vMinutes) + _
                        CInt(vSeconds)

if err.number <> 0 then
        msgbox "Error #:" & err.number & " Description:" & err.description & _
            "Source:" & err.source, 0, "Error in ConvertStringtoTotalSeconds!"
end if

End Function  ' End of function ConvertStringtoTotalSeconds
```

ANALYSIS When the script is run after this change, the message box specifically highlights which piece causes the error. Figure 17.11 illustrates that the Cint function, when applied to a string that contains non-numeric characters, causes VBScript to generate an error. This is the cause of the original run-time calamity first encountered at the start of the lesson.

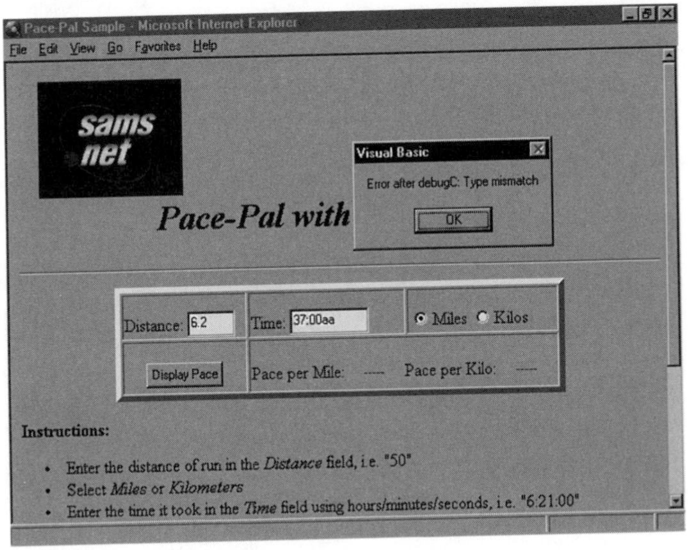

Figure 17.11.

Output from the first message box trace after the error, with trace on decomposed statements.

Ensuring That the Bug Is Dead

Once you know the cause of the bug, fixing it is usually easy. First, decide what type of fix you want to put in place. In most programs, like Pace-Pal, many solutions are available. For example, Pace-Pal could immediately check that data entered by the user is in the correct format, and demand that the user re-enter the data if it is invalid. Or Pace-Pal could check the data and drop illegal extra characters without telling the user. Or Pace-Pal could simply convert any invalid data to 0 and let the user know. The possibilities are many.

For the sake of simplicity, the last solution mentioned is used in this example. Although this solution isn't necessarily the best way to handle the fix when viewed in the context of the whole program, it does eliminate the error. A check for invalid data is made right before the problem statement. If invalid data is found, the user is informed and all times are forced to be 0. Since this is a legal numeric representation, the type conversion problem is avoided and no error occurs. This solution is shown in Listing 17.11.

Listing 17.11. The fix that our trace pointed us to!

```
' If there is invalid string data, warn the user
    '    and reset data to prevent more errors
    if (not IsNumeric(vHours)) or (not IsNumeric(vMinutes)) _
       or (not IsNumeric(vSeconds)) then
       msgbox "Time contains character when digits expected. " & _
           " Please respecify!", _                vbOKonly,"Invalid time"
             vHours = 0
             vMinutes = 0
             vSeconds = 0
       end if


    ' Return total seconds value
    ConvertStringtoTotalSeconds = CInt(vHours) + CInt(vMinutes) +
CInt(vSeconds)

    if err.number <> 0 then
       msgbox "Error #:" & err.number & " Description:" & _
           err.description & _
           " Source:" & err.source, vbOKOnly, "Error in _
           ConvertStringtoTotalSeconds!"
       end if

End Function   ' End of function ConvertStringtoTotalSeconds
```

17

ANALYSIS   With this fix, the program will be robust enough to continue even if a user enters invalid input. The resulting message box is shown in Figure 17.12. The program will inform the user of the error, substitute a time of 0 in place of the input, and calculate a pace of 0 seconds per mile.

The next step after inserting the fix is to verify that it worked. In this case, that verification is relatively easy. This fix addresses a type-conversion error that prevented Pace-Pal from calculating a final pace. Since the code that checks the error status is still in place at the end of the procedure, simply rerun the procedure. If you don't get an error message, you know the type conversion error has been eliminated. Likewise, the fact that a pace of 00:00 shows up in the pace text box indicates a complete calculation. So in this case, verifying that the fix really solves the problem is relatively easy. For some bugs, you may have to add more trace statements or variable analyses after the fix is in place to verify that it had the intended results.

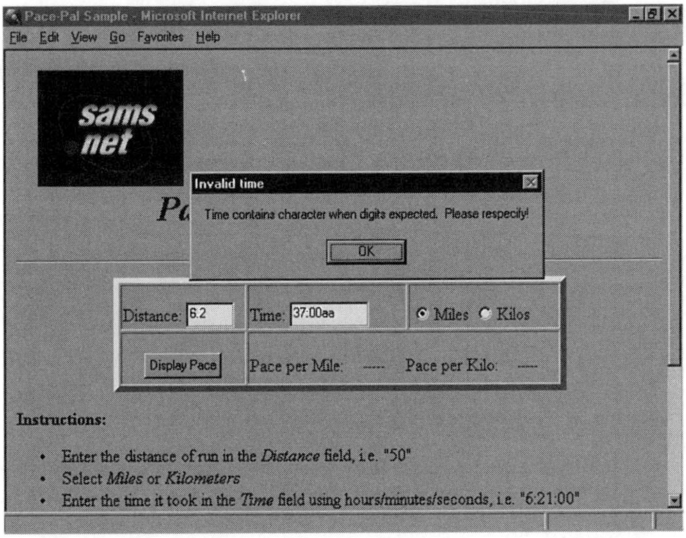

Figure 17.12.

User feedback from the bug-proofed Pace-Pal.

It is important to note that this fix keeps the program from crashing when the user enters an invalid time such as 37:12AA. However, a similar problem still exists in the code with distance rather than time. If the user enters 6.2AA rather than 6.2 miles, a type-conversion-induced run-time error will result from a different procedure in Pace-Pal that calculates the final pace. Because the type of problem present in dealing with time is also present in dealing with distance, more than one fix is needed in Pace-Pal to address all the areas where this type of problem occurs. This, it turns out, is very common in debugging, especially in data-handling code. If you find a bug in one place, check for it in other areas of the program too. If wrong assumptions or coding techniques led to problems once, they very likely will lead to problems again.

If you think you have a problem area that you need to check throughout your application, you should be able to pinpoint it quite easily if it results in an error condition. You can use the techniques presented earlier in this lesson. Insert `On Error Resume Next` in every procedure. At the end of every procedure, check the `err` object and print out a message if an error occurred within that procedure. This level of tracing will give you a clear indication of any procedures where the error occurs.

The Do-It-Yourself Trace Debug Window Approach

By now the value of good tracing is probably clear. Good debugging usually comes down to good program tracing. Several approaches to tracing are available. The technique of tracing the flow of every statement by displaying message boxes was presented earlier in today's lesson. This method can be a bit cumbersome since it requires interaction with a series of message boxes each time you do a trace. The technique of simply printing out a message box only if an error has occurred was also illustrated earlier in today's lesson. This approach is quite effective, but there may be times when you want to monitor the flow of your program even if an error has not occurred.

There are many reasons why tracing all statements, even under non-error conditions, can provide a helpful overall picture of what the code is really doing. Understanding the flow of the code and gaining insight into the state of the variables as the code execution progresses will help you better understand the behavior of a program. The more you understand the overall behavior of a program, the better code you can write for it. Likewise, you'll be able to make better intuitive decisions when chasing problems. So what's the best approach when you want to trace normal program flow? As we've already established, the "always display message box" approach can be rather cumbersome. And the "display message box only after error" approach doesn't give the full level of feedback you may be looking for in every case.

What you really need is a separate debug window that lets you peek into the program as it progresses, much like Visual Basic 4.0's debug window. It turns out you can build at least some of those capabilities right into your page with VBScript. You just add a rather large form *textarea* input control at the bottom of your page. Terminology for this type of control varies, but since it is similar to the text box control of Visual Basic 4.0, we'll refer to it as a text box here. A debug text box is typically used as a temporary debug tool, and is removed before you release your final version of the code. But in the meantime, during the script development phase, it can be a considerable help during debugging. Listing 17.12 shows the Pace-Pal HTML source code with an `<INPUT>` tag added to define this type of debug text box. The sample program `Ppalerr5.htm` on the CD-ROM uses this same approach, but additional formats the input controls in a table for better visual presentation on-screen.

Listing 17.12. Adding a form textarea input control to capture debug trace statements.

```
<FORM NAME="frmPace">
<PRE>
<FONT COLOR=BLUE FACE="Comic Sans MS" SIZE=6>
Distance:       <INPUT NAME="txtDistance" VALUE="" MAXLENGTH="5" SIZE=5>
<INPUT TYPE="RADIO" NAME="Dist" CHECKED VALUE="Miles" _
onClick=SetDistance("Miles") > Miles
<INPUT TYPE="RADIO" NAME="Dist" VALUE="Kilos" onClick=SetDistance("Kilos")>Kilos
Time:             <INPUT NAME="txtTime" VALUE="" MAXLENGTH="11" SIZE=11>
in minute:second format
<INPUT TYPE=BUTTON VALUE="Display Pace" SIZE=30 NAME="Calc">
Pace per Mile: <INPUT NAME="txtPaceMiles" VALUE="" MAXLENGTH="5" SIZE=5> _
Pace per Kilo: <INPUT NAME="txtPaceKilos" VALUE="" MAXLENGTH="5" SIZE=5>
Debug Window: <TEXTAREA NAME="txtDebug" ROWS="10" COLS="60" >
</TEXTAREA>
</FONT>
</PRE>
</FORM>
```

17

ANALYSIS The text area control, which has been named txtDebug in this example, provides a convenient place to log trace information. You can add code to your script to display debug information in this control wherever you want logging to take place in your program. As a matter of fact, if you want, you can print debug information after each and every script statement. This logging takes place in an unobtrusive manner and doesn't require the interaction of the message box. You can even provide variable and code location information when you display information in the txtDebug control. An example of Pace-Pal modified to use this style of tracing is shown in Listing 17.13.

Listing 17.13. Tracing program flow and variables with form textarea input control.

```
document.frmPace.txtDebug.Value = document.frmPace.txtDebug.Value & _
    "Prior to assignment, vSeconds =" & vSeconds & vbCrLF
    ' Return total seconds value
    ConvertStringtoTotalSeconds = CInt(vHours) + CInt(vMinutes) _
         + CInt(vSeconds)
document.frmPace.txtDebug.Value = document.frmPace.txtDebug.Value & _
    "After assignment, vSeconds =" & vSeconds & vbCrLf
```

ANALYSIS When Pace-Pal is run with these modifications, a clear trace appears in the txtDebug text area control as the program progresses. A sample of the trace is shown in Figure 17.13. This trace can provide great insight into code behavior. Another advantage of storing trace output in the txtDebug control is that you can use this information to review your program history even after your script execution completes. For example, assume that your script generates 200 lines of trace information in response to a button click. After the block of code associated with the button click completes, all this information will still be available in the txtDebug control. You can scroll through the data and reconstruct what happened to the script by looking at this trace. Notice that the variable vbCrLf is used here. This is declared to contain the standard line separator characters according to the conventions described on Day 4, "Creating Variables in VBScript."

Figure 17.13.

Output from the textbox trace.

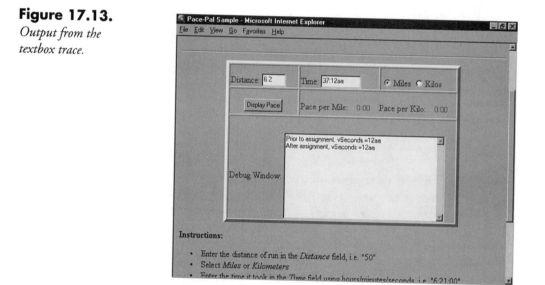

Building Your Own Trace Routines

The technique of logging trace statements to a text box control is handy, but you can make it even more convenient. The statements that log information are not difficult to understand, but they are a bit lengthy. Also, you want to ensure that you take the same approach with every log statement. If you generate one type of trace information in one area of code, and then generate trace information in another format somewhere else in your script, it will be more confusing to analyze the trace results. So it would be more convenient to simply call an easy-to-use subroutine every time you want to log trace messages. That way, the subroutine could contain the code to handle all aspects of logging the trace information.

An example of a trace debug subroutine is shown in Listing 17.14. This procedure just takes a string, which is provided as a parameter at the time the procedure is called, and adds that string to the current contents of the text box control. This procedure may be called many times from different locations in the program. The string, which is provided as data to this procedure, should describe the program from which the call is made in order to provide a meaningful trace history. For clear output, new information provided by the trace procedure should be displayed as a new line in the text box. That is the purpose of the vbCrLf constant variable seen in the listing. vbCrLf is a variable for the intrinsic VBScript constant containing the carriage return/line feed characters that cause a new line to be generated. The assignment statement appends the new information after the existing contents of the text box control. Then, a carriage return line feed is appended to the end of that. Any information that follows will appear on a new line.

Listing 17.14. The definition for a simple trace routine.

```
sub DebugMsg(Info)
'-----------------------------------------------------------
' Print debug message to textarea used for debug display
    document.frmPace.txtDebug.Value = _
        document.frmPace.txtDebug.Value & info & vbCrLf
end sub
```

ANALYSIS Using this type of subroutine doesn't just save you from repeatedly typing the same trace code. It also ensures that all trace output is generated in a standard, consistent manner. After all, every trace message comes from the same place with this approach. Then the rest of the code simply makes use of this common subroutine wherever traces are needed. Listing 17.15 shows an example of Pace-Pal, modified to use calls to the trace procedure to carry out a trace.

Listing 17.15. The call to a simple trace routine.

```
DebugMsg "Prior to assignment, vSeconds =" & vSeconds
    ' Return total seconds value
    ConvertStringtoTotalSeconds = CInt(vHours) + CInt(vMinutes) _
        + CInt(vSeconds)
DebugMsg "After assignment"
```

ANALYSIS Because any expression can be passed for subsequent display to DebugMsg, you have the flexibility to send information about any variable and have that recorded with your program trace. Notice that in the first call to DebugMsg, the descriptive string passed to the procedure contains the contents of a variable as well as indicates the location where the call was made. The benefits of this type of flexible trace are tremendous. You can monitor the changes in variables as your program executes, and monitor the current location and progression of the code. You can gain very keen insights from the program monitoring this trace procedure provides.

NOTE

You may have noticed that the calls to the debug trace procedure are not indented, unlike the rest of the program. This is a convention that can be used to make temporary calls stand out. All the debug trace calls here are temporary calls only. Normally, you add them just to aid your debug efforts during design time and remove them prior to releasing your final product. The practice of left-aligning the debug statements makes it easy to spot the statements and remove them later on.

Sample Variant Variable Analysis Routine

The information provided by the DebugMsg procedure is good, but even that might not tell you everything you want to know. If you're chasing a problem in a script, it may not be enough to just see the program flow. You might even use DebugMsg to display the contents of a variable, and find it still doesn't quite fill you in on the whole story of the state of your program. One other piece of the picture that can be very important is determining what subtype of data a variable represents, as well as the current value of that data.

For example, a variable that prints out as 23 in the trace log may be stored in a variant variable with subtype string, or a variant variable with subtype integer. You learned about variant subtypes on Day 4. For some types of problems, it can be quite important to understand which subtype data representation a variable currently has. If you write elegant code to look at the variant subtype and interpret it for logging, the code can be rather lengthy. It's certainly not something you would want scattered all over your program. Fortunately, you can apply the same trace procedure solution to this problem. An expanded trace procedure can be defined to provide a "power trace." This procedure not only accepts a descriptive parameter indicating the program location, it also accepts a parameter that contains a variable to analyze. The procedure will then log an informational string to the text box control based on these parameters. Part of the information logged in the text box control displays the program location. The other portion reflects the value and subtype of the variable. An analysis of the variable is carried out to determine the subtype of the variant. This type of debug procedure provides a very detailed and powerful trace history. An example is shown in Listing 17.16.

Listing 17.16. The definition for a variant variable analysis routine.

```
sub VarAnalyzeMsg(InfoMsg, VarToAnalyze)
'-----------------------------------------------------------
' Print debug info message to textarea used for debug display, and
'    printout type and value of VarToAnalyze
```

17

```
dim VarMsg ' Used to build up info about VarToAnalyze

' Determine type of variable
'   Note: If this code was in Visual Basic 4.0,
'     the Vb intrinsic constants such
'     as vbEmpty could be used instead of hardcoded values
'     (not defined in beta VBScript)
select case VarType(VarToAnalyze)
    case 0    ' vbEmpty
        VarMsg = "Empty"
    case 1    ' vbNull
        VarMsg = "Null"
    case 2    ' vbInteger
        VarMsg = "Integer, Value=" & VarToAnalyze
    case 3    ' vbLong
        VarMsg = "Long, Value=" & VarToAnalyze
    case 4    ' vbSingle
        VarMsg = "Single, Value=" & VarToAnalyze
    case 5    ' vbDouble
        VarMsg = "Double, Value=" & VarToAnalyze
    case 6    ' vbCurrency
        VarMsg = "Currency, Value=" & VarToAnalyze
    case 7    ' vbDate
        VarMsg = "Date, Value=" & VarToAnalyze
    case 8    ' vbString
        VarMsg = "String, len=" & len(VarToAnalyze) _
            & " Value=" & VarToAnalyze
    case 9    ' vbObject
        VarMsg = "OLE Automation Object"
    case 10   ' vbError
        VarMsg = "Error"
    case 11   ' vbBoolean
        VarMsg = "Boolean, Value=" & VarToAnalyze
    case 12   ' vbVariant
        VarMsg = "Non-OLE Automation Object"
    case 13   ' vbDataObject
        VarMsg = "Byte, Value=" & VarToAnalyze
    case 17   ' vbByte
        VarMsg = "Byte, Value=" & VarToAnalyze
    case 8194 ' vbArray + vbInteger
        VarMsg = "Integer Array, Ubound=" & Ubound(VarToAnalyze)
    case 8195 ' vbArray + vbLong
        VarMsg = "Long Array, Ubound=" & Ubound(VarToAnalyze)
    case 8196 ' vbArray + vbSingle
        VarMsg = "Single Array, Ubound=" & Ubound(VarToAnalyze)
    case 8197 ' vbArray + vbDouble
        VarMsg = "Double Array, Ubound=" & Ubound(VarToAnalyze)
    case 8198 ' vbArray + vbCurrency
        VarMsg = "Currency Array, Ubound=" & Ubound(VarToAnalyze)
    case 8199 ' vbArray + vbDate
        VarMsg = "Date Array, Ubound=" & Ubound(VarToAnalyze)
```

continues

Listing 17.16. continued

```
            case 8200 ' vbArray + vbString
                VarMsg = "String Array, Ubound=" & Ubound(VarToAnalyze)
            case 8201 ' vbArray + vbObject
                VarMsg = "Object Array, Ubound=" & Ubound(VarToAnalyze)
            case 8202 ' vbArray + vbError
                VarMsg = "Error Array, Ubound=" & Ubound(VarToAnalyze)
            case 8203 ' vbArray + vbBoolean
                VarMsg = "Boolean Array, Ubound=" & Ubound(VarToAnalyze)
            case 8204 ' vbArray + vbVariant
                VarMsg = "Variant Array, Ubound=" & Ubound(VarToAnalyze)
            case 8205 ' vbArray + vbDataObject
                VarMsg = "vbDataObject Array, Ubound=" & Ubound(VarToAnalyze)
            case 8209 ' vbArray + vbByte
                VarMsg = "Byte Array, Ubound=" & Ubound(VarToAnalyze)
            case else
                VarMsg = "Unknown"
        end select

    VarMsg = "...Var type is " & VarMsg
    ' Print to textarea used for debug trace, must use vbCrLf
    '    to advance lines
    document.frmPace.txtDebug.Value = _
        document.frmPace.txtDebug.Value & InfoMsg & vbCrLf
    document.frmPace.txtDebug.Value = _
        document.frmPace.txtDebug.Value & VarMsg & vbCrLf
end sub    ' VarAnalyzeMsg
```

NOTE

Style Considerations

If you're really alert, you may have noticed that a check is made to see if the variable is represented in several storage types that VBScript does not support. These include currency and arrays of nonvariants. It's true that VBScript variants do not represent these subtypes of data. However, the VBScript documentation indicates that the VarType can return values for any of these types. This is probably just a carryover from VBA and Visual Basic 4.0, which do support these additional types. Since it doesn't hurt to check for these extra types, and since it could even provide added insight if there were an internal VBScript error that resulted in a bad type, these checks are left in here. This also makes for *upward-compatible* code that can be ported to VBA or Visual Basic 4.0 programs without change.

ANALYSIS   A modified sample of the familiar Pace-Pal example is shown in Listing 17.17. Pace-Pal has been modified to make calls to the VarAnalyzeMsg routine. These calls have been added both before and after the statement that earlier samples showed was the problem statement. Since there are three variables involved in the problem statement, vHours, vMinutes, and vSeconds, all three should be inspected prior to the problem statement to help determine the cause of the problem. Therefore, three different calls to VarAnalyzeMsg are used, one to analyze each specific variable. Likewise, the same three calls to VarAnalyzeMsg are made after the problem statement. This is to ensure that none of the variables has unexpectedly changed value or subtype.

NOTE

You can pretty well determine by looking at the code involved in the Pace-Pal problem area that no variables will be changed after the problem statement. However, the poststatement calls to VarAnalyzeMsg ensure that you are not making any mistaken assumptions about values not changing. This is a good standard debugging practice to follow, and the calls are included here to illustrate that point. You should scientifically verify the contents of variables during debug rather than making potentially faulty assumptions. If you've decided that a full trace is in order, you can never assume that a value will not change. It is always best to check debug information both before and after a given statement. Even if you think that nothing will have changed, there is always a chance that you're wrong, and the extra debug procedure costs you only the time it takes to enter it.

17

Listing 17.17. The call to the variant variable analysis routine.

```
Call VarAnalyzeMsg("Analyzing vHours prior to ConvertString",vHours)
Call VarAnalyzeMsg("Analyzing vMinutes prior to ConvertString",vMinutes)
Call VarAnalyzeMsg("Analyzing vSeconds prior to ConvertString",vSeconds)

    ' Return total seconds value
    ConvertStringtoTotalSeconds = CInt(vHours) + CInt(vMinutes) + _
        CInt(vSeconds)

Call VarAnalyzeMsg("Analyzing vHours after call to ConvertString",vHours)
Call VarAnalyzeMsg("Analyzing vMinutes after call to ConvertString",vMinutes)
Call VarAnalyzeMsg("Analyzing vSeconds after call to ConvertString",vSeconds)
```

NOTE

> The source file for the Pace-Pal program modified to contain the change shown here is available on the CD-ROM under `ppalerr5.htm`.

ANALYSIS The modified Pace-Pal program with the `VarAnalyzeMsg` trace statement generates the output shown in Figure 17.14. The `txtDebug` text box trace area is filled with meaningful trace information that can help you understand the behavior of the program. Although this trace facility might not be as powerful as the trace capabilities built into other languages such as Visual Basic 4.0, it does give you ample power to get to the root of just about any VBScript–generated error.

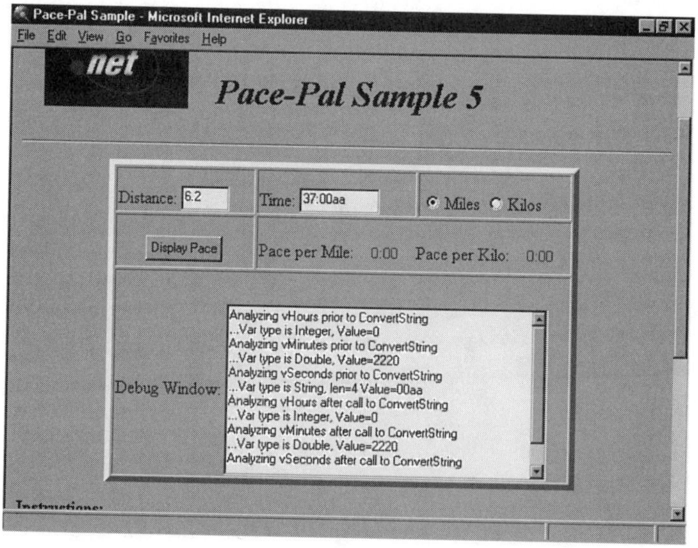

Figure 17.14.

Output from the variant variable analysis routine.

Error Handling to Include in Your Final Script

Much of the focus of today's lesson has been on tracing your program to eliminate a bug. The debug code changes made to trace code are typically removed before you make a final version of your Web page available to your users. The `On Error Resume Next` and `err` object techniques illustrated, though, have some purposes in final non-debug code-based pages as well. They are essential if you are trying to make the final version of your Web pages as robust as possible for your end users. The worst thing you can subject a user to is a cryptic run-time error. It is much better to insert code that tells VBScript to proceed past the errors without alarming your user. `On Error Resume Next` and the `err` object can be used to accomplish this.

You can add code statements to check for errors in every procedure and to analyze what type of error occurred using the err object. Based on the type of error, your code can take many different approaches that will make things easy on the user. Code can hide errors from users if the errors are minor. You might choose not to inform the user of an internal VBScript error if it is something you can correct in code and if the user does not need to know about it. If the error was caused by user data, as was the case with Pace-Pal, you might ask the user to re-enter some input or repeat an action. In other cases, there may be no recovery path, but at least you can present the user with a more friendly, explanatory message than that which VBScript would produce. Likewise, you can gracefully bring the script to a halt rather than have it abort on the user immediately as it would if VBScript handled the error directly. The end result in all these cases is a higher quality of scripts for your user.

More Reasons Why VBScript Can Be Tough to Debug

But wait, there's more (as if it weren't tough enough already)! We've got no debug environment; we've got a language where a multitude of run-time problems, such as type conversions, are waiting to strike if you don't use it just right! Just as you're about finished with the day, you hear, "But wait, there's more!" There are still a few more challenges to debugging VBScript that haven't been covered yet. It's important to be aware of these additional challenges, not so you will spend sleepless nights worrying about them, but so you will have a broad view of what to expect as you start to chase VBScript-related problems.

VBScript is what is sometimes called a "glue" language. It is great at gluing many components together to provide a powerful programmatic interface. You can easily weave a masterpiece of ActiveX controls, Java applets, intrinsic form controls, and OLE automation components into one tapestry when building your script. However, opening the door to such easy integration of components also opens the door to potential problems with them. A third-party control may have a bug in it. The Java applet provided by your co-worker may be riddled with hideous logic errors. The possibilities for problems are endless. And if your VBScript program incorporates those pieces, the problems will be visible to the user through your program. When such a problem occurs, the user considers it your script's problem. Then it falls to you, the debugger, to isolate areas of code to prove that a problem is caused by one specific component.

And now the good news that will save you from those sleepless nights: The very same skills discussed in this lesson that will help you hone in on VBScript errors will also help you hone in on component-related errors. You still need to trace through the program, isolating the problem to one specific area of the code. You still may need to display variable values, or even component property values, to monitor the state of the program before and after potential component-related problem statements. You still may need to decompose one larger

VBScript statement involving components into a series of smaller statements to isolate the problem. In every case, the same tools and techniques already discussed still apply.

The Moral of the Story

The best advice to give for debugging and error handling would be, "Don't make mistakes!" However, the outcome is no more probable than if you told the sun to rise in the north and set in the south. Mistakes are an inherent and unavoidable part of today's programming model. If you're a programmer, you will be making plenty of them. A big part of the task of producing VBScript programs is getting the bugs out and making your programs shield the user from the bugs. The real moral of the story, then, is to apply these debug, trace, and error-handling techniques vigorously. Make use of debug tracing and variable analysis routines like those provided in this lesson. They will add both efficiency and consistency to your debugging. Keep your eye open for good debugging tools. VBScript debug tools are currently far behind those for Visual Basic 4.0, but this language is still in its infancy, and you can expect support to increase. For now, scripts may take longer to debug than programs in other languages due to the lack of tools. But with patience, strategy, and some of the techniques discussed in this lesson, your debugging sessions can still be highly effective.

Summary

Today's lesson provides important debugging techniques that can be applied to syntactic and semantic errors. Syntactic errors are problems caused by incorrectly specifying your programs. Syntactic problems typically cause run-time error messages, and therefore are often relatively easy to spot and address. Semantic errors arise when you incorrectly lay out your program logic. These do not cause run-time errors, but rather just lead to bad results. Spotting and correcting semantic errors can be more of a challenge in many cases.

There are several key features of the language that specifically aid in dealing with errors:

- ☐ `On Error Resume Next`
- ☐ `err.description`
- ☐ `err.source`
- ☐ `err.number`
- ☐ `err.clear`
- ☐ `err.raise`

VBScript provides a means to turn off the automatic generation of run-time error messages to the user and prevent the subsequent script termination. The `On Error Resume Next` statement accomplishes this. If you have used this statement in a procedure, then when an error is encountered in that procedure the program will continue without displaying an error message. The state of the error can be checked by using the err object's number, source, and description properties. These properties provide insight into the error code of the last error, the software component responsible for the error, and a text description of what that error was. The clear method can be used to clear the err object and set it back to its initial state as if no error had yet occurred. The raise method can be used to generate a run-time error to be caught by a higher level procedure or displayed to the user.

Tracing techniques can be of value in analyzing all types of errors. The easiest method is to simply insert a line of code that displays a message box after each statement and observe which message boxes are displayed. A more elegant approach is to use On Error Resume Next so that any run-time errors will not be fatal. Then, check the status of the err object after each critical call and only print out a message if that call caused an error. Yet another approach is to print out trace messages to a debug-specific form control such as an input text area control. Then you have what is essentially a window into the flow of the program.

If you're doing a lot of debugging, you'll want an even more powerful debug repertoire. You can obtain this by building your own debug routines. These routines can write trace information to a text area control, or even perform detailed variable analysis, displaying variable values and subtypes. A debug routine is easier to insert in your code than direct debug statements in some respects. This is because the debug logic is supplied just in one place, and the calls to the routine ensure consistency of debug approach throughout your program. Sample debug routines are provided in this lesson.

VBScript does not have a powerful set of debug tools like some languages do (such as VBScript's older cousin, Visual Basic 4.0). However, there is enough in the language to craft your own effective debug approach. The most important tools, however, are the same ones you supply for any language you must debug—your own persistence and patience.

Q&A

Q Suppose you have *not* used the On Error Resume Next statement in your source code, so that errors are addressed in the default manner. Is there any value to checking the err.number error code indicator at the end of each function to see if errors have occurred?

A No! Although you might think you are being a good, conscientious programmer by diligently checking error codes, if you didn't have an On Error Resume Next in your code, you'd be going through the motions for no reason. The On Error Resume Next statement tells the VBScript run-time interpreter to keep chugging along even if an error is encountered. If you *haven't* used this statement, then as soon as VBScript hits an error, it will generate a run-time error and bring your program to a screeching halt! The err.number check at the bottom of your function will never be reached.

Q Assume that you have used `On Error Resume Next` so that the program can continue if an error is encountered, and you can carry out error analysis at the end of your function. What is more helpful feedback to print out in a message box in your error analysis, `err.Number` or `err.Description`?

A Generally, `err.Description` is more helpful because it describes the cause of the problem. Of course, the description can sound rather vague at times (such as `type conversion error`), but that is more helpful than simply a numeric code. The numeric code can be helpful when users call in problems to a technical support person, because users generally can pass on a number correctly but often paraphrase and inadvertently distort text messages. In this respect, printing out both `err.Number` and `err.Description` is often the best approach when considering technical support needs. They are just two ways of describing the same problem: in terms of descriptive (or semi-descriptive) English, and in terms of a numeric code assigned by Microsoft.

The numeric code can come in very handy if you have to deal with the problem programmatically. If you need to write program logic to check if a certain type of error has occurred, it may be easiest to simply check `err.number` to see if the error code is the one you want to specially handle.

Q Can you use the err object to ignore certain errors and inform the users of others?

A Yes, if you couple it with `On Error Resume Next`! If you've used `On Error Resume Next` previously in the procedure, or at the top of your script, VBScript will valiantly continue after encountering an error (after it updates the err object for you). Then, at some later point in your code, you can have code statements that inspect this value and take action based upon it if it indicates the specific error you are concerned about. Assume, for example, that you don't want to tell your user about divide-by-zero errors because you'll just supply a default result in those cases; however, you want to inform them of any other problem. The following code allows you to do just that:

```
if err.number = 11 then
    ' Divide by zero err code is 11, so supply default
    '    result in this case
    ResultVar = 100
else if err.number <> 0
    ' Any other errors, let user know
    msgbox "Warning, an error has occurred," & _
        " please report it to tech support: " & _
        err.Description, vbOKOnly, _
        "Error Detected In Mortgage Calculator"
end if

'....normal processing....
```

Q **Okay, so I decide I want to screen out any type-mismatch errors and let my users know about them, but don't want to tell them about other errors. How do I find out what the error code for the type-mismatch error is?**

A The easiest way is to write a simple piece of test code. You actually *want* to put a bug in your code for once using this approach! It's actually kind of fun! Your test code should cause the error to happen, and then you can print out the err.number value in a message box to figure out what the code is and apply it to other programs. Now you know what the error code will be when it occurs under real conditions! For example, use this code to figure out what error number VBScript uses for a type mismatch:

```
On Error Resume Next
Dim b
b = "dog" * "cat"
msgbox "I caused an error! And I'm not sorry! Err number is " _
    & err.number & _
" and description is " & err.description, vbOKOnly, _

"Pinpointing an Error Code"
```

These error codes are, for the most part, the same as those used in Visual Basic 4.0 and VBA. At the time of this printing, no consolidated source of documentation seems to exist, but it is easy to generate this yourself for VBScript errors. Simply write a program that loops through and prints every error:

```
count = 0
do while count <= 65535
    ' set the error code
    count = count + 1
    err.Number = count
    ' Print out the corresponding error message for this error code
    txtErrorList = txtErrorList & err.Description & vbCrLf
loop
```

Workshop

Trace the flow of an entire program by logging a trace message to a form textarea input control after each statement. You learned how to use this technique today. Use one of your own programs to trace, or use the Pace-Pal program used in this lesson.

Use a statement like the following to add the textarea input control that will be used as your trace window:

```
<FORM NAME="frmTestLog">
Debug Window: <TEXTAREA NAME="txtDebug" ROWS="8" COLS="60" ></TEXTAREA>
</FORM>
```

Then, after every normal program statement, add another statement right after it that will print a log message to the debug window you have defined. Use a variable declared to be the intrinsic Visual Basic constant vbCrLf to cause each log message to be generated on a new line. A sample declaration of this and other intrinsic constant-variable declarations can be found on the CD-ROM in shared\tools\constant.txt. The following code shows an example of using vbCrLf:

```
dim vbCrLf : vbCrLf = chr(13) & chr(10)   ' Causes line break in text

document.frmTestLog.txtDebug.Value = _
    document.frmTestLog.txtDebug.Value & _
    "After statement such and such…" & vbCrLF
```

Quiz

NOTE

Refer to Appendix C, "Answers to Quiz Questions," for the answers to these questions.

1. Take a look at the following conditional expression. Assume that you want to trace its logic. Insert the necessary trace statements to fully understand the run-time logic flow of the conditional. (There are many different ways to achieve this, so there is not just one correct answer!) Here's the code:

```
If a > 3 then
    b = c + 1
else
   if a = 1 then
      b = c + 4
   else
      if < -2 then
         b = c + 7
      end if
   end if
end if
```

2. Assume that you've just had the sobering experience of seeing a Type mismatch error pop up in front of you. After some intense words with your computer and some focused troubleshooting, you isolate the problem to this statement:

```
r = q / p
```

Show the trace logic that you could add to help analyze the state of these variables and determine the problem.

Day 18

Advanced User Interface and Browser Object Techniques

There are a lot of ways to make pages active. You can use scripts to interact with the user, control objects, and even generate HTML on the initial document. After all, the concept of a scripting language is to extend the capabilities of the page. But in addition to providing new functions, VBScript lets you do old things better. This is particularly true of image handling. What happens when a user clicks on one area of an image to trigger some action? With a traditional page, you had to make use of image maps with server-side assistance to provide a response. VBScript, on the other hand, lets you respond immediately. With the new layout control, you have a powerful range of capabilities. Other controls greatly enhance the user experience as well. What if you have a page with plenty of graphics to load? In days past, you were pretty much limited to providing a hypertext link and loading the graphics on demand. With VBScript, you not only can trigger a link from code, you can even cause graphics to be preloaded well before a page that needs them is displayed.

Today's lesson outlines these techniques. It looks at processing clicks on an image to determine exactly which area was clicked on. This lesson checks out the method for linking to another page through code. You'll examine techniques for preloading graphics. Building from these samples, you'll explore an approach for using all these techniques together. Then you will get an overview of the entire browser object capabilities. Finally, you'll get a look at what you can do with the powerful layout control with 2-D control from a script. Not only will this information allow you to have more powerful scripts, but it may also cause you to rethink your entire Web page approach. Smart scripting, with these techniques and others like them, lets you do the old tried-and-true page presentation methods better than before, as well as add exciting new capabilities to your pages.

2-D Forms, the Layout Control, and the ActiveX Control Pad

If you've spent much time designing Web pages, you know that a great deal of patience is a prerequisite for the task. It can often be tedious work to lay out and position the HTML elements and any associated controls on a Web page to achieve best visual results. An evolving World Wide Web Consortium draft standard would make this task much easier. The standard provides a framework for precisely specifying the position of elements on pages. This approach to page layout is sometimes called 2-D layout since it deals with two-dimensional placement of elements on pages. This means that when you design your form you can precisely specify where on a page any given element should be positioned. You won't have to worry about breaks, meticulous alignment issues, or relying on tables to position elements side by side where you want them. Instead, you could simply indicate the x and the y position of elements. Then the element would be laid out in a two-dimensional space on that page or frame. Script languages such as VBScript can take great advantage of this. The script program can query the position of elements or reposition elements.

2-D layout techniques are rapidly evolving. Microsoft has already provided an interim strategy to carry out this type of Web page development. This strategy is based on a `layout` control. An object declaration for the layout control looks similar to other object declarations:

```
<OBJECT CLASSID="CLSID:812AE312-8B8E-11CF-93C8-00AA00C08FDF"
ID="Layout2" STYLE="LEFT:0;TOP:0">
<PARAM NAME="ALXPATH" REF VALUE="Layout2.alx">
</OBJECT>
```

You incorporate the `layout` control into your page. If you use the ActiveX Control Pad tool, it is automatically inserted in response to a menu item request. If you include a `layout` control in a page, then the `layout` control in turn references another data page with an ALX file (ActiveX layout file). The `layout` control uses this data file to determine how to place

18

components, generate HTML, and associated scripts on the part of the main page that it is designated to control. The `layout` control can work with 2-D location specifications that are in its data file. These attributes are properties of elements that the `layout` control recognizes. Therefore, the elements that the `layout` control has control over can be defined in a 2-D manner at design time. The layout control can even provide for specifying "Z-order," or the layering relationships between multiple elements.

A sample ALX file is on the CD-ROM in file `Layout2.ALX`. You can open it in a standard text editor to inspect it. The page that incorporates this data file through the layout control is `Layout2.htm`. You can run this page to see an example of what can be accomplished with the `layout` control. The sample shows an image that is moved about the page in response to user events. Overlapping images are also used. Be sure to click on the avatar heads to initiate the sample! VBScript code moves the heads around the Web page in response to the user's selection of directional arrows. You can observe the layering capabilities of the `layout` control through the behavior of the heads as they move about the screen. The head on the first avatar will be layered on top of the directional arrows as it moves across them. The head on the second avatar will be layered below the arrows when it moves across them.

NOTE

> One very powerful feature made possible by the layout control is that it provides for overlaid elements. For example, a control with a transparent background can be placed on top of an image control and the user can see the image underneath. Along with the much-improved capabilities for handling 2-D and layering issues with the layout control comes better handling of issues such as transparency that make it easy to build impressive solutions in the Layout Editor. At the time of this printing, many impressive sample programs using layout control technology were available for viewing on the Microsoft site. Go to `www.microsoft.com/intdev` and do a search on `layout control` for further details.

18

Microsoft has a development tool that works in conjunction with the layout control to allow for easy creation of the data file. The Microsoft ActiveX Control Pad can be used to edit pages. The corresponding Layout Editor lets you define ALX files in a visual fashion. The editor provides easy access to controls, including an `image` and a `hotspot` control. The `hotspot` control is actually implemented as a transparent label. You can drag elements onto a layout form, position them, and get a feel for the visual results immediately. This is much like the traditional form-based design of Visual Basic. Then with the integration power of the `layout` control, this layout form data is integrated into your page at run-time. What if you want VBScript code to interact with elements in the layout file? You simply associate VBScript with them in that file, using exactly the same methodologies you have seen so far!

The ActiveX Control Pad Layout Editor and the layout control are available from Microsoft's Web site. Check www.microsoft.com/intdev for the latest availability information.

With the power of the layout control and the ActiveX Control Pad Layout Editor you can move into the new era of Web page authorship. Your VBScript skills move right there with you. This style of Web page design leads to very rich, sophisticated Web pages. The role of VBScript is even more important with this new style of page design because the pages that are produced will certainly become more sophisticated, full functioned, and in many cases more like traditional applications. These trends will all increase the need for good scripting solutions.

The layout control approach itself is very likely an interim solution. It can be expected that eventually what is now known as the layout control will become an intrinsic part of the browser, and eventually the shell and operating system environment. In the not too distant future the standard approach for working with pages will be very much like that of Visual Basic. You will be able to work from a form or collection of forms, associating code with the visual objects that you see.

Along with these capabilities, the Microsoft ActiveX Control Pad also provides an editor that can be used for editing VBScript. This editor not only provides basic editing support, it also has a facility for easy insertion of object definitions. A sample page on the CD-ROM, Page1.htm, was produced with just the ActiveX Control Pad and contains notes on its usage. The tool facilitates creation of pages and scripts in many ways. You can easily paste in a label control, for example, without having to remember all the syntax. Also, a stand-alone utility called Acid was available at the time of this printing on the Microsoft Web site. This achieves much the same purpose of inserting object definitions, but can be used independently with any environment that allows you to paste. VBScript is very much affected by the availability of such tools. One of the unique aspects of VBScript is that it is first and foremost an integration language. It is intended to be used to integrate components and interact with environments. Therefore, any tools that make it easier to use VBScript can be expected to greatly increase its use and adoption.

Loading Graphics in Advance with the ActiveX preload Control

Just about every Web page user has experienced the frustration of staring at a not-quite-ready page as the graphics are downloaded from the server. Even with a high-speed link to the Internet, the wait for images to be downloaded can be a nuisance. For those with lower-speed modem links, waiting for graphics has become a new 20th century form of self-inflicted torture.

VBScript and a special ActiveX control now make it possible to alleviate some of this suffering. An ActiveX preload control can be used in Web pages and optionally controlled from code to load graphics before they are required. To appreciate how this works, imagine that a user is to be presented with two Web pages. The first Web page is a welcome page for the Virginia Happy Trails Running Club, a regional running club organization. The second page contains results from the club's annual Bull Run 50 Mile trail ultramarathon race. Included on that page are several high-resolution photographs of runners during the race.

The user can be expected to first spend time on the welcome page, reading over the detailed greeting, club history, club philosophy, and scheduled events. Traditionally the computer sits idle during this time while the user spends several minutes reading the screen. Only after this period of time will the user proceed on to the race results page. Once the race results page is loaded, the user must wait a couple minutes as the large photographs are downloaded from the server. Then he can view the final results page.

The user's pattern of interaction in this instance is

1. View the welcome page (while the computer does nothing in the background)
2. Advance to the results page
3. Wait for the results page graphics to download
4. View the results page

The computer does nothing in the background, which means that as the user is viewing the page, nothing else is really going on in that user's computer. A more efficient Web page would take advantage of the time the user spends reading the first page to have the computer start downloading some of the graphics that will be needed for the next page. The graphics can be downloaded without the user even realizing that the download is taking place. It happens automatically and transparently to the user as he reads the first page. Once he proceeds to the second page, the graphics are already available locally. The user experiences no wait; he can start viewing the second page immediately. This new model of interaction is

1. View the welcome page (while the computer downloads the next page's graphics in the background)
2. Advance to the results page
3. View the results page immediately

Obviously, the second approach is much nicer for the user. So how do you make it happen? The ActiveX preload control makes it possible. The preload control lets you specify the URL location of an image file to download and allows you to tell the control when you want that download to occur. The preload control is added to a page by including its object declaration, just as the objects from Day 10, "An Introduction to Objects and ActiveX Controls," were added. The declaration to add a `preload` control object named `preGif` is shown in Listing 18.1.

Listing 18.1. The declaration for a `preload` control that downloads a GIF file.

```
<OBJECT

ID=preGif
classID="clsID:16E349E0-702C-11CF-A3A9-00A0C9034920"
width=1
height=1
>
<PARAM NAME="URL" value="massive.gif">
<PARAM NAME="enable" value="0">
</OBJECT>
```

ANALYSIS This control will never be seen by the user. A `preload` control is not visible on the page. It goes about doing its work out of sight. It has two object attributes that are of significance—`classID` and `ID`. The `classID` identifies this object definition as that of a `preload` control. The `ID` assigns a name to this `preload` control that you can refer to from your code.

NOTE Currently `classID` is identified in terms of a rather cryptic-looking number. You can expect to eventually be able to identify a `classID` by a classname instead. Check the book update pages, described in Appendix B, "Information Resources," for an up-to-date summary of this and any other enhancements as VBScript, ActiveX, and Browser technology evolve.

Next comes the list of parameters, which are essentially properties of the `preload` control. There are two main properties you must be concerned with. The first is the URL property. This property identifies the file that is to be downloaded. If you have an image file contained in the same directory as the main page itself, for example, you simply supply the filename in the URL parameter. If the file to be downloaded resides at a different server location, you can specify the full URL name.

The next property is the `enable` property. This property controls when the download starts. When `enable` is set to 1, the download will commence. When it is set to 0, no download occurs. You can use the `preload` control by itself, without any code, by taking advantage of this property. To do this, you would simply include the control declaration in your HTML source code and set the `enable` property to 1. Then as soon as the page is loaded, the control will begin downloading the desired file.

Alternatively, you can write your code to turn on the download at some specific point. You might do this if the user is at a page where he is not likely to proceed further, and you have provided a button for the user to indicate his intentions in advance if he will continue. Then all your users don't have to have the download happen; just those who request it. In response to a button click, for example, code could set the `enable` property to 1 to cause the download to begin. An example of such code is shown in Listing 18.2.

Listing 18.2. Starting the download by turning on the `enable` property.

```
Sub cmdPreload
    ' The user clicked this button to indicate they plan to continue
    ' on to the next pages when they are done reading this page,
    ' so start downloading the next page graphic now.
    preGif.enable = 1
end Sub
```

ANALYSIS   The `preload` control downloads data in anticipation of a user proceeding to a subsequent page that uses the data. As the user views the page, the download continues. The only sound the user might notice while viewing the original page is the occasional hit on his hard disk as the data downloads. At some point, the user will likely click on the link that advances him to the next page. When he gets to that next page, the data is already available. At least some of the data for the page will already be cached, and the user will be able to view the page more quickly. This approach has the most user impact for larger files. The bigger the file, the better it is to shield the user from the load time.

NOTE   It's very important to note that the `preload` technique applies to any kind of file that's included as part of a Web page. You can `preload` audio files, movie clips, or VRML files, as well as images. As a matter of fact, the benefits of preloading these other file types are potentially more noticeable, because they tend to be larger. For the sake of simple, clear examples, this lesson focuses primarily on using the control with image files.

Setting `enable` on (to 1) in code or in the object definition raises some interesting considerations. You could always start the background download for the next page as soon as the user loads the current page. Of course, there is no guarantee that the user will proceed to the next page. As a matter of fact, he may back up or select a hypertext link to a different page. Then the graphics download was wasted effort; it was never needed at all. How costly is this wasted effort? Most likely, the user will never know the difference. But on the other hand, a download is extra work for the system. That means if the user stops viewing the current page and tries to carry out some other task on his system, part of the computer's resources are already occupied on a download that the user couldn't care less about.

So although the user won't usually notice the difference, he could. And he might not appreciate a lot of unnecessary preloads. He might even view it as downright impolite. Alternatively, you could force the user to click on a button at the start of the page to indicate whether he thinks he will continue to subsequent pages. That way, you need only turn on preloading for users who stand to benefit from it. Once again, though, you run the risk of imposing on the user a bit. Clicking on a preload button is an extra step. And for less experienced users, who might be unclear on the concept of downloads and separate image files, it may even be a very confusing step.

The best solution, however, can be implemented only with certain types of pages. Suppose you have a page that has lots of interaction with the user. Information is collected through input controls and buttons, and feedback is provided through labels, message boxes, input boxes, graphs, or other means. Based on the level of interaction, a script can ideally assume at some point that the user will continue to further pages. For example, assume that a page lets a user price different car package options. If the user tries several packages, the script could assume that the user will likely view a linked page that shows what that car line looks like. The script could trigger the preload of the images for that page in the same event that prices a package. The next page image, which the user probably will proceed to, starts to get downloaded even as the user continues to price his options. He's none the wiser that the download has started. When he proceeds to the link to view the car a couple minutes later, he marvels at how quickly the page, laden with snazzy images of the car, pops up on the screen.

Unfortunately, the ideal cases don't present themselves very often. When you use the `preload` control, you generally must make a subjective choice about the best time to start the preload. There are no right or wrong answers; rather, the answer depends largely on the type of page and its expected usage flow.

Since so much of a user's time is spent waiting for images to load, it is probably better to overuse than underuse this control. If a graphic image was already previously downloaded to the user's computer during the session, it will simply be pulled from the browser cache (temporary local storage) rather than pulled across the network.

It is often helpful to know when a preloaded image is completely downloaded. That way, you can give the user a visual cue that the next page is ready, or perhaps initiate another in a series of image downloads. Fortunately, the `preload` control provides an event for just such a

18

purpose. A `Complete` event is generated after an image download finishes. You can supply code to deal with a `Complete` event just as you have for other events covered earlier in this book. You simply define a procedure with a special name. That name consists of the control name, followed by an underscore, and then the event name. The event procedure for the `preload` control, which was defined in Listing 18.1, is shown in Listing 18.3.

Listing 18.3. The `Complete` event for the `preload` control.

```
sub preGif_Complete
    MsgBox "Graphics for the next page are downloaded.",_
        vbOkOnly + vbInformation, "Next page ready"
end sub
```

Another event that can be generated by the `preload` control is the `Error` event. The `Error` event will occur when certain types of error situations arise. Your script can use this event to let the user know that problems have occurred during a download. A script could even perform some types of error recovery, such as linking the user to a different page when an error occurs. (This can be done with `Location.URL`, which you'll learn more about later today). An example of the error event is shown in Listing 18.4.

Listing 18.4. The `Error` event for the `preload` control.

```
sub preGif_Error
    MsgBox "An error occurred downloading graphics for the next page. ",_
        vbOkOnly + vbInformation, "Next page not ready"
end sub
```

The `preload` control provides one method that may be of use. It is the `AboutBox` method, which is supported by most of the other ActiveX controls. You can use this to provide the user with a way to verify the version of the control he is using. For example, the code in Listing 18.5 could be associated with a command button. It calls the `AboutBox` method to allow a user to verify his current control level.

Listing 18.5. The `AboutBox` method for the `preload` control.

```
sub cmdVersionCheck
    ' Let the user see the details on this control
    preGif.AboutBox
end sub
```

18

Caching Considerations When Using `preload`

When you use `preload`, you may have a difficult time convincing yourself of its benefits. This is because a browser's caching does such a good job that it can fool you into thinking your downloads are nearly instantaneous. Browser caching means that your browser stores pages and the files those pages require in temporary locations on your hard drive when a page is first loaded. When you return to that page later, the necessary files can be directly reused, rather than downloaded across the network. If you're testing the `preload` control, keep this caching aspect in mind. Caches can be emptied to force a load across the network. However, make sure you fully understand all your cache options before attempting to empty it, and remember that the user of your page will enjoy these caching benefits as well. However, `preload` may not be providing as big a benefit as you imagine on frequently used pages. The big advantage of `preload` is on first-time page loads. Then, depending on a user's browser cache settings, he may be reloading the file from cache rather than across the network anyway.

Putting `preload` to Work in Your Script

All you need to do to use `preload` is insert the `preload` object in your script, assign a file to the URL of the control, and turn its `Enabled` property on. Then you need a secondary page that uses the file loaded on the first page. Today's workshop provides an example of how to use `preload`. Figure 18.1 shows the first page that puts `preload` to work.

Figure 18.1.

The first page of a preload sequence (from today's workshop).

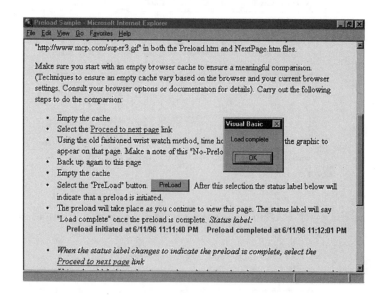

Figure 18.2 shows the secondary page that has reduced load time because the image on the page is loaded when the first page is presented.

Figure 18.2.

The second page of a preload sequence (from today's workshop).

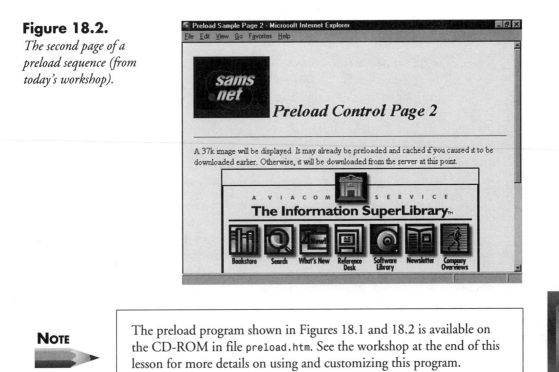

The preload program shown in Figures 18.1 and 18.2 is available on the CD-ROM in file `preload.htm`. See the workshop at the end of this lesson for more details on using and customizing this program.

18

Maintenance Considerations When Using `preload`

You can make your pages more impressive with `preload`. In the ideal world, images, audio files, and avi movie files can be waiting and ready to go as your user smoothly flows from one page to another. Your user perceives that he has better performance than ever, and it's all thanks to your insightful page and script authorship. But there are some downsides, too. When you use a preload to prepare data for a page yet to come, you are making an assumption about one page leading to another. As your pages are modified, it will take more effort to make sure this relationship is maintained. If the name of a preloaded file on the second page changes, it not only requires changing the HTML source code there, but will also require a change on the first page that preloads the graphics. Because there is no automatic indication of these types of relationships, more burden is placed on the author to ensure that such links are properly maintained. The polished, professional impression that can be conveyed through preloaded pages is worth the price. Just make sure you understand the pitfalls as well as the benefits, and you can put `preload` to work for your pages.

Anchor Clicks on Images and Text

It used to be that quite a bit was involved in making your page react to a user's clicks on an image. The page itself couldn't begin to deal with this situation. HTML had no native intelligence to support reacting to the clicks. Instead, it could send the click information back to the server if it knew that image was preplanned to be a *map*, having different regions for the user to click on. Once the information got back to the server, a map file was needed to help associate the clicked area with the corresponding action. This map file would tie the desired action to a script or resulting page. And finally, the end result page would make its way back across the network to be displayed in the user's browser.

Quite a lot of action and overhead resulted from one little click! Then along came VBScript. VBScript can still provide the action, but eliminates the overhead. You can provide a *smart page* that reacts to clicks without leaning on a server across the network. As a matter of fact, you can even do more! You can write code that reacts to mere movements of the mouse even without clicks. And when the clicks do occur, you can redirect the destination link through your script. All you need is the VBScript image click, `MouseMove` events, and the code you write to go with them.

The magic that lets you get this degree of control is the ability to reference an anchor object. An *anchor* is indicated by the `<A>` tag and allows you to specify a hypertext link for the entity that follows the tag. You can supply an anchor to an image or a text string. Then, when the user clicks on that image or text string, the referenced page is loaded into the browser. This hypothetical anchor, for example, links the user to a page called `Suds.htm` when the user clicks on the graphic `EmptyStein.gif`:

```
<A HREF="suds.htm"> <IMG SRC="EmptyStein.gif"></A>
```

This anchor carries out the same link when the user clicks on the text string `Tell me more`:

```
<A HREF="suds.htm"> Tell me more!</A>
```

The Anchor ID

You can associate an ID with the anchor link. The ID allows you to do a wonderful thing: reference the anchor from your source code! More specifically, it lets you reference anchor events. If you have a named anchor link and you supply appropriately named procedures in your code, your script can deal with two very important anchor-link events—the `MouseMove` and the `Click`.

First, take a look at the following example of providing an ID for an anchor. This is an example of an image anchor for which an ID has been provided. The name, in this case, is `lnkPicture`:

```
<A ID="lnkPicture" HREF="../shared/vbperf.htm">
<IMG SRC="../shared/jpg/picture.jpg" WIDTH=450 HEIGHT=300 BORDER=20></A>
```

18

The following lines show a text anchor that links to an image. The anchor associated with the image is named lnkText:

```
<A ID=lnkText HREF="../shared/jpg/picture.jpg">
Note: You can detect mouse moves on text links like this one too!</A>
```

The Anchor MouseMove Event

Once you have an ID for an anchor, you just have to supply the event procedure in your script using the normal event procedure naming approach. The first part of the name is the anchor ID, then an underscore, and then the event you want to handle in the script. MouseMove is one event that the anchor generates. This event is triggered any time the user moves the mouse over an anchored area, regardless of whether it's a text anchor or an image anchor. When the MouseMove event occurs, it passes the current x and y coordinates of the mouse into the procedure as well. It is up to you to decide what to do within your script routine if you handle this event. Listing 18.6 shows an example of a script procedure that handles a MouseMove event for the lnkPicture anchor.

Listing 18.6. The MouseMove event procedure for an image anchor.

```
Sub lnkPicture_MouseMove(shift, button, x, y)
' This event is called whenever the mouse moves over the linked image to
'     generate a new label caption depending where the mouse moves.

    ' Remember the last position moved to, so we can see where we are if
    '    a click occurs. (The click event doesn't get passed x/y values)
    s_CurrentX = x
    s_CurrentY = y

    ' Check to see if mouse has moved into hot zone on the picture
    If InZone(x, y,  205, 199, 253, 250) Then
        ' The mouse is on the book
        lblWeSay.caption = "This is recommended reading for serious VB_
                            programmers."

    elseIf InZone(x, y,  154, 111, 169, 118) Then
        ' The mouse is on Tim's mouth
        lblWeSay.caption = "Hi, I'm Tim. I like tennis, cockatiels, " & _
            " and integrating components with VB, the nastier the better."

    elseIf InZone(x, y,  304, 126, 320, 130) Then
        ' The mouse is on Keith's mouth
        lblWeSay.caption = "Howdy, I'm Keith. I enjoy running on trails, " &_
            " going to the park with the kids, and writing VB programs at 4AM."

    Else
        lblWeSay.caption = ""
    End If
End Sub
```

18

NOTE

The anchor `MouseMove` event currently passes four parameters to the subroutine that is defined for it: a shift indicator, a button indicator, the x position, and the y position. You have seen how the x and y positions are used. At the time of this writing, the shift and button parameters were not fully supported. A `1` is always returned in the shift parameter, and a `0` is always returned in the button parameter. You may want to check the Microsoft Web site at `www.microsoft.com/intdev` to check if this support is added down the road.

The x and y coordinates that are passed to the event routine indicate the position of the mouse *within* the anchor area. The leftmost side will be `0` for the x value, and x values will increase to the right. The top of the anchor area will be `0` for the y value, and y values will increase from top to bottom. Figure 18.3 shows the x and y values for various areas of an image of two disheveled programmers.

Figure 18.3.

x and y values, as interpreted by anchor event.

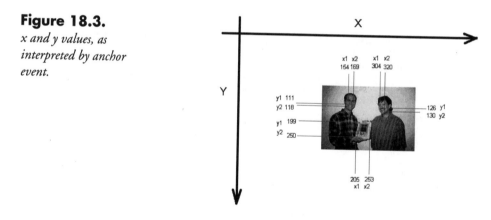

In the code in Listing 18.6, the x and y values are stored in a global-scope variable. This is because the anchor's `Click` event, which is considered next, does not receive any x and y parameter information with it. So by always remembering the last place the mouse has moved in a global variable, other areas of the code, such as the anchor `Click` event, know exactly where the mouse is when they are called.

Another interesting aspect of handling x and y values is the way you can use them to determine exactly which area of an image the mouse is on. The code in Listing 18.6 is carrying out checks to see if the mouse is over specific areas of the picture. The corresponding Web page is shown in Figure 18.4.

Figure 18.4.

A Web page with a script that processes anchor `MouseMove` *and* `Click` *events.*

NOTE

The program shown in Figure 18.4 is available on the CD-ROM in file `mousetrk.htm`.

18

This Web page displays one message in a label control if the user's mouse moves over the book in the picture. It displays a different message in the label if the mouse moves over the mouth of either of the disheveled programmers. If the mouse moves onto any other area of the image, the label will be blanked out so no message is displayed. The code in Listing 18.6 makes this logic pretty clear. A series of checks is carried out to see where the mouse currently is with respect to the predefined zones of the book or the mouths. The zones are outlined in Figure 18.3.

NOTE

If you are laying out your own anchor image handling and need to identify the edges of your boundaries, just use code like that of Listing 18.6. When the mouse is clicked anywhere on the anchor image, a message box pops up, giving the x and y coordinate. If you click on the two opposite corners of a desired zone and note the x and y positions, that is all you need to define your zone.

A function call is used to determine whether the current x and y values fall within a specific zone. The function call accepts a parameter for the current x and y position, as well as the x and y pairs for the upper-left and lower-right corners of the zone. The definition for this function, called InZone, is shown in Listing 18.7.

Listing 18.7. The InZone function.

```
Function InZone(CurrentX, CurrentY, rx1, ry1, rx2, ry2)
' This function returns true if the supplied Current x/y parameters are within
'    the box defined by parameters rx1, ry1, rx2, ry2

    If (CurrentX>=rx1) AND (CurrentX<=rx2) AND (CurrentY>=ry1) AND _
        (CurrentY<=ry2) then
            ' It's in the box
            InZone = vbTrue
        else
            ' It's not in the box
            InZone = vbFalse
        end if

End Function
```

ANALYSIS   With the MouseMove event in this function, you can provide the user with any type of feedback in response to any area of the image. You could, for example, display a state map and provide the name of any county that the mouse moved over. You could display a picture of your old broomball team, and display the name of each player the mouse moved over. The possibilities are many. And if you're a seasoned Web page author, you'll appreciate the fact that you can provide this feedback with only local script processing. No server intervention is required.

The Anchor Click Event

The anchor Click event is generally the one that triggers heavy-duty action. Regardless of what you do in the event procedure you supply, the browser will react to the click on a link. After your event procedure completes in reaction to a click, the browser will load a linked page in response to an anchor click.

You define the OnClick event procedure in your script with the ID of the anchor, an underscore, and then OnClick. Listing 18.8 shows the OnClick event for the anchored image of the disheveled programmers.

18

Listing 18.8. The `OnClick` event procedure for an anchored image.

```
Sub lnkPicture_OnClick
' This event is called whenever a click occurs on the image.
'    It will link to a different page depending on where the click was.

        ' Show the user where the click was first.
        msgbox "You clicked at X position " & s_Currentx & " & _
                " and Y position " & s_Currenty, 0, "Image Click Feedback"

        ' The link has a target destination supplied in the <A> tag, but change
        '      to the Macmillan Publishing destination if the book area was_
               clicked on.
        '      Otherwise the default location will be used.
        If InZone(s_CurrentX, s_CurrentY, 205, 199, 253, 250) Then
              location.href = "http://www.mcp.com"
        End If
End Sub
```

ANALYSIS   When the `Click` event occurs, a message box is generated to show the x and y position of the click. This makes use of the x and y values that were preserved from the most recent `MouseMove` on the image. This will always indicate the click position, since the mouse must be at the last place that was dealt with in the `MouseMove` event. If the mouse had been moved after that event, another `MouseMove` event would have occurred and caused the global x and y values to be modified again. The most recent values are therefore guaranteed to be current.

Redirecting a Link to Another Location

The last portion of the code in Listing 18.8 illustrates one of the most useful anchor interactions. This is the ability to implement an image map on an anchored image, to process mouse clicks and to redirect subsequent page links right from your code. Most users are accustomed to interacting with large image maps, where they can click on different areas of an image to select a link to another page. This has traditionally required server-side communication, maps, and scripts to derive which region of an image the click was indicating. As the example shows, that ability is now available from within a script. All that's needed to round out the image map model is the means to cause a specified link to take place. And that capability is provided by the `location.href` property.

The location entity can be thought of as an intrinsic document-level object. No special action is required to define it. The HREF parameter of the object specifies the URL of the link. Assume that you have specified an HREF attribute within <A> tags. When you click on an anchored image, this attribute is the target destination unless, that is, this target destination is overridden by the `Click` event handler for the anchored image. The `Click` event takes place after the user clicks on the anchored image but before the browser attempts to load the associated URL indicated in the HREF attribute. Therefore, the event handler is executed during a brief window of time in which the URL can be reassigned before the browser reacts and loads the next page. The event handler can modify the anchors HREF attribute by setting location.href to some other URL.

The sample in Listing 18.8 illustrates this approach. When the Click event occurs, a check is made to see if the click was within the area of the book that the disheveled programmers are holding. If the click was within this zone, then location.href is reassigned to be http://www.mcp.com. The browser will load this page, which is the Macmillan Computer Publishing home page. On the other hand, if the click did not fall within this zone, no assignments are made to location.href. In this case, the HREF attribute is still the same value that was specified in the original HTML for the anchor:

```
<A ID="lnkPicture" HREF="../shared/vbperf.htm">
<IMG SRC="../shared/jpg/picture.jpg" WIDTH=450 HEIGHT=300 BORDER=20></A>
```

So if the HREF attribute is not overridden by the event-handling procedure, the browser will proceed normally and load the page associated with the anchor. The ../shared/vbperf.htm page would be loaded in response to such a click.

Since you can assign location.href from your code before an anchored link takes place, you have the ability to specify a link dynamically. Your code can make a decision on where to link to after the user clicks on a page. This decision and subsequent redirection can occur without any intervention from the server.

There are many reasons you might want to control a link location from your script. Perhaps you want to direct the link based on values supplied in other fields on a page. For example, assume you have a clothing store page and a user indicates through a radio button choice that he prefers spring fashions. Then you can link him to the spring fashion page rather than the winter fashion page when he clicks on the Sales Info part of an image. Or maybe you author a page for a convention center. Your welcome page provides a general overview of the facility. But if the user clicks on the hypertext link Today's Meetings, you could present different information based on the time of day. If your script detects that it is early morning, you might link to a page of morning activities. And if it detects it is afternoon, you can link to the afternoon page. Of course, you'd want to give all users some way to see all activities, as well, but this could be handled by an additional link.

Another possibility is related to the preload control discussed earlier. You can define an anchor link over an image to go to a subsequent page. The HREF link target for the image is initially specified as a nonexistent location. As soon as the user moves the mouse over that image, the script event procedure can start the preload control's downloading of the relevant file. The script's preload control Complete event can set a global variable to indicate that the preload has finished. When the user clicks on the image, the code Click event handler can check the global variable to see if the required graphic for the next page is fully loaded. If it is, the link can be assigned to `location.href` and the preload can complete. If it is not, no valid link is provided, and the user receives a message telling him that the next page is not yet ready to be viewed. This may not be a standard technique you'd want to apply to every page. But in certain situations, such as a textbook page with a link that leads to a sample page with a large audio file, this technique could make for a much more pleasant user experience. The user won't be confronted with viewing a page that is not yet able to do anything for him.

Directly Linking to Another Location

So far, the focus has been on redirecting links. But what is actually going on is a little different. When you set `location.href`, you cause that link to take place and that page to be loaded. It doesn't matter if you do it in response to an anchor click or just in response to a plain old command button click with no relation to an anchor at all. When you tell it to happen, that page will be loaded. Listing 18.9 shows code that loads a page from the `Click` event of a button.

Listing 18.9. Directly linking to another location.

```
sub cmdK_Onclick
    location.href = "http://www.mcp.com"
end sub
```

An infinite range of possibilities is opened by this capability. You can cause another page to load in response to anything, from anywhere in your code! Since VBScript gives you access to the events of an anchor and provides an object to direct its link, you have full control over the flow of pages based on the current conditions of a page. As a matter of fact, you can control the progression of pages even outside an anchor. No difficult server code or customized browser is required. Your pages can become as smart and responsive as you care to make them.

Browser Objects

In this book's first 17 days of learning about what you can do with VBScript, the focus has been on two different layers. One is the core capabilities of the VBScript language. This consists of aspects of the language itself. For example, language keywords such as `if` and `dim` are supported directly by the VBScript interpreter. This language will be consistent whether you use VBScript hosted in the Internet Explorer browser, in some other browser, in the Internet server, or even in some application that supports VBScript not related at all to the Web. Then the focus turned looked at objects defined externally to the browser, including ActiveX controls. Objects can be controlled by VBScript because the host environment makes it possible. Support in the Internet Explorer browser and its interface with the VBScript interpreter lays the framework for letting your VBScript access such objects. If you use VBScript in another host environment such as a different browser or a non-Web-related application, it may very well provide the same support. On the other hand, it may not. There is no requirement in the VBScript language definition that dictates that every host must provide this capability.

Clearly, the host environment makes a difference in what you can do with VBScript. There is one more area yet to consider: objects the host itself exposes. You have already seen many such objects today, including the location and document objects. The Internet Explorer, which is the host primarily focused on in this book, provides VBScript with access to information about itself and with interfaces to control its own behavior through objects such as the document object. These capabilities relate to different ways the browser handles information and provides support for generating and viewing that information. The Internet Explorer provides access to this browser information by making available several intrinsic browser objects. This is not a unique concept. Other browsers such as Netscape Navigator expose a range of objects to JavaScript. For the most part the objects exposed by Microsoft Internet Explorer to JavaScript and VBScript are the same as those exposed to JavaScript by other browsers. This means that intrinsic objects in scripting are likely to be very consistent from browser to browser. However, it is important to realize that the intrinsic objects exposed by the browser are not an inherent part of the VBScript language. If you work with VBScript hosted in other environments, these objects may not be available to you, but if you're in another browser host, odds are they will be.

The real power of VBScript is its ability to integrate objects and easily script together solutions around these building blocks. In that respect, it is very important to realize which objects are available for you to use from the browser. These can become an important part of your scripting arsenal and lead to more powerful pages for your end user.

Objects exposed by the Internet Explore browser consist of the window object, the document object, the element object, the frame object, the history object, the frame object, the script object, the anchor object, the element object, the form object, and the navigator object. With these objects you can do many things. From your code you can link to other pages. You can detect the version of the browser that is being used. You can respond to mouse movements and clicks on link areas. You can work with the browser history list. You can even find out the name of the referring page for the current page. In other words, you can tell the page that your user visited before he linked to the page that contains you VBScript. You can also use these objects to provide control over multiple frames from your code. The following script statement, for example, could reside in a script in a currently displayed frame page and update the contents of another visible frame:

```
parent.frames(1).document.writeln "<HTML><BODY><h2> You can " & _
 generate HTML to a page!</h2></BODY></HTML>"
Parent.frames(1).document.close
```

NOTE

> A frame is an independent HTML window created through the <FRAMESET> and <FRAME> tags. You can find more details on frames from any HTML reference, including Microsoft's online documentation at www.microsoft.com/intdev. The parent keyword references the parent window of the current frame. That window contains a collection of all existing frames created underneath it. The first is referenced as parent.frames(0) and the second as parent.frames(1). The document keyword indicates the document object belonging to that frame. Writeln is a method of the document object that you can use to generate HTML content to a page, and close is a method used to conclude the document changes.

The possibilities are limitless. A good representative summary of these intrinsic browser objects appears in the sample program Browser.htm on the CD-ROM. This page includes samples of script control between frames and various ways to advance from one page to another and determine information ranging from the browser version to the last date that a page changed. A table of some of the key properties and methods of the browser objects appears on this page. Browser.htm will serve as a good initial reference point to the browser objects for you. A detailed discussion of all the objects would be very lengthy, given the range of capabilities. Refer to Microsoft's documentation for the comprehensive documentation. However, the samples you have seen so far today, as well as the samples you can inspect in Browser.htm, should be enough to get you off to a good start on creating your own sophisticated scripts.

Summary

Today you have examined ways to provide what have been coined "smart pages." These pages use special scripting so that they can preload files for subsequent pages and respond to mouse movements and clicks on anchored images. A script can even select links based on dynamic conditions of the page when an anchored link is selected.

The ActiveX preload control provides the means to preload files. Preloading a file for a subsequent page can take place in the background while a user views a current page. Then, when the user moves to the subsequent page, he will not have to wait for that file to be downloaded from the server. The preload control can start loading a file in advance for a subsequent page as soon as a parent page is loaded. On the other hand, it can be declared through its object definition so that it doesn't start preloading the file until code triggers it. A script can make decisions on whether to preload a file based on the user's other interactions. In cases where a preload occurs, the user will have the perception of better performance. The `preload` control even provides a complete event so a script can detect when the download of a file is complete and notify the user that the next page is ready.

Another aspect of pages that you can easily control through VBScript is the anchor. The anchor defined through HTML can be specified with an ID attribute. This name is then used in VBScript to refer to events of the anchor. The `MouseMove` event occurs whenever the mouse moves over the anchored image or text. The `MouseMove` event is accompanied by parameters that provide the current x,y location of the mouse. These parameters can be used directly or stored for later reference by the `Click` event. The `Click` event occurs whenever the anchor is clicked on. The `Click` event is not provided with any parameter information. `Click` event code that needs to make decisions based on the current mouse position can do so by looking at the mouse position last stored by the `MouseMove` event.

One of the important features of the anchor control in VBScript is that you can override an anchor's target link from code. You do this by setting the `location.href` property. The URL specified in `location.href` is the page that the browser will load. A script doesn't even have to react to an anchor event to do this. The `location.href` property can be set from anywhere in the code and will cause the specified link to take place. So you can build your own links anytime, anywhere, for any reason, in your scripts!

All these capabilities add up to provide a very high degree of control over the most important aspects of pages—links, anchors, and associated files. Links let you control the flow of pages. A file is anything an anchor points to, such as an image, an audio file, or a subsequent HTML page. You can load server files, link files, and respond to user interaction with anchors and file links. Smart pages that do more for the user, without any server intervention, are the end result.

Q&A

Q **What code statement would you use to start the download of an audio file from a `preload` control named `preKeithsYodeling`?**

A `preKeithsYodeling.enable = 1`

Q **Can the anchor `MouseMove` event be used just with image links, and not text links?**

A No, you can use it to track text-link mouse movements as well.

Q **As the mouse moves around in an anchored image, does just one `MouseMove` event occur, or do many?**

A Many `MouseMove` events occur. The `MouseMove` event is generated every time a mouse movement is detected, so as you move the mouse around in an image, a series of calls to it will be made.

Q What if I want to write code that changes the caption of a label just the first time the mouse moves across an image, but I don't want to update it over and over?

A Use a static variable to keep track of how many times the event procedure has been called. Check the value each time the event is called. The first time through, when this variable is 0, set the caption. If the value is not 0, it has already been set in a previous call, so no action is required.

Q What attribute do you use to name an anchor so your code can reference it?

A The ID attribute, which is specified within the anchor <A> tag.

Q Can I set location.href from a regular procedure, or does it have to be within an anchor-related procedure?

A You can set location.href from a regular procedure. No anchor association is required. This means you can cause another page to be loaded anywhere in your script.

Workshop

Compare how long it takes a page to load normally with the time required to preload the main graphic file using the ActiveX preload control. Use the preload.htm and nextpage.htm files that are on the CD-ROM that accompanies this book. The pages generated by these files are shown in Figures 18.1 and 18.2.

Customize this solution to work with your own graphic. These files reference the graphic image http://www.mcp.com/super3.gif. Replace all occurrences of this file reference in both files to reference your graphic image instead. Use the largest file possible to make the preload and no-preload differences stand out.

Instructions for carrying out the comparison of preload and no preload appear on the page displayed by preload.htm. Study the script events from the preload.htm listing in Listing 18.10 before viewing the page. Then, when you view the page, see if you can mentally match up the page feedback to the events you examined.

Listing 18.10. preload.htm source code.

```
<SCRIPT LANGUAGE="VBS">
<!--
sub cmdPreLoad_OnClick
    lblStatus.caption = "Preload initiated at " & now
    preGif.enable = 1
end sub
```

continues

Listing 18.10. continued

```
sub PreGif_Complete
    lblStatus.caption = lblStatus.caption & "     Preload completed at " & now
    msgbox "Load complete"
end sub

sub PreGif_Error
    msgbox "Error detected"
end sub

sub cmdCheck_OnClick
    msgbox preGif.enable
    preGif.AboutBox
end sub
-->
</SCRIPT>


<!-- --------------- Preload Control -------------------------->
<OBJECT
ID=preGif
classID="clsID:{16E349E0-702C-11CF-A3A9-00A0C9034920}"
width=1
height=1
>
<PARAM NAME="_extentX" value="1">
<PARAM NAME="_extentY" value="1">
<PARAM NAME="URL" value="http://www.mcp.com/super3.gif">
<PARAM NAME="enable" value="0">
</OBJECT>
```

Quiz

NOTE

Refer to Appendix C, "Answers to Quiz Questions," for the answers to these questions.

1. Assume that you have an anchor declaration such as the following:

   ```
   <A HREF="http://www.mcp.com" ID=lnkBooks>
   <IMG  ALIGN=BOTTOM SRC="../shared/jpg/samsnet.jpg" BORDER=2></A>
   ```

   Show the name of the declaration that would be required to handle the Click event for this anchor.

18

2. Show the anchor declaration that would be required to handle the `MouseMove` event for this anchor:

```
<A HREF="http://www.mcp.com" ID=lnkBooks>
<IMG  ALIGN=BOTTOM SRC="../shared/jpg/samsnet.jpg" BORDER=2></A>
```

Be sure to include parameters.

3. Show the statement you would need to add to the `Click` event in the answer to question 1 to redirect the link. You want the link to proceed to page `http://www.microsoft.com/vbscript`.

Day 19

Dynamic Page Flow and Server Submittal

So far, the discussion of VBScript has focused solely on the scripts that relate to the page running on the client computer without much regard to the Web server. The server has another role that goes beyond just downloading pages or components. VBScript code in a page can, in some cases, certainly affect what happens on the server. Understanding this role can be just as important to deploying full-fledged active Web page solutions as understanding VBScript fundamentals. Client-side validation of server-bound data and server-side application processing in response to that data is the topic of the second half of today's lesson.

The pages that are downloaded from a server to your client computer often are intended to serve simply as front ends for collecting data. The data is then provided to the server for storage or subsequent processing. It might seem at first that VBScript is just a periphery player in the server-side communication because so far, this book has focused on how you can use VBScript for stand-alone pages independent of the server. However, VBScript can serve as the basis of the front end for data validation and final submittal of the data to the server to ensure clean data and thereby enhance server performance.

Today's lesson will cover the server front-end and back-end arrangements in enough detail that you understand all the issues involved. You will see how to validate form data in your script and how to initiate the submission of form data to a server within your script. You will probably encounter your own situations where you will need to write scripts that interact with the server. Today's lesson will show you how to do it successfully with an awareness of the big picture.

The Advantage of Validating Server-Bound Data

For some time, HTML has had a model for collecting data on a page and submitting it to a server. Although that model is evolving with the help of technologies such as VBScript, the concepts are still much the same. Input control fields collect data from the user. Two specific HTML definitions are required for the page to submit that data to a program on the server. The input controls must be defined within a form so that the data from them can be submitted together as one data set. Some specific action must trigger the submittal, which is accomplished through an input control that is similar to a regular command button but has a type of submit.

Consider the form definition further. When the data is provided to the server, the server must be able to tell which program to submit that data to. After all, the server can't just assume the data should be added to a database or saved in a file or ignored. That is why the form tag has an ACTION attribute, which specifies the program on the server that processes the input from the client. These server-side programs that process page data in the past have commonly been called *scripts*. In addition, the form tag definition sets a method attribute to indicate how the information should be passed from the client back to the server.

All the details of this interaction are beyond the scope of this book, but it is important to have a feel for some of the technologies involved. In the past, the primary protocol for supplying data back to the server and launching a script was *CGI*, or Common Gateway Interface. This is still in broad use today. In addition, another technology called *ISAPI*, or Internet Server Application Program Interface, is rapidly emerging. This approach can be much faster than CGI on Windows systems because an ISAPI-launched program works in the same address space as server software. What this really means is that it can be significantly faster. A related technology called *IDC*, or Internet database connectivity, can even result in direct database interaction through the use of a template file.

NOTE

You can also use VBScript on NT Server with the Internet Information Server Web server software. The focus of this book is illustrating its use through the browser, so this topic is not considered in detail here. However, the same VBScript core syntax rules and language fundamentals that we have covered here apply in that environment as well.

Although there are technical differences in the way these approaches are implemented, the concept is the same from the standpoint of your page and your code. When the user clicks a submit button on the form, the browser submits all the input fields on the form as well as the action parameter back to the server. The server activates the specified application and provides the field names from the form and their associated data to it as well.

It is then up to the application to respond to the request. Typically, the CGI or ISAPI application on the server might store the information from the page into a database. It might also generate another page to download to the client. These tasks are accomplished with assistance from the Web server. Typically, the CGI or ISAPI application will generate one long string for a page. This string contains all the tags that make up the Web page to be sent to the client. The server takes care of passing that data through the HTTP protocol back to the client. All this interaction happens fairly transparently to the user. From the perspective of the end user, she supplies some data and submits it, and suddenly, another page appears.

Some examples can help illustrate the process and also lead to the specific way that VBScript comes into play. First consider Listing 19.1, which shows a simple form definition on a page.

Listing 19.1. Form definition.

```
<form name="frmOrder"
     action="/scripts/oleisapi.dll/Order.clsOrder.ProcessOrder" method="GET">
Your Name: <input name="txtName">
Street Address: <input name="txtAddress" >
City: <input name="txtCity">
State: <input name="txtState">
Zip: <input name="txtZip">

<input name="cmdOrder" value="Submit Order">
</form>
```

19

NOTE

Usually, the data in the form would be presented in a more visually attractive format, such as with each element placed in the cell of an HTML table. For the sake of simplicity, the example is shown without any of these frills.

ANALYSIS Note that a submit button is defined at the bottom of the form. When the user selects the submit button, the browser automatically submits the form to the server. No VBScript code or any kind of code is required to make this happen! This is part of the HTML form and submit element definition. The server will receive data that includes the string `/scripts/oleisapi.dll/Order.clsOrder.ProcessOrder`. Also appended to this string is other information about the contents of `txtName`, `txtAddress`, `txtCity`, `txtState`, `txtZip`, and the form method attribute. The string `/scripts/oleisapi.dll/Order.clsOrder.ProcessOrder` tells the server to pass this request to the ISAPI OLE automation director, `/scripts/oleisapi`. (OLE automation is a method of communicating that some applications, including those generated by Visual Basic 4.0, can respond to.)

`oleisapi` is actually a dynamic link library on the server system. `oleisapi` starts the requested program. It can locate the requested program because it is registered in the system registration database as an OLE automation server. `Order.clsOrder` specifies the DLL name and class of the program intended to handle this request. `ProcessOrder` specifies the method of this program that will be initiated. `oleisapi` initiates the `Order.clsOrder.ProcessOrder` method, passing it two important parameters. The first is the data from the Web page in one long string. The second parameter is used by `Order.clsOrder` to supply a return page that `oleisapi` will direct back to the server and subsequently back to the client.

NOTE

This discussion focuses on an NT Server Web server solution, but the general concepts will largely apply to other environments as well.

Listing 19.2 shows the code for the `Order.clsOrder.ProcessOrder` method. This is Visual Basic 4.0 code, not VBScript. I show it here because it gives you a good, representative idea of what a server-side application might do with data from a page.

Listing 19.2. A server application called in response to page form submittal.

```
Public ProcessOrder(strRequest as String, strResponse as String)
    Dim strName as String
    ' Extract the name from the data that came from the page
    strName = GetNameField (strRequest)
```

```
' See if a valid name was supplied
if len(strName) = 0 then
    ' Name is missing, can't process the order.
    '     Generate a page scolding the user
    strResponse = <html><head><h1>The name is missing!</h1>" & _
        </head><body><p>Please supply a valid name with the order!" & _
        </body></html>"
else
    ' Store order info from page in database
    StoreInDB (strRequest)
    '     Generate a page confirming to the user
    strResponse = <html><head><h1>Order Confirmation</h1>" & _
        </head><body><p>Thanks for placing the order with us!" & _
        </body></html>"
end if

'Add the standard header that is needed when sending new page from
'    the server to the browser to the front of the response string
    strResponse = "Content-Type: text/html" & vbCrLf & vbCrLf & strResponse
End Sub
```

ANALYSIS   The comments in this code segment provide a pretty good overview of what the code is doing. The code calls a user-defined procedure to return only the name field from all the string information that originated from the page. It makes a check to see if a name was supplied. If the name is missing, the code assigns to a string a series of HTML tags that make up the new pages. If the name is present, the order is stored in the database by calling a user-defined procedure. The page is built in a string with HTML tags thanking the user. Then the code adds a required header to the response string to indicate that HTML text format data is returned. The ProcessOrder method procedure then terminates, and the server returns the response string to the client. The client receives the new page, which came from an application-generated string rather than a file. Of course, the end user doesn't realize the difference; he just sees that a result page has arrived from his original query.

Consider the flow of this interaction when the user forgets to supply a name while specifying an order on the original Web page, as illustrated in Figure 19.1.

The request went all the way to the server, which then detected the missing name, so no data was saved. The response page went back to the user. There's a little bit of overhead, considering that nothing was saved in the database. The interaction involved the user's time, network communication, and server processing time, all for the end result of no change to the server database.

Now you can finally see an alternative implementation where VBScript comes to the rescue! Suppose that you define exactly the same form, but you add a block of code to the page, as shown in Listing 19.3.

19

Figure 19.1.

Server validation of bad input.

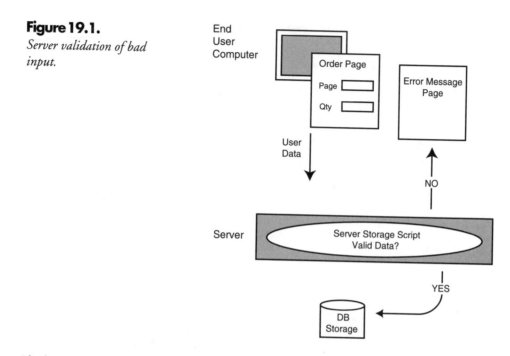

Listing 19.3. VBScript page-resident validation.

```
<script language="VBScript">
<!--
    sub cmdOrder_OnClick
    ' Submit order if the request is valid

    ' Make sure user has supplied name before submitting order to server
    if len(document.frmOrder.txtName) = 0 then
        ' No name was supplied, order won't be submitted
        MsgBox "You must supply a name.",vbOKOnly, "Can't submit order"
    else
        ' Order OK, submit it to server
        document.frmOrder.submit
        MsgBox "Order was submitted. Thanks.",vbOKOnly, "Confirmation"

    end if
    end sub
-->
</script>
```

ANALYSIS The comments in this code once again provide pretty full details on what transpires. If the text box string has a length of 0, no submittal takes place. How is that accomplished? You simply don't select the form's submit method. If you had no VBScript event handler, the browser would submit all data automatically. If you supply code for the Click event of a submit-type input button, the data is not submitted unless you explicitly call the form's submit method. You can see the use of this method in the `Else` branch of the conditional. If the name is present, the data is submitted. Once the form is submitted, the code executes the same process of launching the server application that was described earlier.

There are other ways to deal with the submittal as well. You could have declared the `cmdOrder` button to be a special HTML submit button by setting its type to `"TYPE=SUBMIT"` in the `<INPUT>` tag. Then when the user clicked on the button, the form would automatically be submitted. However, if you use such a submit button, you could also plug your own routine into the form's `OnSubmit` event before it is submitted:

```
<FORM ID="YourForm" LANGUAGE="VBScript" OnSubmit="YourVBFunction"
ACTION="serversidescript">
```

If you use such an event handler, you must set an event return code at the end of the event handler to tell the browser how to proceed. The language the browser expects is a string starting with `return`. So you'd end with `MyForm.OnSubmit = "return YourVBFunction()"`, for example. Your function would do the validation and return `True` if the submit were to proceed or `False` if it weren't. At the time this book was printed, the `OnSubmit` event was not yet fully supported.

Whichever way you implement the solution, the advantages gained through validation are great. The code in Listing 19.3 has done something very significant: It has eliminated the need for any server-side validation. The Visual Basic code that stores data in the database no longer needs to check whether a name exists. It will only be called if valid data was first verified by the VBScript code that resides at the client computer. This saves processing time on the server when the data is saved. You use fewer lines for error-checking code. Better yet, consider what happens when an error does occur. Before, you had communication from the client to the server, processing on the server, and communication from the server to the client just to generate an error message to the user. Now, all that occurs is the client-side processing by the VBScript code. That generates the error message directly. All the network traffic, not to mention the user wait for the network and the server-side processing, is completely eliminated!

Figure 19.2 shows the flow for this interaction. Compare Figures 19.1 and 19.2, and observe the difference in approaches. This is a very simple, scaled-down example of the advantages of placing the validation load on VBScript rather than the server. Even this simple example shows significant savings.

As you can see, even though VBScript performs the processing on the client, it can have a close association with any programs on the server that might process data from the page. VBScript can execute front-end validation processing before form data is submitted to the server. It can screen out bad data or modify questionable data before submitting it to the server. The front-end processing reduces server load, network load, and even user wait time in the event that the data is bad and it must generate a reply. When this happens, VBScript can provide feedback right away without the server program generating a response and sending it back.

19

Figure 19.2.

VBScript form validation flow.

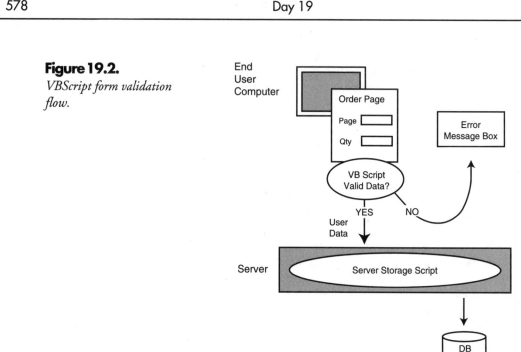

Of course, when you develop software in this manner, you must plan the scripts in conjunction with the server-side software. It does little good to have a script validate data if it's not validating it according to the right rules. Generally, this kind of in-sync planning of server application and script works out well because the server application must be planned in concert with the form anyway. VBScript can lead to a smoother performance from the entire server when you use it to perform the type of validation described here.

Reducing Traffic by Scripting Dynamic Pages

The previous example looked at eliminating overhead by avoiding the traffic in validating a page. Consider another kind of savings: What if you have a sequence of several pages the user must traverse in the process of collecting data? The traditional approach would be similar to Figure 19.3.

In this flow, each page leads to the other after it arrives at the server. The user must supply some data on each of three consecutive pages. The data for each page goes to the server, a server application saves the data to the database, and then the next page is generated and sent back to the user's client computer. This continues for each of the three pages. If the server finds errors during data validation, it must generate even more pages, and the flow shown in Figure 19.3 becomes even more complicated. To keep things simple, assume all data is okay for this discussion, but recognize that if there were data validation problems, the communications overhead would be even greater.

Figure 19.3.

A sequence of several pages with server interaction on each.

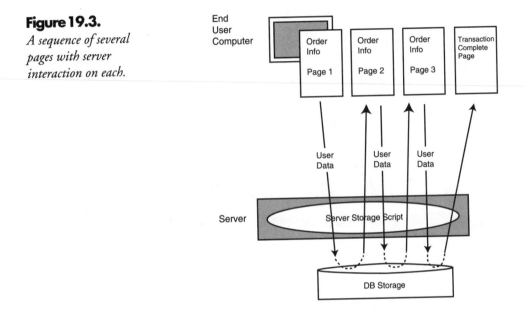

As you probably expected, VBScript provides a way to address this type of scenario and slice out the overhead, too. Figure 19.4 shows the flow you can achieve with VBScript.

Figure 19.4.

A sequence of one page due to VBScript validation and flow control on the original page.

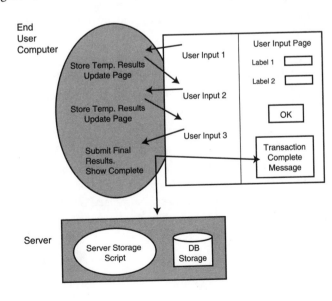

19

VBScript dynamically controls the flow with this approach. This requires some special thought about which controls to use on a page. For this example, assume that the user must supply two fields on each page. You define a page with two text box input controls contained within a form, each preceded by a label. The form also has a submit input button. In addition, you add a label at the top of the page.

The first page is loaded with all label captions set relative to the first page. The caption on the submit button is assigned to read Next Page. The user supplies data in two fields and clicks the Next Page button. Script logic in the OnClick event for the button now controls the segue to the next page. The heading label and the labels by each text box are filled with new text to simulate page 2. The information that the user supplied in the two text boxes is tucked away into two script scope variables so that the script can easily retrieve it in a short while. A count variable is updated to indicate the user is now on page 2.

Now, the user interacts with page two. She might even have the perception that a new page was downloaded—after all, it looks different! She supplies two more pieces of information and clicks Next Page. Again, the OnClick event makes everything possible. From the count variable, it is clear to the script that page 2 is being processed. The heading label and the labels by the text boxes are updated with new captions appropriate to page 2. The caption on the button is now changed from Next Page to Submit because all the data will be complete after the next click. The count variable is incremented. Again, the text box values are retrieved and stored in different script-level variables.

Finally, the user completes the third page. She enters the final two fields of data and clicks Submit. At this point, the code in the OnClick handler can tell that this is the last page to process because the count variable is now 3. After validating the data, the script submits the form by invoking the form's submit method and presents the user with a message box indicating this action.

The code must take one more action first before submitting the form. Did you notice it? After the user clicks Submit, the text boxes contain only two of the user's six responses. The rest are stored in variables, but input controls are the only easy way to communicate responses back to the server. No problem. You can use any format you want when supplying the form input fields. Use whatever convention the server-side application is expecting.

The VBScript code can do some data "massaging" or transforming to ensure that all the user's input takes the journey to the server. The VBScript code simply appends two of the variables onto each text field, separated by & for easy parsing. Each text field ends up containing the entries for three fields. Then the user selects Submit, and the data goes to the server. Listing 19.4 shows the code segment to handle this final page of the sequence.

Listing 19.4. Handling the final user input.

```
sub cmdOrder_OnClick
   static intPageMode

   ' Check to see what simulated page is being processed
   if intPageMode = 0
      '. . . code here to handle cases of other page modes
   elseif intPageMode = 3 then
      ' Last page, submit the data

      ' Consolidate data from prior pages so it all travels with form fields
         document.frmOrder.txtField1 = document.frmOrder.txtField1 & _
            "&" & varA & "&" varB
         document.frmOrder.txtField2 = document.frmOrder.txtField2 & _
            "&" & varC & "&" varD

         ' Submit the data to the server and tell user
         document.frmOrder.submit
         MsgBox "Your order has been submitted, thanks!", _
            vbOKOnly, "Confirmation"

         ' Now put the user back at page 1 in case they want to do
         '    another order
         intPageMode = 1
         ' Reset the labels that are beside the text boxes, and the button
         lblField1.caption = "FirstName:"
         lblField2.caption = "LastName:"
         document.frmOrder.cmdOrder.Value = "Next Page"
   end if
end sub
```

ANALYSIS   This example illustrates a very powerful concept. An interaction that would usually require several pages and involve considerable network time is reduced to just a single page. Instead of sending data to a server application three times in the process of making the order and causing three different database changes, the script makes only one submittal after the user has supplied all the data. The user's waiting time is drastically reduced. For any validation problems, feedback to the user is immediate. It's a complete and total victory over the old approach.

Well, almost total. The VBScript approach has a couple slight disadvantages, too. This approach does require additional script coding. The coding is not always really clean or clear if you're handling a large number of fields. Page aesthetics might suffer to some degree. It will be harder to dynamically simulate three drastically different pages unless they are generic in appearance.

Still, these disadvantages are minor compared to the advantages of the overhead and time saved. Good planning and design can make this kind of script approach easy to put in place. You can use many tools to help make a single page take on a changing character. You can use labels to change captions. Text boxes can change multiple lines of displayed text. You can use

19

the New control covered on Day 11, "More ActiveX Controls," to hide or show images by changing display dates. Button captions can be modified between simulated pages. You can change the color of a label from one simulated page to another to highlight differences between pages. Message box and input box functions can provide a high level of user interaction. By taking this approach, you are really moving the page more in the direction of an application and further from the original Web page model of a static piece of text. The end result is good for the user. Better interactions and better responses are the net gain from using VBScript to simulate a series of pages. It won't work out in every case, but keep your eyes open for situations where you can apply this. When it does present itself as an opportunity, you can take advantage of it.

Summary

Today's lesson looks at server-related VBScript issues. Although VBScript performs processing on the client, it has a close association with any programs on the server that might process data from the page. VBScript can carry out front-end validation processing before form data is submitted to the server. This saves on server load and also eliminates unnecessary network load and user wait time in the event that the data is bad and not ready to be stored. In that case, the user-level notification can occur immediately from the client-based VBScript, rather than wait on the server to detect the problem and provide a response.

It is important to keep the role of VBScript clear when considering NT Server solutions because Visual Basic can be involved in several areas of the solution. VBScript is supported in the Internet Explorer and other browsers to provide client-side solutions. You can also use VBScript with Internet Information Server to serve as a scripting language for various server-side tasks, although that is not the focus of this book. In addition, you can use Visual Basic to generate OLE Automation Server DLLs residing on the server that can be called in response to form input on a page. The mechanism for calling such programs is using ISAPI to call the `oleisapi` DLL on the server. `oleisapi` is specified as the form action parameter on the page itself. Other server technologies include IDC, which makes generating server data from a database very easy, and the standard CGI, or Common Gateway Interface. CGI programs that are triggered on the server from a page are commonly called scripts. Future versions of Visual Basic will support using that language to produce ActiveX controls. Then, you can distribute Visual Basic–produced controls. With the multiple layers of Visual Basic in various Internet solutions and the use of script at several levels, there is quite often confusion among people who are not well versed in these technologies. Now, you can lead the way in shedding light on this confusion!

Today's lesson concludes by examining strategies to reduce the number of pages downloaded from the server by replacing several static pages with one dynamic page. The controls and techniques that greatly facilitate this include the label control, the text box, the message box function, and the input box function. In addition to these controls and techniques, careful thought is required to plot out the optimal strategy for the right mix of function, scripting, and downloaded pages.

Q&A

Q **Does VBScript enable you to have any interaction with the input buttons of the submit type?**

A Yes, you can have code in an OnClick event for the submit button. You can use this code to perform field validation and control whether the code is submitted. If you supply code for the OnClick event button, the script must call the form's Submit method if the determination is made that the data is valid and should be passed on to the server.

Q **What are the advantages of using VBScript in your Web page to validate data, rather than relying on the server to do it?**

A When your script validates data before submitting it to the server, you avoid all the overhead of unnecessary network communication if the data turns out to be invalid. In addition, you spare the server from doing the validation work, thus lightening the load on its CPU. This can be an important consideration, especially when the server tends to be overloaded anyway.

Q **Name two user interface techniques that you can use to provide dynamic page feedback. These techniques enable you to use only one changing page for a user interface rather than multiple pages.**

A The possibilities include using labels or text boxes for feedback, as well as feedback and interaction through input boxes and message boxes.

Workshop

Explore many Web pages on the Web. See if you can find page sequences where a flow of several pages could be reduced to one page if the pages were more active and dynamic.

Quiz

NOTE

> Refer to Appendix C, "Answers to Quiz Questions," for the answers to these questions.

19

1. The following code is intended to perform a validation check that confirms that a user is 18 or over before processing a job application. If the user age is 18 or over, then the form input should be submitted to the server. The current code has an omitted statement that prevents the submission from taking place. Add the missing statement so the submittal occurs when data is valid:

```
<HTML>
<HEAD>
<script language="VBScript">
<!--
sub cmdApply_OnClick
' Process the application by submitting to server if data is valid

    ' Make sure the user age is 18 or over
    if document.frmApply.txtAge.value < 18 then
        MsgBox "Sorry youngster, you're not old enough to apply!", _
            vbOKOnly,"Can't take app"
    else
        MsgBox "Application processed", vbOKOnly, "Confirmation"
    end if
end sub
-->
</script>

<HR>
</HEAD>

<BODY LEFTMARGIN=10 TOPMARGIN=20 TEXT=#000000
 LINK=#FF0066 VLINK=#330099 ALINK=#000000>
<FONT FACE="ARIAL" SIZE=2>
<CENTER>
<em>Enter your information:</em>
<BR>

<!------ Job Application Form ------------------>
<form name="frmApply" action="/scripts/oleisapi.dll/ HumanRes.JobApp.TakeApp"
    method="GET">
Name: <input name="txtName">
Address: <input name="txtAddress" >
Age: <input name="txtAge">
Job Desired: <input name="txtJob">
<input  value="Apply" name="cmdApply">
</form>

</BODY>
</HTML>
```

2. Modify the correct code from Question 1 so that it only submits the form if the user is over 18 and supplies a name.

Day **20**

Porting Between Visual Basic and VBScript

If you're a Visual Basic programmer, you likely were pretty excited when you heard about VBScript, which is derived from Visual Basic. The ability to write active Web pages in a language already near and dear to your heart is an appealing one. By some claims, Visual Basic is close to being the world's most widely used programming language, if it's not there already. So many programmers welcome the familiarity of VBScript. Even more, a lot of programmers have likely thought of how great it would be to move much of their existing Visual Basic code into their VBScript Web pages. This is a great way to achieve code reusability, enhance the power of your Web pages, save your company money, and show the boss that all the Visual Basic products you've been working on in the past are even more valuable then she suspected.

Today's lesson addresses the issues of moving code between Visual Basic and VBScript. The languages are indeed blood relatives—closely enough related that code portability is a feasible option. In fact, VBScript is said to be a strict subset of Visual Basic for Applications (the core Visual Basic technology behind the

VBA in Visual Basic 4.0, Office, Excel, and other products) and 100% upward compatible to VBA. When you hear these claims you might start to think that moving code between Visual Basic environments is hitch free. However, this is not entirely true.

There are many differences to be aware of between the languages. The nature of the port makes a big difference, too. It is much easier to take a VBScript application to Visual Basic then to take a Visual Basic application to VBScript. In the first case you're taking code from a language subset and moving to an environment where there are even more language choices. In the second case, you're taking code from a full implementation of the language and moving it to an environment where language choices are much more limited. Unfortunately, the more difficult port direction is the more likely one because there is already a large body of Visual Basic code available that could be exploited in VBScript.

Differences in various host environments can complicate matters as well. Currently, the Internet Explorer 3.0 browser makes available a wide variety of intrinsic objects such as document and location objects that your VBScript code can manipulate. Someday, they will likely become a standard part of Windows, but for now you'll find that the available environmental objects vary between your standard Visual Basic application interface and your VBScript browser hosted interface.

It's a fair expectation that translation-tool products may emerge to aid in porting code. Short of that, however, porting code between the two will take a mixture of both experience and plain old elbow grease. An understanding of many of the differences between the language set and subset is provided here to help you in your future porting work. Just as importantly, understanding what's not in VBScript but is in its parent language will give you a better overall perspective on the focus and capabilities of this language. For that reason, it is still well worth your while to read this chapter even if you don't have background in Visual Basic or don't plan to port any code. You'll come away with a better understanding of what VBScript is all about.

How Do Visual Basic and VBScript Compare?

VBScript is derived from Visual Basic or, to be more technically accurate, VBA, the Visual Basic engine. The language syntax and behavior are taken directly from VBA. When you consider how the syntax and capabilities of these two languages relate, it helps to picture a domain graph. Visualize a circle that represents all the language elements and functions in Visual Basic. Then picture another circle that represents all language elements and functions in VBScript. Where these circles intersect is the commonality between the languages. The best case for portability would be if the languages were identical and the circles directly overlapped, as in Figure 20.1.

20

NOTE

When *Visual Basic* is used in the discussions that follow, it refers to the common Visual Basic language supported in the Visual Basic development product and Visual Basic for Applications, the engine behind it. VBA is also used to provide Visual Basic support in products such as Word, Excel, and others. By contrast, *VBScript* refers specifically to the language syntax that is supported by the VBScript language interpreter and environments such as Internet Explorer, which host it.

Figure 20.1.

The ideal overlap of Visual Basic and VBScript.

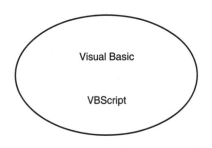

This best-case compatibility is far from what actually exists, and there are good reasons why it couldn't exist. It can be assumed that many goals shaped the development of VBScript and the decisions about what would go into it. Some of these goals have been stated at past Microsoft developers' conferences, and the impact on the language is clear. One goal was to have a secure script language. This meant that there could be no way for a script to directly carry out interaction with the user's system beyond the relatively narrow confines of the Web page it controlled. Therefore, the traditional file input/output (I/O) of Visual Basic was removed and so were the data access and the clipboard objects. Another goal was to have a light-footprint language. A language that took significant space in memory or had overhead that slowed it wouldn't do. VBScript is a slimmed-down version of Visual Basic, with many functions not provided. It is a safe bet that the goal of sleekness of solution accounts for some of what wasn't provided.

A further goal might have been to create a script language that is easy to use and appropriate for scripting tasks. The broad and extensive language of Visual Basic is great for sophisticated corporate applications that must share database information and business rules in a client/server fashion, and it provides many features that facilitate creation of such enterprise solutions. It also provides a considerable level of compatibility with older versions of BASIC, all the way back to pre–Visual Basic versions of BASIC. However, a broad range of language constructs and backward compatibility to older BASIC programs are not important for a script language. A script language can best fulfill its purposes if it is very easy to use and

20

understand. Web page authors will be most likely to apply it to enhance their pages. So it is a fair guess that the desire to keep it simple and straightforward also played a part in shaping VBScript, and it accounts for the fact that only key functions of Visual Basic are included rather than a lot of fluff.

So you can picture VBScript as a proper subset of Visual Basic. You might expect VBScript to include just some of what's in Visual Basic with no other changes or additions. The figure for this scenario is shown in Figure 20.2.

Figure 20.2.

The relationship of VBScript to Visual Basic is much like this figure.

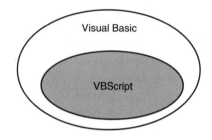

This is still not quite the full picture, however. There are some approaches you can take in VBScript code that are not directly supported by today's Visual Basic. In a couple isolated areas there are slight differences in the way statements work. The following statement, for example, dimensions an array of 10 elements addressable by indexes 0 through 9 in Visual Basic and an array of 11 elements, addressable by indexes 0 through 10 in VBScript:

```
dim MyArray(10)
```

The minor language-specific differences that exist today between the beta VBScript and Visual Basic 4.0 are few and likely will be resolved by subsequent product releases. VBScript is derived from the newest version of VBA, Visual Basic for Applications 5.0, on which the next version of Visual Basic itself is expected to be based. Then the relationship of the released products in the Visual Basic family line will be truly subset-to-set.

In most cases, however, the differences encountered in a port are not due to the language syntax itself. The differences are because certain elements you can reference make sense only in the context of a Web page. A document object or location object makes sense to reference when dealing with a Web page, but they have no equivalent in the 4.0 version of Visual Basic, for example.

However, the differences can't be ignored if you're sharing a lot of code between environments. Another perception of how the languages relate, when you consider that some objects you are likely to use in VBScript are specific to the browser environment, is reflected in Figure 20.3. The languages have a subset relationship, but the intrinsic object model offered by the

20

host environment keeps it from being a true subset. There is a lot you can do in Visual Basic that can be done directly in VBScript, and there are some intrinsic objects you can use in VBScript that you will not find directly available in Visual Basic.

NOTE The differences between object models and host environments will quickly fade as some of Microsoft's future vision unfolds. Eventually, the independent browser concept will disappear as any document, whether local or remote or an ActiveX application written to document specs, is simply hosted by the Windows operating system shell.

Figure 20.3.

The representation of the relationship of VBScript to Visual Basic when the intrinsic object model is considered.

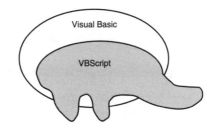

Finding Differences When You Port Code

You might need to move Visual Basic code to your VBScript Web pages to take advantage of your existing code. On the other hand, once you write some scripts, you may need to go in the other direction. A procedure you have defined in VBScript might be of use in a non-Web–targeted Visual Basic program, so you may be moving code to Visual Basic. In either case, you want a way to detect differences between the environments. You can find many differences by looking for the program incompatibilities documented in this lesson. This can be a tedious process, and it's always possible you won't catch them all when initially modifying source code for a conversion. If any slip by during a conversion, you'll likely discover them as you make the conversion, try your test code, and receive grumbling error messages from the language processor!

If you're moving from VBScript to Visual Basic, the task is relatively easy. First of all, you're moving from a smaller domain of the language to a larger one. For the most part, you're adding potential syntax you can use rather than taking away syntax as you move the code into Visual Basic. Many of the scripts will port with no problems at all, and for those that do introduce problems, the Visual Basic development environment will be a tremendous help in your porting activity. It can flag syntax errors effectively even before the program runs. If porting issues have introduced run-time errors, Visual Basic offers a rich set of debugging capabilities, including a built-in trace facility, to help you hunt down those errors.

20

If, on the other hand, you are moving from Visual Basic to VBScript, your task will be considerably more difficult because you are moving from a larger language domain to a smaller one. Many aspects of the language supported in Visual Basic are not supported in VBScript, so you may have a lot of code to remove or syntax to modify. You cannot make dynamic link library calls, including Windows API calls, from VBScript, and these often are heavily used in Visual Basic. There is no easy way to automatically highlight the differences, although it can be expected that future tools may come along to partially automate the task. If problems are introduced by the port or if you miss converting a nonsupported keyword, the debugging task can be daunting. You may simply be rewarded with a script that provides a cryptic run-time error, or worse yet, gives no run-time error and just doesn't work. You have little at your disposal to help you track down these problems. As you learned on Day 17, "Exterminating Bugs from Your Script," no standard VBScript debug environment is available. Some of the techniques described on Day 17 can help you build your own debugging capabilities into the script, but this takes time and effort.

NOTE

At the time of this writing, few tools are available to aid in such tasks. It is likely that over time, a richer set of tools will develop to make porting easier. Information at `www.doubleblaze.com` may describe availability of some such tools in the future.

It is important to have a good understanding of what is supported in VBScript and what is not before attempting to port. The guidelines here serve as a good starting point, and Appendix A, "VBScript Syntax Quick Reference," can supplement the guidelines. Your ultimate authority of what constitutes legal VBScript syntax is currently available right over the Web. Microsoft's VBScript language reference can be reached at `http://www.microsoft.com/vbscript`. In addition, whenever you do any code porting to VBScript, you should allow time for lots of painstaking adjustments and testing. Lots and lots of testing! Finally, you should keep in mind that in many cases, there will be no way to do a direct port. If your Visual Basic program makes extensive use of file I/O and the clipboard, you have no easy VBScript alternative. Instead, you have to reset your porting expectations or redefine your script goals. Visual Basic to VBScript porting can work well in many cases, as long as you can avoid the *gotchas*, which are covered next in detail.

Syntax Elements in Visual Basic 4.0 but Not in VBScript

Because so much of Visual Basic is not in VBScript, it is rather difficult to succinctly summarize it all in one table. The summary here is not intended to be a complete guide, but it does highlight some of the differences. The discussion that follows starts by looking at some major areas that are not supported. This is followed by a table that briefly presents some of the specific keywords that are not a part of VBScript.

Constants

VBScript does not support constants. An easy (although somewhat time-consuming) workaround does exist. Simply declare the constants as variables and assign them a value initially. VBScript also does not support the intrinsic constants of Visual Basic. These are constants starting with a vb prefix that are automatically defined and refer to values expected by Visual Basic functions. These intrinsic constants must likewise be explicitly declared as variables and assigned a value. A file on the CD-ROM, under subdirectory \shared\tools\constants.txt, contains a text file that you can use to copy and paste sample declarations for many frequently used intrinsic constants. The good news is that the constant values expected by most functions are the same between Visual Basic and VBScript. For example, the same value you use to request a Yes/No message box in Visual Basic is also used in VBScript.

File I/O

File I/O is not supported under VBScript. This is an area for which no direct easy workaround exists. Information that persists from one session to another would be saved on the server with the normal Web page model. One possible solution to consider is whether it makes sense to have the information that would normally be saved to the file submitted through CGI to be saved on the server. You could resort to a control to handle storage needs if you can find one commercially available or create your own. It is likely that eventually third-party ActiveX controls may evolve to address more of these needs, for those willing to sacrifice the *nonwritable* security by incorporating such controls into their programs.

20

Database Support/Data Access Objects

The situation here is much like that of file I/O. This support is not present in VBScript. You should consider whether the database activity can be replaced by CGI interaction with a server-controlled database.

Classes and Property `let`/`get`/`set` Procedures

Classes and the properties and methods that go with them, including the ability to define `let`/`get`/`set` procedures, are not supported in VBScript. Painful though it may be, the necessary workaround is to restructure code into a standard procedure/variable model when moving it to scripts.

Financial Functions

The advanced financial functions are not available in VBScript. If you need a certain function, you can program it yourself as a function call in your script. It may take quite a few lines of script, however.

String Functions

Most string functions in Visual Basic are provided in an old-style syntax that uses a string ($) designator on the end of the function, as well as the new style without it. For example, you can use `Left` or `Left$` to extract the left portion of a string, and `Mid` or `Mid$` to extract a substring from a string. The functions work the same regardless of the method used. VBScript only supports the standard method (such as `Left`) and not the syntax that ends with $, such as `Left$`. The porting workaround is quite easy for this one—just make some global changes to get rid of the $ string designator.

Variable Types

VBScript supports only variant variables, as you learned on Day 4, "Creating Variables in VBScript." This means that all nonvariant declarations in your Visual Basic code must be changed to variant declarations. Visual Basic code by experienced programmers rarely makes use of variant declarations. In Visual Basic, it is generally considered poor programming to rely too heavily on variants. Since the values of variant variables are not explicitly typed, programs based on variant variables are more likely to contain bugs by taking on a data representation the programmer didn't intend. For the same reason, changing variables from explicit types to variants as you move them to code can introduce changes in the behavior of programs. Therefore, any such changes should be examined carefully. Unfortunately, since most programs are variable-centric, a lot of changes and checking are usually necessary.

One example of the type of change to be aware of is shown in the Visual Basic Calculation program in Listing 20.1.

Listing 20.1. The Visual Basic Calculation program with standard nonvariant declarations.

```
Dim a As Single
Dim b As Integer
Dim c As Integer
a = 0.045
b = 10

c = a * b
MsgBox c
```

ANALYSIS   When the code is run, the value 0 is displayed in the message box. Assume that you port this code to VBScript, converting the declarations to variants, as in Listing 20.2.

Listing 20.2. The VBScript Calculation program with variant declarations.

```
Dim a
Dim b
Dim c
a = 0.045
b = 10

c = a * b
MsgBox c
```

ANALYSIS   When this seemingly identical code is run in the script, the value 0.45 is displayed because a Variant variable makes some assumptions for you. Since the result variable c is a variant, it can take on any data subtype form. When the calculation is carried out and the interpreter sees that a single-precision (decimal-point–based) number is used, it assumes that it is the type of data representation it should use for the result variable c as well. The variable c is not forced to use an integer representation as it was in the first example.

To successfully port the code to VBScript, you would need to carry out an additional piece of code modification, shown in Listing 20.3.

20

Listing 20.3. The VBScript Calculation program with variant declarations and `Cint`.

```
Dim a
Dim b
Dim c
a = 0.045
b = 10

c = Cint(a * b)
MsgBox c
```

ANALYSIS The use of the `Cint` function explicitly forces the result to be represented as an integer in the variant variable. In the example shown here, this doesn't seem too critical. After all, it was just displaying a message box. It doesn't matter much if it shows a `0` or a `0.45`. Assume that the software is calculating some financial data or some medical analysis for you; in this case, the difference in such data type representation could be significant indeed.

As you can see from this example, the only way to make sure your variables work as intended, once you port them over, will be to check all statements that use those variables, line by line, or exhaustively check a truly representative range of all program outcomes. Either way, the conversion of your data types to variants can mean a lot of work for you when you carry out a code port.

Intrinsic Objects—Print, Clipboard, and Debug

In Visual Basic you can use the print object to print, the clipboard object to move data to and from the clipboard, and the debug object to provide a trace of your programs to the debug window. No equivalents exist in VBScript for these techniques. If you are using the clipboard just to move data back and forth within your own program, you could use global variables instead. Similarly, you can build your own debug window through a text box or list box control and write to it in a manner similar to that of the debug control. You learned about this technique on Day 17. No documented intrinsic way to print a page from VBScript is available at this time. However, keep in mind that the user can always manually trigger a print of a page from the browser menu.

NOTE   Any application in Windows can be written so that it exposes its objects. In other words, it can make certain interfaces to control its behavior publicly available for other applications to use. It is possible that some browser environments of the future might expose objects

20

that allow a page to be printed, or it could be possible to write an advanced ActiveX control that could be included in a page to capture a bitmap of the browser and deliver it to the printer. So keep in mind that with most of the "can't do in VBScript" restrictions highlighted here, there is almost always a way to make it happen with enough programming. However, the capabilities mentioned here are neither native to VBScript nor easily achievable with the currently exposed browser objects. And if you do resort to outside help from a control in your script page, the browser will alert users with a security notification if they have their browser set to the secure option.

Error Handling, `Gotos`, and Labels

Visual Basic provides rich error-handling capabilities. You can direct code to go to a specific area of error-handling code when an error occurs through the use of `On error Goto <LabelName>` statements. VBScript doesn't provide this flexibility. `Gotos` and labels are not supported at all. You can specify `On error Resume Next` to tell the VBScript interpreter to continue processing after an error occurs. You can't automatically route the flow of the code for error conditions. If you wish to do this, you must explicitly check an error code immediately after a call, as described on Day 17. The bottom line is that if you've used good, robust error handling in Visual Basic, you are going to have to reassess and restructure it in VBScript.

Program Control

Many ways to control the execution of your program and interact with other programs are available in Visual Basic. These include the use of `DoEvents`. Under Windows 95, you can use this statement to tell the system to give your app a turn at responding to events other than the currently executing area of your code. Under Windows 3.1, which doesn't inherently support multitasking, this statement causes the operating system to give other apps a turn at responding to events rather than responding to your currently executing code. VBScript provides no such control. With VBScript, as long as your code is running, no other interaction can occur with the page or the browser. The Microsoft Internet Explorer browser notices if code executes for an unduly long time and gives you a chance to interrupt it.

Similarly, Visual Basic statements that let you control other apps are not supported in VBScript. `Shell`, `AppActivate`, and `Sendkeys` can be used to drive another application in Visual Basic. DDE functions, a means of dynamic data exchange communication, can be

20

used in Visual Basic to communicate with another application. Visual Basic lets you make dynamic link library calls, including Windows Applications Program Interface calls that can control the behavior of virtually every aspect of the Windows environment. No equivalent functions exist for any of these in VBScript, very likely due to the secure scripting philosophy with which VBScript was designed. You cannot use a script for these purposes using the standard VBScript language.

Other Syntax Not Supported

Many broad areas that are not supported in VBScript have been covered in this lesson; however, some other syntax features that are not supported are summarized in Table 20.1. Refer to the Visual Basic language reference help file that comes with Visual Basic for more details on these statements and functions. Keep in mind that this table does not represent everything that is not supported in VBScript; it simply adds to the list of what has been covered so far. It would be difficult to cover every single nuance of all the differences, but this list is fairly comprehensive and will give you a good starting point. At the time of this printing, a more comprehensive list was also available at Microsoft's Web site under www.microsoft.com/vbscript.

Table 20.1. Partial list of Visual Basic syntax with no VBScript equivalent.

Add

AddItem

AppActivate

Arrange

Arrays (setting low bounds so indexing starts at other than 0)

Beep

Boolean (must use variant)

Byte (must use variant)

CCur

Chr$ (note that Chr is supported)

Circle

clipboard object

Cls

Command

Command$

Conditional compiler directives

Const (must use variables to simulate constants)

Count

Currency (use variant to represent decimal-based money amounts)

Cvar

CVDate

Currency data type (use variant to represent decimal-based money amounts)

Date statement (allows program to set current date)

Date$ (date function to display date is supported)

Debug.Print

Declare (can't use dynamic link libraries [DLLs])

DefType

Dim x As New TypeName

DoEvents

Double (use variant)

Drag

End

EndDoc

Environ

Environ$

Erl

Error (the err object is supported)

Error$ (the err object is supported)

Fixed-length strings (use variant variable length string)

Format

Format$

GetObject

Global

GoSub...Return

Goto

20

continues

Table 20.1. continued

Hide

IfTypeOf x Is TypeName

InputBox$ (Inputbox is supported)

Integer (use variant type)

IsMissing

Item

Lcase$ (Lcase is supported)

Left$ (Left is supported)

Like

Line numbers and labels

LinkExecute

LinkPoke

LinkRequest

LinkSend

Literals:

    Real numbers with scientific exponentiation, such as 1.746E+100

    Date-specific formats such as #7/6/62# (assign 7/6/62 to a variant)

    Type characters, such as VarI%

Load

LoadPicture and SavePicture

Long (use variant)

Lset statements

Me

Mid$ (Mid is supported)

Mid statements (Mid as a function is supported)

Move

NewPage

Object (use variant to represent objects such as Hypertext Markup Language [HTML] forms)

On Error...Goto (On Error Resume Next is supported)

`On Error...Resume` (`On Error Resume Next` is supported)

`Option Base`

`Option Compare`

`Option Private Module`

`ParamArray`

`Optional`

`Point`

`PrintForm`

`Print`

`Private` (module level)

`Pset`

`Public` (module level)

`OBColor`

`RGB`

`Refresh`

`Remove`

`RemoveItem`

`Resume` (only support is for `On Error Resume Next`)

`Right$` (`Right` is supported)

`Rset` statements

`Rset` (strings)

`Rset` (structs)

`Scale`

`SendKeys`

`Set x = New TypeName` (`Set x = ObjName` is supported)

`Set/Let/Get` (property procedures not supported, but `Set x = ObjName` is)

`SetFocus`

`Shell`

`Show`

`Single` (use variant)

20

continues

Table 20.1. continued

Space$ (Space is supported)

Spc

Stop

Str$

StrConv

Str, Val

String$

Tab

TextHeight and TextWidth (for printing, graphics)

Time$ (Time is supported)

Trim$, Ltrim$, and Rtrim$

Type...End Type

TypeOf

TypeName

Type suffixes (%,$,!, and so on)

Ucase$ (Ucase is supported)

Unload

Use of explicitly named arguments such as KeithTest (argument1:=4)

With...End With

Zorder

Other Visual Basic and VBScript Differences

You have seen that many Visual Basic keywords and constructs are not supported in VBScript. VBScript has a few other differences from Visual Basic as well. These are discussed in the following sections.

Arrays

Arrays always start at an index of 0 in VBScript. In Visual Basic, you have the option to define the lower bound. In addition, you get a different number of array elements with the same declaration in Visual Basic and VBScript. This Visual Basic declaration gives you 10 elements that can be referenced from code by index numbers 0...9:

```
Dim CountArray(10)
```

This VBScript declaration gives you 11 elements that can be referenced from code by index numbers 0...10:

```
Dim CountArray(10)
```

You may have noticed that both lines are the same. That's not a typo! The declaration just works differently under Visual Basic 4.0 and VBScript. (As discussed earlier today, this difference is likely to disappear with future product releases that are based on the new VBA 5.0 engine.) Fortunately, in this case the porting impact going to VBScript is relatively small. The VBScript declaration will give you an extra array element, but your code can work as before without change. The extra element can simply go unused without interfering with existing code unless you use the Ubound function to determine the upper bound of an array when looping, assigning values, and so on. If so, you could have trouble with your code. The recurring porting theme is that you need to check everything carefully.

Intrinsic Browser Objects

As mentioned earlier in today's lesson, Visual Basic supports many objects that VBScript does not. These include the clipboard object, debug object, and data object. However, VBScript can also take advantage of objects not directly available to Visual Basic. The Internet Explorer environment provides VBScript with access to location, document, navigator, and other objects discussed on Day 18, "Advanced User Interface and Browser Object Techniques." Typically, major design assessment will be required if you discover that code to be ported has relied on such objects. The browser does support intrinsic objects such as a command button, a text box, and others covered on Day 8, "Intrinsic HTML Form Controls," and Day 9, "More Intrinsic HTML Form Controls," that are very similar to the standard controls in Visual Basic. Property lists will be similar for these controls, but not identical in every respect. However, if you stick to relatively simple standard uses of these controls, porting difficulty should be minimal.

20

Multiple Form Architecture

Perhaps one of the most challenging porting problems is moving Visual Basic programs that make heavy use of underlying forms. VBScript under Internet Explorer now offers a somewhat equivalent model with its Layout Control forms interface. This, coupled with Internet Explorer's incorporation of 2-D layout for HTML, makes it possible to position elements and controls anywhere on a page in a formlike fashion. This approach is discussed in more detail on Day 18. If you have a Multiple Document Interface application under Visual Basic, you won't have a direct equivalent under VBScript, although you can use Internet Explorer's frames, also discussed on Day 18, to build a slightly different kind of multiple windows. The best bet is to reassess the entire user interface and determine whether you can best represent a series of Visual Basic forms with the Layout Control approach, through a progression of Web pages, the display of input and message boxes from a script, or the display of varying labels. In any event, some user interface redesign may be in order if you are porting code that includes a nontrivial user interface to VBScript. Over the long run, it is possible that the form model between Visual Basic and VBScript may merge with subsequent releases of the product and the operating system.

Summary

Today's lesson addresses issues that are likely to be of concern when moving code between Visual Basic and VBScript. VBScript provides a powerful Web page programming capability, and it is also closely related to what is one of the world's most widely used languages—its parent language Visual Basic for Applications. A natural result is that programmers will look to porting code between the environments for maximum payback of coding efforts. Considering the differences between Visual Basic and VBScript can be valuable even for programmers who have never used Visual Basic and who just program in the script environment. Knowledge of what's *not* in VBScript but is in the parent language helps provide a broader view of the language and a greater overall understanding of what it can best accomplish.

Differences between the languages are described throughout today's lesson. VBScript is largely a subset of Visual Basic. There are some intrinsic Internet Explorer objects available to VBScript that are not directly available to Visual Basic. Likewise, Visual Basic supports some objects and many language aspects that are not present in VBScript. This means that special care must be taken in moving code between the environments. Therefore, the easiest ports are those where Visual Basic code is converted to VBScript. But these are not always pain-free. Incompatibilities are very likely to arise, and they can range from the very obvious to the very subtle. Because VBScript has no dedicated development environment, debugging scripts that have been converted is often a challenge. Tracking down porting problems and language differences can be especially time consuming. A good understanding of the language differences smoothes the process.

Many specific language differences are addressed. VBScript provides access to some elements that Visual Basic does not. For example, you can use the document and location objects in VBScript but not in Visual Basic. In some cases, Visual Basic and VBScript support the same elements, but they work slightly differently. A `Dim ArrayName(n)` statement allocates 0 to n elements in VBScript but just 0 to n-1 elements in Visual Basic 4.0.

Today's lesson addresses many areas of Visual Basic that are not supported in VBScript, including the clipboard object, print object, application control statements such as `shell`, `AppActivate`, `SendKeys`, data access objects, and file I/O. Guidelines are presented to smooth the porting process. The best tool to aid in porting code, however, is simply a strong understanding of both languages and experience with both. It is important to keep the code compatibility in perspective. Even though there are some pitfalls to moving code between these environments, the two languages are still so closely related that improved programs and great productivity savings can result for those willing to tackle such ports.

Q&A

Q **Which of the following are available in VBScript?**

clipboard object

`Err` object

`Shell` statement

printer object

A Only the `Err` object is available in VBScript. The rest of the items are specific to Visual Basic and not supported in VBScript.

Q **Because VBScript is a subset of Visual Basic, does that mean that any VBScript program will work as-is when recompiled as a Visual Basic program?**

A No. Many scripts may be upward compatible from VBScript to Visual Basic. However, some will be affected by slight differences in the languages. These include areas such as different indexing for array declarations and the presence of script-specific objects such as the document object, for example. VBScript syntax is a subset of Visual Basic, but host environment objects are not.

Q **Can VBScript write to a temporary file, since regular file I/O is not supported?**

A No. The current version offers no direct file I/O capabilities of any type.

20

Workshop

1. If you are a Visual Basic 4.0 programmer, pick a sample program to study in the Visual Basic `samples` directory that is under the Visual Basic 4.0 main directory. Run the program and inspect its source code. Assess how much of the sample is portable and how much is not, based on the guidelines in this chapter. Then try to

make the code work in VBScript. Was the porting more effort than you had estimated? This is often the case with such porting projects.

2. This workshop can be carried out even if you do not have prior experience with Visual Basic. Review the areas described in this lesson that are highlighted as those that Visual Basic supports and VBScript does not. Assess whether any of these are traits that would be useful in your Web pages and scripts if the support had been provided. Then think about why the support is not there for a feature. Was it likely omitted to make VBScript more secure, to keep VBScript more lightweight, or just to make implementation of VBScript happen sooner? If you consider these angles, you'll come away with a broader appreciation of VBScript.

Quiz

NOTE

Refer to Appendix C, "Answers to Quiz Questions," for the answers to these Quiz questions.

1. Suppose you're porting a Visual Basic program over to VBScript. The original Visual Basic program makes frequent calls to DLLs you wrote that carry out company-specific calculations. What strategies can you use to get your VBScript code to provide the same functionality as that of the original BASIC code, considering that this DLL dependency exists?

2. Refer to the following Visual Basic code:

```
Const TAX_RATE = 0.04
Const ITEM_PRICE = 25
Dim intUnits as Integer
Dim intCost as Integer

' Calculate the total cost
intUnits = InputBox("How many units do you wish to purchase?")
intCost = (ITEM_PRICE * intUnits) * TAX_RATE
```

Several of the statements in this code will not work when ported to VBScript. Can you identify them?

3. Rewrite the code from question 2 so that it is VBScript compatible.

Day 21

Security, Stability, and Distributed Source Control Issues

You've made it to the last day! It's appropriate to end by tackling one of the most far-reaching issues—security. The reason security concerns exist at all in the context of VBScript and the World Wide Web is that pages bearing VBScript are foreign visitors arriving at a client computer from a server. A common fear is that maliciously or incompetently designed pages that a user unwittingly encounters could wreak havoc on the local computer. Today's lesson addresses these concerns and discusses the features of the VBScript and server-supplied component model that reduce these risks.

At the end of today, which marks the completion of three full weeks of VBScript material, you will have full knowledge of how to create and deploy effective VBScript scripts. You'll have a good understanding of the many issues such as security that might shape some of your scripting and component integration strategies. Once you complete today's lesson, creativity and ingenuity will be your guides to script creation from this point forward in your VBScript experience. Unleashing experience, ingenuity, and creativity to produce better, active documents is what VBScript is all about.

Stability Issues

When you download a page from the Web, you download all the code along with it. As you interact with that page, code could be executed at any time while you're barely aware of the fact. Think of the material covered so far in the first 20 days of study to imagine some of the ways this could happen. You click an anchored image, and code that was written to respond to image clicks is launched. A timer is started as soon as the page loads, and after you stare at the page for 10 seconds, the timer expires. Unbeknownst to you, the timer event code starts to execute in the background.

There's no getting around the fact that unless you personally inspect the source of each and every page you ever load across the Internet, you're really taking it on blind faith that a page is valid. You have some good reasons to have such faith, but it helps to understand them to think about some of the potential security risks. Such risks include the possibility of catastrophic script errors, script viruses, or erroneous or malicious ActiveX controls. I consider each of these areas in turn with an explanation of why you don't have to lose too much sleep over such risks.

NOTE
> The material that follows should put your mind considerably at ease about the security of Web pages. However, the security arena today has a lot of gray areas. It will probably be some time before the Internet has a unified security front. In the meantime, keep in mind that there is always, in theory, a remote potential for disaster to strike because trouble is, by definition, surprises that you don't foresee.

Guarding Against Catastrophic Error Scripts

One risk of loading a Web page across the network is that the code contained in it might cause some terrible error when it runs on your system. Consider a hypothetical worst-case situation that highlights some of the risk involved. Suppose you put your new Web pages on the company's brand new Web server. One of the pages includes a script that you wrote to calculate travel expenses. As luck would have it, the script has a bug. When you click the command button to request the sum of all the daily expenditures on an expense report page, the script attempts to calculate the total price by looping through each day. Because of a bug in the `While` conditional, this loop loops forever rather than terminate after the specified number of days.

Suppose that you rather hastily placed this page on your company's Web server without testing it thoroughly. Meanwhile, your company's CEO takes advantage of a quick break in his overseas meeting to update his travel expense account information from his laptop. He connects his laptop to the phone system, makes a few clicks, and finds your Web page in front of him. His presentation package software is also cached in his browser, full of pages for the presentation he is about to give. As the CEO nervously waits out the break, he enters the last few days of meal information into your page. Then, he clicks a calculate button, launching the calculation code. He waits and waits and waits. He starts to think of alternate career paths for the programmer who provided this page if he has to reboot his system. Just in the nick of time, a message box pops up. It knowingly proclaims, "This page contains a script that is taking an unusually long time to finish. To end this script now, click Cancel." Although the CEO is still a bit miffed at not completing his expense report, he is relieved at the graceful recovery. In fact, he reminds himself as he turns his attention to his presentation that he'll have to commend his programming staff for their foresight in checking for such circumstances and avoiding catastrophe.

The credit really should go to the browser, however. The message is generated by the Internet Explorer browser when it detects a long period of inactivity in the script. This is a natural safeguard that's built in to the browser's support of the script language. Its purpose is to keep any page's script from locking up the browser with infinite processing.

Listing 21.1 shows an example of code that causes this type of infinite loop. This code is intended to add up the value of every prime number from 1 to 1000 when a calculate button is selected. However, the script has an error. The `intCount` counter variable is incorrectly incremented at the bottom of the loop. Therefore, the script will never reach the loop's exit condition of `intCount >= 1000`. The program keeps right on looping endlessly unless something comes along to make it stop.

Listing 21.1. Code with an endless loop.

```
<SCRIPT language="VBScript">
<!--
' Total count from calculation

sub cmdStart_OnClick
' Adds up value of every number evenly divisible by 3; from 1 to 1000.

    Dim intCount ' Current number to analyze
    Dim intTotalCount ' Cumulative total
```

21

continues

Listing 21.1. continued

```
     ' Act on every third number, adding to total if divisible by 3
     do while intCount <= 1000

         ' Add to the total count if the number is divisible by 3
         if (intCount mod 3) = 0 then
             intTotalCount = intTotalCount + intCount
         end if

         intCount = count + 1
     loop

     lblStatus.Caption = "Grand total is " & intTotalCount

end sub

-->
</script>
```

NOTE

> The page with this program, infinite.htm, is available on the
> CD-ROM that comes with this book.

When this code is executed, the loop keeps repeating continuously because the wrong name
is used to increment the loop counter. The browser, however, notices that the script is
executing for an unusually long time. After about 25 seconds, the browser presents a message
box notifying the user of this fact and giving him the option to cancel the script altogether.
Figure 21.1 shows the message box that results from running the script in Listing 21.1.

NOTE

> Listing 21.1 purposely showed incorrect code with an infinite loop to
> illustrate the browser recovery that takes place. For the algorithm in
> Listing 21.1 to function correctly, you'd need to replace the line
>
> intCount = count + 1
>
> with the line
>
> intCount = intCount + 1
>
> and then everything would work just fine.

Figure 21.1.

A message box indicating that the program has been running for a long period of time.

As the infinite loop example shows, you can hang an individual script on a page, but you can't easily hang the browser itself. Even more importantly, you can't write a script that hangs the computer. The language is designed to be robust. VBScript cannot get into situations where it could inadvertently harm the systems it is running on. The programming constructs responsible for some of the more serious errors in many languages that could interfere with other programs are simply not present in VBScript. There are no pointers to memory to misuse. There is no memory management to mishandle. There is no capability to interact with system messages or for that matter, even to call system routines. In the Windows environment, this means that you cannot make dynamic link library calls, including Windows Application Programming Interface (API) calls, from VBScript. A lot of the more complex operations that a normal Windows program can perform simply can't be done in VBScript. VBScript is all the safer for it.

Even when a script does go bad, such as in the infinite loop example, the browser and the operating system provide an added layer of protection. Simply put, any ill effects of poor VBScript programming will almost always affect only the page itself and not anything else. This is by design. Few users would want to download Web pages laden with VBScript if they risked hanging their browsers or their systems with every such page. With the robustness of VBScript, users can download pages that use it with no such concerns.

21

Security Issues

The VBScript language is designed to be error proof, as the last section discusses. It's also designed to be vandal proof. Just as no user wants to download potentially mistake-prone pages, no user wants to download pages that pose a risk of bringing viruses onto the local system.

Guarding Against Malicious Scripts

Suppose VBScript had a command such as FormatHardDrive. (It doesn't, but just suppose it did!) A mischief-minded hacker could put a page on the Web and advertise it as "Free Tips on VBScript." If the function existed, he could provide a page that looked normal but made use of code like that in Listing 21.2.

Listing 21.2. A script function that does not exist but would be dangerous if it did!

```
<Script Language="VBScript">
' Startup code
  FormatHardDrive
  msgbox "You've been vicitimized"
</script>
```

If you could write this code, Web users would be pretty helpless. Any page could potentially contain such a hidden surprise. The only way to find it would be to inspect all the code before the page was ever loaded.

VBScript provides a limited, safe function set for exactly this reason. Web page users can take comfort in the knowledge that VBScript does not support any dangerous function calls. As a matter of fact, even many capabilities that you might not regard as dangerous are not present. There is no standard file support. You cannot use the clipboard from VBScript. Direct dynamic link library declarations that give access to other libraries and Windows Application Program Interface calls to carry out operating system–level functions are not allowed.

It all adds up to a language that you cannot easily manipulate for malicious purposes. One cannot say "never" with absolute certainty about anything, but most experts agree that VBScript offers little in the way of capabilities to interfere with the whole system. The biggest security threat with VBScript comes with the components that it can integrate. Integrated components such as OLE automation objects and ActiveX controls are separate pieces of code not written in VBScript. These components could, in theory, pose risks, depending on how

21

they were written; they can use DLL calls and Windows API calls and delete files. However, you have a good model for dealing with these components, which is addressed in the next section.

Safe Components

The real security risk in downloading a script-based Web page is the components it uses. Like the famed Trojan Horse of old, the components can come along for the ride with the page and then perform malicious deeds when a script calls them. After all, VBScript is restricted by the domain of its language from getting into trouble. You can write a component in other languages, such as C++, that have no such restrictions. Whenever a script calls such a component, that code gets a chance to execute. This would seem to be a security hole in the script-based Web page model, but these concerns have an answer.

When you download a page that brings components with it, you are informed by the browser what those controls are. You can choose whether to accept them onto your local system. How can you ever trust a component that you didn't write? An entire system is in place to certify components by providing a trail of ownership. A component provider is not likely to intentionally package a virus-laden component and distribute it when the company name is clearly identified with a product; you can expect that the same assurance will apply when an Internet component has a trail. A business that produces a component must submit it to an authorized lab for certification, which grants a unique digital signature to be embedded in that component. This does not necessarily mean that you will never find bugs in a component. It does mean that you can track the code back to the original development company. It also means that if any changes occur in the component after it leaves the original developer, the browser will warn you before downloading it.

Certified code is called *signed* code, meaning it has a unique digital signature that the certification lab granted. The certification lab, called a *certificate authority*, documents the code submittal and the company producing it and then grants a digital certificate. This identification number is used to help identify the component in the future. The software provider then takes the digital certificate and encrypts it into the software product using an encryption password, or *key*.

Now the software can be distributed. Whenever a user downloads the code, the browser can use a different public key supplemented by a Windows 32 API function call in the Windows environment to verify that the component has a valid certificate. This can also detect if any changes have occurred in the component since it was released from the vendor. If no signature is present on a component, a user can still choose to download it. They can also download a component with an invalid signature, although it would probably be foolhardy to do so

21

because this could indicate component tampering or viruses. Although the first implementation of this approach is currently available on Windows 32-bit platforms, it is intended as a cross-platform approach in the long run.

Only that specific component will carry that digital signature. As a result, you know what you're getting when you download the component. A component that is backed by a certified digital signature is one that is traceable, recognizable, and tested. How will this affect your VBScript code? When you consider which controls to integrate to make your active pages, it is probably a wise strategy to choose certified components. Today, this procedure is not yet fully in place, and most Web page users don't give it a lot of thought. Eventually, viewing a page that warns of noncertified components might be regarded as a risky move that only the most daring users care to take!

> **NOTE**
>
> You can find information about certification process and implementation techniques by searching http://www.microsoft.com/intdev and reviewing information in the ActiveX Software Development Kit (SDK) available for download there. If you have questions on the state of certification of a commercial ActiveX component, it is recommended that you check with the vendor.

The Internet Explorer browser will alert you to the potential download of any component. Then you make the decision of whether to assume the risk of download based on your familiarity with the control. Most people are much more likely to risk trying a certified component traceable back to the vendor than to take a chance on a page laden with controls of questionable origin. The browser pops up a dialog box that asks you whether you want to download the control. You can turn this feature off in the browser.

If you select View | Options from the menu, choose the Security tab, and then select the Programs button, you see a dialog box that lets you specify whether you want Expert security, Normal, or None. If you choose Expert, you'll get warnings about any page that has a control. Normal will just automatically prevent the controls from doing damage by not utilizing them on the page. If you choose None for open Internet cruising, you're doing the equivalent of driving without a seat belt. You may get along just fine taking your chances, and the odds may be highly in your favor, but there's always a chance you could be hit head-on by a rogue control. The potential damage that could be done in these unlikely circumstances is certainly enough to cause an Internet fatality and a good conversation piece among your Internet-savvy co-workers. The None setting is by far the most convenient to the Web page user. You must weigh the familiarity and trust you have in the pages you'll be viewing against this convenience. What's this all mean to you as the VBScript developer? Your users will face the

21

same decision, and the degree of safety of controls and components you incorporate into your script solutions may determine whether those pages are utilized. Building your pages on known, certified controls is the answer.

Distributed Source Control

Now that I've addressed issues of security, you can feel more at ease making use of the pages and components that come to you from the server. You know that you can't cause too many problems accidentally with your code and that other programmers can't cause you too many problems accidentally or intentionally. How about protection for the source code of your scripts? Perhaps you're a consulting firm, and you have a page that provides feedback to users on adjusting sensitive electronic equipment. Customers come to you just because you offer this service. The code in your page uses some algorithms based on constant values that took you many months to research and perfect. Those algorithms are also proprietary to your company, for if other consultants had access to the logic, they would offer the same services. Listing 21.3 shows such a hypothetical page and its script.

Listing 21.3. A page with proprietary code.

```
<HTML>
<HEAD>
<TITLE>Ken and Jasper's WiseOne Engineering</TITLE>

<H1>
<A HREF="http://www.mcp.com"><IMG  ALIGN=BOTTOM SRC="wiseone.jpg" BORDER=2></A>
<EM>Ken and Jasper's WiseOne Engineering</EM>
</h1>
<HR>
</HEAD>

<EM>Enter the reading on Gadget 1 and we'll give you the adjustment factor</EM>

<SCRIPT language="VBScript">
<!--

sub cmdAdjustment_OnClick
' Calculate the adjustment factor based on Gadget 1 reading
    dim dblTemp1 ' Hold intermediate result

    ' Use our secret constants to get the adjustment factor
    dblTemp1 = Cdbl(txtGadget.value) * 23.015
    ' Then apply some more of our secret constants to do the Tim adjustment
    if dblTemp1 > 20 then
        dblTemp1 = dblTemp1 / 31.3
    else
        dblTemp1 = dblTemp1 / 15.7
    end if
```

continues

21

Listing 21.3. continued

```
        lblStatus.Caption = "The adjustment factor is " & str(dblTemp1)

end sub


-->
</script>



<center>
Enter gadget 1 value here:<input name="txtGadget1">
<h3>Click here to do the adjustment</h3>
<input type="button" name="cmdAdjustment" value="Adjustment">
</center>
<BR><BR><BR>
<!-- -------- Label Control to Display Status --------------------->
<OBJECT
classid="clsid:99B42120-6EC7-11CF-A6C7-00AA00A47DD2"
id=lblStatus
width=750
height=16
align=middle
hspace=5
vspace=0
border=0
>
<param name="angle" value="0" >
<param name="alignment" value="3" >
<param name="BackStyle" value="0" >
<param name="caption" value="">
<param name="FontName" value="Arial">
<param name="FontSize" value="16">
<param name="FontBold" value="1">
</OBJECT>


<HR>

<center>
<address>
Copyright 1996
By Ken and Jasper's Wiseone Engineering and Tim Associates<br>
3100 Ginnyemmaben Lane
Lisakaylaryanville, Mi 11111
</address>
</center>
</BODY>

</HTML>
```

The code is not secure in this case. Notice how easy it is to spot the top-secret constants in this code (even if a comment didn't call attention to them). The company's proprietary knowledge is there for everyone—including competitors—to view. Anyone who looks at your page can view your script by selecting the View Source option of her browser. This is quite different from the programs generated by most sophisticated languages. Usually, traditional programs are distributed as files of bytes to be executed or interpreted, and you cannot read them easily, if at all. The ease of viewing a Web page source is generally a nice feature because it helps developers quickly pick up new techniques and learn from one another's pages. However, this stops feeling like a nice feature as soon as you complete your first Web page that you want to share with the world without sharing the script source code behind it.

How can you protect this code? Your options are rather limited today but are rapidly expanding. As long as your Web page has standard VBScript code, it's there for the viewing and the taking. Legal or ethical considerations might discourage people from taking a competitor's code, but from a strictly technical aspect, anyone who can view your page in the browser also has the capability to view and lift the code in your page. The still-evolving network etiquette and attitudes of users are oriented toward very open sharing. Because the Internet and World Wide Web began and prospered on the concept of openness, a widespread attitude is that the source code of any page is fair game to view, investigate, and even incorporate.

NOTE

> The software development industry and one's personal satisfaction in being a part of it will remain strongest if all programmers seek to maintain the highest ethical standards in crafting their programs. Be sure to pay careful attention to copyright issues and seek permission from other page owners before incorporating any pieces of programming from another Web page into your own. (This guideline should be coupled with common sense. It does not apply to intentional sample code, of course. Help yourself freely to any of the code you find in these sample pages—you don't have to e-mail us to ask if you can use it in your solutions!)

Better solutions for protecting VBScript do exist. One alternative is to move your code to an ActiveX control or a Java applet object and distribute that with your page. The objects are distributed as files of bytes to the client computer rather than as easily read text. Of course, this is not always a very attractive option because it can involve a fair amount of work. However, it is expected that the next version of the regular Visual Basic product will allow generation of ActiveX controls, so at least it will be easier to make this migration. Listing 21.4 shows a modified page after the proprietary code of Listing 21.3 was replaced by a customized ActiveX control.

21

Listing 21.4. A page where the proprietary code has been moved to an ActiveX control.

```
<HTML>
<HEAD>
<TITLE>Ken and Jasper's WiseOne Engineering</TITLE>

<H1>
<A HREF="http://www.mcp.com"><IMG  ALIGN=BOTTOM SRC="wiseone.jpg" BORDER=2></A>
<EM>Ken and Jasper's WiseOne Engineering</EM>
</h1>
<HR>
</HEAD>

<EM>Enter the reading on Gadget 1 and we'll give you the adjustment factor</EM>

<SCRIPT language="VBS">
<!--

sub cmdAdjustment_OnClick
' Calculate the adjustment factor based on Gadget 1 reading
    dim dblTemp1 ' Hold intermediate result

    ' Use our custom-made ActiveX control to get the adjustment factor
    ctlOurControl.GadgetReading = txtGadget.value
    dblTemp1 = ctlOurControl.GetAdjustment

    lblStatus.Caption = "The adjustment factor is " & str(dblTemp1)

end sub

-->
</script>


<center>
Enter gadget 1 value here:<input name="txtGadget1">
<h3>Click here to do the adjustment</h3>
<input type="button" name="cmdAdjustment" value="Adjustment">
</center>
<BR><BR><BR>
<!-- ----------- Label Control to Display Status -------------------->
<OBJECT

classid="clsid:99B42120-6EC7-11CF-A6C7-00AA00A47DD2"

id=lblStatus
width=750
height=16
align=middle
hspace=5
vspace=0
border=0
>
<param name="angle" value="0" >
```

```
<param name="alignment" value="3" >
<param name="BackStyle" value="0" >
<param name="caption" value="">
<param name="FontName" value="Arial">
<param name="FontSize" value="16">
<param name="FontBold" value="1">
</OBJECT>


<!-- -------- Custom Control to Calculate Adjustment ---------------------->
<OBJECT

classid="clsid:99B42120-6EC7-11CF-A6C7-00AA00A47DD2"

id=ctlOurControl
width=750
height=16
align=middle
hspace=5
vspace=0
border=0
>
<param name="Gadget1" value="20" >
</OBJECT>

<HR>

<center>
<address>
Copyright 1996
By Ken and Jasper's Wiseone Engineering and Tim Associates<br>
3100 Ginnyemmaben Lane
Lisakaylaryanville, Mi 11111
</address>
</center>
</BODY>

</HTML>
```

If you compare Listing 21.3 and Listing 21.4, the risk of including proprietary code is clear. When it's in the script, it's there for all to see. When it's moved to an ActiveX control, others might be able to use the control to get the same results from your page, but they cannot view the source code itself. Moving key code to a control also facilitates reusability. If you've used the control in 20 pages and you have to change a constant, you can just update one control. If you used direct VBScript code without a control, you'd need to make a change in 20 places. For key issues such as security and maintainability, you might sometimes decide to move part of your script solutions to controls. Generally speaking, though, the flexibility and quick development of coding in VBScript probably justify keeping as much code as possible at the script level.

21

You can also use the Layout control described on Day 18, "Advanced User Interface and Browser Object Techniques," but then your code will not be as easily viewable. When the user selects View | Source from the browser, he will see the page that includes the Layout control, not the code defined within the Layout Editor. Because this technology is still in early beta, this may be handled differently on subsequent releases. There is a long-term solution that is likely to be even better: An evolving standard would place a tag at the top of the page that indicates, among other things, whether the source of a page can be viewed. If it is designated as private, the browser would not display the source code behind it even when the user selects View | Source. There are always ways to defeat security, however. These technologies are perhaps more prone to interception than having code in a control, and you might not want to have your company fortune depend on them.

Fortunately, the vast majority of VBScript writers are probably not too concerned with these source code privacy issues. Most code makes pages active and glues together the operation of components, but the code doesn't often have corporate knowledge embedded within the script. However, VBScript is so quick and easy to use that you might find a greater cumulative body of knowledge reflected in the collective scripts of all your Web pages. Be aware that wherever your script visits, its source code visits as well!

Summary

Today's lesson addresses the robustness and safety of HTML-related scripts written in VBScript. The browser will detect any long-running scripts that might be stuck in a loop, notify the user, and halt the script. The language itself provides few means to get into trouble. VBScript has no file I/O, no clipboard control, no memory management, and no memory pointers for this reason. This makes it a safer language that is highly unlikely to introduce errors affecting other programs. Viruses pose another risk to the integrity of the user's browser environment. The same language restrictions that apply to VBScript to reduce the likelihood of accidental errors also reduce the possibility of viruses.

The only potential for serious problems with a script is through the components it integrates. You can download components along with a page and the script that uses them from a Web server. Because components are written in languages other than VBScript, all safety bets are off. However, components can also be certified. A certification means that the control has been examined, tested, and provided with a digital signature that uniquely identifies it across the industry. You can use certified controls with a high degree of confidence that you are safe from risk.

Q&A

Q What happens when VBScript gets into an endless loop? Will the script keep running until the browser runs out of memory?

A No. The browser will detect that the script has been running for an inordinate period of time and present you with a message box to cancel the script.

Q If you need to communicate with another task in the Windows environment from VBScript, is it better to use a dynamic link library call, share information through the clipboard, perform simple file I/O, or redesign your script?

A The first three approaches will not work because none of the technologies mentioned are supported under VBScript. The best bet is to rethink the design of the script. Perhaps you can merge the tasks that must communicate into one page. Maybe server-side communication through submitting data to a server program you write is a better approach. In any case, VBScript will not support these communication activities directly.

Workshop

Write your own endless loop program for experimental purposes as described earlier today. Because this is a script where you have intentionally introduced a problem, make sure not to distribute it on your server. Even though you don't expect any other side effects, practice safe computing. Make sure all other programs of importance are closed before you do these tests.

Load the page with this script into the browser. Start the loop and observe how long it takes the browser to detect the long-running script, notify you, and halt it. Do you think this behavior could interrupt any correctly functioning scripts? Write a large calculation loop (that is not endless) and time it. Observe whether it comes in under the browser "endless activity" detection time. Most practical applications should complete their work well under this time line.

Try to use other programs at the same time the code is running. See if you observe any noticeable effect on the performance of those other applications. Generally, you won't see much impact, but certain operations can cause a ripple. For example, a script that heavily stresses memory could make a noticeable impact. Extensive allocation of very large strings through repeated string assignments to grow the string longer and longer is one such case.

21

Quiz

NOTE

Refer to Appendix C, "Answers to Quiz Questions," for the answers to these questions.

1. List two normal aspects of a traditional Windows programming language not in VBScript whose absence could be said to make VBScript a more secure environment.

2. Why is it safest to use certified controls in a script?

21

WEEK 3

In Review

This week you learned about a broad range of issues, all of which are important to being a top-notch VBScript developer. You rounded out your repertoire this week by learning about all the advanced functions of VBScript in areas such as string handling, date usage, and math. Then you tackled key strategic areas that are essential to sophisticated script development. Among these areas are debugging techniques, advanced user interface considerations, validation and server techniques, porting code, and security. Now that you have reached the conclusion of this week's chapters, your arsenal of VBScript techniques is complete. Although the learning never stops as evolution marches ever forward with advanced software technologies, you have now gained a state-of-the-art, fundamental knowledge of what VBScript is all about.

Where You Have Been

A lot of important ground was covered this week as you completed the quest to obtain full VBScript knowledge in all nuances of the language. Day 15 covered working with strings through a variety of string functions. Working with math and dates was introduced on Day 16. Day 17 took a look at exterminating bugs from your script, and Day 18 showed you how to use advanced user interface techniques in your script. Active document strategies were covered on Day 19. Day 20 discussed porting between Visual Basic and VBScript. Finally, the week ended with a look at some very important security and server considerations on Day 21. You are now ready to use scripts to produce your own active pages. With the techniques you have picked up along the way, you can fully exploit this leading-edge technology. You can create fast, powerful scripts with an ease and flexibility that was unheard of a short time ago in the industry. Of course, many more changes are probably coming in the days ahead, including new World Wide Web–related standards, continuing evolution of the Windows environment, and advancements in many page- and document-related technologies. You can rest fairly assured of two things in the days ahead: Change is constant, and your VBScript scripting knowledge will probably be of use in many of the still emerging areas, as well as in the pages you write today. Happy scripting!

APPENDIX

A

VBScript Syntax Quick Reference

VBScript is composed of a great deal of syntax you need to keep straight. You will probably use many elements of the syntax so often that you will easily remember what they do. However, even an experienced programmer uses some of the syntax elements infrequently. When you come across those elements in your code or strain to remember if you have the syntax exactly right, a good reference can serve as a welcome relief.

Languages such as Visual Basic 4.0 come complete with a very useful context-sensitive help facility. VBScript provides no such inherent support. It is a hosted language that comes along for the ride with the environment that supports it, such as a browser. It is not a separate product with its own development environment and the help that is typical of such an environment. You can turn to other places for help on the Internet, however. At the time of this writing, Microsoft had a very helpful VBScript language reference that could be reached at `http://www.microsoft.com/vbscript`.

This appendix is intended to supplement the VBScript information available from the Web location. Unlike some of the other language references available, the information in this appendix is presented in an alphabetical fashion, intermixing functions, statements, intrinsic constants, and major properties in the same list. A brief description of each element is provided, but it's not enough to replace the official reference material—just enough to give you a quick, high-level understanding of what that element does.

You'll develop a common way to refer to information as you work your way through a new book or sample programs. You might find a language element that is unfamiliar, but all you need to do to quickly get back on course is see a brief description of what it does and find out if it is a property, function, or other type of construct. This appendix can serve as a quick first resort for such information.

Table A.1. Summary of VBScript syntax.

Symbol	Type	Description
+ (addition)	Operator	Adds two numbers together. You can also use this to concatenate strings.
' (comment indicator)	Keyword	What follows this symbol on the line is a comment.
" (double quote)	Keyword	Shows the start and end of a literal string.
& (string concatenation)	Operator	Performs the concatenation of two string expressions.
/ (division, floating point)	Operator	Divides two numbers and returns a floating-point result.
\ (division, integer)	Operator	Divides two numbers and returns an integer result.

Symbol	Type	Description
= (equals)	Comparison	Checks whether two expressions are equivalent.
^ (exponent)	Operator	Raises a number to the power of an exponent.
> (greater than)	Comparison	Checks whether the left-side expression is greater than the right-side expression.
>= (greater than or equal)	Comparison	Checks whether the left-side expression is greater than or equal to the right-side expression.
< (less than)	Comparison	Checks whether the left-side expression is less than the right-side expression.
<= (less than or equal)	Comparison	Checks whether the left-side expression is less than or equal to the right-side expression.
_ (line continuation character)	Keyword	Indicates that the current line continues onto the next line.
* (multiplication)	Operator	Multiplies two numbers.
- (subtraction or indicator)	Operator	Finds the difference between two numbers; or, when applied to one operand, treats it as a negative value.
: (colon)		Indicates line separation, as in `A = A + 1 : B = C + 1`.
<> (not equal)	Comparison	Checks whether two expressions are not equivalent.
Abs	Function	Returns the absolute value of a number.
And	Logical operator	Performs a logical conjunction on two expressions.
Array	Function	Returns a variant comprising an array.
Asc	Function	Provides the character code corresponding to the first letter in a string as a return code.
AscB	Function	Like Asc, but returns the first byte rather than the first character of a string.
Atn	Function	Provides the arctangent of a number as a return code.

continues

Table A.1. continued

Symbol	Type	Description
Call	Statement	Calls a procedure.
CBool	Function	Provides as a return code an expression that has been converted to a variant of subtype `Boolean`.
Cbyte	Function	Provides as a return code an expression that has been converted to a variant of subtype `Byte`.
CDate	Function	Provides as a return code an expression that has been converted to a variant of subtype `Date`.
CDbl	Function	Provides as a return code an expression that has been converted to a variant of subtype `Double`.
Chr	Function	Provides as a return code the character associated with the ASCII code. This function can return 1 or 2 bytes.
ChrB	Function	Returns the byte associated with the ASCII code.
Cint	Function	Provides as a return code an expression that has been converted to a variant of subtype `Integer`.
Clear	Method for the `Err` object	Results in resetting all of the `Err` objects properties to a no-error state.
CLng	Function	Provides as a return code an expression that has been converted to a variant of subtype `Long`.
Cos	Function	Provides as a return code the cosine of an angle.
CSng	Function	Provides as a return code an expression that has been converted to a variant of subtype `Single`.
CStr	Function	Provides as a return code an expression that has been converted to a variant of subtype `String`.

A

Symbol	Type	Description
CVErr	Function	Provides as a return code a variant of subtype Error containing a user-provided error code.
Date	Function	Returns the current system date.
DateSerial	Function	Provides as a return code a variant of subtype Date for the given month, day, and year.
DateValue	Function	Provides as a return code a variant of subtype Date for the given string.
Day	Function	Provides as a return code a whole number of 1 through 31, representing the day of the month for the given date string.
Description	Property for the Err object	The string that describes the current error.
Dim	Statement	Declares variables.
Do...Loop	Statement	Repeats a block of code while a condition is True or until a condition becomes True.
Empty	Literal	Signifies that a variable is uninitialized.
Erase	Statement	Reinitializes fixed-size array elements and frees the storage space of dynamic arrays.
Err	Object	Provides information about run-time errors.
Eqv	Logical operator	Performs logical equivalence for the two expressions provided as operands.
Exit Do	Statement	Exits a Do...Loop code block.
Exit For	Statement	Exits a For...Next code block.
Exit Function	Statement	Exits a function.
Exit Sub	Statement	Exits a procedure.
Exp	Function	Returns e (the base of natural logarithms) raised to a power.
Fix	Function	Provides the integer portion of a number as a return code; if the number is negative, it provides the first number greater than the operand.

continues

Table A.1. continued

Symbol	Type	Description
For...Next	Statement	Repeats a group of statements a designated number of times.
For Each...Next	Statement	Repeats a group of statements for each element in an array or a collection.
Function	Statement	Declares a procedure-level block of code that returns a value when called.
HelpContext	Property for the Err object	The context ID in a corresponding help file for the current error.
HelpFile	Property for the Err object	The corresponding help file for the current error.
Hex	Function	Provides as a return code a string representing the hexadecimal value of a number.
Hour	Function	Provides as a return code a whole number from 0 through 23, representing the hour of the day.
If...Then...Else	Statement	Executes a group of statements, depending on the value of an expression.
Imp	Logical operator	Performs a logical implication on the two operands provided.
InputBox	Function	Displays a dialog box with a prompt, appropriate buttons, and an input text box and then returns the input text and button response to the calling program.
Int	Function	Provides the integer portion of a number as a return code; if the number is negative, it provides the first number less than the operand.
InStr	Function	Provides the position indicator of the first character of the target string within the search string.
InstrB	Function	Provides the position indicator of the first byte of the target string within the search string.
Is	Operator	Compares two object reference variables.

A

Symbol	Type	Description
IsArray	Function	Provides as a return code a `Boolean` value signifying whether a variable is an array.
IsDate	Function	Provides as a return code a `Boolean` value signifying whether an expression can be converted to a date.
IsEmpty	Function	Provides as a return code a `Boolean` value signifying whether a variable has been initialized.
IsError	Function	Provides as a return code a `Boolean` value signifying whether an expression is an error value.
IsNull	Function	Provides as a return code a `Boolean` value signifying whether an expression contains no valid data (`Null`).
IsNumeric	Function	Provides as a return code a `Boolean` value signifying whether an expression can be evaluated as a number.
IsObject	Function	Provides as a return code a `Boolean` value signifying whether an expression represents an OLE automation object.
LBound	Function	Provides as a return code the smallest available subscript for the stated dimension of an array.
Lcase	Function	Provides as a return code a string that has been converted to lowercase.
Left	Function	Provides as a return code a specified number of characters from the left side of a string.
Len	Function	Provides as a return code the number of characters in a string or the number of bytes required to store a variable.
LenB	Function	Provides as a return code the number of bytes in a string or the number of bytes required to store a variable.

continues

Table A.1. continued

Symbol	Type	Description
Log	Function	Provides as a return code the natural logarithm of a number.
Ltrim	Function	Provides a string that has leading (leftmost) spaces removed.
Mid	Function	Provides as a return code a described number of characters from a string.
Minute	Function	Provides as a return code a whole number from 0 through 59, representing the minute of the hour.
Mod	Operator	Divides two numbers and returns only the remainder.
Month	Function	Provides as a return code a whole number from 1 through 12, representing the month of the year.
MsgBox	Function	Shows a given prompt in a message dialog box with a button and returns the user's button response.
Not	Logical operator	Checks for logical Not equivalent condition.
Nothing	Literal	Removes reference and frees memory.
Now	Function	Returns the current setting of your computer's system date and time.
Null	Literal	Indicates no valid data state, as opposed to Empty, which indicates no data was ever assigned.
Number	Property for the Err object	The numeric error code for the current error.
Oct	Function	Provides as a return code a string representing the octal value of a number.
On Error Resume Next	Statement	Indicates that if an error occurs, control should resume at next statement.
Option Explicit	Statement	Indicates that variables must be declared.
Or	Operator	Performs a logical disjunction on two expressions.

A

Symbol	Type	Description
Raise	Method for the Err object	Forces a run-time error to be raised.
Randomize	Statement	Starts a sequence for the random-number generator.
ReDim	Statement	Allocates or reallocates storage space and declares dynamic-array variables at the procedure level.
Rem	Statement	Used to include comments in a program. The single quote, which achieves the same purpose, is used more often.
Right	Function	Provides as a return code a described number of characters from the right side of a string.
Rnd	Function	Provides a random number as a return code.
Rtrim	Function	Provides a string that has trailing (rightmost) spaces removed.
Second	Function	Provides as a return code a whole number from 0 through 59, representing the second of the minute.
Set	Statement	Assigns an object reference.
Sgn	Function	Provides as a return code an integer disclosing the sign of a number.
Sin	Function	Provides as a return code the sine of an angle.
Source	Property for the Err object	The source of the error for the current error.
Space	Function	Returns the given number of spaces.
Sqr	Function	Provides as a return code the square root of a number.
Static	Statement (Procedure-level)	Declares a persistent variable. Contents will be retained from one call to the next.
StrComp	Function	Returns a value signifying the outcome of a string comparison.

continues

Table A.1. continued

Symbol	Type	Description
String	Function	Returns a repeating character string of the number of characters described.
Sub	Statement	Declares procedures that do not provide a return code.
Tan	Function	Provides as a return code the tangent of an angle.
Time	Function	Returns a variant of subtype Date showing the current system time.
TimeSerial	Function	Returns a variant of subtype Date comprising the time for a specific hour, minute, and second.
TimeValue	Function	Returns a variant of subtype Date containing the time.
Trim	Function	Provides as a return code a duplicate of a string without leading spaces (LTrim), trailing spaces (RTrim), or both leading and trailing spaces (Trim).
Ubound	Function	Provides as a return code the largest available subscript for the indicated dimension of an array.
Ucase	Function	Returns a string that has been converted to uppercase.
Val	Function	Returns the numbers enclosed in a string. Not supported in current beta.
VarType	Function	Returns a value disclosing the subtype of a variable.
vbAbort	(See footnote*)	Applies to the MsgBox function; Value = 3 indicates abort.
vbAbortRetryIgnore	(See footnote*)	Applies to the MsgBox function; Value = 2 displays Abort, Retry, and Ignore buttons.
vbApplicationModal	(See footnote*)	Applies to the MsgBox function; Value = 0 indicates that the application is modal. The user must respond to the message box before continuing work in the current application.

Symbol	Type	Description
vbArray	(See footnote*)	Applies to the VarType function; Value = 8192 indicates array.
vbBoolean	(See footnote*)	Applies to the VarType function; Value = 11 indicates Boolean.
vbByte	(See footnote*)	Applies to the VarType function; Value = 17 indicates byte.
vbCancel	(See footnote*)	Applies to the MsgBox function; Value = 2 indicates cancel.
vbCr	(See footnote*)	General purpose; indicates carriage-return character.
vbCritical	(See footnote*)	Applies to the MsgBox function; Value = 16 displays critical message icon.
vbCrLf	(See footnote*)	General purpose; indicates carriage-return and line-feed characters.
vbCurrency	(See footnote*)	Applies to the VarType function; Value = 6 indicates currency.
vbDataObject	(See footnote*)	Applies to the VarType function; Value = 13 indicates non-OLE automation object.
vbDate	(See footnote*)	Applies to the VarType function; Value = 7 indicates date.
vbDefaultButton1	(See footnote*)	Applies to the MsgBox function; Value = 0 indicates the first button is the default.
vbDefaultButton2	(See footnote*)	Applies to the MsgBox function; Value = 256 indicates the second button is the default.
vbDefaultButton3	(See footnote*)	Applies to the MsgBox function; Value = 512 indicates the third button is the default.
vbDouble	(See footnote*)	Applies to the VarType function; Value = 5 indicates a double-precision, floating-point number.
vbEmpty	(See footnote*)	Applies to the VarType function; Value = 0 indicates empty.

continues

A

Table A.1. continued

Symbol	Type	Description
vbError	(See footnote*)	Applies to the VarType function; Value = 10 indicates error.
vbExclamation	(See footnote*)	Applies to the MsgBox function; Value = 48 displays the warning message icon.
vbFalse	(See footnote*)	General purpose; indicates Boolean value represented by 0.
vbFriday	(See footnote*)	Applies to the Weekday function; Value = 6 indicates Friday.
vbIgnore	(See footnote*)	Applies to the MsgBox function; Value = 5 indicates ignore.
vbInformation	(See footnote*)	Applies to the MsgBox function; Value = 64 displays information message icon.
vbInteger	(See footnote*)	Applies to the VarType function; Value = 2 indicates integer.
vbLf	(See footnote*)	General purpose; indicates line-feed character.
vbLong	(See footnote*)	Applies to the VarType function; Value = 3 indicates long integer.
vbMonday	(See footnote*)	Applies to the Weekday function; Value = 2 indicates Monday.
vbNo	(See footnote*)	Applies to the MsgBox function; Value = 7 indicates no.
vbNull	(See footnote*)	Applies to the VarType function; Value = 1 indicates null.
vbObject	(See footnote*)	Applies to the VarType function; Value = 9 indicates OLE automation object.
vbObjectError	(See footnote*)	Indicates an object-generated error.
vbOK	(See footnote*)	Applies to the MsgBox function; Value = 1 indicates OK.
vbOKCancel	(See footnote*)	Applies to MsgBox function; Value = 1 displays OK and Cancel buttons.
vbOKOnly	(See footnote*)	Applies to the MsgBox function; Value = 0 displays OK button only.
vbQuestion	(See footnote*)	Applies to the MsgBox function; Value = 32 displays warning query icon.

A

Symbol	Type	Description
vbRetry	(See footnote*)	Applies to the MsgBox function; Value = 4 indicates retry.
vbRetryCancel	(See footnote*)	Applies to the MsgBox function; Value = 5 displays Retry and Cancel buttons.
vbSaturday	(See footnote*)	Applies to the Weekday function; Value = 7 indicates Saturday.
vbSingle	(See footnote*)	Applies to the VarType function; Value = 4 indicates single-precision, floating-point number.
vbString	(See footnote*)	Applies to the VarType function; Value = 8 indicates string.
vbSunday	(See footnote*)	Applies to the Weekday function; Value = 1 indicates Sunday.
vbSystemModal	(See footnote*)	Applies to the MsgBox function; Value = 4096 indicates system modal. All applications are suspended until the user responds to the message box.
vbThursday	(See footnote*)	Applies to the Weekday function; Value = 5 indicates Thursday.
vbTrue	(See footnote*)	General purpose; indicates Boolean value represented by -1.
vbTuesday	(See footnote*)	Applies to the Weekday function; Value = 3 indicates Tuesday.
vbUseSystem	(See footnote*)	Applies to the Weekday function; Value = 0 uses the NLS API setting.
vbVariant	(See footnote*)	Applies to the VarType function; Value = 12 indicates variant.
vbWednesday	(See footnote*)	Applies to the Weekday function; Value = 4 indicates Wednesday.
vbYes	(See footnote*)	Applies to the MsgBox function; Value = 6 indicates yes.
vbYesNo	(See footnote*)	Applies to the MsgBox function; Value = 4 displays Yes and No buttons.
vbYesNoCancel	(See footnote*)	Applies to the MsgBox function; Value = 3 displays Yes, No, and Cancel buttons.

continues

Table A.1. continued

Symbol	Type	Description
Weekday	Function	Returns a whole number showing the day of the week.
While...Wend	Statement	Performs a series of statements as long as a given condition is True.
Xor	Logical operator	Performs logical exclusion on the operands.
Year	Function	Returns a whole number showing the year for the date string representation.

*The symbols with the vb prefix are values expected by various VBScript functions. In Visual Basic these are intrinsic contants. In VBScript, you must declare these as variables if you wish to treat them as constants since there is no direct constant support.

APPENDIX

B

Information Resources

One book can take you a long way, but eventually, you're bound to have more questions or wonder about more related topics than can be addressed in several hundred or even several thousand pages. That's when the World Wide Web's virtually unlimited capability of browsing for information can be a great asset. With the help provided here to point you in the right direction, you should be able to find abundant online information on all aspects of VBScript and related technologies.

The URLs that appear here were active at the time of writing. There is no guarantee that they will still be current at the time you read this because links and sites may change with time. This information will at least give you a taste of the wealth of VBScript-related information available on the Internet and provide a starting point for further online research. The information that follows is divided into two sections: discussion of where you can find the home pages for any needed updates for the examples used in this book and a larger section that discusses URLs for a variety of helpful VBScript or related technology sites.

Update Information for This Book

All the samples used in this book are available on the CD-ROM that comes with the book. That should be your first avenue for exploring the scripts further. Make sure you start with `default.htm` on the CD-ROM. This will provide you with an overview page that provides links to all other topics and sample programs. However, we might need to update some of these samples over time. Some examples may be revised as the product evolves. In such cases, these files might be available over the World Wide Web at the site listed here. In addition, we'll maintain a list of any late-breaking announcements relevant to the book. Check these sites for current availability at the time you read this; there is a good chance that you will find they are active and contain some information of interest. Your best bet is to investigate and see what's there!

Sams.net Home Page

```
http://www.mcp.com
```

This URL will take you to the home page for Macmillan Computer Publishing USA. From here, you can select Sams.net and navigate to the Sams.net home page. Check the book topics there to see if any relevant updates to the samples in this book exist under the official location.

DoubleBlaze Software Consortium Home Page

```
http://www.doubleblaze.com/vbs21day
```

This URL is another potential source of information on any updates to the book. Information on VBScript tools may be available as well under `www.doubleblaze.com`.

DoubleBlaze Software Consortium is a small, independent software research and development company of Mr. Brophy. Mr. Koets and his Cockatiel Software company have close affiliations with DoubleBlaze as well. So if you want to see what the authors are up to and if they have any books coming up, this is the place to go. You quite likely will find general information on VBScript tools, and maybe even a cartoon on the site from time to time.

The Internet Services Provider

B

For more information on CNS Internet Services, an Internet service provider that offers services ranging from Internet connections to Web page hosts, refer to `http://gr.cns.net`. CNS offers, among other services, Web page hosting if you need a place for your scripts to live on the Internet.

General Information Resources

The following is an index of just some of the multitude of information resources related to the World Wide Web, Web page development, and VBScript.

Carl & Gary's Visual Basic Home Page

`http://www.apexsc.com/vb`

General Visual Basic information.

CGI Specification

`http://hoohoo.ncsa.uiuc.edu/cgi/interface.html`

Information on the Common Gateway Interface specification.

Lynx

`http://www.cc.ukans.edu/about_lynx/`

Information on the Lynx browser.

Macmillan Computer Publishing

http://www.mcp.com

Information from Macmillan Computer Publishing, including a link to Sams.net, publisher of leading Internet-related books such as *Teach Yourself Java in 21 Days* and *Teach Yourself VBScript in 21 Days*.

Microsoft

http://www.microsoft.com/intdev

Microsoft provides a variety of information and Internet products from the Web site. Microsoft's products in this arena are evolving rapidly, and locations of information change from time to time. The best strategy to get any kind of information, unless noted otherwise, is to start at www.microsoft.com/intdev. Then, from the Internet Developer's area, use the search boxes to search for your topic of interest. That's the most reliable way to dig up the pages you need quickly!

Microsoft ActiveX Control Kit

http://www.microsoft.com/intdev

At this site you can get ActiveX controls that you can download and install on your system, which enables you to run scripts that utilize these controls with your browser. Eventually these controls will likely be installed with the browser and a separate download may not be necessary.

Microsoft Internet Download Toolbox

http://www.microsoft.com/intdev

From this location you can reach a summary of available Internet tools that you can download over the Web.

Microsoft Internet Explorer

http://www.microsoft.com/ie/

The browser for downloading and related information.

Microsoft VBScript Information

http://www.microsoft.com/vbscript

General VBScript information from Microsoft.

Microsoft VBScript Language Reference

http://www.microsoft.com/vbscript/us/vbslang/vbstoc.htm

VBScript language reference pages from Microsoft.

NCSA Mosaic

http://www.ncsa.uiuc.edu/SDG/Software/Mosaic/NCSAMosaicHome.html

The browser for downloading and related information.

Netscape

http://home.netscape.com

From here you can reach the Navigator browser for downloading and related information.

Unofficial VBScript Information Page

http://home.sprynet.com/sprynet/bjjohnson/vbs.htm

Summary of VBScript resources from Brian Johnson.

Visual Basic CGI Programming

http://website.ora.com/devcorner/db-src/index.html

Approach for writing back-end Visual Basic and Access programs using Windows CGI, from Bob Denny.

VBScript Observations and Samples

http://www.doubleblaze.com

Under this URL you can reach an area of VBScript observations and samples collected in the course of research and experimentation. Availability and degree of information will vary over time.

B

World Wide Web Consortium (W3C) Drafts

http://www.w3.org/pub/WWW/TR

A list of W3C working drafts in general.

W3C Objects: "Inserting Objects into HTML" Working Draft

http://www/w3.org/pub/WWW/TR/WD-object.html

The W3C draft standards on "Inserting Objects into HTML."

APPENDIX

C

Answers to Quiz Questions

Day 1

1. The World Wide Web has become one of the most popular services on the Internet, since it allows users to view Web pages. Another very popular Internet service is FTP, since that service allows Internet users to send and receive files on the Internet. The ability of Web pages to allow you to use FTP is a marriage of two of the most popular Internet services today.

2. Web pages are built using the Hypertext Markup Language, or HTML. Other languages such as VBScript and CGI can be used to make Web pages more powerful in ways that HTML cannot.

3. VBScript is *not* a part of HTML, but HTML can include a tag that will tell the browser to allow VBScript code to execute. When VBScript code is placed within HTML code, a special "tag" is used that tells HTML to allow another language to be run. The Web browser is responsible for figuring out what that other language is and passing control to it. Thus, when a VBScript is embedded in an HTML document, the Web browser passes control to the VBScript interpreter.

Day 2

1. The most significant capability a scripting language affords a Web page is the ability of the user to interact with the Web page. This means that the user can manipulate the various controls, objects, and components on the Web page, and the code that executes when those controls are manipulated accomplishes the user's goals.

2. VBScript can work with and help integrate together intrinsic HTML controls such as text box controls and buttons; Java applets; ActiveX controls such as rotating labels, charts, and timers; OLE controls, or OCXs, such as calendars, status bars, and other specialized controls; and embedded OLE objects, such as spreadsheets, graphics programs, and word processors.

3. The VBScript code that comes along in a Web page cannot directly access any files on the client's computer. This prevents a Web page from making any modifications to sensitive files on the user's computer. VBScript is also very safe in that it doesn't give programmers the ability to create unrecoverable crashes by virtue of its language syntax.

4. VBScript was derived from Microsoft Visual Basic. A limited set of commands and functions were taken from Visual Basic. This makes it easy for those who already know Visual Basic to use VBScript—plus it leverages all the benefits of Visual Basic to the Internet.

5. All you need is a browser that supports Visual Basic Script, which typically includes the Visual Basic Script run-time interpreter. Then, you are ready to use any page

containing Visual Basic Script. If you are going to develop Visual Basic Script programs as well, you need a simple text editor to edit HTML documents. Armed with these tools, you can write and use Web pages that contain Visual Basic Script code.

Day 3

1. To state it in quite simplified terms, all you need in each case is for the tool to have access to the VBScript runtime interpreter, along with the ability of the software tool to recognize when it needs to pass control to the runtime interpreter.

2. In addition to Internet Explorer, technologies such as Next Software, Inc's WebObjects, Microsoft's Internet Information Server, and Active VRML will take advantage of VBScript. Many browsers do or will support VBScript, as well as many OLE controls designed for creating browsers or implementing that technology. Because the Internet is changing so quickly, the list is growing rapidly. In our opinion, most browsers will eventually support VBScript, but at the time of this writing, the majority of Web users were not yet on VBScript–aware browsers. Refer to the references in Appendix A, "VBScript Syntax Quick Reference," to obtain up-to-date information.

3. This code listing illustrates the "barebones" structure of an HTML document that uses VBScript. Note that all the HTML sections have starting and ending tags associated with them:

```
<HTML>
<HEAD>
</HEAD>
<BODY>
<SCRIPT LANGUAGE="VBScript">
<!--
… VBScript code goes here
-->
</SCRIPT>
</BODY>
</HTML>
```

Day 4

1. The data type of VBScript variables is called the variant. Using the variant, you can store data of all the fundamental data subtypes listed in this lesson. The data subtypes you can store include the integer, long, byte, Boolean, single, double, date, and string data types.

2. Here's the answer:

```
Dim Name
Name = "Tim Koets"
```

C

3. Here's the answer:

```
If IsNumeric(Age) = False Then
    MsgBox "The size must be a number. Please enter it again."
End If
```

Day 5

1. The answer is shown in the following code segment. The Web page, named
    `05quiz01.htm`, is contained on the CD-ROM that accompanies this book:

```
<HTML>

<TITLE>Chapter 5 Quiz #1</TITLE>

<H1><A HREF="http://www.mcp.com"><IMG  ALIGN=BOTTOM SRC="../shared/jpg/_
            samsnet.jpg" BORDER=2></A>
Converting Inches to Feet</H1>

<BODY>

<HR>

<CENTER>Feet    <INPUT NAME="txtFeet">
<INPUT TYPE=BUTTON VALUE=" Convert " NAME="cmdConvert"></CENTER>

<HR>

<center>
from <em>Teach Yourself Visual Basic Script in 21 Days</em> by
<A HREF="../shared/keith.htm">Keith Brophy</A> and
<A HREF="../shared/tim.htm">Tim Koets</A><br>
Return to <a href="..\default.htm">Content Overview</A><br>
Copyright 1996 by SamsNet<br>
</center>

<SCRIPT LANGUAGE="VBScript">
<!-- Option Explicit

    Sub cmdConvert_OnClick()
        Dim Inches, Feet
        Feet = txtFeet.Value
        Inches = Feet * 12
        MsgBox "There are " & Inches & " inches in " & Feet & " feet."
    End Sub

-->
</SCRIPT>

</BODY>

</HTML>
```

2. The answer is shown in the following code segment. The Web page, named
    `05quiz02.htm`, is contained on the CD-ROM that accompanies this book:

```
<HTML>

<TITLE>Chapter 5 Quiz #2</TITLE>

<H1><A HREF="http://www.mcp.com"><IMG  ALIGN=BOTTOM SRC="../shared/jpg/_
              samsnet.jpg" BORDER=2></A>
The Ticket Stand</H1>

<BODY>

<HR>

<PRE>Name                           <INPUT NAME="txtName"></PRE>
<PRE>Number of Tickets              <INPUT NAME="txtTickets"></PRE>
<PRE>Row Number (1 for front row) <INPUT NAME="txtRow"></PRE>

<CENTER><INPUT TYPE=BUTTON VALUE=" Get Cost " NAME="cmdCost"></CENTER>

<HR>

<center>
from <em>Teach Yourself Visual Basic Script in 21 Days</em> by
<A HREF="../shared/keith.htm">Keith Brophy</A> and
<A HREF="../shared/tim.htm">Tim Koets</A><br>
Return to <a href="..\default.htm">Content Overview</A><br>
Copyright 1996 by SamsNet<br>
</center>

<SCRIPT LANGUAGE="VBScript">
<!-- Option Explicit

   Sub cmdCost_OnClick()

      Dim Cost
      Dim Ticket_Count

      Ticket_Count = txtTickets.Value

      Cost = 20.00                ' Base price

      If txtRow.Value = 1 Then
          Cost = Cost + 4.00      ' Add $4 for front row
      End If

      Cost = Cost * Ticket_Count  ' Get cost for all tickets
      Cost = Cost + Cost * 0.03   ' Add 3% commission
      Cost = Cost + Cost * 0.08   ' Add 8% sales tax

      MsgBox "Your total cost is " & Cost

   End Sub

-->
</SCRIPT>

</BODY>

</HTML>
```

C

3. a. 36

    b. 2

    c. -1

    d. True

    e. False

Day 6

1. If...Then—This control structure is used to make decisions. If the condition is satisfied, the code that follows the If...Then statement is executed.

    A simple example of its use is

    ```
    If Result = True Then
        MsgBox "The result is true."
    End If
    ```

    For...Next—This control structure is used to repeat a block of code nestled between the For and Next statements based on some condition.

    A simple example of its use is

    ```
    For x = 1 to 100
        age(x) = 0
    Next
    ```

    Do...Loop While—This control structure is used to repeat a block of code while the condition is true.

    An example of its use is

    ```
    Do
        age(x) = 0
        x = x + 1
    Loop While x < 100
    ```

2. Here's the code:

    ```
    YearBorn = InputBox("What year were you born in?  ")
    If YearBorn < 1890 Or YearBorn > 1990 Then
        MsgBox "The year you have entered is invalid."
    End If
    ```

3. Here's the code:

    ```
    Proceed = False
    Do
        YearBorn = InputBox("What year were you born in?  ")
        If YearBorn < 1890 Or YearBorn > 1990 Then
            MsgBox "The year you have entered is invalid."
        Else
            Proceed = True
        End If
    Loop Until Proceed = True
    ```

Day 7

1. A function, which is called differently from a subroutine, returns a value to the code that calls it. Functions must be set equal to a return value:

```
Answer = MyFunction(A, B, C)
```

A subroutine, on the other hand, isn't set to a variable. It can be called like

```
MySubroutine A, B, C
```

or

```
Call MySubroutine(A, B, C)
```

2. It is impossible for a procedure to change the value of a variable passed to it unless it gets its own copy. Because the variable A was passed to the function by value, the function GetHypotenuse has its own copy, which is modified within the function. The original variable, however, has exactly the same value it had before the function was called.

3. The correct code listing is shown below. The code was in error because the function CalculateCost modified the two variables passed to it. Those variables were passed by reference, not by value, which is illegal.

```
Sub cmdTest_OnClick()

    Dim Base_Cost
    Dim Total_Cost
    Dim Tax

    Tax = 5      ' Michigan sales tax (5%)

    Total_Cost = CalculateCost(Base_Cost, Tax)

    txtResult.Value = "The total cost is $" & Total_Cost

End Sub

Function CalculateCost(ByVal Cost, ByVal Tax)

    Tax = Tax / 100

    Cost = Cost + Tax * Cost

    CalculateCost = Cost

End Function
```

The solution to the problem is to pass the two parameters in by value so that the function has its own copy of the variables. That way, it can modify the variables as it needs to. The new code listing shows the necessary changes.

Day 8

1. The textarea control is different in many ways. First, it gives you a two-dimensional area in which to place text. Unlike the text control that only has a one-dimensional SIZE attribute, the textarea control lets you adjust its dimensions with the ROWS and COLS attributes. Finally, the textarea control has a starting and ending tag, whereas the text control has a conventional input tag.

2. The following simple Web page, which is named Quiz8-02.htm on the CD-ROM, contains a textarea control and a button. The user enters the products into the textarea control and clicks the button as shown:

```
<HTML>

<HEAD>
<TITLE>Chapter 8 Quiz #1</TITLE>
</HEAD>

<BODY>
<H1>
<A HREF="http://www.mcp.com"><IMG  ALIGN=MIDDLE SRC=".._
/shared/jpg/samsnet.jpg" BORDER=2
HSPACE=20></A>
<EM>Chapter 8 Quiz Answer</EM></h1>
<HR>

<H2>Product Information</H2>

<FORM NAME="MyForm">

<P>Please enter all of the products you would like information about
in the space below. Then, click on the button and you will be
presented with a series of Web pages detailing your selections.
<HR>
<PRE><TEXTAREA NAME="txaProducts" COLS="60" ROWS="10"></TEXTAREA></PRE>
<P><INPUT TYPE="BUTTON" NAME="cmdGetInfo" VALUE=_
"Get Product Information">

</FORM>

<HR>

<center>
From <em>Teach Yourself VBScript in 21 Days</em><br>
by <A HREF="../shared/info/keith.htm">Keith Brophy</A> and
<A HREF="../shared/info/tim.htm">Tim Koets</A><br>
<br>
Return to <A href=Back08.htm>content overview</A><br>
Copyright 1996 by SamsNet<br>
</center>

<SCRIPT LANGUAGE="VBScript">
<!-- Option Explicit
```

```
Sub cmdGetInfo_OnClick()
    MsgBox "The products you're requesting information on_
            will be sent to you momentarily."
End Sub

-->
</SCRIPT>

</BODY>
</HTML>
```

All you need to do next is pass the products to the server and get the information back to the user. You'll learn more about how to do that on Day 19.

Day 9

1. The primary difference is that with a radio button, the user can only select one of several choices. With a check box, the user can select as many of the choices as he wants. Both are useful depending on the circumstances. One important impact this has on your VBScript code is that you can reference the checked property of a check box. A radio button, on the other hand, must be handled through code associated with the OnClick event to know which button the user selected.

2. The text control: You use this control to accept strings from the user in a simple box on the screen.

   The button control: The button control provides a 3-D button the user can click to perform some operation usually designated on the caption of the button.

   The textarea control: This is similar to a text control, but the area the user can enter text into is bigger than one line.

   The radio button control: You commonly use radio buttons to present a series of choices to the user where the user can select only one choice.

   The check box control: Check boxes enable the user to select one or more choices from a list.

   The password control: Use the password control in place of the text control when you want the text entered in the box to be masked so that the user can't see it.

   The reset control: Use the reset control when you want to provide a way for the user to reset a Web page to when loaded. This is especially handy if the user is unable to reload a page from the browser or other software he is using.

   The submit control: This control is a button that, when clicked, sends the contents of an HTML form to a Web server. Use this when you are using CGI to communicate with a server.

The combo control: The combo control is used to present the user with a list of items, of which the user may decide to select one or more items. Use this when you are unsure of the type and number of items you will have, since the combo control lets you select them dynamically.

The select control: The select control provides the user with a list of items much like a menu. Use it to produce a dynamic list of items, only allowing the user to select one item.

The hidden control: The hidden control is like a text control, except that it's invisible. Use it to store data on a Web page instead of in a variable. This could be useful when you wish to transfer data from one scripting language to another or for an easy way to store data being transmitted across a Web server.

3. The answer to this quiz question is provided on the CD-ROM that accompanies this book. Figure C.1 shows the file, which is named convert.htm.

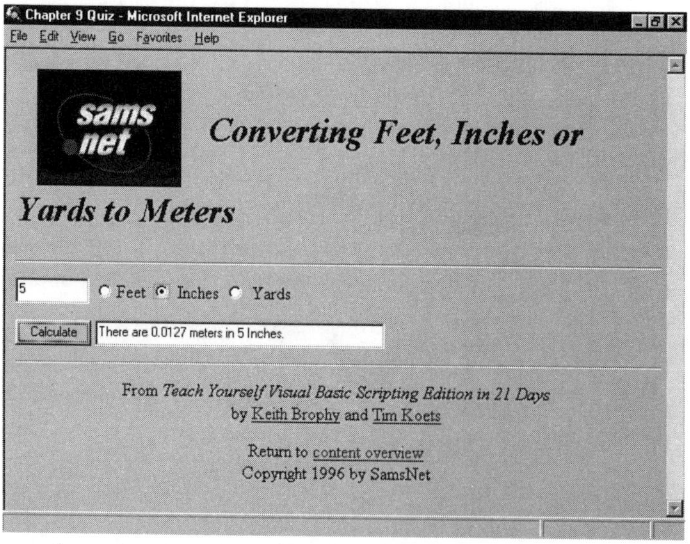

Figure C.1.

A Web page that converts feet, inches, or yards to meters.

The following segment shows the source code for the Web page:

```
<HTML>

<HEAD>
<TITLE>Chapter 9 Quiz</TITLE>
</HEAD>

<BODY>
<H1>
<A HREF="http://www.mcp.com"><IMG  ALIGN=MIDDLE
SRC="../shared/jpg/samsnet.jpg" BORDER=2 HSPACE=20></A>
<EM>Converting Feet, Inches or Yards to Meters</EM></H1>
<HR>
```

```
<INPUT TYPE="TEXT" NAME="txtNumber" SIZE="10">

<INPUT TYPE="RADIO" NAME="optUnits" CHECKED
  OnClick="SetUnits('Feet')"> Feet
<INPUT TYPE="RADIO" NAME="optUnits"
  OnClick="SetUnits('Inches')"> Inches
<INPUT TYPE="RADIO" NAME="optUnits"
  OnClick="SetUnits('Yards')"> Yards
<P>
<INPUT TYPE="BUTTON" NAME="cmdResults" VALUE="Calculate">
<INPUT NAME="txtResult" SIZE="50">

<HR>
<center>
From <em>Teach Yourself VBScript in 21 Days</em><br>
by <A HREF="../shared/info/keith.htm">Keith Brophy</A> and
<A HREF="../shared/info/tim.htm">Tim Koets</A><br>
<br>
Return to <A href=Back09.htm>content overview</A><br>
Copyright 1996 by SamsNet<br>
</center>

<SCRIPT LANGUAGE="VBScript">
<!--
    Dim Units

    Units = "Feet"

    Sub SetUnits(NewUnits)
       Units = NewUnits
    End Sub

    Sub cmdResults_OnClick()

       Dim Number
       Dim Result

       Number = txtNumber.Value

       If Units = "Feet" Then
           Result = Number * 0.3048
       ElseIf Units = "Inches" Then
           Result = Number * 0.00254
       ElseIf Units = "Yards" Then
           Result = Number * 0.9144
       End If

       txtResult.Value = "There are " & Result & " meters in " &_
                         Number & " " & Units & "."

    End Sub

-->
</SCRIPT>

</BODY>
</HTML>
```

The solution uses a script-level variable called Units that tracks the user-selected units. Whenever the user clicks a radio button, the subroutine SetUnits proceeds to change the script-level Units variable. Then, when the user clicks Convert, the script uses the appropriate multiplier in a conditional expression to obtain the result. This example shows how to effectively use intrinsic HTML controls, procedures, conditional structures, and script-level variables to accomplish the task.

Day 10

1. The following is the code:

```
<SCRIPT LANGUAGE="VBSCRIPT">
<!--
sub lblTester_Click
    lblTester.Caption = "Kenny Jasper"
end sub
-->
</SCRIPT>
```

2. The following is the code:

```
If (lblTester.Angle >= 20)and (lblTester.Angle <= 40) then
    lblTester.Caption = "Brooke"
else
    lblTester.Angle = lblTester.Angle + 10
end if
```

Day 11

1. The following is the code:

```
Sub MyTimer_Time
    ' Check to see what the current interval is
    if MyTimer.Interval = 2000 then
        MyTimer.Interval = 1000
    elseif MyTimer.Interval = 1000 then
        MyTimer.Interval = 500
    else
        MyTimer.Enabled = 0
    end if
end sub
```

2. The following is the code:

```
MyItem.date = "7/6/62"
```

By setting the suppression date back in time, you ensure that the code will consider that the suppression date has already been reached, and the graphic will not display.

Day 12

1. The following code segment shows the answer. Notice that because the Java applet resides at a different location from the current page, you must provide CODEBASE. CODETYPE and the associated apology message are optional.

```
<OBJECT
        ID="jvaGifts"
        CLASSID="java:Birthday.Logs"
        CODETYPE="application/java-vm"
        CODEBASE="http://www.mcp.com/javastuff/"
        HEIGHT=100
        WIDTH=100
    >
<PARAM NAME="MaxSpend" VALUE="200">
A java applet is used on this page but your browser does not support that.
</OBJECT>
```

2. `jvaGifts.MaxSpend = "300"`

Day 13

1. Indentation is used to show the hierarchy of the code under the conditional checks. Good variable names indicate the type and the purpose of each variable. The combination of these changes results in a much more readable program:

```
vAge=txtage.value
If IsNumeric(vAge) then
    if vAge < intGENERATION_X_AGE Then
        msgbox "Dude, prepare to surf!"
    Else
        msgbox "Welcome - Prepare to enter our Web page"
    End If
Elseif vAge = "unknown" Then
    msgbox "you must supply an age to proceed"
Else
    msgbox "please supply a valid age"
End If
```

2. The following code segment shows the two event scripts merged into one consolidated script:

```
<script Language="VBScript">
sub lblFeedback_click
    msgbox "Feedback label has been clicked"
end sub
Sub cmdCalculate_OnClick
    msgbox "Button has been clicked"
End sub
</script>
```

Day 14

1. The solution involves prompting the user with a Yes/No message box and, if the
   user responds yes, generating the `<H2>Extra Hints<H2>` tag with `document.write`.
   Here's the solution:

```
<HTML>

<HEAD>

<TITLE>Brophy & Koets' Teach Yourself VBScript - Quiz 1 Solution</TITLE>


</HEAD>
<BODY>

<SCRIPT LANGUAGE=VBS>
<!-

    dim rc              ' Stores return code value
    rc = msgbox("Do you want extra hints to be displayed on this page?", _
          vbYesNo + vbQuestion,"Setting up the page")

    if rc = vbYes then
        ' Show Big Spender Page
        Spender = vbTrue
        document.write "<H2>Extra Hints</H2>"
        ' ... more document.write statements to display hints could go here
    end if
-->
</SCRIPT>
<! Regular HTML statements that are always carried out could follow... -->
<H3>Welcome to the Question Page</H3>
<p>Q1. What eats lots of oranges and has 80,000 legs?
<p>Q2. Why is the grass green?
<BR>
<BR>
<p>A1. The field in the Boston Marathon
<p>A2. If it was white you couldn't tell if a polar bear was in your lawn!

</BODY>
</HTML>
```

2. Since the page is generated sequentially, the script will be carried out in the order
   in which it is encountered. Moving the script between the question and answer
   statements causes it to be carried out, and Extra Hints to be generated on the page,
   in that sequence. When the user responds affirmatively, he will see the Extra Hints
   text right after the question area on the Web page. Here's the solution:

```
<HTML>

<HEAD>

<TITLE>Brophy & Koets' Teach Yourself VBScript - Quiz 2 Solution</TITLE>
```

```
</HEAD>
<BODY>

<! Regular HTML statements that are always carried out could follow... -->
<H3>Welcome to the Question Page</H3>
<p>Q1. What eats lots of oranges and has 80,000 legs?
<p>Q2. Why is the grass green?
<BR>
<SCRIPT LANGUAGE=VBS>
<!-

    dim rc              ' Stores return code value
    rc = msgbox("Do you want extra hints to be displayed on this page?", _
            vbYesNo + vbQuestion,"Setting up the page")

    if rc = vbYes then
        ' Show Big Spender Page
        Spender = vbTrue
        document.write "<H2>Extra Hints</H2>"
        document.write "<p>Q1. Think about 26.2 miles"
        document.write "<p>Q1. It involves an animal"
        ' ... more document.write statements to display hints could go here
    end if
-->
</SCRIPT>
<BR>
<p>A1. The field in the Boston Marathon
<p>A2. If it was white you couldn't tell if a polar bear was in your lawn!

</BODY>
</HTML>
```

3. Use the `vbDefaultButton2` intrinsic constant to cause the second button to be highlighted:

```
rc = MsgBox ("Do you want poor Fred to bike 68 miles by himself?", _
    vbYesNo + vbDefaultButton2, "Biking Question")
```

Day 15

1. The following is the code:

```
if StrComp(txtDepartment.Value, "Accounting", 1) = 0 then
    ' Accounting department has been entered
else
    ' Accounting department was not entered
end if
```

Note that the non-0 third parameter to `StrComp` instructs the function to carry out a match that is not case sensitive.

2. Many variations of this code would carry out the algorithm. The key is to loop through the string, using `InStr` to check for an occurrence of `Brown` and advancing

the start position for InStr each time through the loop. The following is the solution:

```
dim blnDone    ' indicates when the string count is complete
dim intCount   ' counter of how many times Brown is detected in string
dim intFoundPosition  ' the position where Brown is found in string
dim intCurrentPosition  ' the next position to search for Brown in string

' Initialize variables to start looking at string
blnDone = vbFalse
intCurrentPosition = 1

' Continue to advance through string until done
' condition no more Brown's are found
do while not blnDone
    ' Find where the next Brown is
    intFoundPosition = InStr(intCurrentPosition, _
      s_strBorrower, "Brown")
    ' See if Brown was found
    if intFoundPosition = 0 then
        ' No more Brown's are in string so the search is done
        blnDone = vbTrue
    else
        ' Brown was found, increment count and prepare
        ' to search again after this one
        intCount = intCount + 1
        intCurrentPosition = intFoundPosition + len("Brown")
    end if
loop
msgbox "Brown borrowed the book " & intCount & " times. "
```

Day 16

1. Here's the answer:

```
Dim dtmNow
' Get current time
dtmNow = Now()
if s_dtmEvent < dtmNow then
    msgbox "Registration deadline is passed."
End if
```

2. Int always truncates left on the number line. Fix truncates toward the number line. Cint rounds to the nearest even number. Here are the numeric results:

   Line 1: -6

   Line 2: -5

   Line 3: -6

3. Here's the answer:

```
dim intCounter, intLeftOverPlayers

for intCounter = 1 to 1000

        intLeftOverPlayers = _TotalPlayers Mod 9
next

msgbox intLeftOverPlayers
```

Day 17

1. One sequence of trace messages you can use is to insert a trace in every condition:

```
If a > 3 then
    b = c + 1
    MsgBox "After b= c + 1", vbOKOnly , "Debug-Time Trace"
else
  if a = 1 then
      b = c + 4
      MsgBox "After b= c + 4", vbOKOnly , "Debug-Time Trace"
  else
      if < -2 then
          b = c + 7
          MsgBox "After b= c + 7" vbOKOnly , "Debug-Time Trace"
      end if
  end if
end if
```

2. The key is to inspect the values of the variables and the variable type of the variables:

```
dim strVarP, strVarQ, strVarR

' Retrieve the subtype and value of each of the variables and then display_
it.
'    vbCrLf is used to separate lines in the output message.
strVarP = "(P) Subtype = " & VarType(P) & "  Value = " & P
strVarQ = "(Q) Subtype = " & VarType(Q) & "  Value = " & Q
strVarR = "(R) Subtype = " & VarType(R ) & "  Value = " & R
MsgBox  strVarP & vbCrLf & strVarQ & vbCrLf & strVarR, vbOKOnly, "Debug
Variables"

r = q / p
```

This code will print the value and subtype of each variable. This trace code must be inserted *before* the problem statement. If you inserted it after the problem statement, the runtime error would occur first and your trace statement would never be reached (unless you used On Error Resume Next).

The statements will print the variable's current value as well as the subtype, but nothing will be displayed when printing the value of an empty or a null variable. In some cases, the subtype of the variable may be empty or null. If so, the value returned by the VarType function will provide you with this information. (See Day

4 for a full discussion of VarType capabilities.) For other subtypes, the standard subtype and value of the variable are displayed.

With this information on each variable involved in the equation, you should be able to pinpoint the cause of any type of error that occurs. Inspection of this information would show that one of the variables being used in the division has an underlying subtype of double (VarType = 5) and the other has an underlying subtype of string data (VarType = 8). The remaining variable has a subtype of empty (VarType = 0), but that could be correct since that is the result variable and perhaps no values have yet been assigned to it. The fact that a string is being used in the division, however, should be enough to tell you there is an errant code assignment somewhere, and lead you to other areas of the code to find the culprit. One potential cause of such a problem could be code like the following:

```
dim p, q, r

p = 1.3
q = "a"
 .
 .
 .
r = q / p
```

This type of error is obvious if the statements are clustered together, but if the assignments are not in the vicinity of the division statement, then analyzing variables is usually a necessary first step to knowing where to look for the cause of the problem.

Another way to carry out the same type of analysis would be to use the VarAnalyze procedure. This procedure provides the same capabilities as the code snippet above, but the procedure itself generates information each time it is called. The procedure also provides a verbal description of the VarType (such as empty) rather than just the numeric value. If the VarAnalyze procedure were used, the trace would appear like this:

```
' Retrieve the subtype and value of each of the variables and then display_
it.
'    vbCrLf is used to separate lines in the output message.
VarAnalyze ("Contents of  p prior to the division: ", p)
VarAnalyze ("Contents of  q prior to the division: ", q)
VarAnalyze ("Contents of  r prior to the division: ", r)

r = q / p
```

Day 18

1. The name is formed by joining the anchor name with the OnClick event:
```
sub lnkBooks_OnClick
...
end sub
```

2. The name is formed by joining the anchor name with the `OnClick` event:

```
sub lnkBooks_MouseMove (s, b, x, y)
...
end sub
```

3. You can redirect the link with the location object's HREF property. Just assign the Uniform Resource Locator address of the page you wish to visit to `location.href`.

```
sub lnkBooks_Click
    location.href = "http://www.microsoft.com/vbscript"
end sub
```

Day 19

1. You must supply a statement with the form submit method, by making the one-line modification as shown in the following code:

```
' Make sure the user age is 18 or over
if document.frmApply.txtAge.value < 18 then
    MsgBox "Sorry youngster, you're not old enough to apply!", _
        vbOKOnly,"Can't take app"
else
    document.frmApply.Submit
    MsgBox "Application processed", vbOKOnly, "Confirmation"
end if
end sub
-->
```

2. The following is the modified code:

```
<!--
sub cmdApply_OnClick
' Process the application by submitting to server if data is valid

    ' Make sure the user age is 18 or over
    if document.frmApply.txtAge.value < 18 then
        MsgBox "Sorry youngster, you're not old enough to apply!", _
            vbOKOnly,"Can't take the application"
    elseif len(document.frmName) = 0 then
        MsgBox "Sorry, we can't take an application from just nobody!",
            vbOKOnly,"Can't take app"
    else
        document.frmApply.Submit
        MsgBox "Application processed", vbOKOnly, "Confirmation"
    end if
end sub
-->
</script>
```

Day 20

1. VBScript cannot make use of DLLs, so the option of using the DLL in the code is out. You could rewrite the DLL code into an ActiveX control if you have a language such as C++ that can generate these controls. Then you could make use of

that from within your VBScript for the same purpose, or you could rewrite the DLL code into script subroutines, which are themselves a part of the script. This approach is likely to be too cumbersome if there is too much code in the DLL. Most likely the ActiveX control strategy is the quickest path to reach the same level of function in the script as the original program.

2. (a)VBScript does not support constants, so TAX_RATE and ITEM_PRICE must be declared as variables. (b)VBScript only supports the variant variable type, so the variable declarations for intUnits and intCost must be modified accordingly. (c)The value assigned to intCost will no longer be an integer under VBScript. Under VBScript the variable will have to be declared to be of type variant because that's the only type supported. Because a variant can assume any type, the variable will assume a single type (decimal point number) after this assignment.

3. The following is the code, modified to work for VBScript:

```
dim TAX_RATE
dim ITEM_PRICE
Dim intUnits as Integer
Dim intCost as Integer

' Set up constant values
TAX_RATE = 0.04
ITEM_PRICE = 25

' Calculate the total cost
intUnits = InputBox("How many units do you wish to purchase?")
intCost = (ITEM_PRICE * intUnits) * TAX_RATE
' Store cost in its integer representation
intCost = cInt(intCost)
```

Day 21

1. Any language features that relate to external communication and control fall into this category. They include normal file input and output, clipboard support, printer object support, dynamic link library calls, calls to system application programming interfaces, and object linking and embedding (OLE) communication.

2. Commercial controls with the highest level of certification have been verified by an independent certification laboratory to be free of malicious intent. This does not mean they are bug free, but it does imply an overall level of general soundness. Likewise, if a control is certified, it carries with it a digital signature so that the creator of the control is clearly and uniquely identified. This provides a trail of accountability if any problems occur.

INDEX

Building an Intranet

—Tim Evans

Building an Intranet is the first book to focus on using Web technology to provide information for a company internally. The reader will learn how to choose hardware and software, how to set up a secure Web server, and how to make his company's applications Web aware. The CD-ROM contains source code from the book and valuable utilities. Learn how to design, build, and deploy information and applications within an organization!

$55.00 USA/$77.95 CDN User level: Casual–Accomplished
ISBN: 1-57521-071-1   720 pages

Teach Yourself Java in 21 Days

—Laura Lemay, et al.

Introducing the first, best, and most detailed guide to developing applications with the hot new Java language from Sun Microsystems. The CD-ROM includes the Java Developer's Kit. This book provides detailed coverage of the hottest new technology on the World Wide Web and shows readers how to develop applications using the Java language. Includes coverage of browsing Java applications with Netscape and other popular Web browsers.

$39.99 USA/$56.95 CDN User Level: Casual – Accomplished – Expert
ISBN: 1-57521-030-4   500 pages

Teach Yourself Web Publishing with HTML in 14 Days, Premier Edition

—Laura Lemay

This book teaches everything about publishing on the Web. In addition to its exhaustive coverage of HTML, it also gives readers hands-on practice designing and writing HTML documents. The CD-ROM is Mac and PC compatible and includes applications that help readers create Web pages using graphics and templates. Readers will learn how to upload their page to a server and how to advertise. Design, create, and upload your Web page to a Web server for the world to see!

$39.99 USA/$56.95 CDN User Level: New – Casual – Accomplished
ISBN: 1-57521-014-2   840 pages

Visual Basic 4 Unleashed

—Various Authors

Provides the reader with a comprehensive reference to virtually all the topics that are used in today's leading-edge Visual Basic applications. The CD-ROM contains complete source code from the book, a screen saver, a resource monitor, a game, and more. Includes complete coverage of all the new features of the latest version of Visual Basic, advanced programming topics, component-based programming, using other APIs and software, and database programming. Features a special project section focusing on developing different types of applications.

$49.99 USA/$70.95 CDN User Level: Casual – Accomplished – Expert
ISBN: 0-672-30837-1   1,224 pages

HTML and CGI Unleashed

—December and Ginsburg

Targeted to professional developers who need a detailed guide and have a basic understanding of programming. Provides a complete, detailed reference to developing Web information systems. Covers the full range of tools— HTML, CGI, Perl, and C editing and conversion programs, and more—and how to create commercial-grade Web applications.

$49.99 USA/$70.95 CDN User Level: Accomplished – Expert
ISBN: 0-672-30745-6   864 pages

Peter Norton's Guide to Visual Basic 4 for Windows 95

—Peter Norton

This guide teaches readers how to use Visual Basic to create powerful applications without all the technical jargon. Provides a hands-on overview of the entire programming environment. Explores advanced topics, such as linking to C and Windows directly, creating custom controls, and connecting to other Windows applications. Covers dialog boxes, buttons, a mouse-driven paint program, and advanced data handling.

$39.99 USA/$56.95 CDN User Level: New – Casual – Accomplished – Expert
ISBN: 0-672-30615-8   944 pages
Replaces Previous Edition: ISBN: 1-56686-093-8, $39.95 USA/$55.95 CDN

Database Developer's Guide with Visual Basic 4, Second Edition

—Roger Jennings

This book shows developers how to optimize their applications for desktop and client/server databases, write queries in ANSI SQL and Access SQL with Visual Basic code, and create front-end databases using MIDI forms. Disk contains a data dictionary application, cross tab query generator, multiplatform graphical front end, and DDE and OLE applications with Excel 5. Provides in-depth coverage of networking issues surrounding databases. Explains how to use third-party, data-aware custom controls to add flexibility to applications.

$59.99 USA/$84.95 CDN User Level: Accomplished – Expert
ISBN: 0-672-30652-2   1,152 pages
Replaces Previous Edition: ISBN: 0-672-30440-6, $44.95 USA/$62.95 CDN

Teach Yourself JavaScript in a Week

—Arman Danesh

Teach Yourself JavaScript in a Week is the easiest way to learn how to create interactive Web pages with LiveScript, Netscape's Java-like scripting language. It is intended for non-technical people and will be equally of value to users on the Macintosh, Windows, and UNIX platforms. Teaches how to design and create attention-grabbing Web pages with JavaScript. Shows how to add interactivity to Web pages.

$39.99 USA/$56.95 CDN User Level: Accomplished – Expert
ISBN: 1-57521-073-8   576 pages

Add to Your Sams.net Library Today
with the Best Books for Internet Technologies

ISBN	Quantity	Description of Item	Unit Cost	Total Cost
1-57521-071-1		Building an Intranet (book/CD-ROM)	$55.00	
1-57521-030-4		Teach Yourself Java in 21 Days (book/CD-ROM)	$39.99	
1-57521-014-2		Teach Yourself Web Publishing with HTML in 14 Days, Premier Edition (book/CD-ROM)	$39.99	
0-672-30837-1		Visual Basic 4 Unleashed (book/CD-ROM)	$49.99	
0-672-30745-6		HTML and CGI Unleashed (book/CD-ROM)	$49.99	
1-56686-093-8		Peter Norton's Guide to Visual Basic 4 for Windows 95 (book)	$39.95	
0-672-30615-8		Database Developer's Guide with Visual Basic 4, Second Edition (book/CD-ROM)	$59.99	
1-57521-073-8		Teach Yourself JavaScript in a Week (book/CD-ROM)	$39.99	
		Shipping and Handling: See information below.		
		TOTAL		

Shipping and Handling: $4.00 for the first book, and $1.75 for each additional book. If you need to have it NOW, we can ship product to you in 24 hours for an additional charge of approximately $18.00, and you will receive your item overnight or in two days. Overseas shipping and handling adds $2.00. Prices subject to change. Call between 9:00 a.m. and 5:00 p.m. EST for availability and pricing information on latest editions.

201 W. 103rd Street, Indianapolis, Indiana 46290

1-800-428-5331 — Orders   1-800-835-3202 — FAX   1-800-858-7674 — Customer Service

Book ISBN 1-57521-120-3

Build it and they will come...

Email **Support** **Service**

Speed **YOU** **Web**

Design **cgi** **Hosting**

...maintain it and they will stay!

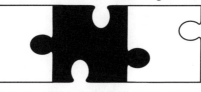

Campbell Network Systems • 820 Monroe NE • Grand Rapids, MI 49503

1.888.694.INET (4638)

http://www.cns.net

DoubleBlaze Software Consortium

"Thriving on the beta edge."

Get the scoop on VBScript and leading VBSript
development tool solutions.

Stop by and visit us at www.DoubleBlaze.com

☞

(but bring a VBScript-compatible browser with you)

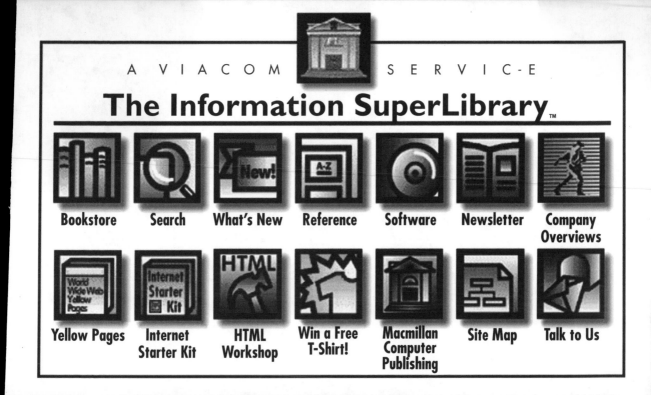

What's on the Disc

The companion CD-ROM contains all the source code and project files developed by the authors.

Windows NT Installation Instructions

1. Insert the CD-ROM disc into your CD-ROM drive.
2. From File Manager or Program Manager, choose Run from the File menu.
3. Type `<drive>\install` and press Enter, where `<drive>` corresponds to the drive letter of your CD-ROM. For example, if your CD-ROM is drive D:, type `D:\INSTALL` and press Enter.
4. Follow the on-screen instructions in the installation program. Source code files will be installed to the `\TYVBS` directory unless you choose a different directory. Installation also creates a Program Manager group named Teach Yourself VBScript.

Windows 95 Installation Instructions

1. Insert the CD-ROM disc into your CD-ROM drive. If the AutoPlay feature of your Windows 95 system is enabled, the Installation program will start automatically.
2. If the Installation program does not start automatically, double-click the My Computer icon.
3. Double-click the icon representing your CD-ROM drive.
4. Double-click on the icon titled Install.exe to run the installation program.
5. Follow the on-screen instructions in the installation program. Source code files will be installed to the `\TYVBS` directory unless you choose a different directory. Installation also creates a Program Manager group named Teach Yourself VBScript.